Reading and Learning to Read

Reading and Learning to Read

Jo Anne L. Vacca
Richard T. Vacca
Kent State University

Mary K. Gove
East Cleveland Schools

Scott, Foresman and Company

Glenview, Illinois   Boston   London

To Our Parents . . .
  Joseph J. and Anne M. Lynott
  William and Pauline Vacca
  John R. and Thelma L. Kratochvil

Library of Congress Cataloging-in-Publication Data

Vacca, Jo Anne L.
  Reading and Learning to read.

  Bibliography: p.
  Includes index.
  1. Reading (Elementary)   2. Language arts
(Elementary)   I. Vacca, Richard T.   II. Gove,
Mary K.   III. Title.
LB1573.V32   1987   372.4   86–33772
ISBN 0-673-39185-X

ISBN 0-673-39185-X

45678910-RRC-908988

Acknowledgments

Chapter 3

  Box 3.2 Recommendations from the Joint Committee on Reading and Pre-First Grade. Reprinted with
permission of the International Reading Association. From "Reading and Pre-First Grade: A Joint
Statement of Concerns About Present Practices in Pre-First Grade Reading Instruction," *The Reading
Teacher,* April 1977.
  Figure 3.1. Writing Samples from Three Four-Year-Olds. Reprinted with permission of Jerome C.
Harste and the International Reading Association. Figure 1 from "Children's Language and World:
Initial Encounters with Print," Jerome Harste, C. L. Burke, and V. A. Woodward from *Reader Meets
Author/Bridging the Gap: A Psycholinguistic and Sociolinguistic Perspective,* J. A. Langer and M. T. Smith-
Burke, editors.

(Continued on page 518)

Preface

The completion of *Reading and Learning to Read* brings to mind the saying, "It's not the big things in life that cause us difficulty; it's the little ones." After putting the finishing touches on these fifteen chapters, one small task remained: We were to furnish our editor, Mylan Jaixen, with a "one- or two-sentence description" of our book. One or two sentences? To describe a five hundred-page book? Backed into a corner, we tried to capture the essence of what *Reading and Learning to Read* is all about. You know—when the teacher says, "Just give me the main idea of the book in your own words." All right . . .

Reading and Learning to Read is a comprehensive, readable text intended to stimulate both prospective and practicing elementary teachers to reflect on what they do and why they do it. How beliefs about reading influence the way you work with children in instructional settings is presented in the context of language and literacy learning.

Essentially, we ask readers of this book what they believe and value about reading and learning to read. Underlying the content is our own belief that teachers are instructional decision makers. Whether beginning or practiced, teachers, like their students, rely on pertinent experiences and background knowledge. In neither the delivery of instruction nor the process of learning to read do we start out tabula rasa. In both situations the *connections* make the difference.

Teaching and learning alike require connecting the known to the unknown. Whether you are a preservice or inservice teacher, apply the techniques of anticipation and prereading preparation, both of which play a major role in comprehension, to the subject of this text. Ask three pivotal questions of yourself right now: (1) What do I already know about reading? (2) What do I believe about how children learn to read? (3) What do I need to know about reading instruction? We hope to make you think about your own belief systems, and to show how these beliefs are connected to models, approaches, and instructional strategies.

The five-part structure of *Reading and Learning to Read* assists readers in taking an ongoing inventory of their own store of knowledge and experiences while incorporating new knowledge about language and literacy. Part One, "Thinking

About Reading," places reading in the larger context of language and literacy learning. Through interviews about our beliefs we begin to connect what we believe with what we do in the classroom and with various approaches to instruction. In Part Two, "The Roots of Literacy," we discuss early literacy and beginning reading and writing instruction. Learning to write is as natural to children as learning to read. Rather than teaching reading and writing as separate curricular entities, teachers can teach them in tandem within a natural learning environment. Part Three, "Selecting Strategies," is an up-to-date presentation of three critical aspects of reading instruction in the elementary school: comprehension, vocabulary development, and word identification. The heart of contemporary reading instruction is comprehension. We have approached comprehension instruction from an active, meaning-making stance, much like our approach throughout *Reading and Learning to Read*. Part Four, "Vehicles for Instruction," emphasizes the instructional decisions teachers make in selecting materials. Here we aim to build understanding of literature in the reading program, basal readers and other instructional materials, content area reading, and computers as tools for developing literacy. Finally, in Part Five, "Making Decisions," we conclude our discussion of the major considerations influencing teachers as they strive to assess reading behavior, organize effective classrooms, and meet individual student needs. We also include wide-ranging information on types of assessment, diagnostic teaching, effective classrooms, individualized reading, and children with special needs.

Our position throughout the book is that reading involves meaning in the transaction between reader and author. Similarly, *reading instruction should be purposeful, meaningful, and enjoyable.* As teachers we share a mutual goal with the young readers we hope to influence: to build our strengths as we grow in independence and understanding.

Successful readers rarely read every single word of a text in order to comprehend it. You will no doubt spend more time on some sections of *Reading and Learning to Read* than on others. Fortunately for all of us, some key individuals did read every word in this volume. We especially thank the following reviewers for their dedicated professionalism and support: Jane Hansen of University of New Hampshire, Taffy Raphael of Michigan State University, Walter Prentice of University of Wisconsin, Peggy Ransom of Ball State University, Elizabeth Sulzby of University of Michigan, and Leo Schell of Kansas State University. More thanks to our production editor, Janice Friedman of Little, Brown, and a grateful tip of the hat to our editor, Mylan Jaixen.

J.V., R.V., and M.G.
Kent, Ohio

Brief Contents

Part I: **Thinking About Reading** 1

Chapter 1   *Reflections on the Reading Process*   2
Chapter 2   *Approaches to Reading Instruction*   30

Part II: **The Roots of Literacy** 53

Chapter 3   *Early Literacy Experiences*   54
Chapter 4   *Beginning Reading Instruction*   76
Chapter 5   *The Writing Road to Reading*   102

Part III: **Selecting Strategies** 139

Chapter 6   *Reading Comprehension*   140
Chapter 7   *Vocabulary Knowledge and Concept Development*   172
Chapter 8   *Word Identification*   204

Part IV: **Vehicles for Instruction** 233

Chapter 9   *Bringing Children and Literature Together*   234
Chapter 10   *Basal Readers and Instructional Materials*   264
Chapter 11   *Bridging the Gap Between Children and Content Area Textbooks*   304
Chapter 12   *Computers and Literacy*   338

Part V: **Making Decisions** 373

Chapter 13   *Assessing Reading Behavior and Performance*   374
Chapter 14   *Managing and Organizing the Effective Classroom*   410
Chapter 15   *Adapting Instruction to Meet Individual Needs*   450
Appendixes   485
Bibliography   503
Index   521

Contents

Part I: Thinking About Reading   1

Chapter 1   Reflections on the Reading Process   2

Different Theories, Different Instructional Practices   5

Changing Perspectives on the Reading Process   6

Linguistic, Cognitive, and Social Influences 7   Models of the
Reading Process 10   How Do Models of Reading Differ? 13

Thinking Reflectively About Reading   16

Interpreting the Interview 17   Descriptions of Conceptual
Frameworks of Reading 20   Rating Your Conceptual Framework of
Reading 22   What Does the Conceptual Framework of Reading
Tell You? 22

Summary   25

The Workshop   26

In the Classroom 26   In the Field 27

Chapter 2   Approaches to Reading Instruction   30

Holistic vs. Subskill Approaches   34

Reading: Skill or Skills? 36

Range of Approaches   38

Individualized-Prescriptive 39   Basal Reading 42   Language
Experience 43 Individualized-Personalized 43

Instructional Strategies   44

How Practices Reflect Beliefs 45   Reflecting on the Teaching
Episodes 48   Deciding on Strategies 49

Summary   49

The Workshop   50

In the Classroom 50   In the Field 51

Part II: The Roots of Literacy   53

Chapter 3   Early Literacy Experiences   54

Reading Begins at Home   56

Learning to Read Naturally   59

Longitudinal Studies of Early Readers **59**   Individual Case
Studies **62**

Instructional Implications for Kindergarten and First Grade   63

Creating a Home-Centered Environment **64**   Reading to
Children **66**   Sharing Books **66**   Repeating Favorite
Stories **67**   Providing Assistance with Reading **67**

Language Experiences   69

Talking, Creating, Singing, and Dancing **70**   Role-Playing and
Drama **72**

Summary   73

The Workshop   74

In the Classroom **74**   In the Field **74**

Chapter 4   Beginning Reading Instruction   76

Readiness to Read   79

Instructional Beginnings   80

Learning What Reading Is All About **82**   Learning About Sounds
in Words **88**   Procedures for Segmenting Sounds in
Words **90**   Recognizing Letters **92**   Learning About the
Language of Instruction **93**

Assessing Readiness for Reading   94

Observing Reading and Reading-like Behavior **94**

Summary   97

The Workshop   97

In the Classroom **97**   In the Field **100**

Chapter 5   The Writing Road to Reading   102

How Writing Develops   105

Progressing from Scribbling to Writing **106**   Building on Emerging
Competence: The Case for Invented Spellings **110**   Creating a
Natural Learning Environment **115**

Getting Started   117

Establishing a Routine for Writing **117**   Establishing Classroom
Guidelines and Procedures **119**

Guiding Children Through the Writing Process   121

Strategies for Rehearsing **122**   Drafting, Revising, and
Editing **125**   Publishing, Displaying, and Sharing Writing **132**

Summary   136

The Workshop   137

In the Classroom **137**   In the Field **138**

Part III: *Selecting Strategies*   139

Chapter 6   *Reading Comprehension*   140

Building a Schema for Stories   142

Elements in a Story Grammar **143**   Is It Necessary to Teach Story
Structure? **148**

Building and Activating Schema   150

Advance Organizers **152**   Student-Generated Questions **154**

Guiding Interactions Between Reader and Text   157

Directed Reading-Thinking Activity **157**   Inferential Strategy **160**

Using Questions to Promote Comprehension   161

Questions as a Springboard to Discussion **161**   Alternatives to
Questions **162**   Classifying Questions According to Cognitive
Function **163**   Question-Answer Relationships **165**

Summary   170

The Workshop   170

In the Classroom **170**   In the Field **171**

Chapter 7   *Vocabulary Knowledge and Concept Development*   172

Vocabulary Knowledge and Concept Development   174

The Relationship Between Vocabulary and Comprehension   175

Experiences, Concepts, and Words   177

Words Are Labels for Concepts **177**   Words and Concepts: A
Closer Look **179**   Class, Example, and Attribute
Relations **179**   Definitional and Contextual Knowledge of
Words **182**   Some Principles to Guide Vocabulary Instruction **183**

Strategies for Vocabulary and Concept Development   186

Relating Experiences to Vocabulary Learning **187**   Developing
Word Meanings **191**   Classifying and Categorizing Words **193**

Summary   201

The Workshop   203

In the Classroom **203**   In the Field **203**

Chapter 8   Word Identification   204

  Key Terms Related to Word Identification   207

  The Role of Sight Words in Learning to Read   208
    Should Words Be Taught as Wholes? **209**   High-Frequency
    Sight Words **210**   Teaching "Key Words" **211**

  The Role of Context in Learning to Read   214
    Context Analysis **215**   Using Context to Decide If a Word
    Is Important **217**

  The Role of Phonics in Learning to Read   218
    The Content and Language of Phonics **219**   Some Suggestions
    for Teaching Phonics **223**   Instructional Activities **226**

  Toward Oral Reading Fluency   228
    Echo Reading **228**   Simultaneous-Listening-and-Reading
    (SLR) **228**   Repeated Readings **229**

  Summary   230

  The Workshop   231
    In the Classroom **231**   In the Field **232**

Part IV: Vehicles for Instruction   233

Chapter 9   Bringing Children and Literature Together   234

  Helping Children to Want to Read   237

  Surrounding Children with Literature   240
    Selecting a Classroom Collection of Books **240**   Listening
    to Literature **243**   Story Telling **246**   Helping Children
    Find and Share Books **248**

  Allocating Time for Silent Reading   251
    Putting SSR into Action **253**   SSR for Beginning Readers and
    Less Able Readers **254**   Multiplying the Benefits of SSR **255**

  Encouraging Response to Literature   257
    Implications for Aesthetic Reading **258**

  Summary   261

  The Workshop   261
    In the Classroom **261**   In the Field **262**

Chapter 10   Basal Readers and Instructional Materials   264

  Historical Background   267
    1683: A Strong Bottom-Up Approach **268**   Basal Readers
    as We Knew Them **269**

  Basal Programs of the Eighties   273

Characteristics of Basal Readers   279

Appearance **279**   Illustrations **279**   Procedures for Analyzing
Stereotypes **281**   Language Style **281**   Workbooks **282**
Lesson Framework **283**

Making Instructional Decisions   285

Designing Alternative Lessons **286**   Comprehension Strategy
Lesson for Second-Graders **287**   Vocabulary/Comprehension
Strategy Lesson **289**

Instructional Materials   290

Beliefs About Reading and Instructional Materials **292**   Selecting
Reading Materials **292**   Evaluating Reading Materials **294**
Teacher-Made and Student-Produced Materials **297**

Summary   300

The Workshop   301

In the Classroom **301**   In the Field **302**

Chapter 11   *Bridging the Gap Between Children and Content
Area Textbooks*   304

Why Are Textbooks Difficult to Read?   306

Factors in Judging the Difficulty of Textbooks **307**   Using
Readability Formulas **308**

Textbook Organization   313

External Organization **313**   Text Structure **316**

Helping Students Read Textbook Assignments   318

Activating and Building Background Knowledge **318**   Guiding
Reader-Text Interactions **323**   Reinforcing Vocabulary and
Concepts **326**   Study Strategies **328**

Developing Units of Study   332

What's Involved in Unit Planning **333**   Putting a Unit to
Work **334**

Summary   335

The Workshop   337

In the Classroom **337**   In the Field **337**

Chapter 12   *Computers and Literacy*   338

Computers and Reading   341

CAI Programs **341**   CAI for Teaching Reading Skills **351**
Literature, Computer Style **353**

Computers and Writing   354

Connecting Writing and Reading **354**   Word Processing: A
Powerful Scaffold **356**

Guiding Stages in the Writing Process 362
Programs for Rehearsing 362 Programs for Editing and
Proofreading 365 Sharing and Publishing 368

A Comment on Evaluating Computer Programs 370

Summary 370

The Workshop 371
In the Classroom 371 In the Field 371

Part V: Making Decisions 373

Chapter 13 Assessing Reading Behavior and Performance 374

Toward a Corroborative Framework for Decision Making 377

Formal Assessment 378
Standardized Tests 378 Criterion-Referenced Tests 383

Informal Assessment 384
Informal Reading Inventories 385 Analyzing Oral Reading
Miscues 389 The Cloze Procedure 394

Diagnostic Teaching 396
Observing 399 Interviewing 401

Summary 406

The Workshop 407
In the Classroom 407 In the Field 407

Chapter 14 Managing and Organizing the Effective Classroom 410

Characteristics of Effective Classrooms 413
Discipline 414 Time on Task 415 Direct
Instruction 417 Evaluation of Students 419

Teacher Behavior 420
As the Principal Sees It 421 As the Student Sees It 424
As the Teacher Sees It 426

Individualizing Instruction 426
Individualized Instruction: Confusions and Misunderstandings 427
What Is Individualized Instruction in Reading? 429 Influences
of Individualized Instruction 430

Putting It All Together: Classroom Organization 432
Creating a Physical Environment 432 Ideas for Getting
Organized 434

Classroom Scenarios 442
Scenario 1: Beginning Reading with "The Gingerbread Man" 443
Scenario 2: Primary-Grade Experiences and the
Microcomputer 446 Scenario 3: Intermediate-Grade
Classroom Newspaper 447

Summary   448

The Workshop   449
In the Classroom 449   In the Field 449

Chapter 15 Adapting Instruction to Meet Individual Needs   450

What Does It Mean to Adapt?   453

Working with Colleagues to Meet Special Needs   454
Networking 455   Mainstreaming 457

Adapting Instruction for Gifted Readers   457
Who Are Gifted Readers? 457   Instruction for Gifted Readers:
Avoiding Some Instructional Traps 458   Reading Instruction for
Gifted Readers 459   Networking and Teaming to
Enhance Instruction 462

Adapting Instruction for Children with Learning Disabilities   463
Who Are the Learning Disabled? 463   Reading Instruction for
the Learning Disabled 464   Networking and Teaming to
Enhance Instruction 467

Adapting Instruction for the Linguistically Diverse   467
Who Are the Linguistically Diverse? 469   Reading Instruction
for Linguistically Diverse Learners 470   Networking and Teaming
to Enhance Instruction 473

Adapting Instruction for Bilingual Learners   473
Who Are Bilingual Learners? 474   Reading Instruction for Bilingual
Learners 476   Networking and Teaming to Enhance
Instruction 481

Summary   481

The Workshop   483
In the Classroom 483   In the Field 483

*Appendix A Guidelines for Analyzing Conceptual Frameworks
of Reading Interviews*   485

Appendix B Newberry Award Books   489

Appendix C Caldecott Award Books   491

Appendix D A Bibliography of Predictable Books   493

*Appendix E Computer Programs for Reading Instruction and
Addresses of Publishers*   496

Bibliography   503

Index   521

Part I

Thinking About Reading

Chapter 1

Reflections on the Reading Process

"You are what you believe." As a teacher, your beliefs and assumptions about reading and learning to read are reflected in your actions and interactions with children in an instructional context. In this chapter, you are invited to thoughtfully consider what you believe and what you do (or will do) in the name of reading instruction. As you reflect, you should recognize, first of all, that life in the classroom is complex. What you do to make sense out of that complexity—and why—are closely related. One of teachers' greatest sources of frustration is doing things they neither understand nor believe in. In this book our goal is to help you, the teacher, develop rationales for teaching reading effectively.

*I think my students learn to read by talking, listening, reading, and writing
about things important to them.*

Arch, a first-grade teacher

*I want my students to read what's on the page—so I don't allow oral reading
errors to go by unnoticed.*

Jim, a fifth-grade teacher

My goal is to help children become independent readers.

Margaret, a sixth-grade teacher

*I tell my students not to let one word bug them, that they might be able to
know the story without knowing that one word.*

Helen, a second-grade teacher

*My first-graders learn to read by learning letters and their sounds and then
by learning to blend these sounds into words.*

Linda, a first-grade teacher

The quotations above reflect the teachers' different instructional emphases. In the
pressured world of teaching, it's easy to lose sight of what we believe about
children, reading, and how children learn to read. Yet reflecting on *what we do*
and *why we do it* is one of the best tools we have for improving instruction.

A major premise behind this book is that teachers hold beliefs and make
assumptions about the reading process. These beliefs and assumptions influence
the way we work with children in instructional contexts. Some teachers, such as
Jim (quoted above), emphasize accurate identification of words. Others, like
Helen, place much less importance on accuracy in word recognition. Some teachers
believe that students learn to read through specific skills such as "blending sounds"
into words. Others agree with Arch, whose students learn to read by "talking,
listening, reading, and writing about things important to them." Yet just about
every teacher we've ever talked to agrees with Margaret's reflection on the main
goal of instruction: to teach children to become independent readers. The
differences among teachers reflect varying approaches in getting students to read
on their own.

"What is reading?" Naturally, pre-service and in-service teachers' responses
will vary greatly. Background knowledge, teaching experience, previous study,
perspectives, and attitudes influence your answer. Nevertheless, whether you are
preparing to teach or are already in the field, chances are you are forming or have
formed "theories" about reading and learning to read. Your statements about
reading and reading instruction reflect these theories.

Many of you prudently might suggest that you are "eclectic." If something has potential for the classroom, you'll probably use it. Our expectation in writing this book is that you will be involved continually in a process of developing rationales for what "works."

You need only to observe teachers of reading in action or talk to them about instructional concerns to recognize that every teacher operates in the classroom with what we call an *implicit theory of reading*.

While few would argue that nothing is as practical as a good theory, we embrace the notion, "There's nothing so theoretical as a good practice." An implicit theory of reading is very often manifested in practice as you plan for instruction, select instructional materials and strategies, evaluate students' reading, and in general, give help during instruction. In this chapter we consider the relationship between *explicit* and *implicit* theories of reading and learning to read. Moreover, we help you to think reflectively about your own beliefs and the assumptions you make about reading instruction.

DIFFERENT THEORIES, DIFFERENT INSTRUCTIONAL PRACTICES

What teachers do to make sense out of the complexity of their classrooms—and *why* they do it—is the departure point for this chapter. Read how Arch and Linda, two first-grade teachers, handle the complexity of learning to read in their classrooms.

Arch is an oddity at Clark Lane Elementary School. Not only is he the only male first-grade teacher in the district, but he is also the self-acknowledged "renegade" of the instructional staff at this school. By his own admission Arch doesn't do anything by the book.

The "book" in Arch's case is the teacher's manual of the basal reading program that is used extensively by the other teachers at Clark Lane. Arch eschews basal reading instruction as prescribed in the manual in favor of what he calls "invitations" to learn. He invites his first-graders to explore and experience with him the uses of oral and written language in a variety of instructional situations. Early in the year, for example, Arch's class will read "anything that's real and important to the kids": signs, box top labels, and most importantly, their own writing. His pupils write (and dictate) a lot. They also listen to Arch read and engage in discussions about stories before "ever getting into any kind of formal reading instruction. You know . . . identifying letters and words . . . learning the skills of reading."

Arch places little importance on his students' recognizing every word as they read. He says, "I tell my students not to let one or two words prevent them from reading; that they might be able to understand what the story is about and to enjoy it without identifying all of the words."

Linda is also effective at what she does: teaching six-year-olds to read. But her approach is decidedly different from Arch's. She believes quite strongly that beginning readers must start with sound-letter correspondences, translating print into speech. Other than occasional "experience charts" in the first weeks of the school year, Linda doesn't even attempt to introduce writing until most of her children make the monumental "click" between the black squiggly marks on a page and the sounds they represent.

Of the "click," Linda says, "You can't miss it. It's a joy to watch." When she sees children making the connection between print and speech, Linda begins to aim for mastery. She teaches sound-letter correspondences thoroughly. She believes in having beginning readers "overlearn" decoding skills to the point where they can use them automatically in translating print to speech.

Linda says, "My students learn to read by blending sounds into words and putting words together into sentences." She explains why: "I think it is important for students to overlearn their consonant and vowel sounds so that they can recognize each word." Comprehension is important to Linda as it is to Arch, but the two differ in perspective. Linda feels the most important instructional activity is for children "to read by themselves, to read to learn new information." However, to get to this point she believes her students "must have word attack skills to learn to read."

Both Arch and Linda operate from predominantly different belief systems about learning to read. Yet they share a common purpose. Each works hard to produce able, self-confident readers. Yet they welcome first-graders to the world of learning literacy in school in starkly contrasting ways. What Arch does reflects a language-centered view of reading and learning to read. What Linda does reflects a skills-centered view.

Different views of reading often result in and support different instructional concerns and practices. Figure 1.1 shows the links among several key concepts in this book. It illustrates how explicit theories of reading found in the literature and supported by empirical study influence the implicit views of reading held by teachers. In turn, views of the reading process influence teaching: for example, the plans we make, our instructional decisions, the way we interact with children during instruction. Moreover, our actions in the name of instruction influence children's reading, their concepts of reading, and their attitudes toward reading.

Additional factors that may influence our thinking about reading should not be discounted. For example, our memories of learning, methods courses, school policies, curriculum guidelines, the beliefs of colleagues and administrators with whom we work closely, the book publishing and testing industry, and pressures from the community contribute to our beliefs and assumptions. Teachers become more consistent in their practices as they examine what their implicit theories have in common with explicit theories of the reading process.

CHANGING PERSPECTIVES ON THE READING PROCESS

Part of the challenge of reading instruction concerns the elusive nature of the reading process. Who can ever really *know* a process as complex as reading? The best we can do is develop explicit theories that organize knowledge and research

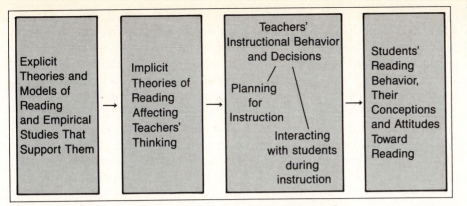

Figure 1.1 Relationships Among Key Concepts in This Book

about reading into a system of assumptions, principles, and procedures. Theories allow us to predict and explain phenomena which otherwise are unexplainable. Over the years new knowledge and views on the reading process (and how it works) have resulted in changing perspectives on the reading process.

Reading and learning to read, for example, have been explained from a cognitive perspective. Reading is a thinking process and should be taught and thought of as such. Yet viewing reading and learning to read strictly from a cognitive perspective is not sufficient.

People think and learn through using language. Reading is as much a language process as it is cognitive in nature. Goodman (1986) put the matter of language learning this way: "Language enables us to share our experiences, learn from each other, plan together, and greatly enhances our intellect by linking our minds with others of our kind. . . . Written language greatly expands human memory by making it possible to store far more knowledge than the brain is capable of storing. . . . Written language links us with people in faraway places and distant times, with dead authors" (pages 11–12).

Learning to read needs to be viewed from the perspective of learning to use written language effectively. Children are language users; for them, learning to read is inherently social. If children perceive little use of written language, then they will have a difficult time learning to read and write. However, if written language is meaningful, then the *situation* in which it is used allows children to discern what reading and writing are all about.

Linguistic, Cognitive, and Social Influences

Cognition and language are critical components in human development. Although the acquisition of language is a complex process, many children understand and use all of the basic language patterns by the time they are six years old. The child's apparent facility with language is best understood by recognizing the active relationship between cognition and language.

Jean Piaget (1973) spent most of his life observing children and their interactions with their environment. His theory of cognitive development helps to explain that language acquisition is influenced by more general cognitive attainments. As children explore their environment they interpret and give meaning to the events that they experience. The child's need to interact with immediate surroundings and to manipulate objects is critical to language development. From a Piagetian view, language reflects thought and does not necessarily shape it.

Lev Vygotsky (1962, 1978), the acclaimed Russian psychologist, also viewed children as active participants in their own learning. However, at some point in their early development, children begin to acquire language competence; as they do so, language stimulates cognitive development. Gradually they begin to regulate their own problem-solving activities through the mediation of egocentric speech. In other words, children carry on external dialogues with themselves. Eventually external dialogue gives way to inner speech.

According to both Piaget and Vygotsky's views, children must be actively involved to grow and learn. Merely reacting to the environment isn't enough. An important milestone in a child's development, for example, is the ability to analyze means-end relationships. When this occurs children begin to acquire the ability to use language to achieve goals.

Observe the nonlanguage activity of infants. Babies learn to scream or point whenever they want something. Parents rarely ever misunderstand a baby's "wants." But later, as infants grow into toddlers, they learn to use language as an instrument for their intentions: "I want . . ." becomes a favorite phrase. No wonder M.A.K. Halliday (1975) described oral language development as a "saga in learning to mean." Children learn to act and interact in meaningful ways. Learning to mean is a powerful drive. As children learn what language can do for them, they begin to learn its form. Each child's "saga" highlights the commonsense notion that language is social.

The Social Bases for Language.   In the child's first several years, skill in spoken language develops naturally and easily. Children discover what language does for them. They learn that language is a tool that they can use and understand in interactions with others in their environment. They also learn that language is intentional; it has many purposes. Among the most obvious is communication. The more children use language to communicate, the more they learn the many special functions it serves.

Halliday (1975) viewed language as a reflection of what makes us uniquely human. His monumental work explored how language functions in our day-to-day interactions and serves the personal, social, and academic facets of our lives. Frank Smith (1977) expanded Halliday's functions of language by describing ten of its uses. He proposed that "the uses to which language is put lie at the heart of language comprehension and learning." The implications of this proposition for learning to read will become apparent throughout this book.

The ten uses of language are described below (Smith, 1977, page 640):

1. *Instrumental:* "I want." (Language as a means of getting things, satisfying material needs.)
2. *Regulatory:* "Do as I tell you." (Controlling the behavior, feelings, or attitudes of others.)
3. *Interactional:* "Me and you." (Getting along with others, establishing relative status. Also, "Me against you"—establishing separateness.)
4. *Personal:* "Here I come." (Expressing individuality, awareness of self, pride.)
5. *Heuristic:* "Tell me why." (Seeking and testing knowledge.)
6. *Imaginative:* "Let's pretend." (Creating new worlds, making up stories, poems.)
7. *Representational:* "I've got something to tell you." (Communicating information, descriptions, expressing propositions.)
8. *Divertive:* "Enjoy this." (Puns, jokes, riddles.)
9. *Authoritative/contractual:* "How it must be." (Statutes, laws, regulations, agreements, contracts.)
10. *Perpetuating:* "How it was." (Records, histories, diaries, notes, scores.)

Children recognize the meaningfulness of written language once they become aware of its uses. As Halliday (1975) noted, if children have difficulty learning to read, it is probably because beginning instruction often has had little to do with what they have learned about the uses of oral language.

Psycholinguistics and Reading. A psycholinguistic view of reading and learning to read combines an understanding of how language works with how humans learn. A reader acts upon and interacts with written language in an effort to make sense out of an author's message. Reading is not a passive activity, but an active thinking process that takes place behind the eyes. The reader searches for information cues from the text and constructs meaning. As we explain in more detail later in the chapter, language is made up of three systems: *semantics* (meaning), *syntax* (grammar), and *graphophonemics* (letter-sound correspondence). When systems of language are isolated from one another, learning to read becomes more difficult than it needs to be.

Sociolinguistics and Reading. A sociolinguistic perspective helps us to view the reading process as a transaction between reader and author. Reading is a "give-and-take" exchange between an author, who must have a sense of the audience, and a reader, who must read with a sense of the author.

Because reading is uniquely human, learning to read requires sharing, interaction, and collaboration. Parent/child, teacher/child, and child/child relations and participation patterns are essential in learning to read. To what extent do children entering school have experience operating and communicating in a group as large as that found in the typical classroom? Children must learn the ropes. In many cases, kindergarten may be the first time when children must follow and respect the rules that govern how to operate and cooperate in groups. They must know not only how and when to work independently versus share and participate with one another; they must also learn the rules that govern communicative behavior.

Communicative competence, as defined by Hymes (1974), develops differently in children because they have not all had the same set of experiences or opportunities to engage in communication in the home or in the community. Some preschoolers have acquired more competence than others as to *when to* and *when not to speak,* and as to *what to talk about, with whom, where,* and in *what manner.* As hard as it may appear from an adult perspective, the sociolinguistic demands on a five- or six-year-old are staggering.

Since a large part of learning to read will depend on the social context of the classroom, opportunities must abound for discussions and conversations among teacher and child and children and other children. Within this context, children must show: (1) an eagerness to be independent; (2) an unquenchable zest to explore the new and unknown; (3) the courage to take risks, try things out, experience success as well as some defeat; and (4) the enjoyment of being with others and learning from them (Gans, 1963).

Kay, a kindergarten teacher with over twenty-five years of professional experience, confided in us her "secret" for teaching reading: "A hug for every child and lap-time whenever it's needed." Every child has a need for acceptance, love and affection, and individual attention. Certainly children differ in their emotional make-up and feelings of worth. But no child needs ever to experience overwhelming failure or rejection in learning to read.

Models of the Reading Process

Explicit theories are "operationalized" by reading models. Models of the reading process often depict the act of reading as a communication event between a sender (the writer) and a receiver of information (the reader). Generally speaking, language information flows from the writer to the reader in the sense that the writer has a message to send and transmits it through print to the reader who then must interpret its meaning. Reading models have been developed to describe the way readers use language information to construct meaning from print. *How* a reader translates print to meaning is the key issue in the building of models of the reading process. This issue has led to the development of three classes of models: *Bottom-Up, Top-Down,* and *Interactive.* A brief definition of each type of reading model follows.

Bottom-Up Models of Reading. These are models of reading that assume that the process of translating print to meaning begins with the print. The process is initiated by decoding graphic symbols into sounds. Therefore, the reader first identifies features of letters; links these features together to recognize letters; combines letters to recognize spelling patterns; links spelling patterns to recognize words; and then proceeds to sentence, paragraph, and text level processing.

Top-Down Models of Reading. These models of reading assume that the process of translating print to meaning begins with the reader's prior knowledge. The process is initiated by making predictions or "educated guesses" about the meaning of some unit of print. Readers decode graphic symbols into sounds to "check out" hypotheses about meaning.

Interactive Models of Reading. These are models of reading that assume that the process of translating print to meaning involves making use of both prior knowledge and print. The process is initiated by making predictions about meaning and/or decoding graphic symbols. The reader formulates hypotheses based upon the interaction of information from semantic, syntactic, and graphophonemic sources of information.

The terms "top-down," "bottom-up," and "interactive" are used extensively in the fields of communication and information processing. When these terms are used to describe reading, they also explain how language systems operate in reading.

The Semantic System. Meaning is at the core of the reading process. Semantic information reflects the background knowledge and experiences, conceptual understandings, attitudes, values, skills, and procedures a reader brings to a reading situation.

Children use their experiences to give meaning to new events and experiences. *Schema* is a technical term used by cognitive psychologists to describe how humans organize and store information in their heads. *Schemata* (the plural of *schema*) have been called "the building blocks of cognition" (Rummelhart, 1982) and "a cognitive map to the world" (Neisser, 1976) because they represent elaborate networks of concepts, skills, and procedures that we use to make sense of new stimuli, events, and situations.

For example, do you possess the semantic information needed to interpret the following passage?

The procedure is quite simple. First you arrange things into different groups. Of course, one pile may be sufficient depending on how much there is to do. If you have to go somewhere else due to lack of facilities that is the next step, otherwise you are pretty well set. It is important not to overdo things. That is, it is better to do few things at once than too many. In the short run this may not seem important but complications can easily arise. A mistake can be expensive as well. At first the whole procedure will seem complicated. Soon, however, it will become just another facet of life. It is difficult to foresee any end to the necessity for this task in the immediate future, but then one can never tell. After the procedure is completed one arranges the materials into different groups again. They can be put into their appropriate places. Eventually they will be used once more, and the whole cycle will then have to be repeated. However, this is part of life. (Bransford and Johnson, 1973, page 400)

Upon first reading, Bransford and Johnson's passage may seem difficult to understand unless you were able to activate an appropriate schema. How many of you recognized that the passage had to do with washing clothes? Once a schema for washing clothes is activated, the words and phrases in the passage take on new meaning. Now try rereading the passage. Upon rereading, you will probably react by saying, "Aha! Now that I know the passage is about washing clothes, it makes sense!" Ambiguous words such as "procedure" and word streams such as "A mistake can be expensive" are now interpreted within the framework of what you know about washing clothes. The more you know about washing clothes, the more comprehensible the passage becomes. When readers activate appropriate schema, *expectations* are raised for the meaning of the text. Your expectations for the passage above help you to anticipate meaning and to relate information from the passage to existing knowledge.

The more we hear, see, read, or experience new information, the more we refine and expand existing schemata within our semantic language system. The illustration in Figure 1.2 below shows how this happens when a reader interacts with text information.

The Syntactic System. Besides having semantic knowledge, readers possess knowledge about how language works. *Syntactic information* is provided by the grammatical relationships within sentence patterns. In other words, readers use their knowledge of the meaningful arrangement of words in sentences to help construct meaning from text material.

The arrangement or order of words provides important information cues during reading. For example, although children may be able to read the words,

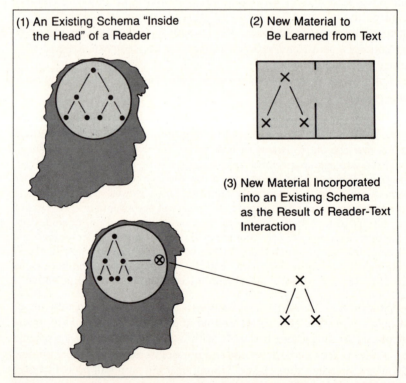

Figure 1.2 Schematic Representation Showing the Connections Made Between New Information and an Existing Schema

"*ran race the quickly children the,*" they would make little sense out of what they read. The meaning is not clear until the words are arranged like so, "*The children quickly ran the race.*" In addition, a reader uses syntactic information to anticipate a word or phrase which "must come next" in a sentence because of its grammatical relationship to other words in the sentence: "I saw a red _____." Most children reading this sentence would probably fill in the blank with a noun, because they intuitively know how language works.

The Graphophonemic System. The print itself provides readers with a major source of information: the graphic symbols or black squiggly marks on the page represent the relationship between speech sounds and letters. The more experiences readers have with written language, the more they learn about regular and irregular sound-letter relationships. Experienced readers acquire sufficient knowledge of sounds associated with letter symbols that they do not have to use all the available graphic information in a word in order to decode or recognize it.

How Do Models of Reading Differ?

Models of reading attempt to describe how readers use semantic, syntactical, and graphophonemic information in translating print to meaning. It is precisely in these descriptions that bottom-up, top-down, and interactive models of reading differ. Figures 1.3 and 1.4 *generally* show the flow of information in each kind of reading model. Note that the illustrations are general depictions of information processing during reading and do not refer specifically to models such as those found in *Theoretical Models and Processes of Reading* (1985).

Bottom-Up Models. As illustrated in Figure 1.3, the process of deriving meaning from print in bottom-up models is triggered by graphic information embedded in print. This is why bottom-up models are described as being "data driven." Data in this case are the letters and words on the page. A prototype model for bottom-up processing was constructed by Gough (1976), who attempted to show what happens in "one second of reading." In Gough's model, reading involves a series of steps that occur within milliseconds in the mind of the reader. The reader takes one "linguistic step" after another, beginning with the recognition of key features in letters and continuing letter-by-letter, word-by-word, sentence-by-sentence until reaching the top: the meaning of the text being read.

The reading model by Laberge and Samuels (1976) is also essentially bottom-up. However, the Laberge-Samuels model incorporates the idea of *automaticity*. The concept of automaticity suggests that humans can attend to only one thing at a time but may be able to process many things at once so long as no more than one requires attention. Automaticity is similar to putting an airplane on automatic pilot and freeing the pilot to direct his or her attention to other things.

In reading, *decoding* and *comprehending* vie for the reader's attention. Readers must learn to process graphophonic information so rapidly that they are free to direct attention to comprehending the text material for meaning.

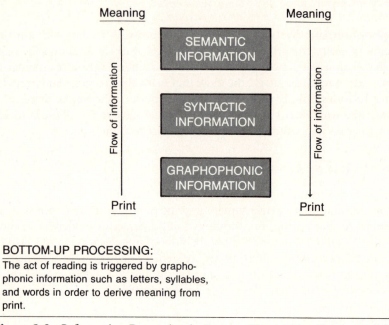

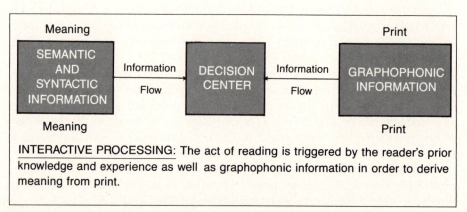

Figure 1.3 Information Processing in Bottom-Up and Top-Down Models
of Reading

Figure 1.4 Information Processing in Interactive Models of Reading

The young reader is similar to the novice automobile driver. When learning to drive a car, the beginner finds the mechanics of operating the automobile so demanding that he or she must focus exclusively on driving. However, with practice the skilled driver pays little conscious attention to the mechanics of driving and is able to converse with a passenger or listen to the radio. Likewise, the beginning reader must practice decoding print to speech so rapidly that decoding becomes "automatic." As beginners become more fluent in decoding, they can devote their attention to comprehending the writer's message.

Top-Down Models. Top-down models emphasize that information processing during reading is triggered by the reader's prior knowledge and experience in relation to the writer's message. Obviously there are no pure top-down models because readers must begin by focusing on print. As opposed to being "data driven," top-down models are said to be "conceptually driven." That is to say, ideas or concepts in the mind of a reader trigger information processing during reading. As Frank Smith (1979) put it, "The more you already know, the less you need to find out" (page 15). In other words, the more readers know in advance about the topic to be read, the less they need to use graphic information on the page.

To get a better idea of how reading is "conceptually driven," read the following story:

Flan and Glock

Flan was a flim.
Glock was a plopper.
It was unusual for a flim and a plopper to be crods, but
Flan and Glock were crods. They medged together.
Flan was keaded to moak at a mox. Glock wanted to kead
there too. But the lear said he could not kead there.
Glock anged that the lear said he could not kead there
because he was a plopper.

Although you've never heard of Flan and Glock nor know what a flim or a plopper is, it is not difficult to interpret from this short story that Glock was discriminated against. How did you figure this out? Your knowledge of capitalization may have led you to hypothesize that Flan and Glock are proper names. Knowledge of grammar, whether intuitive or overt, undoubtedly helped you to realize that flim, plopper, crods, and mox are nouns and that medged and keaded are verbs. Finally, your knowledge of the world led you to predict that since the lear said, "Glock could not kead there because he was a plopper" Glock probably is a victim of discrimination.

Note that these interpretations of the story are "educated guesses." However, both prior knowledge and graphophonic information were required to make these guesses. From our perspective, reading is rarely totally top-down or bottom-up. A third class of models helps to explain the interactive nature of the reading process.

Interactive Models. Neither prior knowledge nor graphophonic information is used exclusively by readers. Interactive models suggest that the process of reading is initiated by formulating hypotheses about meaning *and* by simultaneously decoding letters and words. According to Kamil and Pearson (1979), readers assume either an active or passive role, depending upon the strength of their hypotheses about the meaning of the reading material. If readers bring a great deal of knowledge to the material, the chances are that their hypotheses will be strong and that they will process the material actively, making minimal use of graphophonic information. Passive reading, on the other hand, often results when readers have little experience with and knowledge of the topic to be read. They rely much more on the print itself for information cues.

Effective readers know how to interact with print in an effort to understand a writer's message. Effective readers adapt to the material based on their purposes for reading. Purpose dictates the strategies that readers use to translate print to meaning. Two of the most appropriate questions that readers can ask about a selection are, "What do I need to know?" and, "How well do I already know it?" These two questions help readers to establish purposes for reading and formulate hypotheses during reading. The questions also help decide how to *coordinate* prior knowledge and graphophonic information.

Note that the models of reading just described don't take into consideration the social nature of reading and learning to read. In this sense, they're incomplete. However, models are useful in some respect in helping you to reflect on your beliefs and assumptions about reading instruction.

THINKING REFLECTIVELY
ABOUT READING

Your beliefs about how students learn to read lie on a continuum between concepts that reflect bottom-up models of reading and concepts that reflect top-down models of reading. By participating in the Conceptual Framework of Reading Interview, you will get a general indication of where your beliefs about learning to read lie on the continuum illustrated in Figure 1.5.

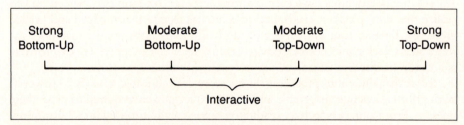

Figure 1.5   Beliefs About Reading Fall on a Continuum

If you are a pre-service teacher studying reading for the first time, you may find it difficult to answer some of the questions in Form A. However, we encourage you to respond to all of the questions based on whatever sources of knowledge and beliefs you currently hold about the reading process and how it should be taught. Knowledge sources may include your own school experiences, observations in the field, experiences as a reader, and previous study. Toward the end of the semester, you may wish to respond to the interview questions again. This will provide a good measure of the growth you have made in thinking about reading and learning to read. Stop reading now; study the directions and respond to Form A or Form B of the Conceptual Framework of Reading Interview in Box 1.1.

Interpreting the Interview

In order to determine your conceptual framework of reading, study the descriptions below of a Bottom-Up Conceptual Framework of Reading and a Top-Down Conceptual Framework of Reading. Then compare each answer to the interview questions to the descriptions given. Each response should be judged to be *bottom-up* (BU), *top-down* (TD), or *not enough information* given to clearly determine if it is bottom-up or top-down (NI).

One way to analyze the responses to the interview is to ask, "What unit of language is emphasized in the response?" The smallest units of written language are letters; the largest unit, the entire selection. Think of written language as concentric boxes. In Figure 1.6, the largest box is the entire text selection. It could be a story, a poem, an article on the Civil War. This unit of language is made up of *paragraphs,* which are made up of *sentences,* which are made up of *words,* which are made up of *letters.*

Now ask yourself as you judge your responses, "What unit of language did I stress?" For example, if you said that your major instructional goal "is to increase students' ability to associate sounds with letters," then the unit of language emphasized suggests a bottom-up (BU) response. Bottom-up responses are those that emphasize *letters* and *words* as the predominant units of language.

On the other hand, a top-down response (TD) would be appropriate if you had said that your major instructional goal is to "increase students' ability to read library books or other materials on their own." In this response, the unit of language involves the entire selection. Top-down responses emphasize sentences, paragraphs, and the selection itself as the predominant units of language.

An example of a response that does not give enough information (NI) is one in which you might have said, "I tell the student to figure out the word." Such a response needs to be probed further during the interview by asking, "How should the student figure out the word?"

There are sample responses for each question and their ratings in Appendix A, "Guidelines for Analyzing the Conceptual Frameworks of Reading Interview," in the back of the book. These responses are summaries of those given in the study in which the Conceptual Framework of Reading Interview was validated (Gove, 1981).

BOX 1.1
Conceptual Framework of Reading Interview

Directions: Select *Form A* of the interview if you are preparing to become a teacher. Select *Form B* of the interview if you are presently a teacher. Read each question, thinking in terms of *your own* classroom: whether it is the one in which you plan to teach or the one in which you now teach. As you respond to each question, explain *what* you (would) do and *why* you (would) do it.

FORM A: PRE-SERVICE TEACHERS

1. You have just signed a contract for your first teaching position in an elementary school. Which goals for reading instruction do you feel most confident in making progress in during the school year?

2. Suppose a student is reading orally in your class and makes an oral reading error. What is the first thing you will probably do? Why?

3. Another student in your class is reading orally and doesn't know a word. What are you going to do? Why?

4. You have read about and probably tried out different kinds of strategies and activities for teaching students to read. Which ones do you feel will be the *most* important in your classroom? Why?

5. What kinds of activities do you feel your students should be involved in for the *majority* of their reading instructional time? Why?

6. Here are the typical steps in the Directed Reading Activity (DRA) as suggested in basal reader manuals: (1) Introduction of Vocabulary, (2) Motivation or Setting Purposes, (3) Reading, (4) Questions/Discussion after Silent Reading, (5) Skills Practice for Reinforcement.

   Rank these steps in order from *most* important to *least* important (not necessarily in the order you will follow them).

7. Is it important to introduce new vocabulary words *before* students read a selection? Why or why not?

8. Suppose your new students will be tested to give you information to help you decide how to instruct them in reading. What would this diagnostic test include and what kind of information would you hope that it gives you about your students?

9. During silent reading, what do you hope your students will do when they come to an unknown word?

10. Look at the oral reading mistakes which are underlined below on these transcripts of three readers. Which of the three readers would you judge as the best or most effective reader (Harste and Burke, 1977)?

channel   channel

READER A   I live near this <u>canal</u>. Men haul things up and down the <u>canal</u> in big boats.

2. candle

1. ca   candle

READER B   I live near this <u>canal</u>. Men haul things up and down the <u>canal</u> in big boats.

2. channel

1. ca   cannel

READER C   I live near this <u>canal</u>. Men haul things up and down the <u>canal</u> in big boats.

FORM B: IN-SERVICE TEACHERS

1. Of all the goals for reading instruction that you have in mind as a teacher, which one(s) do you think you have made good progress toward accomplishing this year? Explain why.

2. What do you usually do when a student is reading orally and makes an oral reading error? Why?

3. What do you usually do when a student is reading orally and doesn't know a word? Why?

4. You probably use different kinds of strategies and activities in teaching reading. Which ones do you feel are the *most* important for your students? Why?

5. What kinds of activities do you feel students should be involved in for the *majority* of their reading instructional time? Why?

6. Here are the typical steps in the Directed Reading Activity (DRA) as suggested in basal reader manuals: (1) Introduction of Vocabulary, (2) Motivation or Setting Purposes, (3) Reading, (4) Questions/Discussion after Silent Reading, (5) Skills Practice for Reinforcement.

   Rank these steps in order from *most* important to *least* important (not necessarily in the order you follow them).

7. Is it important to introduce new vocabulary words *before* your students read a selection? Why or why not?

8. Suppose your students were tested to provide you with information which helped you decide how to instruct them in reading. What did diagnostic testing include and what kind of information did it give you about your individual students?

9. During silent reading, what do you hope your students do when they come to an unknown word?

10. Look at the oral reading mistakes which are underlined on the transcripts of three readers. (These are the same as on item 10 of the pre-service form). Which of these three readers do you judge as the best or most effective reader?

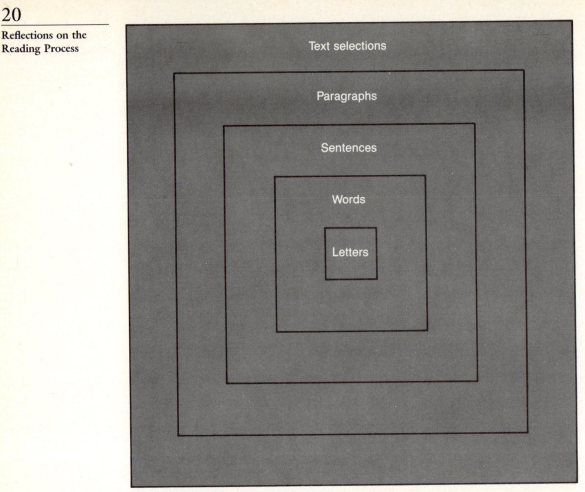

Figure 1.6 Units of Written Language

Descriptions of Conceptual Frameworks of Reading

A Bottom-Up Conceptual Framework. Teachers who have a bottom-up conceptual framework believe that students must decode letters and words before they are able to derive meaning from sentences, paragraphs, and larger text selections. Consequently, they view reading acquisition as mastering and integrating a series of word identification skills. Letter/sound relationships and word identification are emphasized instructionally. Because recognizing each word is believed to be an essential prerequisite to being able to comprehend the passage, accuracy in recognizing words is seen as important. If you hold a bottom-up conceptual framework, you may consider the practice of correcting oral reading errors as important in helping children learn to read. Or you may believe that helping students to read a passage over and over or to read orally into a tape recorder are important instructional activities because they develop accurate word recognition. Teachers who hold bottom-up conceptual frameworks of reading emphasize the teaching of subskills in a sequential and orderly manner.

A Top-Down Conceptual Framework. Teachers who hold this framework consider reading for meaning an essential component of all reading instructional situations. Therefore, they feel that the majority of reading/language arts instructional time should involve students in meaningful activities in which they read, write, speak, and listen. They may also emphasize the importance of students choosing their own reading material and enjoying the material they read. Sentences, paragraphs, and text selections are the units of language emphasized instructionally. Since recognizing each word is not considered an essential prerequisite to comprehending the passage, word errors during oral reading may not be corrected. Instead, you may advocate noninterference during oral reading or encourage a student to use the context or meaning of the passage to determine unrecognized words.

Table 1.1 summarizes the beliefs defining the bottom-up and top-down conceptual frameworks of reading.

TABLE 1.1

**Beliefs Defining Bottom-Up and Top-Down Conceptual
Frameworks of Reading**

	Bottom-Up Conceptual Framework of Reading	Top-Down Conceptual Framework of Reading
Relationship of Word Recognition to Comprehension	Believe students must recognize each word in a selection to be able to comprehend the selection.	Believe students can comprehend a selection even when they are not able to recognize each word.
Use of Information Cues	Believe students should use word and sound-letter cues exclusively to determine unrecognized words.	Believe students should use meaning and grammatical cues in addition to graphic cues to determine unrecognized words.
View of Reading Acquisition	Believe reading acquisition requires mastering and integrating a series of word recognition skills.	Believe students learn to read through meaningful activities in which they read, write, speak, and listen.
Units of Language Emphasized Instructionally	Letters, letter/sound relationships, and words.	Sentences, paragraphs, and text selections.
Where Importance Is Placed Instructionally	View accuracy in recognizing words as important.	View reading for meaning as important.
Evaluation	Think students need to be tested on discrete subskills.	Think students need to be tested on the amount and kind of information gained through reading.

Rating Your Conceptual Framework of Reading

After you have judged each response to the interview questions using the guidelines in Appendix A, check the appropriate column on the rating sheet below for each interview probe.

Rating Sheet for Conceptual Framework of Reading Interview

Interview Probe	Rating Scale		
	BU	TD	NI
1. Instructional goals			
2. Response to oral reading when reader makes an error			
3. Response to oral reading when a student does not know a word			
4. Most important instructional activity			
5. Instructional activities reader should be engaged in most of the time			
6. Rank ordering of steps in a reading lesson			
7. Importance of introducing vocabulary words before students read			
8. Information from testing			
9. How a reader should respond to unfamiliar words during silent reading			
10. Rationale for best reader			

An overall rating of your conceptual framework of reading is obtained from the chart below and shows where you fall on the beliefs about reading continuum in Figure 1.5, page 16.

Rating Chart

STRONG BOTTOM-UP   gave zero or one top-down response (the rest of the responses are bottom-up or not enough information)

MODERATE BOTTOM-UP   gave two to four top-down responses

MODERATE TOP-DOWN   gave two to four bottom-up responses

STRONG TOP-DOWN   gave zero or one bottom-up response

What Does the Conceptual Framework of Reading Tell You?

Often teachers may vary in the connections they perceive between their instructional practices and assumptions about learning to read. In addition, some teachers are not aware of how specific practices are theoretically related. Analyzing your responses to the Conceptual Framework of Reading Interview is one way to see such relationships.

Meet several teachers whom we interviewed and who reflected on *what* they do to teach children to read and *why* they do it.

Connie is a first-grade teacher with over fifteen years of teaching experience. Here's what she says in examining her beliefs about reading and instructional practices.

In examining my beliefs, methods, and techniques as a reading teacher . . . I find that I have probably always held an interactive view of reading. However, I do feel that I began teaching closer to the bottom-up end of the beliefs continuum and have been moving slowly and steadily toward the top-down end. Now that I better understand what I have been doing, I feel much better about myself as a reading teacher.

Somehow, my undergraduate courses on how to teach reading seem merely a distant jumble of experience charts for language development or creative writing and diphthongs and digraphs for reading instruction. When I first began teaching, I remember relying heavily on the detailed directions in the teacher's manual, and using the basal materials supplied by the district. Frequently we were told to use the basal program as it was written. This reflected mostly a "bottom-up approach" to instruction. And this was how I taught.

Throughout the years, while still following the teacher's manuals in the various basal programs fairly closely, I find myself doing more and more "top-down activities" without fully realizing why they seem to work for my students and me. I can recall many times when the basal program just didn't seem to be working with certain students and I would try most anything to improve my students' reading ability and their enjoyment of books.

I remember one year when I was teaching first grade that I had a small group of students that were not learning to read well in the basal program. The teacher across the hall had the same problem so I combined her students with mine for a special reading class. Every Friday we would write a story or news report on chart paper with each child's contribution beginning with his name. Quickly I would copy our story on a duplicating master and make copies of it. Each student received a copy with his own sentence underlined. Surprisingly, they could read their sentences and their reading ability began to improve.

Although I still do teach phonics as part of reading instruction, I try to encourage my students to read much more than what is in the basal program. I worry less about their mastery of all of the word-attack skills. I try to plan activities which increase the students' enjoyment of reading as well as their reading ability. Sharing their reading and writing through the use of pictures, murals, tapes, filmstrips, "TV" productions and other student-made materials helps meet this objective.

Although I cannot see abandoning the basal reading program, the idea of combining the language experience approach with the basal program makes a lot of sense to me.

Helen teaches in the primary grades. Her main instructional goal has been for each child to make as much growth in reading as possible. Here is what she reflected on after taking part in the Conceptual Framework of Reading Interview:

I want children to have a good attitude toward reading and enjoy reading. Children must realize that reading is a necessary skill for survival and for seeking knowledge.

I teach each reading group differently, depending on the needs of the group. Introduction of vocabulary is very important to the low ability reading group. I go over new vocabulary with the average group and spend time on the words that are unfamiliar to them. The above average reading group may already know the words or have the necessary skills for sounding out the words, or use context of the sentences to help them.

Using a basal reader is only one of the tools I use to teach reading comprehension and other reading skills. Reading cannot be separated from the other language arts. Writing, speaking, and listening are all a part of a total reading program. A primary reading program should give as many opportunities as possible to read. So I introduce my students to many types of literature so that they will want to continue to read for their own personal satisfaction. Some other activities I use are sustained silent reading time, games, chart stories, creative writing using personal interests and experiences, listening skills, poetry, dramatic, and art activities.

The school library is an important part of what I do. I involve parent volunteers and high school students to listen to the children's book reports each week. This activity uses comprehension skills, oral reading, speaking skills, and, many times, written language skills.

Keeping a log of the children's reading creates excitement among the children. Last year each child had a booklet titled "Treasure Chest of Reading." Each nine weeks they had a picture of a treasure chest. For each book they read and reported on they received a paper coin. The book's title was printed on the coin and glued on the treasure chest. The volunteer kept a written record of the books read and commented on their comprehension and their oral reading. At the end of the year the children had a complete list of the books they had read during the school year.

Ken had taught fifth- and sixth-graders for six years. He makes the assumption that all of his students need to become critical thinkers. Here's what he says:

The emphasis of my instruction lies in three or four areas. I allow an abundance of time for the act of reading, both silently and orally, which permits practice and skill development if needed. I provide exposure to a wide variety of reading material (fiction, nonfiction, poetry, magazines, newspapers, etc.). I also engage my students in a wide variety of activities designed to develop their comprehension skills as well as their critical thinking abilities. Most important, however, I find that a child will blossom and learn to read more efficiently if he has a positive self-concept. One of my main functions as a teacher is to feed as much positive reinforcement and guidance to my students. The child must believe that I care for him as an individual, so I must do this not only in an individualized way, but in a personalized way. The child must get the message that I believe that he is a unique being within the group setting.

As students often model teacher behavior, I attempt to show my students that I value reading through my actions. As well as engaging in the activities already mentioned, I read to my students on a daily basis, read with them when they have been given a reading assignment, and have my own personal reading material in class to read during silent reading time. I do spend some time in skill development when I feel it is necessary for the task at hand (or the level and needs of the student).

Lana is a pre-service teacher who is about to begin her student teaching experience. The interview was conducted toward the end of her reading methods course. Here's how she reflected on some of the questions from the interview.

I feel it is very important for students to "read for meaning." I will put heavy emphasis on comprehension activities in my classroom instruction. I truly believe, that regardless of the grade level of the students, comprehension is a must. Students need to understand what they are reading . . . the whole reading process seems useless to me unless students can understand, think about, and apply what they have read.

The first thing I will do when a child makes an oral reading error is to look at how serious the error is without necessarily correcting the student. Perhaps the error is very slight and doesn't interfere with the meaning of the passage. If the error is serious, such as a word that doesn't make sense in the passage, then I may ask the child to look at word clues or context clues.

The only time that I feel it's important to introduce vocabulary before a reading selection is when there are no possible ways for a student to use context clues, surrounding words or prior knowledge to "figure out" the word. If I feel the word is extremely difficult, or unfamiliar, or a name that is pronounced in French or Spanish, then I would introduce the word in some form of pre-reading vocabulary instruction. I feel that basal readers introduce too many vocabulary words in pre-reading instruction. I want to challenge the children to determine unknown words. I don't want to underestimate the students' potentials nor do I want them to underestimate their own potential.

Throughout this book we urge you to recognize that instructional decisions and practices are theoretically related. We encourage you to make the connections between your beliefs and practices and to expand your repertoire of instructional strategies. Moreover, we contend that teachers of reading should reflect a strong interactive view of the reading process. This view recognizes the definite interplay between the reader and the text and the situation in which learning occurs.

The way to discover the implicit theory that each of us has about reading is by talking about *what* we do and *why* we do it or by observing one another in a teaching situation and asking *why* we did what we did. In this sense, all teachers are theorists because they make instructional decisions daily.

SUMMARY

In this chapter we reflected on our beliefs about reading and how they relate to decisions we make about reading instruction. We proposed that teachers' implicit theories of reading are manifested in their daily instruction. We asked *what* teachers do and *why* they do it. Because we believe that all teachers are theorists in that they have reasons for their instructional decisions, we examined the reading process from a cognitive, linguistic, and social perspective and described three models that involve the processing of language information. Finally, and most importantly, we analyzed our conceptual frameworks of reading and shared in the personal reflections of four teachers.

Models of reading serve a useful purpose to anyone seriously interested in improving classroom instruction in reading. They help connect the theory with the practice. Models—bottom-up, top-down, and interactive—attempt to describe *how* readers use semantic, syntactic, and graphophonic information in translating print to meaning.

These descriptions of models, in turn, help us compare our beliefs with various theories of reading. We are better able to recognize that our instructional decisions and practices are related to our beliefs. It is important to take this first step—unveiling what we already believe—before we take further steps to improve the reading instruction we will deliver.

THE WORKSHOP

In the Classroom

Within the context of your reading methods class, the activities that follow will help you think about, extend, and apply some of the major ideas presented in this chapter.

1. Decide which of the statements listed below are more likely to be agreed with by teachers who hold moderate to strong bottom-up views of reading, and which are more likely to be agreed with by teachers who maintain moderate to strong top-down views of reading. In the space provided next to each statement, mark *B-U* to represent a bottom-up perspective of reading and *T-D* to signify a top-down perspective. In small groups, share your individual responses and elaborate on the reasons for your choices.

    _____ Learning to read is a process involving the mastery of various reading skills.

    _____ Precise word identification is a prerequisite to understanding what is read.

    _____ Proficient readers are likely to misread some words in a passage because they are constantly trying to predict what comes next.

    _____ Words are easier to read in the context of a sentence or paragraph than in isolation.

    _____ An effective reader is one who rapidly recognizes words in a reading selection.

    _____ Children's oral reading errors should always be corrected whenever the errors are made in an instructional situation.

2. Develop a position paper in support of either (a) or (b) below. The position you take should be based on what you have read in the chapter, outside readings, and your own experiences and observations.

    a. First-grade children need to be taught by practices consistent with a bottom-up view of reading.

    b. First-grade children need to be taught by practices consistent with an interactive to top-down view of reading.

3. Suppose a high school student interested in becoming a teacher asked you what you were studying in this textbook. How would you explain the concepts below in words that the high school student would understand?

reading process   implicit theories
psycholinguistics   schema
sociolinguistics   models of reading
functions of language   automaticity

Share your explanations with other members of the class.

4. Reflect on how you learned to read, the reading habits you have formed, home and school influences on your reading development, and the kinds of reading you do. Prepare an autobiographical sketch that captures these personal memories. How did you learn to read? What home reading experiences do you recall? What kinds of instructional activities and practices were you involved in as an elementary school child? Which ones do you recall fondly? Which, if any, do you recall with regret? In retrospect, what belief systems and views of reading and learning to read did your elementary school teachers seem to hold? Were you effectively taught how to handle the variety of reading tasks you are faced with in the real world? Share your autobiographical sketch with other members of the class. What differences in reading development and attitude are evident? What similarities exist?

In the Field

1. Using the conceptual framework of reading interview (Box 1.1), interview an elementary school teacher of reading. Analyze the teacher's implicit theories of reading as suggested in this chapter.

2. Observe an elementary school teacher teaching reading. (You may wish to watch the teacher interviewed in the above field exercise.) Record what you see and hear during reading instruction time. Based on the instructional practices you have observed and the interactions recorded between teacher and students, characterize the teacher's view of reading. If you observed the same teacher that you interviewed, explain whether her or his instructional practices and interactions with students are consistent with her or his conceptual framework of reading.

3. Interview several elementary school children at different grade levels to determine their perceptions of reading. Ask questions such as those from interviews developed by Kraus (1983) and Burke (1978).

   a. Suppose someone from another planet happened to land on earth and, seeing you reading, said, "What are you doing?" You would probably answer, "I'm reading." That person might then say, "What is 'reading'?" How would you reply?

   b. What would you do to teach someone to read?

   c. Who is the best reader you know? What makes him or her a good reader?

   d. How did you learn to read?

   e. What did your teacher or you do to help you learn?

   f. What do you do better in reading now than you could at the beginning of the year (or last year)?

   g. Your teachers do a lot of things to help children learn to read.

      (i) Tell me about the one thing that one of your teachers did that helped you *the most* to learn to read.

      (ii) Tell me about one thing that any one of your teachers did that did *not* help you very much.

h. If you're reading all by yourself and you come to a word you don't know, what do you do? Why? What do you do if that doesn't help? Why?

What concepts of reading do the children you interviewed seem to have? Do these concepts appear to differ according to children's grade levels? If so, in what ways? Share your interview findings with other members of the class.

Chapter 2

Approaches to Reading Instruction

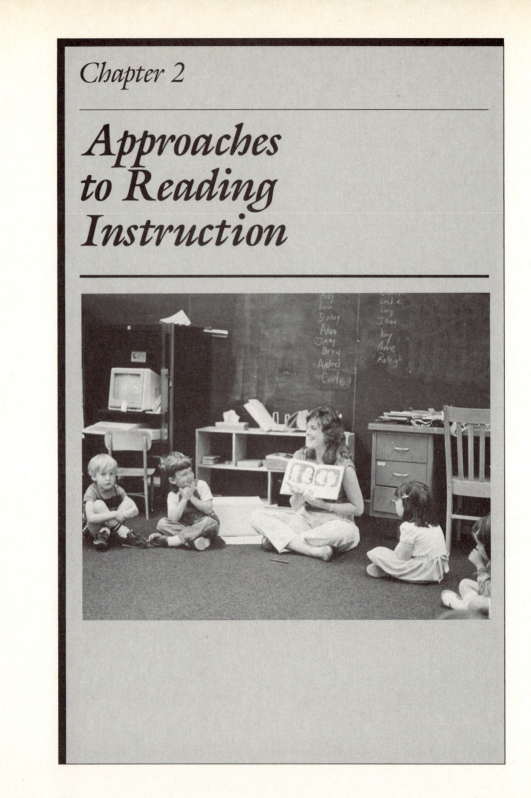

Approaching reading instruction brings to mind the following: "How do you catch a unique rabbit?" "You 'neak up on him." The parallel between this bit of humor and approaches to reading instruction is that regardless of the complexities involved in teaching children to read, teachers must find ways to do exactly that every day. It's all in the attitude: the mind-set, or expectation, of success in capturing the often-elusive prey. Teachers who have high expectations for children are confident that their approach to reading instruction will bring positive results. As you read this chapter, trace the connection between your own beliefs and major approaches to reading instruction. The goal of instruction, after all, remains fairly constant: children reading independently with purpose, understanding, and enjoyment.

I explained to Madeline's teacher on parent night that she was in the top group last year, but her fourth-grade teacher, Ms. Flynn, didn't let them go into the next level book when they finished because it was only April. If Madeline can pass the test, she'll be moved up.

Lee, mother of a fifth-grader

The kids work only on the skills they need. With these new prescription reading modules I can put my hands on materials they need on their own level.

Mrs. Winkley, a fourth-grade teacher

The whole class voted last week to study small furry animals for the next month. So, we are collecting pictures, stories, poems, books, models—everything we can find about the topic.

Mr. Kline, a fourth-grade teacher

What are the major approaches to reading instruction used in today's elementary classrooms? The three teachers mentioned above—Ms. Flynn, Mrs. Winkley, and Mr. Kline—each represent rather distinct instructional approaches. The overriding concern of Madeline's teacher is that students be placed in the appropriate level within the structure of the basal series the school is using. Skipping stories—let alone books at any given level—is frowned upon by teachers who ascribe to this logic. The basal reading approach is adhered to in Madeline's school; both parents and teachers have become comfortable with the norms that go along with it.

The next teacher, Mrs. Winkley, would say that her approach is an individualized one. She is providing, almost on a one-to-one basis, instruction on identified subskills to certain students. These skills have been prescribed by a pre-test analysis and coded in the accompanying boxes of materials for a fairly easy and systematic retrieval. Mrs. Winkley's students are mastering prescribed reading skills on an individual basis.

Interestingly, Mr. Kline describes his approach, too, as individualized. Although student consensus resulted in the whole class selecting furry animals for a month's instruction, individual students may opt to spend more or less time on a particular book or, for example, art project. Some may decide to produce book reports on fictional furry characters while other students trace the history and habits of the black squirrels' immigration to Kent, Ohio, from Canada. Mr. Kline's students are personally using their reading skill on an individual basis.

In Chapter 1 we uncovered some of our implicit *beliefs* about reading and learning to read, made them more explicit as we talked about them, and related them to *models* of the reading process. We took two of the three steps necessary to connect theory to practice: to relate our beliefs with instructional decisions. Now, we're ready to take a third step in which we try to understand approaches to reading instruction. In Figure 2.1 the process we are following is illustrated.

As we first began to analyze our beliefs, it became apparent that they were

Step 1	What are your *beliefs* about how students learn to read?
↓ Step 2	How do your beliefs reflect *models* of reading?
↓ Step 3	What are the major *approaches* to reading instruction?

Figure 2.1 Connecting Theory to Practice

not static and therefore were not easy to compartmentalize. We felt more comfortable placing them on a continuum from an emphasis on the letter (smallest unit of language) to an emphasis on the whole text selection (largest unit of language). Second, we examined our beliefs according to how they might correspond to models that theorists have constructed of the reading process. Again, we put them on a continuum, this time ranging from strong bottom-up to strong top-down. Figure 2.2 depicts these exercises.

   In this chapter, we continue this reflective process as we learn about approaches to reading instruction. There are major *approaches* that differ in degree and, hence, lend themselves to examination on a third continuum in Figure 2.3.

   Approaches to reading instruction range from subskill to holistic; these concepts will be explained in this chapter's first section. Next, the various kinds of approaches to instruction will be explained and related to each other on the subskill-holistic continuum. Each major approach is presented in a separate chapter later in this text: language-experience, basal reading, and individualized (as both prescriptive and personalized). In the third section of this chapter, instructional

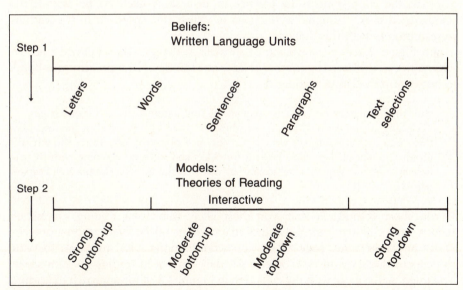

Figure 2.2 Analyzing Beliefs & Models

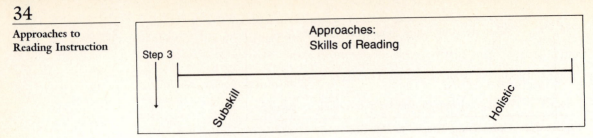

Figure 2.3 Analyzing Approaches

approaches will be distinguished from instructional *strategies*—the heart of decision-making—and the topics of the remaining chapters in this text.

HOLISTIC VS. SUBSKILL APPROACHES

Two formulas succinctly describe holistic and subskill approaches to reading instruction. Do you take the approach that reading is the equivalent of the sum of the teachable skills? Or do you take the approach that reading is greater than the sum of teachable skills?

FORMULA 1. $R = S_1 + S_2 + S_3 + \ldots S_n$

FORMULA 2. $R > S_1 + S_2 + S_3 + \ldots S_n$

If you chose formula 1, then you probably think that reading successfully presumes the acquisition of a "finite but rather large number of relatively distinct and specifiable abilities" (Estes and Johnstone, 1977, page 893). You would want materials for your students to practice or drill skills likely to be assessed on standardized tests. It might seem logical to depict this approach to the learning to read process with this drawing.

In Figure 2.4, the sequencing of subskills is depicted as a railroad track on which one tie is followed by another as far as one travels. This approach corresponds to bottom-up models of reading .

> with their emphasis on subskills, sequencing and automaticity at various stages. . . .
> "Teaching to weaknesses" is a set of objectives, one for each skill of interest; place
> them in a logical sequence; write a test for each objective; administer the test to a
> group; examine skill profiles, looking for peaks and valleys; beginning with the ear-
> liest skill in the sequence, remediate all the weaknesses. . . . (Kamil and Pearson,
> page 15)

If you chose formula 2, then you most likely think that reading successfully requires that children learn "strategies characteristic of the fluent reading process" (Estes and Johnstone, page 893). You would want topical materials for your students to discuss with each other what they have been reading to learn about. You might agree more with the depiction in Figure 2.5 of the approach to learning to read.

In Figure 2.5 the holistic expansion of reading skill through selected themes is depicted as a spider web in which strands grow both vertically and horizontally from a central core. This approach corresponds to top-down models of reading.

> ... "teaching to strengths" approach. That is determine those components of the reading process in which a student demonstrates proficiency. A teacher's greatest instructional concern becomes helping children develop resources for making meaning hypotheses on their own. For example, language-experience stories [and] text-previewing activities require students to make predictions (Kamil and Pearson, pages 15–16).

Underlying your preference for a holistic approach or a subskill approach to reading instruction is a question of enormous significance to the teaching of reading: Should reading be taught as a skill or as a set of separate subskills?

Figure 2.4 Subskills Sequencing

Figure 2.5 Holistic Expansion

Reading: Skill or Skills?

Is reading a skill, or is it a set of subskills? John Downing (1982), a noted reading researcher, wondered if reading could be defined as one or the other of these. He reasoned that if reading could be classified as either a skill or as a set of subskills, then all that is known in psychology about the nature of a skill and subskills could be applied to reading. As Downing surveyed the psychological literature, he found a comprehensive definition of a skill provided by McDonald (1965): "From a psychological point of view, playing football or chess or using a typewriter or the English language correctly demands complex sets of responses—some of them cognitive, some attitudinal, and some manipulative." McDonald stressed that it is not merely a matter of motor behavior. The player must also understand the game, enjoy playing it, and have appropriate attitudes about playing the game. McDonald went on to state: "The total performance . . . is a complex set of processes—cognitive, attitudinal, and manipulative. This complex integration of processes is what we usually mean when we refer to 'skill' (page 387)."

Downing (1980) pointed out that psychologists have technical terms for a part of a skill, that is, *subskills* or *subroutines*. Maybe that is what these reading skills are. What do psychologists mean by "subskills" or "subroutines" of a skill?

Does the skill of reading have subskills or prerequisite skills that students need to be able to perform in order to read? Downing (1980) made a very strong statement about the so-called reading skills described in many reading method texts: "These bits of alleged behavior touted by the 'accountability-behavioral management system movement' (Artley, 1980, page 547) mostly have no basis in objective data from studies of actual reading behavior. In other words, these so-called 'reading skills' are largely mythical (page 535)."

Taking a more moderate stance than Downing, Samuels (1976) believed that it may be possible to determine a true hierarchy of subskills in reading. However, he admitted, "Despite the fact that . . . commercial reading series, with their scope and sequence charts, order the reading tasks as if we did know the nature of the learning hierarchy in reading, *the sad truth is that the task is so complex that a validated reading hierarchy does not exist* (page 174, emphasis added)."

Yet all basal reading programs—in fact, just about all published reading programs—have scope and sequence charts which are lists of "skills' to be taught. When these scope and sequence charts or management systems are compared, there is little agreement as to sequence. Some first-grade and kindergarten programs begin with the alphabet and then proceed through consonant sound/letter association and then begin introducing vowel sound/letter association. Others begin with rhyming elements and graphic shapes and then present some words and sound/letter associations. Likewise, there is little agreement to be found when comparing lists of skills of different commercial publishers for middle- and upper-grade reading programs. Stennett, Smyth, and Hardy (1975) reviewed a number of published reading programs and concluded *"none provide a sound rationale or adequate documentation for either the relevance of their skill content or the sequence of instruction* (pages 223–224, emphasis added)."

Several research studies have tested the validity of subskills of reading. These studies were empirical attempts to determine if skills such as "determining the number of syllables" are prerequisite subskills for reading as well as to determine if readers need to have these skills in order to read. McNeil (1974) tested 150 children aged seven to nine on competence in oral reading and fifteen subskills in word attack. Three subskills were *not* found to be prerequisites and a fourth was on the borderline of being classified as not being a prerequisite skill. Four other subskills were identified as "possibly necessary but not sufficient." The seven remaining subskills had been mastered by nearly all the competent readers and by only a few incompetent readers. McNeil pointed out, however, that it is possible that competent readers acquired these subskills after or as they learned to read, not as a prerequisite to reading.

When studies similar to this are conducted using mathematics skills such as the ability to add a two-digit number to a one-digit number, with regrouping, prerequisite skills are identified. For example, if students cannot add 43 + 9, they are unable to perform some of the prerequisite skills such as being able to add two one-place numbers, knowing the addition facts, or knowing how to regroup. Much of mathematics seems to be a set of subskills. Thus teaching children a set of prerequisite mathematical subskills will help them solve math problems. The skill of reading, though, is different from mathematics. The relationship between sets of subskills and the act of reading is not as clear-cut.

When Jeanne Chall wrote *Learning to Read: The Great Debate* (1967), the current debate focused on whether readers should be taught by a "code emphasis" approach (another name for a phonics approach) or by sight words at the beginning stages (which was labeled a "meaning emphasis" approach). Chall reviewed a large number of studies and came to the conclusion that phonics or decoding needs to be emphasized from the very beginning.

No sooner had publishers printed new "code emphasis" basal readers than the debate heated up again. A group of reading educators led by Kenneth Goodman (1973) conducted studies that demonstrated that the argument was much more than "code versus meaning emphasis." The argument was one of whether to approach reading instruction as a set of subskills or to teach reading as a communication process using whole language.

In the 1970s, the major research had little to do with the study of reading instruction. Instead, *reading as a process* dominated research (Vacca and Vacca, 1983). Because of the emphasis on basic research, teachers have been in the midst of an information explosion that has contributed to unprecedented theorizing and research on the reading process. By and large, work in psycholinguistics, socio-linguistics, and cognitive psychology has focused on reading as the search for and interpretation of meaning in print.

Drawing from this growing body of basic research, many reading educators maintain that reading needs to be taught as a language process and not merely as the sum of various phonic and comprehension subskills. Reading, taught as an active process of deriving meaning, is the major emphasis for approaches on the holistic side of the continuum.

In the mid-1980s, two major national reports verified that reading and learning to read are more involved processes than some educators believed. Reading is "a complex skill . . . a holistic act" according to the Commission on Reading's *Becoming a Nation of Readers* (1985, page 7). Instructionally speaking, this report later advised that " . . . no matter how children are introduced to words, very early in the program they should have experience with reading these words in meaningful texts" (page 43). The second report, *What Works: Research About Teaching and Learning*, recommended "direct experience with written language as requisite for reading" (1986, page 9).

In summary, views of reading instruction as mastering sets of subskills or as involving students in a holistic process can be traced to our beliefs as well as theories of reading discussed in Chapter 1. The view of learning to read by mastering subskills is based on the bottom-up belief that reading acquisition is mastering and integrating a series of word recognition and comprehension subskills. On the other hand, the view of reading instruction as creating opportunities for students to be involved in the holistic process of reading is based on the top-down and interactive belief that students learn to read through meaningful activities. These activities include reading, writing, speaking, and listening about things important to them. What, then, are the major approaches taken by teachers to create opportunities for their students in reading? This is addressed in the next section.

RANGE OF APPROACHES

The range of approaches to reading instruction may include several approaches within the subskill to holistic continuum. Reasonably speaking, however, a major approach should meet these two basic criteria: First, it is observable in actual

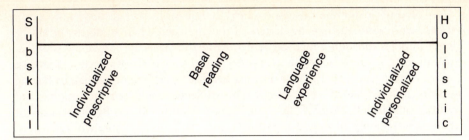

Figure 2.6   Range of Approaches

classroom instruction around the country; second, it is derived from a theoretical base that is top-down, bottom-up, or interactive. Adhering to these criteria, there are four major approaches to reading instruction: individualized-prescriptive; basal reading; language-experience; and individualized-personalized. Figure 2.6 illustrates their relative positions on the subskill-holistic continuum.

The term *individualizing reading instruction* has come to mean two very different approaches to teachers. One kind of individualization is associated with a bottom-up theory: Heavy emphasis is placed on prescribing linguistic and other sequential subskills. Another kind of individualization is associated with a top-down theory: Heavy emphasis is placed on personalizing instruction through literary genres. Consequently, the term *individualized reading* refers to two distinct approaches.

Basal reading occupies the central and broadest position on the continuum. Basal reading programs come the closest to an eclectic approach. That is, within the basal reading program itself some elements of the other approaches are incorporated. Yet basal reading programs, built on scope and sequence foundations, traditionally have been associated with bottom-up theory. This association has been modified over the years with the addition of language experience and literature activities.

Language experience, located on the holistic side of the continuum, is tied closely to an interactive or a top-down theory of reading and writing. This approach is often considered a kind of beginning reading approach, although adaptations and extensions into intermediate and middle grades are becoming more evident in classrooms.

Individualized-Prescriptive

This type of individualized instruction is often favored by teachers who devote large chunks of the reading period to work on phonics or linguistics. They focus on sound-letter relationship instruction advocated by linguists such as Bloomfield and Barnhart in *Let's Read: A Linguistic Approach* (1961). While there are some variations in the teaching procedures offered by the programs labeled *linguistic,* the stress by and large is on small language units such as letters, syllables, spelling patterns, and words.

The Bloomfield-Barnhart method (1961) emphasized that reading instruction should begin with teaching the letters of the alphabet. Then students should be taught phonics through a method similar to *analytic phonics*. In analytic phonics, students learn sound-letter relationships by seeing how parts of words sound alike and are written similarly. For example, teachers may teach the digraph *sh* by having students compare "*sh*ell" and "da*sh*." The students would see the graphic and auditory similarities in "di*sh*," "fi*sh*," and "wi*sh*." Bloomfield and Barnhart thought letter-sounds should be taught in sentence contexts, while comprehension was of secondary importance in the early stages of reading. Bloomfield and Barnhart believed that the major emphasis in beginning reading instruction should be on decoding, that is, associating the phonemes or sounds of our language with their most regular grapheme representations, or letters or groups of letters.

Fries is another linguist who endorsed this approach and co-authored a basal reader series, the *Merrill Linguistic Readers,* in 1966. Other linguistic programs published at about the same time include *SRA Basic Reading Series* (1964) published by Science Research Associates, the *Linguistic Readers* (1965) published by Harper & Row, and *Programmed Reading* (1963), a programmed linguistic series published by McGraw-Hill.

These programs include stories written so that there is a gradual introduction and numerous repetition of specific sound-letter relationships. The readers were comprised of sentences such as "The fat cat sat on the mat" and "The car was parked in the market." Patterns that were considered simpler such as the "cat, hat, mat" pattern were introduced before more difficult ones such as the "car, park, market" pattern.

Other linguistic programs advocated *synthetic phonics* rather than the analytic phonic approach. Whereas in the analytic phonic method students break words down into grapheme-phoneme (letter-sound) units, in synthetic phonics students build words up letter-by-letter. In using the synthetic phonic method, teachers show beginning readers that "c" goes with a /k/ sound, "a" goes with an /a/ sound, and "t" goes with a /t/ sound. When these phonemes or minimal sound units are blended together, the child would read "c-a-t — cat." This is where the term *sound it out* comes from. In using synthetic phonics, students "sound out" words in a letter-by-letter fashion.

The *Lippincott Basal Program* (1968) emphasized the teaching of synthetic phonics. *The Distar Program,* in use since the late seventies, also gives teachers explicit directions for teaching students by the synthetic phonics method.

Another characteristic associated with an individualized-prescriptive approach is *skills management*. Often, this involves the purchase and use of commercially boxed skill cards organized into prescription modules such as those Mrs. Winkley referred to at the beginning of this chapter.

Let's take a minute and look into Mrs. Winkley's fourth-grade class. It is September and Mrs. Winkley is eager to meet her students and begin teaching her favorite subject, reading. The week before school started, she and her colleagues attend an in-service class on a recently adopted skills management system to be used with their basal reader. During the in-service Mrs. Winkley hears that the school system is working toward adopting some "basic minimal standard" in both the teaching of mathematics and reading. In doing this, the school system will become more "accountable" for the students' education.

After a coffee break, the in-service program leader got around to what Mrs. Winkley wanted to know — how to actually use this skills-management system in her classroom. A list of behavioral objectives was given to her as well as mastery tests that were to be used to periodically test the students' performance on the set of objectives or subskills. She was told students have "mastered" a reading skill if they were able to correctly answer 80 percent of the items testing that skill. For each reading skill, she was given a list of workbook pages, ditto sheets, games, and other activities to use to drill students who had not mastered the reading skill, that is, had not passed the mastery test for that skill. Mrs. Winkley even was given a set of cards for each skill that could be sent home to get parents involved in drilling the child on needed skills.

After some consideration, Mrs. Winkley decided the skills management system made a lot of sense. She remembered last year teaching her middle reading group the skill of determining how many syllables were in words. She had drilled the whole group of students on this reading skill. Some of the students already seemed to know how to do this; others in the group struggled. "With this management system," she thought, "I will be able to know which students need to be taught particular skills and which students won't need further instruction in them."

Skills management systems usually include a sequentially ordered set of skills written as objectives, sets of tests to measure these objectives, directions for determining what level of achievement constitutes mastery, and resource files of specific workbook pages, dittos, games, and other activities that can provide instruction and practice for each of the skills. These systems also have a method of organizing and reporting which skills students have or have not mastered.

In addition to *phonics instruction* and *skills management,* a third characteristic is becoming associated with an individualized-prescriptive approach: *computer assisted instruction.*

Since the early 1980s, computer assisted instruction (CAI) has become a "hot topic" in the education business. With increasing advances in computer technology, schools are being supplied with microcomputers. Futurists envision that individual classrooms will one day have several terminals connected to a larger computer that serves the entire school. This school computer will be connected to a CPU serving the school district.

In the future, students will have access to microcomputers in schools similar to those presently under development at the Xerox Research Center in Palo Alto. These microcomputers are being designed to store and allow students access to the equivalent of an encyclopedia of information, to create artistic creations or musical compositions (Mason, Blanchard, and Daniel, 1983).

Books will *not* become obsolete and neither will teachers. Rather, microcomputers are another tool that teachers can use in teaching as discussed at length in Chapter 12. Books and the microcomputer terminals will simply be recognized as two sources of information for both students and teachers to use.

Specialized devices such as Speak-N-Spell, Speak-N-Read, the Talking Picture Book, and Alphamaster are beginning to appear in classrooms. Such battery-powered reading devices may become more widely accepted than their predecessors, plug-in devices that were hampered by inadequate wiring in many of our school buildings. By 1990, videodisc systems should become widely available in schools (Mason, Blanchard, and Daniel, 1983). TV monitors and videodiscs, similar to movie projectors of the 1970s, will be used by some teachers and not used by others.

Individualized instruction is presented from a historical perspective in Chapter 14. As a major approach to reading instruction it is observable in elementary classrooms in phonic lessons, skills practice, and some forms of computer assisted instruction. Individually prescribed instruction, akin to programmed learning, emanates from bottom-up models of the reading process.

Basal Reading

Basal reading programs, the dominant approach to classroom reading instruction, are examined at length in Chapter 10. Teachers who traditionally use the reading lesson or story with a small group of students during a specified time in a regular location are most likely to use the basal reading approach. They constitute the majority in terms of numbers of classroom teachers around the country using a particular approach.

Modern basals have management systems. Scope and sequence charts display skills to be taught and a timetable of levels that are keyed to grade levels. Another basic feature of basals programs is controlled vocabulary, which is especially evident in the early grades. This means that children are to be taught certain vocabulary words that appear in the basal stories. Both of these aspects of basal reading programs, the list of subskills to be taught in the scope and sequence charts and introducing students to the vocabulary words prior to each story, are evidence of bottom-up assumptions. These assumptions are that students learn to read by learning subskills and that students need to be able to pronounce words in a selection to be able to comprehend it.

In addition to having scope and sequence charts and controlled vocabulary, basal reading series outline a standard lesson framework with slight variations in differing basal programs. The Directed Reading Activity (DRA) is the common label for the lesson framework in basal series. The DRA has four major instructional components: (1) motivation and background building, (2) guided reading, (3) skill development and practice, and (4) follow-up and enrichment. These components are discussed in Chapter 10 and are important because they are based on interactive assumptions that students learn to read by reading, writing, and talking about meaningful topics. As a major approach to reading instruction, basal reading is easily observable in elementary classrooms in small reading groups. It spans a large segment on the subskills-holistic continuum due to its relationship to both bottom-up and interactive theories of reading. Basal reading, frequently described as eclectic, runs the gamut from word attack skills practice to extended and meaningful reading, discussing, and writing.

Language Experience

Teachers often use Language Experience in combination with other approaches to reading instruction. Language Experience is also, however, a major approach to teaching reading to children from kindergarten through second and into the intermediate grades. This approach is examined in several chapters throughout this textbook.

The Language Experience Approach (LEA) includes more than recording the ideas of first-graders after they have taken a trip to the school nurse or the zoo. It is planned and continuous activities such as individual- and group-dictated stories, building word banks of known words, creative writing activities, oral reading of prose and poetry by the teacher and students, directed reading-thinking lessons, investigating of interests using multiple materials, and keeping records of student progress.

Russell Stauffer (1970) and Roach Van Allen (1974) have been strong proponents of LEA. Allen has summed up the theory behind the language experiences from the young reader's point of view: What I think about, I can talk about; what I can say, I can write or someone can write for me; what I can write, I can read; and I can read what other people write for me to read.

Teachers who subscribe to LEA have common viewpoints about children and their language. For example, they probably would agree that children's oral and written expression is based on their sensitivity to classroom and home environments. Further, they would support children working with their *own* language.

Thus the Language Experience Approach is based on the idea that language should be used to communicate thoughts, ideas, meaning. It is very much an interactive approach to teaching reading. As such it is placed on the right side of the subskills-holistic continuum. Teaching strategies that are part of LEA are interspersed throughout this book. How to use dictated stories and word banks, the directed reading thinking procedure with comprehension strategies, and ways to extend children's writing and reading into more writing and reading are just a few examples of LEA-related instruction.

Individualized-Personalized

The individualized-personalized type of instruction is used by teachers who want to provide for individual student differences in reading abilities and at the same time focus on meaning, interest, and enjoyment. Veatch and Acinapuro (1966) designed a program for individualizing reading and articulated the "how-to's" of this approach. In this approach teachers encourage their students to personally select their own trade books (another name for popular books). The teacher has conferences once or twice per week with each student. During these conferences students might be asked to read aloud parts of the book they had read which they especially enjoyed. Teachers take notes on the type of miscues students make as they read. Also, students discuss with teachers words with which they had difficulty. The overall emphasis of the individualized program as described by Veatch and

Acinapuro is on meaning and on having students apply and extend the ideas in their reading.

Some proponents of the individualized reading program contend that reading skills should *not* be taught; they argue that these skills will be learned as the child reads (Farr and Roser, page 146). The main thrust of the individualized approach, even as explained in the 1960s, is that importance is placed on reading for meaning and for enjoyment. Studies report that children in classes in which the individualized approach to reading is used read more and read a greater variety of materials than children in other classes. Further, they read more for their own enjoyment and interest (McDonald et al., 1966).

In the late 1970s and early 1980s articles suggesting a literature base reappeared in reading instruction journals. The development of a literature base is the core of the personalized individual approach. Students are surrounded with books, and time is set aside for reading and talking about books. The teacher reads books to students and helps them read some of those same books as well as other books. Students act out and make things they read about.

In classrooms using literature in this way children delight in the exploits of Curious George, Madeline, Encyclopedia Brown, and Pippi Longstocking. The rationale is that an important part of classroom life should be *reading*: reading literature that makes children wonder, weep, laugh, shiver, and gasp.

Pieces of literature are used as springboards for writing. Children can write differing endings for stories or incidents in their own lives that reflect similar conflicts to ones about which they have read. Students also look at story structures such as the repetitive structure in "The Three Little Pigs" and devise stories using the same kind of structure. Further, the conflicts between characters in literature can be used to help students gain insights into their own life situations. Students are encouraged to write about these also.

Self-selection of trade books or literature books is part of personalizing reading through the individualized approach. Teachers hold conferences with individual students about the books they are reading. Other forms of organization are also used. For example, a group of students read and respond to the same piece of literature. Or students read different books with similar themes and then share and compare insights gained. Reading instruction delivered in this way emanates from assumptions about the reading process that are interactive and top-down. Thus the "other" side of the individualized-prescriptive approach is an individualized-personalized one which falls on the holistic side of our approach continuum. It depends on teachers who know children's literature and classroom organization. These are discussed at length in Chapters 9 and 14, respectively.

INSTRUCTIONAL STRATEGIES

We have connected theory to practice in this chapter by moving from our beliefs to models of reading and then to approaches for reading instruction. The final step is inserted in Figure 2.7 to illustrate the whole process we are using to connect theory to practice in teaching reading.

Step 1	What are your *beliefs* about how students learn to read?
↓	
Step 2	How do your beliefs reflect *models* of reading?
↓	
Step 3	What are the major *approaches* to reading instruction?
↓	
Step 4	Which instructional *strategies* will you decide to use?

Figure 2.7 Connecting Theory to Practice

Strategies are the key to reading instruction; they are the hour-by-hour, day-by-day evidence of what is really happening in the classroom. In Chapter 14 we present a discussion of how teachers individualize instruction through their selection of strategies and allocation of time to those strategies. In Chapter 15, our emphasis is on how to adapt instruction to meet children's special educational needs.

Often, teachers don't have a voice in choosing the major approach to instruction in their school. For instance, the district as a whole or their particular school may have recently adopted a new basal series and committed the entire staff to an in-service series on how to manage these materials. In fact, it would be more unusual today to find a school in which each teacher has the option of independently deciding which approach to use. It's only when teachers decide on specific strategies—that is, tactics or plans or practices—that they are making actual planning decisions about reading instruction.

Unlike the broader term, *approaches,* strategies for instruction are specific ways of providing direct and indirect instruction in reading. Some teachers employ dozens of strategies throughout the week's reading instruction; others tend to rely on a favorite few. Whatever the number of strategies in their repertoire, teachers tend to act consistently in the classroom. Although they may say that they prefer a variety of strategies, rarely do they mix strategies relating to opposite beliefs and theories of reading. Instead, practices reflect teachers' beliefs about reading.

How Practices Reflect Beliefs

Teachers' actions in their classrooms reflect their beliefs about reading and learning to read. To illustrate how differences in beliefs become evident in instruction, Gove designed a study (1982) of four teachers, who had differing beliefs about reading, using the same approach—basal reading.

The four teachers were chosen because when interviewed they produced clear reasons for *why* they followed specific practices. For example: "I do this because students need to learn the sounds that go with letters to be able to learn to read;" or, "I do this because recognizing each word in a story is not necessary to understand the story." Though these four teachers did not use the terms *bottom-up, top-down, subskills,* or *holistic,* they each were aware of differing philosophies for teaching reading; each advocated a preferred philosophy.

All four of the teachers taught in self-contained classrooms. Three taught second grade and one taught third grade. Three taught in an urban school system that used a single basal reader instructional program. One taught in a suburban school system that had a multibasal program. Two of the teachers had taught for five years, one for fifteen years, and one for seventeen years. All of the teachers were viewed as competent by their principals. The teachers showed interest in their students and seemed to have established good rapport with them.

The teachers were all given the same story, "War on Small Deer," and told to teach it as they would normally teach such a basal story. They each selected students to be in the teaching episodes, which were videotaped. Now let's examine the portions of teaching episodes of the four teachers which illustrate their differing approaches.

PAT

Pat began the lesson by holding up flash cards of phonograms like "ou," "ay," and "ui." She and the students chanted the sounds and rules associated with the letter clusters flashed. Pat then stated that the students were going to read a story, "War on Small Deer." She then led a discussion with the students on the phonogram "ar" in the word "war." They talked about how /ar/ is in the word "warm." The students then read the story and discussed with Pat what happened in the story. After this, Pat and her students did some "body spelling" which was devised by Pat. "Body spelling is a tool to break down words. It gives them power to sound out words," she said. "It helps readers who reverse letters."

In "body spelling" a word, the students touch a part of their body for each "sound" in the word. If the beginning sound is a single consonant, the students touch their left shoulders, saying the beginning sound. If the beginning sound is a blend, they touch their left ear. For the middle sound in the word, they touch a middle part of the body, that is, they would touch the top of their head for a short vowel. For the ending sound, they touch their right ear or shoulder depending on if the sound is a single consonant or a blend. She and the class have decided on further body spellings for such aspects of sound-letter associations as digraphs like "oo" and what to do for two- and three-syllable words.

CHRISTINE

Christine began the lesson by having her students pronounce and discuss the meaning of two vocabulary words from the story, "crocodile" and "huge." She also had the students read and discuss from a list of "past time words," words such as "want-wanted," "roar-roared," "push-pushed." Christine then showed the students a picture of a crocodile and asked them what they knew about crocodiles. She asked if they had ever played a trick on somebody; whether they would like to play a trick on a crocodile; and, if so, what trick they would like to play. Christine then asked the students what they thought would happen in the story and asked the students to read it. Like Pat, she led a question and answer recitation after students read the story. After the recitation, Christine had the students find descriptive words in the story like "small," "huge," and "dark."

JENNY

The third teacher who taught the story was Jenny. She began the lesson by asking her students to look over the story and find words with which they "might have trouble." Jenny wrote a sentence on the board containing each of the "trouble words." Then for each of the words she read "her sentence" from the board; asked students questions about letter clusters in the words and about the shape of the word; asked students to write the word and trace over it as she pronounced it. Finally, she asked the students to make up and write a sentence containing the word and the meaning of the word discussed.

Next Jenny showed the students a picture of a crocodile as Christine had done and discussed with the students their views of crocodiles. Then Jenny asked her students to listen to her read the story to find out what Small Deer wanted and how he tricked the crocodile. After some discussion of the plot of the story, Jenny asked her students to read the story silently and to keep in mind what happened in the story and to decide if they thought Small Deer was a person or an animal. Jenny and her students discussed the story further. Then Jenny and her students dramatized the story.

MARGARET

The fourth teacher, Margaret, did not begin the lesson by introducing specific words. Rather, she had her students think of words that would fit into the sentence "I saw a _____ at the zoo." The students mentioned animals such as *monkey, elephant, lion,* and *giraffe.* Margaret then asked them to read the sentence, filling in the blank with these animals. She next put the word "catch" on the board and asked why "catch" could not be put in the sentence. One of the students responded that "catch" wouldn't make sense in the sentence.

Margaret introduced the story by saying, "I have a story I'd like to share with you." She confided later that she wanted the students to construct as much as possible of the story through reading. For this reason, she did not give a lot of information about the story before the students began reading. In setting purposes for reading, Margaret said, "I'd like you to read the first paragraph to yourself. Keep in mind who is in the story and what they're starting out in the story doing."

Near the beginning of this teaching episode, as the students were reading, Margaret discovered that Kevin did not recognize three words that were important to the content of the story. At this point she wrote sentences on the board putting the words "river," "crocodile," and "water" in predictable contexts so that Kevin would recognize them. For example, she asked Kevin to read the sentence, "I will swim in the *river,*" and asked, "What makes sense in the sentence and begins with an 'r'?" With this help Kevin was able to recognize the word "river."

Then the students and the teacher read the story paragraph by paragraph, stopping to summarize what they knew about the story. In this way, the plot of the story was discussed. Margaret completed the lesson by asking the students to illustrate parts of the story.

Reflecting on the Teaching Episodes

Pat, Jenny, Christine, and Margaret did have similarities in how they taught the lesson. They all used aspects of the directed reading activity—introducing vocabulary or sound-letter associations, building background for reading, setting purposes for reading, reciting, or discussing the story, and extending with activities after the reading and discussing. The middle portions of all the four teaching episodes were also very similar. All four teacher-students groups discussed the plot of the story after the students had read the story.

Consider how the different instructional practices of the four teachers reflected their beliefs about how students learn to read, even though all of them used the same instructional approach: basal reading. Pat and Christine held bottom-up beliefs about how students learn to read. They believed that students learn to read by learning word recognition skills and that students need to recognize all the words in a selection to be able to read the selection. Christine, however, was somewhat more moderate in her practices than was Pat. These belief systems were uncovered during interviews *before* the videotaping.

Jenny and Margaret, on the other hand, held moderate top-down or interactive beliefs about learning to read. They emphasized listening, reading, writing, and talking about meaningful topics. Jenny was somewhat more moderate in her practices than was Margaret. The belief systems of Jenny and Margaret were also categorized *before* they were videotaped.

These teaching episodes can be further analyzed by considering which units of language the teacher focused on at the beginning and end of the episodes. At the beginning of the session, Pat and her students chanted sounds and rules that go with *letter clusters*. Christine and her students discussed the pronunciation and meaning of vocabulary *words* chosen by the teacher and made a list of "past time" *words*. Jenny focused her students' attention on *words* chosen by the students that they might have trouble with and had the students put these words in *sentences*. Margaret focused her students' attention on how to approach *words in context*.

Thus the teachers who held bottom-up beliefs emphasized letter clusters and words, and the teachers who held interactive/top-down beliefs emphasized words in context and the meaning of the story. This was true even though all four teachers were using the basal reading instructional approach with its directed reading activity format.

In practice, the instructional approach used is not as important as *what teachers do* and which strategies they select. Harste and Burke (1977) related their contact with a teacher they had previously observed conducting a directed reading lesson. The teacher said that when Harste and Burke next observed, she would be doing a "language experience" lesson. When the observers arrived, the teacher and her class composed the following story about a class trip to the zoo:

We went to the zoo.
We saw lots of animals.
We saw a monkey.
We saw a tiger.

We saw a duck.
We had lots of fun.

Harste and Burke reported that it was fascinating watching the teacher use LEA in this manner. No matter what the children actually said, the teacher transformed their language into the type of sentences shown in the dictated story above! The language of the story resembles the language in many pre-primer basal readers. When the class had finished the story, the teacher wrote the word *we* on the chalkboard. She then asked the children to identify the number of times the word *we* was used in the story. She followed the same procedure with the word *saw* and the word *a*.

This teacher apparently believed that it is important for students to recognize each word in the selection and that they learn to read by learning to recognize words. Even when using the Language Experience Approach, she focused her students' attention on recognizing the words in the story—not on the class trip or the meaningful experiences of the student. Although this teacher was using an approach that we classified as interactive, her instructional strategy emphasized bottom-up concerns.

Deciding on Strategies

If teachers are to be decision-makers, it is essential that they concentrate on careful planning when it comes to selecting strategies for reading instruction. This is, after all, the essence of *teaching,* a process of making and implementing instructional decisions to increase the probability of learning (Hunter, 1977).

Deciding on which strategies to use may sometimes be a spur-of-the-moment decision. When time permits, however, teachers prefer to make thoughtful decisions about instructional strategies. They deliberately plan to use certain strategies based on: (1) the students' interests and concerns; (2) cues to strategy needs that the teacher picks up from evaluation of student work; (3) the teacher's knowledge of the strategies that facilitate reading development, and the context in which learning to read takes place.

SUMMARY

The connection between theory and practice in teaching reading has taken us through a four-step process in Chapters 1 and 2. After eliciting our own beliefs about reading, we studied several models or theories of the reading process and matched our beliefs to them. This resulted in the idea of a continuum ranging from bottom-up to top-down rather than separate categories of beliefs or theories. Approaches to instruction, introduced in this chapter, follow a similar pattern.

The four major approaches to reading instruction fall on a continuum from subskills to holistic: individualized-prescriptive (linguistic; skills management), basal reading, language experience, and individualized-personalized (literature). They correspond to bottom-up, interactive, and top-down theories as well as individual belief systems. Yet when it comes to the daily delivery of instruction, the approach is not as critical as the strategies used during instruction.

Instructional strategies, the actual tactics selected and put into practice by teachers, are the determinants of the type of reading instruction experienced by students. Hence, to understand what is going on in the classroom one must consider specific teaching strategies rather than more general approaches to reading instruction. Teachers in practice make decisions about strategies: These strategies consistently reflect teachers' beliefs about reading.

THE WORKSHOP

In the Classroom

1. Check the statements in the following list that you agree with. In small groups discuss your responses to the statements with one another.

_____ The approach to reading is not as important as the instructional decisions a teacher makes or the strategies used for instructional purposes.

_____ A child learns to read by reading, not by learning individual skills presumed to be operating during reading.

_____ There's no one best way to teach reading.

_____ Teaching reading holistically is a nice idea, but it isn't practical given the realities of classroom instruction.

_____ It isn't feasible to use basal readers to individualize reading instruction.

2. Complete the study chart below, using information from the chapter, class notes, and out-of-class readings suggested by the instructor.

Reading Approaches	Theoretical Base	Provisions for Skill Development	Advantages	Limitations
Basal				
Language-experience				
Individualized-prescriptive				
Individualized-personalized				

3. Collect samples of language-experience stories dictated or written by first-graders. Analyze the stories for content and language. What do these stories suggest about children's oral language development? How does the content of the stories compare to the content of beginning reading materials in a basal program?

4. Study the scope and sequence charts of several basal reading programs. In what ways are the charts alike? How are they different, especially in terms of the skills emphasized for instruction? What rationale does each basal program provide for its scope and sequence in the development of skills?

In the Field

1. Interview a teacher who uses children's literature regularly to teach reading. Determine how the teacher encourages children who don't want to read; keeps track of what each child is reading and how he or she is progressing in reading; and encourages children to respond to what they read.

2. Observe a reading group throughout the entire sequence of a basal reading lesson. The sequence may take one to several days to complete. Watch to see what happens before the reading of a story selection, during the reading, and after the story is finished. Record what both the teacher and students do throughout all aspects of the instructional sequence. Analyze the notes you take and respond to these questions:

    a. What did the teacher do with vocabulary before, during, and after the story?
    b. How did the teacher build and sustain motivation throughout the lesson?
    c. If the students read orally, what did the teacher do when oral reading errors were made?
    d. What learning activities did the teacher engage the students in?
    e. What appeared to be the teacher's main instructional emphasis before, during, and after the story?

Part II

The Roots of Literacy

Chapter 3

Early Literacy Experiences

The concept of "wellness" is quickly becoming a part of our national consciousness. Television news features and popular magazine articles suggest that there will be increasing emphasis on preventive medicine in the years ahead. "Holistic" health specialists are educating the public on avoiding illness. There are parallels, we believe, between the pursuit of wellness in today's society and the pursuit of literacy. A healthy environment for learning to read and write is one in which young children are immersed in language—both oral and written. In this environment, preschoolers develop a "set" for literacy. We have a lot to learn from early readers and writers. Young children should ease into reading and writing naturally, thereby avoiding the need for "correction" at some later point. This chapter provides a dose of preventive medicine, in the form of early literacy experiences of young children who find learning to read and write as natural as learning to talk.

I'm gonna learn (how to read) when I go to school.

Michael, age four and a half

I want my child taught how to read in kindergarten. The sooner the better!

Louise, mother of a preschooler

I was afraid to teach Ray anything about reading before he entered school. I didn't want to do the wrong things. You know, teach him things that would interfere with the way he started learning to read in kindergarten and first grade.

Janice, a parent

Beginnings are important. When it comes to learning to read, a good beginning is often considered one of the most important factors in the prevention of reading failure. Therefore issues related to beginning reading instruction—for example, the concept of readiness as it applies to learning to read—have been the subject of much debate and controversy for at least fifty years. Such debate has sometimes perplexed both preservice and experienced classroom teachers.

Consider Pikulski's (1978) astute observation on readiness for reading:

Hundreds of articles have been written about reading readiness, and hundreds of experiments have been conducted in an effort to better understand what it is, how it can be measured and what can be done to develop it. Yet the debate continues. . . . *How can a classroom teacher, usually a kindergarten or first-grade teacher, deal with the concept of readiness with thirty or sixty children when the so-called experts can't agree?* (page 192, emphasis added)

This chapter won't settle disagreements or bring to closure current debates.

Learning to read underscores the importance of understanding how children develop literacy and the ability to use written language in reading and writing. In this chapter we tackle important issues related to the early reading development of children before they enter school and the implications of such development for beginning instruction. What do the kindergarten and first-grade teacher need to know about children's preschool knowledge of and experiences with reading? How can we make the child's first encounter with formal reading instruction smooth and profitable?

READING BEGINS AT HOME

The roots of reading begin at home. Nevertheless, most children enter school with expectations that they're "gonna learn how to read." It doesn't matter to Michael (the four-and-one-half-year-old friend whom we quoted above) that he already reads many signs—"STOP," for example, and "ZOO"—which have a great deal of meaning to him. It also doesn't matter that Michael "knows" most of the alphabet by name and often "reads along" by reciting favorite passages from bedtime stories that his mother and father read to him. Nor does it matter that Michael's mother still chuckles over his behavior at around the age of two when he first recognized a McDonald's billboard from the back seat of the family car. Michael "oohed" and "aahed" and chanted, "Stop! Stop! Hungry, Mommie."

Michael doesn't grasp the significance of these events because he is on the threshold of starting school. Nor does his mother recognize the importance of these abilities. Despite Michael's observable reading and reading-like behaviors at home, there remains a trace of uncertainty on his mother's part. Although the groundwork has been laid for Michael to continue to grow as a reader, his mother expresses some concern as to whether he'll achieve success in learning to read. She is sure that he will but adds, "We'll wait and see."

Need Michael's mother assume a "wait and see" attitude? A child such as hers grows up immersed in a print-oriented world. Children see written language all around them—in books, supermarkets, department stores, fast food restaurants and on television, signs, and a variety of printed materials from *TV Guide* to labels on household products. Print is everywhere. When aren't children confronted with written language in some form in their immediate environment? The child may also see parents, brothers, sisters, and others using written language to some degree—whether to read recipes, follow directions, do homework, solve problems, acquire information, or enjoy a story. The plethora of print that confronts young children on a day-to-day basis plays a subtle but important role in their desire to understand written language and use it for personal and social means.

Today's preschooler acquires much more intuitive and conscious knowledge about print and its uses than most adults would imagine. James Hymes (1958) was emphatic in his observation that reading "sells itself" to the preschool child because written language is in the "limelight" constantly. Everyday living "beats the drums" for reading with a bombardment of print that no formal program of instruction could ever match.

Michael, our preschool friend, already knows a lot about print and has had some valuable early reading experiences. In this respect, he's not so different from many children his age. In other ways Michael is also fairly typical. He's loved, healthy, curious, active, and not overly intelligent, independent, or outgoing for his age. Yet children are unique. Good teachers know this and know how to rally instruction around the differences in children.

The differences in children should weigh heavily in planning initial reading experiences and selecting appropriate teaching strategies. Individual differences, however, need not suggest a separate or unique program of instruction for each child. An individualized reading program is as much a state of mind as it is a fixed or specific approach to instruction. How teachers go about individualizing says more of their beliefs about reading and learning to read than it does about any specific method.

However, individualized instruction sometimes gets translated narrowly to

BOX 3.1

Something to Think About:
Kid-Watching at the Supermarket

In our undergraduate reading classes we ask students to observe young children learning about reading in natural settings. One of our students, Meg, plans on teaching in the primary grades. She decided to "shadow" unobtrusively a mother and her two children as they shopped in the local supermarket. Here's what Meg observed and recorded in her "field notes":

> The mother pushed the shopping cart with the younger of the two children sitting in the child seat. I learned that the two children were named Brian and Kate when overhearing the mother talking in line. Brian was around 14 months old and Kate about 3 or 4 years old. Kate sat on the bottom shelf of the cart. When the mother stopped in the produce area, she said to the children, "Look at the bananas. Don't they look good?" Brian looked at the bananas and said, "Bananas." The mother continued in an easy, slow voice to comment on the color of the bananas and what she planned to use them for. At this time, I decided to observe Kate more closely.
>
> As her mother went up the dairy aisle, Kate walked between the cart and her mother. As Kate walked around the store, she asked questions like "what's this?" pointing to specific items on the shelves. Her mother would always answer her and explain about the item if more questions were asked. At one point, a can was thrown out of the cart by Brian while the mother was looking over the cereals. She walked over to the cart, picked up the thrown can, and asked Kate what had happened. Kate pointed to Brian saying, "He threw it." The mother then asked Kate to find that cereal that she was looking for. (I couldn't hear what kind.) Kate roamed the aisle looking for the cereal and eventually found it. Throughout shopping Kate was quite active and inquisitive. She would look at items in the store and always wanted to know more about them. For some products she would finger the letters on the box or can and ask, "What does this say, Mommy?"

Think about Meg's observations. What do they tell you about the uses of language? In what ways does the older child demonstrate knowledge of written language? How does the mother's interaction with the children support and encourage language learning?

mean "learning small things in small steps," where each child gets the same program "except for some differences in pacing (Moffett, 1975)." Our job, first and foremost, is to establish classroom conditions in which individual learning takes place during literacy instruction. Individual learning shouldn't be confused with individualized instruction. Holdaway (1979) argued that it's impossible to determine the right level, content, pace, and style of learning for each child, each day. This is why individual learning in this book means the teacher sets the conditions for learning by giving enough differential help through instruction for each child to learn to read and write successfully.

LEARNING TO READ NATURALLY

Some children learn to read naturally. They acquire the ability to read through a process that can best be described as trial and error learning. These early readers make discoveries about written language in a low-risk atmosphere that is relatively free from anxiety and criticism. In school, however, the stakes are usually high and the risks involved in reading are great. The margin for error isn't what it was at home, especially if the emphasis in school is on learning through memorization, analysis, and recitation. Many beginning reading tasks in curricular programs are organized into "skill hierarchies" based on "bottom-up" instructional models. As a result, children are introduced to reading instruction with emphasis on the smallest possible print units—letters, for example. For those children who have little background experience with print, confusion mounts quickly in what often becomes a high-risk learning situation. Therefore, we must ask, "What can the teacher learn from studying how preschool children read without apparent instruction?"

Holdaway (1979) contended that children are as predisposed to learn to read naturally as they are to learn to speak because they are immersed in both oral and written language. They develop a "set for literacy." The irony, however, is that many adults are unaware of the child's immersion in a print-dominated world:

> The amount of written language confronting a child can come as a surprise to an adult who normally pays only passing attention to it. But adult readers have learned to ignore this plethora of print, while to an inquiring, learning child it must be a stimulating situation (Smith, 1976, page 298).

Perhaps this is why most adults form the expectation that learning to read is a function of formal instruction in schools. Does a similar expectation exist for a child's growth and development in spoken language? Of course not. Most parents play an important role in the oral language development of their children. Yet few, until recently, have begun to believe that learning to read begins through interaction with parents and significant others. The foundations of literacy are built upon children's social and linguistic interaction with their world and the significant persons in it.

Longitudinal Studies of Early Readers

There have not been many longitudinal studies of early readers. But the findings of reported studies have been enlightening and hold many implications for learning to read in kindergarten and first grade.

In a nutshell, studies of early readers indicate that learning to read is strongly associated with positive home environments. Teale (1978) identified four factors that have been repeatedly associated with the learning environments of early readers:

The Availability and Range of Printed Materials. Early readers have access to a variety of easy reading materials in the home. Not only do young readers have easy availability to extensive book collections at home, but they also tap into the local library. Moreover, early readers are attracted to reading *anything* that interests them in their immediate print environment, from labels on cans to TV supplements in local newspapers to cookbooks, telephone directories and bus timetables. As Teale observed, ". . . children come to reading through a variety of printed materials as diverse as books and Vicks bottles" and ". . . each child has a variety of interests . . . (page 926)."

Reading Is "Done" in the Environment. While books, billboards, and cereal box labels are all potential sources for reading in a young child's environment, Teale repeated what has been emphasized in this book: ". . . this potential [for reading] will remain unrealized unless the child learns what function print in the environment serves (page 926)." In this respect, reading aloud to children is repeatedly mentioned in studies as an important contributing factor in the learning environment of early readers. In addition, early readers' homes are frequently characterized by one or more parents and older siblings who read regularly.

The Environment Facilitates Contact with Paper and Pencil. Early readers apparently spend significant amounts of time expressing themselves through scribble writing, drawings, copying words, and inventing spellings for words. Writing is an important, often underestimated, factor in learning to read. As Teale put it, ". . . a positive environment for learning to read would certainly facilitate the child's scribbling cum writing (page 929)." We pursue this point in Chapter 5.

Those in the Environment Should Respond to What the Child Is Trying to Do. The quality of interaction that the child has with the "significant others" in his or her home environment—parents, older siblings, grandparents, aunts and uncles—plays heavily in reading development. Often, however, assistance in learning to read is not consciously given. Instead, significant others such as parents read to children repeatedly (and read certain stories over and over) and *answered the questions that children asked about reading*. What better way to help the child make the connection that print is meaningful than to respond to the question, "What does this say?" as the child points to a printed page.

Inquiries into emergent reading behavior have focused on the question: Why do some children learn to read easily and naturally without the apparent benefit of formal instruction in school? Delores Durkin (1966), for example, reported two pioneering studies of early readers. In *Children Who Read Early*, she described one longitudinal study conducted in Oakland, California over a six-year period and another in New York City over a three-year period. She identified 49 beginning first-grade children from more than 4,400 whom she classified as early readers. These children could read at least 18 primary-level words from a list of 37; had obtained a score of at least 1 on a standardized reading test; and had not received school instruction in reading prior to first grade. Durkin gathered diverse sets of information on each child with respect to family backgrounds, preschool experiences, personal characteristics, intelligence, and reading achievement.

Of the questions she asked parents, two provided revealing responses: "How did your child first show an interest in reading?" "Can you remember what might have encouraged the interest?" Two excerpts from the case studies of Jack and Jean provide some insight into Durkin's findings:

Jack: Jack was described by the mother as "terribly active"—as a child who "always has to be doing two or three things at a time." It was at this point . . . that the mother mentioned how Jack was "always, always writing," even while he watched favorite television programs. She said she herself was unaware of Jack's ability to identify written words until he began reading aloud some of the advertisements on television. She said his recognition of the same words on food products in the grocery store was "a source of great delight for him." At the time, she said, Jack was about four. (page 120)

Jean: The mother . . . referred to Jean's early interest in books, and to the way she had enjoyed being read to "ever since she was about a year old." The mother mentioned that both she and her husband were "avid readers," and that both enjoyed reading to the children . . . The mother also recalled how she used to buy "little books for the children in the supermarket" . . . it was these books in particular that excited Jean's curiosity about the names of letters. This interest, the mother explained, was followed by attempts to write the letters. The mother said she gave Jean help with printing "whenever she asked for it (page 123)."

Several major findings emerged from Durkin's work. First, early readers as a group keep their advantage in reading achievement over nonearly readers of the same mental age. Second, an early start, contrary to popular opinion at the time, did not result in academic injury and was particularly valuable for those children at a lower range of intelligence. Third, early readers come from diverse family backgrounds. Nevertheless, parents were remarkably alike in showing a genuine willingness in helping with reading and responding to children's questions about print. Parents had a high regard for reading and read to their children regularly. Moreover, early readers showed a preoccupation with scribbling, drawing, and writing. Durkin called these readers "paper and pencil kids." Finally, reading aloud to children provided the spark that created an interest in reading and led to children's curiosity about words and sensitivity toward written language.

In *Young Fluent Readers*, Margaret Clark (1976) traced the development of thirty-two children in Scotland over several years who found learning to read as natural as learning to speak. Her conclusions were similar to Durkin's: For example, few parents of early readers made a deliberate effort to teach their children to read. Instead, they conveyed their enthusiasm for print through constant modeling—by themselves reading in the presence of children and by reading children's favorite stories aloud to them.

Clark especially underscored the role of "everyday print" in the child's learning to read: "Although these early reading experiences for some of the children were in books from which they had enjoyed stories, for some of the children the print in their immediate environment played an important role. This was particularly true of the boys who showed interest in signposts, car names, captions on television and names of products at the supermarket" (page 51).

In addition, Clark described the local library as one of the striking features in the lives of the early readers. Extensive use of the local library was encouraged by parents initially but later sustained by the children themselves. Clark concluded that parents or other significant persons in the lives of early readers help them become sensitive to written language and to understand the act of reading. She captured the essence of the adult's roles: "A number of the fluent readers had available an interested adult with time to devote to them at the stage when they were interested in reading—either to read to them, talk with them, or answer their questions" (page 102).

Individual Case Studies

Jane Torrey (1969) painted a vivid portrait of a young child whose early literacy development was described by his mother as a "gift received directly from God." John was the middle child in a black family of five. His father was a truck driver and his mother a hospital maid. Both parents had limited educations (neither completed high school) and lived with their children in a subsidized housing project in a large southern city. When John entered kindergarten (before the age of five), he was alreading reading and writing fluently. His kindergarten teacher soon discovered that he was interested primarily in reading and writing. At this point the school asked Torrey to work with John, to observe his reading ability and "help him put his skills to good use."

In Torrey's discussions with John's mother, many of the environmental factors already described as having a strong associations with learning to read were again identified. As she tutored John at his home three hours a week for four months, Torrey kept a record of her observations.

John delighted in seeing words emerge in print. When he encountered words that he could not write or type himself, he took great pleasure in dictating stories to Torrey and watching her transcribe his language on paper. Also, during oral reading John showed no sign of "word calling," but always read in a conversational tone. Even though he had developed his own rules for "sounding out" unfamiliar words, John preferred to ask Torrey about those words he did not know. Torrey observed that John treated written language as an alternative to spoken language. He seemed to expect print to represent meaning.

During oral reading, John's performance could not always be described as "word perfect"; that is to say, some of the words he read aloud deviated from the words in the text selection. For example, a portion of text that began, "You may help Uncle Wiggly a hop along," was read by John, "Help Uncle Wiggly a hop along." John's dialect affected his production of oral language during reading. For example, if the text said, "When do you go to school?" John read, "When you go to school?" In Chapter 15 we will examine the instructional implications of linguistic diversity. For now, however, consider Torrey's observation that John read for meaning, not to pronounce the words on a page per se. Instead, he learned to express the author's meaning in "his own way" during oral reading. Torrey concluded that John learned to read naturally because "he asked the right questions" about the relationships between spoken and written language. His questions were not concerned initially with the isolated features of print such as letters or letter clusters. Instead, his inquiries related to: "How does something I say look in print?" or "What does that print say?"

This last finding echoes the conclusions of two other researchers who observed and studied the early literacy development of their own children. Glenda Bissex (1980) and Bonnie Lass (1982, 1983) kept detailed diaries of their sons' reading and writing development. Both children, Paul Bissex and Jed Lass, had a fascination with print. In Paul's case, reading and writing appeared to develop concurrently. At age four, he clearly recognized the connection between writing and reading. For example, when he read his writing, complete with *invented spellings*, Paul explained: "Once you know how to spell something, you know how to read it" (page 1). As his mother noted, Paul developed multiple strategies because of his use of invented spellings: "Paul seemed to be asking himself not only 'What does this word *sound* like?' and 'What does this word *look* like?' but 'What does this mean?'" (page 102). In Chapter 5, we will explain the concept of invented spellings and its implications for writing.

Jed Lass's literacy development paralleled Paul's and John's in many respects. All three preschoolers were driven to make meaning from print. Caution, of course, must be exercised in generalizing the findings of individual case studies to the literacy learning of all preschool children. The young people we describe, however, provide certain insights for teachers of beginners. Reading for preschool children is as natural and as important an activity as play. For preschool readers, learning to read might best be considered a form of play. Young children clarify and master many physical, social, and intellectual skills through repeated play experiences. And so it is with reading. The more repeated and meaningful experiences that children have with written language, the more they clarify and begin to exercise some control over the processes involved in learning to read.

The very first clarification that preschoolers appear to make is in the relationship of speech to print. Somehow early readers become aware of and understand the connection between spoken and written language; that language is comprised of utterances (words and sentences) that correspond with similar units of print. Reading instruction in school cannot make much sense to children unless they first make the connection between print and speech. Furthermore, early readers learn how to manage and regulate their reading through the many experiences they have with print. They do so by exploring and experimenting with written language. As a result of their trial and error interactions with print, young children probably learn on their own to figure out and construct the rules which govern the skills involved in reading.

Ideal conditions for learning to read or write may not exist for all children. What, then, do some of the insights above hold for initial school experiences?

INSTRUCTIONAL IMPLICATIONS FOR KINDERGARTEN AND FIRST GRADE

Reading instruction in kindergarten today is more the rule than the exception. In 1977 a statement of concerns about present practices in pre-first-grade reading instruction was issued by a joint committee made up of members from seven national and international professional educational associations.* The concerns expressed by the committee reflect the highly formalized, structured instructional practices that run counter to natural language learning and the development of the "whole child." The recommendations of the committee listed in Box 3.2 highlight provisions for a *language-centered* curriculum for beginners. Not only do we support a language-centered curriculum but also underscore the need for an instructional environment for learning to read that is *home-centered*.

Creating a Home-Centered Environment

Insights from the early reading experiences of preschool children have yet to fully influence beginning reading in schools. Instruction for five-year-olds should not be a carbon copy of practices that are appropriate for older children or that emphasize drill, repetition, and memorization. Instead, the beginner in kindergarten needs supportive, meaningful situations in learning to read. In this respect, there is much to be learned from the behavior of parents of preschool readers.

A teacher of beginners should consider focusing reading instruction around the "natural" methods of parents whose children learned to read before school entry. A home-centered environment for reading places less attention on instructional methods and more emphasis on individual attention and a warm, accepting relationship between child and teacher. A home-centered learning environment in school establishes ideal conditions for learning to read in much the same way that the home environment of the child establishes ideal conditions for learning to speak.

Don Holdaway (1972) described some of the characteristics of a natural language learning environment which operates efficiently in a preschooler's mastery of oral language:

1. *Young children are allowed to develop in their own way and at their own rate using language functionally to meet their needs.*

2. *Parents are positive and rewarding in their reception of most responses that children attempt.* In learning oral language, children have a built-in support system provided by parents that does not stress criticism or correction but allows for trial and approximations.

3. *Parents demonstrate tremendous faith and patience.*

4. *Parents do not create competitive situations in which children learn language.* Parents may compare a child's performance with what he or she did yesterday or a week ago but rarely do they make close comparisons of their child's performance with another child.

---

* Sponsors of the joint statement of concerns and recommendations for the improvement of reading in pre-first grade included the American Association of Elementary/Kindergarten/Nursery Educators, the Association for Childhood Education International, the Association for Supervision and Curriculum Development, the International Reading Association, the National Association for the Education of Young Children, the National Association of Elementary School Principals, and the National Council of Teachers of English.

BOX 3.2

Recommendations from the Joint Committee on Reading in Pre-First Grade

1. Provide reading experiences as an integerated part of the broader communication process that includes listening, speaking, and writing. A language experience approach is an example of such integration.

2. Provide for a broad range of activities both in scope and in content. Include direct experiences that offer opportunities to communicate in different settings with different persons.

3. Foster children's affective and cognitive development by providing materials, experiences, and opportunities to communicate what they know and how they feel.

4. Continually appraise how various aspects of each child's total development affects his/her reading development.

5. Use evaluative procedures that are developmentally appropriate for the children being assessed and that reflect the goals and objectives of the instructional program.

6. Ensure feelings of success for all children in order to help them see themselves as persons who can enjoy exploring language and learning to read.

7. Plan flexibility in order to accommodate a variety of learning styles and ways of thinking.

8. Respect the language the child brings to school, and use it as a base for language activities.

9. Plan activities that will cause children to become active participants in the learning process rather than passive recipients of knowledge.

10. Provide opportunities for children to experiment with language and simply to have fun with it.

11. Require that pre-service and in-service teachers of young children be prepared in the teaching of reading in a way that emphasizes reading as an integral part of the language arts as well as the total curriculum.

12. Encourage developmentally appropriate language learning opportunities in the home.

5. *Children learn in meaningful situations that support the language being learned.*

6. *Children have models to emulate. Because the language learning process is innately rewarding, they spend much of their time voluntarily practicing.*

It is evident from the case studies reported in the previous sections that many of the conditions necessary for language learning were operating in the lives of early readers. Teachers of reading beginners must approximate these ideal conditions in their classrooms. Consider, then, establishing some of the hallmarks of a home-centered environment for learning to read.

Reading to Children

There is no better way to create a love for books than by reading to children. Reading to children sparks their imagination and gives them a sense of wonder. According to Cramer (1975), reading to children will help them appreciate the gift of literature, develop and enrich their own language, and build implicit concepts about reading and writing.

Reading to children helps them learn to read in subtle but important ways. It is through reading that children develop a schema or sense for stories. In Chapter 6, we discuss fully the role of *story structure* in learning to read and how children can use their schema for stories to comprehend material. A story schema is developed early in the lives of children who have been read to frequently. Moreover, reading to children provides models for writing as they develop a sense of plot, characterization, mood, and theme.

Cramer (1975, pages 461–462) provided valuable guidelines for reading to children:

1. *Plan each day's reading selection in advance.* Normally one should have certain days reserved for the reading of a continuing story. It is also useful to reserve at least one day a week for a special selection—poetry, surprises, or readings designed to mesh with other daily or weekly classroom activities.

2. *Select reading material best suited for the children being read to.* Keep in mind age and interest levels. Many teachers choose to consult various sources in selecting appropriate books.

3. *Interpret the mood, tone, and action of the passage being read.* Don't be afraid to be dramatic. Inhibition, shyness, or fear of making a fool of oneself often prevents teachers from entering into the drama of a story.

4. *Differentiate the reading-to-children time from the directed-reading-and-listening-activity time.* It is neither necessary nor desirable to make the reading-listening time into a structured lesson. The primary objective is enjoyment.

5. *When reading a narrative that will be continued the next day, stop at a point that is likely to invite anticipation for the next episode.* Judicious use of this device can have a positive effect on attendance and sustained high interest level in the selection being read.

Jim Trelease's *The Read-Aloud Handbook* (1985) is an invaluable resource for parents and teachers who want to make reading to children a regular routine. Not only does Trelease provide the "do's and don'ts" of reading aloud, but he also gives a "treasury" of read-aloud books—annotated references that can be used to make reading come alive for children.

Sharing Books

Reading to children is an important way of sharing books. The act of sharing books with children provides invaluable stimulation for relating speech to print. Almost all of the early readers in various studies came from book-oriented homes.

Reading to and with children captures their fascination with print. They progress from sheer delight in the human experience of story sharing to recognition that the pictures in books "tell a story" to awareness that those black squiggly marks (not the pictures on a page) have a direct association with spoken language.

Holdaway (1979) devised a teaching strategy called the *shared book experience* to incorporate the facilitating features of the bedtime story. The idea behind the strategy is to use a "big book" (usually constructed by the teacher with 24″ by 15″ pages). The "big book" allows all the children in the class or in a small group to participate actively in the reading of the story. Because the print and illustrations are large enough for all the children to see, the teacher captures their attention immediately and focuses instruction around key goals. For example, the teacher should read the story aloud often enough so that children learn it by heart. The story then becomes the basis for discussion and language-related activities (i.e., story dramatization) as well as teaching children about directionality and other print-related concepts.

Whether a teacher uses a "big book" format or not, sharing books is an invaluable experience for beginners. In Chapter 9, we explore ways to book share.

Repeating Favorite Stories

Repetition of favorite stories and eventually "memory reading" play a crucial role in the child's understanding that print is supposed to sound like language. The phenomenon of memory reading involves the child recalling and rehearsing favorite segments of stories by heart. Young children learn to use a variety of strategies to achieve some sense of independence over their favorite stories. As part of sharing books and reading aloud, the teacher should be ready and willing to read and reread favorite books and to invite children to participate as much as possible. The language patterns of the books should be predictable, melodic, and rhythmic. In Chapter 9 we will have more to say on predictable materials and book choices for young children.

Some adults are quick to point out that children who memorize stories are just pretending to read, just "going through the motions." Pretending, however, shouldn't be discouraged. In fact, imitation establishes good models. The reading-like behaviors associated with an imitative stage in reading provide children with important early book experiences. Just consider some of the print concepts they learn: Books have pages; the pages can be turned; books have a right and wrong way up; the pictures help to tell a story; books are a source of enjoyment and pleasure.

Providing Assistance with Reading

Parents of early readers answer questions when their children ask for assistance. The parent usually follows the child's lead, not vice versa. Children choose their own activities and materials, and when questions arise, a parent or a significant other is there to help out.

One of our preservice students who is studying to be an elementary school teacher observed her two children, Ben and Matt, interact with each other just before bedtime. The brothers share the same bedroom and often read bedtime stories together. Ben is eight years old and Matt is five.

Ben: Matt, pick out a story. (Matt proceeds to do so while Ben plays with the dog.)

Matt: Ben, can I read the big words?

Ben (points to the book): Are these the big words?

Matt: Yeah, those words.

Ben: Why don't I read the black words and you read the red ones? OK?

Matt (points to book): You mean these?

Ben: Yeah.

Matt: But I don't know all the words.

Ben: Well, I'll just help ya—OK?

Matt: Okay. I'll try. (Matt sighs and the story begins.) Will you help me with that? (Matt points to a word on the page.)

Ben: "Scissors."

Matt: "Scissors."

Ben: Yeah, good. That's right. (The story continues until Matt reads the word "fish" for "goldfish.")

Ben: No. What kind of fish?

Matt: Goldfish?

Ben: Yeah, good. (Ben points to a picture of the goldfish. After a while Ben gets tired of giving Matt hints about the words.)

Ben: Can I read the rest?

Matt: Yeah, but I want to read the last page.

Ben: OK. (Ben reads the book until the last page.) Are you goin' to read this?

Matt: Yeah. (Matt attempts the last page and does fairly well with Ben's occasional assistance.)

Ben: Good, Matt! You're learnin' to read real well.

Matt has acquired knowledge of written language and has developed concepts of reading by being immersed in stories from a very early age. He is learning how to read *by* reading—with Ben, his parents, and on his own. Matt seeks assistance when he needs it and doesn't recognize such help as corrective or critical.

Hoskisson (1975) recommended a strategy that he devised called *assisted reading* which combines all of the features of home-centered learning: reading with children; sharing books; repeating favorite stories; memorizing text; and providing assistance as needed. Parents or teachers can easily adapt the three stages associated with the strategy.

STAGE 1.   Read to children and have them repeat the phrases or sentences after the person doing the reading. This encourages memorizing. It is sometimes referred to as *echo reading* because children are to repeat the phrases and sentences exactly as they were read. It is during echo reading that children are working out the connection between print and speech and developing a concept of *word*.

STAGE 2.   This stage begins when children recognize that some of the words occur repeatedly in stories they are reading. At this point, the teacher can leave out some of the words that they think children know. The children fill in the blanks left as they read.

STAGE 3. Children enter this stage of assisted reading when they do most of the reading and the teacher fills in the words the children may not know or may have trouble recognizing. The goal is to maintain as smooth a flow of the reading as possible. When children hesitate or seem unsure of a word, supply the word rather than asking them to "sound it out" or requiring them to practice word identification strategies.

LANGUAGE EXPERIENCES

Young children need to have the time and space to explore language in order to clarify its uses and gain facility in its production and reception. Children who experience language and its intricacies take giant steps on the road to becoming literate.

It is no coincidence that many preschool readers are also early writers. They have a strong desire to express themselves in symbolic terms through drawing, scribbling, copying, and, ultimately, producing their own written language. Exploring written language through paper and pencil helps children form expectations that print is meaningful.

Harste, Burke, and Woodward (1982) demonstrated how much knowledge children between the ages of three and six actually have about the purposes and form of written language. For example, when asked "to write everything you can write," three four-year-olds from different countries produced, organized, and identified print that reflected their native languages (English, Arabic, and Hebrew). The writing samples of Dawn, Najeeba, and Dalia (reproduced in Figure 3.1) show that these preschoolers have more knowledge about print than adults might have anticipated.

According to Harste and his collaborators, Dawn's scribbles look undeniably English. When Najeeba finished her writing she said, "Here, but you can't read it, because it is in Arabic." Najeeba went on to point out that in Arabic one uses

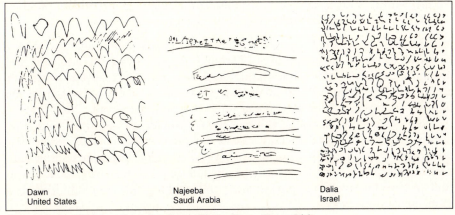

Dawn
United States

Najeeba
Saudi Arabia

Dalia
Israel

Figure 3.1 Writing Samples from Three Four-Year-Olds

"a lot more dots" than in English. Dalia is an Israeli child whose whole writing bears the predictable look of Hebrew. Kindergarten and first-grade children build on their knowledge of written language by participating in planned and spontaneous writing activity. In doing so they acquire knowledge about reading *by* writing.

In the remainder of this chapter and in Chapters 4 and 5 we show how beginners can explore the natural relationship between writing and reading through language experiences and independent writing.

Talking, Creating, Singing, and Dancing

The main feature of a language experience approach is that it embraces the natural language of children and uses their background experiences as the basis for learning to read.

Language experience activities in beginning reading instruction permit young children to share and discuss experiences; listen to and tell stories; dictate words, sentences, and stories; and write independently. The teacher can revolve language experiences around speaking, listening, visual expression, singing, movement, and rhythmic activities.

Use conversation to encourage individual or group language experience stories or independent writing. A language experience story is one, as we explain in the next chapter, that is told by the child and written down by the teacher for instructional purposes.

1. *Talk about everyday sights and occurrences.*
2. *Provide problem-solving tasks* (for example, making a milkshake) or highly motivating situations (for example, making peanut butter and jelly sandwiches) to elicit oral language.
3. *Tell stories through pictures.* Wordless picture books are particularly useful for stimulating language development through storytelling and creative writing.
4. *Discuss enjoyable occasions* (e.g., birthdays, holidays, special events such as the World Series, the class picnic).
5. *Use visual experiences to stimulate conversation* (e.g., television, book illustrations, art work). Visual expression through art activity, in particular, provides exciting opportunities for language experiences.

Use art as a vehicle for personal expression. Artistic expression represents a powerful force in children's lives. Through various forms of aesthetic and manipulative activity, children learn that there are many ways to express what they are thinking or feeling. What children draw, paint, or sculpt today can be the basis for what they talk or write about tomorrow and, then, read.

Every classroom for young children should provide enough space to do and display art projects. Art materials should include crayons, colored chalk, clay, playdough, paints, felt-tip pens, scissors, paste and glue, paper, newsprint (un-printed newspaper), and an assortment of junk (e.g., straws, wire, boxes, soap bars, toothpicks, Styrofoam, pipe cleaners, and anything else that might lend itself to manipulative activity).

1. *Cut cross-sections of vegetables such as carrots, potatoes, lettuce, and broccoli for vegetable printing.* Vegetable printing requires tempera paint and a few paper towels folded into a shallow container to create a "stamp pad." Children dip the cut vegetables into the pad—and then print. They can also print designs on old cloth and old sheets or create "scrolls" using window shades.

2. *Vary vegetable printing with "thing printing" in which children discover that ordinary objects produce a variety of shapes and textures.* Use keys, sponges, paper clips, leaves, sticks, and clothespins for "thing printing"—and then observe the language that children use to describe their creations.

3. *Create sculpturing opportunities in which children model materials of a manipulative nature.* Try potato sculpting. Children are encouraged to figure out how to attach objects such as straws, toothpicks, pipe cleaners, wire, yarn, and anything else to a potato to create an organized form. Box sculptures also produce interesting organizations. Children build forms out of boxes, and then spray or brush paint their creations for added effect.

Singing, dancing, and other rhythmic activities are valuable means of expression in their own right. Such activities can also be linked easily and naturally to reading and writing instruction. For example, you can:

1. *Encourage "readalongs" as children sing familiar and favorite songs.* Create large "cue cards" that contain the lyrics to the songs. As children sing, the teacher directs their attention to the lyrics. She moves her hand across the card, left to right, top to bottom, pointing under each word, and synchronizing her movement with the music.

2. *Create new lyrics for familiar songs that have a highly repetitive pattern.* In one kindergarten class, the children changed "Old MacDonald Had A Farm" to "Old MacDonald Had an Amusement Park." Imagine the "new" lyrics that were contributed by the children!

3. *Play the "magic circle" game.* Children cross through a three- or four-foot circle on the floor. At random intervals children are stopped in the circle. When stopped, a child must follow directions given by the teacher. For example, "Imitate a lion," or "Pretend you are walking the plank on a pirate's ship."

4. *Create dances that tell a story.* Songs such as "The Eensy Weensy Spider" can be used to encourage movement and interpretation through dance.

5. *Improvise "movement stories" inspired by poems and familiar stories.* Chenfeld (1978) suggested that as you read with students, include movement as a way to further express and interpret the reading material. Children make fine choreographers creating spontaneous movement sequences for "The Gingerbread Man" or "Peter Cottontail" and other action stories.

6. *Stretch the imagination through games that involve basic rhythms such as walking, hopping, running, and marching.* Ask children, for example, for different types of walks such as slow walks, fast walks, graceful walks, or angry walks. Permit children to create their own walks and demonstrate them to classmates.

Role-Playing and Drama

Young children delight in pretending. Role-playing and dramatic activities in a beginning reading program not only stimulate the imagination but also provide many opportunities to use language inventively and spontaneously.

Role-playing affords children the chance to approach ordinary or unusual events and situations from different perspectives and points of view. Children begin to recognize that there are different levels and uses of language appropriate for different situations. Role-playing can be adapted easily to stimulate writing and to enhance reading comprehension throughout the elementary grades.

The objective of drama in the classroom is self-expression. Children "play along" in structured and unstructured situations. *Dramatic play* activities require very little planning and involve unstructured, spontaneous expression such as pretending to be a leaf falling from a tree or an astronaut going to Mars. *Creative drama*, on the other hand, is more structured in the sense that children often have definite parts to play as they act out a favorite story or event. Props, costumes, and scenery may be called for. A third kind of dramatic activity, *pantomime*, involves wordless communication in which children use their bodies to translate reality and convey meaning.

The teacher should have a dress-up area for dramatic activities. Because drama is so unlike traditional classroom activities, the teacher's approach, much like a parent's, is one of continuous encouragement and facilitation. Consider some of these language experiences.

Use children's literature for drama. Folk tales such as *Little Red Riding Hood* or *Henny Penny* provide simple plot structures and clearly defined characters. Action-filled poems can be valuable for pantomime and movement activities.

Engage children in problem situations as a start for spontaneous dramatic activity. Rose (1982) suggested these problems:

1. You have been called at school to go home immediately.
2. You are waiting in line at McDonald's or Burger King and are very hungry. On two occasions people get ahead of you. What do you do the third time it happens?
3. You have just broken your mother's pearl necklace and the pearls are scattered on the floor. You are picking them up when your mother enters the room.
4. You run into the police station to report that your bicycle has been stolen. The police seem to doubt your story .

Aurand Harris, one of the leading playwrights for children, advocated that children recognize differences between telling and writing a story and acting in and writing a play (*Bright Ideas,* 1984). Beginners should experience the joy and language stimulation from acting in plays adapted from good stories (folktales, nursery book rhymes, fables, and the like). Moreover, as they get older, children can collaborate on playwriting and acting. The following features are essential to the development of children's plays:

1. The play must be an adaptation of a good story.
2. The characters must be interesting and likable.
3. There must be one *main* character.
4. The main character must want or need something and in the end that need must be met.
5. The other characters must relate to the main character.
6. Events should follow in a chronological order.
7. Action must move rapidly and be exciting.
8. The play should have positive values and an optimistic outlook.

So far, we have scratched the surface in presenting some of the implications of early reading for beginning instruction. However, in the next chapter we continue the discussion.

SUMMARY

In this chapter we dealt with the developmental aspects of reading acquisition in relation to some children's early reading behavior. We inquired into the nature of beginning reading instruction by looking at preschoolers' knowledge of and experiences with print. Children bring much to reading. Topics ranging from physical factors to a child's cognitive and language background were presented. Several studies of early readers led us to focus on two intertwining areas: first, the natural process of learning to read; and second, implications for the very beginning of instruction.

Young children use what they have learned and experienced daily to make sense out of new events and experiences. As they build positive associations with books through such natural activities as the bedtime story, children are developing a "set for literacy." Preschoolers are immersed in a world of meaningful print; they exhibit early reading behaviors well before they enter a classroom. What kinds of experiences, then, are needed to get the kindergarten child off to a good start?

Readers at the beginning of their instruction benefit from a curriculum that is both home-centered and language-centered. Home-centered refers to those supportive, individual situations in which the warm, accepting, and patient relationship develops between teacher and child. Reading to children, sharing books, and assisting with reading are among the activities that easily transfer from parents to teachers. Language-centered refers to those experiences in which children explore spoken and written language through planned and spontaneous activities. Speaking, visual expression, singing, movement and rhythmic activities, role-playing, and drama are all instructional devices for teachers who want to approximate ideal conditions for learning to read in their classrooms.

THE WORKSHOP

In the Classroom

1. Discuss the questions below in small groups:
    a. Why do some preschoolers develop a "set for literacy" and others do not?
    b. What are some instructional implications for the statement made by Lass (1982), "Although parents often try to imitate teachers, perhaps the modeling should be reversed"?
    c. Why should learning to read and write be as natural as learning to walk and talk?

2. Choose a popular children's story and make a "big book." Then prepare a lesson that involves reading the big book story aloud, discussion, and dramatization. Share your big book lessons with others in the class.

3. With another class member, participate in a role-playing situation around the following scenario: The principal of an elementary school is adamant in the belief that children in kindergarten must receive very formal, structured instruction in learning to read. As a member of the committee that composed the Joint Statement of Concerns and Recommendations for the Improvement of Reading in Pre-First Grade (see page 65 to refresh your memory), you have been asked by a group of concerned parents to meet with the principal. Your task is to convince the principal to support a natural language-learning environment in the school's kindergarten. The role-playing begins as you introduce yourself in the principal's office. . . .

In the Field

1. Refer to Box 3.1, "Kid-Watching in the Supermarket." Observe a preschool child or group of children learning about reading and writing in a natural setting. Unobtrusively record what you see and hear as the child (children) interacts with written language. What do your notes tell you about the child's use of language? In what ways does the child demonstrate knowledge of written language? If an adult was observed interacting with the child, how did the adult's behavior support and encourage language learning?

2. Observe a kindergarten or first-grade class during language arts or reading time. Note what the teacher does, the amount of time spent on instructional activities, and the kinds of learning activities initiated during instruction. Use these questions to analyze your notes:
    a. Were children read to or were stories told to them? If so, how much time was spent in listening to stories? Describe the instructional situation and how children responded to it.
    b. Describe situations in which a child was given encouragement and support—perhaps with a hug or an accepting word—within the learning situation.
    c. Did children spend time completing worksheets? How much time was spent on worksheets? Describe the nature of the exercises in the worksheets and children's participation in the instructional situation.
    d. Did children spend time scribbling, drawing, or writing? If so, how much time was spent in activities such as these? What did the children draw or write? Describe the instructional situation and children's participation.

e. Describe the classroom discourse and language interactions that occurred during instruction. What were the topics of talk and conversation between teacher and children and children and other children?

After you analyze your notes, compare your findings with those of other members of the class. What conclusions can be drawn from the experience?

3. Read a children's story to a group of beginning readers, following the guidelines given in this chapter. Describe the experience and assess its instructional value in promoting literacy.

Chapter 4

Beginning Reading Instruction

"Ready or not—here I come!" How often have you heard young children at play using this rallying cry as they engage in a game of "tag" or "hide-and-go-seek?" *"Ready or not"* has also been the rallying cry heard in making decisions about children's initial school experiences with reading. Are they ready to read or not? The question, in many respects, isn't the best one to ask. Raising it invariably means that some children are delayed in beginning instruction until they have had readiness training. Such delay suggests that some children are non-readers when they come to school and others are readers. In this chapter, we present a different view: one based on a developmental perspective of learning to read.

I read somewhere that in several European countries they don't even begin teaching reading until a child is seven. Is seven better (to begin teaching children to read) than five or six?

Grace, a kindergarten teacher

Nowhere does a knowledge of the reading process play a more significant part in the development of literacy than in children's first encounter with reading instruction. How we view and assess readiness for reading, plan beginning reading experiences, and interact with children during instruction will build a sturdy bridge between their varied interests, backgrounds, and skills and the initial confusion that they often experience during instruction.

Because of the insights gained from studying early readers, one camp of reading professionals argues ardently against the very concept of readiness. They contend that learning to read depends on a positive environment in the home and begins from the time children hear their first nursery rhymes and stories. Therefore, the acquisition of reading should be as natural as oral language development, given ideal learning conditions.

Another camp of reading professionals holds firmly to the belief that readiness for reading is largely a result of maturation. To paraphrase a popular expression about wine, children cannot come of reading age before their time. Put another way, they must reach a certain level of physical, mental, and emotional maturity to profit from teaching. Therefore, reading readiness actually means a *best time* to benefit from beginning instruction.

We see value in both positions. Decisions related to readiness for reading should take into account both the environmental and maturational backgrounds of children. The danger comes when either the environmental or maturational position is embraced to the extreme. For example, learning to read should be as natural as learning oral language. But we cannot dismiss or minimize the importance of beginning instruction and teacher support, especially when the home environments of children have been less than ideal. What happens in the classroom impacts on children's emerging skills and concepts of reading, as well as their motivation to read. All children need good models, invitations to learn, and support in their development toward proficient reading, much of which they can get from effective teachers.

The notion of a best time to benefit from reading instruction should not translate into one-dimensional indicators of reading readiness such as a child's mental maturity or a score on a readiness test. It was popular in the 1920s and 1930s to view children as having "ripened" to a stage where they might benefit from reading instruction. The importance of mental age, supported by the views of Morphett and Washburne (1931), served as the chief indication of ripeness. For many years a 6.5 mental age became the benchmark upon which to decide matters of instruction. With a mental age of 6.5 etched in stone, some faulty practices came into being. According to Farr and Rosner (1979): "The impact of a requisite mental age took the form of delayed instruction and promoted a near blanket application of reading-readiness workbooks. With these workbooks, which included activities that were often only busy work and were not related to learning to read, some first-grade teachers marked the passage of time from school entrance until most of the children reached the prescribed readiness level of 6.5 years of age" (page 89).

Strict adherence to a score on a reading readiness test can be as misleading an indicator of when to begin teaching reading as mental age can be. Determining a child's potential for learning to read is too complex an issue—involving social, cognitive, linguistic, affective, and physical factors—to reduce it to a test score. Readiness for reading means different things for different children. Reliance on a readiness test score tends to minimize the differences in children and negate a developmental view of learning to read.

A persistent question has focused on whether or not to delay reading instruction for children entering school. However, with new knowledge emerging on early reading and literacy development, a different question is being asked: Should a separate program of readiness instruction be offered apart from beginning reading?

READINESS TO READ

The question of *when* to begin instruction has social and cultural overtones. Why, for example, did Louise, the mother we quoted in the previous chapter, develop the strong expectation that her son Tommy be taught to read in kindergarten? Was it the result of the article in a popular women's magazine that she alluded to during our interview with her? Or is it out of her fear that the slightest lag in Tommy's development as a reader will only put him behind the educational eight ball in later grades? Or could it be, as Farr and Rosner (1979) have suggested, that the reading ability of American children is such a highly prized skill that Americans "have equated reading with success more than any other nation" (page 88)?

Whatever the reason, community and social pressures have changed the face of children's first experiences with reading instruction in school. Formal reading programs in kindergarten are more the rule than the exception. Yet several child development experts such as David Elkind (1981), believe the push for reading instruction in kindergarten has been more to meet the needs of parents than of children. Elkind even coined the expression, "the hurried child," to describe the general tendency in today's society to treat children as miniature adults. Children, Elkind argues, are rushed into adulthood.

Are American children pushed too quickly into reading instruction? We raise the question for more than rhetorical effect. Americans have come to expect nearly all children to start learning to read in school at ages five or six. Grace, the kindergarten teacher we quoted to begin this chapter, was expressing her concern when she asked whether it was better for schools to begin teaching children to read at age seven (as is the case in Sweden, for example) rather than at ages five or six.

The answer to Grace's question lies in an understanding of reading as a developmental process which begins before children even step foot in school. The term *readiness* signifies that children are prepared to learn something about reading. Therefore, the question of age isn't as important as, "What does the child already know about print? What reading behaviors and interests does the child already exhibit? What does the child need to learn?"

Answers to the three questions above will demonstrate that readiness for reading is not a period of time in which children progress from non-reading behavior to beginning reading. A predominant view of readiness for reading has been to treat it as a period of transition extending over several weeks or months. According to Clay (1979) a transitional view of readiness upholds the notion that children gradually change from nonreaders to beginning readers. At best, such a view pays lip service to a developmental concept of reading. It leads to the unwarranted assumption that children bring little, if anything, to school in the way of knowledge about and experience with print. Most children are bound to have some knowledge of print and book experiences prior to school, as limited as they may seem in some cases.

No wonder, then, that such a staunch advocate for cognitive readiness as P. David Ausubel (1968; 1978) maintained that if he had to reduce all of educational psychology to one principle, it would be this: "The most important single factor influencing learning is what the learner already knows (page vi)."

On the job, then, readiness for reading means matching the child with the instructional task at hand. Readiness for reading always needs to be considered relatively. It depends on *what* is taught and *how* it is presented. Therefore, in planning reading instruction for five- and six-year-olds, a basic principle should guide our actions: Rather than thinking about getting children "ready" for reading, consider what must be done to get reading instruction "ready" for children.

INSTRUCTIONAL BEGINNINGS

This day of all days—the first day of school—is usually hot and muggy, but full of anticipation and excitement nevertheless. Thoughts of kids from previous years go through Sandra's mind as she sips coffee in the faculty lounge a half-hour before the children arrive. This is Sandra's fourth "first day" as a teacher. She's just as nervous as her very first day and as full of expectation as her children. She knows what to do. She has learned gradually, on-the-job, although she credits her undergraduate program with doing much to prepare her to be a competent teacher. Sandra is ready more this year than she was the year before. She knows that she must anchor the teaching of reading in knowledge of what children bring to instruction, how they learn, and how language works.

An instructional program for reading beginners should incorporate recent developments in the study of the reading process as well as new insights into early reading behavior. Beginning instruction should reflect knowledge of how children acquire reading ability developmentally. And it should take into account children's acquaintance with and knowledge about print. Planning instruction appropriately requires knowing where children are in their awareness of concepts related to print, their interests in reading and learning to read, and their preschool book experiences. For this reason, Aulls (1982) proposed five levels that categorize children's "acquaintance with print." These levels provide a framework for decisions related to instruction:

1. *Children who have no acquaintance with books, sentences, words, or letters.* They show very little interest in producing or receiving information from print.

2. *Children who have some acquaintance with books and their use, with phrases or sentences, with words or with letters.* They show an interest in acquiring information from print at some level.

3. *Children who understand the concepts necessary to handle a book meaningfully.* They can follow along as a book is read; they can read some words; they can identify or match most upper- and lowercase letters; and they definitely show an interest in having books read to them or in trying to read them aloud themselves.

4. *Children who can already read parts or all of the contents of one or two simple books.* They can read parts of a book that have been read to them several times after an interval of several days, and they show an interest in producing print as well as attempting to read it.

5. *Children who exhibit consistent interest in reading books on their own.* They have read at least three books and can reread them with little or no help; they indicate the ability to sound out some words as the occasion arises and, by pointing, can distinguish words from letters in a line of print. These children regularly show their growing knowledge of print by spontaneously exploring books or labels on foods, et cetera.

Aulls maintained that the broad purpose of beginning instruction is to bridge the gap between children's knowledge of language and their level of acquaintance with print. Therefore at the very beginning of instruction, teachers need to know where to start. Consider these instructional goals:

1. Motivate children to want to learn to read.

2. Help children acquire some understanding of what reading and learning to read are all about.

3. Encourage children to write (a topic dealt with in depth in the next chapter).

4. Involve children in reading pictures.

5. Interest children in listening to stories with emphasis on interpreting what is heard and gaining familiarity with "book language."

6. Teach about directionality; left-to-right, top-to-bottom orientation of written language.

7. Teaching the meaning of *word* and the function of space in establishing boundaries between words.

8. Teach children the meaning of terms that figure in reading instruction.

9. Teach children to discriminate visually among letters and words.

10. Teach children the names of letters.

11. Teach children to use their knowledge of language to predict words that "must come next" in a sentence.

12. Teach children to recognize words that they are interested in learning or that occur frequently in meaningful contexts.

13. Teach children letter-sound correspondences.

The thirteen goals listed above are not sequential in the sense of having to accomplish one before proceeding to another. In fact, several may be accomplished in combination or simultaneously. However, the translation of these goals into instructional activities and strategies lies in having a developmental perspective of beginning reading.

A child doesn't learn to read overnight. Nor, as we have shown, do children learn all that they need to know entirely in school to be able to read. Concepts of literacy develop gradually. As children progress, certain kinds of learning are necessary. These types of learning precede and accompany beginning reading behavior.

Learning What Reading Is All About

First of all, the child must be able to figure out what spoken language and written language have in common. Without learning the relationship between speech and print, the beginner will never make sense of reading or achieve independence in it. Earlier we suggested that reading often to children, repeating favorite bedtime stories, and providing opportunities to draw, scribble, and interact with print in the immediate environment are some of the ways that children naturally learn to make sense out of reading and its uses. Nevertheless, many five-year-olds enter school with only vague notions of the purpose and nature of reading. They are not yet aware that what is said can be written; that written language is comprised of words and sentences; or that reading involves directionality, attending to the spacing between words, punctuation cues, and other conventions of print. There are several ways of going about this important instructional task.

The Uses of Written Language. From the beginning of their school experience children must learn that the value of reading or writing lies in its uses as a tool for communicating, understanding, and enjoying. A five-year-old or a seventy-five-year-old should engage in reading and writing for real reasons and in real situations. Effective teachers make their own opportunities. Consider, therefore, teaching about the uses of written language when any interesting or natural occasion arises in the classroom.

ITEM: The teacher and children are gathered around the guinea pig cage discussing their new pet. The teacher is explaining the food guinea pigs eat and is showing the children the food they will be feeding the pet. One of the children remembers that the class goldfish died because too much food was put in the bowl. The teacher suggests that the class make a sign to put on the package telling the right amount of food and a chart to put near the cage to be checked on the day he is fed. She discusses the reasons these written records will help (Taylor and Vawter, 1978, page 942).

Situations such as the guinea pig scenario evolve naturally in the classroom. Nevertheless, seizing the opportunity to help children recognize the value of reading and writing requires a certain amount of awareness and commitment. For example, Taylor and Vawter (1978) illustrated how two teachers approach an everyday event differently. As children prepare for a field trip to a farm, one kindergarten teacher passes out name tags routinely and without explanation. Another teacher, however, poses a problem to be solved by the children: "If the farmer wants to ask one of us a question, how can we help him to know our names?" Through give-and-take discussion, the children offer solutions that range from "tell him," to "I don't know," to "wear our names." As the discussion progresses, the teacher passes out the name tags, suggesting that names are written so that someone can read them and that writing a name helps to identify someone.

In Chapter 1 we outlined the uses of oral language. These language functions can and should be adapted to print at the beginning of instruction. Not only will children become aware of the purposes of written language, but many of the activities outlined below build word awareness. Therefore beginners should be introduced to some of the more obvious uses of print.

In general, the classroom should reflect a living example of written language put to purposeful ends. Fill the classroom environment with print to suit specific instructional goals. Print should be evident everywhere in the form of labels for classroom objects, simple messages, rules, directions, and locations where specific activity takes place such as a story reading area or art center. Specifically, consider these uses of written language:

Perpetuating Uses. Show children how to bridge the gap between time and space through print, or *perpetuate*. To do this, *keep records and charts of daily activity.* For example, Durkin (1980) recommended charting the weather for the week. Develop a chart with the days of the week running across the top. Slots for fitting cards are available under each day. Children use words to describe the day's weather.

Monday	**Tuesday**	**Wednesday**	**Thursday**	**Friday**
awful	foggy	sunny	_____	_____
rainy	cloudy	clear	_____	_____
sticky	dark	dry	_____	_____

Post the names of room helpers for each week. Each morning, make a point of going to the chart and having the children identify who will help the teacher for the day.

Vote or poll children on various classroom events or activities and tally the results. For example, ask children for some suggestions for naming the new pet rabbit. List the names, limiting the voting to three or four possible choices, and tally the results for the children to see.

- ☐ Thumper
- ☐ Whitey
- ☐ Long Ears

You can also *send messages and use children as messengers to deliver notes to other teachers or to parents.* Explain the purpose of the note and why you wrote it. Or *display notes from the principal congratulating children for work well done.* Also post thank-you notes, letters, the school lunch menu for each day, as well as a host of other forms of communication.

Finally, *keep a classroom scrapbook, beginning from the first day of school and including important events throughout the year.* Use Polaroid pictures, magazine pictures, et cetera, and record the importance of each event.

Regulatory, Authoritative/Contractual Uses. Show children how print can be used to control and direct behavior, establish rules, and agreements. To do this, *list classroom rules and use print to give directions such as lining up for the bus or going to the library. Establish "official" written contracts with children for various classroom activities,* i.e., *clean-up after art activities, taking milk count for the week.*

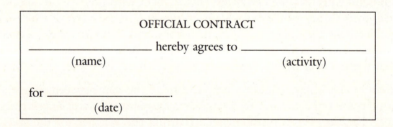

OFFICIAL CONTRACT

_____ hereby agrees to _____
     (name)   (activity)

for _____.
       (date)

Teachers can also *make recipe charts for cooking projects.* The charts may have pictures and words explaining what to do. Pictures can depict *ingredients* such as flour, sugar, or eggs (cut from a magazine advertisement) or *processes* (sketch of eggs being broken). Finally, *follow directions with clue cards that use pictures and simple words or play scavenger hunt using simple messages to direct the hunt.*

Instrumental Uses. Children should learn that print can be used to express personal needs. Teachers can *list materials needed to participate in various activities:*

Art	*Music*	*Building*	*Planting*
clay	bells	wood	seeds
scissors	shakers	glue	water
paint	piano	cardboard	pots
brushes	record player	blocks	tools

Write (dictate) Christmas lists or birthday wishes. Use signs to invite children to participate in various activities:

It's storytime!

Line up for the playground.

Diversion Uses. Demonstrate the value of print as a tool for enjoyment, or *diversion. Read aloud to children on a daily basis.* Also consider story-telling. (In Chapter 9 we will explain a variety of reading aloud and story-telling procedures and activities.) In particular, introduce children to humorous and nonsensical literature. Consider such classics as Dr. Seuss's *Cat in the Hat* (1957) and others, Mayer's (1968) *The Billygoofang*, Pincus's *Tell Me a Mitzi* (1970), and Krauss's *The Backward Day* (1950). Read to children those that you especially enjoy.

Tell puns, jokes, riddles, brain teasers, and the like. For example, ask children, "What's white and can be poured in a glass?" Record responses. Or consider posting a riddle and joke on a section of the bulletin board, with the answer or punchline written on the inside flap.

What is black and white and red?	(Picture of skunk and bottle of catsup)	A skunk who sat in catsup.

Use simple language patterns to introduce children to the rhythms of language. Later in the year use "patterned" stories and poems to model language patterns in writing. These patterned stories are highly predictable, enjoyable, and repetitious enough that children are naturally attracted to them. Bill Martin's *Instant Readers* or Dr. Seuss's materials develop children's sensitivity to hearing language. For example, as in these lines by Dr. Seuss (1960):

One fish, two fish.
Red fish, blue fish.

This one has a little star.
This one has a little car.

As the year progressed in one kindergarten class, children were creating their own writing by dictating familiar patterns to the teacher:

One bear, two bear.
White bear, brown bear.

This one has a big red nose.
This one has big fat toes.

Personal Uses. Children need to learn that written language can be used to express individuality, pride, and awareness of self—a *personal* use of language.

Develop a "this is me" book for each child. The book is bound and contains the child's drawings and description of self and family. The first page might begin, "This is me." The child draws a self-portrait. Other pages may include: This is my family, this is my pet. My favorite game is _____. My favorite book is _____. I like _____. I want to be _____. My best friend is _____.

In a similar vein, *write "me" cards that tell the names of pets, favorite toys, books, colors, television programs, or movies. Write names of places of interest, places recently visited, or exciting places to explore in the community.*

As children develop letter and sound awareness, have them suggest self-descriptive words for each letter in their names: jolly; open; happy; nice. *Ask children for "best" words and write on the blackboard.* Then read them to other members of the class. *Write words that name special people, such as family members, friends.* Then attach a photograph of the person to accompany the name.

Language Experience Stories. What more appropriate way to help children understand what reading is all about than to show them how language is transcribed into print. A language experience story is just what it implies—an account that is told aloud by a child and printed by another person. In the beginning of instruction there are numerous ways to involve children in producing experience stories. For example, many of the suggestions for teaching about the uses of written language in the previous section can serve to stimulate the child's dictation or, for that matter, a group-dictated story. Not only does an experience story vividly show the relationship between speech and print, but it also introduces children to the thrill of personal authorship.

This doesn't mean that children shouldn't engage in independent writing experiences. However, when language experience stories are coupled with regular writing time, children make great strides in learning about written language. Some argue that language experience activities are superfluous in light of the recent emphasis on writing process. (Read Chapter 5 for an extended discussion.) We disagree. From a learning-to-read perspective, young people will benefit greatly from *both* language experience and writing.

The value of language experience lies in the physical ease by which text is produced *to achieve reading instructional goals.* When a child dictates, the physical burden of writing is removed. This often results in more of a child's ideas being put in print than otherwise possible in beginning situations. In Chapter 5, we advocate regular, ongoing writing activity from the first day that children enter school. Dictated language experience stories should be phased out as children's independent writing fluency increases.

Steps to Follow in Producing Language Experience Stories. A child can dictate a complete story, or several children can collaborate on an account by contributing individual sentences. In either case, the first step is to provide a stimulus (a classroom guinea pig, pictures, concrete objects, an actual experience a child has had) that will lead to dictation. Whatever the stimulus, it should be unusual and interesting enough for children to want to talk about it and to remember it two or three days later when the dictation is reread.

As children dictate, it's important to keep their spoken language intact. Therefore, write down exactly what is said regardless of whether grammatical differences exist in the dictated account or sentences are less than complete. By capturing language just as it is spoken, the teacher preserves its integrity and insures the child's total familiarity with the print to be read.

Once the story is written down, the teacher should read it aloud several times, carefully but steadily moving left-to-right, top-to-bottom, and pointing to each word or a line as it is read and then sweeping to the next line. Next the account should be read in unison with the teacher continuing to model left-to-right, top-to-bottom orientation to print.

A dictated story need not be long. It can represent free-flowing language or controlled responses elicited by guiding questions. Suppose students were conversing about their summer activities. The teacher might say, "Let's tell each other what we did on our summer vacations." Jim begins, "I went fishing for the first time." As he says this, Mrs. Phillips, the kindergarten teacher, writes on an "experience chart" (a large pad of newsprint):

Jim said, "I went fishing for the first time."

The other children contribute to the story with Mrs. Phillips writing each contribution beginning with the child's first name. The account was dictated as follows:

Jim said, "I went fishing for the first time."
Dory said, "We went to my grandma and grandpa's in Florida."
Tony said, "I didn't do nothing but swim."
Sheila said, "My family and me fished too."
Michele said, "I went to Sea World."

Examine what Durkin (1980) suggested can be accomplished with reading material from a language experience story. Depending on one's instructional goals, the teacher can:

1. Motivate children to want to read.

2. Personalize instruction.

3. Demonstrate the connection between spoken and written language.

4. Demonstrate left-to-right, top-to-bottom orientation of written English.

5. Demonstrate that the end of the line does not always mean the end of a thought.

6. Demonstrate the value of written language for preserving information, ideas, and feelings.

7. Teach the meaning of "word" and the function of space in establishing word boundaries.

8. Teach the function of capitalization and punctuation.

In Mrs. Phillips's case, the story was read three times as the children watched her move left-to-right, top-to-bottom. Next, they read the story aloud two more times as she continued to model left-to-right orientation. She then had each child read his or her contribution, directing the children to "read it the way you said it." As a child read, she moved her hand along the bottom of each line coordinating pointing with the child's voice. She also read in unison with each child.

Mrs. Phillips wanted to build confidence among her readers as she unobtrusively provided them with valuable learning opportunities. In addition to a "reading experience" she also spent time engaging the children in building the concept of "word." First, she read the entire story in a natural speaking manner, pointing to each word as it was read. By suggesting to the children that they read their individualized contributions, she reinforced word understanding. Mrs. Phillips also asked the children questions such as, "Which word appears the most?" and discussed how space separates one word from another. Finally, Mrs. Phillips asked the children to draw an illustration for the sentence or part that each contributed to the account. These illustrations were then pasted around the chart as they were completed and posted on a bulletin board where other class members might read them.

Learning About Sounds in Words

While language experience stories help children discover that the string of sounds in spoken language can be broken down into units of print made up of words and sentences, they must also learn that a word can be separated into sounds and that the segmented or separated sounds can be represented by letters. Such learning involves the beginnings of *phonic analysis*. In Chapter 8, we examine more closely issues related to phonics. For now, however, note that a *phone* is defined as the smallest sound unit that is identifiable in spoken language. While phones describe all the possible separate speech sounds in language, they are not necessarily represented by the letters of the alphabet. *Phonemes,* however, are minimal sound units that can be represented in written language. That is to say, phonemes are sounds which correspond to letters of the alphabet. Hence, the term *phonic analysis* is used here generally to refer to the child's identification of words by their sounds. This process involves the association of speech sounds with letters. In the beginning of reading instruction, key questions that need to be asked are, "Is the child able to hear sounds in a word? Is the child able to recognize letters as representing units of sound?"

One of the first indications that children can analyze speech sounds and use knowledge about letters is when they invent their own spellings during writing (Read, 1975; Henderson and Beers, 1980). Invented spellings, as we discuss in Chapter 5, are a sure sign that children are beginning to be conscious of sounds in words.

In Table 4.1 study the invented spellings from several samples of writing from three kindergartners.

In the case of Monica, Tesscha, and James, their spellings reflect varying levels of sophistication in hearing sounds in words and in corresponding letters to those

TABLE 4.1

Spellings of Three Kindergartners

Word	Monica's Spelling	Tesscha's Spelling	James's Spelling
monster	monstr	mtr	aml
united	unintid	nnt	em3321
dressing	dresing	jrasm	8emaaps
bottom	bodm	bodm	19nhm
hiked	hikt	hot	sanh
human	humin	hmn	menena

sounds. Gentry and Henderson (1980) contended that Monica demonstrates the most phonological awareness and James the least. A perusal of Monica's list of words indicates that she has learned to distinguish sounds in sequence and can correspond letters directly to the surface sounds that she hears. Tesscha has also developed an awareness of sounds and letters, although this awareness is not as evident or developed as Monica's. James is the least ready of the three to benefit from sound/letter instruction. The fact that he uses numbers for letters is indicative of his confusion and lack of letter and word awareness. For James (and other five- and six-year-old children at a similar level of performance) analyzing sounds in words and attaching letters to those sounds is beyond his present conceptual reach. Making initial reading tasks too abstract or removed from what James already knows about print won't help him to progress in reading.

Children get confused easily when taught to identify sounds in words or correspond letters to sounds if they have not yet developed a concept of what a word is. Likewise, the level of abstraction in recognizing a word is too difficult for children if they have yet to make any global connection that speech is related to print. From an instructional point of view, a beginning reading program that starts with a strong "bottom-up" premise, introducing letter recognition and speech-to-print rules to all children, puts the proverbial cart before the horse, especially for five- and six-year-olds who have yet to acquire basic understandings about written language. Certainly this doesn't mean that program goals for studying words, analyzing sounds in words, or recognizing correspondences between sounds and letters are not worthwhile. However, they must be put into perspective and taught to beginners in meaningful contexts and as the need or opportunity arises.

Hearing Sounds in Words. The Russian psychologist Elkonin (1973) argued that one of the critical features in learning to read is for the child to hear sounds in sequence in a word. In American schools, teachers of beginners gear instruction so that children go from *letter recognition to sound association*. However, Elkonin's work shows that making the correspondence between sounds and letters is easier if children are first aware of the number of sound segments in a word.

Separating sounds in words has been referred to as *phonemic segmentation*. The following procedures can be incorporated into individual or small-group instruction, once children are identified as ready to benefit from training in phonemic segmentation. In order to benefit from such instruction, children must have already developed strong concepts of print as "talk written down" as well as a concept of "word." Because the initial stages of training in segmenting a word into sounds is totally aural, children need not be aware of letters to profit from this type of instruction. Eventually, children learn to attach letters to sounds that are separated.

Procedures for Segmenting Sounds in Words

1. *Give the child a picture of a familiar object.* Below the picture is a rectangle divided into squares according to the number of sounds in the name of the object. Remember that a square is required for every sound in a word, not necessarily every letter. For example, if the picture were of a boat, there would be three squares for three sounds:

b	oa	t

2. *Next, articulate the word slowly and deliberately, allowing the child to hear those sounds that can be naturally segmented.* Note that research has shown that it is easier to hear syllables than individual phonemes in a word (Liberman, Shankweller, Fischer, and Carter, 1974).

3. *Now, ask the child to repeat the word, modeling the way the teacher has said it.*

4. *Continue to model.* As a word is articulated, show the child how to place counters in each square according to the sounds heard sequentially in the word. For example, take the word *boat*. As the teacher articulates each sound, place a counter in the square:

5. *Walk the child through the procedure by attempting it together several times.*

6. *Show another picture; then the word.* Ask the child to pronounce the word and separate the sounds by placing the counters in the squares. The teacher may have to continue modeling until the child catches on to the task.

7. *Phase out the picture stimulus and the use of counters and squares.* Eventually the child is asked to aurally analyze words independently.

In time, the teacher should combine phonemic segmentation with letter association. As the child pronounces a word, use letters and letter clusters instead of counters in the squares. Ask, "What letters do you think go in each of the squares?" At first, write in the letters for the child. Clay (1979) suggested that the teacher accept any correct sound/letter correspondence the child gives and write it in the correct position as the child watches. She also recommends that the teacher prompt the child with questions such as: What do you hear in the beginning? What do you hear at the end? What else do you hear? What do you hear in the middle?

Hearing sounds in words is no easy reading task for five- and six-year-olds. The research of Liberman and her associates (1977) pointed out that preschool and kindergarten children have a more difficult time of segmentation tasks than do first-graders. As we suggested earlier, helping children to sound out words and learn sound/letter correspondences may be premature if they have not made the connection between speech and print or developed a good sense of what a word is.

For those beginners who can profit from sound separation and show an interest in instruction, we strongly recommend that the teacher move quickly from the training task described above to application in "real" situations. The writing of children is a natural occasion to apply phonic analysis principles to purposeful activity. To illustrate, Cramer (1978) provided an account of how one teacher helped a first-grade child to approximate the spelling of a word *needed* for writing. The teacher/child interaction went like this:

Jenny: Mrs. Nicholas, how do you spell *hospital*?

Mrs. Nicholas: Spell it as best you can, Jenny.

Jenny: I don't know how to spell it.

Mrs. Nicholas: I know you don't know how to spell it, honey. I just want you to write as much of the word as you can.

Jenny: I don't know any of it.

Mrs. Nicholas: Yes, you do, Jenny. How do you think *hospital* starts? (Mrs. Nicholas pronounced hospital distinctly with a slight emphasis on the first sound, but she deliberately avoided grossly distorting the pronunciation.)

Jenny (very tentatively): h-s.

Mrs. Nicholas: Good! Write the *hs*. What do you hear next in *hospital*? (Again Mrs. Nicholas pronounced the word hospital distinctly, this time with a slight emphasis on the second part.)

Jenny (still tentatively): p-t.

Mrs. Nicholas: Yes! Write the *pt*. Now, what's the last sound you hear in *hospital*? (While pronouncing the word "hospital" for the last time, Mrs. Nicholas emphasized the last part without exaggerating it unduly.)

Jenny (with some assurance): l.

Mrs. Nicholas: Excellent, Jenny, *h-s-p-t-l* is a fine way to spell *hospital*. There is another way to spell *hospital,* but for now I want you to spell words you don't know just as we did this one.

In the next chapter we explore invented spellings further and their relationship to reading and writing. Because Mrs. Nicholas was willing to tolerate misspellings in a beginning situation, Jenny benefited. Not only did she have an opportunity to apply her knowledge of sound/letter correspondences, but Jenny also had the opportunity to test the rules that govern English spelling in an accepting environment.

Recognizing Letters

Letter recognition has been a well-established predictor of first grade success in reading (Durrell, 1958). However, studies by Ohnmacht (1969) and Samuels (1972) showed that teaching children to master the recognition of letters does not necessarily help them to become better readers at the end of the first grade. Therefore, teachers of beginning reading should not assume that the relationship between letter naming and reading success is *causal*. The ability to recognize letters and to succeed in reading probably results from a more common underlying ability. Venezky (1978) contended that letter recognition scores on a reading readiness test can be interpreted as a sign of general intelligence or positive home experiences and a child's early exposure to print.

No doubt, today's five-year-old brings more letter knowledge to beginning reading instruction than the five-year-old of a decade ago. Television plays a big part in this phenomenon. Children's programs such as *Sesame Street* and *Electric Company* are largely responsible for increasing children's letter awareness.

The kindergarten teacher should capitalize on children's knowledge of letters in a variety of ways. Plan instruction in letter recognition around daily classroom routines and activities. Also help children discriminate small but significant differences among letters—not necessarily in isolated activity, but in meaningful written language contexts. Traditionally visual perception tasks have involved letter identification and discrimination. While these tasks are more justifiable than discrimination activities involving geometric shapes, the teacher should move quickly to letter recognition and discrimination within words and sentences. Consider these instructional tasks:

Discuss letters in the context of a language experience story, or "key words" which children recognize instantly because they are personal and meaningful. (See Chapter 8 for a discussion of key word instruction.) For example, ask children to find at least one other child in the room whose first name begins with the same letter as theirs does. If a child can't find a match, ask the class to "brainstorm" some names that begin with the same letter as the child's name. Write the names on the board for discussion and analysis.

Use alphabet books. Every kindergarten class should have a collection of alphabet books. Ask children to find the page that a certain letter is on. Compare and contrast the illustrations of the letter in the different books. Ask children to illustrate their own rendition of the letter. Over time the class can develop its own alphabet book.

Target a letter for discussion. Have children search for the letter on labels of cans and other commercial products ("Special K," for example), in magazines, newspapers, and other sources of print. Children can make a letter collage by cutting the letters they find, arranging and pasting them onto a big construction-paper letter that the teacher has made.

Tie letter recognition to writing. Begin with each child's name. Encourage children to write their names by tracing copies of the letters or writing independently. Ask children to count the number of letters in their name, examine names for repeating letters, and so on.

Create letters through art activities. Art is a very important part of the child's school experience. It gives children the opportunity to learn that there are many ways to express thinking, feelings, and point of view. Art also heightens children's awareness of their physical environment, involving them through the manipulation of different materials and the development of visual and sensory capacities. For this reason, one small but significant form of expression might be to create letters through drawing, finger painting, sculpting, and making collages such as the letter poster described above.

Learning About the Language of Instruction

In the past several pages some educational jargon has been introduced to classify and label important instructional concepts: for example, *phonic analysis* and *phonemic segmentation*. While an attempt has been made to define specialized terms in context, some confusion may still exist as to the meaning of these terms. In the same way, the "language of reading instruction" has also been used quite freely, that is, *reading, sounds, letters, syllables, words,* et cetera.

Developmentally, if children are to succeed in reading, they must acquire and understand the "language of reading instruction." That is, they must learn the terms and labels that are needed to talk about reading and carry out reading tasks. What, for example, is the child's concept of "reading"? Of a "word"? Of a "letter" or "sound"? Does the child confuse "writing" with "drawing" and "letter" with "number" when given a set of directions? Without a knowledge and understanding of these terms, cognitive confusion mounts quickly for the child (Downing, 1979). The teacher's job is to make explicit what each child already knows implicitly about written language.

Instructional terms are understood gradually by children and are best taught through examples. Recognize early on that when a child gives a wrong answer it may be the result of unawareness of the language of instruction. Because it's easy to use terms that might be misunderstood, beginners shouldn't necessarily be expected to know terminology to succeed at various reading tasks. In time they gradually learn most of the important terms through instruction. Yet by the end of the first grade, some terms may still remain fuzzy for some children. It's important, therefore, to be wary of giving directives that rely too heavily on the language of instruction.

As can be seen from the strategies and activities that have been presented, a basic instructional principle for beginning reading is to *teach for the task.* In other words, beginners should be involved in learning to read in reading-like situations where they are exposed to print from the first day they come to school. We have avoided suggesting instructional practices that are not directly tied to actual reading tasks. Readiness-building activities that are isolated from print have little to do with learning to read. Written language, therefore, should always be the vehicle by which we prepare children for reading, no matter if such preparation includes visual discrimination, left-right progression, or concepts of language.

ASSESSING READINESS FOR READING

Another important instructional principle for beginning reading is to assess a child's preparedness for learning to read by providing abundant, varied opportunities to begin to read. In short, *assess through teaching* and then adjust instruction appropriately for individual children.

Reading readiness assessment is often treated ritualistically at the beginning of each school year. Children usually are given a standardized reading readiness test to determine if they are ready for the school's reading program. The limitations in using a readiness test score for such determinations have already been discussed. While most standardized tests attempt to evaluate those prereading skills and abilities that are related to success in beginning reading, they are limited by the test author's views concerning which variables are essential for success in reading. Compare the subtests of the six leading standardized readiness tests on the market today in Table 4.2.

Although it may be difficult in some cases to determine the nature of some of the subtests by their title, it's easy to recognize that some of them are more directly related to tasks involved in learning to read than others. Nevertheless, almost all of the subtests that are related in some way to learning to read are predicated on a bottom-up view of the reading process. Therefore, if the reading experiences that you plan for beginners are broader in scope than those tasks suggested on readiness tests, it is imperative that informal assessment through teaching and observation reflect the instructional conditions in your classroom.

Observing Reading and Reading-like Behavior

Beginning teachers can evaluate children's readiness for reading through a wealth of information garnered from the day-by-day classroom interactions that occur. The teacher, however, has to tune in to children's reading behavior. You must be a good listener and observer. Through many of the instructional activities that have been suggested in this and the previous chapter, important information will emerge to help make instructional decisions. For example, as you interact with children, ask yourself these questions as suggested by McDonnell and Osburn (1978).

Do children attend to the visual aspects of print? If I am reading a story, can the child tell me where to start and where to go next? Is the child able to point to words as I read them, thereby demonstrating knowledge of directional patterns of print? Does the child understand the concepts of words and letters? Can he/she circle a word and letter in the book? To eliminate the good guesser, this ability should be demonstrated several times.

TABLE 4.2

Comparison of Subtests from Standardized Readiness Tests

Name of Test	Subtests
Clymer-Barrett Prereading Battery	Recognition of letters; matching words; discrimination of beginning sounds in words; discrimination of ending sounds in words; shape completion; copy a sentence.
Gates-MacGinitie Reading Tests—Readiness Skills	Listening comprehension; auditory discrimination; visual discrimination; following directions; letter recognition; visual-motor coordination; auditory blending.
Harrison-Stroud Reading Readiness Profile	Using symbols; making visual discriminations; using the context; making auditory discriminations; using context and auditory clues; giving names of letters.
Lee-Clark Reading Readiness Test	Matching; cross-out; vocabulary and following directions; identification of letters and words.
Metropolitan Readiness Tests	Word meaning; listening; matching; alphabet; numbers; copying, draw-a-man.
Murphy-Durell Reading Readiness Analysis	Phonemes; letter names; learning rate.

Do children use their intuitive knowledge of language? Can the child look at a picture book and invent a story to go with the pictures? Does the invented story, when the teacher begins to write it down, indicate the child is using a more formalized language that approximates the language used in books (book talk) rather than an informal conversational style? Does the child recognize that the print and the pictures are related? Can the child "read the words" of a memorized text such as a nursery rhyme, even though the spoken words are not completely accurate matches for the print? Is this recall stimulated or changed by the pictures?

Are children beginning to show signs of integrating visual and language cues? Is he/she beginning to read single sentences word by word, pointing to each word with a finger while reading? Can the child use all the cues available to a reader: the predictability of language, word order, a beginning sound, and an appropriateness to context while reading? Does he/she stop and correct, without prompting, when a visual-vocal mismatch occurs?

Does the child expect meaning from print? Does he/she demonstrate that a message is expected by relating a sensible story?

These questions easily lead to the development of checklists that can help the teacher make systematic evaluations. The checklist in Box 4.1 provides a representative example of one checklist that can be used for this purpose.

An integral part of informal assessment is to also consider children's back-

BOX 4.1

Checklist for Beginning Reading Behaviors

Name: _____   Date: _____

Skill Area	Seldom or Never	Usually	Always
A. Basic Literacy Concepts			
1. Recognizes the uses of written language			
2. Demonstrates left-right progression			
3. Recognizes sentences			
4. Recognizes words			
5. Recognizes letters			
6. Recognizes sounds			
B. Uses of Language			
7. Interested in communicating ideas			
8. Uses variety of words			
9. Invents story to go with pictures			
C. Integrates Skills			
10. Begins to read sentences word-by-word			
11. Begins to use information cues			
12. Self-corrects without prompting			

ground. The checklist in Box 4.2 lends good insight into what to observe related to a child's cognitive, language, social, emotional, and physical development.

SUMMARY

In this chapter we explored the relationship between readiness and beginning reading. The readiness program should not be thought of as an all-or-none phase of instruction that precedes beginning reading. If reading is viewed developmentally, then teachers will make use of children's preschool experiences with and knowledge of print to get beginners started in reading. The principle behind instruction is to teach for the task of reading. In other words, beginning reading should center around reading-like situations rather than on activities that are unrelated to having children interact with printed language.

Three strands of instruction characterize beginning reading. First, children should participate in instructional activities in which they learn what reading is all about. To this extent, we showed how to incorporate several language functions which lend themselves to print into instructional practices. Through these activities children will learn that the string of sounds in spoken language can be broken down in units of print made up of words and sentences. Moreover, they should engage in instruction in which they learn that a word can be separated into sounds and that these separated sounds can be represented by letters. Finally, a third phase of beginning instruction should center around children learning about the language of instruction. They must learn the terms and labels that are needed to talk about reading and carry out reading tasks.

We emphasized informal assessment over a standardized reading readiness testing because informal assessment provides teachers with daily judgments of children's preparedness and progress in beginning reading situations. Assessment through teaching and observation yields valuable information about a child's abilities as well as about the teaching methods that seem to be easiest and of greatest interest to individual children.

THE WORKSHOP

In the Classroom

1. Suppose that you were to conduct a book interview with a young child to determine the child's level of acquaintance with print. What questions would you develop to tap the child's knowledge about books and print? Develop a set of questions to use both before and during reading. Compare your questions with those of others in the class.

2. Consider Bob's present level of acquaintance with print. Bob is an active kindergartner who loves to be "on the move," playing with games and building blocks. He will sit to hear a good book, but when asked to follow along he doesn't know where to begin. Sometimes he points to the top right side of the page,

BOX 4.2
Reading Readiness Checklist

Always | Sometimes | Never

Cognitive Development

1. Does the child understand basic concepts of size (big-little), direction (up-down), and sequence (first-last)?

2. Does the child understand simple classification?

3. Can the child complete simple analogies involving opposites (e.g., hot : cold :: big : _____)?

4. Can the child make reasonable predictions for how a story might end?

Experiential Background

5. Has the child traveled out of state?

6. Has the child been to a zoo?

7. Has the child been to a library?

8. Does the child play regularly with other children?

9. Does the child have a hobby or special interest?

Language Development

10. Does the child have labels for concepts related to his environment (e.g., objects, actions, and places)?

11. Can the child tell a story or describe a personal experience accurately?

12. Does the child articulate clearly?

13. Does the child recognize that words often have multiple meanings?

14. Does the child understand common figures of speech?

15. Does the child recognize the connection between an anaphoric term and its antecedent (e.g., John is tall. *He* is also fat.)?

Emotional Development

16. Does the child seem happy and well adjusted in school?

17. Can the child accept a setback?

18. Does the child begin and finish a task without constant supervision?

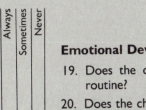

Emotional Development (continued)

19. Does the child adjust well to new tasks or changes in daily routine?
20. Does the child have a positive self-concept?

Social Development

21. Does the child take turns with others?
22. Does the child share when appropriate?
23. Does the child listen without interrupting others?
24. Can the child submerge himself in a group activity?

Physical Development

25. Does the child show evidence of visual problems?
26. Does the child show evidence of auditory problems?
27. Can the child sit quietly for a reasonable length of time when appropriate?
28. Can the child do simple exercises and related motor tasks (e.g., jumping jacks, skipping, and bouncing a ball)?
29. Does the child seem alert and well nourished?

Attitude Toward and Interest in Reading

30. Does the child ask about letters, words, and other printed symbols?
31. Does the child choose to look at books on his own?
32. Has the child grasped the relationship between oral and written language?
33. Does the child listen attentively and with enjoyment to books read aloud?

Source: From Harris, L. A., and Smith, C. B. (1980). *Reading instruction: Diagnostic teaching in the classroom* (3rd ed.). New York: Holt, Rinehart & Winston, 121–122. Reprinted by permission.

sometimes to the middle of the page. Design several classroom experiences with print from which Bob may benefit.

3. Examine a readiness-to-read test. What are the essential readiness skills assessed by the test? Critique the test, applying the major ideas presented in this chapter.

4. Devise a set of classroom activities which would help children understand the following uses of language: perpetuating, regulatory, instrumental, personal, divertive.

In the Field

1. Conduct book interviews with kindergarten and first-grade children. Use the questions that you developed from the classroom workshop activity suggested above. Then classify each child's level of acquaintance with print, using Aull's categories outlined in this chapter. Share your findings with class members.

2. Poll several kindergarten and first-grade teachers on their views of reading readiness. What is their concept of readiness to read? Do they subscribe to a separate program of readiness instruction? What do they value as children's first school experiences with reading?

3. Plan and teach a lesson to a small group of children in which the children dictate an experience story. Plan the language experience activity by deciding how best to stimulate the story and how to involve children in further literacy learning once the story is written.

Chapter 5

The Writing Road to Reading

Anne Frank's words from The Diary of a Young Girl *echo some of the important themes of this chapter: "I am the best and sharpest critic of my own work. I know myself what is and what is not well written. Anyone who doesn't write doesn't know how wonderful it is . . . I want to go on living after my death! And therefore, I am grateful . . . for this possibility of developing myself and my writing, of expressing all that is in me . . . I can recapture everything when I write . . . So I go on with fresh courage; I think I shall succeed, because I want to write!" Writing must serve the functional needs of children. In classrooms across the country, young people* want to write *because they believe they have something worthwhile to say. They know that if writing is for anything, it is for reading. In this chapter we explore literacy development from the perspective of writing. How children develop as writers has a significant impact on learning to read.*

Writing is like talking to your best friend.

Eric, a first-grader

Writing is a dance in the sun.

Christi Ann, a second-grader

Writing is knowing.

Maria, a fourth-grader

Writing is meeting the person in me I never knew.

Mike, a seventh-grader

Listen to the voices of Eric, Christi Ann, Maria, and Mike. They define writing in unique ways—as self-expression, communication, thinking, and learning. Their words may not be the same, but their definitions suggest an awareness of the functions that writing serves in their lives. They know, perhaps intuitively, that writing is an act of composing; a process of discovery; a powerful way to understand and be understood.

This chapter is about children's writing and the strong bonds that exist between learning to write and learning to read. Youngsters like Eric, Christi Ann, Maria, and Mike probably have learned as much about reading by writing as they have learned about writing by reading. In this chapter, we find out why.

Writing and reading have been described as two sides of the same process (Squires, 1984). Yet in many elementary schools, writing and reading are strangers to one another, isolated and taught as separate curriculum entities. In many schools, teachers have followed a much-traveled road to literacy instruction. Along the way, reading and writing are taught separately and sequentially. The premise underlying this instructional path is that reading ability develops first, and writing ability follows. Nevertheless, with new knowledge about literacy development emerging daily, teachers are recognizing that when young children are engaged in writing, they are using and manipulating written language. In doing so, children develop valuable concepts about print and how messages are created.

There is compelling evidence to suggest that writing and reading abilities develop concurrently and should be nurtured together. Carol Chomsky (1970; 1979) was one of the first language researchers to advocate that children write first, and read later. She contended that writing is a beneficial introduction to reading because children acquire letter and word knowledge through invented spellings. Marie Clay (1979) has also supported the powerful bonds between writing and reading. She views reading and writing as complementary processes. Literacy development demands that children engage in reading and writing concurrently.

In Robert Frost's poem, "The Road Not Taken," a traveler stands undecided before two roads diverging in the wood. Which one should the traveler take?

Both are appealing. Weighing one against the other, the traveler decides to take the less-traveled road which is grassy and wanting in wear. The choice turns out to be a good one, for as the traveler reflects:

I shall be telling this with a sigh
Somewhere ages and ages hence:
Two roads diverged in a wood, and I—
I took the one less traveled by,
And that has made all the difference.

Teaching always involves decisions and choices. With what is known today about the way children develop literacy, teachers of beginners may find themselves in a position similar to the traveler's in Frost's poem.

In this chapter you'll journey on a less-traveled road: the writing road to reading. The road is paved in the knowledge that young children are language learners who are actively involved in their own literacy development before entering school. Certainly, some preschoolers have been more actively involved than others through social interaction with the significant others in their lives. As we have shown in Chapter 3, reading and paper and pencil activities play a major role in that social interaction. Moreover, in Chapter 4, the transitions from preschool literacy development to beginning instruction were highlighted. In this chapter, we explore how children develop as writers and how to create environments which support development and learning.

Who knows? The writing road to reading may make all the difference in how children approach literacy tasks in school and use reading and writing in their lives.

HOW WRITING DEVELOPS

Some preschoolers such as those described in the studies by Durkin, Clark, Torrey, and Bissex (described in Chapter 3) are prolific with pencil and paper. Others are just as handy with crayon, ink marker, or paint brush. Sometimes a convenient wall or refrigerator door substitutes nicely for paper. The common denominator for "paper and pencil kids" is a strong desire and need for self-expression and communication.

The noted Russian psychologist Lev Vygotsky (1962) suggested that an infant's gestures are the first visible signs of writing: "Gestures are writing in air, and written signs frequently are simply gestures that have been fixed." Calkins (1986) explained Vygotsky's point with this example: "The urge to write begins when a baby, lying in her crib, moves her arms, and we draw close to the crib, our faces lighting into smiles. 'She's waving to us,' we say. Because we attach meaning to what could be called meaningless gestures, the gestures assume meaning. Babies learn the power of their gestures by our response to them" (page 35). As infants learn about the power of signs and symbols, there is, in Vygotsky's words, "a fundamental assist to cognitive growth."

Klein (1985) distinguished between the terms *writing* and *written expression*. Written expression comes earlier than writing. Scribbles and drawings are examples of written expressions *if* they have symbolic meaning to the child. The difference, then, is in the child's ability to produce units of written language, that is, letters, words, sentences. For Klein, a working definition of writing should include written expression: writing is the *"ability to employ pen or pencil and paper to express ideas symbolically so that the representations on the paper reflect meaning and content capable of being communicated to another by the producer"* (pages 3–4). How youngsters move from various representations of written expression to units of written language is a natural and important evolution.

Progressing from Scribbling to Writing

Scribbling is one of the primary forms of written expression. In many respects, scribbling is the fountainhead for writing and occurs from the moment a child grasps and manipulates a writing tool. Children take their scribbles seriously, if Linda Lamme's quotation from a scribbler is any indication: "Dat's not a scrwibble. It says, 'What's for dinner, Mom?' " Lamme (1984) has described the progression of scribbling in children's writing development in her excellent handbook for parents.

Early Scribbling. Early or "uncontrolled" scribbling is characterized by children making random marks on paper. Evidence of early scribbling can be gathered for most youngsters before their first birthday. Very young children who scribble soon learn that whatever it is that is in their hands, it can make marks. Early scribblings, according to Lamme, compare with babbling in oral language development (see Figure 5.1).

Since early scribbles are not representational (they do not convey meaning), parents and teachers should suppress the urge to ask a child, "What is that?" Instead, encourage a child to get markings on paper without pressure to finish a piece of work or tell what it's about.

Controlled Scribbling. Movement away from random scrawls becomes evident in the scribbles of children as they begin to make systematic, repeated marks—such as circles, vertical lines, dots, and squares as in the example in Figure 5.2.

Controlled scribbling occurs in children's written work between the ages of three to six. The marks are often characterized as *scribble-writing* in the sense that the scribbles are linear in form and shape and bear a strong resemblance to the handwriting of the child's culture. Recall, for example, Dawn's, Najeeba's, and Dalia's scribble-writing in Chapter 3.

Scribble-writing stands in contrast to *scribble-drawing* which is more pictographic in expression. Children use drawing as a means of written expression. According to Klein (1985), *"Drawing is possibly the most important single activity that assists both writing development and handwriting. It is critical to the child's evolving sense of symbol, and it directly assists muscle and eye-hand coordination development"*

Figure 5.1   An Early Scribbling Sample

(page 40). Children between the ages of four to six use drawings or pictographs as a form of written expression in their work.

Name Scribbling. Name scribbling is an extension of scribble-writing. Scribbles become representational to the child-writer: The scribbles mean something. At this point, parents or teachers should begin to model writing and write with children. This is where the language experience activities described in the previous chapter play an important role in the writer's development. Make cards, lists, or signs with child-writers; label things. Have children dictate stories as you write them as well as encourage independent writing.

When children differentiate between drawing and scribbling as means of written expression, they begin to make great strides in their knowledge of print. Name scribbling underscores this differentiation and results in the formation of valuable concepts about written language; namely, that markings or symbols represent units of language such as letters and words, which in turn represent things and objects that can be communicated by messages.

Four-year-old Matthew Padak is a young writer. His scribble-writing in Figure 5.3 was developed as a thank-you note to two of the authors of this book. What do you notice in Matthew's writing?

When his mother asked Matthew to read the thank-you message aloud, he

Figure 5.2 Example of Controlled Scribbling

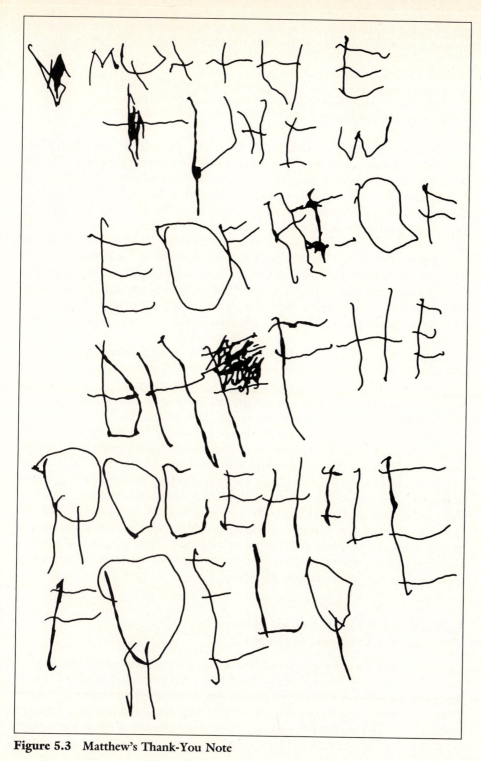

Figure 5.3 Matthew's Thank-You Note

approximated a speech-to-print match. That is, he matched *his spoken words to the letters and marks on each line of print.* Here's what he read line by line:

> This is Matthew Padak
> speaking, Rich Vacca
> and JoAnne Vacca. Thank you
> for coming to our house.

What does Matthew's written expression tell us about his development? First, Matthew is acutely aware of the message-sending function of writing. He has developed a "message concept." Through his many encounters with print in his environment, Matthew has also developed alphabet letter awareness. He knows, too, some of the conventions of writing peculiar to the English language. Writing, for example, moves from left to right, then back to the left at the end of a line, and from top to bottom on a page. Also, Matthew has developed an awareness of audience—in this case, the Vaccas. His thank-you message is direct and to the point. In case you're wondering what the two solid markings are that appear at the beginning and end of the first line, Matthew's explanation is both sensible and pragmatic: "That's where they (the Vaccas) can put the nails through." In other words, when the Vaccas display Matthew's thank-you note on their bulletin board, they'll know where to place the thumb-tacks!

Matthew's note is also revealing by what it doesn't reflect. At age four, Matthew's writing doesn't indicate word awareness (i.e., that words are comprised of letters and are separated from one another by "boundaries" or white spaces). Matthew might be called a "one-letter speller." A letter or several letters on each line of text may represent a word, phrase, or entire sentence.

As Matthew continues to grow as a writer, his writing will become increasingly more sophisticated. He will develop a concept of word and a knowledge of sound-letter correspondence. We are confident that Matthew will soon be writing words and sentences with the aid of invented spellings. Spelling invention will give way to convention as he gains greater knowledge and control of sound-letter relationships. Other writing conventions, such as punctuation and capitalization, will also evolve with continued writing experiences in an environment that encourages growth and supports Matthew's literacy development. How parents and teachers view the conventions of writing, particularly invented spellings, in beginning situations is crucial to writing development.

Building on Emerging Competence: The Case for Invented Spellings

Invented spelling is a name given to children's misspellings before they have learned the rules of spelling. Most children don't begin school having mastered sound-letter correspondence. Yet as we have shown in the previous chapters, children come to school having varying degrees of knowledge about the structure of written language. Young Paul Bissex's case in Chapter 3 is a good example of how a child, through his use of invented spellings, expected his writing to make sense and have meaning. As his mother noted, quoting Piaget: "Children have real understanding of that which they invent themselves" (Bissex, 1980, page 203).

In Chapter 4, we briefly examined the invented spellings of three kindergartners, Monica, Teescha, and James. Recall from that discussion that invented spellings signal to teachers that children are beginning to analyze speech sounds in print. By first grade, for example, most children know something about letters. They may know the names and shapes of some letters. Others may make associations between sounds and letters.

During the past decade, spelling researchers have explored the developmental relationship between spelling ability and reading and writing (Read, 1971, 1975; Clay, 1979; Bissex, 1980; Henderson and Beers, 1980). From their work it is clear that young children apply systematic strategies to relate speech sounds to print. These strategies are applied through definable developmental stages. These stages, adapted from Gillet and Temple (1986), are broadly defined below.

Prephonemic spelling. Once children know some letters, they begin to experiment with the relationship between the letters and their sounds. One early concept that develops is that there is a one-to-one correspondence between the initial consonant or final consonant of a word and the words. The word *back* is spelled with a *B* or *sink* with a *K*. This concept is gradually expanded to include the consonant boundaries of word. For example, ML = *mail* and DR = *dear*. Matthew, whose thank-you note is illustrated in Figure 5.3, is an early prephonemic speller.

Phonemic spelling. At this stage, vowels begin to appear in children's invented spellings. Six- and seven-year-olds learn to sound their way through a word making sound-letter matches as they write. There is still a tendency to use a one-to-one match although it is now much more refined than in the previous stage. For example, MAL = mail; ESTR = Easter; COT = coat; SRPRIS = surprise. Note that long vowels are represented with the corresponding letter name. Often, logical substitutions are made for short vowels, such as SEK = *stick* or JRAS = *dress*.

Transitional spelling. As a result of extended opportunities to read and write in and out of school, children begin to abandon the notion that there has to be a one-to-one match between a spoken sound and a graphic symbol. They now actively search for chunks or patterns of letters that represent spoken sounds. They begin to develop greater spelling awareness by observing the CVC pattern, that is, GET; the CVVC pattern, that is, MALLE = *mail*; DAER = *dear;* CEAP = *keep;* the CVCe patterns, that is, TAKE = *take*; LIKE = *like*; CAER = *care*.

Conventional spelling. By the third grade children have developed many accurate notions of how to spell words which conform to the standard rules of the language. They use correct spellings more and more often in their attempts to communicate.

Examining Bobo's Spelling Development. Bobo is an "average" second-grader in Sharon Piper's class. A regular classroom event in Mrs. Piper's room is journal writing. Early in the school year, Bobo's journal entries indicated that he was using several systematic strategies in his writing. His entries on October 27 and 28, for example, indicated that he was employing both a letter-name strategy (*cam* for *came*) and what Henderson and Beers (1980) described as a transitional strategy showing awareness of lax vowels and the *e* marker (*scerry* for *scary*; *guey* for *guy*).

Mrs. Piper decided to follow Bobo's development as a speller by examining words that recurred through different entries over time. Here's what she discovered:

today

Nov. 3	to daey
Nov. 20	taooday
Dec. 3	teay
Jan. 5	today

yesterday

Nov. 19	ewastdoaday
Dec. 11	yesdday
Feb. 5	yesterday

opening my presents

| Dec. 14 | opting my poisis |
| Dec. 18 | opning my pisins |

coming

Dec. 17	ciming
Feb. 4	caming
Feb. 11	comming
Apr. 16	comeing

snow

Nov. 20	sarrow
Dec. 9	sniwing
Jan. 18	snowing

tomorrow

Nov. 7	tamarro
Apr. 28	tomorrowe
Apr. 29	tomrrow

vacation

| Dec. 7 | waicing |
| Dec. 16 | facishin |

outside

Nov. 5	altt
Nov. 20	aitsadd
Dec. 9	awtside
Jan. 21	owtshd
Feb. 24	outsid
May 3	outside

All of the examples above show progress toward a correct form. The important point, however, is that Bobo's progress reveals how children *invent* and *reinvent* spellings as they experiment with written language. Chomsky (1970) pointed out that the child doesn't *memorize* spellings, but instead, reinvents them each time in order to more closely approximate correct spelling. Invention, then, reflects that spelling is a process that is refined over time and that children have little trouble making the transition to conventional spelling when they have many opportunities to write freely.

Advantages of Invented Spelling. The gradual sophistication in children's invented spellings should be celebrated by teachers and parents as a display of intelligence and emerging competence with written language. When "correct spelling" isn't an obstacle in the path of young writers, they are free to get their ideas down on paper. Invented spellings help children place ideas before notions of correctness. Every primary teacher knows the interruptions that can occur in class when youngsters constantly ask for the correct spelling of practically every word they don't know. What we sometimes fail to recognize, however, is that children probably seek correct spellings because they perceive that the teacher values accuracy in their writing. When children are bound by notions of correctness, the writing process comes to a halt. Classroom writing becomes a laborious undertaking rather than a liberating act.

A supportive classroom environment encourages children to try to spell words as best they can during writing. The first rule in a class of beginners should be not to ask for spelling help. Instead, encourage children to "try their best."

In Pip Stein's first-grade class the children write on the first day of school and every day thereafter. In the beginning some of her students choose to draw first and then "try their best" to put what they draw in words. These early writing forays, as you might expect, reflect various stages of invented spelling. Of course, some children just draw, and that's okay in Mrs. Stein's class. In these instances, she encourages them to *draw and tell*. Sometimes, she serves as a "secretary" to preserve what a child says. She views her role as secretary as a "bridge" in children's writing development—especially for those students whose literacy experiences at home have been limited.

Many of Mrs. Stein's students use invented spellings to produce writing that they "share" with others. The share session provides a natural occasion for reading. In one such session, late in November, Leon shared his drawing and writing (displayed in Figure 5.4). He first told about the picture. A "rock star" is on stage performing in front of a packed audience. Leon isn't the star. He's the rock singer's agent! In sharing his piece of writing, everyone sensed Leon's enthusiasm as he read:

> This boy did it. He have a big show and he will work for me. He will be, be, be, be on T.V. He will go for it. Now go.

A supportive environment allows children, like Leon, to play and experiment with written language without the restrictions imposed by demands for accuracy and correction.

Sowers (1982) listed the advantages of not placing a premium on accuracy:

1. Children build independence because they don't have to ask for every word they don't know.

2. By emphasizing ideas rather than correctness, children become fluent in their writing. They can "elaborate and play on paper" without interruptions.

3. Children move efficiently through the stages of spelling development when they have opportunities to apply strategies about sound-symbol correspondences at their own pace and level of sophistication.

4. Children develop control and responsibility for their writing by taking risks and trying out the "rules" that they are forming about spelling. As Sowers noted, "The worst outcome of an unsuccessful invention is that communication stops temporarily." But if the invention succeeds, so does the child: "Real rewards await the child who writes fearlessly about a FROSHUS DOBRMN PENSR instead of a BAD DOG" (page 48).

Figure 5.4 Leon's Writing Sample

The whole idea behind encouraging spelling invention is to build on the emerging competence of the beginner. As children put their ideas ahead of concerns for correct spelling, they will develop confidence in their ability to write; they will recognize the value of taking risks. Putting words down on paper isn't easy, but as children approach writing confidently they will do so much more fluently and powerfully.

Creating a Natural Learning Environment

In school, children develop fluency and power in their writing when they have occasions to write freely about things that are important to them. This is why a positive attitude toward invented spellings contributes greatly to children's writing development. Concerns for the form and mechanics of writing are important but must be viewed from a developmental perspective. The first order of concern in the classroom should be on the exploration and development of topics that matter to young writers.

Since the mid-1970s Donald Graves and his colleagues have conducted research on the writing processes of elementary children. Extensive field work in primary grade classrooms, for example, has yielded valuable insights into the influence of the learning environment on writing development.

Graves (1975) found that *informal* learning environments increased the volume of writing produced by seven-year-olds. Not only did they write more; the young children in Graves's research also took greater control over and responsibility for their writing under informal conditions for learning. They needed much less external motivation to write from their teachers and less supervision. Graves also observed that when children selected their own topics, the quality and volume of writing dramatically increased as young writers became engrossed in the content of their writing.

An informal classroom environment for writing has much in common with the characteristics of a natural learning environment outlined in Chapter 3. First of all, in an informal classroom context, young writers are encouraged to develop in their own way and at their own rate. Teachers are positive and rewarding in their reception of children's written work. A "built-in support system" surrounds the learner. There is tremendous faith and patience that children will develop as writers. A willingness to wait permeates the writing environment, especially at times when some children seem to be at a plateau or even regressing in their writing ability. Criticism and correction give way to children's trial and error forays into writing. In a natural learning environment, teachers and children celebrate the experience of writing and sharing their work with one another.

Examine Ron Cramer's (1978) suggestions for encouraging classroom writing:

1. *Use children's experiences and encourage them to write about things that are relevant to their interests and needs.* Children must choose topics that they care about. Yet a fear that teachers often harbor is that students will have nothing to say or write about if left to select their own topics. Rarely is this the case. Children want to write. But before they begin, they should have good reason

to believe that they have something to say. How can you help? Guide students to choose topics which they have strong feeling about; provide opportunities for topic discussion and brainstorming before writing; show students how to plan and explore topics by using lists, jotting notes, and clustering ideas.

Not only must children recognize that they have something worthwhile to say, but they should have good reason to believe that they will succeed. As Cramer (1978) noted, it's fruitless to force children to write on assigned topics for which they can generate little enthusiasm or background knowledge.

2. *Develop sensitivity to good writing by reading poetry and literature to children.* Young writers need to listen to written language. In Chapter 9, we explain ways to bring children and literature together. Although literature is a mirror that reflects good writing to children, Cramer is quick to point out that the writing of other children also serves as a powerful model. Sharing good literature and children's writing helps young writers feel that they are capable of producing similar work.

3. *Invent ways to value what children have written.* Children need praise and response, the two mainstays of a built-in support system for classroom writing. Sharing writing-in-progress is an important way to insure classroom response. Displaying and publishing writing is another.

Children's writing reflects the functions of written language. Children, like adults, don't engage in writing for the sake of writing. Because their efforts are purposeful, their writing must result in products. Later in this chapter, we explain ways to value children's products through publication. Certainly one of the best ways to value writing and reading is through bookmaking. Nowhere do children build a sense of authorship better than by writing and illustrating their own books.

4. *Guide the writing personally.* As children are writing, you should circulate around the room to help and encourage. As Cramer put it, writing time is no time to perform other tasks. *Conferencing*, then, becomes the primary means of response and feedback in the writer's environment. Teacher-student and peer conferences help to create a collaborative, noncompetitive atmosphere in which to write, try out work in progress, and share what has been written with others.

5. *Write stories and poetry of your own and share them with your students.* Sharing your writing with students or discussing problems that you are having as a writer signals to children that writing is as much a problem-solving activity for you as it is for them. What better way to model writing than to "let students in" on the processes you use as a writer. Children need to know that writing is as exciting for you as it is for them.

6. *Tie writing in with the entire curriculum.* Content area activities may provide the experiences and topics that can give direction and meaning to writing. Writing to learn will help children discover and synthesize relationships among the concepts they are studying in social studies, science, mathematics, art, music, and health. The connections between reading and writing are especially meaningful when children explore concepts through written language.

7. *Start a writing center in your classroom.* A writing center represents a place where young writers can go to find ideas, contemplate, or read other children's writing. The center should be well-equipped with: lined paper of various sizes and colors; lined paper with a space for a picture; drawing paper of all sizes; stationery and envelopes; tag board; index cards; a picture file; pencils, colored pencils, crayons, and magic markers; paper clips; white glue and paste; paper punches; book display stands; dictionaries; reference materials such as magazines and encyclopedias; a classroom library for students' writing; and an address file of book authors, sports figures, celebrities, and magazines that print students' work. A writing center isn't a substitute for having a classroom program where children work every day at developing the craft of writing. Instead, the center is a visible support that enhances the writing environment in your classroom.

GETTING STARTED

Getting started with writing process instruction is challenging (and sometimes unsettling) because there isn't a prescribed formula or prepackaged curriculum to implement. In the beginning, your efforts will consist mainly of trial and error learning. One of the keys for making the writing process work is to establish a routine that leads to orderly and productive classroom activity.

Establishing a Routine for Writing

No two writing process classrooms look the same; nor should they. Instructional routines and procedures vary from classroom to classroom. However, classrooms often have certain characteristics in common.

One classroom characteristic is that children have freedom of movement. Allowing them to choose where they want to write contributes to the writing environment. Many will choose to write at their desks or a nearby writer's table. Some may opt for the writing center or a private area of the room designated "The Writer's Nook" or "The Writer's Hideaway." Arrange the room so that movement and easy access to classmates are possible. Access to classmates, in particular, will become an important part of trying out work in progress, sharing drafts, and holding peer conferences.

A second characteristic involves continuity from day to day. It's crucial to establish a regular writing time that children will come to expect and anticipate. Set aside forty-five to sixty minutes every day, if possible, for writing. This is not to suggest that children shouldn't be encouraged to write at other times of the day. However, it does suggest a set time for writing that will provide students with a sense of continuity and regularity.

When there's a "special time" for writing every day, children learn to anticipate writing *when they are not writing* (during lunchtime, on the playground, or at home). Writing, in Nancy Atwell's words, becomes habitual: "In situations where students can't write every day, three days each week are enough for developing the habit of gathering and considering ideas for writing. And I think the three days should be regular and consecutive—e.g., every Monday, Tuesday, and Wednesday—this provides the sense of continuity and routine writers need" (Atwell, 1985, page 37).

As part of the routine of writing, the functional needs of the developing writer should be taken into account. Instructional routines should encourage *occasions to write*. These occasions serve specific purposes and lead to various forms of writing. For example, Wolf and Vacca (1985) argued that the occasions below give students a real sense of audience and purpose.

Pen pal arrangements with other classes within the building

Pen pal arrangements with a class from another school within the city

Pen pals in other cities or countries

"Secret" pen pals who leave messages to each other in the classroom

Writing for a school or class newspaper

Writing for a school or class literary magazine

"Author of the Week" Bulletin Board which features a different student writer each week

Entering writing contests within the community

Providing opportunities for students to read pieces of writing over the school's public address system

Weekly "radio broadcast" on the school's "P.A." system

Arrangement with a younger class for students to read selected pieces of writing

Arrangements with a day care center for students to read selected pieces of writing

Many displays of student writing within the classroom and in the corridors of the school

Video taping of students reading their pieces of writing

Slide presentations with student-authored scripts

Play festivals featuring student-authored scripts

Student-written communication for requests for change within the school

Student-written correspondence used in search of information for a research topic

Student-made publicity for school events

Student-written speeches for school assemblies and programs

Young author festival to highlight student-authored books

Student-written speech as a character from a story or from social studies

Daily journals and diaries (real and imaginary)

Biographical sketches based on interviews or research

Letters requesting free material (many items listed in *Free Stuff for Kids*, Meadowbrook Publishing Co., Deephaven, MN 55391)

Song writing

Reviews of movies or television programs

Student-written directions on how to do something

Writing cartoon scripts (pages 25–26)

Important occasions for writing are created when you connect literature and content-area learning to writing. Reading to write serves a powerful functional need on the part of students.

Another integral part of the routine of classroom writing involves the use of folders. Process-centered classrooms often contain a box of writing folders which become the focal point of activity. The writing folders contain almost everything that children write during the school year. Each child has a writing folder (usually a legal-size manilla folder) to store written work. The folders are housed in a brightly decorated cardboard box or in a filing cabinet within easy reach of the children.

Some teachers recommend using two writing folders: a *daily folder* which contains a child's immediate work-in-progress; and a *permanent folder* for completed and abandoned pieces of writing. The permanent folder has at least two important purposes. First, it documents students' writing development during the school year. Children (as well as parents or the principal) can study their progress and the changes that have occurred in their own writing. They enjoy reading and reviewing the topics they've written about and the types of writing they've completed. Teachers find that folders are invaluable for helping students better understand the writing process. Second, when students accumulate their writing, they can see the investment that they have made. The folder, then, helps to build a sense of pride, accomplishment, and ownership. It is a visible record of a child's growth as a writer.

Establishing Classroom Guidelines and Procedures

A process-centered classroom should be guided by rules and procedures that set clear expectations for behavior and interaction and give children a sense of structure and stability. Rules or guidelines will emphasize different things in different classrooms. Yet you may want to consider some of the following:

When engaged in drafting, writers shouldn't be disturbed. There will be plenty of time to talk with one another about your writing and to share work-in-progress.

Talk is an important part of writing, but there are limits set on the number of persons who share with one another at any one time.

All classroom writing is kept in folders which are housed in a box located in an easily accessible place in the room.

The class writes and shares every day (Graves, 1982).

Along with these guidelines, classroom procedures establish a predictable structure for writing.

The Mini-Lesson. Begin each day's writing time by providing students with the structure they need to understand, develop, or use specific writing strategies, or to give them direction in planning their writing or revising drafts. The mini-lesson, as the name implies, is a brief, direct instructional exchange (usually no longer than ten minutes) between the teacher and the writing group (which may include the whole class). The exchange isn't a substitute for individual guidance, but instead, is meant to get students started or to address specific problems or needs. For example, a mini-lesson can help to: stimulate topic selection; brainstorm ideas and rehearse for writing; illustrate "interesting" vs. "dull" writing; model literary style by reading passages from literature; illustrate good sentence structure; illustrate good paragraph structure; teach and/or model strategies for revision; teach a mechanical skill.

Calkins (1986) provided several in-depth examples of different types of mini-lessons that she has seen used by elementary teachers.

The Writer's Workshop. The writer's workshop follows a mini-lesson and is the actual time students spend "in-process," whether they're collecting information, drafting, revising, or editing their work. For part of this time, you may find yourself working on your own writing. In addition, your role is primarily to facilitate the workshop by responding to the needs of writers as specific situations demand.

Two plans that teachers have followed in facilitating the writer's workshop are outlined below:

Plan #1

  I. Mini-Lesson (3-10 minutes)

 II. The Writer's Workshop
    A. Circulate to help individuals (10 minutes)
    B. Work with children in a group conference (15 minutes)
    C. Hold scheduled individual conferences (15 minutes)

III. Group Share Session (10 minutes)

Plan #2

  I. Mini-Lesson (3–10 minutes)

 II. The Writer's Workshop
    A. Write with class (5–10 minutes)
    B. Circulate to help individuals (10–20 minutes)
    C. Hold scheduled individual conferences (10–15 minutes)

III. Group Share Session (10 minutes)

The Group Share Session. The main purpose of the share session is to have writers reflect on the day's work. "Process discussions" focus on concerns implicit in the following questions:

How did your writing go today? Did you get a lot done?

Did you write better today than yesterday?

Was it hard for you to keep your mind on what you were writing?

What do you think you'll work on tomorrow?

What problems did you have today?

Calkins (1983) provided these guidelines to facilitate sharing:

RAISING CONCERNS   A writer begins by explaining where she is in the writing process, and what help she needs. For example, a child might say, "I'm on my third draft and I want to know if it's clear and makes sense," or, "I have two beginnings and I can't decide which is best."

READING ALOUD   Usually, the writer then reads the writing (or the pertinent section) out loud.

MIRRORING THE CONTENT AND FOCUSING PRAISE   The writer then calls on listeners. A classmate begins by retelling what he has heard, "I learned that . . ." or "Your story began . . ." Sometimes a listener may begin by responding to praising or showing appreciation for the writing.

MAKING SUGGESTIONS   Questions or suggestions are then offered about the concern raised by the writer. Sometimes other things will come up as well.

Besides reflecting on the day's writing, reserve the share session for celebrating finished work. Ask volunteers to share their writing with an audience. The "author's chair," a strategy we discuss in the next section, is an integral part of the sharing experience. The celebration that children take part in reflects their "payoff" for the hard work that writers go through to craft a piece of writing to satisfaction.

GUIDING CHILDREN THROUGH THE WRITING PROCESS

In a process-centered classroom, children quickly become aware that writing evolves through steps and stages. These stages have been defined by different authorities in different ways. In this book the stages include: rehearsing, drafting, revising and editing, and publishing. The stages in the writing process aren't neat or orderly. No wonder they have been described as *recursive*. Writing, as Lindemann (1982) noted, is "a messy business, rarely in real life as tidy as textbook descriptions portray it. We don't begin at step one, 'find a topic,' and follow an orderly sequence of events to 'proof-reading the paper.' Certainly, we plan what we want to say before we begin drafting, but the act of writing generates new ideas and shapes new plans" (page 23).

Strategies for Rehearsing

Rehearsing is everything that writers do before the physical act of putting ideas on paper for a first draft. "Getting it out" is a useful mnemonic because it helps us to remember that rehearsal means activating background knowledge and experiences, getting ideas out in the open, and making plans for approaching the task of writing.

The rehearsal stage has also been called *pre-writing*, a somewhat misleading term because "getting it out" often involves writing of some kind (e.g., making lists, outlining information, jotting notes, or freewriting in a journal). Regardless of terminology, rehearsing is a time to generate ideas, stimulate thinking, make plans, and create a desire to write. In other words, rehearsing is what writers do to get "energized"—to explore what to say and how to say it: "What will I include? What is a good way to start? What is my audience? What form should my writing take?"

The teacher's job is to make students aware that the writing process must *slow down* at the beginning. By slowing down the process, you will help them discover that they have something worthwhile to say and that they want to say it.

There are many ways to rehearse for writing: talking, reading to gather information, brainstorming and outlining ideas, role playing, doodling, drawing, cartooning, jotting down ideas, taking notes, interviewing, and even forming mental images through visualization and meditation. Space limits us from exploring each of these strategies in depth. Instead, our focus will be on two areas of rehearsal: (1) talking about topics and (2) freewriting.

Choosing and Talking About Topics. Young writers need to try out their topics and explore ideas with the teacher, with other children, or with people who know something about the topic. Talking is the springboard by which students discover and choose topics for writing. Atwell (1985) described several procedures for initiating, modeling, and valuing self-selection:

1. *Have students (in pairs) interview one another.* These interviews occur early in the school year and are designed around open-ended questions about family, friends, likes and dislikes, earliest memories, hobbies, skills, fears, holidays, and personal favorites (books, movies, poems, athletic teams, etc.). First, model one or two interviews with students as the class observes the exchange of ideas. Such interviews are ice-breakers. Then make lists of questions available to students for the interviews. They can choose some or all of the questions to ask. The interviewers take notes on the interviewees and then reverse roles. The ideas generated from the interviews are then transferred to "My Ideas about Writing" lists that the students keep in their writing folders.

2. *Allow students to initiate topic conferences with the teacher.* When a student is stuck and can't find a topic, he may ask for a topic conference. You can guide

him toward self-selection by "talking through" the selection process. Ask questions that tap into the child's world. As you talk, the student jots down ideas for consideration. Ask questions that lead to conversation: What is special about you? What are you good at? What is important to you? Who makes you feel happy? Sad? Angry? What's one thing that you could teach to someone else? Questions such as these let students know that you support and affirm that they have something to say.

3. *Model self-selection*. Atwell decribed an approach that works well for her. Here's what she recommends. First, describe to the class three or four topics that you have considered writing about for the day's session. Tell how you thought about these topics the night before in anticipation. Propose, then reject, those topics that may be too broad or which you know little about. As you share reasons with the class, zero in on the one topic that you know a lot about and really want to write on. Now that you have modeled your own selection process, have students sit silently for two or three minutes, thinking about topics they might like to write about. Then, in pairs, the students describe to each other the ideas that came to mind. Allow each student to talk for about three minutes then change roles. The entire class then re-groups and several volunteers describe the topics they have discovered.

Freewriting in Journals. When journals are part of the writing environment, children use them to write about anything they please. A journal is a goldmine for generating ideas and a place to record thoughts and feelings. Journals bring children in touch with themselves. All forms of written expression and types of writing are welcomed in journals—from doodles to comments to poems to letters, and finally to written conversations between child and teacher.

Freewriting in journals, as the strategy implies, means that writers are "free" to express themselves without pretense or anxiety over form and correctness. Journals can be used to generate ideas which, in turn, may be used to draft more elaborate pieces of writing. Freewriting has also been called *expressive writing* (Britton et al., 1975). Tammy Lynn, a second-grader, illustrates what James Britton meant by expressive writing in her journal entry in Figure 5.5.

If journals are to be used to generate ideas, you must set aside time to read and respond to children's entries on a regular basis. Because child and teacher enter into a personal relationship through the vehicle of the journal writing, there are, as we have seen, many occasions to "dialogue" in writing. According to Gambrell (1985), the "dialogue journal" emphasizes meaning while providing natural, functional experiences both in writing and reading. Child and teacher use dialogue journals to converse in writing. Your responses to children's entries may include comments, questions, and invitations to children to express themselves.

Gambrell suggested these guidelines for using dialogue journals in the classroom:

1. Use bound composition books. (Staple appropriate writing paper inside a construction paper cover. Paper should be large enough for several journal entries so children see the developing dialogue.)

September 20, 1983
 mRs. piper we have
Bunk beds and my sister
fell of and harT her head and
arm. it was bresed bad but she
still wenT to school and my
mom Told me if i wanted to
sleep on the Top becuse
every cuple munts my mom
puts up plain beds and
we take torns and it was
kristys torn but she fell
off

Figure 5.5 Tammy Lynn's Journal Entry: An Example of Expressive Writing

2. To motivate students, tell them journals are like letters. They will write to you and you will write back. Encourage writing about any topic of interest or concern to them.

3. For best results, write daily. Set aside a special time for writing and reading. For children in grades one and two, 10 minutes might be appropriate, whereas older children may need 20 minutes.

4. Focus on communication. Do not correct entries; instead, model correct forms in your response.

5. Respond in a way that encourages written expression such as, "Tell me more about . . . ," "I'd like to know more about . . . ," "Describe . . . ."

6. Dialogue journals are private. Convey to students that they belong to the two of you, but they may share if they wish. Sharing should always be voluntary.

Drafting, Revising, and Editing

"Getting it down" is an apt way to describe drafting. Once writers have rehearsed, explored, discovered, planned, talked—and done whatever else it takes to get ideas out in the open—they are ready to draft a text with a purpose and an audience in mind. If students are well rehearsed, first drafts should develop without undue struggling. The Writer's Workshop provides the in-class time for first draft writing. As children draft, the teacher regulates and monitors the process. For example, while students are writing, the teacher shouldn't grade papers or attend to other nonrelated chores. Instead, you are either writing yourself or keeping writers on task.

Drafting, then, is a good time to confer individually with students who may need help using what they know to tackle the writing task. Serve as a sounding board; ask probing questions if students appear to be stuck.

How's it going?

What have you written so far?

Tell me the part that is giving you a problem. How are you thinking about handling it?

I am not clear on _____. How can you make that part clearer?

Are you leaving anything out that may be important?

What do you intend to do next?

How does the draft sound when you read it out loud?

What is the most important thing that you're trying to get across?

A first draft, once completed, is just that—a writer's first crack at discovering what he or she wants to say and how he or she wants to say it.

Each interaction that occurs when a writer seeks *response*, either from the teacher or another writer in the class, constitutes a *conference*. Simply stated, a conference may be held by a writer when he or she needs feedback for work-in-progress. The conference may last five seconds or five minutes depending on the writer's needs. However, once a student decides to rework a first draft, conferencing becomes a prominent aspect of revision and editing.

Conferencing. When writers work on a second or third draft, they have made a commitment to rewrite. Rewriting helps students to "take another look." This is why good writing often reflects good rewriting.

To conduct a teacher-child conference, you must learn to define your role as listener. Graves (1982) noted that when conducting a conference, the child leads and the teacher intelligently reacts.

To elicit clarification in a piece of writing, you might focus the conference with a specific question or two appropriate to the writer's needs.

The following general steps will help you conduct a conference:

1. The writer reads the draft out loud.

2. The teacher listens carefully for the meaning of the draft.

3. The teacher then *mirrors the content* ("Your draft is about . . . "); *focuses praise* ("The part I liked the best about your draft is . . . "); *elicits clarification* ("Which parts are giving you the most trouble?" "What are you thinking about doing to solve your problem?"); *makes suggestions* ("I think you should work on . . . "); and *seeks writer's commitment* ("Now that we have talked, what will you do with the draft now?").

To illustrate how effective a conference can be in helping a child to revise, Wolf (1985) described her work with Jessica, a second-grader. Jessica's first draft, displayed in Figure 5.6, is a fluent but rambling piece on a topic that evolved from a social studies lesson on the problem of pollution in big cities.

In this draft, Jessica's content is remarkable; her voice is strong. In conference with the teacher, Jessica realized that her ideas "jumped around." She would need to help the reader to keep the ideas straight. So here's the strategy that she and the teacher worked out: Jessica used a green marker to underline all those ideas about factories and how they pollute the air. Then she went back and used a red marker to underline all those things about how pollution made people and animals sick. Jessica mentioned to the teacher that she also wanted to include her mother's problems with pollution. As a result, she underlined all of those ideas with a yellow marker. She then rewrote a second draft, putting all the ideas underlined in green together, all the ideas underlined in red together, and all the ideas underlined in yellow together. The conference was a perfect opportunity to discuss paragraphing and the idea of indentation. Jessica's second draft is displayed in Figure 5.7.

Teachers who conference regularly with students quickly realize two things: (1) it's an overwhelming, if not impossible, task to conference with every student who needs feedback during a day's writing; and (2) the class must assume responsibility for providing response to fellow writers.

"Peer conferencing" provides an audience for a writer to try out work-in-progress. A child may arrange during the writer's workshop to "hold a conference" with another child, if it doesn't interfere with the other child's writing. In addition, time might be set aside for peer conference teams to meet.

Pollushein! By Jessica

I hate pollushun! It comes from fackters. They pollut the air. Pollushun can make you sick! I sujest you stay away from pollushun! Every day fater ys pollut the air even more. When I go to teleto I go in a car. We see Lots of fackters polluting The air. We see all sorst of fackterys. facktery chimnis are what pallut the air If thay wod tink about other pepill.

Figure 5.6 Jessica's First Draft on Pollution

(continues)

Maybe if thay wod spend ther
money on geting their chimneys
clean the peopill won't
have to wach the air.
for the dascusting things in
it. Like my mom
she works down town
All so cars and
turuks polluth the air
When my mom parcks
her car she walks
To her offices. Whill
she is walking to her
ofies she smels the discust
ing smells in the air
When facktters dump ther junck

Figure 5.6   Jessica's First Draft on Pollution (continued)

in Lakes thay are polluting The Waters

That is how fish dig and pepell can't go swiming in That Lake! for thas resans pepell shoud not pollut the are and water! The end

Figure 5.6 Jessica's First Draft on Pollution (*continued*)

A peer conference team consists of two, three, or four members. At first, a team responds to a writer's draft from questions that the teacher has prepared and modeled through class discussion, demonstration, and individual student conferences.

What did you like best about this paper? What worked very well?

Was there anything about this piece of writing that was unclear to you?

What feeling did this piece of writing convey to you?

Where in the paper would you like to see more detail? Where could the writer show you something instead of telling you about it? In other words, where could the writer use more description?

Editing. During revision, students will be messy in their writing. In fact, they should be encouraged to be messy. Show them how to use carets to make

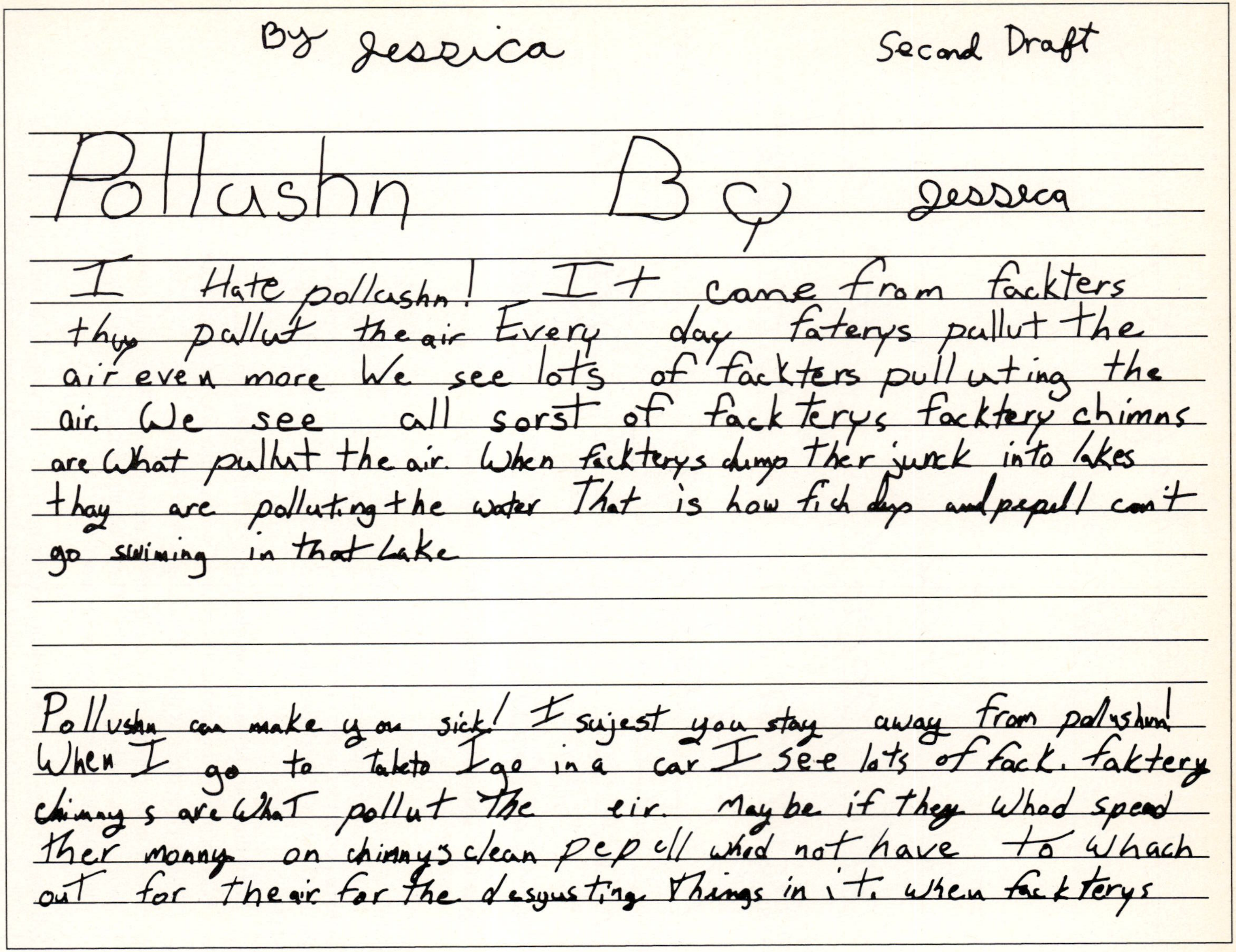

Second Draft

By Jessica

Pollushn
By
Jessica

I Hate pollushn! It come from facktrs thay pollut the air. Every day facktrys pullut the air even more. We see lots of facktrs pulluting the air. We see all sorst of facktrys. Facktery chimns are what pullut the air. When facktrys dump thr junk into lakes thay are polluting the water. That is how fish dyp and pepull cant go swiming in that lake.

Pollushn can make you sick! I sujest you stay away from pollushn! When I go to takto I go in a car I see lots of fack. faktery chimnys are what pollut the air. Maybe if they whod speed ther many on chimnys clean pepoll whod not have to whach out for their far the desgusting things in it when facktorys

Figure 5.7 Jessica's Second Draft on Pollution

dump ther junk in the Lakes they are polluting the water that is how fish dye pepell cant go swiming in that lake.

If thay wod think about other pepell. maybe if thay wod spend ther mony on getting ther chimnys cleand then pepell wod not have to woch the air for the disscusting thing in it. Like my mom she works down town allso cars & trucks pollut the air. when my mom parks her car she walcks to her offes. she smelld the disgusting tings in the air!

Figure 5.7 Jessica's Second Draft on Pollution (*continued*)

insertions, and allow them to make cross-outs or to cut and paste sections of text, if necessary. The use of arrows will help students show changes in the position of words, phrases, or sentences within the text.

Once the content and organization of a draft are set, children can work individually or together to edit and proofread their texts for spelling, punctuation, capitalization, word choice, and syntax. Accuracy counts. "Polishing" or "cleaning up" a revised draft shouldn't be neglected, *but students must recognize that concern for proofreading and editing comes toward the end of the writing process.*

Children should edit for those skills that are appropriate for their ability and stage of development as writers. An editing conference should provide a *focused evaluation* in which one or two skill areas are addressed. If children have edited their writing to the best of their ability, the teacher may then edit the remainder of the piece for spelling and other conventions.

Publishing, Displaying, and Sharing Writing

If writing is indeed a public act, then it's meant to be shared with others. Writing is for reading—and children learn quickly to write for many different audiences. When young writers have a sense of their audience, the task of writing becomes a real effort at communication.

The pride and sense of accomplishment that come with authorship contribute powerfully to the development of writers. As Kerby and Liner (1981) noted, publishing involves the ego; it provides a strong incentive for children to keep writing and rewriting. But more than anything else, publishing in the classroom is fun. Consider the following vehicles for displaying, sharing, and publishing student work.

Oral Presentations. We recommend the frequent use of read-aloud sessions as a way of sharing and celebrating writing. In this way, all children will at one time or another have an opportunity to read their work to the group. The Share Session described earlier creates the opportunity to present. Establish a tone of acceptance during oral readings of finished work. Having a child read a completed piece of writing from the "author's chair" is one way to celebrate authorship because it dignifies the hard work and effort that has been put into the writing.

Bookmaking and Class Publication. Young people take great pride in writing and illustrating their own books. Often, book writing provides the impetus and the reason for the writing to be important enough for the hard work that goes into the final product. Writing a book creates a meaningful context and a natural motivation for youngsters to revise and edit stories for content, organization, complete sentences, interesting words, and correct spelling. Young writers are especially inspired to write books when children's literature is shared with them on a regular basis—a topic we explain thoroughly in Chapter 9. They are also eager to make books when they can choose the type of book they want to write. Some possibilities for bookmaking are given in Table 5.1.

Class-produced newspapers, magazines, anthologies, and books are excellent ways to publish student writing. Have students involved in all phases of the publication's production. We suggest that children participate not only as writers, but also work in groups to assume responsibility for editing, proofreading, design, and production. Production of a class publication need not be elaborate or expensive. Dittoed publications have the same effect on student writers when they see their work in print.

Class Displays. Display student writing. As Kirby and Liner (1981) found, ". . . a display of finished products attracts attention and stimulates talk and thinking about writing" (page 217). Establish an author's day or a reading fair in which students circulate around the room reading or listening to as many pieces as they can. In their book, *Gifts of Writing* (1980), the Judys outline numerous formats for "one-of-a-kind publications." These publications "preserve" the writing in a variety of forms.

Publishing for Real Audiences. Letters, community publications, commercial magazines, and national and state contests are all vehicles for "real world" publishing outside of the classroom and school. Letters, in particular, are valuable because there are so many audience possibilities.

In addition to letters, the local newspaper, PTA bulletin, or school district newsletter sometimes provides an outlet for class-related writing activity. Commercial magazines and national, state, local, or school writing contests also offer opportunities for publication. Commercial magazines and writing contests, of course, are highly competitive. However, the real value of writing for commercial publication lies in the authenticity of the task and the real world audience that it provides. Several magazines that publish the work of young writers are listed below:

Chart Your Course. P.O. Box 6448, Mobile, AL 36660. Material by gifted, creative, and talented children. Ages 6–18.

Child Life. The Children's Better Health Institute, 1100 Waterway Blvd., Indianapolis, IN 46206. Ages 8–10.

City Kids. 1545 Wilcox, Los Angeles, CA 90028. Ages 11–14.

Cobblestone: The History Magazine for Young People. 20 Grove Street, Peterborough, NH 03458. Each issue devoted to a particular theme. Ages 8–14.

Cricket. Box 100, LaSalle, IL 61301. Note: Considers *only* material that complies with current contest rules and descriptions (see each issue for current contest rules). Ages 5–13.

District: Young Writers Journal. 2500 Wisconsin Ave., N.W., #549, Washington, DC 20007. For District of Columbia students and residents only. Ages 9–14. Currently in planning stages. Write for information.

Ebony Jr.! 820 S. Michigan Ave., Chicago, IL 60605. Specializes in material about blacks. Ages 6–12.

Paw Prints. National Zoo, Washington, DC 20008. Specializes in wild exotic animal conservation and other animal-related material. Ages 6–14.

TABLE 5.1

Ideas for Making Books

Type of Book	Sample	Construction
Shape Books Stories about animals, objects, machines, people, etc.; poems; nursery rhymes; innovations	I Like girls / TALL TALES / Bubbles	Make pages in the shape of your book. Bind together with staples, masking tape, or lace with yarn.
Ring Books Group stories; word fun; poems; collection of poems	BOOKS / morgan Bil	Punch holes in pages and use notebook rings or shower curtain rings to bind together.
Stapled Books Individual stories; group contributions; alphabet books; word books; poems	thE SiLLy KiD!	Pages and cover are stapled together, then bound for added durability with masking tape.
Fold-out Books Poems; patterns; sequence; stories		Pages folded accordion-style and then stapled or glued to covers.
Bound Cloth Books Poems; collections of poems; stories that have been edited and prepared for printing		(See extended directions on next page.)

Extended Directions for Bound Cloth Books

Supplies: 1 piece of lightweight fabric (approximately ½ yard), several needles, white thread, white paper, dry mount tissue, cardboard, masking tape, an iron, and an ironing area

1. Each child should have 6 or 7 sheets of paper. This will give him a finished book with 10 to 12 pages, but will not be too difficult to sew. Fold each sheet of paper in half (one-by-one). (Fig. 1).

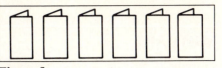

Figure 1

2. Bring the sheets together and sew along the fold. *Hint:* Start on the outside of the fold so the knot is not seen when finished. (Fig. 2).

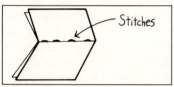

Figure 2

3. Cut out the fabric to measure 12″ × 15″. Prepare some templates from cardboard for students to use as guides. (Fig. 3).
4. Spread out the materials as pictured. (Fig. 3).

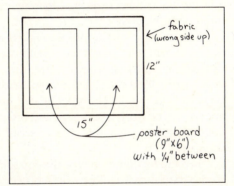

Figure 3

5. Fold the edges of the fabric over the two boards and tape in place at the corners. (Fig. 4).

Figure 4

6. Now, make a sandwich using the cover, then a piece of dry mount tissue (8½″ × 11″), then the sewn pages, and iron in place as pictured. Iron only on the endpapers since the pages can be scorched. (Fig. 5).

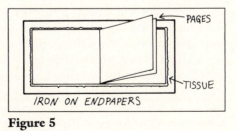

Figure 5

Sprint. Scholastic, Inc., 730 Broadway, New York, NY 10003. Publishes student writing based on assignments in its previous issues. For students aged 9–11.

Stone Soup. P.O. Box 83, Santa Cruz, CA 95063. Ages 6–12.

Wee Wisdom. Unity Village, MO 64065. Ages 6–13.

SUMMARY

Learning to write is as natural to children as learning to read. Recent research has resulted in compelling evidence that suggests that reading and writing develop concurrently. Rather than teaching reading and writing as separate curricular entities, they should be taught in tandem.

Written expression precedes writing in the sense that the latter reflects children's ability to produce units of written language. Nevertheless, an inclusive definition of writing underscores the ability to use a pen or pencil (or another appropriate writing tool) and paper to express ideas symbolically. Children are engaged in writing when their markings represent meanings that they are capable of communicating to others.

The ability to write progresses from early, uncontrolled scribbles (which do not have symbolic value) to scribble writing and drawing. When young people differentiate drawing from writing, they are able to makes rapid progress in their writing development. The random markings of toddlers, for example, gradually begin to become more differentiated and controlled. The scribbles take on the appearance of written language and often reflect implicit knowledge of text. When young children engage in "name scribbling," they have developed a concept of message.

Invented spellings mirror the emerging competence of young writers. Spelling studies reveal that children develop consistent strategies and that their spellings progress through stages: *prephonemic*, *phonemic*, *transitional*, and *conventional*. This progression shows that children invent and reinvent spellings as they experiment with written language. There are many advantages for encouraging invented spellings in beginning situations. When correctness isn't emphasized, children build independence; develop fluency, spelling rules, and phonic knowledge naturally; and assume ownership and responsibility for their writing.

One of the keys to writing development in classrooms rests with the environment that teachers create. Natural environments for learning provide encouragement and a built-in support system. There is tremendous, patient faith that children will develop as writers. Time for writing, response to writing, and ownership of one's own writing are the hallmarks of a natural learning environment.

Getting started with writing process instruction is challenging. Teachers must establish a routine for writing. For example, there should be time to write every day, freedom of movement in the class, and occasions to write. Writing folders should be the focal point of the classroom writing program. Process-centered classrooms allow for great flexibility, but not anarchy. Guidelines need to set clear expectations for behavior and interactions within the classroom.

In process-centered classrooms, students are encouraged to choose topics that matter to them and to rehearse for writing through talking, reading, brainstorming, and other "prewriting" strategies. Talking and journal writing, in particular, will help children discover and select topics for writing.

Drafting, revising, and editing are commonplace occurrences in process-centered classrooms. Throughout the stages of writing, children need response—from the teacher and other children. Conferencing is the vehicle by which teacher and writers respond to one another in order to try out work and get ideas to improve their drafts. Revision means that the writer will "re-see" or "re-think" a piece. Once the content of writing is set, then editing becomes a major responsibility of the writer. Editing means preparing the writing for an audience. It involves "polishing" by attending to such matters as spelling, punctuation, and usage.

Publishing provides the payoff for the hard work that goes into the writing process. Finding ways to value writing is crucial. Some suggestions include: providing the author's chair; sponsoring class publications, book making, oral presentations, contests; and advising about submission to magazines that publish student work.

THE WORKSHOP

In the Classroom

1. Develop a writing autobiography as suggested by Anthony L. Manna (1986). Think back to when you were a young child and try to recall the first time you engaged in writing something. Start with your earliest memory and trace your journey as a writer up to and including the present time. Think about:

teachers	settings
assignments	grades
advice	topics
feelings	habits
senses	idiosyncrasies

   Let these questions guide you:
   a. What are some words that come to mind when you think of "writing" in relation to your school experiences?
   b. Who were the teachers that mattered? That didn't matter?
   c. Do you like to write?
   d. Do you, or would you, like to teach writing?
   e. What are your most effective characteristics as a writer?
   f. Your least effective?
   g. Have you ever written anything you were proud of? What is it?
   h. When, where, and how do you usually write?
   i. What is your most effective characteristic as a teacher of writing?
   j. Your least effective?
   k. What are some good and bad experiences you've had as a writer?

   Add whatever comments you'd like in order to make a portrait of yourself as a writer. Focus on what your personal journey shows you about the way writers develop—or don't develop. What does your experience show you about novice writers who are learning how to write? In what ways will your autobiography influence the way you teach writing? What advice would you give to teachers of writing?

2. Design a process-centered writing lesson. Use what you have learned about the writing process and effective strategies to aid that process. Be sure to touch on these issues:

   a. What pre-writing activities will you use in order to be reasonably sure that students will have something to say when they begin to write?

   b. How will you provide for in-process response to the writing?

   c. How will you provide for growth in mechanics and editing? Which skills will you try to develop?

   d. How will you arrange for the writing to reach an audience?

   e. How will you handle management problems such as finding time for the writing, keeping kids on task, arranging the classroom environment, evaluating the work, and so on?

   You may design a lesson to be completed in several days or one that will take a week or two. Discuss the content of your lessons with other members of the class.

3. Analyze the invented spellings of first-, second-, third-, and fourth-graders from writing samples that you have collected or from those provided by your instructor. What are the developmental stages of spelling of the children whose writing you have analyzed? What does an analysis of spelling tell you about each child's knowledge of words and sound-letter relationships? How would you design instruction to help each of the children continue to grow and develop as spellers?

4. Brainstorm ways to connect reading and writing during instruction. Share your ideas with others in the class.

In the Field

1. Observe an elementary school teacher during writing instruction time, taking notes on what the teacher says and does. What provisions does the teacher make for writing instruction? Is the teacher's approach to writing process- or product-

   centered? Prepare a report in which you analyze the lesson and present it to the class.

2. With a small group of children from an elementary grade and using one of the techniques suggested in the chapter, model how to self-select topics for writing. Report on the success of the teaching experience. What would you do differently the next time you modeled topic selection? What would you do the same?

3. Conduct a writing process conference with an elementary student who has just completed a draft. (Consider some of the suggestions in this chapter for conducting the conference.) Describe what happened during the conference. What did you learn from the experience?

4. Help a group of elementary school children make a book for publication. Decide on the type of book to make, using either the suggestions in this chapter or others from Judy and Judy's *The Gifts of Writing: Creative Projects with Words and Art* (New York: Scribner's, 1980).

Part III

Selecting Strategies

Chapter 6

Reading Comprehension

140

During a college reunion several years ago Lucy, a former roommate, asked, "What do you teach?" "Reading," we said, whereupon Lucy related a rather sad story of her nine-year-old son's problems with reading. We noted that many youngsters have problems similar to her son's, but they respond well to planned, meaningful experiences in reading and writing. Just as we were explaining that such experiences are designed to promote comprehension, Lucy interrupted by saying, "Oh, he can comprehend okay; he just can't read." Needless to say, we weren't on the same wavelength with Lucy; our concepts of reading differed. As you study this chapter, you will know that its title is not an afterthought. The title is "Reading Comprehension," not "Reading and Comprehension."

Reading is learning stuff you didn't know before.

> *Ronnie, a fifth-grader*

Reading is thinking about the story and figuring it out.

> *Janice, a third-grader*

Reading is talking about the story. You read it, you know. And then tell about it.

> *Lyle, a first-grader*

Who claims to read without comprehension? Our position throughout this book has been that reading involves meaning in the transaction between reader and author. Without comprehension, the act of reading is an empty, vacuous event. Each chapter in Part III deals in one way or another with strategies that help children grow as comprehenders. Children's earliest home experiences with print are often purposeful, meaningful, and enjoyable. Should school experiences be anything less?

In the past two decades, reading researchers have taken dead aim on understanding the reading process, with comprehension the bullseye. Fueled with federal funding, major research projects have undertaken to better understand how readers comprehend written discourse. As a result, more is known theoretically and practically about comprehension today than ever before. With this knowledge has come a renewed commitment to teaching comprehension as a thinking process.

The explanations of the reading process in Chapter 1 suggested that meaning doesn't lie hidden in the text. The text provides cues that help the reader to construct meaning. Meaning is derived from the transactions that occur between the reader and the writer of the text. Reading comprehension is an active process that takes place behind the eyes. How the human brain processes text information is the key to meaning making. From an *interactive* point of view, information processing is often triggered by the knowledge the reader brings to print. Readers build meaning by connecting new knowledge to knowledge they already possess.

Not only must students use background knowledge to comprehend, but they must also bring into play knowledge about the text itself. As readers mature, they become more sophisticated in recognizing the ways which text selections are organized in expository and narrative writing. To engage in reading as a meaning-making activity, readers must search for and find structure in everything they read.

BUILDING A SCHEMA FOR STORIES

Most authors aren't in the habit of writing carelessly or aimlessly. They impose structure on their writing. Perceiving structure in text material improves learning and retention. When students follow relationships in a reading selection, they're in a better position to construct meaning and to distinguish important from less important ideas and events. In Chapter 11, we show how to help students recognize text structure in content area reading materials. In this section, however, attention is paid to the underlying elements that comprise the structure of simple, well-told stories.

Stories are basic to any school's reading curriculum. Because stories are central to children's reading development, much time and effort have been spent attempting to understand how stories are comprehended. A child's knowledge of stories begins to develop at an early age. In Chapters 3 and 4, we explained how children hear and tell simple stories and then read and view them in both home and school experiences. Children learn implicitly that well-told stories are predictable. There is an underlying structure that all simple stories appear to have in common. As children develop a *story schema*, they begin to sense "what comes next."

A "simple" story actually isn't as simple as it might appear on the surface. During the past decade it has been shown how complex the underlying structure of a story can be. Attempts have been made to identify the basic elements that make up a well-developed story (Mandler and Johnson, 1977; Thorndyke, 1977; Stein and Glenn, 1979). These efforts have led to the development of several variations of *story grammar*. Just as sentence grammar provides a way of describing how a sentence is put together, story grammar helps to specify the basic parts of a story and how those parts tie together to form a well-constructed story. What do most well-developed stories have in common? While individual story grammars may differ somewhat, most would agree that a story's structure centers around *setting* and *plot*.

Elements in a Story Grammar

The setting of a story introduces the main character (sometimes called the *protagonist*) and situates the character(s) in a time and place. The plot of a story is made up of one or more *episodes*. A simple story has a single episode. More complex stories may have two, several, or many episodes as well as different settings. Each episode is made up of a chain of events. Although the labeling of these events differs from story grammar to story grammar, the following elements are generally included:

a beginning or initiating event: either an idea or an action that sets further events into motion.

internal response (followed by goal or problem): the character's inner reaction to the initiating event, in which the character sets a goal or attempts to solve a problem.

attempt(s): the character's efforts to achieve the goal or alleviate the problem. Several attempts may be evident in an episode.

an outcome(s): the success or failure of the character's attempt(s).

resolution: the long-range consequence that evolves from the character's success or failure to achieve the goal or resolve the problem.

a reaction: an idea, emotion, or a further event that expresses a story character's feelings about success or failure of goal attainment/problem resolution or that relates the events in the story to some broader set of concerns.

The events in the story form a causal chain. Each event leads to the next one as the main character moves toward goal attainment or problem resolution.

With the elements of story grammar in mind, read the story below, "People of the Third Planet," and analyze its structure. To help you "map" the story's structure, use the chart in Figure 6.1 on page 146. Write in the spaces provided on the chart what you believe to be the major story parts, including the setting and chain of events.

People of the Third Planet
by Dale Crail

The silver flying saucer came down silently and landed in a parking lot in a small town on earth. It was one o'clock in the morning, and the streets were dark.

Slowly a section of the saucer slid open. Two creatures from another world stepped out. For a moment they thought no one was near. Then they noticed a line of figures standing before them.

One creature whispered to the other, "Over there I see some people of the Third Planet. But they do not come forward to greet us. Perhaps this is not the time to tell the people of the Third Planet about our world."

The other creature shook his head. "No, our orders are clear. Now is the time. We must approach these earth people and arrange a meeting with their leader."

He stepped forward and began to speak. "People of the Third Planet—or Earth, as you call it. We greet you in peace. We are messengers from a world that is millions of years older than your own. We wish to establish a peaceful link between our two worlds and exchange ideas with you. We would like to speak to someone of importance on your planet. Please direct us to such a person." No one in the line of figures moved. They did not even seem interested in the space creature's words.

After several seconds the creature stepped back and whispered to his friend, "These earth people act as if they do not understand what I am saying. How can that be? We monitored their radio signals and listened to them speak. I am sure we are using their language correctly."

"Stay calm," said the other creature. "I will speak to them."

He raised his voice and said, "Earth friends! Perhaps you are frightened by our sudden appearance. Or perhaps you do not fully understand our message. I assure you that it is of the greatest importance. It is necessary that we speak to the leader of the Third Planet. Please tell us where we may find this person."

The figures remained absolutely still.

"We will not harm any of you," the space creature went on. "We only wish to talk with your leader. But—if you do not cooperate—we will be forced to take one of you with us for questioning."

Not one figure moved or said a word.

The creature from the saucer began to get angry. He clenched his fists and whispered to his friend, "Apparently these Earth people will not tell us anything. Let us take one aboard. We will force the Earth person to speak."

He shouted at the figures standing before him, "You have left us no choice! We will have to use force."

He was amazed that even these words had no effect. The figures did not turn and run. They did not move at all.

In a fury he raced up to the first figure in line and said, "You are my prisoner. March forward to the saucer!"

Nothing happened.

Then he hit the figure hard, but still the figure did not move.

"It is no use," he said. "I cannot force this Earth person to walk. It is as if the Earth person has roots that go deep into the ground."

"Use your ray gun!" his friend yelled. "Cut the Earth person away from the Earth that these people love so much."

There was a single flash of fire from the space creature's gun. The Earth person fell noisily to the ground.

Even then none of the other figures moved.

This was more than the space creatures could believe.

"People of the Third Planet!" the first creature said. "We greeted you in peace, and you did not answer us. We captured one of your people, and you did not stop us. You are strange people with no feelings for anyone. Farewell, people of the Third Planet. Farewell."

The two creatures put the captured figure into their saucer and then climbed in themselves. With a sudden flash of light the flying saucer took off from Earth.

A police car was coming down the street just as the saucer flashed up into the sky.

"What was that?" one of the police officers asked.

"Looked like an explosion in the parking lot," his partner said. "Better see what happened."

The car raced toward the lot and screeched to a stop. The driver jumped out and flashed his light and found the officer down on one knee, pointing to a metal base that was still hot to the touch.

"Someone sliced off this thing," the police officer said. "Did a neat job of cutting too. But what for? They could only get away with a few pennies. Why would anyone want to steal a parking meter?"

Now that you have completed the chart, compare your mapping of the story parts with the chart on the next page. Although there will undoubtedly be some differences in the way the story parts are interpreted, there will probably be a fair amount of similarity in what constitutes the elements of story grammar in "People of the Third Planet."

Knowing the underlying elements of a story benefits both teacher and students. You can use story organization to plan instruction more effectively and to anticipate the problems students might have in following a specific story's action, especially if it lacks one or more story elements. Students, on the other hand, can build and use story schema to better understand what they read. The closer the match between the reader's story schema and the organization of a particular story, the greater the comprehension is likely to be. This is why a *story map* is an important planning tool in the hands of teachers.

Mapping a Story for Instructional Purposes. An analysis of a story's organizational elements strengthens instructional decisions. Beck (1979) and her associates recommended creating a *story map* as a way of identifying major structural

Story Structure for "People of the Third Planet"

Setting		Chain of Events
Time and Place: A small town parking lot at one o'clock in the morning.	Two creatures land in the parking lot in a silver flying saucer and step out.	
Beginning event that initiates the action		The two creatures see a line of figures standing before them. They assume that the figures are earthlings or people from the Third Planet, the name by which they call Earth.
Internal response and goal/problem		The two creatures want to tell the people of the Third Planet about the world from which they come. They decide to approach the earthlings in the parking lot to arrange a meeting with the leader of the Third Planet.
Attempt(s) and outcome(s)		One of the creatures greets the earth people but there is no response. The second one raises his voice in greeting and still there is no response. Then one of the creatures says he will use force and take one of them aboard for questioning. Still there is no response. The creature further tells the first person in line to march into the saucer. No response. He hits the earth person. No response. The creatures finally detach the earth person from the ground with a ray gun. They take the captured figure aboard the saucer and leave saying the earth's people have no feelings for anyone.
Resolution		Police come by and see the remains of an explosion in the parking lot and discover a parking meter is gone.
Reaction		The police wonder why anyone would steal a parking meter since they'd only get a few pennies.

Figure 2 Story Structure for "People of the Third Planet"

Setting		Chain of Events
Time and Place:	**Character(s):**	
The beginning event that initiates the action		
Internal response and goal/problem		
Attempt(s) and outcome(s)		
Resolution		
Reaction		

Figure 1 A Chart for Mapping Story Structure

elements—both explicit and implicit—underlying a story to be taught in class. A chart such as the one in Figure 6.1 helps you to map the relationships that exist among the major events in a story. Once these relationships are established, they form the basis for developing a line of questions that will help students grasp the story parts under discussion. According to Beck, students should thoroughly understand the general framework of the story before broader, evaluative questions can be considered.

The generic questions below are easily applied to specific stories. As you examine these questions, consider how you would adapt them to "People of the Third Planet."

SETTING   Where did the story take place? When did the story take place? Who is the main character? What is _____ like? What is _____'s problem? What did _____ need? Why is _____ in trouble?

INTERNAL RESPONSE AND GOAL/PROBLEM   What does _____ decide to do? What does _____ have to attempt to do?

ATTEMPTS AND OUTCOMES   What did _____ do about _____? What happened to _____? What will _____ do now? How did (*the attempt*) turn out?

RESOLUTION   How did _____ solve the problem? How did _____ achieve the goal? What would you do to solve _____'s problem?

REACTION   How did _____ feel about the problem? Why did _____ do _____? How did _____ feel at the end?

When students have responded to questions related to the story line, engage them in discussion centered around other important aspects of the story such as its theme, character development, or the reader's personal response to the story.

THEME   What is the moral of the story? What did you learn from the story? What is the major point of the story? What does this story say about (*unusual truth*)? Why do you think the author wanted to write this story?

CHARACTERS   Why do you think (*character*) did that? What do you like about (*character*)? Dislike? Does (*character*) remind you of anyone else that you know?

PERSONAL RESPONSE   Is there anything you would have changed in the story? How did the story make you feel? Happy? Sad? Angry? Bewildered? Was there anything about the story that didn't make sense?

Not only is story mapping useful for planning questions, but it also provides you with information about "break points" during reading. A break point occurs whenever students are asked to stop in-class reading to discuss story content. When and where to stop reading, as we will explain later in this chapter, is one of the most important decisions you can make when guiding a *directed reading-thinking activity*.

Is It Necessary to Teach Story Structure?

We don't advocate teaching story elements for the sake of teaching story elements. Such practice can turn out to be as mindless as teaching reading skills for the sake of reading skills. However, making children aware of the predictability of a well-developed story is appropriate, especially if the children don't appear to use story schema during reading. You can put story structure to good use in the classroom when there is access to reading materials that are written around recognizable story structures. Moreover, avoid using narrative selections which masquerade as stories. These so-called stories go nowhere; they're incomplete and severely lacking in one or more story parts.

The following activities and suggestions will help students build a sense of story and reinforce their awareness of story structure.

Read, Tell, and Perform Stories in Class. There is no better substitute for building experience with stories or extending students' knowledge of how stories are put together than to read, tell, and perform stories in class on a regular basis. These types of experiences with stories are as paramount in the upper grades as they are in the beginning grades. In Chapter 9, we will emphasize the nuts and bolts of storytelling. In earlier chapters, we explained the importance of reading aloud, story writing, and dramatic activities. Language experiences such as these are integral to the development of concepts related to literacy.

Don't Teach the Language of Story Grammar as an End in Itself. Although children need to be aware of the language of instruction, avoid teaching jargon for the sake of learning technical terms. Children develop story schema gradually and implicitly, mainly through direct experience and interaction with stories. However, when teaching story parts explicitly to children, use language that is simple and familiar. For example, instead of asking a child to identify the "initiating event" in the story, you may want to phrase the question in more familiar language such as, "What happened in the beginning of the story to get things started?"

Build on children's concepts of *problem* and *trouble*. You might ask, "What does trouble mean? Have you ever been in trouble with a parent or a friend? What kind of trouble happens in stories you have read? How did (*the main character*) get into trouble? How did (*the main character*) get out of trouble?"

The concept of trouble is closely related to the central problem in a story. Moldofsky (1983) concluded that most fiction in the elementary and middle grades revolves around a problem. Because the problem gives coherence to a story, it is probably one of the most important story parts for readers to recognize. For this reason, build on students' sense of problems in their own lives. Categorize the types of problems that they have experienced (e.g., problems related to needing, wanting, feeling, etc.). Then relate problem areas to stories children have read and will read.

Show Relationships Among Story Parts. Diagrams and flow charts depicting the relationships that exist among events in the story give children a visual image

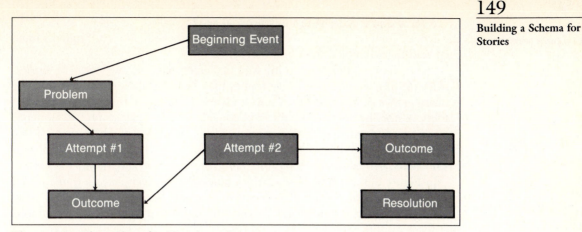

Figure 6.2   Flow Chart for Mapping a Story

of how stories are organized. Gordon and Braun (1983) suggested giving students copies of a diagram minus the story information. As information is discussed related to the story parts depicted on the diagram, students can write what is said on their own copies.

Pearson (1982) claimed that children as young as eight are successful, with much teacher modeling, at representing a story in a flow chart. Flow charting can take many different forms such as the one illustrated in Figure 6.2.

The value of diagramming or flow charting lies in the discussions that take place before, during, and after the activity. Discussions should revolve around the relationships of one event to another. The goal behind a discussion is to make students consciously aware that events in story form a causal chain. With much teacher-led discussion, modeling, and guided practice, many students beginning in the second or third grade will grasp how to diagram story parts and make flow charts on their own. Once this is the case, have students share their products with one another. Rather than emphasize accuracy during sharing sessions, ask for reasons and rationales. Encourage speculation and risk-taking. Also, allow students the opportunity to revise or alter their individual efforts based on the discussion.

Reinforce Story Knowledge Through Instructional Activities. In addition to activities like flow charting, children's understanding of story structure can be extended through varied instructional tasks. Whaley (1981) suggested two activities: *macro-cloze stories* and *scrambled stories*.

A "macro-cloze story" is based on the same principle that operates for a cloze passage (see Chapter 13 for a fuller explanation). A teacher constructs cloze material by deleting single words from a passage. Children are then given copies of the cloze passage and are required to supply the missing words. When constructing a macro-cloze story, instead of omitting single words, delete one or more parts from the story. The deleted portion(s) of text may be a sentence, several sentences, or an entire paragraph in length. Reproduce copies of the story with lines drawn to show where the text deletions have occurred. Students should then read the story and discuss the necessary information orally or in writing.

A second instructional task involved an activity called "scrambled stories." As the activity implies, a story is separated into its parts and jumbled. Students must then read the scrambled story and reorder it.

"Story frames" present a third way of heightening an awareness of stories. Fowler (1982) showed how story frames may be particularly appropriate in the primary grades or in situations where students are at risk in their development as readers. A story frame provides the student with a skeletal paragraph: "A sequence of spaces tied together with transition words and connectors which signal a line of thought." Fowler identified five story frames, each with a different emphasis: *plot summary, setting, character analysis, character comparison,* and the story's *problem.*

In Figure 6.3, examine how Chris, a nine-year-old, completed a frame which centered on the story's central problem. As students become familiar with using story frames, you may want to involve them simply in writing summary paragraphs that focus on different elements of the story.

Building a schema for stories is an important aspect of comprehension instruction. No less important is how children activate and use schemata in general to predict and anticipate meaning during reading. Prediction and anticipation are valuable tools for helping students read for meaning. In the next section, we explore how strategies related to prediction and anticipation help remove potential roadblocks to comprehension.

BUILDING AND ACTIVATING SCHEMA

A common sense imperative emerges from a schema theory of reading comprehension: help students act upon and interact with the main ideas of a reading selection *before* encountering them in print. The value of *pre-reading preparation* lies in helping comprehenders recognize what they know and what they need to find out more about. Two pivotal questions that readers must ask as they approach a reading selection are, "What do I already know about the reading selection?" and, "What do I need to know?"

"What do I already know?" agitates thinking. Readers must learn how to take inventory of their own store of knowledge and experiences. Helping children reflect in this manner is crucial from an instructional point of view. For one thing, it's a great confidence booster to know that you know something about a subject to be encountered in print. One of the challenges of teaching is convincing children that they know more about a text than they often give themselves credit for.

On the other hand, "What do I already know?" helps children recognize what they don't know, *but* will learn more about from reading. When faced with a text selection, they may lack an *available* schema for comprehending the material. Here's where background building activities will help develop a frame of reference for children to handle incoming information in text. In the next chapter, the "Cone of Experience" is explained within the context of concept development. Edgar Dale (1969), the cone's originator, provided valuable insights into building real and vicarious experiences for reading and learning tasks. When children lack a schema for reading, concrete, extended discussions focused on the key ideas

In this story the problem starts when _____ Jack's
mother finds out that they
ran out of food.

After that, _____ Jack sold the cow
for a cuple of magic beans

Next, his mother threw them
out the window and they
grew into a giant stalk. . Then,
Jack climbed the stalk and
stole the magic goose from the giant. . The

problem is finally solved when _____ the giant
dies and the goose lays golden
eggs _____. The story ends _____
when they live happily ever after.
Chris—age 9

Figure 6.3 Example of a Completed Story Frame

before reading should be the rule and not the exception. The use of film, video, pictures, and filmstrips are excellent experience builders.

Although children may have a schema for reading they may fail to bring it to bear as they read. Maturing readers are often unaware that prior knowledge is of any consequence in the reading process. However, when strategically engaged in exploring what they know and what they need to know, young readers soon recognize the importance of establishing goals and plans for reading. Searching for answers to questions such as, "What do I need to know?" leads to prediction making and goal-directed behavior.

As you study the strategies and activities below, note that additional procedures are recommended in Chapter 11 for building and activating schema.

Advance Organizers

To prepare children conceptually for ideas to be encountered in reading, help them link what they know to what they will learn. An *advance organizer* provides a frame of reference for comprehending text precisely for this reason—to help readers make connections between their prior knowledge and new material. Swaby (1983) defined advance organizers as involving teacher-directed attempts to clarify and organize students' thinking "in such a way that they know what information they already have that will be important and helpful in comprehending incoming information . . . . Any effort by a teacher to prepare students conceptually for incoming information by hooking the major concepts of the new information to the concepts already possessed by the learners can be interpreted as an advance organizer" (page 76).

There's no one way to develop or use an advance organizer. In Chapter 11, for example, we show how to arrange key concepts into a *structured overview* (also called a *graphic organizer*) to get students ready for content area reading assignments. Advance organizers may also be developed as *written previews* or as *verbal presentations*. Whatever format you decide to use, an advance organizer should highlight key concepts and ideas to be encountered in print. These should be prominent and easily identifiable in the lesson presentation. Another key feature of an advance organizer activity should be the explicit links made between the children's background knowledge and experience and the ideas in the reading selection.

An advance organizer may be developed for narrative or expository text. Use it for difficult text selections, when the material is unfamiliar to students because of limited schema. Construct an advance organizer by following these guidelines:

1. Analyze the content of a reading selection, identifying its main ideas and key concepts.

2. Link these ideas directly to children's experiences and storehouse of knowledge. Use real-life incidents, examples, illustrations, analogies, or anecdotes to which student readers can relate.

3. Raise questions in the organizer that will pique interest and engage students in thinking about the text to be read.

BOX 6.1

Advance Organizer for the Reading Selection
"Understanding the Language of a Dog"

MAIN IDEA OF PASSAGE TO BE READ	Dogs and human beings are alike in an important way. We both use "language" to communicate messages to others. A dog uses a unique language.
BUILDING AND SHARING PRIOR KNOWLEDGE AND EXPERIENCES	When you think of our "language," what comes to mind immediately? *Probably words.* Using words in speaking and writing is one way to communicate a message to someone else. But try to think about how you sit or stand when you're angry or pouting. Can someone get the message you're trying to communicate just by looking at you? How about when you're nervous or excited? How else do we show others what we're feeling or thinking about without using words? (Discuss the other elements of body language.) Does anyone ever tell what your pet is thinking or feeling? How? (Discuss student responses. Compare examples.)
MAKING THE CONNECTION BETWEEN PRIOR KNOWLEDGE AND THE PASSAGE TO BE READ	Use what we have just discussed to read the passage for today. Look for specific ways in which a dog can communicate with you, or other animals.

Study the advance organizer in Box 6.1 and then read the selection that follows.

Understanding the Language of a Dog

Dogs may not use words to tell how they feel, but they do use parts of their bodies to talk. This is called "body language." When you wave to someone, you are using body language. When a dog wags its tail, it is using body language, too.

Most dogs have a strong sense of *territoriality*. This means they are protective of things that belong to them, including their living space. A dog may feel quite strongly about its bed, a favorite toy, or the backyard. And it is the dog's sense of territoriality that makes it communicate through its body.

A dog may use its body to say many things. By bowing down, wagging its tail, barking, or holding out one front paw, the dog may be saying, "Let's play." When the dog crouches down and rolls over on its back, it means, "Come closer." And if the dog scratches at you with a paw, it may mean, "I want something."

A dog may use body language to warn you away from its territory. To do this, the dog may show its teeth, stick its ears up, growl, or hold its tail out stiffly. This means, "Stay away." The dog may growl, crouch, lower its tail, and flatten its ears against its head. This means, "Better stay away. I'm not sure about you."

As we suggested earlier, the key to a successful advance organizer lies in the discussion that it initiates. Children must participate actively in making the links between what they know and what they will learn. Much will be lost if they are assigned to read (or listen or view) an organizer without the opportunity to act upon it within the context of their own experiences.

Student-Generated Questions

When students learn to ask questions before, during, and after reading, they put themselves in the strategic position of generating their own organizers for learning. Showing children how to ask questions is no easy task, because it cuts against the grain of typical classroom discourse. As early as first grade, children learn two of the main rules that usually govern classroom talk: (1) The teacher talks in questions; (2) the students talk in answers. The following techniques and strategies alter the rules of classroom interaction by promoting students' self-questioning behavior.

Active Comprehension. Whenever children are engaged in a process of generating questions throughout reading, they are involved in active comprehension. According to Singer (1978), teachers encourage active comprehension when they *ask questions that elicit questions in return*. A first-grade teacher, for example, might focus attention on a picture or illustration from a story or book. Instead of asking, "What is the picture about?" the teacher poses a question that gets questions in response: "What would you like to know about the picture?" In return, students might generate questions which focus on details, main idea, or inferences from the illustration.

Ms. Mayer, a sixth-grade teacher, read the opening paragraph of *The Best Christmas Pageant Ever* to her class:

> The Herdmans were absolutely the worst kids in the history of the world. They lied and stole and smoked cigars (even the girls) and talked dirty and hit little kids and cussed their teachers and took the name of the Lord in vain and set fire to Fred Shoemaker's old broken-down toolhouse.
>
> The toolhouse burned right down to the ground, and I think that surprised the Herdmans. They set fire to things all the time, but that was the first time they managed to burn down a whole building.
>
> I guess it was an accident. I don't suppose they woke up that morning and said to one another, "Let's go burn down Fred Shoemaker's toolhouse" . . . but maybe they did. After all, it was a Saturday, and not much going on.

She then asked, "What more would you like to know about the Herdmans?" As her sixth-graders responded, Ms. Mayer wrote their questions on the chalkboard:

Why were the Herdmans so bad?
Did they enjoy setting fire to the toolhouse?
Did they feel guilty after the toolhouse burned down?

Not only do these questions stimulate interest and arouse curiosity, but they also draw students into the story. In the process, students' reading behavior will be more goal-directed. That is, they will read to satisfy purposes which *they* have established, not the teacher.

Nolte and Singer (1985) explained that teachers can show students how to generate their own questions for a story by adhering to a "phase-in, phase-out" strategy. Phase-in, phase-out simply means that you gradually shift the burden of responsibility for question-asking from your shoulders to students'. A good deal of this strategy involves modeling question-asking behavior and making students aware of the value of questions before, during, and after reading. The following plan will ensure a smooth transition from teacher-directed questions to student-generated questions. Although the steps in the plan were recommended for nine- and ten-year-old students, they can easily be adapted for younger or older readers.

1. Discuss the importance of asking questions as you direct students' comprehension of a story.

2. Model the types of questions that can be asked about central story content, including setting; main character; problem or goal; and obstacles encountered while attempting to resolve the problem or achieve the goal resolution.

3. As you work through a story, ask questions that require questions in response, for example, "What would you like to know about the setting of the story? The main character?" "What would you like to know about what happened next?" Spend several class periods guiding question-generation in this manner.

4. Divide the class into small groups of four to six children. One student in each group is designated to serve in the role of "teacher" by eliciting questions from the other members. Circulate around the room to facilitate the group process. Spend several class periods in small group question-generation. Allow several minutes toward the end of each class period for "debriefing" with students, for example, "How did the questioning go? Were there any problems? Why does question-asking make a story easier to read?"

5. Have students work in pairs, asking each other questions as they read.

6. Have students work on their own to generate questions. Discuss the questions they raised as a whole group.

In following these steps, Nolte and Singer found that training students to ask questions resulted in superior comprehension on the part of nine- and ten-year-olds as compared to nine- and ten-year-olds who did not receive such training.

Reciprocal Questioning. Reciprocal Questioning, or *ReQuest* as it is also called, was created for remedial instruction (Manzo, 1969). Yet this strategy can easily be used in any situation requiring reading to help students think as they read. *ReQuest* encourages students to ask their own questions about the material being read.

Should you use *ReQuest*, consider these steps:

1. Introduce ReQuest to students in their reading groups.

2. Both the students and the teacher silently read a common segment of the reading selection. Manzo recommended one sentence at a time for poor comprehenders. This may also be appropriate for beginning readers. Consider varying the length of reading for older students. For example, both teacher and students begin by reading a paragraph.

3. The teacher closes the book and is questioned about the passage by the students.

4. Exchange roles. The teacher now asks students questions about the material.

5. Upon completion of the student-teacher exchange, the next segment of text is read. Steps 3 and 4 are repeated.

6. At a suitable point in the text, when students have processed enough information to make predictions about the remainder of the assignment, the exchange of questions stops. The teacher then asks broad questions such as, "What do you think the rest of the assignment is about?" "Why do you think so?"

7. Students are then assigned the remaining portion of the selection to read silently.

8. The teacher facilitates follow-up discussion of the material.

The *ReQuest* procedure also works well in groups when you alternate the role of student-questioner after each question. By doing so, you will probably involve more students in the activity. Also, once students understand the steps and are aware of how to play *ReQuest*, you may also try forming *ReQuest* teams. A *ReQuest* team composed of three or four students challenges another *ReQuest* team.

Whenever students are asked to generate questions, some will not know how to do so. Others will ask only literal questions during ReQuest because they don't know how to ask any others; they don't know how to ask questions that will stimulate inferential or evaluative levels of thinking. One way to deal with these situations is to provide a model that students will learn from. Your role as a questioner should not be underestimated. Over time you will notice the difference in the ability of students to pose questions and in the quality of questions asked.

Your Own Questions. Another schema-based strategy involving self-questioning is called *Your Own Questions*. As the name implies, this strategy helps students set purposes for reading and directs their reading behavior. They are encouraged to generate questions and then search the reading situation for answers. Here's how *Your Own Questions* works:

1. Have students preview a title and pictures and/or listen to or read a portion of text from the beginning of a selection.

2. Encourage students to write or ask as many questions as they can that they think will be answered by reading the remainder of the selection.

3. Discuss some of the questions asked by the students before reading. Write the questions on the board.

4. Students then read to see if questions are answered.

5. After reading, which questions are answered? Which weren't? Why not?

Your Own Questions teaches children to approach reading material inquisitively. Discussing student-generated questions before reading raises expectations and helps to determine what content readers judge to be important. The strategy, then, is similar to *ReQuest* and *Active Comprehension* in that it allows readers to achieve self-defined goals.

GUIDING INTERACTIONS BETWEEN
READER AND TEXT

On the road to reading maturity, young readers need to become aware of and skilled at recognizing when shifts in thinking occur during reading. The shift may involve an author's transition to a new topic, changes in setting, twists in the plot, and so on. Or the author may put demands on the reader's ability to make inferences. For whatever reason, many youngsters run into trouble while reading because they don't know *how* or *when* to adjust their thinking as a particular reading selection demands.

Suppose you were teaching a class in which most of the students had appropriate background knowledge for the reading selection. Discussion before reading activates schema, and students approach the selection with anticipation of what lies ahead in the material. But somewhere during reading, you sense that the readers are having trouble understanding the story. Some look confused as they read. A couple raise hands to ask for clarification. Others just plow ahead— whether they're comprehending is anyone's guess.

Readers sometimes get lost in a welter of details or bogged down in the conceptual complexity of the selection. The prereading activity that you initiated at the beginning of the lesson, while necessary, wasn't sufficient to maintain readers' interactions with the text. As a result, they're able to process only bits and pieces of information but fail to group in any coherent way the author's intent and message. How can you help?

Assigning questions *after* reading may help to clarify some of the confusion but does little to show readers how to interact with the author's ideas *during* reading. This is why guiding reader-text interactions is an important part of comprehension instruction. In this section, we explain two strategies that teachers have found useful for this purpose. In Chapter 11, additional procedures are suggested.

Directed Reading-Thinking Activity

The *Directed Reading-Thinking Activity* (DR-TA) builds critical awareness of the reader's role and responsibility in interacting with the text. The DR-TA strategy involves readers in the process of predicting, verifying, judging, and extending thinking about the text material. Throughout this process, the teacher agitates thinking by posing open-ended questions. The learning environment for DR-TA lessons must be supportive and encouraging so as not to stifle or inhibit students' participation. For example, never refute the predictions that children offer. To do so is comparable to pulling the rug out from under them.

"Think time" is important in a DR-TA lesson. We suggest that you pause several seconds or more for responses after posing an open-ended question. If there's silence during this time, it may very well be an indication that children are thinking. So wait and see what happens.

To prepare a DR-TA for a story, analyze its structure first. Map the story as we suggested earlier. Once you have identified the important story parts, decide on logical stopping points within the story. In Figure 6.4, we indicate a general plan that may be adapted for specific stories.

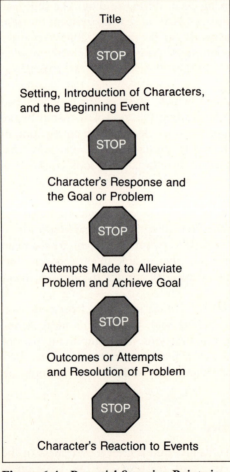

Figure 6.4 Potential Stopping Points in a DR-TA

Linda Fleckner, a sixth-grade teacher, used the DR-TA to guide reader text interactions for the short story, "People of the Third Planet." Earlier you were invited to map the elements of this story. Study the dialogue that occurred between Ms. Fleckner and two students at the beginning of the lesson:

Ms. F.: (*Writes title on the board before assigning the story.*) What do you think this story's about?
Student: It's about outer space.
Ms. F.: Why do you say that?
Student: Because it's about a planet . . .
Ms. F.: (*Writes the prediction on the board.*) Let's have some more predictions.
Student: This is about space, I think. But something happens on Earth.
Ms. F.: Why do you think it's about Earth?
Student: Earth is the third planet from the sun, right? (*Ms. F. writes the prediction on the board.*)

Comments: First note that Ms. Fleckner used two open-ended questions and resisted posing additional questions to clarify students' predictions. In doing so, she set a tone of acceptance and didn't turn the question-response exchange into an interrogation session. In addition, she wrote the predictions on the board. Later, she returned to the predictions and asked students to verify their accuracy, reject them outright, or modify them in light of information gained from reading.

After five or six predictions about the title were written on the board, Ms. Fleckner assigned the first segment of text. Students read through the story's initiating event (the first eight lines from the story on page 144). Study the exchange that followed with the student who predicted that the Third Planet was Earth:

Ms. F. (*pointing to the chalkboard*): Well, how did some of your predictions turn out?
Student: I was right. It's about Earth.
Ms. F.: You certainly were! So what do you think is going to happen now that the space ship has landed on Earth?
Student: War will break out. Someone's going to report the space ship. The Creatures are going to come out and capture the people.
Ms. F.: Why do you say that?
Student: Because that's what happens in the movies.
Ms. F.: That's a possibility! (*She turns her attention to the class and asks for other predictions.*)

Comments: Initial predictions are often off-the-mark. This is to be expected since students' predictions are fueled by background knowledge and experience.

The DR-TA begins with very open-ended or divergent responses and moves toward more accurate predictions and text-based inferences as students acquire information from the reading. Compare the DR-TA to the Inferential Strategy, which also makes substantial use of students' ability to use background knowledge and make predictions.

Inferential Strategy

The *Inferential Strategy* was designed for elementary children, especially those in the primary grades (Hansen, 1981). Unlike the DR-TA, the Inferential Strategy does not require stopping points throughout the reading selection. Instead, it relies on several questions *prior* to reading and discussion afterward.

Consider the following steps in the Inferential Strategy:

1. Analyze the content selection for important ideas central to the material. Before assigning the class to read the material, select three ideas that are important or might be difficult to understand.

2. Plan prereading questions. Develop *two* questions for *each idea* identified in the content analysis. One question is posed to tap background knowledge relative to the idea; the other, prediction. For example: (*Background*) How do you react when you feel uncomfortable in a social situation? (*Prediction*) In the selection you are about to read, Tim feels unsure of himself on his first blind date. How do you think Tim will react when he meets his date?

   Ask students to write predictions before discussion takes place.

3. Discuss responses to background and prediction questions *before* reading. Discuss both students' previous experience with the topic and their predictions for the selection.

4. Upon finishing the prereading discussion, assign selection to read.

5. After reading, relate predictions to what actually happened in the selection. Evaluate the three or four ideas that motivated background and prediction questions.

For example, in Mrs. Conti's second-grade class, the children read a story from their basal reader (Jovanovich, 1974). "The Lion and the Mouse" contained the following story line:

SETTING	A happy little mouse is running and jumping in the grass in the morning.
BEGINNING EVENT	The mouse gets lost in the grass and is picked up by a lion who says he wants to eat him.
INTERNAL RESPONSE	The mouse is frightened; he wants to be set free.
ATTEMPT	The mouse promises to help the lion if the lion will set him free.
OUTCOME	The lion laughs in disbelief, but decides to let the mouse go free.
RESOLUTION	The lion gets caught in a net and the mouse chews him free.
REACTION	The lion is grateful—a little mouse helped him after all.

Mrs. Conti chose three ideas around which to ask background questions and prediction questions: (1) A kindness is never wasted; (2) everybody needs someone; (3) you can use your head to get out of trouble.

Study the background and prediction questions that Mrs. Conti asked for the third idea: (*Background question*) All of us have probably been in trouble at some time—maybe with a friend, a brother or sister, or a parent. Sometimes we have to use our heads to get out of trouble. What are some of the things that you have done to get out of trouble? (*Prediction question*) In this story, a mouse got caught by a lion who wants to eat him. What do you think he'll do to get out of trouble?

During the prereading activity, the children shared their answers to the questions. They had much to contribute. They then read the story in its entirety. After reading, the predictions that were made were compared with inferences derived from the story.

The kinds of questions asked in the DR-TA and Inferential Strategy help to guide reader-text interactions and promote comprehension. In the next section, we explain in more detail how you can use questions to help children to search for meaning in text.

USING QUESTIONS TO PROMOTE COMPREHENSION

Questions are only as good as the context in which they're posed. If questions fail to create an active, problem-solving environment for readers, then much will be lost in the transactions that occur among you, the students, and the text. If questioning is to promote reading comprehension, it must first and foremost serve as a springboard to conversation and discussion.

Questions as a Springboard to Discussion

Whereas recitation is concerned chiefly with recall and regurgitation of what has been read, discussion initiates thinking by going beyond right answers to inference making, reaction, and evaluation. Dillon (1983) maintained that the ultimate goal of discussion is to have students add to their knowledge or judgment on the matter being discussed. Therefore questions should be based in perplexity. There should be a "gnawing" inside each student to explore, clarify, and find out more. If this is the case, certain principles must be inherent in classroom behavior, including orderliness, mutual trust and respect for one another, and the right to maintain or hold differing opinions and points of view.

A good discussion has no hidden agenda: There are no predetermined conclusions to reach. As a result, the discussion hinges on teacher modeling and class reflection. A few questions—carefully planned to provide direction—are the rule, not the exception. Plan key questions in advance by writing them in clear, understandable language. Avoid "rapid-fire" question-answer exchanges or asking questions "off the top of your head." Otherwise, discussion will soon wither. Three types of questions at key points in a discussion will keep students on task: (1) a preliminary question to identify a problem or issue; (2) a question or two to clarify or redirect the discussion; and (3) a final question or two that ties together loose ends or establishes a premise for further discussion.

One way to get a discussion off to a good start is by asking a question about a perplexing situation or establishing a problem to be solved. If you are working with a story, raise an issue related to the central problem, or theme. From time to time, it may be necessary to refocus attention to the topic by piggy-backing on comments made by particular students: "Tim's point is an excellent one. Does anyone else want to talk about this?" During small group discussions, a tactic that keeps groups on task is to remind students of time remaining in the discussion. Keeping the focus or redirecting a discussion is one time when you may want to ask a question to "clarify the question." You may want to ensure that students understand a particular student's comment. Often, keeping the discussion focused will prevent the class from straying from the task.

Alternatives to Questions

Dillon (1983) explained several alternatives to questions to stimulate student thought and response and to encourage participation.

Declarative Statement. Instead of using a question, express a thought that has occurred to you in relation to what a student has just said. The effect of a straightforward statement in response to a student's comment is to have the student and others examine your thinking instead of trying to guess what's in your head. As Dillon put it, a question says, "Supply this bit of information and then stop." In contrast, statements invite further response and enhance student thought.

Reflective Restatement. Sometimes it is valuable to "mirror" the content of a student's response. A reflective restatement, then, lets the students know that you are listening and informs them of the extent of your understanding of what is being said. Restate by saying, "I get from what you say that . . ." or "So you think that . . . " (Dillon, 1983, page 31). What you'll find, more often than not, is that a student will agree with your reflection and then elaborate.

State of Mind. At certain points in a discussion share with students your state of mind. For example, if you are confused by a student's point, say, "I'm sorry, I'm not getting it" or, "I'm confused about what you're saying." At other points in the discussion, you might wish to express your state of mind by pondering what has been said: "I was just thinking about what you said. Could it be that . . . "

Deliberate Silence. According to Dillon (1983), "Deliberate silence is the most intriguing alternative to questions and one of the most effective" (page 38). He suggested that when a student finishes a response, or falters, you might consider maintaining a deliberate silence for three to five seconds. Often, the silence results in the student extending his or her comments or another student will enter into the discussion. To be effective at the use of silence, you must practice timing. One second can seem like an hour in a teacher-student exchange; three seconds, an eternity. However, a minimum of three seconds is necessary for silence to be noticeable.

Classifying Questions According to Cognitive Function

Given the appropriate context, questions can trigger a full range of intellectual activity. No wonder questioning has long been considered one of the most critical skills in a teacher's repertoire. Hilda Taba (1975) can hardly be faulted for hyperbole for asserting that questions are "by far the most influential single teaching act." As the result of Taba's research as well as the research of others, it is almost axiomatic to assert, *what we ask is what we get*. That is, if readers are asked predominantly inferential and evaluative questions, they're more likely to make inferential and evaluative responses. Question-asking, on the other hand, that seeks recall and recognition from children will result in exactly that. This is why Aulls (1978) noted that "low level questions may be doing very little to enhance students' reading comprehension growth" (page 3).

Many classification schemes have been proposed since the 1950s (Bloom, 1956; Guilford, 1956). Over the years these schemes or taxonomies have been simplified for classroom use. In reading, for example, you can engage children in a full range of cognitive function by using "levels of comprehension" to plan and guide instructional activity.

Levels of Comprehension. Readers respond to meaning at various levels of abstraction and conceptual difficulty. Herber (1978) has contended that a "levels" view simplifies comprehension while still dealing with the complexity of intellectual activity that is associated with more detailed and intricate classification schemes such as Bloom's or Guilford's. Although skills are assumed, levels of comprehension emphasize the interaction of comprehension skills within a broader cognitive framework:

Literal Level. When children interact with text at the literal level they "are reading the lines." The literal level has been described as "gist reading" because the reader must, at a minimum, understand what the author says.

Interpretive Level. Recognizing what the author says is necessary, but not sufficient, for making meaning from print. Children must learn to search for implicit or intended meaning. In other words, they must "read between the lines" to infer what the author means or is trying to say. The interpretive level involves convergent thinking and also includes Bloom's notion of "comprehension." The important difference between literal and interpretive reading is in how the reader manipulates information. At the literal level, recognition and understanding of the author's main ideas and details are essential. However, to interpret, the reader must recognize the relationships that exist among the main ideas and details and use these relationships to make inferences and draw conclusions about the author's intentions and implicit meaning.

Applied Level. The applied level involves divergent thinking and includes analysis, synthesis, application, and evaluation. The reader reacts to text in terms of its relevance and significance. Reading at the applied level deals with questions such as "So what?" "What does the information mean to me?" "Does it make sense?" The reader is functioning "beyond the lines" and is involved in creating new insights about the material.

Question Continuum. Cunningham (1971) proposed that teachers view question-asking along a continuum from narrow to broad. Indeed, questions have the potential to stimulate thinking, but the level of comprehension you want students to function at depends on the type of question asked. "Narrow" questions, for example, prompt literal understanding and inferential thinking. "Broad" questions lead to applied responses and engage readers in creative and evaluative thinking. The narrower the question, the more convergent the answer; the broader the question, the more divergent the response. Figure 6.5 illustrates the range of questions on the continuum.

Narrow and broad questions can be easily identified from the continuum. The narrowest questions on the continuum involve processing text information at a literal level. Often this means recognizing *who, where, what, when,* or *how many.* Narrow responses are usually signaled by words such as *define, list, name,*

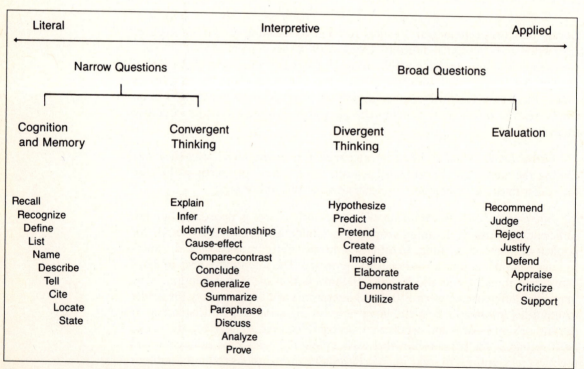

Figure 6.5   Question Continuum

quote, and *describe*. Convergent questions are also narrow but tend to move toward the broad question side of the continuum because students are involved in more complex cognitive activity at an interpretive level. To make inferences, readers must focus or converge on information from the text and identify or infer textual relationships such as cause-effect and likenesses and differences. They must use information from different parts of the text to interpret the author's intended meaning.

Broad questions are divergent and evaluative. They invite application, personal response, and reaction. As Aulls (1975) noted, "Usually broad questions lead to unpredictable responses because more than one response is always possible" (page 12). Not only are responses to a broad question at different applied levels possible, but they must be encouraged. The rationale behind broad questions is to show students how to use or react to information that is explicitly or implicitly dealt with in a reading selection.

Classification schemes have tended to categorize questions apart from the reader and the text. However, the current emphasis is on posing questions within the context of both the reader's background knowledge and the text itself. Pearson and Johnson (1978) proposed that the type of question asked to guide comprehension should be based on the *information readers need to answer the question*. As a result, teachers must help students become aware of likely sources of information as they respond to questions.

Question-Answer Relationships

When designing questions at different levels of comprehension, special attention should be given to the most likely source of information the reader needs to answer the question. Certain narrow questions can be thought of as *textually explicit* because they promote recall or recognition of *information actually stated in the text*. Other narrow questions are *textually implicit* because they provoke convergent thinking. Readers must search for text relationships and think about the information presented. If students are to integrate ideas within a text, then textually implicit questions are likely to be the most useful. Finally, broad questions usually place the reader's knowledge of the world at the center of the questioning activity. Such questions are *schema-based*. Students must rely on their own resources as well as the text to solve problems, discover new insights, or evaluate the significance of what was read.

Question-Answer Relationships (QARs) were proposed by Raphael (1982, 1986) to help learners know what information sources are available for seeking answers to different types of text questions. Through this strategy, readers become more sensitive to the different mental operations and text demands required by different questions. As a result, teachers and students become cognizant of the three-way relationships that exist among the question, the text to which it refers, and the background knowledge and information at the reader's disposal. QARs enhance children's ability to answer comprehension questions by teaching them how to find information they need to answer questions. Explicit instruction will make students sensitive to two information sources where answers can be found.

The first information source is the TEXT. Some answers to narrow, textually explicit questions can be found *right there* in the text. Other answers from the text, however, demand a *think and search* strategy on the part of students. That is, convergent or textually implicit questions require students to *search* the text for information and to *think* about the relationships that exist among the bits of information found.

The second information source is the READER. Broad questions signal to the reader that you are on your own. The text may help, but answers must come from inside readers' heads. As you can see, the use of *Right There*, *Think and Search*, and *On My Own* are mnemonics to help readers recognize question-answer relationships.

Procedures related to learning QARs can be taught directly. Direct instruction involves training, which will vary with the age and sophistication of the reader in your class. Study the five-day training period that a third-grade teacher used to make her students more sensitive to QARs.

Day 1: Introduce QARs and Begin Training. Mrs. Miller showed students a chart containing a description of the three basic strategies for finding answers to questions: *Right There*, *Think and Search*, and *On My Own*. The chart was displayed in a prominent spot in the room and children were encouraged to refer to it whenever needed during instructional reading activities.

Once the children were familiar with QARs, Mrs. Miller continued to build an awareness of question-answer strategies by assigning three short passages which were no more than two to five sentences in length. Each passage was followed by a question. For example:

1. Timmy Turtle was very sad. He wanted to play with the other turtles. But they were all up on the bank. "I would give anything in the world to be up on that bank," said Timmy. The other turtles went up the bank all the time, but Timmy just didn't try.

   Why didn't Timmy try to go up the bank?

2. Penny wasn't much of a hen, but she was good at one thing. She could get the boy and his mother out of bed. When the sun came up, Penny flew to the top of the house. First, she would spin around. Then she would sing a little song.

   Why did Penny sing when the sun came up?

3. Beavers like to build their houses in the water. They like to live where the water is not too shallow. When the water is too shallow, beavers build a dam out of small trees and twigs. The dam goes from one bank to the other, making a pool in the shallow water. Then the beavers can build their house.

   Where do beavers like to build their houses?

Mrs. Miller's third-graders weren't required to answer the questions. Instead, the class discussed the differences between a *Right There* question and answer,

Think and Search question and answer, and an *On My Own* question and answer. Mrs. Miller encouraged students to use the chart and she reinforced their responses with clear and complete explanations.

Once the children reached consensus about the QARs (Passage 1 = On My Own, Passage 2 = Think and Search, Passage 3 = Right There), they practiced identifying questions in a similar manner with several more short passages of about the same length. Using this approach, students soon caught on to the difference between QAR categories. With some classes, however, this phase of training may take more than a day to accomplish.

Day 2: Continue Practice. Mrs. Miller began the second day of training by assigning several short passages. She provided one question for each QAR per passage. In addition to the passage and question, the children were given the answer to the question and the correct identification of the QAR. An example from the worksheet prepared by Mrs. Miller is illustrated below.

> Joe, Mike, and Terry were getting ready to play baseball on the school playground. Joe kicked the ground. He was having a temper tantrum. "It's no use," Joe said, throwing down his bat. "We're no match for the other team. I bet if we do play, we won't win!"
>
> *Question: How does Joe feel?*
> *Answer: Angry, upset*
> *QAR: Think and Search*

In comparing the passages, Mrs. Miller wanted her students to decide why some of the questions, such as the one in the example above, represented one QAR category and not another. After the discussion, she gave students a passage with questions and answers, only this time the students had to identify the QAR for each. Discussion followed with more clarifications made.

Directions: Draw a line from each QAR to the question and answer that matches it.

Jimmy put some paper on a stool. With steady hands, he made the paper into a hat. The baby was looking at what he was doing. She didn't think about her toothache. He put the hat on his head. She smiled a little.

RIGHT THERE   1. What did Jimmy put on the stool?

paper

THINK AND SEARCH   2. What is one thing you can do to make your mother or father happy? *I would do something nice, like clean my room.*

ON YOUR OWN   3. What kind of boy do you think Jimmy is?

Kind, cares about the baby

Day 3: Review and Work with Longer Passages. On the third day of training, Mrs. Miller reviewed what the children had learned thus far about QARs. She once again referred them to the chart if they needed to figure out one QAR from another. She then assigned a longer passage (about 100 words) with five questions (at least one each from the QAR categories).

Students were asked to work in groups to decide: (1) the QAR for each question, and (2) the answer for each question. When students completed the task, each group reported its work to the whole class. Discussion and explanations followed.

Upon completion of the small group work, children were then assigned to individually complete another passage, about the same length, with five questions. Again, they were required to identify the QAR categories and formulate answers for the questions. An example from Mrs. Miller's training packet follows:

Why Are Some Days Cloudy?

In one place, a boy goes outside and looks up at the dark sky. He says, "It looks snowy today."

Not too far away, a girl looks up at the sun. She says, "It is going to be a fair day today. There are no clouds in the sky."

And in a place not too far from the girl, a man goes out of his house. He feels drops of water on his face and hair. He says, "I will need a hat today to keep my hair dry."

How can the same day be snowy, fair, and rainy in three places? Why does a sunny day sometimes become cloudy? Why does a cloudy day sometimes become snowy or rainy?

Air is a gas that can't be seen. It is all around us. As it moves, it takes in drops of water. When the air has little water in it, the sky is fair and we can feel the sun. When the air takes in too much water, rain or snow will begin to fall.

1. What kinds of days do you like best?

   QAR: _On My Own_

   Sunny. They make me happy.

2. Why does the man need a hat?

   QAR: _Right There_

   To keep his hair dry.

3. How do you feel on a sunny day?

   QAR: _On My Own_

   Happy

4. When air takes in too many drops of water, what begins to fall?

QAR: _Right There_

Rain or Snow.

5. Why does a sunny day become cloudy?

QAR: _Think and Search_

Water goes into the air.

Days 4 and 5: Apply QARs. As part of the basal reading lesson, Mrs. Miller had her students use what they learned about question-answering strategies to answer qustions after reading. For each question, children followed the format below:

What did Mary find on the beach?

_____ Right There

_____ Think and Search

_____ On My Own

Answer: _____

_____

Why did Mary's father say, "We can't get such things for the house right now?"

_____ Right There

_____ Think and Search

_____ On My Own

Answer: _____

_____

Once children have become accustomed to using different information sources for different types of questions, several modifications can be made. For one, you might ask children to create their own questions for a reading selection—two for each QAR category. They then supply the answers to the questions as they understand them. Another alternative is to have students create questions, but leave one question unanswered from the Think and Search category and one from the On Your Own category. They then form groups of two, switch papers, and try to answer one another's questions. In this way, each question-maker gets to hear the view of another student on convergent and broad questions. Another modification involves class discussions. During question-answer exchanges, you can begin a question by saying, "This question is *right there* in the text." Or,

"You'll have to *think and search* to find the answer in the text." Or, "You're *on your own* with this one."

As students become sensitive to question-answer relationships, you will find it easier to guide reader-text interactions. Not only will readers develop strategies for responding to questions, but they will also realize that they have an active role to play in comprehending text selections.

SUMMARY

In this chapter, we approached the heart of contemporary reading instruction—comprehension—from an active, meaning-making stance. After examining the elements of story grammar, strategies were discussed for building and reinforcing children's awareness of a story's underlying structure. There is, however, no substitute for building children's experiences with stories (and developing concepts) by reading, telling, listening, and performing them on a regular basis.

Instructional activities and strategies were described for building and activating readers' schema. Prereading preparation, if anything, involves engaging children in exploring what they already know and what they need to know in order to comprehend text effectively. Advance organizers and student-generated questions activate background knowledge and create a set for comprehending reading material.

Two major strategies, the Directed Reading-Thinking Activity (DR-TA) and the Inferential Strategy, are useful in helping to guide reader-text interactions. Both involve the use of prediction and background knowledge and engage children actively in constructing meaning and making inferences during reading.

Without doubt, questions promote comprehension. They should serve as springboards to discussion and reflection. Modeling question-asking behavior is crucial to reading comprehension instruction. Question-Answer Relationships (QARs) sensitize readers to sources of information where answers to questions can be found. QAR strategy aids in providing explicit training through explanation, modeling, demonstration, practice, and application.

THE WORKSHOP

In the Classroom

1. Choose a story from a basal reader and construct a story map, using a chart similar to the one suggested in the chapter. Then examine the story map to determine where to create "breakpoints" in planning a DR-TA. Try out the DR-TA with an appropriate group of elementary school students and report on the lesson.

2. Construct a story map from another narrative selection, then design a lesson to reinforce or extend students' schema for stories. The lesson might include the "macro-cloze" or "scrambled story" activities suggested in the chapter. Finally, field-test the lesson with a group of students at the appropriate grade level.

3. Working with several class members, make plans for teaching a reading selection. First, decide on the selection to use and develop a story map. Then brainstorm comprehension instructional activities appropriate for the selection and think of ways to guide comprehension before, during, and after reading. Last, group members should try out the lesson independently with students at the appropriate level and then reconvene as a group to discuss results.

In the Field

1. Discuss with a group of children a story they have just read, and tape-record the conversation. Analyze the discussion to see if you followed these key guidelines to keep students on task: (a) asking a preliminary question to identify a problem or issue; (b) inserting a question or two as needed to clarify or redirect the discussion; and (c) posing a final question or two that tied together loose ends or established a premise for further discussion. Also check to see if you used declarative or reflective statements, state of mind queries, or deliberate silence as alternatives to questions.

2. Choosing different grade levels, observe three elementary school classrooms during reading instruction time. Take notes on what the teacher does to facilitate comprehension. Also watch what students are doing when they are not working directly with the teacher: Are they completing worksheets, reading selections longer than one or two sentences or a paragraph in length, or writing about what they have read? Are they involved in any other instructional activities? Relate what you see to ideas presented in this and previous chapters.

3. Plan and then teach a comprehension lesson for a small group of elementary school students which revolves around one or more of the following strategies: Active Comprehension, ReQuest, and the Inferential Strategy.

Chapter 7

Vocabulary Knowledge and Concept Development

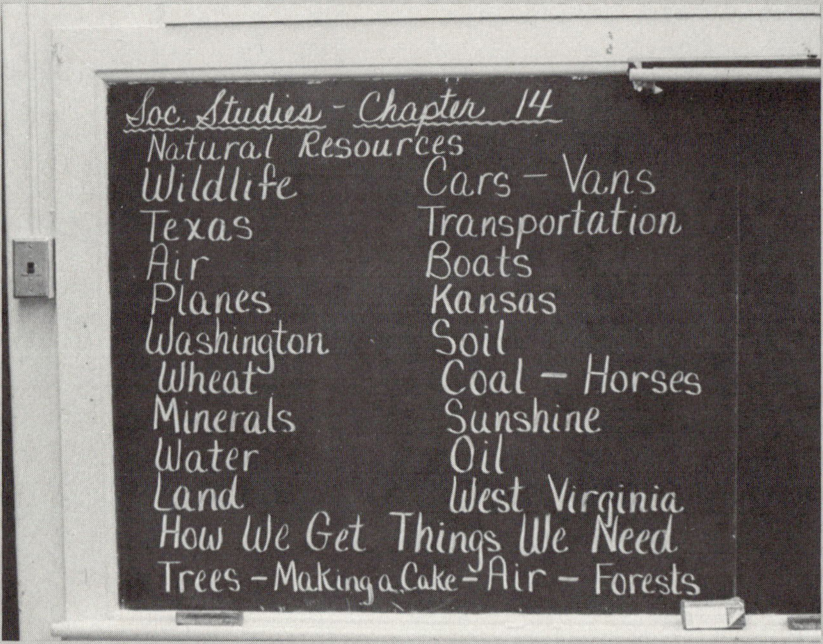

"Good teachers begin the day's reading lesson by preparing children for the story to be read—introducing new words and concepts they will encounter." Pretty strong words. They come from the United States Department of Education publication, What Works *(1986). Some educators may argue that vocabulary instruction involves more than introduction and preparation for story reading. Nevertheless, directives such as the one above, supported by research findings, underscore the connections between vocabulary knowledge and reading comprehension. In this chapter we explore these connections and examine how to teach words in depth. It's no accident that we devote an entire chapter to developing vocabulary and concepts. From our perspective, it's essential that teachers provide substantive and interesting strategies to build children's word knowledge and expand their concepts. After all, it's what works. . . .*

I know Coke is made from coal but it still tastes good.

Alita, a fifth-grader

Sometimes I don't understand what I'm reading because the words are too hard. You know, I don't know what they [the words] mean.

Joe, a fourth-grader

I like words.

Cindy, a first-grader

I don't have the time to spend on vocabulary instruction.

May, a third-grade teacher

VOCABULARY KNOWLEDGE AND CONCEPT DEVELOPMENT

Mrs. Osborne has taught fifth-graders in the *same* school and in *same* classroom for nineteen years! You may question, as we did, whether she has ever gotten tired of being surrounded by the same four walls year in and year out. However, the question never occurred to Mrs. Osborne. She thanks her students for that. Just when she thinks she has experienced everything there is to experience as a teacher, something new or different is bound to happen in the classroom.

Part of the joy of teaching for Mrs. Osborne is the uncertainty of what children will do or say. She still shakes her head in disbelief as she tells how she once initiated a unit on coal resources in the United States. As part of getting students ready for the unit, Mrs. Osborne introduced the "important vocabulary" because she was aware of the relationship that exists between knowledge of word meanings and reading comprehension. One of the terms she introduced was *coke*. In discussing its definition, she reminded the class not to confuse *coke* with the soft drink bearing the same name. Sure enough, however, when she was grading the unit test, Mrs. Osborne discovered Alita's postscript at the bottom of her test paper: "P.S.: I know *coke* is made from coal, but it still tastes good."

Alita's postscript is as real as the problems teachers face daily in developing vocabulary knowledge and concepts in their classrooms. In a nutshell, the practical problem and challenge is one of teaching vocabulary words *well enough* to enhance children's comprehension of written language (Beck and McKeown, 1983). If children are not readily familiar with most words they meet in print undoubtedly they will have trouble understanding what they read.

Although the confusion over the meaning of *coke* is innocent enough, it highlights how children use language and build concepts. Other than the initial discussion of the words, Mrs. Osborne assumed that children would develop an understanding of *coke* and the other terms in the unit from such staple activities as defining the words and writing them in sentences. She did little else instructionally

unit. Nevertheless, as Alita's postscript demonstrates, students must not only be able to define words, but must also experience unfamiliar words in frequent, meaningful, and varied contexts. A major premise of this chapter is that *definitional knowledge* is necessary, but students must also develop *contextual and conceptual knowledge* of words in order to comprehend fully what they read.

Mrs. Osborne was only partially correct in her assumption that vocabulary learning entails defining and using words in sentences. Students need to have many opportunities to "experiment" with words. The more that they encounter vocabulary in as many language contexts as possible, the more they will come to know and use words.

Opportunities to experiment with words abound. Every time a decision is made by a student-writer as to which word is "best" in a piece of writing, vocabulary learning takes place. Mark Twain said that the difference between the right word and the almost-right word is the difference between lightning and the lightning bug. Children develop sensitivity to the "right word" when they have many occasions to write—an important point discussed in Chapter 5. Children also experiment with words whenever they hear unfamiliar words read aloud in a piece of literature or encounter new words while reading. They develop an "ear" for language and an "eye" for the images created by language.

Protheroe (1979) suggested that good authors consciously try to use new vocabulary in ways that will become familiar to the reader. An author, for example, will build an array of familiar contexts in which to place a difficult word so that students will nod their heads and say with some confidence, "Yeah, yeah, I know what that word means!" A concern in this chapter is with developing in children the "yeah, yeah, I know that word!" attitude. What instructional opportunities can be provided to influence the depth and breadth of children's vocabulary knowledge? What are the instructional implications of vocabulary for reading comprehension? How do students develop the interest and motivation to want to learn words? To answer these questions, we must first recognize that vocabulary development in the classroom is neither accidental nor incidental. It must be orchestrated carefully not only during "reading time" but also throughout the entire day.

THE RELATIONSHIP BETWEEN VOCABULARY AND COMPREHENSION

The relationship between knowledge of word meanings and comprehension has been well documented by researchers and acknowledged by children. Joe, a fourth-grader we quoted to begin the chapter, had little difficulty recognizing that he does not understand what he's reading when the words get too hard—that is, when he does not understand what the words mean. The seminal work of F. B. Davis (1944) and other researchers such as Thurstone (1946) and Spearitt (1972) have consistently identified vocabulary knowledge as an important factor in reading comprehension.

Various explanations are used to account for the strong relationship between vocabulary and comprehension. Anderson and Freebody (1981) proposed three hypotheses: *aptitude, instrumental,* and *knowledge*.

The *aptitude hypothesis* suggests that both vocabulary and comprehension reflect general intellectual ability. A large vocabulary as measured by test performance is a solid indicator of verbal and mental ability (Wechsler, 1958). Vocabulary, therefore, has been one of the most robust measures of aptitude and intelligence. The relationship between vocabulary and comprehension is explained this way: The more intellectually able the student, the more he or she will know the meanings of words and, therefore, comprehend better while reading. Children with large vocabularies have a built-in advantage because they often possess superior mental and verbal agility.

It is best to guard against the pessimistic (if not fatalistic) attitude that only "smart kids" can acquire words easily—or that only the most intelligent child profits from direct instruction in vocabulary. Vocabulary knowledge, while a strong correlate of intelligence, is not necessarily innate. A child's environment and experiences are crucial in learning concepts and words. A home and school environment that fosters wide reading and varied language experiences provides the building blocks for vocabulary and concept development. A classroom environment that promotes direct and systematic vocabulary instruction influences the depth and breadth of children's vocabulary growth.

The *instrumental position* establishes a causal chain between vocabulary knowledge and comprehension. The case for an instrumental hypothesis can be defended on the following grounds: If comprehension depends in part on knowledge of word meanings, then vocabulary instruction ought to influence comprehension. Simply stated, knowing words plays an instrumental role in understanding text.

The instructional implications of the instrumental hypothesis are straightforward. Teach word meanings well enough and students will find reading material easier to comprehend. Unfortunately, vocabulary instruction research has provided contradictory evidence on this effect. Pany and Jenkins (1977), Schacter (1978), and Tuinman and Brady (1974) showed that vocabulary instruction has little effect on comprehension performance. However, more recent studies by Stahl (1983) and Beck, Perfetti, and McKeown (1982) showed that when *enough* words from reading selections are taught in *depth* prior to reading, comprehension is facilitated.

Unlike the aptitude and instrumental hypotheses, the *knowledge hypothesis* suggests that vocabulary and comprehension reflect general knowledge. In other words, students with large vocabularies related to a given topic also have more knowledge about that topic, which in turn produces better comprehension. Vocabulary knowledge is viewed more or less as a signal that a reader is likely to possess more background information and conceptual knowledge to understand a text. Closely tied to a schema view of reading, the knowledge hypothesis proposes that vocabulary words must be taught within a larger framework of concept development.

Vocabulary is cumulative. People learn new words throughout life as they learn new information. Vocabulary words ought to be learned within the framework of acquiring new knowledge. As Anderson and Freebody (1981) suggested, "Every serious student of reading recognizes that the significant aspect of vocabulary development is in the learning of concepts not just words" (page 87).

We believe that all three hypotheses have merit in helping to understand the relationship between word knowledge and comprehension. In planning vocabulary instruction, we would do well to borrow from each explanation. Surely the implications of the aptitude hypothesis signal the importance of reading aloud to children and immersing them in written language. Wide reading experiences develop a facility with written language.

Moreover, the instrumental and knowledge explanations have many instructional implications that we address in the remainder of this chapter. Words need to be taught directly and well enough to enhance comprehension. Students must have quick access to word meanings when they are reading. Quick access can be achieved through a variety of strategies that make use of children's definitional, contextual, and conceptual knowledge of words.

Before examining instructional strategies, the relationship among children's experiences, concepts, and words needs to be explored. What are concepts? What does it mean to know words?

EXPERIENCES, CONCEPTS, AND WORDS

One way to define *vocabulary* is to suggest that it represents the breadth and depth of all the words we know—the words we use, recognize, and respond to in meaningful acts of communication. *Breadth* involves the size and scope of our vocabulary; *depth* concerns the level of understanding that we have of words.

Vocabulary has usually been classified as having four components: *listening, speaking, reading,* and *writing*. These components are often said to develop in breadth and depth in the sequence listed. Five- and six-year-olds, for example, come to school already able to recognize and respond to thousands of spoken words. Children's first vocabulary without much question is listening vocabulary. However, as a child progresses through the school years, he or she eventually learns to identify and use as many written as spoken words. By adulthood, a person's reading vocabulary often outmatches any of the other vocabulary components.

For this reason, it is more or less assumed that listening and speaking vocabularies are learned in the home, whereas reading and writing vocabularies fall within the domain of school learning. Although this assumption may hold generally, it creates an unnecessary dichotomy between "inside" and "outside" school influences. It is much safer to assume that both home and school are profoundly influential in the development of all components of vocabulary.

Words Are Labels for Concepts

Although words are labels for concepts, a single concept represents much more than the meaning of a single word. It might take thousands of words to explain a concept. However, answers to the question, "What does it mean to know a word?" depend on how well we understand the relationship among words, concepts, and experiences. Understanding this relationship provides a sound rationale for teaching vocabulary within the larger framework of concept development.

Concepts are learned through our acting upon and interaction with the environment. Edgar Dale (1969) reminded us how children learn concepts best: through direct, purposeful experiences. Dale's Cone of Experience in Figure 7.1 depicts the levels of abstraction from the most concrete, nonverbal experiences beginning at the base of the cone to the most abstract and removed experiences at the tip of the cone—verbal symbols. For a child who has never eaten a *banana split*, the most intense and meaningful learning would occur via a trip to an ice

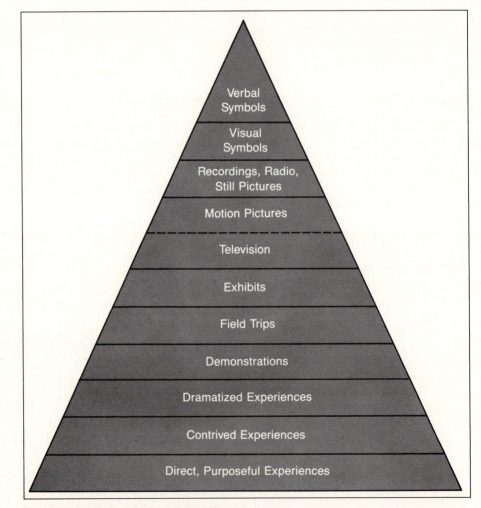

Figure 7.1 Dale's Cone of Experience

cream parlor! The relationship of experiences to concepts and words sets the stage for an important principle of vocabulary instruction: In order to learn new or unfamiliar words it is necessary to have experiences from which concepts can be derived.

Words and Concepts: A Closer Look

One way of thinking about a concept is that it is a mental image of something. By "something," we mean anything that can be grouped together by common features or similar criteria—objects, symbols, ideas, processes, or events. In this respect, concepts are similar in nature to schemata.

Concepts are synonymous with the formation of categories. We would be overwhelmed by the complexity of our environment if we were to respond to each object or event that we encountered as unique. So we invent categories (or form concepts) to reduce the complexity of our environment and the necessity for constant learning. Every canine need not have a different name to be known as a dog. Although dogs vary greatly, the common characteristics that they share cause them to be referred to by the same general term. Thus in order to facilitate communication, we invent words to name concepts.

Scan a page from any dictionary and you will encounter word after word after word—most of which represent the names of concepts. The only place that these words stand alone is on a dictionary page! In your head, concepts are organized into a network of complex relations. Suppose, for example, you were to fix your eyes on the word *baboon* as you scanned the entries in the dictionary. What mental picture comes to mind? Your image of *baboon* probably differs from that of another person. Your background knowledge of *baboon*, or the larger class to which it belongs known as *primates*, will very likely be different from someone else's. So will your experiences with and interests in baboons, especially if you are fond of frequenting the zoo or reading books about primate behavior. The point is that we organize background knowledge and experiences into conceptual hierarchies according to class, example, and attribute relations. Let's take a closer look at these relationships.

Class, Example, and Attribute Relations

Note that we suggested that concepts are organized into a network of complex relations. What do we mean by *complex relations*? We stated earlier that the concept *baboon* is part of a more inclusive class called *primates*, which in turn is a member of a larger class known as *mammals*, which in turn is a member of an even larger class of animals known as *vertebrates*. These *class relations* are depicted in Figure 7.2.

Class relationships in any conceptual network are organized in a hierarchy according to the *superordinate* and *subordinate* nature of the concepts. For example, in Figure 7.2 the superordinate concept is *animals*. There are two classes of animals known as *vertebrates* and *nonvertebrates* which are in a subordinate position in the hierarchy. However, *vertebrates* is superordinate in relation to *amphibians, mammals,*

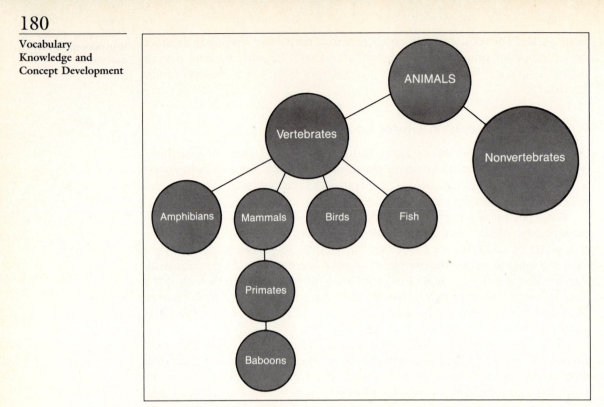

Figure 7.2   An Example of a Concept Hierarchy

birds, and *fish* which, of course, are types or subclasses of vertebrates. To complete the hierarchy, the concept *primates* is subordinate to *mammals* but is superordinate in relation to *baboons.*

By now you have probably recognized that for every concept there are examples of that concept. In other words, an *example* is a member of any concept under consideration. A *nonexample* is any instance that is not a member of the concept under consideration. Class/example relations are reciprocal: *Vertebrates* and *nonvertebrates* are examples of *animals. Mammals, birds, fish,* and *amphibians* are examples of *vertebrates. Primates* is one example of *mammals,* and so on.

To extend this discussion, suppose we were to make *primates* our target concept. In addition to baboons, what are other examples of primates? No doubt, *apes, monkeys,* and *Homo sapiens* come quickly to mind. These examples can be shown in relation to each other.

Note that the examples of primates listed in Figure 7.3 are not exhaustive of all possible primates that we could have listed. Nevertheless, we might ask, "What do baboons, apes, monkeys, and Homo sapiens have in common?" Answers to the question would force us to focus on relevant *attributes,* those traits, features, properties, or characteristics that are common to every example of a particular concept. In other words, the relevant attributes of primates refer to the character-

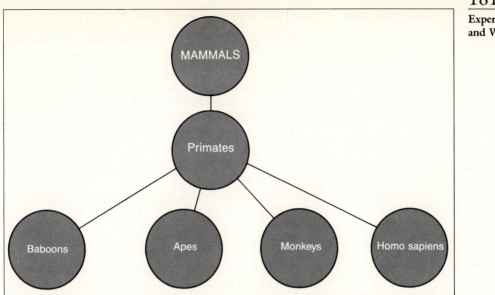

Figure 7.3 **Class/Example Relations for the Target Concept** *Primates*

istics that determine whether baboons, monkeys, apes, and Homo sapiens belong to the particular class of mammals called *primates*. An attribute is said to be *critical* if it is a characteristic that is necessary for determining class membership. Some attributes are called *variable* if characteristics within a class are shared by some but not all examples of the class.

All primates, from baboons to human beings, have certain physical and social characteristics, but not every primate shares each of these features. Nearly every example of a primate can grasp objects with its hands and/or feet. A primate has nails, rather than claws. Vision is a primate's most important sense. Most species of primates live in groups, but some live alone. A social group is often considerable in size and highly organized. Primates have the capacity to communicate with one another by means of signals based on scent, touch, vision, and sound. And, of course, primate infants depend to a large extent on their mothers.

This discussion began when we asked you to form a mental image of *baboon*. The clarity with which you were able to picture *baboon* in your mind depended, as you may have surmised, on how well you were familiar with the characteristics of primates in general and baboons specifically. Baboons, apes, monkeys, and *Homo sapiens* share common characteristics, but they are also different.

In what ways are baboons similar to other primates? How are baboons different? These are important questions in clarifying your concept of baboon and sorting out the relations that exist among the various examples. Concept learning involves to a large extent the search for and listing of attributes that can be used to distinguish examples from one another and to distinguish examples from nonexamples.

Definitional and Contextual Knowledge of Words

To define a word is to be able to identify the features or attributes of the thing, event, or quality that it designates. Looking up words in a dictionary and using them in sentences is one way of defining words—but not the *only* way. Smith and Johnson (1980) provide alternative routes that direct students away from the possible boredom associated with having to always look up words in a dictionary and write their definitions. Here are several of their suggestions:

USAGE	Define each word by using it in a sentence.
SYNONYM	Define each word by writing another word that has a similar meaning.
ANTONYM	Define each word by writing a word that has a meaning opposite to the word.
CLASSIFICATION	Define each word by indicating its semantic features. *Example:* Lunch is a light meal served at midday.
EXEMPLIFICATION	Define each word by providing examples, a picture, or the specific object.
COMPARISON	Define each word by providing an example and a statement of how the example differs from the referent. *Example:* An ocean is like a lake but larger.

The more definitional knowledge that children possess, the greater their conceptual understanding of words. Definitional knowledge has been defined as the knowledge of the relations of a word to other known words (Stahl, 1982). It is quite possible that students will bring a global sense of the meaning of some words but be unable to list specific features or attributes. Such words are in children's "twilight zone." They have heard a word, maybe even have seen it in print, but they have not had enough direct or vicarious experience with it to process it's meaning beyond a superficial level.

Other words students will know well. Not only will they comprehend a word's meaning, but they will be able to generate novel sentences or use a word in a variety of language contexts. In short, not only is definitional knowledge brought into play, but also *contextual knowledge*. Readers who use contextual knowledge are able to recognize fine shades of meaning in the way words are used. They know the concept behind the word label well enough to realize that concept in different contexts.

The meanings of words will always be approximate and indefinite when they reside outside of a sentence or meaningful context. As Artley (1975) put it, "It is the context in which the word is embedded rather than the dictionary that gives it its unique flavor" (page 1072).

The broad goal of vocabulary instruction is to build students' definitional and contextual knowledge of words that have a high degree of *relevancy* and *utility*. That is to say, vocabulary development in the classroom should focus on high probability words, those that children will encounter in print throughout the year or use frequently in various modes of communication. Guidelines for establishing vocabulary programs throughout the elementary grades follow.

Some Principles to Guide Vocabulary Instruction

Consider five principles to guide the teaching of vocabulary in elementary classrooms. These principles aren't absolutes; however, they provide guideposts that evolve from common sense, authoritative opinion, and recent research and theory on the relationship between vocabulary knowledge and reading comprehension.

Principle 1. *Select a large percentage of words for teaching that children will encounter while reading.* Readers can tolerate not knowing some words while reading and still comprehend the text selection. So when introduced to and taught relatively *few* new words prior to a reading selection, chances are that vocabulary instruction will not lead readers to better comprehension. However, when vocabulary learning is centered around acquiring a large percentage of words from actual selections that will be read in class, comprehension is likely to be enhanced (Stahl, 1982; Beck and McKeown, 1983). Which words are the best choices for vocabulary instruction? Which aren't?

Words shouldn't be chosen for instructional emphasis just because they are big, unusual, or obscure. A reader learns to use "monitoring" strategies, such as those we discuss in the next chapter, to overcome such obstacles. Nor should difficult words be chosen if they do not relate to the central meaning or important concepts associated with passage content. Teaching obscure, archaic, or difficult words just because they are obscure, archaic, or difficult is not necessarily a legitimate reason for instruction. In fact these words will probably be seen in print quite rarely or used by children very infrequently. Words such as these should be avoided because they have very little long-term payoff.

Instead, consider the following for instructional emphasis:

Key words. Key words come directly from basal, literature, or content text selections. These words convey major ideas and concepts related to the passage content and are essential for understanding to take place. Key words need to be taught, *and taught well*, because they present definite obstacles to comprehension that cannot be overlooked by the reader.

Useful words. Useful words have the kind of relevancy and utility that we alluded to earlier. Children encounter useful words repeatedly in a variety of contexts. In some cases, a child may be familiar with useful words, having been taught or introduced to them in earlier stories or units, or in previous years. However, it cannot be assumed that these words are "old friends"; they may be mere acquaintances.

Interesting words. Interesting words tickle the imagination and create enthusiasm, excitement, and interest in the study of words. Words that have unique origins, tell intriguing stories, or have intense personal meaning for students make good candidates for instruction. Children can get "hooked" on words through the study of interesting words! This is, as we suggest shortly, the basis for another important principle of vocabulary learning and instruction.

Vocabulary-building words. Classroom instruction should include words that lend themselves readily to vocabulary building skills. Vocabulary building skills allow children to seek clues to word meanings on their own. Words should be selected for instruction that will show students how to inquire into the meaning of unknown words—through structural analysis (drawing attention to word parts) or context analysis (Vacca and Vacca, 1986).

Principle 2. *Teach words systematically and in depth.* Rather than teach many words superficially, give students frequent and varied encounters with selected words to ensure that they learn them well. A recent study of two basal reading programs examined the strategies used to develop vocabulary (Beck et al., 1979). The researchers concluded from their analysis of lesson plans and materials that neither the frequency of encounters with words presented nor the instructional strategies used were adequate to ensure that words were learned well. For example, new words introduced for a selection rarely were repeated in subsequent selections or in practice and reinforcement materials. Moreover, the strategies recommended for teaching meanings provided little more than a definition or an example of the word used in a context.

If words are to be learned well, they must be used repeatedly and manipulated in different ways by students. A variety of vocabulary strategies and activities, which we detail in the next section, can be incorporated in the vocabulary program to cover a range of tasks, including defining; generating oral and written sentences; dramatization; and gamelike tasks involving speed of response. When children have opportunities to manipulate words in many ways, they will gain a richer understanding of the words and more flexibility in using them. This leads to a third guideline for teaching vocabulary.

Principle 3. *Teach different kinds of information about words until the learner has reached an established level of knowledge.* Strategies for instruction should build definitional and contextual knowledge. Moreover, children need to learn words in relation to other words. Therefore teach vocabulary within the context of concept development and relate information about words to children's background knowledge and experiences.

Children need to experience how words "work" in different contexts. Teaching words in context helps children capture the subtleties of language and shows them how to realize a concept when used in different contexts. In the next chapter, strategies are recommended to help students identify the meaning and pronunciation of words through the use of context.

When words are studied in context, enough information should be provided within the sentence or passage to help readers identify meaning. However, the most important aspect of context instruction may very well be in having students apply their personal knowledge about the meaning of a new word in a written or oral response. For example, in the context strategy employed in Gipe's study, she provided three-sentence exercise passages such as the following:

It was hard to see the *beacon* in the thick fog. We knew we would get lost without the *beacon* to guide us. A *beacon* is a light that helps guide you or warn you of danger. Where have you seen a *beacon* that is a warning sign? (Gipe, 1980, pages 399–400)

The final question in the context exercise required that students process the meaning of *beacon* within the framework of a personal association.

Principle 4. *Teach words in relation to other words.* Vocabulary words often are crucially tied to basic concepts. Children, as we have contended earlier, develop definitional knowledge when they are able to relate new words to known words. When words are taught in relation to other words, students are actively drawn into the learning process. They must use background knowledge and experiences to detect likenesses and differences. When words are taught within the context of concept development, children develop a greater sensitivity to shades of meaning associated with words, enabling them to more readily discern the intention of a communication. Rather than students learning words randomly, children should deal with words that are related semantically and belong to categories.

George Henry (1974) outlined four basic cognitive operations associated with learning concepts and words. The first involves the act of joining, or "bringing together." Comparing, classifying, and generalizing are possible through the act of joining. Asking children to explain how words are related or having them sort through word cards to group words together involves the act of joining.

The act of joining has important consequences for vocabulary instruction. Moreover, the act of excluding is another conceptual operation worth considering when teaching words in relation to other words. As the operation implies, children must discriminate, negate, or reject items because they do not belong within the conceptual category. When a child must decide which word does not belong in a set of other words, the process involves exclusion. In this case, a child would search through her background knowledge to distinguish examples from nonexamples or relevant attributes from irrelevant attributes.

So when asked to decide which word does not belong in the list—flower, music, perfume, skunk—upon what set of criteria do you make your decision? One immediate response may have been that *music* doesn't belong since it has little to do with our concept of smell. When engaged in the act of excluding, children are required to distinguish from among words that convey the meanings of a concept.

A third conceptual activity or operation involves the act of *selecting*. A child simply learns to make choices and to explain why based on what he or she experiences, knows, or understands. Synonyms, antonyms, and multiple meaning words lend themselves well to the act of selecting. For example, select the "best" word from those given in the sentence:

Jim's quiet behavior was mistaken for _____.
shyness/modesty/terror

Any of the choices might be acceptable. Yet the value of the activity is in providing a rationale for your choice by judging the worth of several potentially correct answers.

A fourth aspect of thinking conceptually involves the act of implying. Is a child able to make decisions based on if-then, cause-effect relations among concepts and words? Dupuis and Snyder (1983) contended that the most common form of vocabulary exercise using implication is the analogy. They suggest that the act of implying is such a complex cognitive activity that it actually requires the use of joining, excluding, and selecting processes.

Principle 5. *Awaken interest in and enthusiasm for the study of words*. The case too often in elementary classrooms is that vocabulary learning is one of the most deadly dull activities of the school day. Children tend to associate vocabulary instruction with dictionary drill: looking up words, writing out definitions, putting words in sentences. While these activities have some merit, they too quickly become meaningless routine. Children need to know *why* to use dictionaries and *when* to use dictionaries as well as *how* to use dictionaries.

Nevertheless, the excitement about words that the teacher can generate may be the single most important factor in improving vocabulary (Deighton, 1970; Manzo and Shirk, 1972). The teacher's *attitude* toward vocabulary instruction can be contagious. What you do to illustrate the power of words is vital in improving children's vocabulary. Ask yourself whether you get excited by learning new words. Share words of interest to you with students, and tell stories about the origin and derivation of words. As Deighton (1959) argued so convincingly, "A sense of excitement about words, a sense of wonder, and a feeling of pleasure—these are the essential ingredients in vocabulary development" (page 59). To this we add the comment of Cindy, a first-grader we quoted at the beginning of the chapter.

Cindy announced unexpectedly to her teacher, "I like words." Then she flashed her very best "smug mug." You see, Cindy and her classmates had been participating in the dramatization of words. In one of the activities, the teacher, through discussion and demonstration, developed for children the concept of facial expression, or "mugging." With a Polaroid camera in hand she took "mug shots" of her students and placed them prominently on the bulletin board. The children learned to "mug" for the camera by acting out "mug words" (happy mugs, sad mugs, angry mugs, etc.). The very last mug the children learned was the "smug smile of satisfaction," the "smug mug" for short. The teacher explained that when a child knew something that no other person knew or took great pride in an accomplishment, he or she was to flash the "smug mug." On her announcement, Cindy was beaming from ear to ear!

STRATEGIES FOR VOCABULARY AND CONCEPT DEVELOPMENT

Vocabulary instruction should not be neglected in the elementary school classroom. May, the third-grade teacher quoted at the beginning of the chapter, worried that "she doesn't have the time needed to spend on vocabulary instruction." Direct vocabulary teaching need not take more than twenty minutes a day. Moreover, opportunities for incidental instruction and reinforcement arise in content area instruction throughout the school day. Seize upon those natural, teachable moments, and the press for time will not be a major obstacle to providing vocabulary instruction.

Effective vocabulary instruction begins with the teacher's commitment to teach words well. So start slowly, and gradually build an instructional program over several years. We have already recommended that words be selected for emphasis that come from the actual materials that children read during the year: basal and literature selections as well as content area text selections. We further suggest that the program evolve from the instructional implications of the knowledge, instrumental, and aptitude hypotheses discussed earlier. Therefore consider a three-component approach to classroom vocabulary instruction as illustrated in Figure 7.4.

Instructional strategies are not unique to any one component illustrated in Figure 7.4. In fact, strategies for teaching vocabulary should cut across components. Therefore, select strategies based on planning decisions which include: provisions for a variety of activities, the types of information you wish to impart about words, and the depth of processing required to reach an established level of knowledge.

Relating Experiences to Vocabulary Learning

Dale's Cone of Experience, Figure 7.1 on page 178, is a good place to begin in planning and selecting vocabulary strategies which are experienced-based. The more direct, first-hand experiences that students have, the better.

However, in place of first-hand experience, different levels of vicarious experience can establish the bases for vocabulary learning. Vicarious experiences

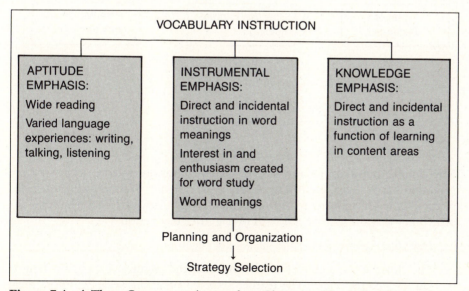

Figure 7.4   A Three-Component Approach to Classroom Vocabulary Instruction

are second-hand experiences, yet valuable in their own right. Dale's Cone of Experience indicates the possibilities that are available in planning experiences that are vicarious: demonstrations, simulations, dramatization, visual and audio media, reading to children, and reading on one's own. We focus on several prototypical strategies to illustrate the possibilities that exist for vocabulary instruction.

Pictures as Experience Builders. Use pictures to stimulate and extend language and help students classify words into categories. Consider these steps:

1. Choose colorful pictures that show action.

2. Ask students to list words that explain the action or describe person(s) in a picture.

3. After many words are written on the board, have students classify them into doing, describing, and naming words.

4. Extend the classification into an experience story or have students write individual stories, as a follow-up lesson.

We observed a first-grade teacher helping children to identify words associated with feelings. Through the course of the lesson she listed on the chalkboard the key concept word and connected three subordinate concepts to it, similar to the diagram below:

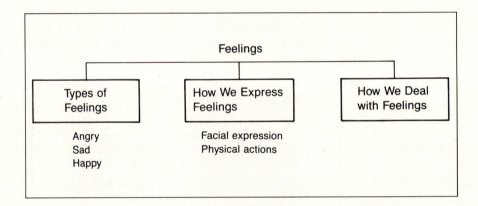

Surrounding the diagram, the teacher displayed various pictures cut out from magazines that showed people expressing different types of feelings. She used the pictures as a springboard to discussion and vocabulary building. Here are the procedures that the teacher followed over a three-day period.

Day One: Construction of the Vocabulary Diagram

1. The children were guided to verbally label the pictures: happy, shy, angry, sad, excited, et cetera. The teacher accepted other answers and wrote them on the board under the pictures.

2. The teacher asked, "What is the name for all of these words?" She read the list of words given. "What are they? Yes, *feelings!*" She wrote the words on the board in BOLD print to begin the diagram.

3. She discussed what clues helped the children decide the feelings of the people in the pictures. Each picture was discussed individually (e.g., "How did you know this boy was sad?"). (The answer might be facial expression, gestures, or actions.)

4. The teacher then asked: "Who has ever felt ＿＿＿＿＿＿＿ ?" and filled in the blank with the words listed on the board (feelings). Pointing to the word as the student voted, she recorded responses (including her own) on the diagram. Do we have the same feelings? Do teachers? parents? brothers? sisters? Is it normal to have these "good and bad" feelings? Discussion followed.

Day Two: Role Playing

5. The children were given situations to encourage them to explore emotions. "How would you look if . . .?

> You have just been pushed by a classmate, and you dropped your books in the mud.
> Your best friend's father has taken a job in another part of the country and the family is moving away. How do you feel?
> You are shopping in a supermarket with your grandfather and you find a quarter in your pocket that you forgot you had.

The teacher asked the students to make up stories about feelings for others to act out, including shyness, fear, love, and anger. Again she had a child point to the word that described the feeling being expressed.

Day Three: Reinforcement

6. The teacher made a Feeling Grab Bag by putting cards with simple pictures and/or words about feeling in the bag. A child selected a card and acted out the feeling for the class to guess. When the correct response was given the child showed the card to the class. If the child could not read the word, the teacher whispered the word in his or her ear.

> Word cards included: *love, sad, shy, fear, anger, excited, surprise, happy,* and *lonely.*

An interesting variation in the use of pictures is to have children form mental pictures through a strategy called the "Key Word Method" (Pressley, Levin, and Miller, 1981). This method involves forming a link between a target vocabulary word and a familiar English word that sounds like part of the target key word. An interactive image between the key word and concept is then formed by the learner. Two steps are involved: (1) Transform the unfamiliar vocabulary word into a familiar English word so that it sounds like the target word (key word). (2) Ask the learner to form a mental image between the key word and the meaning it designates. For example, if you were to learn the Spanish word "carta," which means postal letter, the learner could transform "carta" into "cart" and then imagine a shopping cart transporting a letter. Here are some possibilities for students: *scamper*—have students imagine going camping and running around the tent at night; *struggle*—have students imagine being wrapped up in a rug, frantically trying to escape; *sprint*—have students imagine letters of the alphabet in a 100-yard dash.

Dramatization. Use various forms of dramatization to teach words. Let children have opportunities to conduct "word theatre" performances. In other words, have them perform skits or pantomime words that have been selected for study. Duffelmeyer (1980) hypothesized that an "experience approach" to teaching vocabulary involving dramatization would be more effective in acquiring word meanings than an approach that did not have experience as its base. The procedures he followed can easily be adapted to elementary teaching situations:

1. Before dramatization, pronounce the target word, print it on the board, and ask students to pay close attention to the context in which the word is about to be used.

2. After the dramatization, ask several questions about the skit that are relevant to the target word. After questioning, ask students to volunteer personal experiences that would also convey the meaning of the word.

Consider these provisions for dramatizing words. First write the scripts for students to perform. This entails developing: (1) a setting such as time, place, and characters, and (2) a situation or event that illustrates the meaning or leads to the use of the target word. Second, allow students to rehearse a script in small groups prior to their performance in front of other classmates.

Write the dialogue for students until they become familiar with the activity. Then you need only provide a setting and the situation and direct the students to develop their own dialogue. Eventually, reinforce the meanings of target words by having students create their own settings, situations, and dialogue for dramatization.

Personal Associations. Give students opportunities to relate their own experiences and background to words that they are studying. As we noted earlier in the chapter, relating personal experiences to words may be the most important aspect of vocabulary learning. This is why Manzo (1981) described a "Subjective Approach to Vocabulary" (SAV) as one that invites students to share their own personal images and associations with words as well as record those offered by classmates. In SAV, the teacher writes the target word on the chalkboard, defines it, and gives several examples of the word's use. The students are then invited to share personal experiences or associations with the word: "It is always easier to learn and remember a new word if you can think of some personal experiences or images which you can associate, or picture with it. What thoughts or pictures do you have when you think of __(target word)_?" If children are hesitant at first to respond, the teacher may share a personal experience or image that he or she associates with a word. After sharing personal responses, the teacher directs the students to record the target word in their logbooks, writing its dictionary definition and a short description about their personal image, association, or experience with the word.

Students are able to connect what they know already to the new words. In a similar vein, the *free word association strategy* accomplishes the same objective. Having children participate in brainstorming and other list-generating activities is an excellent way for allowing personal experiences and background knowledge to become the focal point of vocabulary learning. In brainstorming, select any concept word related to an area of study, i.e., horses, nuclear power, seasons, occupations, and so on. Write the word on the board and tell students they have two minutes to write down as many words as they can that relate to the concept. Have several of the children share their word lists with the group. Those students who have fewer than five or six words on their list can make additions as classmates read their word lists. Finally, students can engage in reading or writing activities related to the brainstorming session.

Developing Word Meanings

Earlier we defined the term *definitional knowledge* as the ability to relate new words to known words. The personal association and prediction strategies discussed above are one way of building definitional knowledge. In this section we focus on building definitional knowledge through synonyms, antonyms, and multiple meaning words.

Synonyms are words that are similar in meaning to other words. Antonyms are words that are opposite in meaning to other words. Synonyms and antonyms are useful ways of having children define and understand word meanings. Antonyms, in particular, can demonstrate whether children really comprehend the meanings of new words. Moreover, words that have multiple meanings tend to confuse students, especially when they are reading and encounter the uncommon meaning of a word used in a passage.

Synonyms. Synonym instruction has value when a child has knowledge of a concept but is unfamiliar with its label—the new word to be learned. In such cases, the focus of instruction is to help the student associate new words with more familiar ones. This particular strategy is a good example of the cognitive principle of "bridging the gap" between the new and the known.

For example, a fifth-grade teacher provided a "synonym match" for words that children were studying in a unit on ecology. Several of the matching items in Columns A and B of the activity were:

Column A: New Words	*Column B: Words That You Already Know*
cultivate	change
erode	surroundings
environment	wearing away
modify	work

The children were directed to match the words from Column B with the words from Column A. Discussion followed the activity with students giving reasons for their match-ups. The discussion lead to further clarification of each new term and the realization, as one child put it, that "some words just look hard but really aren't."

In another synonym-related activity, students are given "overworked" or "unimaginative" words in sentences or paragraphs and asked to supply alternative words that will make each sentence or the paragraph more descriptive and interesting. Words such as *nice*, *swell*, and *neat* are good candidates for this type of activity:

> Our trip to the zoo was *neat*. The entire family had a *swell* time. Dad thought that seeing the monkeys on Monkey Island was *fun*. So did I. But Mom *said*, "The monkeys were *okay*, but I liked the reptiles even more. The snakes were *terrific*." We all had a *great* time at the zoo.

This activity, and adaptations of it, can be used as a springboard for children to analyze a piece of their own writing, looking for overworked words and substituting more interesting and precise words.

Antonyms. In addition to matching activities (where students associate the target words with words that are opposite in meaning) and selecting activities (where students select the best choice for an antonym from several listed), consider strategies where children are challenged to work with antonyms in various print contexts.

For example, ask children to change the meanings of advertisements: Change the advertisement! Don't sell the merchandise! Ruin a good advertisement by changing the underlined words to words that mean the opposite.

Examples of Antonym/Advertisement Activity

Today through Tuesday! Save now on this quality bedding. The <u>bigger</u> the size, the <u>more</u> you save.

great
<u>truckload</u>
sale

Just Take Your Purchase To Checkouts & Cashiers Will <u>Deduct</u> 30% Off Ticketed Price

Similar activities can be developed for a target word in a sentence or several new vocabulary words in a paragraph. You may devise an activity in which children work with sentence pairs. In the first sentence, the target word is underlined. In the second sentence, a child must fill in the blank space with an antonym for the target word:

1. The ship sank to the <u>bottom</u> of the ocean.
   The climbers reached the _____ of the mountain.
2. The <u>joyful</u> family reunion never had a dull moment.
   The funeral was the most _____ occasion that I had ever experienced.

Sentence pairs will generate variations of antonyms. Therefore children should be asked to defend their choices. In the first pair of sentences, *top, peak, point* are acceptable antonyms for *bottom*. *Sad, solemn, depressing* are all possible antonyms for *joyful*.

Multiple Meaning Words. Words with multiple meanings give children opportunities to see how words operate in context:

> The *hall* was so long that it never seemed to end.
> The concert took place in a large *hall*.
> The Baseball *Hall* of Fame is located in Cooperstown, New York.

In content area textbooks, children frequently run across common words that have different meanings (*mean, table, force, bank, spring*). These can lead to confusion and miscomprehension. A strategy for dealing with multiple meaning words involves prediction and verification:

1. Select multiple meaning words from a text assignment. List them on the chalkboard.
2. Have students predict the meanings of these words and write them on a sheet of paper next to each term.
3. Assign the reading selection, noting the page numbers where students can find each word in the text reading.
4. Ask students to verify their original predicted meanings. If they wish to change any of their predictions, they can revise the meanings based on how each word was used in the selection (Vacca and Vacca, 1986).

Classifying and Categorizing Words

When children manipulate words in relation to other words, they are engaging in critical thinking. Vocabulary strategies and activities should give students the experience of *thinking about*, *thinking through*, and *thinking with* vocabulary. Working with relationships among words provides this opportunity.

Through the aid of categorization and classification strategies, students recognize that they can classify and categorize words that label ideas, events, or objects. Such strategies involve the processes of joining, excluding, selecting, and implying. Children will learn to study words critically and form generalizations about the shared or common features of concepts. Word sorts, categories, concept circles, semantic feature analysis, and mapping and analogies are activities that help children conceptualize as well as learn and reinforce word meanings.

Word Sorts. The process of sorting words is integrally involved in concept formation. Word sorting is an unbelievably simple, yet valuable, activity to initiate. Individually or in small groups, children sort through vocabulary terms that are written on cards or listed on an exercise sheet. The object of word sorting is to group words into different categories by looking for shared features among their meanings. The strategy can be used effectively at any grade level. According to Gillet and Kita (1979), a word sort activity gives students the opportunity "to teach and learn from each other" while discussing and examining words together.

There are two types of word sorts: the open sort and the closed sort. In the *closed sort*, students know in advance what the main categories are. In other words, they must select and classify words according to the features they have in common with a category. The closed sort reinforces and extends the ability to classify words. *Open sorts*, on the other hand, stimulate inductive thinking. No category or criterion for grouping is known in advance of sorting. Students must search for meanings and discover relationships among words without the benefit of any structure.

A first-grade teacher reinforced the concepts of *hard, soft,* and *rough.* She introduced the class to the "Tammy Touch and Tell" box:

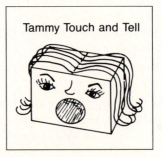

Tammy Touch and Tell

The touch and tell box was filled with objects that felt hard, soft, or rough. The teacher had different children feel the objects in the box and describe to the class how they felt. She then wrote on the board the words used to describe each object. Through discussion of the word list, children decided that perhaps the best words to describe the objects would be *hard, soft,* or *rough.*

The teacher then divided the class into teams of two children. She provided

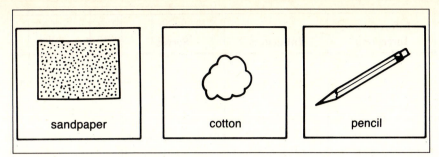

Examples of an "Object Word Card"

each team with an "object envelope." These envelopes contained word cards with the corresponding object pasted above the word. (See the figure above.)

On the board she wrote the words *hard, soft,* and *rough.* Each team was directed to find the word cards in their envelopes and arrange them in a row across the top of their table. Then they were asked to take each object card, read the word, and feel the object. Finally, the children had to place each card underneath the category (*hard, soft,* or *rough*) that described how that object felt. The teacher emphasized the importance of cooperation and teamwork. After the teams had completed this closed sorting activity, they compared and contrasted the ways in which the different teams grouped the object word cards.

For homework, the children went on a home treasure hunt to find some other hard, soft, and rough objects. The teacher explained to the children the rules of a treasure hunt and the kinds of treasures they must try to find. The next day, these collected treasures were used in small group activity and were put on display.

Fifth-grade students participating in a unit on the newspaper discovered the many functions of a newspaper: to inform and interpret, influence, serve, and entertain. A closed sorting task that children participated in involved the completion of the following worksheet in small groups.

Directions: In your groups, place the topics below under the proper headings. You may use a topic more than once. Base your decisions on class discussions and what is found in today's *Plain Dealer* newspaper.

the largest picture on A-1	the Market at a Glance column
Weather Watch	(business)
News Watch	the Transitions column (sports)
the first full-page ad	the Goren on Bridge column
the first Focal Point story	the classified index
legal notices	Funky Winkerbean
the first letter to the editor	display advertising
Dear Abby	death notices
the astrology column	the headline on A-1
the crossword puzzle	

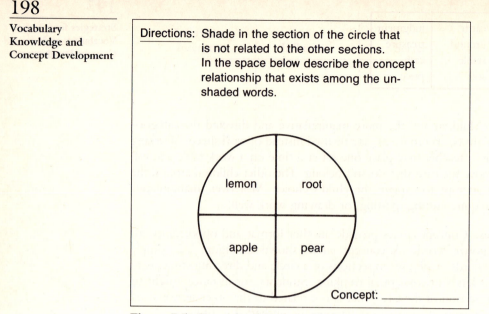

Directions: Shade in the section of the circle that
is not related to the other sections.
In the space below describe the concept
relationship that exists among the un-
shaded words.

lemon   root

apple   pear

Concept: _____

Figure 7.5   Example of Concept Circle

Semantic mapping provides a visual display of how words are related to other words. Early in this chapter semantic mapping was used to make distinctions among class, example, and attribute relations. Similarly, students can use semantic mapping to cluster words belonging to categories and to distinguish relationships among words.

According to Smith and Johnson (1980), the procedures for semantic mapping can be varied to suit different purposes. The first step in the semantic mapping of vocabulary is to select a word central to a story or from any other source of classroom interest or activity. Then write this word on the chalkboard. From this point, vary your procedures depending on your objective for the lesson. For example, ask the class to think of as many words as they can that are in some way related to the word, and jot them down on paper. As students share the words they have written with the class, group the words into categories on the board around the central concept. Have students nominate names for the categories and discuss the category labels, relating students' experiences to the words on the board.

Semantic maps can be elaborately developed or kept relatively simple, depending on the sophistication of the class and grade level. In Figure 7.7, a group of beginning readers developed a concept of "The Five Senses" through a mapping strategy.

The teacher began the map by writing the target concept in the middle of the chalkboard. She then presented the class with a familiar situation: "How often have you known that Mom or Dad was making breakfast even before you got to the kitchen to see or taste it?" The children responded by saying they could smell

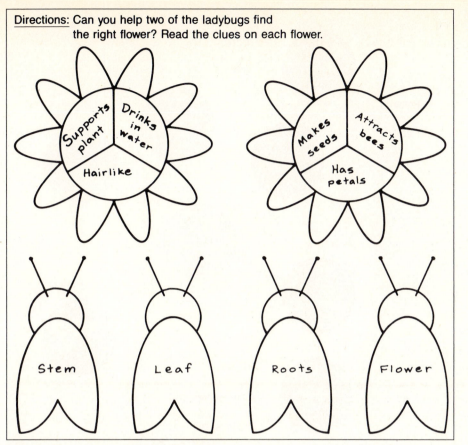

Directions: Can you help two of the ladybugs find
the right flower? Read the clues on each flower.

Supports plant   Drinks in water   Hairlike

Makes seeds   Attracts bees   Has petals

Stem   Leaf   Roots   Flower

Figure 7.6   Variation of Concept Circle

the cooking or hear a parent preparing the breakfast. The teacher praised the
student responses and continued, "You were using your sense of smell and sound
to know that breakfast was being fixed." She then wrote *smell* and *sound* on the
board and connected the words to the central concept.

The children's attention was then directed to the bulletin board display of five
children, each enjoying one of the senses. Through a series of questions, the class
gradually developed the remainder of the semantic map. For example, when the
concept of smell was being developed, the teacher noted, "We call a smell 'scent,' "
and connected *scent* to *smell* on the map. She then asked, "How do you think
flowers smell? What words can you tell me to determine different types of smells?"
As the students volunteered words, the teacher placed them on the map. When
the teacher asked, "When you think of sound, what's the first thing that comes
to your mind?" the children quickly said "noises." The teacher connected *noises* to
sounds. Further discussion focused on types of noises, both pleasant and unpleasant.

**Vocabulary
Knowledge and
Concept Development**

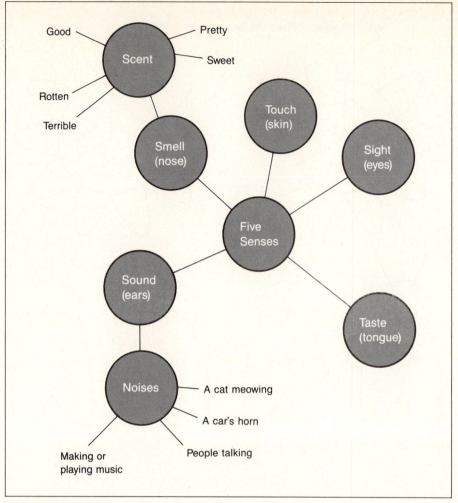

Figure 7.7   A Semantic Map of "The Five Senses"

Analogies. An *analogy* is a comparison of two similar relationships. On one side, the words are related in some way; on the other side of the analogy, the words are related in the same way. Analogies probably should be taught to students beginning in the intermediate grades. If they are not familiar with the format of an analogy, they may have trouble reading it successfully. Therefore, give several short demonstrations in which you model the process involved in completing an analogy.

  1. Begin by asking students to explain the relationship that exists between two words. For example, write on the board a simple class/example relation:

     apple   fruit

Ask, "What is the relationship between the two words?" Explanations may vary greatly but arrive at the notion that an apple is a type of fruit.

2. Explain that an analogy is a comparison of two similar sets of relationships. Write on the board:

> *Apple* is to *fruit* as *carrot* is to _____.

Suggest to students, "If an apple is a type of fruit, then a carrot must be a type of _____." Discuss children's predictions. Provide additional examples.

3. Note that an analogy has its own symbols.

> apple:fruit::carrot: _____.

Point out that the symbol : means *is to* and :: means *as*. Walk students through an oral reading of several analogies, saying: "An analogy reads like this." (Class reads analogy in unison following teacher's lead.)

4. Provide simple analogies at first and gradually increase the complexity of the relationships.

5. Develop analogies from vocabulary used in stories, content area texts, or from topics of interest in the classroom.

Ignoffo (1980) explained the practical value of analogies this way: "Analogies are practical because they carry an implied context with them. To work the analogy, the learner is forced to attempt various . . . procedures that involve articulation, problem-solving and thinking (page 520)."

In Box 7.1, we illustrate some of the types of word relationships from which many analogies can be developed.

SUMMARY

Vocabulary instruction is one facet of reading instruction about which there is minimal controversy. Educators agree that it is possible to extend students' knowledge of word meanings and important to do so because of the relationship between this knowledge and reading comprehension. This chapter explored that relationship, then delved into the instructional opportunities teachers can provide to expand children's vocabulary knowledge and develop their interest and motivation to *want* to learn words.

An important theme of vocabulary instruction was illustrated: the necessity for young readers to have experiences from which concepts can be derived. Guidelines for establishing vocabulary programs throughout the elementary grades were presented. Then, in the chapter's second half, numerous strategies for vocabulary and concept development were presented for teachers to use throughout the school day, in direct instruction as well as in reinforcement activities. For the most part, strategies can be used and adapted for content area instruction—a natural framework for concept development at all ages.

BOX 7.1

Using Word Relationships to Form Analogies

Directions: Study each type of relationship and for each example given, complete the analogy. Then compare your responses with a classmate or colleague.

1. Purpose Relationship

   Examples

   Teeth : Chew   : :   Pen : _____

   Chair : Sit   : :   Knife : _____

2. Part to Whole Relationship

   Examples

   Antler : Deer   : :   Tusk : _____

   Cat : Lion   : :   Dog : _____

3. Synonym Relationship

   Examples

   Small : Tiny   : :   Create : _____

   Copy : Imitate   : :   Large : _____

4. Antonym Relationship

   Examples

   Black : White   : :   Day : _____

   High : Low   : :   Morning : _____

5. Place Relationship

   Examples

   Book : Bookcase   : :   Car : _____

   Flowers : Vase   : :   Clothes : _____

6. Attribute Relationship

   Examples

   Rare : Whale   : :   Common : _____

   Detective : Clue   : :   Scientist : _____

7. Cause and Effect Relationship

   Examples

   Furnace : Heat   : :   Freezer : _____

   Seed : Tree   : :   Egg : _____

THE WORKSHOP

In the Classroom

1. Develop a concept hierarchy similar to the one in Figure 7.3: Decide on a key concept word and include class, example, and attribute relationships in the hierarchy. Share your results with others in the class.

2. Analyze a reading selection for words that children may have difficulty understanding. Use Smith and Johnson's (1980) suggestions presented in the chapter to show how these words can be defined in different ways.

3. Analyze two or three stories in the teacher's manual accompanying a basal reading program. What provisions does the manual make for vocabulary learning and concept development? How do these provisions compare or contrast with the ideas presented in the chapter? Draw conclusions and discuss your analysis with class members.

In the Field

1. Choose any grade level and teach a vocabulary lesson, directing it to a small group consisting of at least four children. The lesson should emphasize one of the following strategies discussed in the chapter: (a) relating experiences to vocabulary learning; (b) developing word meanings using synonyms, antonyms, or multiple meaning words; or (c) developing concepts.

2. Observe a classroom teacher during reading and language arts instruction for several consecutive days. Record the time spent on vocabulary meaning development and the nature of instruction. How much time is devoted to vocabulary learning? What kinds of activities are incorporated in instruction? What conclusions do you draw from your observations?

3. Discuss with several children a semantic map developed around a key concept. How much do the children already know about the concept? What areas require further development?

Chapter 8

Word Identification

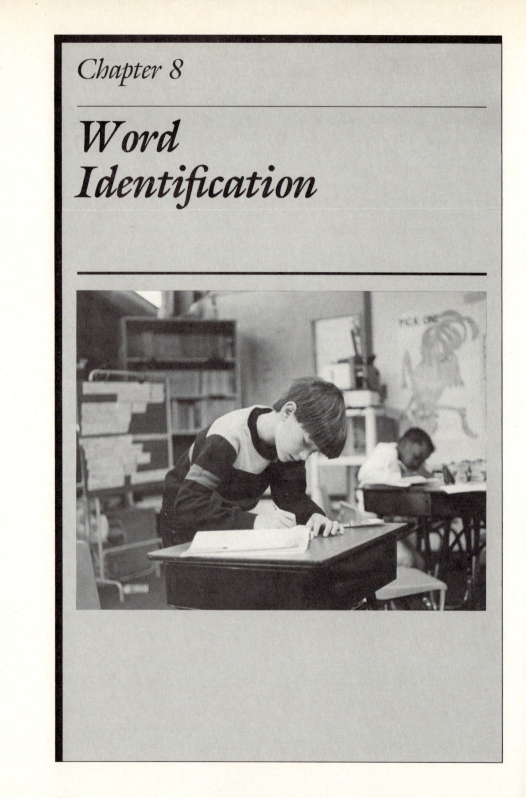

"Sticks and stones will break my bones, but words will never hurt me." Taken literally, there's truth in that old saying. Yet as we go through life we come to realize that some words can indeed "hurt" us; words spoken in anger or fear; words blurted out thoughtlessly; words used incorrectly. Words can be friends, too, and it's this type of relationship we wish for all children as they make their acquaintance with print. Words in their written form *must be attended to by readers*. How readers learn to identify words rapidly and independently provides the focal point for this chapter. How they learn to coordinate various kinds of language information is one of the keys to becoming a fluent reader.

What am I doing? Studying my words.

Jeff, a first-grader

When I come to a word I don't know I sound it out.

Jane, a second-grader

When I come to a word I don't know I try to think of what would make sense.

Sam, a third-grader

When children are asked to explain what they are doing during class time spent on learning to read, their responses will vary. But inevitably the word "words" enters into the discussion. Words are what children usually perceive as the meat of instruction in learning to read. Some children, such as Jeff, say generally that they are "studying words" or "learning new words." Others explain what they do when they come to a word that they don't know. Jane's strategy is to "sound it out." Sam tries to come up with a word that makes sense. Either way, children spend a lot of time and energy working with words.

The same is true for teachers. Johnson and Pearson (1978) argue that words *in their written forms* must be dealt with by readers. *How* teachers invest their time in helping readers identify words is an important instructional question—one that has certainly been the subject of much debate. In some circles, nothing can create a more heated discussion than how words should be taught. "Look-say!" "Intensive phonics!" Terms such as these have taken on good and evil proportions depending on one's perspective. Some reading experts feel strongly that words shouldn't be studied in isolation; nor, they think, should other units of written language such as individual letters or letter combinations. Other reading authorities stress that accurate word identification is an important aspect of learning to read, and that learning sound-letter relationships is the most efficient way to achieve accuracy.

To us the question of teaching children to identify words is not an either "you do" or "you don't" proposition. Much of the time that each of us will invest in teaching children to identify words will depend on what we believe about reading and learning to read. The implicit model of reading that operates in each of our heads influences not only the amount of instructional time given to word identification but also the type of instruction emphasized to help children identify words.

In this chapter we suggest strategies that will result in two broad outcomes of word identification instruction. The first is that children should learn how to deal *rapidly* and *independently* with unfamiliar words. Reading soon becomes tedious, if not overwhelming, when children cannot quickly identify unfamiliar words on their own. Misty, a first-grader, put it this way: "I'm in big trouble if I miss words when I'm reading." Big trouble for Misty probably means not understanding what she reads. According to Cunningham (1979), if word identification requires most of the reader's energy and attention, then comprehension and enjoyment will suffer.

A second outcome of instruction is that readers should develop *multiple strategies* for word identification. Typically, in reading programs, word identification is taught under broad subcategories of instruction such as phonic, structural, and context analysis. The problem arises, however, when these skill areas are taught apart from one another. Readers must learn how to use context along with phonic and structural clues to help identify unfamiliar words while reading. They must learn how to *coordinate* semantic, syntactic, and phonemic information in much the same manner that athletes coordinate muscles to accomplish athletic feats effectively and successfully.

KEY TERMS RELATED TO WORD IDENTIFICATION

A litany of terms have been associated with the act of identifying words: for example, *word attack, word analysis, word recognition,* and *decoding*. These terms have often been used interchangeably to mean almost the same thing. Figure 8.1 illustrates the relationship of these terms to word identification.

Word identification implies putting a name or label on words that are encountered in print. It is a comprehensive term that encompasses the use of meaning as well as phonemic cues to identify unfamiliar words.

As depicted in Figure 8.1, the term *word recognition* suggests a process that involves *immediate identification*. Immediately recognized words are retrieved rapidly from long-term memory. Word recognition is at times used interchangeably

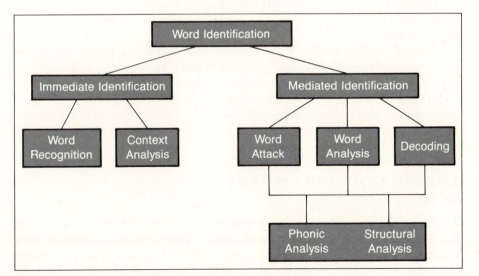

Figure 8.1   Terms Related to Word Identification

with *sight word recognition, sight vocabulary,* or *reading vocabulary*. These terms suggest a reader's ability to recognize words rapidly and automatically. In this chapter we refer to *immediate word identification* to describe rapid recognition. Keep in mind, however, that the process of immediate word identification is far more complicated than recognizing "sight words" on "flash cards." When a word is retrieved rapidly from long-term memory, the process is often triggered by well-developed schema that the reader has developed for a word. Usually the semantic features or physical features (a single letter or letter cluster) of a word will trigger quick retrieval.

Immediate word identification is the strategy used by skilled readers on ninety-nine percent of the printed words they meet. It is also the method used by children when they identify their first words. Often one of the first words children learn to identify in print is their name. Jessica, a four-year-old, can recognize her name printed "Jessica," but may not attend to each individual letter. She recognizes her name because some distinctive feature about it triggers rapid retrieval from long-term memory.

The terms *word attack, word analysis,* and *decoding* imply the act of translating print to speech through an analysis of sound-letter correspondence. These terms somewhat overlap and have been used frequently with what has been commonly referred to as *phonic analysis*.

The terms *phonic analysis* and *structural analysis* differ in an important respect. Whereas phonic analysis deals exclusively with sound-letter associations, structural analysis involves the reader's inquiry into the meaningful parts of words. Analyzing the syllabic and/or meaning-bearing units in a word is a useful tool for word meaning identification.

Both phonic and structural analysis involve *mediated word identification*. Mediation implies that the reader needs more time to retrieve words from long-term memory. The reader does not have in place a well-developed schema for a word: The schema is lacking in either sufficient semantic or physical features for rapid retrieval.

How do skilled readers reach a point where they don't have to rely on mediated word identification strategies? By reading and writing—that's how! As mature readers, we are able to immediately identify or read "by sight" thousands and thousands of words. How did we learn to identify these words? Did we use flash cards to learn them one-by-one? Did we first sound out each word letter-by-letter? Probably not.

THE ROLE OF SIGHT WORDS IN LEARNING TO READ

Teaching children to identify words immediately should not necessarily suggest "look-say" or "flash card" instructional practices. There's more to immediate word identification than flashing a "sight word" card in front of children's eyes and then requiring an instant response. Immediate identification of words is probably the result of *experience with* reading, seeing, discussing, using, and writing words.

Teaching strategies have often fallen within the exclusive domain of *sight word instruction*. However, more than a little confusion has surrounded the teaching of sight words.

The term *sight words* is itself confusing because of its multiple meanings. There are at least three different ways to think about sight word instruction. First, the term has been used to describe instruction centered around words that do not represent common spelling patterns. Words lacking recognizable spelling patterns are classified as "irregular." In other words, they cannot be pronounced according to rules for spelling pattern-to-sound correspondence. Because these words cannot be pronounced in regular fashion, reading educators have tended to recommend that "irregular words" be learned as wholes. Hence the label *sight words*. The word *indict*, for example, might qualify for sight word instruction because the letter cluster *dict* has a variant pronunciation.

Second, the act of *word recognition* and the development of a *sight vocabulary* have been used interchangeably. "Sight words" reflect all the words a reader is able to identify quickly and automatically. To increase the number of "sight words" is actually the goal of all word identification teaching.

A third use of the term *sight words* has been to refer to a relatively small corpus of words which are used with high frequency in running print (sometimes as much as seventy percent of the running words in children's reading material). Some authors have used the term *basic sight words* or *service words* to refer to this collection of words. The *Dolch Basic Sight Words* or the *Fry Instant Words* are two examples of basic sight word lists.

Should Words Be Taught as Wholes?

Several reasons are usually given for beginning word identification with whole words. One is that students learn to recognize words by their configuration (that is, their length and general contour or shape). The configuration of a word, however, has been shown to be a low utility cue in word identification (Levin and Marchbanks, 1965). A word's general contour loses its usefulness because there are many words which have similar configurations.

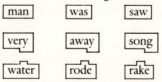

Configuration clues may be more useful for "unusual looking" words. For example, we may speculate that words such as *elephant* and *McDonald's* are quickly identified by young children because of their distinctive shapes:

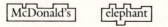

Yet we may also argue that words such as these are identified automatically by a child because they are charged with personal meaning. No doubt some combination of the semantic and graphic features of words helps to trigger instant recognition.

Durkin's rationale for whole word instruction probably makes the most sense (Durkin, 1980). She suggested whole word methodology at the outset of reading instruction on the following grounds: Whole word learning allows children to sense "real reading" quickly. It can also be of greatest interest to most children because they are apt to be familiar with the concept of a *word* rather than linguistic concepts associated with phonics, that is, the child's concept of a *letter* or a *sound*.

High-Frequency Sight Words

Numerous lists of high-frequency sight words have been compiled. Box 8.1, on pages 211–212, contains Edward Fry's Instant Words (1980). According to Fry, the first 100 Instant Words on his list make up half of all written material and the 300 words make up sixty-five percent of all written text.

High-frequency word lists contain a large number of words that are grammatically necessary: words such as articles, conjunctions, pronouns, verbs of being, and prepositions that bind together information-bearing words. These words are called *function words*; they do much to help a sentence function, but they do not get across the meaning of a passage by themselves. Nouns, action verbs, adjectives, and adverbs are *content words*; they supply the content or information of the topic.

Compare the two paragraphs below to get a better idea of how these two types of words work together in running print.

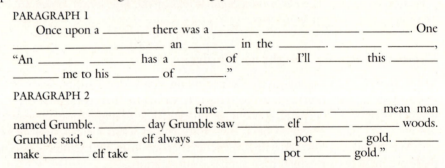

PARAGRAPH 1

Once upon a _____ there was a _____ _____ _____ _____. One _____ _____ _____ an _____ in the _____. _____ _____, "An _____ _____ has a _____ of _____. I'll _____ this _____ _____ me to his _____ of _____."

PARAGRAPH 2

_____ _____ _____ time _____ _____ _____ mean man named Grumble. _____ day Grumble saw _____ elf _____ _____ woods. Grumble said, "_____ elf always _____ _____ pot _____ gold. _____ make _____ elf take _____ _____ _____ pot _____ gold."

When reading paragraph 1, can you tell what the paragraph is about? All of the content or information-bearing words were taken out. When reading paragraph 2, at the very least you know that the story is about a mean man named Grumble and an elf. By studying paragraph 2, you might even have figured out that Grumble wanted to take the elf's pot of gold.

Since content words (information-bearing words) are *not* generally on lists of high-frequency words, what purpose do the lists serve? The rationale is a good one: Beginning readers who can quickly and accurately identify high-frequency function words can more readily read across any line of print. Functions words may be troublesome to young readers because of the similarity of their graphic features. Some children frequently become confused, for example, over words beginning with *wh* and *th* (*that, what; then, when*). Instructional strategies are needed to help children deal with function words to the point of immediate, automatic recognition.

When a teacher prints on a word card the word "elephant" or "desk" or even "run" or "happy," beginning readers have a notion of what these words mean. However, when a teacher prints "is," "only," or "because" on a word card, a first-grade child might wonder what an "only" is. *Function words have very little meaning when they are isolated from the flow of language*. For this reason function words should be taught in the context of sentences, paragraphs, and stories. For example, ask children to distinguish minimal graphic differences between two words by writing the correct word in the blank space provided. Make sure the space is long enough for young writers to fill in the blanks.

We read _____ day.
        every–very

_____ time is it?
What–That

We _____ a cat in the tree.
    Saw–was

_____ do you spell your name?
Now–How

Words such as *every* and *very*, *what* and *that* are *graphically similar*. That is, these words *look* alike. Context-type activities such as the one in the example above sensitized students to minimal differences in words. A reading beginner learns that words that look alike must "make sense" and "sound right" in the context of what is being read.

Sometimes, young readers will habitually mis-identify function words (or content words for that matter) that have minimal graphic differences. A first-grader, for instance, may start a sentence that begins with *Then* by reading the word *When*. This miscue may occur out of habit, probably for no other reason than the fact that a beginner may rely heavily on what is grammatically *familiar*. From a language point of view, a young child is apt to begin more sentences orally with the word *when* than the word *then*. In cases such as this, the child's schema for how language works plus a graphic cue from the word itself contributes to the observed response.

We recommend that children listen to themselves read so that they can develop an "ear" for the kinds of mis-identifications just described. The tape recorder is an invaluable learning resource. As children listen to themselves read aloud, ask, "Does this (the mis-identification) sound right? Does what you just heard make sense?" In the section on the role context plays, we explore additional strategies that will help children monitor reading behavior.

Teaching "Key Words"

One of the quickest and most interesting ways to ease children into reading is through *key word* teaching. Key words are a fundamental aspect of language experience instruction. The concept of "key words" emerges from the work of Sylvia Ashton-Warner (1959, 1963, 1972).

BOX 8.1
The Instant Words

FIRST HUNDRED

Words 1–25	Words 26–50	Words 51–75	Words 76–100
the	or	will	number
of	one	up	no
and	had	other	way
a	by	about	could
to	word	out	people
in	but	many	my
is	not	then	than
you	what	them	first
that	all	these	water
it	were	so	been
he	we	some	call
was	when	her	who
for	your	would	oil
on	can	make	now
are	said	like	find
as	there	him	long
with	use	into	down
his	an	time	day
they	each	has	did
I	which	look	get
at	she	two	come
be	do	more	made
this	how	write	may
have	their	go	part
from	if	see	over

Common suffixes: -s, -ing, -ed

SECOND HUNDRED

Words 101–125	Words 126–150	Words 151–175	Words 176–200
new	great	put	kind
sound	where	end	hand
take	help	does	picture
only	through	another	again
little	much	well	change
work	before	large	off
know	line	must	play
place	right	big	spell
year	too	even	air
live	mean	such	away
me	old	because	animal
back	any	turn	house
give	same	here	point

SECOND HUNDRED (cont.)

Words 101–125	Words 126–150	Words 151–175	Words 176–200
most	tell	why	page
very	boy	ask	letter
after	follow	went	mother
thing	came	men	answer
our	want	read	found
just	show	need	study
name	also	land	still
good	around	different	learn
sentence	form	home	should
man	three	us	America
think	small	move	world
say	set	try	high

Common suffixes: -s, -ing, -ed, -er, -ly, -est

THIRD HUNDRED

Words 201–225	Words 226–250	Words 251–275	Words 276–300
every	left	until	idea
near	don't	children	enough
add	few	side	eat
food	while	feet	face
between	along	car	watch
own	might	mile	far
below	close	night	Indian
country	something	walk	real
plant	seem	white	almost
last	next	sea	let
school	hard	began	above
father	open	grow	girl
keep	example	took	sometimes
tree	begin	river	mountain
never	life	four	cut
start	always	carry	young
city	those	state	talk
earth	both	once	soon
eye	paper	book	list
light	together	hear	song
thought	got	stop	leave
head	group	without	family
under	often	second	body
story	run	late	music
saw	important	miss	color

Common suffixes: -s, -ing, -ed, -er, -ly, -est

What are key words? As Veatch (1979) and her associates described them, "From the first moment a child comes into the classroom she has within herself words that have meaning and feeling for her" (page 19). Key words are charged with personal meaning and feeling for they come out of the experience and background of the young child. According to Veatch, *key vocabulary* learning provides a young child's initiation into the world of literacy.

Teachers can help students identify words quickly through key word instruction. Key words become the core of what might be traditionally called "sight word development." Students learn key words through whole word methodology. The emphasis in learning words as wholes is to tie instruction to meaningful activity: through *seeing, discussing, using, defining,* and *writing* words.

Language experience activities are the most effective way to obtain key words from young children. Veatch suggested these basic steps for obtaining key words:

1. The child tells the teacher the word she wants to learn.

2. The teacher records the word on a piece of tagboard for the child to see, saying the letters as she writes.

3. The child traces the word with his finger and then writes it.

4. The child does something with the word.

5. The teacher reviews words with the child.

Children can do numerous things with *their* words: Draw a picture of them; copy them on the chalkboard; write a story; define the key words; or write them in a "word book" or "personal directory." In addition, the teacher helps children review words intermittently by having the child read words to her or him.

THE ROLE OF CONTEXT IN LEARNING TO READ

As noted in Chapter 3, some preschool children develop an expectation that print should make sense. They have heard stories frequently read to them and are immersed in a language-rich environment. Such young children rely heavily on pictures or other aspects of the immediate situation in deciding what printed words say. Steve, three and one-half years old, was staring at a gum wrapper with PAL written on it. He said, "This says 'gum.'" Was Steve reading? We like to think so. The roots of literacy have begun to take hold for Steve. He has made the association between speech and print.

Steve knows intuitively that reading is supposed to make sense. At his present level of development he makes use of information from his immediate surroundings, the *environmental context* he is in. But as he continues to develop as a reader, he will learn to use with greater sophistication various kinds of *contextual information from the print itself.*

Context Analysis

Readers use context clues to identify words they have heard but may not have experienced visually in print. When readers combine meaning clues with phonic information, they have developed a powerful tool for word identification. Cloze-type activities help to show readers how to use the context of a sentence or passage.

Modified Cloze Passages. Construct modified cloze passages from materials that are at first relatively easy to read. The material used can be stories and poems from basal readers, language experience stories, other written products of the students, or subject-matter texts. Gradually the difficulty of the reading material can be increased. Note that cloze-type materials are available commercially from publishing companies. However, teachers often produce the most effective cloze passages because they are in the best position to gear the material to the needs of their students.

Cloze activities can contain as little as one deletion in a sentence or up to ten to twenty deletions in a passage. There are different deletion systems: *selective word deletion*, *systematic word deletion*, and *deletion of portions of words*. The kind of deletion system used determines what aspects of the passage are focused on as students complete the cloze passages and as they discuss their responses to cloze passages.

Selective Word Deletion. Important nouns, verbs, adjectives, and adverbs can be deleted. These words carry the meaning of the context of what the author is saying. When selected nouns, verbs, adjectives, and adverbs are deleted the focus is on meaningful information from the passage. In addition, vocabulary characteristics of a subject are emphasized. For example, if the subject of a cloze passage is "Going to the Zoo," such words as "yak" and "zebra" are discussed in terms of how their meaning contributed to the meaning of the passage.

Systematic Word Deletion. In this deletion system every *n*th word in a passage is deleted. For example, every fifth, tenth, or twentieth word can be deleted. When such a cloze deletion system is used as a *teaching device*, many function words will be deleted and therefore much of the discussion will consider examples such as, "Bill went _____ the hill." Did Bill go "up," "down," or "around" the hill? The students must deduce appropriate words from the context of the rest of the passage.

Partial Deletion of Words. In this deletion system, every *n*th word or selected word is partially deleted. The following partial deletions can be used: (1) Only initial consonants, initial consonant blends, digraphs, or initial vowels are given and all other letters are deleted; (2) the letters mentioned above plus terminal consonants or terminal consonant digraphs are given and all other letters are deleted; and (3) only consonants are given and vowels are deleted.

Cloze passages in which only the initial letters are given help children understand that initial letter(s) serve to reduce the number of meaningful substitutions available. The discussion of this type of cloze would include how useful the content plus some graphic information can be. The more graphic information given, the more certain the reader will be of what the word is. Study the examples below:

SELECTIVE WORD DELETIONS
     Slim and Shorty were _____ who lived on a big ranch a long way from town. Slim and Shorty had five mules. One day Slim _____, "We're almost out of _____. We have to go to _____. We'll take the _____ to carry the food home."

SYSTEMATIC WORD DELETIONS
     Slim and Shorty began to line _____ the mules. Slim got on the _____ at the front of the line. _____ got on the mule at the _____ of the line.

PARTIAL WORD DELETIONS
     Then Shorty s_____, "How will we get all five m_____ to town?" Slim said, "You w_____ the mules. That way we won't l_____ any."

Cloze with Choices Given. When students find it difficult to complete cloze activities, giving choices for the deleted words makes the task easier. Here are some differing procedures to use in devising the choices for the cloze blanks:

1. The incorrect item, or foil, can be a different part of speech as well as different graphically as in:

   The doctor was _____ that the patient got better so quickly.
             monkey/amazed

2. The foil can be graphically similar to the correct item and a different part of speech:

   The doctor was _____ that the patient got better so quickly.
             amazon/amazed

3. The foil and correct answer can be graphically similar and the same part of speech:

   The doctor was _____ that the patient got better so quickly.
             amused/amazed

4. Three choices can also be given: the correct response, a word of the same part of speech that is graphically similar, and a word of a different part of speech and graphically similar:

   The doctor was _____ that the patient got better so quickly.
             amazed/amused/amazon

A discussion of these particular cloze examples would include a discussion of why a doctor would be more likely to be *amazed* than *amused* by a patient's progress in getting well. Students would also note that, "The doctor was *amazon* that the patient got better so quickly," makes no sense.

Cryptography and Mutilated Messages. Many children enjoy deciphering codes and writing messages in codes. When something is written in code, something has been done to change the graphic display, so context is used to "break the code."

Here are a few ways messages can be mutilated or changed. You and your students can think of more ways. There are also trade books on cryptology that your students can enjoy.

Look red under blue the green table. (Color names are inserted.)

(Bottom of letter is covered.)

Door the open. (Words are scrambled.)

Illustrateathebpoemcondpagedfifty-sixeoffyourgbook. (No spaces are left between words and letter inserted between words.)

Notice that each of these coded messages tells the reader to do something. This is a good way to use codes. Jane, a second-grade teacher, devised some coded messages which led her students on a treasure hunt. Students read directions in coded messages telling them to look specific places, for example, "Look behind the red geraniums." Behind the geraniums was another coded message which told them to look another place. These coded messages finally led them to a treasure.

Using Context to Decide If a Word Is Important

How important is a single word, anyway? This is a question readers need to ask about words they find troublesome. To get this notion across, have students read a somewhat difficult selection. Ask them to put light marks by words that they do not recognize but tell them *not to try to figure them out*. This is actually hard to do! After students have read the selection, ask them to summarize what the author was saying. Then go back and discuss the words the students have marked. Do they know what these words are now? Many of them they will know in spite of the fact that they did not actually try to figure them out. What about the words they are still unable to recognize? Students need to decide, "Are these important to understanding the selection?" If students feel the word is important to understanding the selection, the next order of business is to decide how meaning cues and sound-letter cues can be used to determine what the word is. The point of this lesson, though, is to realize that often a selection can be read and understood without recognizing every word. Students can categorize difficult words that they think are crucial to understanding the selection and those that are not and then discuss why they placed particular words in each category.

Lessons such as this one can be structured to convey the idea that some words contribute more to understanding a selection than others. Also, a teacher needs to encourage students informally to ask themselves about unrecognized words met as they read, for example, "How important is this word to understanding what the author is saying?"

Watson (1978) devised a teaching strategy that she called "Reader Selected Miscues" to help children see that they are in control of making sense out of print. Children should become aware that they have a range of options available to them as readers when they encounter words they don't recognize or, for that matter, something they don't understand during reading.

Steps in Reader Selected Miscue Strategy. The following procedures may be adapted to fit a variety of reading situations that may arise during the course of a school day:

1. Children are assigned to read a selection (fiction or nonfiction) silently and without interruption.
2. When a troublesome word is encountered or something is not making sense, a child inserts a bookmark or lightly marks the page to indicate the problem and then continues reading.
3. When the reading is completed, the children review the things they have marked and select *three* items that caused the greatest difficulty.
4. In addition, the children are asked to explain *how* some of the problems or words that they encountered seemed to "solve themselves" as they continued to read.
5. Finally, the students are to examine passages involving the troublesome words or ideas that they had marked and help each other in clarifying them.

What do readers learn from this procedure? For one thing, they learn that everyone makes mistakes; no one reads "word-perfectly." Readers also see that they are the ones to decide what is hard for them and what comes easily. They see that a portion of a text may be quite readable to some readers and less readable for others, but that everyone meets words or concepts that perplex them. Finally, they see from Reader Selected Miscues that with a "keep-going" strategy, many unknowns will be clarified by the text as they keep reading.

THE ROLE OF PHONICS IN LEARNING TO READ

Phonics is instruction in the relationships between speech sounds and letters. Phonics has a part to play in learning to read. Nevertheless, as Heilman (1977) observed, the *optimum* phonics for children is the *minimum* they need to become independent readers.

The Commission on Reading in *Becoming a Nation of Readers* put the matter of phonics instruction this way: "The goal of phonics is not that children be able to state the 'rules' governing letter-sound relationships. Rather, the purpose is to get across the alphabetic principle, the principle that there *are* systematic relationships between letters and sounds" (page 38). The purpose of phonics, then, is to aid children in continuing their development of knowledge about sound-letter correspondence.

Many children, we have argued, come to school having partial or more fully developed concepts about the *alphabetic principle*. They develop these concepts implicitly through their own efforts at learning to read. Because they are active participants in a literate culture, some children organize for themselves a rich pool of phonic information about letters, sounds, words, and so on. Of course, some children enter school with very little knowledge of the relationships between speech and print.

Once children are in school, writing and reading, as well as phonics, can assist them in continuing to discover *and* rediscover ideas about written language: The continuous flow of speech can be segmented into parts, that is, words. Written symbols called letters represent speech sounds. Words consist of strings of sounds or phonemes. In English, there is not a consistent one-to-one match between each written symbol (grapheme) and each distinct spoken sound (phoneme). Sounds represented by written symbols assist in determining an unknown word. Finally, blending is a process of linking letter sequences with sound sequences. The larger the letter sequence to which a sound sequence can be mapped or attached, the better.

The teacher's job in phonics instruction is to mediate children's language discoveries and rediscoveries by showing them how to use phonic knowledge to assist in the identification of words. Thus the instructional aims of phonics are twofold: (1) to help learners develop and refine a *working knowledge* of how spoken language is coded in writing; and (2) to allow learners to use this knowledge to identify and represent words in print.

Phonics instruction should occur in meaningful language situations. In day-to-day instructional routines, however, phonics has a tendency to get overemphasized in many classrooms. Teachers sometimes find themselves spending an inordinate amount of time on phonics skill sessions that are isolated from continuous, meaningful text. Many lament that they are unable to find time for their students to practice the application of phonic knowledge to relevant reading material. As a result, youngsters can easily form the wrong message about phonics:

Reading = Phonics or "Sounding Out" Words

As the Commission on Reading acknowledged, many of the phonics programs available today "fall considerably short of the ideal." This is why the Commission has called for "renewed efforts to improve the quality of instructional design, materials, and teaching strategies" (*Becoming a Nation of Readers,* page 43). Moreover, the Commission emphasized that phonics instruction shouldn't drag on beyond a child's second year in school. The instructional questions, then, rest mainly with how phonics should be taught and what teachers must know about the content of phonics in order to teach sound-letter relationships sensibly.

The Content and Language of Phonics

In Chapter 2, we introduced the terms *analytic phonics* and *synthetic phonics* to describe the two major approaches to instruction in sound-letter relationships. The analytic method emphasizes the discovery of sound-symbol relationships through the analysis of known words. Analytical phonics is the preferred approach in most basal programs. The steps of the analytic approach proceed from the whole word to a study of its constituent parts. The sequence of instruction usually involves the following steps.

Observe a list of known words with a common phonic element, for example, the initial consonant *t*.

Begin questioning as to how the words look/sound the same and how they are different.

Elicit the common phonic element and discuss.

Have the learners phrase a generalization about the element, for example, all the words start with the sound of the letter *t*. The sound of the letter *t* is /t/ as in top.

The synthetic approach, on the other hand, takes a different route to developing phonic knowledge and skill. It uses a "building block" approach to understanding sound-symbol relationships. The sequence of instruction goes something like this:

Teach the letter names.

Teach the sound(s) each letter represents.

Drill on the sound/symbol relationships until rapidly recognized. Discuss rules and form generalizations about relationships which usually apply to words, that is, when vowels are short or long.

Teach the blending together of separate sounds to make a word.

Provide opportunity to apply blending to unknown words.

There are many similarities between these analytical and synthetic phonics: Both approaches address rules, discuss isolated phonic elements, break words apart, and put them back together again. In so doing, the danger of fragmenting word identification from actual text situations is always present. The challenge to both approaches is the ready application of phonic knowledge to a stream of written language.

Most phonic programs, whether they are based on analytic or synthetic methods or a combination of both, single out *phonic elements* for instructional emphasis. These elements help to distinguish the relationships that exist between speech sounds and letters.

Consonants. Consonants are all the sounds represented by letters of the alphabet except *a, e, i, o, u*. Consonants conform fairly closely to *one-to-one correspondence*. For each letter there is one sound. This property of consonants makes them of greatest value to the reader when attempting to sound out an unknown word. There are some consonant anomalies:

The letter *y* is a consonant only at the beginning of a syllable as in *yet*.

The letter *w* is sometimes a vowel as in *flew*.

Sometimes consonants have no sound as in *know*.

The letters *c* and *g* each have two sounds called "hard" and "soft" sounds:
  Hard *c*: *cat, coaster, catatonic* (*c* sounds like /k/)

Hard *g*: *give, gallop, garbage* (*g* sounds like /g/)
Soft *c*: *city, receive, cite* (*c* sounds like /s/)
Soft *g*: *giraffe, ginger, gym* (*g* sounds like /j/)

Consonant Blends. *Consonant blends* are two or three consonants grouped together, but each consonant retains its original sound. There are several major groups of blends.

l blends: *bl cl fl gl pl sl*
r blends: *br cr dr fr gr pr tr*
s blends: *sc sk sm sn sp st sw*
3 letter blends: *scr spr str squ*

Consonant Digraphs. When two or more consonants are combined to produce a new sound, the letter cluster is called a *consonant digraph*. The common consonant digraphs are:

ch as in *chin*   *ph* as in *phone*
sh as in *shell*   *gh* as in *ghost*
th as in *think*   *-nk* as in *tank*
wh as in *whistle*   *-ng* as in *Tang*

Vowels. Vowels are all the sounds represented by the letters *a, e, i, o, u*. The letter *y* serves as a vowel when it is not the initial sound of a word. Sometimes *w* functions as a vowel, usually when it follows another vowel. There is *rarely a one-to-one correspondence* between a letter representing a vowel and the sound of the vowel. Vowel sounds are influenced heavily by their location in a word and the letters accompanying them. Several major types of vowel phonemes are worth knowing about:

A *long vowel* sound is a speech sound similar to the letter name of a vowel. A *macron* (-) is sometimes used to indicate that a vowel is long. *Short vowel* sounds are speech sounds given to vowel letter names. Short sounds are represented by a brev (˘). The short sound of each vowel letter is evident in the following words:

/a/ as in *apple* or *car*
/e/ as in *exit* or *bed*
/i/ as in *igloo* or *pit*
/o/ as in *octopus* or *hot*
/u/ as in *umbrella* or *hug*

Often when a vowel letter initiates a word, the short sound will be used, for example: *at, effort, interest, optimist, uncle*.

Vowel Digraphs. *Vowel digraphs* are two vowels that are adjacent to one another. The first vowel is usually long and the second is silent. Vowel digraphs include: *oa, ee, ea, ai, ay* as in *boat, beet, beat, bait*, and *bay*. There are notable exceptions: *oo* as in *look*, *ew* as in *flew*, *ea* as in *read*.

Vowel Diphthongs. *Vowel diphthongs* are sounds that consist of a blend of two separate vowel sounds. These are /oi/ as in *oil,* /oy/ as in *toy,* /au/ as in *taught,* /aw/ as in *saw,* /ou/ as in *out,* and /ow/ as in *how.* Generally children do not need to be taught these formally.

Consonant-Influenced Vowels. The letter *a* has a special sound when followed by an *l* as in *Albert* or *tallow.* R-controlled vowels occur when any vowel letter is followed by an *r.* Note *star, her, fir, for,* and *purr.* The power of *r* over vowel sounds is perhaps the most beneficial to point out to children, although in the process of forming their own generalizations about short and long vowel sounds children have probably incorporated r-controlled vowel notions (Heilman, Blair & Rupley, 1986).

Phonograms. *Phonograms* are letter clusters that help to form "word families" or "rhyming words." Letter clusters such as *ad, at, ack, ag, an, ap, ash, ed, et, ess, en, ine,* and *ike* can be used to develop families of words, for example the *ad* family: *bad, dad, sad, fad,* and so on. Phonograms may be one of the most useful phonic elements to teach because they encourage children to map speech sounds onto larger chunks of letters.

Syllables. A *syllable* is a vowel or a cluster of letters containing a vowel, pronounced as a unit. Phonograms, for example, are syllables. The composition of the syllable signals the most probable vowel sound. Take a minute to examine these patterns:

Long vowels	CV	be
	CVe	ate
		like
		rote
	CVVC	paid
		boat
Short vowels	VC or CVC	it
		hot
R-controlled	Vr	art
	CVr	car, her
Digraph/Diphthong Variations	VV	saw, book
		boil, out

These patterns underlie the formation of syllables. The number of syllables in a word is equal to the number of vowel sounds. For example, the word *disagreement* has four vowel sounds and thus four syllables. The word *hat* has one vowel sound, and thus one syllable.

There are three primary syllabication patterns that signal how to break down a word into syllabic units:

The VCCV Pattern. When there are two consonants between two vowels, the word is usually divided between the consonants. Note *hap-pen, mar-ket,* and *es-cape.* However, we do not split up consonant digraphs such as *sh* or *th* or *ng* as in *sing-er, fath-er*. There is a variation of this pattern—the VCCle pattern. A word with this pattern is still divided between the consonants. Note *saddle, bot-tle, rat-tle*, and *pud-dle*.

The VCV Pattern #1. When one consonant is between two vowels the division is before the consonant. Note *re-view, o-pen*, and *be-gin*. Again there is a slight variation with the VCle pattern but still divide before the consonant. For example: *peo-ple, ta-ble, cra-dle*.

The VCV Pattern #2. If using VCV #1 does not result in a familiar word, then divide after the consonant as in *sal-ad* or *pan-el*.

Some Suggestions for Teaching Phonics

Several guidelines will help you to teach phonics. First, be aware of the underlying approach of the phonics program you are using. In practice, teachers tend to use a mixture of both analytic and synthetic approaches. Factors such as the phonic concept to be taught and the nature of the group of children should influence the choice of approach. You need to detect readily the approach underlying a material and then make a judgment as to its appropriateness for the teaching/learning situation.

Children come to phonic instruction with varying degrees of generalization about the way the written language works. Their generalizations constitute a particular level of linguistic awareness as described in Chapter 4. Use formal and informal means to determine children's level of understanding of the units of written language. Informally probe for notions of "word," "letter," and "alphabet" through such activities as: cutting language experience stories into strips and asking individual children to cut off the words; asking children to read stories or messages they have written and to point to the words; having children sort words and letters; discussing the alphabet; having children prepare little story books indicating orally the pages, pictures, words, and so on.

Formally use such tests as: *Concepts About Print Tests: Sand* and *Stones* (Clay, 1979); *Test of Early Reading Ability* (TERA) (Reid, Hresko & Hammill, 1981); *Test of Linguistic Awareness in Reading Readiness* (Downing, Ayers & Schaefer, 1982); *Developmental Spelling Assessment* (Morris & Perney, 1985).

Some phonics information is more important than other phonics information. Commercially prepared reading programs tend to include everything you ever wanted to know about phonics—and more. However, some phonics information isn't worth teaching and learning. For example, children need not spend inordinate amounts of time learning phonic or syllabication rules. To do so is inefficient and unproductive. What is important is that they have many opportunities to segment words into letter clusters that correspond to pronounceable units of speech.

As we showed in Chapter 4, phonemic segmentation is an important word identification strategy. *Blending* is another. Blending is the process of joining together the sounds represented by letters and letter clusters in a word. Essentially the reader links sound sequence with letter sequence. The emphasis should be on directing children to attach sounds to groups of letters. The larger the cluster of letters to which sounds are attached the better. A sight word is an example of a large chunk of letters to which sounds have been attached.

Pat Cunningham (1975, 1976) explained how readers go about breaking multisyllabic words into pronounceable units. Upon encountering an unfamiliar word, they search through their memory of similar looking words and compare the unknown to the known. They do this by segmenting words into letter clusters of the *largest* manageable units. Then readers compare the chunks to known words or familiar letter clusters, looking for recognizable patterns. If the unfamiliar word is in the reader's oral or listening vocabulary, it can be identified. According to Cunningham, readers form and use their own rules for analyzing words through the comparison-contrast process described above.

Whenever possible, children should practice segmenting and blending unfamiliar words that are encountered in a meaningful print context. Remember, phonic instruction at best is designed to help children approximate the pronunciation of unfamiliar words. When approximations occur within a print context, readers can rely on meaning cues as well as phonic information to assist in word identification.

As far as a scope and sequence for phonics instruction, there is no one best model to follow. In general, however, the following sequence appears reasonable (Stoodt, 1981; Tanner, 1983).

1. *Begin with the consonant sounds.*
    Observe initial consonant sound of known words.
    Explore initial consonant substitution.
    Observe final consonant sound of known words.
    Point out the two sounds of *g* and *c*.

2. *Develop an awareness of consonant blends and digraphs.*
    Observe blends and digraphs in initial positions.
    Observe blends and digraphs in final positions.
    Continue to encourage substitution strategies.

3. *Develop knowledge of vowel sounds.*
    Observe the letter patterns associated with common long vowel sounds.
    Observe the letter patterns associated with short vowel sounds.
    Observe vowel digraphs, diphthongs, and r-controlled vowels.
    Develop blending ability as the coordination of sound sequences with letter sequences.

4. *Develop an awareness of syllables and syllabication patterns.*
    Direct attention to larger chunks or groups of letters within words.
    Continue to develop blending ability by having students coordinate sound sequences with larger letter clusters.

When children attempt to figure out unknown words in text, encourage them to use semantic, grammatical, and sound-symbol information. Direct the process by fostering a search for information cues. Help children monitor their searches

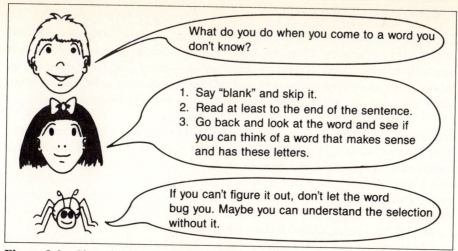

Figure 8.2   Chart for Monitoring Unknown Word

by using a chart similar to the one in Figure 8.2. Explain the procedures on the chart and give children practice using them.

Perhaps the best place for phonics instruction is within a purposeful writing program which in turn is connected to the reading program. Procedures that outline how to integrate phonics instruction with writing are described below (Johnson & Lehnert, 1984).

Step one. Use a shared book experience or the language experience approach on a regular basis. Indirectly teach phonics concepts through these experiences. Note word boundaries, sentences, sounds, and spelling patterns.

Step two. Have children engage in writing activities. Allow them to use invented spellings and to explore sound/symbol relationships through their writing and/or drawing.

Step three. Analyze the children's writing. Note the various spelling stages demonstrated by the children. Form small instructional groups from the analyses. For example, what kinds of phonics information would help to further the phonic knowledge of the first-grader quoted in the following passage?

Daer Ester Bunny,

I would like a srpris for Ester—a real bunny. If I get a real bunny I proms that I wood take care of it.

Note that word boundaries are observed, the *a-e* spelling pattern is honored in the one-syllable words, and the double consonant in the middle of the word *bunny* is correctly used. This child may benefit from some direct instruction about the vowel digraph *ea*. Since the child could spell the word *real* that might be a good place to build from.

Instructional Activities

There are numerous phonic programs, guides, manuals, and prescriptions available to the classroom teacher. All basal reading programs include comprehensive phonic instructional procedures. Where children are concerned, emphasis must be on learning and using phonic concepts, not on mechanistic, rote drill. The activities below are but a few of the many that you can use with beginners.

Listening and Listing. This activity is used extensively in phonics instruction. After students have read or heard a story, draw attention to certain sound-letter associations of specific words used in the text. First, ask children to listen to a sound in a word, such as *b* in *big*. Then point out the letter used to represent the sound. Develop lists of additional words which include that sound. For example: *Bobby, bat, Barbie, buttons, beautiful*. In this way, children begin to make a connection between a symbol and a sound.

The listening and listing activity can be used frequently as children progress from awareness of initial and final consonants to medial consonants to easy-to-hear vowels to hard-to-hear vowels to letter clusters. Listening/listing can be varied in many creative ways to help children notice the significant features of words. One important fact should be kept in mind, however. Use of this activity should be an integral part of a story experience, not an isolated activity.

Word Building. Two common ways in which this activity is used are talking about rhyming words and practicing consonant or vowel substitution.

Poems, songs, and chants provide easy opportunity to listen to sounds in words, to note similarities in rhyming words, and to create innovations in texts. Note how the poem below can be used to have children compose (either through independent writing or dictation) similar rhyming verse:

If you found a dinosaur,
Would you take it by the paw?
Would you say, "Come home with me"?
Would you give it greens for tea?

(From *The Story Box*, 1984, page 2)

Here's how a group of first-graders imitated the poem, working out their version with guidance from the teacher in a language-experience session:

If you found a kangaroo,
Would you make it some stew?
Would you say "How do you do?"
Would you put it in the zoo?

Substitution is a common and useful way of building words. Children first learn to substitute initial consonant sounds to form new words. For example, *dock* can be changed to *lock* can be changed to *rock*. Later children can experiment with substituting vowel sounds. For example, *bet* can be changed to *bit* can be changed to *bat* and so on.

Children need many chances to practice substitution. Try some of these activities:

Use magnetic letters for building words, taking them apart and reconstructing.

Use the blackboard or individual slate boards for rewriting words often.

Use markers, pens, crayons, or paint brush and water to make words.

Use word puzzles or words cut into puzzle pieces.

Use word cards for practice.

When using substitution activities, make sure that children have opportunities to use new words in continuous text at some point. For example, some workbook exercises promote the use of substitution in completing sentences.

Recognizing Patterns. Encourage children to focus their attention on letter clusters when identifying words. There are several activities for this purpose.

Hearing Breaks. Prepare young readers for using letter clusters by directing them to listen for breaks in two- and three-syllable words. For example, for the word *happiness* the children would clap three times for each syllable heard. Indulge in this activity frequently as children encounter multisyllabic words.

Detecting Patterns. As children develop the ability to hear larger units of sounds within words, practice associating letter clusters with sound units. Clay (1979) suggested using strategies such as the following to go beyond the initial consonant:

Scenario: A child is attempting to sound out the word "joking."

Child: j
Teacher: Can you say more than that?
Child: jo - k . . . joke
Teacher: Is the end of joke right?
Child: ing . . . joking
Teacher: Yes. You found two parts to that word, jok—ing. There are many other words like that: pok—ing; tak—ing; hik—ing. Let's go on.

Clay also encouraged a *visual analysis of words* to help children make connections with other words that demonstrate similar letter patterns. For example, when a child encounters an unknown word, ask questions such as the following: Do you know a word that looks like that? What do you think it could be? Do you know a word that starts with those letters? Do you know a word that ends with those letters?

Read and Read Some More; Write and Write Some More. Give children extended opportunities to use phonic knowledge in reading and writing situations.

Allow time to read and to write. Writing and reading put phonic knowledge into action.

TOWARD ORAL READING FLUENCY

Strategies that develop oral reading fluency give beginning readers and high risk readers the feeling of what it's like to read rapidly and fluently. As a result, they begin to recognize a large number of words, especially the high-frequency words. The strategies, *Echo Reading, Simultaneous-Listening-and-Reading,* and *Repeated Readings,* all involve students reading orally in a fluent manner with support. When using each of these strategies, we recommend not focusing the students' attention on words that they aren't able to identify. Also, there's little need to ask comprehension questions after children have read a selection using one of these procedures. Often though, they will comment spontaneously on something that happened in the story and a conversation about the material will occur.

Echo Reading

These steps are appropriate for *Echo Reading:*

1. The teacher and a small group of students read the same selection aloud together in a fluent manner.

2. The students move their pointer fingers along the line of print as they read. This can be likened to a typewriter fluently typing lines of print. It takes some practice with this method to be able to coordinate fingers, eye movements, and oral reading along the line of print.

3. In the beginning sessions, the teacher reads a little louder and slightly faster than the students.

4. Students are urged to read orally with the instructor and not to worry about mistakes made.

5. At times, initial lines or paragraphs can be reread together if students are not comfortable with the fluent oral reading.

6. The first material used with *Echo Reading* should be fairly easy for students to read. Patterned, repetitive stories and language experience stories can be used with students at beginning stages of learning to read. Gradually, stories that are more and more difficult for the students can be used. Students will have favorites that they will want to read together with their classmates and teacher.

Simultaneous-Listening-and-Reading (SLR)

Simultaneous-Listening-and-Reading (SLR) is similar to *Echo Reading.* In both procedures students try to orally read along in a fluent manner. In using *SLR,* instead of reading with a teacher, students read along with a tape recorder or a story on a record. The steps in *SLR* include the following:

1. Students listen individually to tape-recorded stories, simultaneously following along in the written text. They read and listen repeatedly to the same story until they can fluently read the story.

2. Students choose the book or portion of the book in which they want to work. When they are making their selections, the teacher explains that they will continue listening to the same story until they are able to read it fluently by themselves. Students need to choose a book that is too hard to read right away, but not so hard that it is out of range entirely.

3. Students are to listen to their books every day, using earphones and following along in the text as they listen. They need to listen to the whole story through at least once; then they go back and repeat any part they choose to prepare more carefully. They can also record themselves as they read along with the tape or tape-record themselves as they read aloud independently.

4. Every three or four days the teacher listens to the students read orally as much as they have prepared. Students are encouraged to evaluate themselves on how fluently they read the selection they have prepared.

5. Sometimes it takes students a while to get accustomed to working with tape-recorders and at the start keep losing their place in the book. As with *Echo Reading*, it takes practice to coordinate their eyes and ears in following along with the text. Once students become familiar with a story, keeping the place becomes no problem.

6. Chomsky (1976) reported that when students first begin using this method, it may take as long as a month before they are able to read a fairly long story aloud fluently. Students begin taking a much shorter time period, maybe two or three weeks, to be able to read a fairly long story fluently as they become more proficient with *SLR*.

When students are able to read the story fluently without the aid of the tape, they need to receive opportunities to read the story to their parents, the principal, or fellow students. Students using this strategy could not present the story without having a book to follow so they have not really memorized the book. However, a combination of memorization and reading enables students to have an experience of successful, effective, fluent reading.

Another adaptation of *SLR* that increases the ease of using it with groups of children is to have a group of children listen to the same tape at a listening center.

Repeated Readings

The *Repeated Readings* strategy devised by S. J. Samuels (1979) is also designed to develop rapid, fluent oral reading. Here are the steps in using this method:

1. Students choose short selections (50–200 words) from stories that are difficult enough that they are not able to read them fluently.

2. The students read the passage over several times silently until they are able to read it fluently.

3. Samuels suggested that students tape-record their first oral rendition of the passage as well as their oral rendition after practice so that they can hear the difference in fluency. As in using *SLR*, students can be encouraged to evaluate their own fluency after listening to a tape-recording of their oral reading.

Samuels has found that as students read a passage over and over, focusing on reading in a fluent manner, they make fewer and fewer errors, without focusing their attention on specific words.

Lauritzen (1982) proposed two modifications to the repeated reading method that make the method easier to use with groups of students. One modification calls for group rather than individual reading. The second allows for the use of appealing reading selections that contain rhyme, rhythmic language, and predictable patterns.

In presenting the selection, first read the entire story to the group of children. While reading, have them follow the print, either from a book or from a copy on a chart or chalkboard. Next, take turns (teacher first, then children) reading the same portion of text (a line, sentence, or paragraph); the length of the segment to be echoed is determined by the structure of the poem or story. Finally, read the entire selection in unison. At this point, children may read individually, in pairs, or in small groups as many times as they wish. Unison reading can be repeated for several days. If the teacher tape-records the selection, all three methods, *Echo Reading, SLR,* and *Repeated Readings* can be used in an integrated way. The children can *Echo Read* as a group, listen along to the tape for extra practice, and repeatedly read the selection to themselves.

Echo Reading, SLR, and *Repeated Readings* take the struggle and frustration out of moving along in reading a book. These activities give the beginning and inefficient reader the feeling of fluency before the ability has been gained. Students can read a large volume of words using these strategies.

SUMMARY

The underlying premise of this chapter has been that words in their written form must be dealt with by readers. How teachers use instructional time to help readers identify words is important. Two outcomes of word identification instruction were noted. First, readers must learn how to deal rapidly and independently with unfamiliar words. Second, they must develop multiple strategies for word identification.

A distinction was made between immediate word identification and mediated word identification. Immediate word identification is a comprehensive term which encompasses the use of meaning as well as phonic cues to recognize words rapidly. Mediated word identification, on the other hand, suggests that readers need more time to translate print to speech through an analysis of sound-letter relationships.

The role of sight words, context, and phonics was examined within the context of immediate and mediated word identification strategies. Sight word instruction helps readers deal with words as wholes. Learning words at sight involves immediate recognition and is the result of readers' experiences with words in situations involving reading, writing, seeing, discussing, and listening. Strategies for teaching high frequency sight words, function words, and "key" words were presented.

When readers combine meaning cues with phonic cues, they have developed a powerful tool for word identification. This is why readers must learn how to use contextual information to recognize words. Various kinds of contextual activities can be designed to help students coordinate semantic, syntactic, and phonic information. These activities involve cloze-type passages in which target words are deleted from the text. These words can be deleted selectively or systematically depending on the teacher's purposes. Readers must also become aware that a text selection can be read and understood without identifying every word. Context-centered activities such as the "reader selected miscue" strategy help students in this respect.

Phonics instruction helps students to mediate the identification of unknown words. To this extent, it has a part to play in learning to read. Phonics reinforces the alphabetic principle, the principle that there are systematic relationships between sounds and letters. The broad purpose of phonics is to help children continue to develop knowledge about sound-letter correspondence. To this end, we discussed the content and language of phonics, some important principles of phonic instruction, and instructional activities.

Students, especially beginners and those who are at risk, need to develop a feel for what it's like to read rapidly and fluently. As a result, strategies were discussed to involve students in the development of oral reading fluency. These strategies included echo reading, simultaneous-listening-and-reading, and the method of repeating readings. Strategies such as these allow students to recognize a large volume of words rapidly.

THE WORKSHOP

In the Classroom

1. Compare Fry's Instant Words in this chapter to other lists of basic sight words (for example, the Dolch list). What do the lists have in common? Which list do you prefer the most? Why?

2. Analyze the word identification strand of a basal reading program. How is decoding or word identification defined? What are the major components of the strand? How is phonics taught; for example, is phonics taught analytically or synthetically? What provisions are made to help children develop multiple strategies for identifying unknown words? How comprehensively is context taught and reinforced?

3. Now compare the word identification strand with a published supplementary word identification program. How are the two alike? Different? Describe the extent to which the supplementary program is compatible with the basal's word identification program.

4. What should be the role of parents in helping children identify words? Brainstorm ways in which parents can help children with word identification at home.

In the Field

1. Prepare and teach a word identification lesson to a small group of children. Make provisions in the lesson to combine phonics or structural analysis with context usage and application.

2. Collect several samples of writing from a child in primary school. Analyze the writing to determine the child's phonic knowledge. Then interview the child's teacher to determine his or her perceptions of the child's strengths and gaps in phonic knowledge. Does your analysis match the teacher's perceptions? Why or why not?

Part IV

Vehicles for Instruction

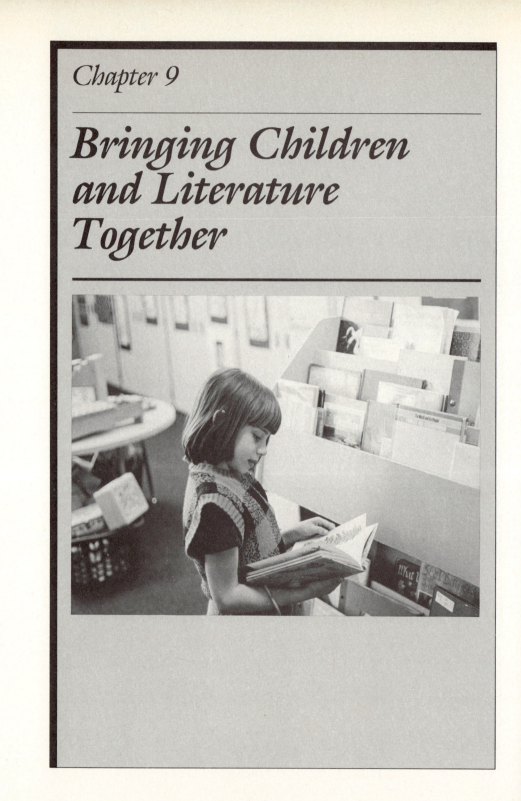

Chapter 9

Bringing Children and Literature Together

Some things just naturally seem to go together: cookies and milk, pen and paper, shoes and socks. Children and books make a natural combination too. If, for example, you were asked to think about a favorite childhood memory connected to reading, what would come to mind? Perhaps you'd think of a title such as Little Women, Anne of Green Gables, David Copperfield, or Rebecca of Sunnybrook Farm. You might even conjure up an image of a character in your mind's eye or a scene or a bit of dialogue that you will never forget. So in a sense, bringing children and literature together carries on an important cultural tradition, satisfies children's cognitive and affective needs, and solidifies their foundation in literacy.

My teacher told the story about the old lady who swallowed the fly. She had a puppet with a stomach you could see, and we could see the animals the old lady swallowed. We helped her tell the story. It was fun!

Jessica, a first-grader

Reading books helps me know that kids have problems too, like me.

John, a fifth-grader

I think it is important for my students to want to read.

Louise, second-grade teacher

I like for my friends to talk to me about books they like. It gets me wanting to read the same books.

Jane, a sixth-grader

Children delight in the exploits of Curious George, Madeline, Encyclopedia Brown, and Pippi Longstocking. And why not? A significant part of classroom reading instruction should revolve around characters and story lines found in literature, if for no other reason than to make children wonder, weep, laugh, shiver, and gasp. What better way to surround young readers with meaningful experiences from text?

At its best, reading is a personal and self-engaging activity. Through reading, children develop not only the ability to reason better but also to feel and to imagine. This is why reading, especially the reading of literature, has been called a "whole brain affair." Reading literature requires analytical thought as well as affective response. Readers must attend cognitively to what is being read. But they must also respond emotionally to the literary text as a whole. These feelings, by and large, are unique and tied to the individual reader's life experiences. As we will explain, emphasizing personal involvement in literature develops in children an imagination, a sense of wonder, and an active participation in the literary experience. To our mind, bringing children and literature together is one of the highest acts of humanity in the classroom.

There are long-term benefits implicit in bringing children and books together on a regular basis. First, reading expands children's experiential backgrounds. Children who have never milked a cow and been awakened by a rooster, or lived in a tenement apartment and played in the alley of a big city, can expand their world through reading. Second, literature provides children with good models of writing. These models are invaluable in children's own writing development and will do much to teach them about the unique characteristics of written language. Third, children "learn to read by reading"—a theme we have repeated throughout this book. When they are encouraged to read books regularly, children are more likely to develop patience with print. In this way, they gain valuable practice in reading. Fourth, when the prime purpose for reading is enjoyment and pleasure, children want to understand what they are reading and are likely to select books with familiar topics, themes, or characters. Natural reading situations are created which will promote students' use of reading strategies. And fifth, wide reading provides opportunities for children to develop vocabulary knowledge. Readers learn the meaning of words by meeting them again and again in a variety of contexts in which they are usually able to figure out the meanings.

Many children will not develop a sense of literature as enjoyment and as a means of understanding the world without deliberate and planned guidance. For this reason, a major goal of a reading program should be to *develop students who choose to read*. In this chapter we consider the dilemma of many teachers who want children to *want* to read, but can't seem to get them "into reading." We also explore ways to immerse children in literature. The reading and telling of stories are essential in developing the reading habit and in helping students find and share books in content subjects as well as "regular" reading times. Throughout the chapter, we emphasize what happens when adults and children support each other in their reading and how the classroom can be a "community of readers."

HELPING CHILDREN TO WANT TO READ

Most teachers want their students to like reading. In fact, the teachers we've known—whether their instruction has reflected bottom-up, top-down, or interactive models—all place importance on developing positive attitudes toward reading. School administrators also emphasize getting students to want to read. Yet children we've observed in many elementary schools don't seem to spend much time reading voluntarily. If this is, as we suspect, a fairly widespread problem, what can teachers do to help students want to read?

Bruckerhoff (1977) surveyed elementary students, asking them to describe their teachers' actions that contributed to positive and negative feelings toward reading. He reported that the teacher activities listed by students that created positive feelings toward reading were *reading to students, serving as a reading model, helping students find books of interest, and telling students that reading is worthwhile*. Teacher actions that the students reported created negative feelings toward reading included requiring students to do extensive book reports, to read uninteresting books, and to read aloud in front of others.

In another study, Brutten (1974) asked elementary students to respond to the following questions: "What has a teacher of yours done to interest you in reading? What could a teacher of yours do to interest you in reading?" Children's responses included *telling interesting stories, showing filmstrips or films about stories, suggesting interesting books, playing records that tell stories, telling only the beginning of interesting stories,* and *preparing teacher and/or student annotated book lists*.

These two studies illuminate some obvious, although at times neglected, things teachers can do to encourage students to read on their own. To these, we add one item: to provide time during the school day for children to read books they choose. In Table 9.1, we list several teacher behaviors that encourage students

TABLE 9.1

Getting Students "into Reading"

Immerse Students in Literature	Use Instructional Time to Show the Value of Reading	Help Students Find and Share Books They Want to Read
Create a classroom climate in which literature is an integral component.	Find classroom time for students to read books of their choice.	Help students find books of interest and on the appropriate level.
Utilize many genres of children's books, including folk tales, poetry, realistic fiction, historical fiction, and informational books.	Model reading behavior and become a reader of children's books.	Tell or read the beginning of interesting stories.
Select and organize a classroom collection of books.	Encourage students to respond to the aesthetic dimensions of literature.	Develop annotated lists of "books worth reading."
Read and tell stories.		
Show films and filmstrips of literature selections.		

to develop the habit of reading. Later in this chapter these behaviors will be discussed and corresponding teaching strategies will be presented.

Heathington and Alexander (1984) found that teachers by and large want their students to enjoy reading but do *not* "put their instructional time" in what they proclaim as important. Heathington and Alexander gave a questionnaire to 101 classroom teachers to ascertain their reactions to several aspects of reading instruction. Attention on the questionnaire was not focused on developing attitudes toward reading per se. The teachers rated the developing of a positive attitude toward reading as a second priority, with developing reading comprehension as their highest priority. These teachers rated developing positive attitudes toward reading as more important than developing phonic abilities, recognition of sight words, word meanings, and oral reading. However, when the teachers assessed the percent of time used for developing these various aspects of reading, they indicated they devoted more time to each of these other aspects of reading than they did to developing favorable attitudes toward reading.

The teachers in this study were also asked how they assessed their students' attitudes toward reading. Twenty-five percent gave no response to this question. Seven percent indicated they made no assessment of their students' attitudes toward reading. It seems likely that almost one-third of the teachers surveyed do not normally think about estimating the degree to which their students' attitudes are positive or negative.

The same teachers were asked to list five activities that they felt contributed most to developing a positive attitude toward reading in their students. "Developing children's skills in reading" was mentioned most frequently as a way to develop positive attitudes toward reading. Next most frequently cited were "providing a variety for interesting, meaningful materials" and "providing opportunities to read aloud." Other ways mentioned included "reading and telling stories," "teacher motivation in reading class," "allowing for creative use of reading," "modeling reading behavior," and "providing time to read."

Notice that two of the three most favored ways to develop positive attitudes related to developing proficiency in reading: developing children's skills in reading and providing opportunities to read aloud. In other words, the teachers seemed to believe that by developing competency in reading, they would develop the love of reading in children. However, this is not necessarily the case. Many children (and adults) develop competency in reading but do not choose to read. Such individuals are in fact *aliterate:* They can read but won't.

Concern for competence is reflected in the comment made by Phyllis, a veteran elementary teacher taking a graduate course in reading. She maintained, "I feel guilty when I read silently with my students. I feel I need to be teaching them skills. I even feel guilty when I read to my students, because I'm still not directly teaching them to read." Probably many teachers feel as Phyllis does—that the major portion of the school day must be spent on skills development with children. Certainly, the skillful development of readers is the raison d'être of instruction. Yet many teachers find it difficult to model purposeful silent reading—a behavior essential to the development of skillful readers—because they do not perceive silent reading as a skill in itself.

Another reason why teachers often do *not* place high priority in their use of time on activities like reading to students and modeling reading behavior is the artificial separation between "story time" and reading instruction, or "work time." Many teachers, especially in the primary grades, read and tell stories to their students. Most children acknowledge that listening to stories is an enjoyable activity. Nevertheless, instructional reading time is not often characterized by the same level of enjoyment. It is often a time when emphasis is placed on doing "skills work." Doing "skills work" usually consists of such things as completing dittoed sheets and workbook pages, reading stories in basal readers, copying the weekly spelling words, or writing them in sentences. In the minds of both teacher and student, story time is distinct from reading instructional time: The two have different purposes, different content and techniques, and consequently, different motivational impact.

Neither children nor teachers should assume that learning to read is more drudgery than pleasure. More often than not, children who have learned to read before they enter school often have been spurred on by the enjoyment of reading. Holdaway (1982, page 293) expressed the phenomenon this way:

> Children who are already reading and writing when they enter school at 5, or who are so ready to learn that they take literacy in their stride, have had a rather different

introduction to the real processes of literacy. Some of their deepest satisfactions for several years have centered around their fumbling but excited attempts to read, write, and spell.

The reading instructional program can be set up so that children will enjoy reading, choose to read over other activities, and naturally get practice at real reading. To do this, teachers need to engage children in literature, then allow and encourage children to choose books that pique their curiosity. Also, teachers need to organize the instructional time to show the importance of reading by modeling purposeful silent reading and by providing time for recreational reading: "By the time they are in the third or fourth grade, children should read independently a minimum of two hours per week" (*Becoming a Nation of Readers,* 1985, page 119). Some instructional strategies to assist teachers with these goals follow.

SURROUNDING CHILDREN WITH LITERATURE

There are some classrooms where children's responses to literature are livelier and more positive than the average and where their choices of books seem to be made with more care. These classrooms are not just happy accidents, but "they are carefully structured environments that reflect a teacher's commitment to literature as a natural medium for children's reading and language learning as well as a source of fun and satisfaction" (Hickman, 1983, page 1). How are these classrooms different from others?

One thing that sets these classrooms apart is that the teachers are enthusiastic about children's literature. Teachers who make a point of talking about their own favorite books or stories or are themselves engrossed in a new title, often find their students wanting to read those same books for themselves. These teachers show personal interest in books in other ways, also. Some teachers share autographed copies of books from their own collections or display book-related items such as ceramic or stuffed toy characters, or posters designed by a picture book artist.

Jill, a first-grade teacher, showed a stuffed rabbit with a blue jacket as she read Beatrice Potter's *Peter Rabbit*. Another teacher told the story of *Little Red Riding Hood* using a doll on which one side was Red Riding Hood and upside-down was a wolf wearing grandmother-type spectacles. However the teacher's enthusiasm is expressed, it helps to create a setting where children know that attention to the world of books is legitimate and desirable.

Selecting a Classroom Collection of Books

A major classroom characteristic that brings children and books together is many carefully selected books. These books come from different sources—the teacher's personal collection, the school library, the public library, and paperback book clubs. While the core collection is permanent, many of the borrowed titles change frequently, so there is always something new to encourage browsing.

Not just "any old book" is in this collection for the sake of quantity. These books are carefully chosen for a variety of reasons as illustrated by Hickman (1983, page 2):

> One teacher of a fourth and fifth grade group, for example, often includes many picture books. She chooses some like Mizumura's *If I Were a Cricket* and Foreman's *Panda's Puzzle* for the special purpose of comparing the artists' way with watercolor; there are others, like Wagner's *The Bunyip of Berkeley's Creek*, just because they are good stories and the teacher thinks the children will enjoy them. The teacher is sensitive to children's interests and books that will have immediate appeal; thus the presence of *Tales of a Fourth Grade Nothing* by Blume, *How to Eat Fried Worms* by Rockwell, and *The Mouse and the Motorcycle* by Cleary. The teacher also recognizes that the students need some books that will stretch their imaginations and abilities, stories of sufficient depth to bear rereading and reflection. Some of the titles chosen for this purpose are Babbitt's *Tuck Everlasting,* Cooper's *The Dark Is Rising*, and Steig's *Abel's Island*. Still others, like Konigsburg's *From the Mixed-Up Files of Mrs. Basil E. Frankweiler*, are available in multiple copies so that small groups can read and discuss them.

One notable feature of book selection is that each title bears some relationship to others in the collection. There may be multiple books by an author or an illustrator or several books that represent a genre such as folk tales. Other connections may be based on a content theme such as spooky things or nature books or survival books.

Choosing Classroom Literature. To be able to choose literature for classroom collections and to give guidance to students as they chose books to read, a teacher needs to be familiar with children's literature. Because children's literature has expanded extensively in the last fifteen years, this is a formidable task.

There are several strategies that can be used to help choose classroom literature. Here are some tips on how not to be overwhelmed as you become familiar with children's literature.

1. *Read and enjoy children's books yourself.* The best way to become familiar with children's books is not to read anthologies or reviews, but to read the books themselves. It is a good idea to keep a card file on the books you have read to jog your memory later. This card file can be used with children to help them in choosing books to read. It can also be used as you share your feelings about particular books with other teachers.

2. *Read children's books with a sense of involvement.* Only by reading books thoroughly can you prepare yourself to share them honestly with children.

3. *Read a variety of book types.* There are various classifications of genres or types of books. By being familiar with specific books in each of the different genres, you can be more helpful when children ask for such things as "a scary mystery" or "someting true to life."

4. *Read books for a wide variety of ability levels.* Children at any grade level vary tremendously in their reading abilities and interests. For example, Carolyn Haywood's *B is for Betsy* is read avidly by some second- and third-graders.

Other children at the same grade levels will be read somewhat more difficult books such as Sobal's *Encyclopedia Brown Lends a Hand* and Blume's *Tales of a Fourth Grade Nothing*. Still others in the same classes may benefit from spending time with picture books such as Maurice Sendak's *Where the Wild Things Are* or Ed Emberley's *The Great Thumbprint Drawing Book*.

5. *Share how your students respond to particular books with other teachers or other university students.* In the San Antonio, Texas, school district, a book reporting system was developed recently. Anyone who read a book and used it with children filled out a review card including a brief summary, a rating, comments on the book's unique value, and recommendations for suggested ability levels. No card was to be turned in unless the book was used with children. Teachers used these cards to help select books for their classrooms. Not unexpectedly, with this teacher sharing system in place, the children read more along with the teachers.

6. *Start by reading several books that are considered by many to be of "good" quality.* Appendices *B* and *C* list the Caldecott and Newberry award-winning books. As you read these and begin using them with children, you will begin to know books to which children in your class will respond favorably.

Determining "Good" Literature. Stewig (1980) explained that the appellation "good" for books for children is a "fragile raft of opinion on the shifting quicksand of taste." The first priority is to choose books that children will like and will read. In order to choose such a collection of books, teachers must be knowledgeable and enthusiastic about children's literature. Through reading children's literature and talking about books with children, teachers learn which books to use in their classrooms. A second consideration is using accepted ways to judge books according to plot, theme, characterization, and setting. In addition, there are a few criteria to use in building a *balanced* collection of books:

1. *The collection needs to contain modern, realistic literature as well as more traditional literature.* In the last few years, some critics have voiced concern about the appropriateness of realism in some of the recent children's literature. Other observers feel realism is justified because it depicts problems children must face while growing up. Each teacher and school must decide whether to include books that deal with divorce, death, and drug use—issues that touch the lives of many of today's children. Traditional literature, which children have delighted in for many years, should also be a part of the classroom collection of books.

2. *The collection needs to contain books that represent different ethnic and minority groups as well as mainstream Americans. The collection also needs to contain stories that depict nontraditional families.* See Chapter 10 for specific criteria useful in evaluating books for stereotyping.

3. *The collection needs to contain books with different types of themes and books of varying difficulty.* The classroom library needs traditional literature, fantasy, poetry, historical fiction, nonfiction, and picture books. Even upper-grade

classroom collections should have some picture books. Picture books often have a good story plot and are one means to get less enthusiastic students "into reading."

There is one more consideration when compiling the classroom collection: the science, art, social studies, and music curricula. Include books on topics that will be studied in these subject areas. Again, make materials on specific topics available in a wide range of reading levels because of different reading abilities of students in one grade level.

Once classroom collections are in place, the literature program itself needs attention. A major part of the program includes reading aloud and telling stories to children.

Listening to Literature

According to Stewig (1980), "most elementary school teachers understand the values that accrue as a result of sharing literature with children" (page 8). Teachers naturally seem to know that there is no better way to interest children in the world of books than listening to stories and poems. In this way, children learn that literature is a source of pleasure. When listening to literature, children have access to stories and poems they could not, or would not, read on their own. Often, once children are excited by hearing a selection, they want to read it for themselves. One study found that reading aloud to fifth-graders for twenty to thirty minutes per day affected both the quantity and quality of their voluntary reading (Sirota, 1971).

Through hearing stories and poems children develop a positive disposition toward books. Cumulative experiences with hearing stories and poems are likely to improve reading comprehension and vocabulary development. A study by Cohen (1968) reported that seven-year-olds who were read to for twenty minutes each day gained significantly in vocabulary and reading comprehension. Listening to stories and poems also can be a basis for group discussion which often leads to shared meanings and points of reference.

For these reasons, literature listening time can be one of the most productive times in the school day. Sharing literature with children is not a "frill." Most primary teachers include time for reading aloud in their schedule. Upper elementary teachers spend less time reading stories to students. Chow Loy Tom (1969) found that approximately forty percent of third- and fourth-grade teachers read aloud to students, while only twenty-six percent of the teachers read to their students in sixth grade. Among the reasons teachers gave for not reading aloud to their students was lack of time. The actual percentages of middle- and upper-grade teachers who read to their students may have changed since 1969. But experience in schools tells us that many upper elementary teachers still do not read to their students on a regular basis.

Upper elementary teachers as well as primary teachers need to see the importance of sharing literature. Some have gradually built up to twenty or thirty minutes a day for reading aloud. They may fill odd moments between a completed activity and the bell with reading to students or schedule it after a recess as a calming down activity. But it is important to note that sharing literature is *not* a "time killer." It is too serious and central to the reading program as a whole to be treated in an offhand way. Time for reading aloud and telling stories needs to be scheduled throughout the week.

Choosing Literature to Read Aloud. What kind of thought and planning go into deciding what literature to share? Why not go to the library, pull some books from the shelf, and, when reading aloud time arrives, pick up a book and read? In classrooms where students become enthusiastic about literature, teachers carefully choose which books to read. They consider the age of the children and what will interest them. They also present different types of literature. Often books read aloud are related to each other in some way. For example, a second-grade teacher read several books by Ezra Jack Keats, *The Snowy Day*, *Dreams*, and *Boggles*. The students soon could recognize a Keats book by its illustrations.

Hickman (1983) noted the example of a fourth-grade teacher who thought her students would be excited by characters that were transformed magically from one type of being to another. She read students tales of magical changes such as *Beauty and the Beast* in Peace's version and Tresselt's retelling of Matsutani's *The Crane Maiden*. Her class also heard Perrault's version of the familiar *Cinderella* and a native American myth, *The Ring in the Prairie,* by Schoolcraft. Last, she read *A Stranger Came Ashore* by Hunter, a fantasy story with magical transformation that is more difficult to understand than the transformations in the preceding stories.

Another teacher might focus on books to demonstrate an assortment of character types.

> In planning experiences with characterization, the teacher chooses books that present a wide variety of characters: male and female, young and old, rich and poor, real and imaginary. The books are read to children and savored. Sometimes the selections are discussed; at other times they are not. Reading occurs each day; the teacher is aware that children may be assimilating unconsciously some of the aspects of successful characterizations exemplified in what they are hearing (Stewig, 1980, pages 62–63).

Folktales in which the plot is generally very important can be read to illustrate simple characterization. Other authors give vivid physical descriptions. Consider this description from Judy Blume's *Are You There God? It's Me, Margaret*:

> When she smiles like that she shows all her top teeth. They aren't her real teeth. It's what Grandmother calls a bridge. She can take out a whole section of four top teeth when she wants to. She used to entertain me by doing that when I was little. . . . When she smiles without her teeth in place she looks like a witch. But with them in her mouth she's very pretty (pages 15, 18).

Teachers can also share with children books in which authors show what the characters are like by describing what they do and how they interact with others.

Even books for the very young do this. For example, in *Sam* by Ann Herbert Scott, Sam tries to interact with his mother, brother George, sister Marcia, and his father, all of whom are too preoccupied with their own concerns. Finally, the family responds. The characters all are developed skillfully by the author and portrayed in subtle monochromatic illustrations by Symeon Shimin. In hearing and discussing such books, children gain an awareness of how authors portray characters.

In classrooms where children get "into literature" teachers carefully choose which books to share with their students and have a reason for reading a particular book to their class. Often they read a series of books that are related in some way.

Preparation for Reading Aloud. Teachers need to prepare for story time. First, before reading a book aloud to the class they should be familiar with the story's sequence of events, mood, subject, vocabulary, and concepts.

Second, teachers must decide how to introduce the story. Should the book be discussed intermittently as it is read, or should there be discussion at the conclusion of the reading? Further, what type of discussion or other type of activity will follow the reading?

Setting the Mood. Many teachers and librarians set the mood for literature sharing time with a story hour symbol. One librarian used a small lamp: When the lamp was lit, it was time to listen. Deliberate movement toward the story sharing corner in the classroom may set the mood for story time. Some teachers create the mood with a record or by playing a piano. As soon as the class hears a specific tune, they know to come to the story sharing corner of the room. Norton (1980, page 335) told of using a small painted jewelry case from Japan. As she brings out the case, Norton talks with the children of the magical stories contained in it. She opens the box slowly while the children try to catch the magic in their hands. The magic is wonderful so they hold it carefully while they listen. When the story ends, each child carefully returns the magic to the box until the next story time.

Introducing the Story. There are numerous ways to introduce stories. The story sharing corner could have a chalkboard or easel with a question related to the literature to be shared, or a picture of the book itself can quickly focus the children's attention. Many teachers effectively introduce a story with objects. For example, a stuffed rabbit may be used to introduce *The Velveteen Rabbit* by Margery Williams. A good way to introduce folk tales is with artifacts from the appropriate foreign country.

You might ask a question, or you might tell the students why you like a particular story or have students predict what will happen in the story using the title or the pictures. You might tell them something interesting about the story's or author's background. It is advantageous to display the book, along with other books by the same author or with books on the same subject or theme. Introductions, however, should be brief and vary from session to session.

Activities After Reading Aloud. Once the stage is set for literature sharing, the teacher needs to read expressively and clearly. There are many different ways to encourage children to respond after hearing a piece of literature. These will be discussed later in this chapter. After some selections, the teacher simply can allow what has been read to sink into the children's minds, allowing children to react privately to what they have heard. Davis (1973, pages 19–21) called this the "impressional approach." The basic idea is that children will take from an experience whatever is relevant to them. Each child will take something from the listening experience. There is no particular reason for the teacher to know precisely what each child gets from each listening experience. Teachers should probably strike a balance between these two approaches. Too many discussions and other follow-up activities may diminish interest; too little will result in a lessened impact of the literature listening.

Story Telling

There are three significant reasons for including story telling in the curriculum.

1. *An understanding of the oral tradition in literature.* Young children in many societies have been initiated into their rich heritage through story telling; today, few children encounter such experiences.

2. *The opportunity for the teacher to actively involve the children in the story telling.* When the teacher has learned the story, he or she is free from dependence on the book and can use gestures and action to involve the children in the story.

3. *The stimulus it provides for children's story telling.* Seeing the teacher engage in story telling helps children understand that story telling is a worthy activity and motivates them to tell their own stories (Stewig, 1978).

Each of the these purposes is important. Children are sure to be spellbound by a well-told story. Close eye contact, the storyteller's expressions, the ingenious props, and the eliciting of the children's participation contribute to the magic. Although we cannot expect everyone to acquire a high level of expertise for a large number of stories, story telling is a skill one can master with practice, a story at a time.

Selecting the Story to Tell. Beginning storytellers should choose selections they like and with which they feel comfortable. Simpler stories are often the most effective for story telling. Stories with which many children are familiar and can help with the dialogue are excellent choices to prepare for story telling to younger children. "The Three Bears," "The Three Little Pigs," and the "Three Billy Goats Gruff" fit in this category. Since ancient and modern fairy tales usually appeal to children ages six through ten, consider stories like "The Elves and the Shoemaker," "Rumpelstiltskin," and "The Bremen Town Musicians." Older elementary children frequently prefer adventure; so myths, legends, and epics like "How Thor Found His Hammer," "Robin Hood," "Pecos Bill," and "Paul Bunyan" tend to be popular choices.

You might select several stories about a certain topic. For example, Norton

(1980, page 334) suggested telling two stories about "forgetting": "Icarus and Daedalus," a Greek legend in which Icarus forgets that his wings are wax, and "Poor Mr. Fingle" (Gruenberg, 1948), who wanders about a hardware store for years because he forgot what he wanted to buy. Caroline Bauer's *Handbook for Storytellers* includes an annotated bibliography of stories by subject as well as recommendations for single stories.

One of the purposes of story telling is to give children an understanding of oral tradition. Even very young children can understand that today stories are usually written down in books, whereas many years ago they were handed down.

An effective way to help children gain this understanding is to tell stories that are similar in plot, such as "The Pancake," from Norse tales included in Arbuthnot's *Anthology of Children's Literature*, *The Bun* by Marcia Brown, and *The Gingerbread Boy*. All of these stories have some kind of personified edible goodie chased by a series of animals and eaten up by the most clever animal. Jane, a kindergarten teacher, read these three stories to her class, then guided her students in making a chart showing how the three stories were alike and different. The class then dictated a story entitled "The Pizza." In the class's story, the Pizza rolled and was chased by the school nurse, some first-graders, and the principal. Its fate, of course, was to be gobbled by the kindergarteners. Through their experiences, the kindergarten class developed a story using elements from their school life, just as storytellers in the oral tradition did from their personal experiences.

Preparing a Story for Telling. The task of memorizing a story may seem formidable. How do teachers spare time for such a task? Stories do not need to be memorized. In fact, the telling is often more interesting if the story unfolds in a slightly different way each time. The following steps are helpful in telling a story:

1. Read the story through two or three times to get it clearly in your mind.

2. List mentally the sequence of events in your mind, giving yourself a mental outline of the important happenings.

3. Reread the story, taking note of the events you didn't remember. Also determine sequences you do need to memorize, such as "Mirror, mirror, on the wall, who's the fairest of them all?" from *Snow White*. Many folk and fairy tales include elements like this, but such passages are not difficult to memorize.

4. Go over the events again and consider the details you want to include. Think of the meaning of the events and how to express that meaning, rather than trying to memorize the words in the story. Stewig (1980) recommends jotting down the sequence of events on notecards; he looks the cards over each time he has a few free minutes. He reports that with this technique it seldom takes longer than a few days to fix the units of action of a story in memory.

5. When you feel you know the story, tell the story in front of a mirror. After you have practiced it two or three times, the wording will improve and you can try changing vocal pitch to differentiate among characters. Also, try changing your posture or hand gestures to represent different characters.

Now that you have prepared the story, decide how to set the mood and introduce it, just as you would before reading a piece of literature. Effective story telling does not require props, but you may want to add variety and use flannel boards and flannel board figures or puppets. These kinds of props work well with cumulative stories containing a few characters. Jessica, a first-grader, told how her teacher had a puppet of "The Old Lady Who Swallowed a Fly" with a plastic see-through window in her stomach. As the story was told, the children delighted in seeing the different animals in the old lady's stomach and helping the teacher tell the repetitive story.

Using Multimedia. In addition to actually telling stories themselves teachers can use story-telling records, filmstrips, and films. No matter how skilled the teacher is at reading and telling stories, the program will be richer if children are exposed to different storytellers' techniques and voices. Many poets and writers have recorded children's favorites like *Where the Wild Things Are* by Sendak as well as Mother Goose rhymes. The Weston Wood Company has produced materials faithful to the literary and artistic quality of the books represented in their films, filmstrips, and cassettes. Random House has a series of filmstrips and cassette tapes about Newberry Award authors that is also worth noting (Tway, 1984, page 314).

Helping Children Find and Share Books

Helping students find books they want to read and arranging for book-sharing are two important ways teachers can encourage students to read. More often than not, a teacher will hear a child moan, "I can't find a book I want to read." Comments like this reveal that students usually do not feel confident in being able to find "good" books by themselves. Earlier we alluded to ways for students to "see" specific books. Teachers can tell exciting anecdotes about authors, provide previews of interesting stories, show films or filmstrips about stories, suggest titles of stories that match students' interests, or compile teachers and/or student annotated book lists. To be able to do these things well, teachers need to be well versed in children's literature and know their students.

In addition to the teacher, there is a second and often even more persuasive source that can help children decide what book to read: their classmates. Peer recommendations make the act of choosing a book more efficient and less risky. As one sixth-grader noted:

> I like it when people recommend books to me. A lot of people will do that—look on the bookshelves and say, "Oh, here's a good book" and show it to me. I like that because it's easier for me. You don't have to search through everything and most of my friends just like the same type of book I like. So, if they find a book, I'll believe them and I'll try it. Normally, I'll like the book (Hepler and Hickman, 1982, page 279).

Recommendations from friends are the primary way adult readers decide what books to read. For many adults, the next best thing to reading a good book is telling someone else about it!

Hepler and Hickman (1982) have proposed the idea of a "community of readers" in talking about how children, in alliance with friends and the teacher, work together in classrooms where school reading does not differ from reading that the rest of the world does. In these classrooms, children spontaneously and informally recommend books to each other and talk over their experiences with books.

The use of students' journals is another effective tool used by teachers to get to know how students feel about their reading and to guide students to "the right book." Jan is a fifth-grade teacher who has her students write daily in a journal. One of her students wrote, "I like it when the whole class reads together. I think it makes me want to read more." Jan responded to this journal entry with, "I'm glad." Another student made the following journal entry: "My favorite book was *Florence Nightingale*. I liked it because of the way she improved the hospitals and made them stay clean. Also she acted differently than any other person I've read about." (Smith, 1982, page 360). In response to this journal entry, Jan suggested the student read other biographies of courageous women.

There is another understanding in the world of adult readers that is communicated to students in classrooms where students are "into reading": If adult readers do not like particular books, we don't finish them. It is common for an adult to say, "I just couldn't get into that book," or "I never finished that biography." Here is some advice written by Lewis Smith to a classroom of readers concerning what to do about books they have difficulty getting through:

> Mark mentioned that he didn't like his version of *Dan Boone*—it didn't pick up his interest, so he stopped reading. That's okay. You should read books you like, because if you spend too long trying to read one you don't like, it may make you doubt reading itself. Jamie asked about this too—she gets discouraged because she reads so slowly. Her mom told her she would get better as she reads more. You do learn to read by reading, and by choosing books that interest you. The books should have some new words, but not so many that they discourage you (Smith, 1982, page 359).

Smith also wrote to the children:

> Don't ever feel bashful about asking a librarian or bookstore person to help you select a book. That's what they are in business to do. And don't hesitate to say, "I need something a little easier," or "I'd like something a little harder." No one can tell you that you ought to be reading something easier or harder. That's your business. But they can suggest good books to try that you don't know about. Instead, look for a book that gives you the feeling, "I don't want to put this down," within the first few pages or a chapter. Many books are like that (page 362).

Smith also encouraged children to ask for suggestions about which books are interesting. But each child needs to decide for him or herself if a book is too hard, too easy, or interesting enough to be read cover to cover. Of course, there are times when students need to be nudged to finish a book or to make the next book they read a bit more challenging.

Problems with Book Reports. In many classrooms, book reporting by students is the main way books are shared. Sam, a sixth-grader, summed up his ideas about book reports this way:

> Book reports are a turn-off. They don't encourage me to read a lot of books because I have to worry about writing something afterward. Lots of time I just choose a short book to get it over with. Once the due date for a book report snuck up on me, and I faked. I just read the book jacket, the beginning and the ending, and then wrote the report. I got an O.K. grade. I don't think Mrs. Rose (that's my teacher) had read the book either.

What can teachers do to keep students from feeling as Sam does? There are, after all, many teachers who believe, "If I don't make my students write a book report, they won't read the book." Quite the contrary is true. In classrooms where teachers are enthusiastic and knowledgeable about children's books and have students participate in book-sharing, children read much more than in the classroom with required written book reports. Speigel (1981) suggested two criteria for classroom sharing of books. First, it must be *completely voluntary*. Second, the greatest amount of time must be spent in *reading,* not in recording books read, giving reports, and completing related art projects.

Although these two criteria make sense to us, there are ways to structure book sharing sessions that provide alternatives to oral and written book reports. Criscuolo (1979), for example, suggested that the class create a book catalog for their room. Students finishing books thought to be of interest to others can write short reactions including why they liked the book, title, author, and where the book can be found (school, classroom, public library). They can draw a picture if so inclined. The catalog could be kept in the file box or held together by rings to allow easy reference. Criscuolo (1977) also recommended that students nominate their favorite books for "academy awards." Nominations for different book categories can be made to the class. For students to be eligible to rank books for a category they would have had to read seventy-five percent of the books in that category. This would act as an inducement for students to read more than one kind of book.

Among the more popular alternatives for children reporting and sharing books with one another are the following:

Make a poster, bookjacket, or other type of illustration that presents an idea central to your topic. For example,

> Design an advertising blurb to sell your book, promote a product, or campaign for a historical figure you have read about.
>
> Draw a caricature of the main character or historical figure you have read about.
>
> Draw a political cartoon you could submit to a newspaper commenting on a topic you have researched.

Make a scrapbook or a collage with pictures and words central to your topic. Then write a short paper explaining the contents of this scrapbook or collage.

If you are reading a book that is historical in nature, make a time line, and list the dates and events of the story in proper sequence. If you are reading a book that is geographical in nature, draw a map and print on it some of the information you have gathered from the book.

Develop a preview of coming attractions. Make a movie trailer or previews of coming attractions for a chapter or a book you have read. Clip pictures or draw your own which show highlights of significant material you have read.

Make a comic strip about a crucial part of the text.

Make a puppet or doll representing the main character and have it deliver a monologue giving personal information about itself.

Make a miniature stage setting for a chapter or scene from material read.

Make a mobile using the words or ideas of the text in such a way that you demonstrate their meanings.

Pretend you're a reporter "on the scene." You are present at a crucial scene from the text. Report what you see and hear. Interview the main character, other characters involved, and imaginary bystanders.

Use costumes and props to dramatize a scene from a book. Be as accurate, yet imaginative, as possible.

Develop a short commercial or editorial on a book you have read and have it videotaped.

If you read a how-to book, make something or perform a demonstration to show the class what you have learned.

Make a list of new and interesting words you have learned from the book. Incorporate these words into a word search or crossword puzzle, complete with definitions, for class members to complete.

When children share books that they have enjoyed, enthusiasm runs high. Coody and Nelson (1982) put it this way: "book sharing that is lively, interesting and informative actually promotes the cause of independent reading . . . To fail to take advantage of the influence of students' peers in the selection, reading, and sharing of library books is to ignore a natural motivating force not found with other methods" (page 50).

ALLOCATING TIME FOR SILENT READING

Students need time in class to develop fluency in silent reading. They need time to develop a patience with print. Putting sustained silent reading (SSR) into action, finding time in the schedule for recreational reading, and eliciting help from administrators and parents in achieving these goals are critical components in setting up a silent reading program.

As explained by Hunt (1970), sustained silent reading is a structured activity in which students are given fixed time periods for reading self-selected materials silently. Here are the essential steps:

1. Each student must select his or her own book.
2. Each student must read silently without interruption for a fixed period of time.
3. The teacher reads along with the students and permits no interruptions.
4. Students are not required to answer content-related questions or give reports or their reactions to what they have read during SSR.

A major reason why a structured reading like SSR is so important is that, despite teacher encouragement, many students *do not choose to read* on their own. SSR provides for all students the kind of reading experience in school that avid readers get on their own—the chance of reading whatever they want to read without being required to answer questions or read orally. In other words, reading for the sake of reading should not be reserved for only the "good" readers.

The overall goals of SSR are (1) to produce students who choose to read *over other activities*; and (2) to encourage students to read voluntarily material selected *by themselves* for information or pleasure. For students to enjoy reading and seek it as an activity we believe they need to participate in structured silent reading during regular class time. Through SSR experiences they begin to see that they can read for extended periods of time and that it is an enjoyable activity.

Even the most reluctant reader will read when a structured period of silent reading is provided. Levine (1984) found that special education high school students who read six to eight years below grade level become engrossed in reading during SSR. In fact, children who say they do not like to read and who disrupt classes will read during SSR.

Learning to read independently is a major benefit. Without SSR, some students may never obtain independence and self-direction in reading and in choosing what they would like to read. Students will read if they are given time to read, if they are permitted to choose their own reading selections, and when what they read does not have to be discussed, labeled, or repeated back to the teacher.

McCracken and McCracken (1978, page 408), who have contributed much to the concept of SSR, have identified seven positive messages about reading that children learn by participating in SSR.

1. *Reading books is important.* Children develop a sense of what the teacher values by noting what the teacher chooses to have them do. Children who spend most of their time completing ditto sheets will perceive completing this "work" as important. Children who read only basal reader-length stories will perceive reading stories five to ten pages in length as important. If teachers want their students to choose to read fully developed pieces of literature, they must provide time for children to read such materials.

2. *Reading is something anyone can do.* Since no one "watches" them, poor readers can make mistakes without worrying. Able readers are "relieved they do not have to prove that they are bright every time they read something" (McCracken,

1971, page 582). When one is allowed to choose one's own material and read at one's own rate, reading is something *everyone* can do.

3. *Reading is communicating with an author.* Reading is often perceived by students as communicating with a teacher if it is only done in situations where short snatches of material are read with reactions then elicited by the teacher. One of the most exciting reactions to SSR we have observed in students is their individual responses to an author's message.

4. *Children are capable of sustained thought.* Many teachers are concerned that students "have short attention spans"; they "don't stick to a task for very long." Students, however, have relatively little trouble sustaining their reading for long periods of SSR. They actually look forward to the extended peacefulness!

5. *Books are meant to be read in large sections.* If basal reading is the main way students participate in reading, they often get the notion that reading involves reading three to ten page segments, not whole selections of literature. In SSR, students get to read larger chunks of material.

6. *Teachers believe that pupils are comprehending.* It is neither possible nor desirable for teachers to know what each student has learned and felt about every story or book read. Students take something away from every reading experience. One way teachers can show students they trust students to learn from reading is not to question them about what they read during SSR.

7. *The teacher trusts the children to decide when something is well written.* When SSR programs are functioning, students are not requested by the teacher to report on what they have read. What often happens is that students will want to share spontaneously what they have read and feel is worth sharing.

Classrooms without voluntary, sustained reading often foster the idea that reading is something to do when forced to and only for short periods of time. Each of these "positive messages about reading" is an important notion to get across if we want students to choose reading over other activities.

Putting SSR into Action

When beginning SSR with your class, talk over with students the rules of SSR and the reasons for having it. When discussing the rules, emphasize that students themselves choose books they want to read. They must be quiet and read during SSR and not move around the room. If they are near the end of a book they need to have a second choice at hand. Many teachers allow students to sit in places other than their desks, but students must decide where to sit before SSR begins. A "Do not disturb" sign on the outside of the classroom door is often helpful.

Initially, begin with short periods of SSR, perhaps five to ten minutes for first- and second-graders and ten to fifteen minutes for third- through sixth-graders. Gradually extend the time up to fifteen to twenty minutes for first- and second-graders and thirty to forty-five minutes for the upper-elementary grades.

A chart could be made to share the purposes of SSR with a class. The teacher might say, "We will learn to enjoy reading more; try a variety of reading materials; learn about new places, new faces and new ideas; get better at reading; learn to concentrate while reading" (Speigel, 1981, page 54).

Some students will be reluctant to participate in SSR at first. Others will be enthusiastic. It is important not to give up the idea quickly. It often takes a month of daily SSR for the more reluctant, restless reader to get into reading for a sustained period of time.

SSR for Beginning Readers and Less Able Readers

The standard procedures for SSR imply that students must already have some degree of reading proficiency before they can participate fully. Nevertheless, it's very important to establish and nurture the habit of sustained attention to a self-selected book in children's *earliest* classroom reading experiences. Hong (1981) has described some procedures for adapting SSR for younger readers in what she called "booktime." Booktime was used with a group of first-graders who had been placed in the lowest reading group in their class. Characterized by their teacher and the reading specialist as having exceptionally short attention spans, the children appeared uninterested in reading and lacked a basic sight vocabulary and word identification skills. Here are the procedures for booktime, which Hong says "evolved gradually as the children made clear what they need and want in their reading environment."

1. Booktime is held at the same time each day so that children come to expect this period as a permanent part of their routine. Repetition of instructions quickly becomes unnecessary. Younger and slower readers will probably have to begin with one to five minutes. With these readers, an eventual ten to fifteen minute session should be sufficient each day.

2. The reading group for booktime consists of five to seven students, rather than a whole class. This contributes to a certain intimacy and allows some sharing without getting too noisy and hectic.

3. Introduction and accessibility of books are critical factors. Booktime assumes the teacher regularly reads aloud to the children. After books are read to the group, they should be placed in the classroom library. The center gradually will accumulate a set of books, each of which will have been introduced to the group in an earlier reading aloud session. This avoids the problem of an individual trying to select a book from a collection of unknown ones. New titles constantly will be added to the center while the less popular or overly familiar ones can be removed.

4. Children select just one book. They may go through several books in one period, but they must peruse only one at a time. And there is no "saving" books by tucking them under one's arm or sitting on them while reading another book.

5. Because children may go through more than one book in a given session,

booktime is best conducted with children sitting on the floor near the book collection, rather than each child's taking a book back to his or her seat. There should be little or no "people traffic" through the reading area. If possible, larger, noisier activities are set on the opposite side of the room.

6. The teacher reads with the children as in standard SSR. But in this situation she or he may also respond to children's questions about print such as, "What's this word?" "Does this say *wait*?" This gives children feedback on their hypotheses about print. They feel encouraged when they hear they've successfully decoded a new word, and they know when they have to revise their conclusions. On the other hand, teachers will want to avoid becoming word-machines, spewing out every unknown word. Children should be encouraged to "read as best they can" and to try to figure out words on their own.

   As in SSR, teachers don't interrogate children either during or after the reading; teachers only respond. With such a limited teacher role, other individuals can help with booktime.

7. Children may read in pairs and talk to each other quietly. The sharing of a book avoids the fuss that comes when two children want the same book. The quiet talk also has educational benefits. It can be quite helpful in reviewing a story (comprehension and sense of story), exchanging reactions and feelings (response to literature), and figuring out some of the text (word identification skills).

8. Children are guided toward treating books with respect. That is, there should be no throwing or rough handling of books. This reinforces the sense of books as something special.

Hong reports that the success of booktime depends upon the quality of the books that are presented. A major criterion is that the plot be clear, well-paced, and predictably sequential. The language should be whole, using complete, natural sentences that create a flow and rhythm. Predictable, patterned books are excellent choices for booktime (see Appendix D).

As the children described by Hong participated in booktime, they became more accustomed to it. They began by focusing their attention on specific books, then developed favorites to which they often returned. The children progressed from a merely general interest and a focus on illustrations toward paying more specific attention to the features of print. After several weeks of booktime, it was not unusual to see the children spend an entire session on the first few pages of a single book, attempting to read the text using a combination of context clues and decoding.

Multiplying the Benefits of SSR

If SSR is to help cultivate the habit of reading, it warrants more than the time the teacher structures for reading. For a successful literature program, students need to read on their own during times other than SSR. What can teachers do to spread the enjoyment found in reading during SSR to reading at other times?

If developing the habit of reading is important, recreational reading should not only be a "when you are done with everything else" activity. Unfortunately, this tends to result in less able readers and children slow in penmanship never getting to choose free reading during classroom time.

Speigel (1981) suggested a number of ways in which teachers can "saturate their daily schedules" with opportunities during which children may choose to read. Teachers can create occasions for free reading time. The following suggestions will help you provide opportunities for free reading time:

1. Read in front of students in moments like waiting for lunch or while supervising a bathroom break.

2. Provide a "settling down" period after lunch, after recess, or after an invigorating discussion. This is a short period when children can choose only activities that involve no moving around or talking. The key to seizing such opportunities is for everyone to have something at hand to read. Teachers can encourage and reward students (with praise) who keep a piece of recreational reading literature at their desks at all times.

3. Bus riders can be urged to take a book on the bus with them.

4. When waiting for an assembly to begin, children may choose to read if the teacher has encouraged them to bring books with them.

Revising the Schedule to Add Free Reading Time. Here's how you can revise your schedule to incorporate free reading time:

1. In the upper elementary grades, one basal reading group a day may do free reading rather than meeting with the teacher in a basal group. The teacher can use the "extra" time for extended work with other groups or with individuals.

2. If each workbook page and ditto sheet scheduled to be assigned is not really important for the students' growth in reading, have children read recreationally instead. If teachers are not sure whether children know how to complete a certain skill page, they can have the children do half the items, either the first half or all even-numbered items. This has several advantages: Students do not waste a lot of time doing something already mastered; they have more time for recreational reading; they are motivated to do their best; and there is less for the teacher to grade.

3. Consider the relative importance of other routinely assigned activities. Do students need to write their spelling words in sentences *every* week? Could a formal spelling lesson be foregone every two or three weeks in favor of free reading time?

Often parents want to help students with their academic progress. However, helping students with workbook pages or with oral reading can become frustrating for both children and parents. Encouraging parents to have short, sustained silent reading times with their children is one way for parents to do something specific that assists their child's school progress but limits the activities to low-pressure, pleasurable interactions. Speigel (1981, pages 57–58) suggests the following schedule for sending a series of newsletters to parents to acquaint them with the recreational reading program of which SSR is a major part:

Newsletter 1 (day 1): Explanation of what a recreational reading program is and how it will work in your class. Schedule of what information will be contained in subsequent newsletters.

Newsletter 2 (day 3): Rationale for having a recreational reading program, with emphasis on how it fits into the basic curriculum. Short statement of support from your principal and reading teacher.

Newsletter 3 (day 5): Suggestions about how parents can help support the program through their efforts at home.

Newsletter 4 (day 7): List of ways parents can volunteer their time in the classroom to support the program.

There is one other person whose support teachers can enlist to promote independent sustained reading—the principal. Teachers need to explain to their principal the importance of a recreational reading program and the need for a large supply of books. The principal can also be invited to participate in classroom SSR, and thus be an important model. This is a good way to convey the idea that reading is important.

ENCOURAGING RESPONSE TO LITERATURE

After reading a book or seeing a movie, we may share the experience by briefly describing the plot. Most often, though, we tell how we felt and why. We point out something in the film or text and/or our personal histories that made us feel the way we did. We give examples from our lives and retell parts of the story. Yet when discussion shifts to the classroom, what usually happens? Often teachers ask questions to elicit a "right answer." Because we have often tried to evaluate what and how much students have understood about the text, teachers spend little time helping students explore, defend, or elaborate upon ideas. In this section, we explore the need to lead students in classroom experiences in which they analyze their *personal* reactions to what they have read. Such action supports a "reader-response theory." In other words, it supports a theory that proclaims that *the reader is crucial to the construction of the literary experience*.

Louise Rosenblatt (1982) was one of the earliest proponents of a reader-response theory. She stated:

> Reading is a transaction, a two-way process, involving a reader and a text at a particular time under particular circumstances. . . . The reader, bringing past experiences of language and of the world to the task, sets up tentative notions of a subject, of some framework into which to fit the ideas as the words unfurl. If the subsequent words do not fit into the framework, it may have to be revised, thus opening up new and further possibilities for the text that follows. This implies a constant series of selections

from the multiple possibilities offered by the text and their synthesis into an organized meaning (Rosenblatt, 1982, page 268).

Rosenblatt took her analysis of reading one step further into implications for classroom literature discussions. In any "reading event," the reader adopts one of two stances: the *efferent stance* or the *aesthetic stance*.

When a reader approaches a reading event with an *efferent stance*, attention is focused on accumulating what is to be carried away from the reading. Readers using this stance may be seeking information, such as in a textbook; they may want directions for action, as in a driver's manual; or they may be seeking a logical conclusion, as in a political article. In an *aesthetic stance*, however, readers shift their attention inward to center on *what is being created during the reading*. Reading is driven by personal feelings, ideas, and attitudes that are stirred up by the text.

In most reading situations, there is both an efferent and aesthetic response to the text. In reading a newspaper article, for example, a reader may take a predominantly efferent stance. But there may be an accompanying feeling of acceptance or doubt about the evidence cited. Although one stance usually predominates over the other in most reading events, the text itself does not dictate a reader's stance. A text is chosen because it satisfies a reader's intended purpose. Rosenblatt's description of what happens in predominately aesthetic reading situations holds direct implications for bringing children and literature together:

> In aesthetic reading, we respond to the very story or poem that we are evoking during the transaction with the text. In order to shape the work, we draw on our reservoir of past experience with people and the world, our past inner linkage of words and things, our past encounters with spoken or written texts. We listen to the sound of the words in the inner ear; we lend our sensations, our emotions, our sense of being alive, to the new experience which, we feel, corresponds to the text. We participate in the story, we identify with the characters, we share their conflicts and their feelings (Rosenblatt, 1982, page 270).

How can teachers encourage aesthetic response to literature?

Implications for Aesthetic Reading

There are several general implications of a reader-response theory for teaching literature.

1. Present texts that clearly satisfy either the efferent stance of gaining information or the aesthetic stance of living through the literary experience.

2. Nurture aesthetic responses to literature over the more commonly promoted efferent responses.

3. Encourage students to pay attention to their feelings and moods as they read or listen to literature.

4. Have students continue the focus of what has been seen, heard, and/or felt by providing opportunities for various forms of expression such as dramatics,

movement, drawing, and painting. These activities allow children to express what caught their attention and stirred either pleasant or unpleasant reactions.

5. Encourage students to respond verbally to the text, but refrain from "testing" students or having them come up with the right answer. Rather, teachers need to guide students back to personal experiences and specific parts of the text to support their reactions.

6. Expect and encourage variation in response to stories and poems. Teachers can have children express personal interpretations of stories or poems. Then children can tell how they arrived at their personal interpretations.

7. Provide students with many experiences in the way authors use characterization or metaphor. Only after many such experiences do teachers need to give students the technical labels "characterization" and "metaphor" to use in their book discussions.

Book-sharing talks are a great way to enhance aesthetic responses to literature. Questioning strategies follow naturally after children have read a story or poem or listened to literature. The following strategies encourage individual responses.

1. Depending on the text, ask questions such as, "Did anything especially interest you? Frighten you? Puzzle you? Seem familiar? Weird?" Have children tell which parts of the text caused these reactions and have them compare these experiences of their real life experiences (Rosenblatt, page 276).

2. Have children tell about the most memorable incident, character, or setting of the book. Children share with each other the specific parts of the text they recalled most clearly after hearing or reading a story (Benton, 1984, pages 268–269).

3. Ask students to tell about the part of the story or character they remember most vividly. Ask, "How did the character(s) feel in this part of the story? Have you ever felt like this? Describe the situation you were in."

4. Read the opening of a story. Immediately afterward tell students to jot down what was going on in their heads—pictures, memories, thoughts—during the reading. The jottings should be in "stream of consciousness" style. Then share the responses and distinguish the common responses from the idosyncratic ones. This shows students that reading has shared elements as well as highly individual ones and that sharing reactions is a valid way of talking about literature (Benton, 1984, page 269).

5. Ask students, "What pictures do you get in your mind's eye of this character, setting, or event? If character X were to come through the door now, what would he/she look like? If you went to the place where the story occurred (setting), what would you see? Why do you say so?"

6. Ask, "What do you feel about this character? This setting? This event? Why?"

7. Ask, "What opinions do you have of this character? Setting? Incident? The way the story was told? Why?"

Using Creative Expression to Respond to Literature. Drama, painting, writing, and drawing are other media through which children can express their reactions in response to literature. Caution is needed, however, to guard against their expending so much time and energy that the "response" to the literature is secondary in importance to the art created by the students. The purpose of creative extension activities should be to draw out the affective response or to further the understanding of the piece of literature.

Improvisation or Dramatics. One very effective way to get children to "live through" a story or part of a story is for them to role play characters in a story. There is evidence that role playing or dramatizations of stories can enhance vocabulary development, reading comprehension, and self-concept (Yawkey, 1980; Pellegrini and Galda, 1982). As children use and experiment with language, their vocabulary expands. Comprehension is developed through the active reconstruction of a story, which brings the characters, setting, and plot from the written page into the minds of the children. The nonjudgmental nature of dramatics makes it enjoyable and can often lead to enhancement in children's self-concepts.

Students assume the character's attitude and view of the world when they role play, choosing a whole story or part of a story they "remembered the most." In role playing children share what specific characters would say, how they would sound, how they would move, and what facial expressions they would have. Children doing the role playing should be the primary decision makers in how the scene should be dramatized. Emphasize to children that more than one interpretation is acceptable. Extreme conflicts in interpretations can be resolved by having students go back to the printed story to support the way they interpreted the story.

Preparing plays for public performance means repeated enactments of the same story and has limited value for developing text comprehension or for encouraging individual reactions to literature. It is probably better to have children improvise or role play many stories than to prepare one story for a public performance.

Visual Arts. There are many ways that children can respond to literature using the many mediums of visual arts—pencil drawings, chalk, crayons, paint, cardboard and paper construction. Teachers frequently have students design book jackets, mobiles, posters, comic strips, or diagrams that illustrate various parts of the story. Often such artwork can be displayed in the classroom to advertise specific books to classmates.

Writing. Besides responding to literature through discussion, dramatizations, and the visual arts, another important way to respond to literature is through writing (discussed in detail in Chapter 5). Writing and the other activities just mentioned bring out differing individual responses and interpretations. In each of the activities we've described, teachers do not believe there is "one right way of responding." Rather, they encourage individual responses to literature and help children connect these to life experiences.

It doesn't take a special teacher to share the richness of children's books with students. However, bringing children and books together requires specific knowledge, skills, and attitudes on the part of the teacher.

Our emphasis in this chapter has been on some of the information, talents, and attitudes that teachers need to create a community of readers. As Rose (1982) acknowledged, "The teacher who wishes to discover the joys of literature must make an emotional commitment as well as an intellectual one" (page 261). We couldn't agree more. Our strong conviction is that teachers of reading—whether in a classroom, resource room, or clinic—pursue the study of children's literature not only during their preservice preparation but also throughout their professional development.

SUMMARY

Immersing children in literature, connecting them with all kinds of books, is a primary goal of reading instruction. We offered a variety of ways in this chapter for teachers to develop students who will choose to read. Specific suggestions for getting students "into reading" were organized into three main areas: immersing students in literature; using instructional time to show the value of reading; and helping students find and share books they want to read.

We considered how teachers, through careful structuring of the classroom environment and selecting a collection of books, can create settings in which children will be involved with literature. Reading aloud, story-telling techniques, and book sharing can result in children reading more in the classroom. To this end, sustained silent reading is critical. For students to enjoy reading and seek it, they need to participate in structured silent reading during regular class time. Rather than offer a few suggestions for implementing SSR, we have presented a comprehensive action plan to incorporate free reading time into the elementary classroom routine.

Finally, we explored ways to help students respond aesthetically to literature. Aesthetic reading helps children participate emotionally in the story, identify with characters, and respond personally to the literary selection.

THE WORKSHOP

In the Classroom

1. Below is a partial list of behaviors often associated with avid reading. Avid readers:

   empathize with characters;
   are enthusiastic about books;
   talk about books with their friends and share their reactions and feelings.

   In small groups, brainstorm additional characterisitics associated with avid readers and then discuss ways in which you would help children develop the kinds of habits and behaviors leading to avid reading.

2. Prepare a story and tell it to several members of the reading class. Follow the

suggestions in this chapter for storytelling preparation. Then, in the field, tell the same story to a group of children. How were the reactions of the two groups similar? How were they different?

3. Examine several children's magazines. How appropriate are they? What appear to be the objectives and content of the magazines? Would you use them for teaching purposes? Explain.

4. Prepare and give a book talk that would motivate others in your class. Report on the experience.

In the Field

1. Interview several elementary school librarians. In what ways do they support the reading development of children and assist the classroom teacher? Compile their ideas and report your findings to the class.

2. Choose a literature selection to read to a group of children. Decide how you will introduce the selection, whether you will discuss the book intermittently as you read it, or whether you will have a discussion at the conclusion of the reading. Also consider how you will lead the discussion. How will you engage children in responding to the selection? Then follow through with the experience. How did the planning match what actually happened during the instructional experience? What changes, if any, did you make as you put the plan into practice?

3. Work with a group of children and guide them in dramatizing a story after they have read it or heard it read aloud to them. The selection could be from either a basal reader or a trade book.

4. Prepare an inventory designed to examine attitudes and/or interests in reading (or use an inventory suggested by your instructor). Administer the inventory individually to several children. Compare their interests and attitudes. Could you have predicted their responses?

5. Collaborate with a classroom teacher to set up a book display that would interest children to read. Use a general theme and introduce some of the books to children. Observe what happens and make notes on the experience.

6. Interview both a primary- and an upper-grade teacher who use SSR regularly. Use the questions below and/or devise questions of your own. Then compare interview responses with those of your classmates.
   a. How often do you conduct SSR?
   b. How do you think your students benefit from SSR?
   c. Can you think of an instance in which specific children have changed in their behavior over a period of time from participating in SSR? Describe the change.
   d. Have you seen any changes in the behavior of restless, reluctant readers over a period of time?
   e. Does your principal or other school personnel participate in SSR? If so, what effect do you think this has?

Chapter 10

Basal Readers and Instructional Materials

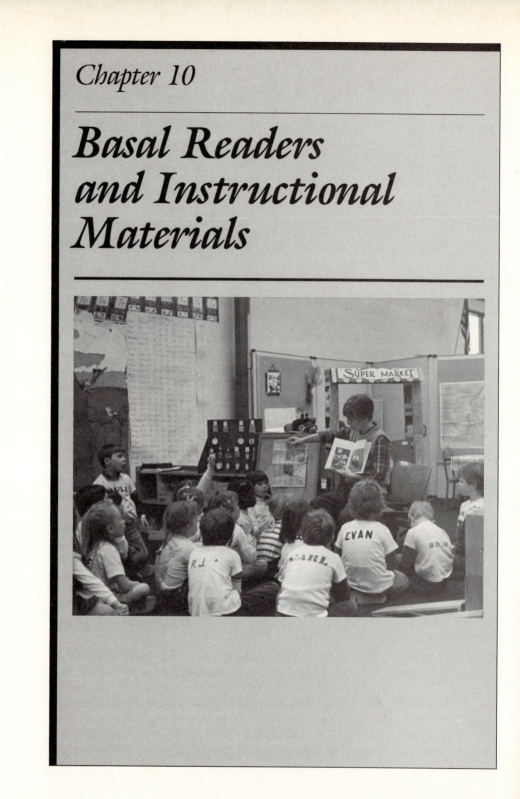

When we think back to our early years in elementary school certain images come to mind: carrying a lunch box, running on the school playground, lining up in alphabetical order, opening our reading book to the right page. Some images, especially those from childhood, stay with us for a long time. As you read this chapter on basal readers and other materials used in reading instruction, you may rediscover some memories from your own elementary classroom experiences. While the terminology may be unfamiliar, the materials lend themselves to basic and thorough descriptions. The chapter integrates many figures and examples, illustrating the pervasive role played by instructional materials. Yet we stress that materials, including basal reading programs, are only the vehicles for instruction. Someone needs to sit in the driver's seat, have a clear route in mind, and take control of the vehicle. That someone is the classroom teacher.

What is my reading program? Well, we use Scott, Foresman.

Betty, a third-grade teacher

There's not enough time to cover everything we're supposed to in one school year.

Joan, a fourth-grade teacher

We purchased a reading series last year and now my teachers are telling me they need supplementary reading materials. What do you suggest?

Lou Herman, an elementary school principal

Our program is complete. It has quality literature selections, total sequential skill development, review and testing, comprehension emphasis, language experience extension lessons. You name it, we have it.

Ann, a sales representative

I'm in the top reading group. We're almost through with our book—the green one with the purple spaceship on it.

Eric, a third-grade student

By far the most popular and widely used kind of material for reading instruction in this country is the *basal reading program*. It has come to be a catchall term, a referent in most discussions about a child's progress and development in reading. Eric, the third-grader above who asserted that he is in the "top group," his parents, and his teacher all know he is doing well in reading. Eric and his counterparts are in the "green book," which signifies that they are in the high achieving group. The students read stories from it, practice skills in a workbook that accompanies it, and (more than likely) bring home a stack of corrected dittos weekly.

Understanding basal reading programs is an important part of understanding and teaching reading. Not only are these programs what most children and parents think about in relation to reading instruction, they are what many *teachers* think of as *the* reading program. Betty, a third-grade teacher, named a particular basal series when asked to describe her reading program. Such a response is more the rule than the exception. Teachers continually reaffirm the importance of basal reading programs. Yet these same teachers have implicit theories about reading, and by the very nature of their job make hundreds of decisions daily about reading instruction in their classrooms.

We cannot dismiss the fact that more than 90 percent of elementary classrooms in this nation contain basal readers. As a consequence, we devote half of this chapter to basal reading programs because, ". . . it is logical that anyone proposing to teach reading in any elementary grade will be better prepared to do so if s/he has a good understanding of those instructional materials (basal reading) and how they are designed to help in the teaching of reading" (Aukerman, 1981, page 2).

While it may be logical to understand basal reading programs—how they can work for you in the classroom—teachers should aim for perspective.

In the first half of this chapter we examine basal reading programs and the instructional concepts that have come to be associated with them. How long have basal readers been used in classrooms? How have they changed over the years? Because the basal programs published today are considered comprehensive, it is essential to study their rationale, organization, components, and lesson frameworks. Most importantly, it is necessary to reflect on how one's beliefs about reading can help the teacher plan or modify lessons in the basal program.

Ironically, the pervasive use of basal readers has not put an end to the problem of insufficient supplementary materials. Principals such as Lou Herman purchase a reading program and sometimes discover they don't have enough materials for students who want to *read*. This reveals two basic lessons regarding materials for reading instruction: (1) supplementary materials are perceived as important to the reading program; and (2) what some teachers think of as supplemental may be the heart of instruction to other teachers, and vice versa.

Hence we devote the other half of this chapter to an analysis of instructional materials, beginning with the *types* of materials available. We will determine how different types of materials correspond to our *belief systems*. Then trends that influence selection of curriculum materials at the district level and current issues will be examined. Several ways of evaluating and selecting commercial materials for classroom use will be suggested. Finally, we'll look into the development of successful teacher-made materials.

HISTORICAL BACKGROUND

Young newspaper readers in the greater Cleveland area were treated to a historical tour of their basal reading books in a news article written especially for elementary-age students and featuring "McGuffey and His Readers." Pictures of William McGuffey, his birthplace, and his writing desk accompanied an actual page reproduction with a story about Bess and her two goats from Lesson XXXIII in the *McGuffey Primer*, the very first book in a series used for reading instruction.

Here's how basal readers were described in the news article so that children could understand what they are all about:

There are many different kinds of basal texts.

How and when words are introduced are carefully planned by experts.

The books come in a series.

The words and stories get longer and harder as the child moves from one level to the next.

Moreover, children were informed that McGuffey first published his series in 1836 and that the readers began with the *Primer* and ended with the *Sixth Reader*. As far as the content of the basal readers was concerned, stories were about everyday life and the rewards of good behavior. Does the content sound somewhat familiar? It should. According to a study by Aaron and Anderson (1981), a remarkable number of values appearing in the readers of the early 1900s appear in today's basals. Although the stories may have changed, Aaron and Anderson acknowledge that "the same virtues are there waiting to be taught" (page 312).

Just as the young Cleveland readers found insightful differences and similarities between their reading material today and the *McGuffey Readers*, teachers also benefit from such comparisons (see Figure 10.1).

1683: A Strong Bottom-Up Approach

The New England Primer, published for American colonists in the late 1600s, followed a rather strong bottom-up model of instruction. The alphabet was taught

---

28   *SECOND READER.*   *SECOND READER.*   29

LESSON XV.

drĕss	hĕard	ŭn′-cle	her-sĕlf′
knīfe	wĭshed	lăd′-der	stō′-ries
wrŏng	strānge	fĭn′-ger	lŏŏk′-ing

WILLIE'S STORY.

One day, when Willie had been reading in his new book, his mother wished him to tell her what he had read in it, and Willie said :

"I read about a little girl who wanted to do just as she liked for one whole day.

"Her mother said she could. So the little girl cut her own bread and butter; but she let the knife slip, and cut her finger.

"Then she ate so much candy that she made herself sick. Then she put on her prettiest dress to play in the garden, and tore it.

"And then she went up a ladder, which her mother never would let her climb, and when she was up very high she heard a noise in the garden.

"It was the dog barking at a strange cat, mamma; and while the little girl was looking around to see what it was, she put her foot on the wrong part of the ladder.

"I mean, mamma, she only put her toe on the round; so her foot slipped, and she fell, and was almost killed.

"That was the end of her day of doing just as she liked."

Write a sentence having in it the word knife.
Write a sentence having in it the word ladder.

Figure 10.1   **Sample Pages from the *Appleton Reader*, 1878** *(From Appleton,* The Second Reader *[New York: American Book Company, 1878].)*

first; then vowels, consonants, double letters, italics and capitals, syllables, and so on were presented for instruction, in that order. There was, however, no such thing as a "controlled vocabulary." Words were not introduced systematically in basal readers until the mid-1800s. Colonial children might meet anywhere from twenty to one hundred new words on one page!

By the mid-1800s, the "word method," silent reading, and reading to get information from content were introduced in basals. The classics, fairy tales, and literature by American authors became the first supplementary reading materials. Colored pictures, attention to children's interests, and the teacher's manual all appeared by the 1920s. It was then that the "work-pad" was used for "seat work" and skills practice in grades one through three.

Basal Readers as We Knew Them

The reading series used in schools in the 1980s are a far cry, both in appearance and substance, from the first readers. Nevertheless, current readers retain many features that were considered at one time or another innovative. Basal reading series have grown noticeably in size and in price. While not necessarily prescribing the bottom-up teaching approach that was used in the 1600s, today's teacher's manual presents a much more serious dilemma for classroom teachers: It often purports to include everything that any teacher will ever need to teach reading.

Publishing companies began to expand and add to their basal reading programs many new components or features around 1925. The "pre-primer," for example, was added to the basal program to introduce beginning readers to the series and build a beginning reading vocabulary (words recognized at sight). Inside illustrations and outside covers also became increasingly colorful. Word lists such as Thorndike's became the standard for choosing vocabulary for the readers.

As the major author for the Scott, Foresman program, William S. Gray was probably responsible for much of the structure associated with the reading instruction that we experienced as children. Workbooks accompanied our reader. First, we worked on skills; then we read for enjoyment. Each book had a different title and much of the story content was supposed to be "realistic" narrative. Whether it was, or is, realistic content is an issue publishers and classroom teachers continue to deal with in this decade.

As the concept of reading readiness became more popular, teachers' manuals contained more detail and readiness books provided opportunities to practice prerequisite skills. One pre-primer multiplied to two, three, or even four pre-primers.

Bottom-up instruction in basal reading programs today depends in part on strict adherence to the scope and sequence of reading skills (see Figures 10.2 and 10.3). This terminology evolved from the 1948 *Ginn Basic Reader's* objective to provide a "vertical" arrangement of skill development and to ensure continuity in skill development (Smith, 1965, page 285). Teachers' editions were keyed to the children's books, and diagnostic and achievement tests such as those in the *Sheldon Basic Reading Series* were developed. Clearly, basal reading programs had become

Scope and Sequence

Module	Language Experience	Comprehension	Vocabulary	Study
1	Exploring entertainment	**C3b-d** Recognizing whole-part relationships: topic, main idea, details (D) **C10c** Recognizing elements of fiction: setting (D) **C13a** Recognizing author's intent: entertain (D) **C8d** Recognizing forms of literature: play (D) **C5a** Recognizing causal relationships: cause and effect (D) **C6b** Recognizing comparative relationships: classifying (D)	**Meanings** (S20b Using library resources: dictionary entries) (D) **Root words** (W74, 75 Recognizing prefixes and suffixes) (D) **Root words** (W75, 80a Recognizing suffixes; recognizing when a final letter **e** is dropped before a suffix beginning with a vowel letter) (D)	**S20b** Using library resources: reference materials (D)
Evaluation		**C5a** Recognizing causal relationships: cause and effect (E) **C6b** Recognizing comparative relationships: classifying (E)	**Root words** (W74, 75 Recognizing prefixes and suffixes) (E)	
2	Discussing story settings	**C10c** Recognizing elements of fiction: setting (R) **C5b** Recognizing causal relationships: predicting outcomes (D)	**Word history** (S20b Using library resources: dictionary entries) (D) **Prefixes** (S20b Using library resources: dictionary entries) (D)	**S21a** Using graphic aids: maps (D)
Evaluation		**C10c** Recognizing elements of fiction: setting (E) **C5b** Recognizing causal relationships: predicting outcomes (E)	**Root words** (S20b Using library resources: dictionary entries) (E)	
3	Classifying pictures of people	**C4b** Recognizing sequential relationships: ideas and events (D) (R) **C15** Making inferences: conclusions (D) **C5b** Recognizing causal relationships: predicting outcomes (M) **C6b** Recognizing comparative relationships: classifying (M) **C15** Making inferences: judgments (R)	**Synonyms** (C1c Using context clues: synonym) (D) (R) **Root words** (W74, 75 Recognizing prefixes and suffixes) (M) **Meanings** (S20b Using library resources: dictionary entries) (R)	**S22b** Organizing information: summarizing (D)
Evaluation		**C4b** Recognizing sequential relationships: ideas and events (E) **C15** Making inferences: judgments (E)	**Synonyms** (C1c Using context clues: synonym) (E)	
4	Discussing the *Odyssey* and the Olympic games	**C6b** Recognizing comparative relationships: classifying (M) **C13b** Recognizing author's intent: inform (D) **C10d** Recognizing elements of fiction: theme (D) **C10a** Recognizing elements of fiction: plot (D)	**Meanings** (S20b Using library resources: dictionary entries) (R) **Synonyms** (C1c Using context clues: synonym) (M)	**S20a** Using library resources: card catalog (D)
Evaluation		**C10d** Recognizing elements of fiction: theme (E) **C10a** Recognizing elements of fiction: plot (E)	**Synonyms** (C1c Using context clues: synonym) (E)	
5	A Checkpoint Module	**C5a** Recognizing causal relationships: cause and effect (E) **C10c** Recognizing elements of fiction: setting (E) **C4b** Recognizing sequential relationships: ideas and events (E) **C6b** Recognizing comparative relationships: classifying (E)	**Root words** (W74, 75 Recognizing prefixes and suffixes) (E)	

Figure 10.2   Scope and Sequence Chart *(From* Winterfall Teacher's Resource Book, *Level 16, Keytext Program [Indianapolis: Economy, 1984], p. xxii.)*

Key to Objectives

○ Exposure prior to major instruction
★ First level of major instruction
△ Subsequent instruction/expansion

□ Maintenance
T Tested in Section Test only
i Tested in a Section Test and the End-of-Book Test
✔ Activities to develop language skills

Level	K	1	2	3	4	5	6	7	8	9	10	11	12	13
Grade	K	R	PP	P	1	2^1	2^2	3^1	3^2	4	5	6	7	8
ld(could), lk(walk), mb(comb)							T★	△	△	□	□	□	□	□
Double ll,nn,rr,ss,zz				T★	T△	△	△	△	△	□	□	□	□	□
Internal						T★	T△	T△	△	T△	T△	T△	△	△
Consonant blends			T★	T△	T△	△	△	△	□	□	□	□	□	□
Initial			T★	T△	T△	△	△	△	□	□	□	□	□	□
Final				T★	T△	△	△	△	□	□	□	□	□	□
Consonant digraphs			T★	T△	T△	△	△	△	□	□	□	□	□	□
Initial (ch,sh,th,wh)			T★	T△	△	△	△	△	□	□	□	□	□	□
Final (ch,sh,th)			○	T★	T△	△	△	△	□	□	□	□	□	□
Phonograms			T★	T△	T△	□	□	□	□	□	□	□	□	□
-un,-at,-an,-et,-ame,-ide,-ick,-op			T★	□	□	□	□	□	□	□	□	□	□	□
-ail,-ose,-ake,-ing			T★	△	□	□	□	□	□	□	□	□	□	□
-eep,-oat				T★	□	□	□	□	□	□	□	□	□	□
-ark,-orn					T★	□	□	□	□	□	□	□	□	□
Uses initial consonant substitution			T★	T△	T△	□	□	□	□	□	□	□	□	□
Vowels														
Short			○	T★	T△	△	△	△	△	□	□	□	□	□
a(had), i(pick), o(got)			○	T★	△	△	△	△	△	□	□	□	□	□
e(let), u(bug)			○	○	T★	△	△	△	△	□	□	□	□	□
Long			○	T★	T△	T△	T△	△	△	□	□	□	□	□
a-e(made), i-e(time), o-e(rope)			○	T★	△	△	△	△	△	□	□	□	□	□
ai(main), ay(hay), e-e(these), ea(eat, please), ee(feed, cheese), oa(toad), u-e(tune)						T★	△	△	△	△	□	□	□	□
e(she), y(by), o(go)							T★	△	△	□	□	□	□	□
ie(tie), oe(toe), ue(true)								T★	△	△	□	□	□	□
Controlled by r					○	T★	△	△	△	□	□	□	□	□
a(dark), e(her), i(girl), o(for), u(turn)						○	T★	△	△	□	□	□	□	□
Less common							T★	T△	T△	T△	□	□	□	□
ea(head), ai (said)							T★	△	△	△	□	□	□	□
i(child), igh(night), o(old)								T★	T△	□	□	□	□	□
oi(oil), ou(out, bought), oy(boy)							T★	△	△	□	□	□	□	□
oo(room, stood), ow(town, show)								T★	△	□	□	□	□	□
au(laugh, caught)								T★	□	□	□	□	□	□

Figure 10.3 Program Scope and Sequence Chart *(From* Sky Climbers, *Level 10, teacher's ed. [Glenview, Ill.: Scott, Foresman, 1985], p. T28.)*

more sophisticated and, to many teachers, *unwieldy*. How would they manage the basal reading program?

Until the 1960s, books in reading series were arranged according to grade placement. Grades turned into levels (anywhere from fifteen to twenty) or, as it became known, the management system. By the 1970s, teachers and curriculum committees in general sought clarification about levels in relation to grades. As a result, publishers now use the term *level* and cross-reference this with its traditional grade equivalent.

As can be seen in Table 10.1, there is more than one level (and book) per grade. Guidelines suggested to help decide at what level book to place pupils entering the program are pupil placement tests and an informal tryout of a book using a one hundred-word selection.

Management systems became necessary when publishers significantly over-hauled their reading series in the 1970s. The majority of textbook publishers added new components, particularly in the area of assessment, such as pre- and post-skill tests, section tests, and end-of-book tests.

The Dick, Jerry, Jane, and Alice that some of us grew up with in the 1940s, 1950s, or 1960s are now part of the past. Today's basal is much more difficult to *label* or categorize with any degree of reliability as was the practice a few years ago. For example, it was not uncommon to have overheard one teacher telling

TABLE 10.1

Scott, Foresman Reading Texts (as of 1985)

Grade	Book	Level
K	*Rise and Shine*	K
1	*Away We Go*	1
	Taking Off	2A
	Going Up	2B
	On Our Own	2C
	Hang On to Your Hat	3
	Kick Up Your Heels	4
2	*Rainbow Shower*	5
	Crystal Kingdom	6
3	*Hidden Wonders*	7
	Golden Secrets	8
4	*Sea Treasures*	9
5	*Sky Climbers*	10
6	*Star Flight*	11
7	*Sun Spray*	12
8	*Moon Canyon*	13

another at a convention book exhibit, "We don't use *Open Court* because it has so little comprehension," or "Harcourt Brace Jovanovich texts are too difficult for our slower readers who need more word-attack work." These remarks seem woefully simplistic to anyone who has had the opportunity to examine and use the latest reading programs. While it's still possible to claim that one program places more emphasis on one area (phonics) over another (comprehension), it's almost impossible to find a reading series that minimizes either.

Sales representatives for basal publishing companies, such as Ann quoted at the chapter's beginning, make large claims for their new programs. Let's find out what these current reading series cover that was advertised in the words of one publisher, "as basic as the sunshine, blue sky, and rainbow."

BASAL PROGRAMS OF THE EIGHTIES

One adjective used over and over to describe basal reading programs through the years is "comprehensive." It still applies.

Most reading series on the market today attempt to satisfy every consumer's appetite when it comes to reading instruction. In order to do that, publishing companies take great care to include certain major components.

Before we look closer at basal reading series and discuss their major components, we should understand several concepts germane to basal instruction.

The terms in Box 10.1 will vary from one series to the next, but it is safe to say that certain components will be found in most programs. Briefly overview some of the major components that are part of almost every basal series.

1. *The readiness program.* Storybooks and workbooks are designed to introduce and develop basic concepts in language, letter-sound relationships, sense of context, following directions, and listening comprehension. *Series r* kindergarten readiness program (Macmillan Publishing Company, 1986), for example, provides numerous preparation materials for kindergarten and first-grade children. In its kindergarten package of supplementary materials, it features: two sets of *Skills Practice Masters; Extra! Books* (independent activities in a magazine format); *ABC Cards*; six *Pick 'n' Play* packs (manipulative materials); *Solo Class Library for Kindergarten* (softcover literature) and *Teacher's Editions for Starting Out*; and *Make Your Mark* (student readers). The readiness programs of all of the major basal series include similar features as well as beginning picture books for children to use some of their readiness skills to interpret pictures.

2. *Pre-primer and primer levels.* New basic sight words are introduced; high-frequency sight words accumulate. Vocabulary and readability are controlled, and experience charts are used to help word recognition. Traditionally, an eclectic phonics approach is favored (sight words, phonic analysis, context analysis, and structural analysis). As many as six levels may be completed by children at the end of the first grade.

BOX 10.1

The Language of Basal Instruction:
Terms Associated with Basal Reading Programs

CODE EMPHASIS

The emphasis of programs from the beginning is on decoding. The content and sequence in teaching sound symbol correspondence is controlled so children can learn quickly how to transform unfamiliar printed words into speech.

CONTINUOUS PROGRESS

Teachers are encouraged to teach students at their reading levels, not necessarily at their grade levels. The instructional materials in a series are prepared for approximately seventeen to twenty levels ranging from readiness materials in kindergarten and first grade to advanced reading materials in seventh and eighth grades. Instead of using one reader in each grade, students may be working in different readers at different levels in the same classroom.

CONTROLLED VOCABULARY

The number of "new" words that students encounter in each reading lesson is controlled. Three ways in which publishing companies control vocabulary in their reading program are: (1) Many high-interest words are used first, followed by the introduction of more abstract words; (2) high-frequency words appear in the beginning, with low-frequency words gradually inserted in the text; (3) words that follow regular spelling patterns are used first, then words with some irregular spelling patterns are used. Words introduced in lower level readers are repeated often in subsequent readers.

CRITERION-REFERENCED TESTS

Informal tests devised by either the publishing company or teacher to measure individual student attainment in skills associated with phonics, vocabulary, and comprehension. The teacher sets the criterion (e.g., 8/10) for adequate performance. The purpose is to assess a reader's performance, regardless of how that performance compares to others taking the same test.

EXTENSION or EXTENDED READING

After the story is read and main parts of the suggested lesson framework are completed, many teachers continue the lesson by using additional activities. Art, music, and writing are

EXTENSION or EXTENDED READING (*cont.*)	catalysts to extend ideas and concepts initiated during the lesson. Questioning at the interpretive and applied levels extends comprehension through group discussion.
INSTRUCTIONAL AIDS	Charts, workbooks, ditto masters, skill-packs, cards, game boxes, and so on are available at various levels of reading series. They are intended to help teachers who are too busy to make their own instructional devices.
LEVELS	Each level provides a sequential arrangement of student books (readers), teacher's editions, and ancillary materials and is built upon those that come before it; each corresponds to grade levels. This ensures more than one book for most grade levels and makes "continuous progress" possible.
MANAGEMENT	The testing program provides teachers with a system to arrange or manage the placement of pupils in different levels of the program. Tests also help identify skills that students need to acquire or strengthen. In addition, tests may indicate that students have mastered skills at one level and should proceed to the next level. Management combines two major elements: behavioral objectives and criterion-referenced tests.
MEANING EMPHASIS	Programs in which reading is taught as a communication process rather than as a series of subskills. They emphasize comprehension more than decoding skills, providing for a variety of word identification methods in different combinations. Meaningfulness of the story content, meaningful ways for children to respond, and integration of language arts activities are some obvious features of this emphasis.
PRIMER	Commonly used in the first grade, this is the book given to children before their first reader.
REINFORCEMENT	To ensure that skills have been learned, exercises involving similar and contrasting examples are used to reinforce the learning. This re-teaching cycle includes the use of extension activities. *(Box continues)*

BOX 10.1 (*Continued*)

The Language of Basal Instruction:
Terms Associated with Basal Reading Programs

SCOPE AND SEQUENCE	This refers to the general plan in basal reading programs for the introduction of skills in a sequential or vertical arrangement and with expanding or horizontally conceptualized reinforcement. Students move up through the levels and across within each level. (See Figures 10.2 and 10.3.)
SKILL BUILDING	Skills (e.g., basic sight vocabulary, conceptual development, listening facility, comprehension) are not presented only once. They are introduced at one level, then repeated and reinforced at subsequent levels with increasing depth. Instruction begins with simpler subskills and follows this design: introduction of a skill, reinforcement of the skill, and review of the skill.
SKILL MAINTENANCE	Recently learned skills are reviewed as necessary to form the base for new learning to occur.
STRANDS	Areas of skills that are developed at increasingly higher levels throughout the program are grouped into strands. Some popular strands of instruction are word identification, vocabulary development, comprehension, reading/study skills, and language arts.
VOCABULARY DEVELOPMENT	To assist children in becoming skillful readers, teachers work to increase students' vocabularies. In order to develop a large number of sight words, new words are introduced, repeated often in the text selections, and more new words are introduced. Phonics and other word analysis skills and meaning-getting strategies using context are employed to continue vocabulary development.
WHOLE WORD METHOD	Words, rather than letters or syllables, are the main instructional unit. Teachers work on the recognition of words, not on sounding out the words.
WORKBOOKS	Children practice reading skills in workbooks that supplement lessons in the text with independent activities. Their purpose is to reinforce skills and concepts that teachers have already taught during the lesson framework with the reader.

3. *Word identification strand.* Skill lessons are provided to teach sight vocabulary and phonics, structural analysis, and the use of context. Students are exposed to new skills, systematically and sequentially, and are tested on them for mastery. Skills may then be retaught and reinforced through additional skill exercises. Some basals, however, do *not* connect the topics of stories in the readers with the word identification program.

4. *Comprehension strand.* Beginning at the early levels, most basal series set specific objectives for comprehension instruction. There are numerous comprehension questions, usually following a routine that continues throughout the book. Questions typically inquire into purpose, motives and acts of main characters, recall of details, and vocabulary usage. There is an effort to incorporate three levels or types of comprehension, from literal to interpretive to critical (especially in the intermediate and upper levels). This decade has brought an increase in questions that encourage prediction making.

5. *Literature.* Science fiction, plays, biographies, short stories, poem, fables, and informational articles are just some of the wide array of literary forms in basal series. Well-known authors have been hired to write stories for several series. Some publishing companies have adapted classic material—a practice criticized by those who prefer leaving the original version intact. The interests of young readers appear to be taken into account (Pieronek, 1980). Animal characters are still popular; they sometimes play subtle roles in the development of children's attitudes toward reading. For example, in an analysis of 170 basal characters portrayed as readers (Snyder, 1979), animals were depicted reading more often than were women!

6. *Language arts.* Listening, writing, composing, grammar, spelling, punctuation, dictionary work, library work, dramatization, and so forth are found in basal programs. These features sometimes appear in connection with another component; for example, a writing assignment accompanies a reading comprehension lesson. Frequently, language arts activities are suggested under enrichment or extension. There may be separate "language" exercises; language development may also be a separate strand. Many basal series combine reading and language enrichment activities in their upper level books.

7. *Management.* According to Aukerman (1981), management programs are an outgrowth of mastery learning and continuous progress curricula. In addition to teacher's manuals, there are many tests, record-keeping aids, in-service training materials, and even letters to parents accompanying complete reading programs. Essentially, these kinds of program components attempt to evaluate children's progress in reading skill development. The teaching method, outlined in the teacher's edition and illustrated in Figure 10.4, is part of this system along with pacing (day-to-day) and time management (pupil text sections matching quarters of the school year).

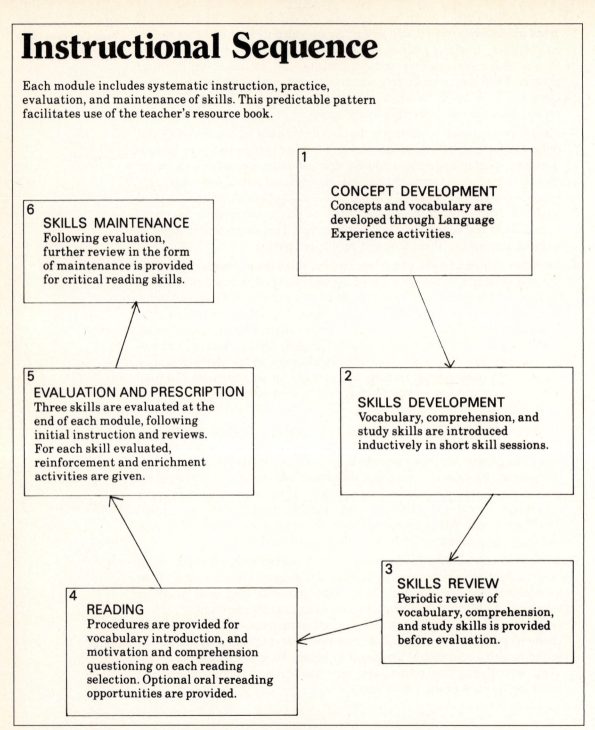

Instructional Sequence

Each module includes systematic instruction, practice, evaluation, and maintenance of skills. This predictable pattern facilitates use of the teacher's resource book.

1
CONCEPT DEVELOPMENT
Concepts and vocabulary are developed through Language Experience activities.

6
SKILLS MAINTENANCE
Following evaluation, further review in the form of maintenance is provided for critical reading skills.

5
EVALUATION AND PRESCRIPTION
Three skills are evaluated at the end of each module, following initial instruction and reviews. For each skill evaluated, reinforcement and enrichment activities are given.

2
SKILLS DEVELOPMENT
Vocabulary, comprehension, and study skills are introduced inductively in short skill sessions.

4
READING
Procedures are provided for vocabulary introduction, and motivation and comprehension questioning on each reading selection. Optional oral rereading opportunities are provided.

3
SKILLS REVIEW
Periodic review of vocabulary, comprehension, and study skills is provided before evaluation.

Figure 10.4   Example of Teaching Method *(From* Winterfall Teacher's Resource Book, *Keytext Program [Indianapolis: Economy, 1984], p. xii.)*

CHARACTERISTICS OF BASAL READERS

More significant than similarities and differences among basal reading programs are the improvements in certain components. The overall physical appearance, literary variety, and reduction of stereotyping deserve special recognition. Other components have become more complex, or thorough, depending on one's viewpoint.

Appearance

Pupil books, teachers' editions (often spiral-bound), supplementary paperbacks, workbooks, duplicating masters, activity books, self-correcting boxed materials, filmstrips, and phonics picture cards are just some of the physical components now available. Many hard-cover pupil readers are identical in cover design and title to the corresponding workbook at that level.

The richness in color and boldness of design are one evidence of publishers' huge monetary investment. It's easy to understand evaluations such as this one written by a graduate student majoring in reading education:

> The attractive appearance, organization, and design of the texts invite children to read and contribute to their motivation. The stunning and delightful illustrations are of high quality, representing a variety of art styles and techniques. The paper, printing and binding are of quality and durability. Illustrations reflect the pluralistic character and culture of the American people.

Illustrations

Illustrations reveal an important growth in the qualilty of basal reading material. One trend is the use of the actual illustrations as reproduced from the original children's literature selection. Many companies intersperse in-house illustrations with some from original sources. Ginn was one of the first companies to feature real children as characters in the stories and in accompanying pictures. First-graders could read about Jim and Beth and Ana and Sara and Ken going to visit a book van or taking a trip to Sea World. This practice is now followed by other companies.

Pictures have come a long way from Dick and Jane in the back yard. These and other stereotypes, so long a part of children's reading material, have undergone radical changes in the last decade. Publishers have in fact occasionally become overzealous in their attempt to show racial minorities, handicapped persons, and senior citizens in all kinds of settings and doing a variety of things. This resulted in the printing of some stories with contrived, unnatural illustrations and characters.

Despite the great effort by basal publishers to expand their readers' exposure to many aspects for our culture, it is critical that teachers do even more. Children need to know *how* to detect the blatant and subtle forms of stereotyping. What are positive instructional opportunities that you can take advantage of with basal readers now that stereotyping is out in the open?

Stereotyping. The illustrations and content of basal readers have made strides in guarding against *stereotyping, tokenism,* and *life-style* oversimplifications. Nevertheless, teachers should continue to be sensitive to these issues as they evaluate and use reading materials, especially basal readers. Some distinctions in terminology are in order.

1. *Stereotyping* is an oversimplified generalization about a particular group, race, or sex, with derogatory implications.
2. *Tokenism* is a minimal, or token, effort to represent minorities. Look for nonwhite characters whose faces look like white ones tinted or colored in.
3. *Life-style oversimplifications* show an unfavorable contrast between minority characters and their setting with an unstated norm of white middle-class suburbia. Look for lack of appropriateness and for exaggerations of reality, such as "primitive" living.

As part of a reading methods course speakers representing several basal reader publishers were invited to give examples of how their materials have been improved and how they have greatly reduced the stereotyping of groups of people. One area the class had studied was sex-role stereotyping. Both boys and girls need to have male and female role models with whom they can identify in a positive way. What have basal companies done in this regard?

The presence of strong female role models was one conclusion of a study of values in basal readers as compared with juvenile periodicals (Aaron and Anderson, 1981). In fact, there were twice as many different female roles in the basals as in the periodicals. Some of the "male" values exhibited in female roles included strength, activity, or power; competitiveness; independence or toughness; a sense of emergency; courage; and smartness, cleverness, or thinking (page 312).

Rupley et al. (1981) examined basals published in 1976 and another group published in 1978 and found some changes in distribution of main character. In those published in 1976, 18.3 percent of the stories were female-dominated; 34.5 percent were male-dominated; and 47.1 percent were classified as "other." In the 1978 editions, 23.5 percent were female-dominated; 25.7 percent were male-dominated; and 50.7 percent were classified as "other."

The class also discussed racism, sexism, ageism, and handicapism. Students thought that they had covered the waterfront until a nutritionist presented some reading materials that are used in schools. There is yet another stereotype, a misrepresentation of an important part of our lives: *foodism*. Where, when, what, and how the characters in stories or films are shown eating can have an adverse, albeit subtle, effect on students. Certainly there is a need to be realistic; people should be shown eating junk foods because they are an accepted part of childhood life. The nutritionist's point was well taken, however: Isn't it important to expose readers to good eating habits and some elements of sound nutrition?

Not only did the class enjoy a good discussion about the merits of pizza and tacos, but the students realized the need to be sensitive to stereotyping in basal materials. A program consultant next involved the class in procedures to use when analyzing basals and other texts for stereotypes, tokenism, and life-style representations. These procedures were adapted from Rudman (1976).

Procedures for Analyzing Stereotypes

1. *Check the illustrations.* Look for tokenism and inappropriate depictions of life-style. Who is doing what?

2. *Check the story line to find out who makes decisions.* Do nonwhite people (or women or senior citizens or those with handicapping conditions) have subservient roles? Do minorities attain excellence and overcome amazing odds, thereby winning acceptance and accolades from white friends? Look also for problems that are personified by minority characters themselves.

3. *Analyze the story's content according to possible effects on self-esteem.* This is one area where teachers can make a difference. Rupley et al. (1981) point out the importance of teachers' correcting misconceptions that may appear in stories, taking into consideration the make-up and backgrounds of children in class when reviewing material in basal stories. If stories are lacking in their portrayal of something real in the lives of children in the class, seek out other materials.

4. *Try to ascertain the author's perspective.* It may or may not be limited if the author is a white male. Does the basal contain stories, poems, and plays written by women and minorities?

5. *Note the setting.* There has been a tendency to locate fictional stories about blacks in the ghetto. If the story takes place in another section of the city, are there whites visible as well as blacks? Are there characters who are part of multi-ethnic populations, and are they drawn as individuals rather than symbols or types?

6. *Note the relationships between people and the descriptions of families.* Is it an intact nuclear family? Is the black mother always the dominant member of the family? What kinds of friendships are described? Are white (or thin or young) friends valued over black (or overweight or old) friends?

7. *Watch for loaded words.* Words that carry overtones of insult are loaded. Such adjectives as "savage," "primitive," "conniving," "lazy," "superstitious," "docile," and "backward" applied to minorities were standard elements of racist stereotypes in the past. Also, look for inappropriate use of dialect. While dialect can be useful in conveying authenticity to a story, it may at times have a negative effect. If it's used as a differentiating mechanism by the author, dialect can cause readers to feel that the dialect *and* the person who speaks it are inferior.

Language Style

The style of written language found in basal readers has been an interest of researchers for several decades. Ruth Strickland (1962) was among the first to verify that children's command of oral language surpassed the language appearing in their basal readers. Investigators of the 1980s continue to find out more about "basalese," a pejorative term for the language style used in basal readers.

A study by Jacobson and Freeman (1981) compared styles of language in five basal series published after 1970 with randomly selected contemporary adolescent novels. The supposition that more variation among informal, formal, and technical styles would occur in novels was not verified, however. Novels did contain more colloquial and slang language while basals contained more technical vocabulary. This implies, again, the importance of teacher assistance. Children need instruction in the different styles of written language: for example, how to recognize them and how to *use* them in oral and written expression. Teachers who want students to enhance their communicative competence need to show children how style of language changes in basal readers and other materials depending on different situations and circumstances.

Another potential problem area in connection with the language of basal readers not reflecting natural language patterns of children was described by Gonzales (1980). In classroom discussions, teachers often try to elicit "basal reader language" from the children. Instead, teachers should accept the children's natural language and encourage spontaneous conversation. The idea is to build on the language strengths of children.

In a recent article on basal readers, Goodman (1986) calls for the use of "real language that is comprehensible and important to the learners" in the earliest selections children are asked to read (page 359). Further, it is a misconception that children's language learning is the result of instruction. Rather, because "language is learned in the course of its use, effective teaching supports and extends learning; it can never control it" (page 361).

Workbooks

Most teachers are interested in workbooks that go along with the basal readers. They have definite opinions about when to use them, how many pages to assign, and so on. Publishing company sales representatives rarely advise that every page of the workbooks be covered. Reading experts, too, frequently advise against making such assignments. Yet the practice persists. Witness this difference of opinion between the author of a recent journal article and an Indiana schoolteacher.

Fitzgerald (1979) reported that workbooks at the intermediate levels are often written several years in readability beyond the basal texts they accompany. She said this can be devastating for students who complete workbooks relatively independent of teacher instruction. Teachers need to know about these deviations so they can make adjustments in instruction. Mossburg (1982), a teacher, replied with "First Grade Teachers Love Their Reading Workbooks," in which she reported results of a questionnaire distributed to one-hundred first-grade teachers. Of the forty respondents, only six used workbooks "strictly for independent work." They were confident that they were using the workbooks correctly. Yet these teachers were "evenly divided as to whether all children should do every page . . . " (page 843). Mossburg argued that Fitzgerald's findings do not apply to the first-grade level.

Osborn (1984) concluded in her report on evaluating workbooks that "all of the hours students spend working in their workbooks have to be considered as a part of reading instruction" (page 33). She recommended that publishers of basal materials devote more planning time to the *integration* of the workbook and the rest of the lesson. Specifically, use new vocabulary from the story in work tasks, and base the majority of work tasks on the reading from the textbook or reader.

These recommendations seem logical, especially in light of a finding of an earlier study at the Center for the Study of Reading (Mason and Osborn, 1981) that students "spent as much or more time working independently in their workbooks as they did working with their teachers." We suggest the following guidelines adapted from Osborn to elementary teachers who are interested in evaluating the effectiveness of workbooks used in the classrooms. To be effective, workbooks should have the following characteristics:

1. They should reflect the most important aspects of what is being taught in the reading program.
2. The level of vocabulary in workbooks should relate to the rest of the program and to students.
3. Workbooks should have instructional language consistent with that used in the rest of the lesson and workbook.
4. Instructions in workbooks should be brief and unambiguous.
5. Workbooks should provide opportunities to practice component tasks prior to performing discriminatory tasks.
6. Workbooks should contain accurate and precise content.
7. Workbooks should provide consistent response modes from task to task which involve reading and writing.
8. Pictures should be consistent with the content of workbooks.
9. Workbooks should be accompanied by brief explanations of purpose.

Lesson Framework

A sales representative with a basal company showed us the features of his company's most recent edition. We asked him a question about the directions in the manual requiring teachers to list vocabulary words on the board before *every* story. However, instead of getting into a discussion of alternatives to this format as we hoped, the sales representative pronounced: "Everyone knows that a *good* teacher presents the words first." We were left thinking about the good teachers we have observed who didn't always present "the words first."

The lesson framework outlined in basal series is fairly standard, with slight variations, across all basals. According to Chaplin (1982) the reading lesson itself is "as indigenous to the elementary classroom as are teachers and pupils" (page 341). The following scenario typically takes place when a group of children enter their "reading circle" for instruction:

> When the group is assembled, the teacher introduces the difficult vocabulary words that will be found in the story. The children are directed to read parts of the story silently and orally. Subsequent to the reading, the teacher checks comprehension through questions based on the story. The length of time devoted to the question and discussion portion of the lesson is usually determined by the number of groups which

the teacher must direct, the constraints imposed by recess or other routine activities, or by the level of enthusiasm that the teacher and/or children have for the story. When the discussion has ended, the children are directed to turn to the workbook pages that accompany the story. Appropriate pages are assigned which the children are told to complete when they return to their seats or at home. The workbook exercises are used to reinforce the word attack and comprehension skills that are pertinent to the story (Chaplin, 1982, page 341).

The *Directed Reading Activity* (DRA) is the most common label for the lesson framework in a basal series. The DRA has four or five major instructional components.

Motivation and Background Building. This aspect of the lesson involves getting ready to read. It is sometimes referred to as the prereading phase of instruction. The teacher attempts to build interest in reading, set purposes, and introduce new concepts and vocabulary. Several procedures may include:

1. Discussion of previous experiences or reading related to the new lesson (connecting the new with the old).
2. Discussion of pictures in the story; making predictions and anticipating content.
3. Discussion of pronunciation and meaning of new words; review of words previously taught.
4. Location of geographical setting if important (map and globe skills).
5. Development of time concepts.
6. Review of important reading skills needed in doing the lesson.
7. Setting purposes for reading.

Guided Reading (silent and oral). Depending on the grade level, the story is often read on a section-by-section basis (primary grades) or in its entirety. Following silent reading, children may be asked to read the story aloud or orally read specific parts to answer questions. The guided reading phase of the lesson focuses on comprehension development through questioning. The questioning techniques of basals are controversial (Durkin, 1978–79). Critics maintain that most questions asked during a DRA lesson *test* comprehension rather than actually show children *how to comprehend* effectively.

Skill Development and Practice. Skill development and practice activities center around direct instruction of reading skills, arranged according to "scope and sequence" and taught systematically. Sometimes this phase of the DRA involves oral rereading, always for a specific skills purpose. Activities and exercises from workbooks that accompany the basal story are used to reinforce skills in broad areas: word analysis and recognition, meaning vocabulary, comprehension, and study skills.

Follow-up and Enrichment. There are many possibilities for follow-up and enrichment activities. Follow-up activities usually rely on additional practice in skill areas. Enrichment connects the lesson to art, music, drama, or creative writing. Follow-up and enrichment may include some of these specific procedures:

1. Creative activities such as dramatization, writing about personal experiences related to the lesson, or the preparation of original projects.
2. Workbook assignments to strengthen specific skills that children may appear to be weak in as a result of doing the lesson. (This involves use of an Independent Practice Workbook to supplement the practice workbook discussed in the previous section.)
3. Additional vocabulary practice.
4. The interpretation of a related experience such as reading a poem or another story on a similar theme.
5. Related reading in other texts and library books.

MAKING INSTRUCTIONAL DECISIONS

The basal lesson can be a tool at our command, or it can command our classroom actions. According to the recent report *Becoming a Nation of Readers* (1985), the latter situation is more frequent: "whether by choice or not, most teachers do rely on manuals" (page 49). Some authorities, such as Kenneth Goodman, believe that something needs to be done about this:

> Once and for all, schools must abandon the quest for teacher-proof materials and the scripted teachers' manuals designed to narrowly control teachers. Teachers, individually and collectively, must determine their own criteria for how they will select and use instructional materials in developing literacy (1986, page 363).

Let's consider how two experienced fourth-grade teachers handle their teacher's manuals. Barbara has been teaching seven years. She follows the lessons in her basal assiduously, lesson-by-lesson and page-by-page from the Teacher's Manual. Her compliance, she suggests, is based on a couple of factors. First, the basal program was put together by reading experts "who know far more than I ever will about reading." We concurred that her observation may in fact be the case but added, "Do these experts know your students as well as you do? Do they know your children's learning and reading strategies? Their needs? Their fears? Or their personal triumphs?" Barbara replied, "Perhaps not. But the lessons must be good or they wouldn't be included in the manual and, besides, they save me hours of planning time."

By contrast, Karen, a fourth-grade teacher with twelve years of experience, follows basal lessons but "reorganizes parts to fit what I think should be taught in my class." We inquired whether her lesson modification required much planning time. Karen replied, "I guess it does, but it's time well spent. I keep what I think is worthwhile and skip some activities because they don't make sense to me. These decisions take very little time. Planning time is consumed when I decide to do something on my own, like develop my own worksheets or devise a game to reinforce skills."

A decision either to adhere closely to the teacher's manual or to modify lessons should be a conscious one. The more teachers become aware of and reflect about *why* and *how* they use basals, the better. Although we avoid putting value judgments on either teacher's attitude, we believe that the process of becoming aware enables teachers to use their knowledge and skills more fully and effectively. Modifications of basal lessons allow teachers to rely on their own strengths as well as those of their students. In the final analysis, teachers should not be faced with an either/or dilemma in using basals to teach reading. Rather, they need to decide where to place instructional emphasis.

It is not unusual to discover very different kinds of reading instruction going on in the same elementary school. Even using just one basal reading program instructional emphasis often varies from teacher to teacher. It is clearly impossible to teach every activity suggested in a basal reading lesson. There isn't enough time in the day; moreover, we wonder whether a teacher would need to do so to produce proficient readers. From an instructional point of view the question is not "Am I going to do everything as suggested in the Teacher's Manual?" The more appropriate question was posed this way by an elementary teacher: "If I'm going to skip parts in the teacher's manual or modify the lesson, I have to have the courage to believe that what I am emphasizing is instructionally worthwhile. So I ask myself, 'What do I need to replace or adapt in the lesson to make it work for me?' "

Designing Alternative Lessons

As teachers of reading become more familiar with instructional options available from this text and others, they are going to try them out in their classrooms. However, they will use alternative strategies *in conjunction with their basal texts*. Further, they may even prefer to follow the basic procedure or steps of the traditional lesson framework and incorporate some alternatives into this structure.

Designing alternative lessons personalizes reading instruction for teachers and students. Consequently, all the whys and hows of designing alternative lessons cannot and probably should not be uncovered. Nevertheless, based on numerous conversations with teachers over the years, there are three major reasons why teachers design alternative reading lessons: (1) the nature of their students as readers; (2) the type of reading material; and (3) the desire to teach comprehension.

Students. Teachers at all grade levels voice concern about two sets of readers in particular: (1) so-called reluctant readers on one end, and (2) gifted readers on the other. Teachers empathize with a third-grade teacher who said it is important that "poorer readers do not become bogged down in working on isolated skills. These readers need to spend time on comprehension too." Gifted students need challenging activities, especially creative activities and those involving higher-level thinking skills. Creative problem solving can and should be used with all groups of readers. In fact, it is just as appropriate for poor readers to partake in problem-solving activities.

Material. Different material makes different demands on the reader. It also provides countless opportunities for teachers to exercise creative judgment. For certain reading groups the objectives of a lesson might actually be better met by omitting parts of the lesson. Sometimes expansion of a component is necessary. If material seems too difficult, it's up to the teacher to facilitate easier management, perhaps with some content area pre-reading strategies such as those in Chapter 11. Stories with some suspense, which lend themselves to making predictions, are of particular value to teachers who regularly alternate the DRA with an alternative lesson structure, the Directed Reading Thinking Activity (DRTA). The first lesson below was designed around this type of material.

Comprehension. As more and more teachers and administrators become aware of the importance of teaching as well as testing comprehension, there is increasing interest in finding new strategies. There has been a definite receptivity on the part of teachers taking in-service workshops and graduate coursework to learn additional strategies for improving their students' comprehension. It seems that more instructional time is spent in college classrooms on the topic of comprehension. As teachers begin to accumulate strategies, they pilot them in their own classrooms and settle on several that work particularly well. The two lessons below were designed by a teacher who testifies to their success in her reading group.

These lessons, which incorporate effective comprehension strategies, follow a similar lesson framework and use basal reader stories as their primary material. They are alternatives for teachers who believe it is possible to replace parts of basal reading lessons without "throwing out" the basal manual.

Comprehension Strategy Lesson for Second-Graders

Preparing. This activity is designed to initially raise curiosity about an assigned story by using second-grade students' prior knowledge and experiences to aid the attainment of concepts related to the reading material. The anticipation guide also serves as a post-reading activity for students to clarify their initial ideas about the meaning of friendship based upon the story author's point of view. Materials needed include copies of the guide as well as "The Popcorn Dragon" (*Lazy Circles*, Economy, 1980, pages 59–68).

Initiating. Begin the reading activity by asking students to respond to questions such as the following: "What is a real friend?" "What might friends do to be helpful or kind?" "How do you know a person is your friend?"

BOX 10.2

Anticipation/Clarification Guide for
"The Popcorn Dragon"

Directions: Place an X under "yes" if you think the statement is true. Put an X under "no" if you think the statement is not true. Do not place any marks in the column marked "story" until *after* you have read the story.

YES	NO	STORY	
_____	_____	_____	1. A friend is always willing to help you.
_____	_____	_____	2. You can't have more than one friend.
_____	_____	_____	3. You can be just as happy when you don't have friends as when you do have friends.
_____	_____	_____	4. Friends always understand how you feel.
_____	_____	_____	5. Sharing with friends can make you feel happy.
_____	_____	_____	6. Friends help one another.
_____	_____	_____	7. Friends should never tell you about things that you do that they don't like.

Involve the students as a class in a short discussion to help each student develop personal ideas about the meaning of friendship.

Moving Forward. Each student should be given a copy of the Anticipation/ Clarification Guide in Box 10.2. Ask students to complete the first two columns marked "yes" and "no" only, or read each sentence to them. Tell them that they will complete the last column *after* they have read the story. After the students have completed the first two columns, initiate a classroom discussion centered around the students' responses *and* the reasons for their responses.

Then, ask students to read the story while thinking about what friendship means to them, and to try to relate their feelings to the ideas in the story. Afterwards, have them complete the last column of the guide marked "story."

Again, initiate a brief classroom discussion about the meaning of friendship as it is presented in the story to permit students to review their original ideas about friendship and clarify their personal ideas.

Closing. You might ask students to write a story about their real friends and real situations. Or have them pretend to be Dianne in the story and write about what they might have done or how they might have felt if they were in the same situation. Another possibility for an expansion activity is to group students in pairs and have a "friend for a day" experience involving the entire class, following this activity with an end-of-the-day discussion on the most important ingredients of the friendship.

Vocabulary/Comprehension Strategy Lesson

Preparing. This activity is designed to be used after an entire third- or fourth-grade class or group has read the story. The activity has a multidimensional purpose of reinforcing and extending descriptive vocabulary as well as aiding comprehension. The building of a word ladder comprises the vocabulary development portion of this activity and the creation of semantic webs will complete the comprehension portion of the activity. Students' background knowledge and prior experiences combine with the existing story schemata to aid both vocabulary development and comprehension. Materials needed include copies of "A Cane in Her Hand" (*Weavers*, Houghton Mifflin, 1981, pages 201–202) and the core question for the semantic web.

Initiating. Begin the activity by helping students, as a class or in groups, generate as many descriptive words as possible about Valerie and her "seeing" problem. The words offered by students need not be inherent in the text itself. Each word should be written on the blackboard under Valerie's name. This word ladder will act as a comprehension catalyst for the remaining portion of the reading activity.

Moving Forward. Each student should be given a copy of the core question from which they will create their own semantic web. Ask students to individually review the descriptive "ladder" words and to relate them to the core question before constructing their own webs (see Figure 10.5). Students should be encouraged to draw inferences from the reading material and include these in their own webs. This portion of the activity should result in personalized visual representation of the interaction between each student's interpretation of the text and the existing story schemata (grammar).

As a class or within groups, students should discuss several webs and the probable reasons for the way the information was organized. Next they should be given the opportunity to change or enlarge their own personal webs.

Closing. As an expansion activity, you may wish to ask students to write about how they might be able to help Valerie if they were one of her neighbors or classmates. Another possible suggestion is to ask students to tell about an imaginary experience in which they help an individual who has a handicap other than a vision problem. A brief discussion should follow the story telling to focus upon

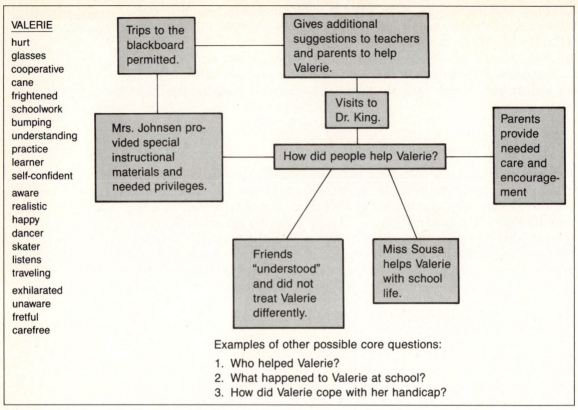

VALERIE

hurt
glasses
cooperative
cane
frightened
schoolwork
bumping
understanding
practice
learner
self-confident

aware
realistic
happy
dancer
skater
listens
traveling

exhilarated
unaware
fretful
carefree

Trips to the blackboard permitted.

Gives additional suggestions to teachers and parents to help Valerie.

Visits to Dr. King.

Mrs. Johnsen provided special instructional materials and needed privileges.

How did people help Valerie?

Parents provide needed care and encouragement

Friends "understood" and did not treat Valerie differently.

Miss Sousa helps Valerie with school life.

Examples of other possible core questions:
1. Who helped Valerie?
2. What happened to Valerie at school?
3. How did Valerie cope with her handicap?

Figure 10.5   Example of a Word Ladder and a Semantic Web

the similar problems all handicapped individuals face and what individuals such as the students can do to help.

INSTRUCTIONAL MATERIALS

Due to the proliferation of reading materials, it is virtually impossible to offer teachers a comprehensive list of current instuctional materials in reading. It's not an exaggeration to say that such a list would be out of date before the ink was dry. It is probably just as well: Teachers must select materials discerningly. How we do that varies according to type of material.

Table 10.2 arrays three major kinds of reading materials: basic instructional materials, supplementary materials, and trade books. Basic materials such as a comprehensive reading program will be used by most children; they will be examined "carefully by school officials and, increasingly, by parent and community groups concerned with maintaining appropriate standards" (Baker, 1979, pages

25–26). Supplementary programs such as multimedia kits will be used as enrichment for some children and reinforcement of basic skills for others. They are much less likely to be scrutinized by selection committees. Trade books, such as library hardcover and paperback books, will be chosen by individual children from the collection selected by librarians, specialists, and the classroom teacher.

The examples provided in Table 10.2 should be expanded as you come into contact with materials. Take some time now to add to our partial listing under the "example" column for basic materials, supplementary high-interest, low-vocabulary materials, and trade books. When you finish the chapter, add others to this list from those you may already be familiar with or new materials you are researching.

Classrooms differ according to the predominant type of material. For example, there are some rooms in which the only visible reading materials are textbooks for reading, science, social studies, and so on. Other rooms evidence racks of paperback books; still others display sturdy cardboard kits with student record books piled nearby. Few classrooms, if any, have the same "mix" of types of reading materials.

One explanation of this phenomenon might be grade level. Lower grades work on different objectives than upper grades. Does this account for the use of one type of material over another? Another explanation might be the reading program of the school district; it's plausible that type of material would be

TABLE 10.2

Types of Reading Instructional Materials

Type	Label	Purpose	Example
I. Basic instructional materials and programs	Basal readers (referred to by publisher's name)	Intended to provide the majority of reading instruction to the majority of students.	Macmillan, Harper & Row, Economy
II. Supplementary programs	Skill kits, high-interest, low-vocabulary series, multimedia packages	Intended to meet special needs such as enrichment, reinforcement of skills; particular groups such as gifted, bilingual-bicultural, and learning disabled.	Signal series (Scott, Foresman) Triple Action (Scholastic) Breakthrough (Allyn & Bacon)
III. Trade books	Library books, popular paperbacks	Individual titles suited to children's interests. Intended for independent reading rather than direct instruction.	Barbara Murphy and Judie Wolkoff, *Ace Hits the Big Time* (Delacorte, 1981) Patricia L. Gauch, *Morelli's Game* (Putnam, 1981) S. E. Hinton, *Rumble Fish* (Dell, 1975)

influenced by program. Certainly, one's use of the basal reading program is closely connected to district curriculum. These are valid explanations, but neither accounts for the teacher's belief system in making decisions about materials.

Beliefs About Reading and Instructional Materials

How do teachers' beliefs about reading correspond to their selection and use of instructional materials for reading? There is no definitive answer to this question. There are many complicating factors that prevent teachers from exercising complete freedom of choice and, hence, prevent us from knowing why certain materials are present in any given classroom. Nevertheless, we believe it is important to consider the relationship between materials used to deliver instruction and the beliefs teachers hold about reading instruction. In other words, it makes sense to assume there is a relationship between what we do and why we do it.

Figure 10.6 illustrates the three major types of reading materials across the continuum of beliefs from bottom-up (on the left) to top-down (on the right). Basal reading programs take up the middle (or moderate) sections of the continuum whereas programmed, prescriptive materials and children's literature books correspond to the bottom-up and top-down quarters, respectively. Supplementary materials span several sections, from flash and skill cards to workbooks to high-interest, low-vocabulary materials.

Differences in beliefs about unit of language to be emphasized are superimposed in the next "layer." Letter-sound emphasis corresponds to materials found in prescription programs with a heavy word analysis component. Whole language emphasis corresponds to materials such as library books and paperbacks without arbitrary skill divisions. This unit of language emphasis is illustrated further by a dotted boundary line for context. Materials involving minimal use of context are on the left whereas materials involving maximal use of context are on the right.

A third layer that we might add is instructional strategy corresponding to these materials. We have initiated this with several basic strategies discussed in other chapters. For example, the DRL corresponds to most basal programs, whereas the DRTA corresponds to many basal reader stories and other stories found in literature and high-interest, low vocabulary materials. Sustained Silent Reading (SSR) corresponds to magazines and trade books: that is, personalized rather than prescriptive materials. What other strategies would you place in one spot or move to several points on this continuum?

Unfortunately, often by the time we step back, look at the types of instructional materials we are using, and relate them to our beliefs and priorities, the materials are already in place. How were they selected in the first place?

Selecting Reading Materials

Many classroom teachers have served on textbook selection committees. A bit of probing reveals the sophistication of the effort: Did teachers use different rating scales for various groups such as parents, teachers, and administrators? Were there

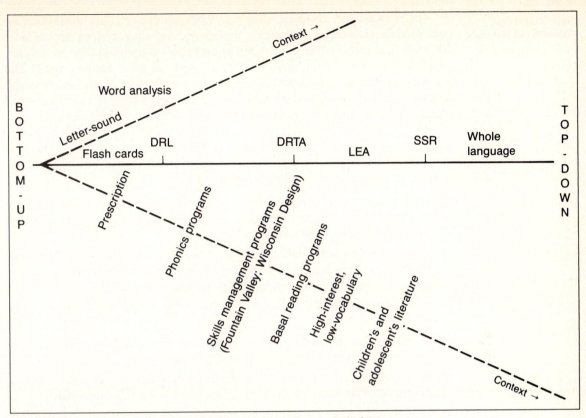

Figure 10.6 **Reading Instructional Materials According to Belief Systems**

presentations by company representatives? Was there piloting of one or two finalists in classrooms over a period of time?

Social trends such as treatment of women and minorities, return to basics, and increasing involvement of parents have varying degrees of impact on curriculum development and materials selection. Depending on the community, other issues need to be considered. Censorship is probably the most pervasive issue because it deals with people's values. The *act of examining publications for objectionable matter* is not the intended mission of most educational materials selection committees. Yet there is a fine line between examining materials for their contribution to instructional goals and banning materials for their conveyance of implicit or explicit messages to students.

A spin-off on the volatile issue of censorship is the increase in media attention given to reading and materials. The morning news, for example, might feature a middle school librarian and her program to bring parents, their adolescents, and adolescent novels together. After reading the novels, parents and kids get together to discuss the books. That evening, the newspaper carries an article about parents objecting to several books on astrology and numerology that were given to their children as part of the Reading Is Fundamental program.

The related issues of literacy, illiteracy (lack of literacy), functional illiteracy (lack of sufficient literacy to function in society), and aliteracy (able to but does not read) are, at this writing, receiving a great deal of attention. Sports stars are coming forward to admit their inability to perform basic reading tasks. The percentage of functional illiterates in the population depends on the article you're reading. Politicians readily adopt adult literacy as a pet project, and local television stations do spots on location at the community's literacy volunteer center.

Trends and issues are important as they directly or indirectly influence curriculum materials selection. We need to keep them in perspective. The next time you are asked to assist in selecting materials, consider these critical questions as guides or criteria to get your committee started:

1. Have you personally evaluated the content of the materials in terms of accuracy of content, level of presentation, and use of level of language? Have you found the materials acceptable in these areas?

2. Does the field testing data reveal on whom the materials were field tested? How many were involved in the use of the materials? In what geographic location were these tests conducted? What were the results?

3. Are authors and publishers readily identifiable within the content of the material?

4. Is there an accompanying instructional guide and, if so, are the curriculum aims, objectives, and instructional strategies presented?

5. Have these materials been used on pupils similar to the pupils in your reading programs? If so, what results were achieved by using these materials?

6. Do you feel you will present these materials with honesty and objectivity?

7. Have members of your district formulated specific ways or methods these materials can be used?

8. Will these materials complement the other instructional messages of your reading programs?

9. Does the material's content present information in a fair and nonbiased manner?

10. Are important concepts reinforced so that there is sufficient repetition of major points?

Evaluating Reading Materials

Reading programs, the most prevalent type of instructional material, are also the most likely to be evaluated by teachers and other groups. Publishing companies have become so attuned to this process that they gear high-power, professional presentations to convince school districts to adopt their particular program. School districts in turn have developed extensive evaluation forms to keep track of and compare the programs' elements.

The brief evaluation form in Box 10.3 illustrates the components that are usually examined and reported on at some length. Note that additional information

BOX 10.3
Textbook Evaluation Profile Chart

Title of textbook	Excellent	Good	Acceptable	Poor	Not included	Not applicable
I. Authorship						
II. Learner verification and revision						
III. General characteristics						
IV. Physical and mechanical features						
V. Philosophy						
VI. Organization of material						
VII. Objectives						
VIII. Subject-matter content						
IX. Readability						
X. Teaching aids and supplementary material						
XI. Teacher's edition or manual						
Total number in each rating classification for all categories						

Additional information:

purpose	interest level	sexism
age level	readability	ageism
grade level	racism	handicapism

at the bottom reflects relatively recent expectations for fair and realistic treatment of people of different races, sexes, and ages as well as the handicapped. This evaluation format applies to textbooks in other subject areas as well as reading and to secondary as well as elementary and middle levels.

Checklists designed to evaluate reading materials of a supplementary nature may be criticized as rather shallow analysis. Their benefits, however, far outweigh this criticism. Checklists are relatively easy to construct; teachers are more willing to spend the short amount of time it takes to develop a list to help them examine materials. Figure 10.7 gives a sample checklist for examining the potential effectiveness of materials; it is one informal evaluation designed by teachers of elementary reading/language.

The evaluation form shown is brief, to the point, deals with teachers' own programmatic goals, and will yield useful information. Unlike more elaborate and

Statement	Yes	No	Unsure
1. Reading materials are consistent with philosophy and goals of the program.	_____	_____	_____
2. Materials are adequate for various phases of the program:			
a. Oral language development	_____	_____	_____
b. Listening comprehension	_____	_____	_____
c. Word recognition	_____	_____	_____
d. Reading comprehension	_____	_____	_____
e. Study skills	_____	_____	_____
f. Recreational reading	_____	_____	_____
3. The materials are:			
a. Interesting and stimulating	_____	_____	_____
b. Easy for children to use	_____	_____	_____
c. Readily available	_____	_____	_____
d. Durable	_____	_____	_____
e. Well organized	_____	_____	_____
f. Cost-effective	_____	_____	_____
4. The materials accommodate the range of reading abilities.	_____	_____	_____
5. I feel adequately prepared to use all materials available.	_____	_____	_____

Additional Comments:

_____

_____

_____

Figure 10.7   Sample Checklist for Examining the Potential Effectiveness of Materials

lengthy commercial evaluation instruments, such checklists can be used by those who actually select and use materials.

Perhaps most critical to analyzing materials is teachers' willingness to try to answer basic questions about their instructional materials. It's better to tackle these questions before purchasing materials because if teachers can't justify the materials they are using, someone outside the classroom may impose other materials on them (Cunningham, 1981). Try to answer these questions about a material that you are interested in buying or are already using:

1. Will this material help meet my instructional goals?
2. How flexible is this material?
3. Does it teach what it says it is teaching?
4. Are the skills taught important to reading?
5. Are the skills taught appropriate for the level of the readers with whom I intend to use the material?
6. Are skills taught at the application level?
7. Are the materials intrinsically motivating?
8. What is the ratio of time spent reading to time spent doing other things?
9. What can I learn from teaching these materials?
10. Is the material worth what it costs (Cunningham, 1981, pages 180–184)?

Teacher-Made and Student-Produced Materials

Have you ever walked into an elementary classroom that resembled the Christmas display window of an F. A. O. Schwartz toy store? The teacher is, to put it mildly, creative and talented at making materials. Many of us are not this gifted, yet we want to generate supplementary materials of the teacher-made variety for our own students. This is a good reason for becoming involved in designing and producing materials. A second and even more practical reason is to help solve a real problem: The classroom is deficient in materials and there is little or no financial support available. *What would you do in a similar situation?*

Do not, cautions Mangieri, "throw in the towel instructionally" (1980, page 20). Instead, realize that we don't often have maximum conditions for instruction. Continue to request funds for what you feel you need and, at the same time, adapt parts of previously used materials and begin to make other materials. "Assume a spirit of adventure about finding and adapting readily available, free and inexpensive materials" (Stahl & Anzalone, page 71).

If teacher-made materials are to retain one of their major attributes—ease in construction—it's important to avoid unnecessary complications. Thus to begin designing and producing your own materials, know the three C's: concepts, content, and clients.

What are the major *concepts* you want (and need) to teach?

How complex is the *content* and how is it organized?

What is its value to your student *clients* and how familiar are they with it?

With knowledge of these criteria at your fingertips, you should be able to design appropriate materials in any of the categories which follow.

Games. One obvious benefit that comes with playing instructional games in the classroom is instant motivation. Games provide a change of pace, even in the classroom where every Friday morning from ten to eleven Concentration or Challenge of Champions or College Bowl is played. There are few surprises in store for the players except one: Who are the winners? Second, games provide skill practice, and "the best way to acquire most skills is to begin early and practice them often" (Harris and Smith, 1980, page 404). Combining these two thoughts produces a good answer to the question "Why are games so popular?" Students reinforce skills and have a good time doing it.

The most typical type of game over the years has probably been flash cards or game board plus word cards. Card games and spin-the-dial or shake-the-dice board games are used to assist students in categorizing, reviewing vocabulary meanings, and sequencing.

The cost of teacher-made games is not necessarily less than commercial materials if durability and professional appearance are taken into consideration (Snyder, 1981). Changing a familiar commercial game or favorite "old" game into a new one is easier to do than starting from scratch. Perhaps more than any other factor, teacher time must be considered. If the game is worthwhile to your students, it's worth spending some time making it. How can you judge the relative importance of the concept being practiced to your students' learning?

One illustration of this might be a teacher who holds a top-down belief about reading and is concerned about what she perceives is an overemphasis on phonics in many commercial materials in her classroom. Her goal was to help her students practice translating visual symbols into meaning. She decided it was worth the time and developed a whole language reading game for her second-graders.

Newspaper. For years, teachers at all levels and in virtually all subject areas have made instructional use of the newspaper. Whether it's looking at classified ads, cutting out comic strips, or actually obtaining a classroom subscription to a major newspaper, students have been exposed to the newspaper as part of their school experience.

Newspapers, like games, generate enthusiasm in the classroom. They also provide a good resource to develop, reinforce, and refine reading-related skills, especially in vocabulary and comprehension. As a bonus, newspapers are a good way to communicate with parents when homework assignments are based on newspapers (Criscuolo, 1981).

Two efficient methods for designing newspaper activities are (1) to begin with a particular competency your students need to work toward and select different parts of the paper for the activities, and (2) to begin with the various parts of the paper and develop activities according to your students' competency needs. The following examples are designed according to the two methods.

From Comprehension Skill to Newspaper Section

I. Remembering (helps students focus on explicitly stated information)
   A. Follow a sports team by recording their progress on sports pages.
   B. Read an article on front page and note the Five W's (who, what, when, where, and why). Write a summary.

II. Inferring (helps students conjecture about what is not explicitly stated)
   A. Examine ads in any section and determine for whom they are intended and how words are used to sell.

III. Evaluating (helps students make and support judgments about what they have read)
   A. Determine the point of view of a sports column or editorial on editorial page. Evaluate that position.

IV. Appreciating (helps students become personally involved as they read)
   A. Read any human interest story in national or local news and respond empathetically in writing.
   B. Write a story or poem in response to a feature story (Degler, 1978).

From Newspaper Section to Reading Skill

I. Lost and Found
   A. Find and read the lost and found ads. Write a story behind one of the ads pretending to be the animal or item lost.

II. Comic Strip
   A. Choose a favorite comic strip character and use as many adjectives as possible to describe the character.

III. Sale Items
   A. Choose an item that you would like to sell. After reading the classified ads to see what kind of information is given, write a four-line ad for the item (Criscuolo, 1981).

The advantages of newspapers range from their minimal cost and constantly renewed supply of ideas to their different reading levels and wide appeal. As the teaching ideas above illustrate, writing instruction as well as reading can be highlighted. One final important benefit of newspapers in the classroom is their natural appeal to the multiple cultures in our society; teachers can use newspapers to help bridge cultural differences (Shields and Vondrak, 1980).

Television. Teachers and parents have become acutely aware in the last few years (Singer et al. 1981) that school-age children spend an average of five hours per day watching television! We are less certain about the relationship between television viewing and the development or hindrance of reading and language arts.

Evidence suggests that a person's television interests serve a purpose just as book interests do; each medium satisfies a different need. For example, Schramm et al. (1961) reported a decrease over time in the use of comic books and radio (fantasy need) while book use remained the same (information need). One survey (Feeley, 1974) of intermediate-grade students revealed associations between reading and information and between television and entertainment; sports viewers read about sports.

An extension of this line of inquiry is whether or not students' preferences for reading or television are related to the *quality* of their reading choices. In a study by Neuman (1982), fourth-, fifth-, and sixth-graders who were classified as "heavy TV–light reading" tended to choose books of lower quality than other groups. It behooves teachers and parents to (1) provide stimulating, high-quality reading materials, and (2) develop television literacy at home and in school.

Learning about advertising techniques, how to make decisions about programs to watch, and the equipment behind the scenes at a television studio are areas in which teachers and parents can intervene. Obtaining scripts of popular programs available from networks, some teachers direct plays from the episodes or organize actual "productions" of TV shows.

Another plus that corresponds to the use of newspapers is that television "exposes children to language not used in their community" (DeHaven, 1983, page 482). It helps them expand their vocabularies and sentence patterns, but most importantly, television takes children to different cultures. In the final analysis, the problem is not one of too much or too little television time. The real problem is the *quality* of that time. Do we use television as an effective way of improving communication, or do we shun it instructionally as a mindless spectator sport? After all, it's not just watching programs such as "Sesame Street" that affect children. A parent's (or teacher's) participation with children can be positive.

SUMMARY

We examined basal reading programs and other types of instructional materials in this chapter, emphasizing the need for teachers to understand and use materials wisely. Beginning with the predominant vehicle for reading instruction in elementary classrooms, we reminisced about the origins of and some instructional concepts that were associated with the use of basals throughout the years. After recalling the books of the Dick, Jane, Jerry, and Alice era, we devoted a section to investigating current reading series.

Basal programs of the eighties, best described as comprehensive, have come a long way. Consequently, we investigated their concepts, language or terminology, and major components. Rather than assigning "pros and cons" to basal reading programs, we concentrated on the significant improvements made in several areas. Their appearance, organization, illustrations, and attempts at improving literature selection and reducing stereotypes are strides made by the publishers. What teachers do with basal readers during instructional time is another matter.

No matter how intimidating it may be to use a basal reading program (and we believe it *is* in many school systems), it's the teacher who provides the reading instruction. Teachers who make daily decisions about children and who elect to spend more class time on vocabulary or comprehension or decoding are molding their own reading program. Teachers who become aware and reflect about why and how they use basals make a list of "pros and cons" obsolete. They consciously emphasize one strategy over another as they take control of reading instruction. Often, and in conjunction with their basal series, teachers modify lessons to individualize for a particular group of students, to capitalize on a type of written material, or to emphasize a skill area. These are teachers who strengthen and take ownership of their basal reading program.

When we considered next the wide assortment of other instructional materials, one question persisted: How do teachers analyze the enormous chunk of classroom materials available for reading instruction? There are current trends and issues that teachers need to consider in relation to materials. They need to differentiate among the types of commercial reading materials and to assimilate criteria for evaluating them. The selection and use of commercial and teacher-made materials affords teachers still another opportunity to choose what is instructionally worthwhile in reading and learning to read.

THE WORKSHOP

In the Classroom

1. Using ideas from the chapter, outside readings, and class notes, complete the study chart individually and then discuss your responses in groups.

	Advantages	Disadvantages
Basal Readers		
Workbooks		
Supplementary Reading Materials		

2. Develop a position paper on whether or not you support the use of basal readers as a major vehicle for reading instruction in the elementary school.

3. Critique a lesson plan in the teacher's manual of a basal reader. What are the strengths of the lesson plan? What aspects of the plan might you emphasize or allow greater instructional time for? In what ways, if any, might you change the plan?

4. Use the questions suggested in the chapter to evaluate a workbook that accompanies a basal reader. Report the results of your evaluation to members of the class.

5. Use the procedures for analyzing stereotypes in this chapter to evaluate stereotyping in either basal or supplementary reading materials. Report the evaluation to other members of the class. Decide how you would handle reading material instructionally that does contain stereotypes.

In the Field

1. Study how a teacher uses and modifies a basal reading approach to instruction. What is the teacher's attitude toward basal instruction? How closely is the teacher's manual followed? How does the teacher use basal workbooks? In what ways, if any, does the teacher deviate from the suggested steps in the manual? What reasons does the teacher give for such changes?

2. Teach a basal lesson to a group of children following the guidelines suggested in the teacher's manual. Reflect on the experience. In what ways were the guidelines effective or ineffective? How would you amend the lesson to fit your instructional needs better?

3. Create an original lesson for a basal story without consulting the teacher's manual. Then try out the lesson with a group of children. Reflect on the experience. Consult the manual and compare the original lesson you developed with the suggested one. What did you learn from the experience?

Chapter 11

Bridging the Gap Between Children and Content Area Textbooks

Teachers will often complain that, after sitting through a lengthy in-service session, they come away with nothing practical, nothing they could use next Monday morning. We had a similar reaction after reading this recommendation from Becoming a Nation of Readers: *"Textbooks in science, social studies, and other areas should be clearly written, well-organized and contain important information and concepts" (1985, page 119). If this is an accurate statement and we already know that few textbooks meet these standards, then what are we to do? Bridging the gap between children and content area textbooks is our answer to the question. Given a practical instructional framework, teachers can help guide elementary students in effectively learning content from texts on Monday . . . Tuesday . . . and after.*

*Today my social studies lesson just seemed to go on and on; the kids weren't
responding. Perhaps the material they had to read was too hard.*

Jim Roberts, a fifth-grade teacher

*Hey Terry, I hope you're in my group today. Mr. Roberts said he is going to
give us one of those reading guides to do during Language Arts.*

Mike, a fifth-grader

When students know how to learn, classroom life is easier for students and teachers
alike. Because the value of reading lies in its uses, reading can be most useful to
elementary children when they are learning how to use content area textbooks
effectively. Reading to learn is the goal of content area reading instruction;
bridging the gap between children and difficult textbooks can make it happen.

Jim Roberts, a fifth-grade teacher, and one of his students, Mike, illustrate in
their own way that reading involves the interaction among teacher, text, and
students. Mr. Roberts recognizes his responsibility for setting the tone and
providing the instructional framework for learning from text. The dilemma comes,
however, in knowing when to shift from "covering material" to putting students
in a position to take charge of their own learning. Students like Mike will find it
difficult to function independently with textbooks if they don't know how to *use
reading to think about content.*

In this chapter we examine how children can use reading to learn content.
What is the role of classroom teachers who teach reading and content material?
While it seems reasonable that you show students how to handle the demands of
textbooks, determining the difficulty of texts is not a simple matter. Teachers need
to uncover the factors that influence text difficulty and also become aware of the
limitations inherent in using readability formulas.

Helping youngsters read textbook assignments so that they can handle
conceptual demands is an important part of content area reading instruction.
Many of the reading strategies presented in the previous chapters can easily be
integrated into content area instruction. When combined with the strategies and
materials presented in this chapter, they serve as models and guides to students
in effectively learning content.

WHY ARE TEXTBOOKS DIFFICULT
TO READ?

Textbooks are such an integral part of schooling that teachers rarely give their
presence a second thought. In some classrooms they blend into the physical
environment, much like desks, bulletin boards, and chalkboards. Yet, teachers
sometimes remark that their textbooks are difficult. When students have trouble
reading content assignments, we are acutely aware of the mismatch between the

reading abilities students bring to text material and the estimated readability of the text.

To compensate for this, some teachers avoid textbook assignments. Instruction revolves around lecture and other activities instead of the textbook. Readings may be assigned but rarely are they discussed in class the next day or included in end-of-unit tests. Some teachers blatantly abandon difficult materials, sidestepping reading altogether as a vehicle for learning. This only compounds the problem.

In lieu of either abandoning difficult materials or avoiding reading altogether, we need to get answers to some very basic questions. How does a textbook meet the goals of the curriculum? Is the conceptual difficulty of the text beyond students' grasp? Does the author have a clear sense of purpose as conveyed to this audience? How well are the ideas in the text organized? With answers to these and other questions, teachers have some basis upon which to make decisions about text-related instruction. Last, but not least, it's an opportunity to exercise their professional judgment.

Factors in Judging the Difficulty of Textbooks

The difficulty of text material is the result of factors residing in both the reader and the text. Therefore, to judge well, you need to take into account several different types of information. A primary source of information is the publisher. Consider the publisher-provided descriptions of the design, format, and organizational structure of the textbook along with grade level readability designations. A second source is your knowledge of students in the class. A third source is your own sense of what makes the textbook useful in learning a particular subject.

The first order of business is to articulate how the textbook will be used. It is crucial to know the textbook's intended function. Will it be used as the sole basis of information or as an extension of information? Will it be one of a number of references? Is it to provide guided activities?

In judging the difficulty of textbooks, you want to find texts that students will understand and want to use. Three crucial areas—understandability, usability, and interestability—should guide assessment and keep it manageable. Irwin and Davis (1980) provided a general textbook readability checklist to help you make decisions about the difficulty of a textbook.

Understandability. The area of understandability provides information about how likely a given group of students is to comprehend the text adequately. This helps you assess relationships between students' own frames of reference and conceptual knowledge and the text information. Has the author taken into consideration the knowledge elementary students will bring to the text? The understandability of the material is influenced strongly by the match between what the reader knows and the text itself.

One way to judge an author's assumptions about students' background knowledge and experiences is, according to Armbruster and Anderson (1981), whether enough relevant ideas are presented in a text to satisfy the author's purpose. For example, many authors will use headings to cue into their purposes for text passages. Convert the headings to questions. If the passage content answers the questions, then the authors have achieved their purposes. Another test of the author's assumptions about vocabulary knowledge is to answer this question from the student's perspective: "If I were a ____ grade student, would the words in the text be beyond my present level of vocabulary knowledge?"

Usability.   The area of usability deals with the presentation and organization of content in the textbook. It helps assess factors contributing to the teacher's day-to-day use of the text in teaching and the student's use in learning. Basically, your response to questions about usability helps decide whether a textbook is *considerate* or *inconsiderate*. Box 11.1 contains a usability checklist of items that are indicators of a considerate text. For example, it may reveal the extent to which relationships among ideas are clear, the logical connection between ideas, and the use of signal words (connectives) to make relationships explicit.

Interestability.   The area of interestability concerns determining which features of a text might appeal to a given group of students. Sometimes it's not possible to identify the real interests of elementary students. Children tend to respond to questions in ways they believe will please teachers. Also, children's interests change from semester to semester, if not week to week. Nevertheless, attitudes toward reading and subject matter instruction form early in the elementary grades. If interest is a motivating factor and a way to improve attitudes, it shouldn't be ignored. As teachers we cannot "make" students interested in a science or math unit, but we can facilitate this.

The more relevant the text, the more interesting it will be to children. Illustrations and pictures should have appeal, and will, when drawings and pictures depict persons they can relate to. Does the cover design and other artwork convey up-to-date, refreshing images? Are print size and face varied? Does the boldface lettering of headings contrast with lightface lettering of the main narrative? Italics and numbering of words and phrases in lists are two other devices that can help make the printed page come alive for elementary students.

Once the information accrues about factors contributing to textbook difficulty, you are in a position to use professional judgment. How the more traditional readability formula can be a complement to a teacher's judgment instead of a substitute for it warrants a closer look.

Using Readability Formulas

When elementary teachers judge instructional content area materials, they frequently use readability formulas. These help *estimate* textbook difficulty and are not intended to be precise indicators. Of the thirty-plus readability formulas available, the most popular ones are relatively quick and easy to calculate. They typically involve a measure of sentence length and word difficulty to ascertain a grade level score for text materials. This score supposedly indicates the reading achievement level students would need to comprehend the material. You do, however, need to be aware of limitations associated with using readability formulas.

Limitations. Readability formulas yield scores that are simply estimates, not absolute levels, of text difficulty. These estimates are often determined along a single dimension of an author's writing style: vocabulary difficulty and sentence complexity, measured by word and sentence length, respectively. These are two variables most often used to predict the difficulty of a text. Nevertheless, they only *indirectly* assess vocabulary difficulty and sentence complexity. Are long words always harder to understand than short ones? Are long sentences necessarily more difficult than short ones?

Keep in mind that a readability formula doesn't take into account the experience and knowledge that even young readers bring to content material. The reader's emotional, cognitive, and linguistic backgrounds aren't included in readability estimates. Hittleman (1973) maintained that readability is actually a moment in time in which a reader's human makeup interacts with the topic, the purposes for reading, and the semantic and syntactic structures in the material. This makes good sense because formulas are not designed to expose the variables operating within the reader. Thus several factors that contribute to a reader's ability to comprehend text are not dealt with: purpose, interest, motivation, emotional state, and environment. This is an important limitation.

Suggestions. Formulas in and of themselves need not be a liability if you follow Nelson's (1978) suggestions for using them:

Learn to use a simple readability formula as an aid in evaluating text material for student use.

Don't assume automatic comprehension will result from matching readability level of material to reading achievement level of students.

Don't assume that automatic reading ease will result from text materials rewritten according to readability criteria. (Leave the rewriting of text material to the linguists, researchers, and editors who have time to analyze and validate their manipulations.)

Do provide materials containing essential facts, concepts, and values of the subject at varying levels of readability within the reading range of your students.

Do recognize that using a readability formula is no substitute for instruction. The elementary teacher still needs to prepare students to read the assignment, guide them in their reading, and reinforce new concepts through rereading and discussion (pages 624–625).

Fry Readability Graph. One fairly quick and simple readability formula is the Fry Readability Graph developed by Edward Fry (1968, 1977). Fry used two variables to predict difficulty and determine grade-level scores for materials from grade one through college: sentence length and word length. The total number of sentences in a sample passage determines sentence length, while the total number of syllables in the passage determines word length.

Three 100-word samples from the selected reading material should be used

BOX 11.1
General Textbook Readability Checklist

	Yes	To some extent	No (or does not apply)
Understandability			
Are the assumptions about students' vocabulary knowledge appropriate? 1			
Are the assumptions about students' prior knowledge of this content area appropriate? 2			
Are the assumptions about students' general experiential backgrounds appropriate? 3			
Does the teacher's manual provide the teacher with ways to develop and review the students' conceptual and experiential backgrounds? 4			
Are new concepts explicitly linked to the students' prior knowledge or to their experiential backgrounds? 5			
Does the text introduce abstract concepts by accompanying them with many concrete examples? 6			
Does the text introduce new concepts one at a time with a sufficient number of examples for each one? 7			
Are definitions understandable and at a lower level of abstraction than the concept being defined 8			
Does the text avoid irrelevant details? 9			
Does the text explicitly state important complex relationships (e.g., causality, conditionality, etc.) rather than always expecting the reader to infer them from the context? 10			
Does the teacher's manual provide lists of accessible resources containing alternative readings for the very poor or very advanced readers? 11			
Is the readability level appropriate (according to a readability formula)? 12			
Usability			
External organizational aids			
Does table of contents provide a clear overview of the contents of the textbook? 1			

Usability (cont.)		Yes	To some extent	No (or does not apply)
Do chapter headings clearly define the content of the chapter?	2			
Do chapter subheadings clearly break out the important concept in the chapter?	3			
Do topic headings provide assistance in breaking the chapter into relevant parts?	4			
Does the glossary contain all the technical terms of the textbook?	5			
Are graphs and charts clear and supportive of the textual material?	6			
Are illustrations well done and appropriate to the level of the students?	7			
Is print size of the text appropriate to the level of student readers?	8			
Are lines of text an appropriate length for the level of the students who will use the textbook?	9			
Is teacher's manual available and adequate for guidance to the teacher?	10			
Are important terms in italics or boldfaced type for easy identification by readers?	11			
Are end-of-chapter questions on literal, interpretive, and applied levels of comprehension?	12			
Internal organizational aids				
Are concepts spaced appropriately throughout the text, rather than being too many in too short a space or too few words?	1			
Is an adequate context provided to allow students to determine meanings of technical terms?	2			
Are the sentence lengths appropriate for the level of students who will be using the text?	3			
Is the author's style (word length, sentence length, sentence complexity, paragraph length, numbers of examples) appropriate to the level of students who will be using the text?	4			

(Box continues)

BOX 11.1 *(Continued)*

General Textbook Readability Checklist

Usability
(cont.)

	Yes	To some extent	No (or does not apply)
Does the author use a predominant structure or pattern of organization (compare-contrast, cause-effect, time order, problem-solution) within the writing to assist students in interpreting the text? 5			

Interestability

	Yes	To some extent	No (or does not apply)
Does the teacher's manual provide introductory activities that will capture students' interest? 1			
Are chapter titles and subheadings concrete, meaningful, or interesting? 2			
Is the writing style of the text appealing to the students? 3			
Are the activities motivating? Will they make the student want to pursue the topic further? 4			
Does the book clearly show how the knowledge being learned might be used by the learner in the future? 5			
Are the cover, format, print size, and pictures appealing to the students? 6			
Does the text provide positive and motivating models for both sexes as well as for other racial, ethnic, and socioeconomic groups? 7			
Does the text help students generate interest as they relate experiences and develop visual and sensory images? 8			

Summary Rating

	Understandability	Usability	Interest
The text rates highest in			
The text rates lowest in			
My teaching can best supplement			
I would still need assistance with			

Statement of Strengths:

Statement of Weaknessess:

to calculate its readability. Grade-level scores for each passage can then be averaged to obtain an overall readability level. The readability graph in Box 11.2 is useful in predicting the difficulty of material within one grade level when the accompanying directions for the Fry formula are followed.

TEXTBOOK ORGANIZATION

The primary purpose of an elementary textbook, whether it's in mathematics, science, English, social studies, or health, is to provide children with information. To make this information accessible, authors organize their ideas and try to tie information together. They make use of external and internal structural features which students in turn need to look for. *External organization* is a textbook's overall instructional design, or its format within chapters as well as at the front and end of the textbook. *Internal organization* is a textbook's pattern of organization, or the interrelationships among ideas in the text. What do elementary teachers need to become knowledgeable about in order to help students gain access to textbook information?

External Organization

Most elementary textbooks contain *organizational aids* to facilitate reading. For example, the preface, table of contents, bibliography, index, and appendix are typical format features. Another name for these aids is front and end matter, including title page, dedication, list of tables and illustrations, and glossary. Books geared for early elementary grades will contain less front and end matter than intermediate-grade texts. Nevertheless, the aids that do tend to be used (especially the table of contents and index) are valuable tools for elementary textbook users.

Helping children use organizational aids to advantage instead of skipping over them is an important step. Certain strategies that teachers can use to focus students' attention on external organizational aids can make the difference between superficial and thoughtful reading. Two interrelated strategies that set the stage for active reading by riveting elementary students' attention on certain cues involve previewing and skimming.

Previewing. A good way to start previewing with a group of children is to model some questions that all readers ask to prepare for reading. *Previewing*, after all, should help students become aware of the purposes for a reading assignment. "What kind of reading are we going to do? What is our goal? Should we try to remember details or look for the main ideas? How much time will this assignment take? What things do we already know about . . . (the solar system, for example)? What do we still need to find out?" These questions prepare children for what's coming. Raising questions and setting purposes is the beginning of efficient processing of information. It calls for further explicit instruction in previewing.

First, select a subject area in which your textbook contains aids that are obviously visual. The textbook writer has incorporated a number of organizational

BOX 11.2
Fry Readability Graph

GRAPH FOR ESTIMATING READABILITY — EXTENDED

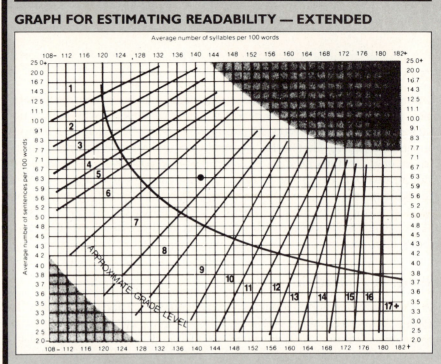

Average number of syllables per 100 words

EXPANDED DIRECTIONS FOR WORKING READABILITY GRAPH

1. Randomly select three (3) sample passages and count out exactly 100 words each, beginning with the beginning of a sentence. Do count proper nouns, initializations, and numerals.

2. Count the number of sentences in the hundred words, estimating length of the fraction of the last sentence to the nearest one-tenth.

3. Count the total number of syllables in the 100-word passage. If you don't have a hand counter available, an easy way is to simply put a mark above every syllable over one in each word, then when you get to the end of the passage, count the number of marks and add 100. Small calculators can also be used as counters by pushing numeral 1, then pushing the + sign for each word or syllable when counting.

4. Enter graph with *average* sentence length and *average* number of syllables; plot dot where the two lines intersect. Area where dot is plotted will give you the approximate grade level.

5. If a great deal of variability is found in syllable count or sentence count, putting more samples into the average is desirable.

6. A word is defined as a group of symbols with a space on either side; thus, *Joe, IRA, 1945,* and *&* are each one word.

7. A syllable is defined as a phonetic syllable. Generally, there are as many syllables as vowel sounds. For example, *stopped* is one syllable and *wanted* is two syllables. When counting syllables for numerals and initializations, count one syllable for each symbol. For example, *1945* is four syllables, *IRA* is three syllables, and *&* is one syllable.

and typographic aids as guideposts for readers. Point out how the table of contents, preface, chapter introductions or summaries, and chapter questions can give readers valuable clues about the overall structure of a textbook or the important ideas in a unit or chapter. Previewing a table of contents, for example, not only creates a general impression, but also helps readers of all ages to distinguish the forest from the trees. The table of contents gives students a feel for the overall theme or structure of the course material so that they may get a sense of the scope and sequence of ideas at the very beginning of the unit. You can also use the table of contents to build background and discuss the relatedness of each of the parts of the book. Model for students the kinds of questions that should be raised. "Why do the authors begin with _____ in Part One?" "If you were the author, would you have arranged the major parts in the text differently? Why?"

To illustrate how you might use the table of contents, study how a fourth-grade teacher introduced a unit on plants in the environment. Ms. Henderson asked her students to open their books to Part One in the table of contents. "What do you think this part of the book ["Plant Competitors"] is about? Why do you think so?" Key words or terms in the table of contents led to these questions: "What do you think the author means by *unwanted plants*? What does *parasite* mean? What do parasites have to do with *nongreen plants*?" Open-ended questions such as these helped Ms. Henderson keep her fourth-graders focused on the material and on the value of predicting and anticipating content.

As these students get into a particular chapter, they will learn how to use additional organizational aids such as the introduction, summary, or questions at the chapter's end. These aids should create a frame of reference for the important ideas in the chapter. They can also survey chapter titles, headings, subheadings, words and phrases in special type, pictures, diagrams, charts, and graphs.

Here are some rules or steps to follow when previewing as Ms. Henderson's students did:

1. Read the title, converting it to a question. ("What are plant competitors in man's environment?")

2. Read the introduction, summary, and questions, stating the author's main points. ("All living things compete with each other; the competitors of useful plants become man's competitors; weeds are unwanted plants; nongreen plants living in or on other plants and animals are parasites; people try to control plant competitors.")

3. Read the heads and subheads; then convert them to questions. ("Competition; weeds; nongreen plant competitors; controlling plant competitors. "How are plant competitors controlled?")

4. Read highlighted print. ("Competitors; nongreen plants; parasites; smut; chemical sprays are very poisonous.")

5. Study visual materials; what do pictures, maps, and so on tell about a chapter's content? (Pictures of mustard plants, destroyed ears of corn, a white pine attacked by tiny nongreen plants, a helicopter spraying a truck farm.)

Until Ms. Henderson's fourth-graders were able to do this somewhat independently, she walked them through the steps many times. She also selected one or two pages from the assigned reading and developed transparencies with some questions her students should ask while previewing. Showing the overhead transparencies to the whole class, she explained her reasons for the questions. Then the students opened their books to another section of the chapter, taking turns asking the kinds of questions she had modeled. Soon they raised some of their own questions while previewing.

Skimming. Learning how to skim content material effectively is a natural part of previewing. *Skimming* involves intensive previewing of the reading assignment to see what it will be about. To help elementary students get a good sense of what is coming, have them read the first sentence of every paragraph (often an important idea). The fourth-graders about to study plant competitors read these first sentences:

> If you had two pet cats and gave one of them some tuna fish, what would happen?
>
> Plants, of course, don't know they are competing.
>
> Even green plants compete with one another for energy sources.
>
> Plants are often weakened by the parasites growing on them.
>
> Many states passed laws to help with the control of weeds.

An effective motivator for raising students' expectations about their assigned text material is to direct them to skim the entire reading selection rapidly, taking no more than two minutes. You might even set a timer and encourage the children to zip through every page. When time is up, ask the class to recall everything they've read. Both teacher and students will be surprised by the quantity and quality of the recalls.

Previewing and skimming are important strategies for helping children develop knowledge of textbook aids and for surveying texts to make predictions. They help get at general understanding as students learn how to "size up" material, judge its relevance to a topic, or gain a good idea of what a passage is about.

Text Structure

The term *text structure* refers to the *internal organization* of text, the patterns of organization or thought relationships in text. If, as Niles (1965) said, students should look for structure in everything they read and know what to do when they find it, what about teachers? First, you need to recognize and understand basic patterns of organization rather than elaborate classification schemes. Second, you must make students aware of patterns of organization and how to look for major thought relationships within patterns.

It stands to reason that the more logically connected one idea is to another, the more likely that the description or explanation will be coherent. Content area textbook authors, seeking to inform, strive to achieve coherency. Hence, they tend to use exposition as their primary style: telling, showing, describing, and explaining. How do authors make these logical connections in expository writing?

Patterns of Organization. Different types of logical connections authors use to link the important and less important ideas are called *patterns of organization*. The main pattern authors use to tie ideas together is located at the "top level" of the content presentation. For example, Meyer (1975) explained that an author may organize content so that there is a *hierarchical relationship* among ideas in the text passage. Therefore, the most important or *superordinate* ideas should be located at the top levels of the content presentation and have many supporting ideas and details below them.

Teachers need to help young readers recognize the major types of patterns used by authors in expository writing. To differentiate important ideas from the less important ones, students should begin to look for the five patterns illustrated below.

1. *Enumeration:* A doughlike mixture comes from the ovens. Rolling machines flatten this dough into very thin slabs. Next, these slabs are treated so that the gum will keep its flavor. Finally, the slabs are cut into sticks, and the sticks are separated, wrapped, and placed into packages. Then the gum is shipped to stores for sale. (Brzeinski, J., and H. Schoephoerster. Test Booklet: *Kaleidoscope*. Fourth grade. Boston: Houghton Mifflin, 1974.)

2. *Time Order:* Fifty years ago, John and Mary were the most popular names in the United States. But today, Jason and Jennifer are the most popular names to be given to children; Amy and Michael are also popular today. In ten years, though, other names will probably be more popular. (Aaron, I., D. Jackson, et al. Workbook: *Hidden Wonders*. Third grade. Chicago: Scott, Foresman, 1981.)

3. *Comparison-Contrast:* There are great differences in population among the fifty states. Seven states have more than ten million people each. Is your state one of those seven? On the other hand, eleven states have fewer than one million people each. Is your state one of those? (Arnsdorf, V., H. Bass, et al. *The World and Its People: States and Regions*. Fourth grade. Morristown, N.J.: Silver Burdett, 1986.)

4. *Cause-Effect:* Long ago when sailors went to sea, they did not have modern instruments to tell them where they were. As a result, once they were out of sight of land, the sailors had to use the sky to tell their location. (Aaron, I., D. Jackson, et al. *Sky Climbers*. Fifth-grade workbook. Chicago: Scott, Foresman, 1981.)

5. *Problem Solution:* There is another way that people might solve the problem of not having enough land. Cities of the future may be built in space. Large space stations may someday hold entire communities. These space cities would make their own fresh air and water. Then people could live far, far away from the earth. (Buggey, JoAnne. *Our Communities*. Third grade. Chicago: Follett, 1983.)

Awareness of Patterns. The older students are, the more they need to become aware of structure in their reading materials. After determining the predominant pattern contained in a text assignment, you can help students find the clues or signals provided by textbook authors to help readers figure out the pattern they are using. A signal may be a word or a phrase that helps the reader follow the writer's thoughts. Common signals or ties which connect ideas to each other are listed in Figure 11.1.

Students will need explicit instruction in how to recognize specific patterns in text assignments if they are to use structure to better understand and remember the material.

HELPING STUDENTS READ TEXTBOOK ASSIGNMENTS

For learning to occur, there must be a point of contact between the reader's knowledge of the world and the ideas communicated by the textbook author. As we explained in Chapter 6, what students know, feel, and believe is a major factor in learning; it helps determine the extent to which they will make sense out of any situation. Thus an instructional goal worth pursuing is to help students "make contact" through a variety of learning strategies that build and activate background knowledge.

Activating and Building Background Knowledge

We noted in Chapter 6 that you can help students learn new ideas by giving them a frame of reference as they get ready to read. A frame of reference is actually an

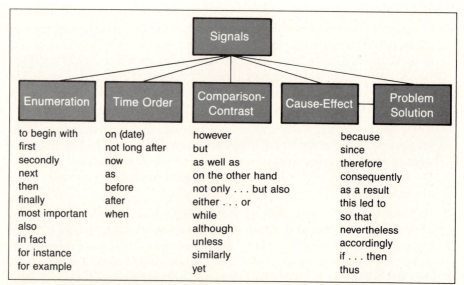

Figure 11.1   Reading Signals

anchor point; it reflects the cognitive structure students need to relate new information to existing knowledge. Helping students organize what they know and showing them where and how new ideas "fit" is essential for learning to take place.

We recommend three activities that serve the dual purpose of providing a frame of reference and raising students' expectations in advance of reading: (1) structured overviews, (2) anticipation guides, and (3) brainstorming.

Structured Overviews. Key concepts or main ideas in the material being studied can be displayed on a *structured overview,* which has also been called a graphic organizer. On it, key technical terms are arranged to show their relationships to each other.

Ms. Mark designed a structured overview to show her third-graders vocabulary in relation to more inclusive vocabulary concepts they would meet in their study of birds. Prior to constructing this preceding activity, Ms. Mark listed the key concepts in her four-week unit, *Birds Are Special Animals.* She then followed the steps suggested by Barron (1969) for developing an overview and introducing it to her students:

1. *Analyze vocabulary and list important words.* Ms. Mark found these key terms in *The Life of Birds,* edited by Donald Moyle:

prehistoric birds	protection
development	language
behavior	ornithology
migration	difference

2. *Arrange the concepts to be learned.* Ms. Mark first chose the word "ornithology" as the most inclusive concept, superordinate to all the others. Next, she classified the terms immediately *under* the superordinate concept and coordinated them with each other.

3. *Add any other vocabulary terms that you believe students understand.* Ms. Mark added terms like "protect," "animals," and "help."

4. *Evaluate the overview.* The interrelationships among the key terms looked like Figure 11.2 and made sense to Ms. Mark and her third-graders.

5. *Introduce students to the learning task.* Ms. Mark created as much discussion as possible among her third-graders as she presented the vocabulary terms. She drew on their understanding and previous experiences with birds as well as on class activities over the previous few days which introduced the unit (e.g., some pre-assessment and an anticipation guide).

6. *As you complete the learning task, relate new information to the overview.* Using this overview as a study guide throughout the "bird unit," Ms. Mark encouraged students to discuss what information was still needed and where it might best be located on the graphic overview.

Anticipation Guides. By creating anticipation about the meaning of what will be read, teachers facilitate student-centered purposes for reading. An anticipation

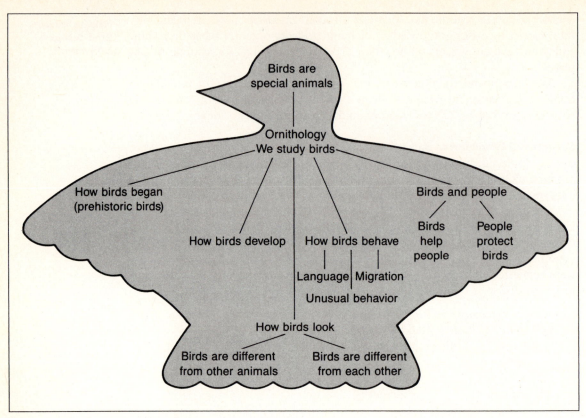

Figure 11.2   Structured Overview

guide is a series of oral or written statements for individual students to respond to before they read the text assignment. The statements serve as a springboard into discussion. Students must rely on what they already know to make educated guesses about the material to be read: They must make predictions.

Let's go back to the fourth-grade class studying about plants in the environment. Their teacher, Ms. Henderson, wanted to help students discuss what they knew and believed about the unit in order to raise their expectations about the content matter before reading the text. Above all, she was determined to involve students actively. Here are the guidelines that Ms. Henderson followed in constructing and using anticipation guides:

1. Analyze the material to be read. Determine the major ideas—implicit and explicit—with which students will interact.

2. Write those ideas in short, clear declarative statements. These statements should in some way reflect the world that students live in or know about. Therefore, avoid abstractions whenever possible.

320

3. Put these statements into a format that will elicit anticipation and prediction making.

4. Discuss readers' predictions and anticipations prior to reading the text selection.

5. Assign the text selection. Have students evaluate the statements in light of the author's intent and purpose.

6. Contrast readers' predictions with the author's intended meaning.

Using these guidelines, Ms. Henderson pinpointed several major concepts, put them in the form of short statements, and wrote each one on the board. After some initial discussion about what students might already know about plants in the environment, Ms. Henderson distributed two three-by-five-inch pieces of construction paper (one green and one yellow) to each child and explained:

> On the yellow paper write "unlikely" and on the green paper write "likely." I will read each of the statements on the board; you will think about it and decide whether it is "likely" or "unlikely." Then, after fifteen seconds, I will say "Go" and you will hold up either your yellow *or* your green card.

The anticipation guide for the above activity included these fifteen statements:

1. A dandelion is always a weed.
2. All plants make their own food.
3. All living things in the environment compete with one another.
4. Plants compete for sunlight.
5. All animals need sunlight.
6. Plants can move around in search of food.
7. Plants compete for space.
8. Plants and animals compete for water.
9. Plants compete with people for energy.
10. People are a parasite.
11. People use their minds to compete.
12. People sometimes pollute the environment to control weeds.
13. People always win in their competition with plants.
14. Science helps people compete.
15. People have always been wise competitors.

The information in each of the statements was developed in two short chapters in the students' text. After each statement or pair of statements, Ms. Henderson encouraged the children to discuss the reasons for their responses with questions such as "Why? "Why not?" or "Can you give an example?"

An interesting example of how an anticipation guide may be used in conjunction with a four-day lesson is contained in Box 11.3. It was designed for use with fourth-graders as an introduction to a unit on primates revolving around the book *The Story of Nim, the Chimp Who Learned Language* by Anna Michel.

BOX 11.3

Anticipation Guide for "The Story of Nim, the Chimp Who Learned Language"

Directions: Read the statements below and place a check next to those that you agree with. Discuss your choices in small groups and explain why you agreed with the statements you checked.

_____ 1. Chimpanzees can imitate what humans do, but attach no meaning to their actions.

_____ 2. Language can be learned by animals in the same way and sequence in which a child learns language.

_____ 3. Humans are evolved from chimpanzees and apes.

_____ 4. Once language is learned, a chimpanzee will forget it and those who taught him given an absence from one or both.

_____ 5. Scientists undertake these projects in order to better understand humans.

_____ 6. Relationships between animals and people aren't as close as those between people and people or animals and animals.

_____ 7. A chimpanzee can use sign language to get what he wants.

_____ 8. An animal in a domestic situation soon forgets all of its natural inborn behaviors and instincts.

_____ 9. Deaf people could understand a chimpanzee trained in sign language.

_____ 10. The best environment for an animal to learn a complex skill such as sign language would be in one with a strict structure and free from distractions.

After the small group discussion, the whole class discusses the trends and ideas that emerged in the groups. These ideas are written on the board in a place where they can remain for a day or two. The book is then assigned in its entirety to be read before the next day's class. Next day, students consider each statement on the anticipation guide again and discuss in small groups the ideas that emerged from reading the text. They compare these with the prereading ideas on the board to identify similarities and differences in the two sets of ideas. Reasons for ideas should be given by students and controversial issues arising might then lead to a debate. For example, "What is the real meaning in a chimpanzee's language acquisition compared with a human child's?"

Brainstorming. The third prereading activity, _brainstorming,_ is especially helpful in getting students to generate ideas they can use to think about the upcoming reading material. The brainstorming procedure involves two basic steps: (1) identifying a broad concept that reflects the main topic to be studied in the assigned reading, and (2) having students work in small groups to generate a list of words related to the broad concept within a specified length of time.

Brainstorming sessions are valuable not only from an instructional perspective, but from a diagnostic one as well. Observant teachers discover what knowledge their students possess about the topic to be studied. It also helps students become aware of how much they know, individually and collectively, about the topic.

Some teachers assign hypothetical problems to be solved before reading a selection, or a real life school-related problem. Others simply select a major concept in the reading material and get students actively involved in brainstorming. Mr. Davis, a sixth-grade teacher, used the latter model to develop a brainstorming activity for a story by Robert Zacks, "The Nest."

Mr. Davis began by telling his sixth-graders they would soon be reading a story called "The Nest." But first, he said, they would work with one of the major concepts of the story, *restrictions*. He divided the class into small groups, using an alphabetical scheme. (Other times he may choose groups or let students form groups with those nearby.) Once the groups were formed, Mr. Davis used a three-step brainstorming activity:

1. In your groups, brainstorm as many ideas as possible in three minutes that relate to the concept *restrictions*. Have one member of your group record the ideas.

2. As a group, put the ideas into categories (groups) wherever they seem to be related. Be prepared to explain the reasons behind the grouping of ideas.

3. Following class discussion on how ideas were grouped, examine your own work again and, using these ideas and others gained from the other groups, make predictions on what you believe the story might be about. Be sure to consider the title of the story somewhere in your predictions.

The activity took approximately twenty minutes and required intermittent teacher direction. Mr. Davis, for example, followed step 1 with a brief oral direction for step 2. Before moving on to step 3, he initiated a class discussion in which groups shared their ideas for grouping ideas into categories and the logic behind the categories. This gave both individuals and groups a chance to react to the varied categories. Although a teacher may offer some suggestions to a group that has bogged down in the categorizing process, we caution that this be done sparingly and only to keep the process going.

After step three in the brainstorming activity is complete and predictions have been generated, the story is usually assigned. It would, however, also be possible to extend the prereading phase. To illustrate, Mr. Davis might have asked students to complete a survey of parents, grandparents, and other adults about the type of restrictions they were faced with in a different generation and which ones bothered them the most.

Guiding Reader-Text Interactions

Many elementary school students will come face to face with difficult text material and have trouble handling the conceptual demands. They need teacher assistance to read this material if they are to learn content from texts. Through the use of teacher-prepared adjunct instructional materials, teachers guide reader-text interactions. Students need structure to handle difficult reading material. *Three-level guides* and *pattern guides* are two adjunct materials that serve as models and guides during reading. They provide structure—a framework for responding to text material and for helping students seek information as they interact with text.

Adjunct instructional materials are developed by teachers to accompany text assignments. For example, the anticipation guide explained in the previous section of this chapter is a type of adjunct material. A guide used in conjunction with text makes learning easier because it helps students comprehend and study text more effectively. When students receive enough support and direction to learn successfully from text, they gain confidence . . . confidence to continue learning.

Three-Level Reading Guides. A three-level guide gives elementary students a "conscious experience" with comprehension levels (Herber, 1978). As they walk through the process, students respond to and manipulate the important explicit and implicit ideas in the material. They gain an opportunity to sense the relatedness of ideas as they move within and among the levels. These levels, which certainly appear to be logically sequenced, are not necessarily "read" in that order by readers. Some readers, for example, may look first for overarching generalizations and not proceed from literal recognition, then to interpretation, and finally to application. This is normal reading behavior because, in reading comprehension, levels are interactive and inseparable.

Mr. Roberts, Mike and Terry's teacher at the beginning of the chapter, wanted to tie in some social studies concepts with the story "Androcles and the Lion" from his students' reading series. He initiated the lesson with a three-minute brainstorming activity in which small groups wrote all the words they knew related to ancient Rome. Next, each group put their words into categories that they copied on the board. Mr. Roberts then introduced the three-level guide in Box 11.4 and directed students, "Read through the story first to get a feeling for what it is about in light of your brainstorming and what you already know." The class read the story silently and then responded to the statements on the guide.

Notice that the guide contains declarative statements that do not require students to produce answers to questions. Instead, Mr. Roberts's students were obliged to make decisions among likely alternatives. Herber and Nelson (1975) supported the notion that it is easier to recognize possible answers than to produce them. Another benefit to using statements is that they can serve as springboards for discussion about content. Mr. Roberts asked his class to share some of their personal experiences of how animals are man's best friends. He also inquired into how the students arrived at the answers they put on their guides. As a concluding lesson activity, Mr. Roberts encouraged some students to write from the point of view of Androcles or the lion, and others to draw or model any of the characters. Were students to "do" guides without the opportunity to discuss and debate responses, the adjunct material would soon deteriorate into busywork and paper shuffling.

Reading guides are not meant to be used with every text assignment every

BOX 11.4

Three-Level Guide to "Androcles and the Lion"

I. Directions: Check the items you believe say what the author says. Sometimes the exact words will be used; other times, substitutes may be used.

_____ 1. The lion roared so loudly Androcles was afraid he would be killed.

_____ 2. After Androcles helped the lion, the lion was so happy he become a friend to Androcles.

_____ 3. In those times, Romans went to the arenas to see these lion-man fights as people today go to circuses and baseball games.

_____ 4. Androcles wasn't afraid because he knew he'd see his friend, the lion.

_____ 5. The people were so touched by Androcles' story that they let him go free.

_____ 6. With their freedom and each other, Androcles and the lion lived happily in Rome for many years.

II. Directions: Put a check on the line beside any of the statements below that you think give the meaning of what the author was trying to say to you.

_____ 1. Animals sometimes show the same kind of behavior for both pain and anger as did the lion.

_____ 2. The friendship of the lion was more genuine than that shown by any man to Androcles.

_____ 3. Runaway slaves deserve what they get.

_____ 4. Ancient people enjoyed crude and shocking forms of recreation.

_____ 5. Even the cruelest of people have compassion for their fellow man.

_____ 6. Freedom to a slave was the best gift he could be given.

III. Directions: To apply what you read means to take information and ideas from what you read and connect them to what you know. Place a check in the blank beside any statement below that can be backed up by any statement from level II or by any of your own past experiences or knowledge gained from studying. Make sure you have reasons for your answers.

_____ 1. Animals are man's best friends.

_____ 2. One good turn deserves another.

_____ 3. At times people can be more cruel than the wildest of beasts.

_____ 4. Freedom is the most important thing that man and beast can possess.

day. The three-level guide is just one instructional aid that helps students grow toward mature reading and independent learning. Its effectiveness increases when students know how to work in groups and how to apply techniques that have been taught clearly. In the final analysis, guides are tools, not tests. Statements in the guide act as prompts that will initiate interaction and reinforce the quality of the reader's response to meaning in text material.

Pattern Guides. The pattern guide is a variation of the three-level guide. It creates a similar experience for students but differs at the literal level. Instead of having students respond to relevant information per se, you can design guide material that allows them to actually experience how the information fits together. As we discussed earlier in this chapter, expository text may be organized according to these major organizational structures: cause-effect, comparison-contrast, time order, enumeration, and main-idea detail. Once students learn how to search for these relationships in text, they are in a better position to retain information more efficiently and effectively and to comprehend material more thoroughly (Meyer, Brandt, and Bluth, 1979).

Mrs. Hahn, a third-grade teacher, followed this teaching sequence when creating and using a pattern guide for "Why Mosquitoes Buzz in People's Ears," a West African folk tale by Verna Aardema.

1. Examine a reading selection and decide on the predominant pattern used by the author.

2. Make students aware of the pattern and how to interpret the author's meaning as part of the total lesson.

3. Provide guidance in the process of perceiving organization through a pattern guide followed by small group or whole class discussion.

4. Assist students who have unresolved problems concerning either the process or the content under discussion.

Mrs. Hahn spent considerable time discussing the predominant pattern (time order) and why her third-graders should search for relationships. She knew that the more children interacted, the more they would be aware of the pattern and how the author uses it. Hence, as her students worked on the pattern guide in Box 11.5, Mrs. Hahn provided feedback to keep them going as well as to clarify their thinking when they reread the story while listening to the record.

Reinforcing Vocabulary and Concepts

Elementary students need many opportunities to use the new word meanings and concepts they're being exposed to in subject areas. They benefit from a language-rich classroom environment in which vocabulary reinforcement materials and activities are available. Furthermore, students usually enjoy the manipulative game-like activities that seem to captivate even the more reluctant students.

When elementary students manipulate technical terms in relation to other terms, they are thinking critically. Vocabulary activities can be designed to give children the experience of *thinking about, thinking through,* and *thinking with* the technical vocabulary of a subject. Working with relationships among technical terms provides this opportunity. For example, a technical term may appear to be totally unfamiliar at a surface level but actually represent a meaning familiar to

BOX 11.5

Pattern Guide for *Why Mosquitoes Buzz in People's Ears*

Read the story *Why Mosquitoes Buzz in People's Ears* by Verna Aardema. After you have read the story, number the sentences below in the order they happen in the story. Check yourself by rereading the story while you listen to the story record.

_____ The mosquito has a guilty conscience.
_____ Mother Owl will not wake the sun.
_____ King Lion learns the truth.
_____ Mother Owl is satisfied and wakes the sun.
_____ One of the owlets is killed.
_____ The mosquito tells the iguana about some yams.
_____ The animals think danger is coming.
_____ The monkey lands on a dead limb.

students. In this situation, associating the new with the known through a matching exercise or word puzzle would be effective.

As a rule, the types of vocabulary reinforcement exercises in Chapter 7 should be first completed individually by students and then *discussed* either in small groups or with the class as a whole. The oral interaction in team learning situations gives more students a chance to use terms. The increased volume in participation creates an atmosphere for reinforcement. Students can exchange ideas, share insights, and justify responses in a non-threatening situation. Barron and Earle (1973) suggested the following procedure for small-group discussion of reinforcement activities:

1. End small group discussion only after the group has discussed each answer and every member of the group understands the reasons for each answer.

2. Encourage the active participation of all group members. A student who has trouble with a particular exercise can still make a valuable contribution by asking questions or asking someone to explain answers.

3. Limit talk to the particular exercise or to related questions.

4. Make sure that students use the words and their meanings in discussing the answers rather than using letters and numbers (e.g., "I think the answer to number 1 is C, 2 is F.")

You may decide to use vocabulary reinforcement activities either before or after reading, depending on the instructional purpose and timing. On the one hand, definitions could be reinforced before reading so meanings can be further developed during the actual reading, while on the other, students' ability to use and manipulate concepts attained from reading would be more easily extended with postreading vocabulary exercises. In either case, you can feel confident that reinforcement activities will enhance students' vocabulary and concept learning.

Study Strategies

Cultivating the right habits and attitudes toward studying is essential, and teachers can help students do this. It is easy for teachers to tell students they "should" study. With the strategies in the rest of this chapter, a teacher can go beyond *shoulds* and show students *how* to study.

Survey Technique. The *survey technique* prepares students for reading through a whole-class overview of the material. The teacher shows students the importance of previewing prior to reading any content chapter—social studies, science, math, health, or a *Weekly Reader* magazine. The survey technique can be used in the primary grades, but is even more effective in upper elementary grades. As with other instructional strategies, decisions must first be made by the teacher about what particular information to emphasize. The six-step procedure may be used with most content textbook chapters containing the following: chapter title, introduction, main headings with subtopics, summary, and review questions. By following the six steps of the survey technique, the class derives an overview or the main idea of the chapter before studying it more intensively.

1. *Use the title*. After reading the title of the chapter with the students, ask, "What do you think you will learn about in this chapter?" "What do you already know about this topic?" "How do you think this chapter relates to the one we just completed?"

2. *Use review questions*. Have students turn to the end of the chapter; then ask a student to read aloud each of the review questions. Students are asked what they think the answer to each question might be. This can be done orally or in writing, individually or in groups. Tierney (1985) and his associates reported that in this step it is not unusual for students to correctly answer 20 to 30 pecent of the questions! In this way, they find out how much they already know on the topic as well as discovering what points the author sees as important.

3. *Use subtitles*. Together with students, note each of the subtitles and devise questions using each of the headings. For example, the heading "Magnetic Poles" could result in the questions, "What are magnetic poles?" The class may develop questions as a whole or in small groups. The questions may be placed on chart paper, the chalkboard, or an overhead projector. The development of such questions results in student-generated probes that are extremely helpful when studying the chapter in detail.

4. *Use graphics*. Pose questions that will lead students to glean information from graphs, charts, and pictures. Suppose the text contained the chart below on the speed of various animals. Ask questions to get students to "read" the visuals to determine information from the chart: "What does the chart tell us?" "What information can we get from the chart?" Or, more specifically, "How fast does a cheetah run?" "How fast does a duck hawk fly?" "How is the chart organized?" "Which is slower, the greyhound or the antelope?"

Sen
way
they
how
illus

1.

2.

3.

4.

I

1. I
a

2. I
r

3. A
e
p

4. V
n
b
st

5. H
st
o
id
a

6. H
T
ex

7. G
en
lir

	Speed (kilometers per hour)
Duck hawk	291
Golden eagle	183
Cheetah	112
Swift	104
Antelope	87
Greyhound	48

5. *Use introductory and summary paragraphs.* Because textbook authors often use introductory and summary paragraphs, ask students to read this information silently. Then discuss how the information in the introduction and summary fits with the information discovered in the first three steps of the procedure.

6. *Identify the main idea.* Based on step 5, have students develop a concise statement of what they think the main idea of the chapter should be. Then have students share their ideas. How are they alike or different? Perhaps a composite main idea can be written on the chalkboard as a guide to reading.

Studying Graphic Aids. Authors have definite purposes in mind when they include *graphics* in their texts. Often charts and tables organize or summarize information developed in the main text. At other times, graphics serve as an example or illustration of points made. Pictures, cartoons, and maps are placed there to encourage readers to relate experientially to the ideas in the text. Not only should graphic aids be surveyed before reading, but also students must learn to study them during reading.

Children often ignore graphic aids in textbooks because they find it difficult to jump from print to visual and then back to the print. This is why they need to read, analyze, and interpret the information in graphic aids just as they do the main body of the text. Open-book discussions, using an overhead projector and focusing everyone's attention on the visual, can be helpful. Those can be done when using the survey technique. As with the other study techniques, teachers can model or "think aloud" how they would go about learning information from a graph or chart. In doing this, ask questions that identify important elements and relationships.

If students need specific information from graphics, three-level guides can be successfully employed. Ms. Gold devised a three-level guide for her fifth-graders for a bar graph on trips made by a steamboat between Natchez, Mississippi, and New Orleans, Louisiana. (See Box 11.6.)

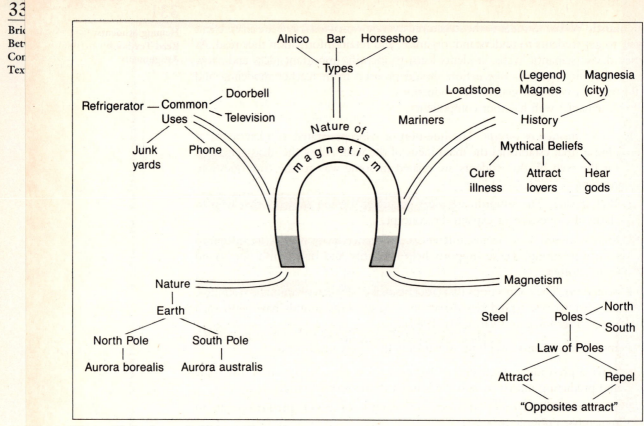

Figure 11.3 Semantic Web on Magnetism

A sixth-grade class used this process to devise a semantic web on the nature of magnetism (Figure 11.3). In this case the class decided to draw a horseshoe magnet for the center of the semantic web instead of the usual circle. Notice also in this web double lines are used for the main web strands. Teachers often use different colors to distinguish the two kinds of strands.

With appropriate modeling, explanation, and experience, students will learn to use semantic webbing as a tool for studying.

DEVELOPING UNITS OF STUDY

At the beginning of this chapter, we proposed two major goals. The first, directed at students, was that they learn how to learn; how to use reading to think about content. The second, directed at teachers, was that they set the tone and provide an instructional framework in the elementary classroom. Planning appropriate frameworks for instruction takes time, but it is time well spent in accomplishing the second goal: It results in a blueprint for making decisions—a workable plan to coordinate instructional activities and materials. In this section we examine some elements necessary for planning a content unit of study at the elementary level.

What's Involved in Unit Planning

Unlike a single lesson, a content unit organizes instruction around a series of lessons that include multiple materials. Rather than excluding the textbook, this means providing more options to coordinate a variety of information sources. This makes sense because "to meet the needs of children, a curriculum must provide experiences that relate to students' personal goals and take into account their interests, purposes, abilities, and maturity" (Coody and Nelson, 1982, page 20). Hence, planning a unit in advance helps you accomplish objectives more efficiently and effectively. You can integrate prereading, reading, and postreading activities in a way that will give students a real sense of continuity.

When making initial decisions about what content to teach, how to teach it, and what theme or topic to use as an organizer, it is helpful to write down the *major concept to be developed*. This is the basis of a content unit. Simultaneously, you should begin listing the main instructional materials and resources. A brief description initiates the unit of study and might resemble this introduction to Ms. Mark's third-grade science unit on birds:

> *Birds Are Special Animals* is intended for a class of third-grade students. The unit will require approximately four weeks of daily sessions. For the first three weeks, the focus will be on activities planned for the entire class. During the last week of the unit, the focus will be on small group and individual projects. The students will use *The Life of Birds,* edited by Donald Moyle, as their main reading source. Supplemental readings from other sources will be assigned throughout the unit. Audiovisual materials will be used as needed to introduce and reinforce concepts. Students will also have access to a variety of materials with which they can explore areas of individual interest. During this unit, the students will have the opportunity to investigate many aspects of ornithology including the evolution of birds, the adaptation of birds to their habitats, and the interrelation of birds and people.

Doing a content analysis is the major part of teacher preparation in the development of a unit of study. After all, it is essential to decide *what is to be learned* in order to establish goals. A content analysis elicits the major concepts and understandings that students should learn from reading the unit materials. Through content analysis, you select the major concepts and decide on the overall learning goals and objectives to be accomplished. According to Earle (1976), it doesn't matter whether these content objectives are stated behaviorally or not. What really matters is that the teacher know which concepts must be taught. Therefore, it's important that the teacher decide on a manageable number of the most important concepts to be gained from the unit. This means setting priorities; it's impossible to cover every aspect of the material that students will read or be exposed to.

For her unit on birds, Ms. Mark identified the following major concepts from her content analysis:

1. The study of birds is called *ornithology*. There are many ways to learn about birds.

2. A chick grows inside an egg in specific developmental stages. Once hatched, the chick continues to grow in a predictable pattern.

3. Birds began to evolve millions of years ago as some reptiles started to fly and grow feathers.

4. Birds are different from other animals. There are other animals that can fly and other animals that can lay eggs, but only birds have feathers.

5. A bird's body is built to make flying possible.

6. Birds are different from each other. They live in different habitats and have different beaks, feet, and colors.

7. Birds behave in many interesting ways. They can find their way over long distances. They have a language. They can learn.

8. Birds and people are important to each other. Birds help people to live in many ways. People need to protect birds if birds are to survive.

Once she had drafted the major content objectives, Ms. Mark then turned her attention to organizing the unit and putting it to work in her third-grade classroom.

Putting a Unit to Work

Ms. Mark used a "branching out" pattern as the organizational framework for her "Birds Are Special Animals" unit. Branching out allowed her the latitude to move from highly structured lessons to less structured ones. At the same time, the movement from single to multiple information sources exposes students to variable instructional materials that may be better suited to their needs and interests. "The heart of a unit," according to Coody and Nelson, "is children's day-to-day learning experiences in the classroom" (page 23). Thus, Ms. Mark *combined* single-text instruction with multiple-text and inquiry instead of relying on just one of the variations shown in Figure 11.4.

As stated in her introduction, *The Life of Birds* would be the main source of information; it helped form the conceptual base which would be extended through a wide variety of assignments. After Ms. Mark compiled lists of audiovisual, fiction, and nonfiction materials at her disposal, she was ready to coordinate the instructional activities. Estes and Vaughan (1985) suggest that teachers number the major concepts in the unit and then use a cross-tabulation system. Box 11.7 depicts how Ms. Mark orchestrated these elements during the first two weeks of the bird unit.

The last two weeks of the unit contained equally rich and varied activities but emphasized more writing than the initial assignments. For example, Ms. Mark capitalized on the classroom experiment of hatching a live chick with the writing activity explained below.

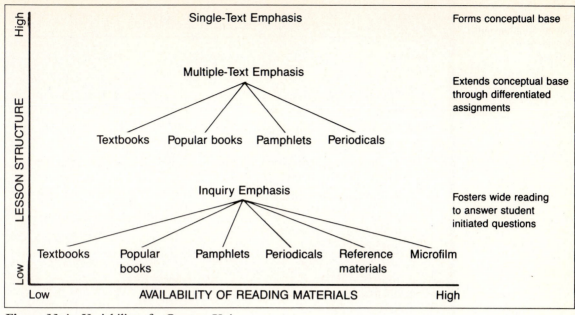

Figure 11.4   Variability of a Content Unit

Our Chick Has Hatched!

After the chick has hatched and the class has decided on its name, each student will write an announcement to his family about the new arrival. The announcement will consist of two parts: (1) statistics of the hatching, and (2) a personal note.

To help the students write the first part, actual samples of birth announcements were brought in by students and the teacher. These were read aloud and posted on the bulletin board. The teacher used these samples to walk the students through the process of announcing birth statistics, including name, date, weight, and length.

When the students had some practice with the first part of the assignment, some additional guidelines were given for writing the personal note. The personal note was not to be longer than one page and it was to focus on the one aspect of the incubation process that most impressed the student.

Developing a unit of study involves deliberate teacher planning to set a tone for students to actively engage in learning around a content theme or topic. It allows a rich opportunity to make reading useful by bridging the gap between children and content area textbooks.

SUMMARY

The value of reading increases as students use it, especially in content areas. This chapter showed ways the teacher can teach and the students can learn *how* to read

BOX 11.7

Cross-Tabulation of Instructional Activities

Activities	Materials Used*	Concepts
1. Introduction to unit	tm	1 2 3 4 5 6 7 8
2. Preassessment: What do we already know?	tm	1 2 3 4 5 6 7 8
3. Vocabulary development: Ornithology	tm	1
4. Anticipation guide: What do you want to know?	tm	1 2 3 4 5 6 7 8
5. Presentation and discussion of unit overview	tm	1 2 3 4 5 6 7 8
6. Brainstorming: How can we learn about birds?	tm	1
7. See filmstrip: *Junior Zoologist: Birds*	av 11	1 4 5 6 7
8. Begin experiment: Incubation of an egg	nf 14: pp. 131–133	2
9. Teacher reads aloud from *A Chick Hatches.* Continues reading appropriate sections as chick develops	nf 5	2
10. Vocabulary development: Inside an egg	tm	2
11. Pattern guide: Our developing chick	tm	2
12. Teacher begins to read aloud *Mr. Popper's Penguins* by R. T. Atwater. Continues reading daily	f 2	8
13. See filmstrip: *Animals and How They Grow: Birds*	av 2	2
14. Begin posting weekly riddle: Mystery Bird	tm	6 7 8
15. Reading: How birds began	nf 15: pp. 8–9	3
16. Vocabulary development: How birds began	tm	3
17. See film: *Looking at Birds*	av 12	4 5 6 7
18. Writing: Our daily record	tm	6 7 8
19. Reading: Seed carryout	nf 6: pp. 20–22	6 7 8
20. Make a seed carryout bird feeder	Student-supplied Teacher-supplied	6 7 8

* Key: av = audiovisual; f = fiction; nf = nonfiction; tm = teacher-made.

content area textbooks. It presented a content-centered approach in which elementary readers apply their reading skills to subject matter from an assortment of material.

Factors involved with the difficulty of textbooks and their organization were explained and a variety of strategies recommended. Examples of the structured overview, anticipation guide, three-level and pattern guide, vocabulary reinforcement activities, and study strategies were included to assist teachers who might like to pilot these instructional techniques in their own classrooms. Also, a workable plan to coordinate an array of instructional activities and materials for third-graders concluded the chapter. Our goal for them and other elementary students remains constant: to function independently—in this case, using reading to think about content.

THE WORKSHOP

In the Classroom

1. Analyze the readability of a content area text selection using the Fry Readability Graph.

2. Analyze an elementary content area textbook using the General Readability Checklist.

3. Plan a content area lesson using a reading selection from a social studies or science textbook. What prereading strategies did you use? How did you guide reader-text interactions? What follow-up or postreading strategies did you decide upon?

4. Construct a structured overview using the procedures suggested in the chapter.

5. Develop a three-level reading guide for a difficult text selection.

In the Field

1. With a small group of children, teach the content area lesson developed in classroom experience #3. Evaluate the lesson. What concepts did the children acquire through reading? How well did you establish purpose and activate a schema for reading? Did you sustain motivation throughout the lesson? What was the most effective part of the lesson? What was the least effective part?

2. In separate lessons, try out the structured overview and three-level reading guide developed in the classroom experiences above. Evaluate your use of these activities.

3. Try out the *survey technique* with a group of children. Evaluate the experience.

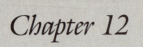

Chapter 12

Computers and Literacy

by Douglas H. Clements

Computers are burgeoning in every aspect of society, and schools are no exception. This chapter demonstrates that every teacher can use computers to enhance instruction of reading and writing. More important than knowledge about "how computers work" is knowledge about how children learn and about how computers can be used to help them learn. In this chapter, you will learn what types of instructional activities computers can provide. Several examples of actual computer reading activities will help you understand how these types differ and which might be best to use in a given situation. You will see how special computer activities can support children's writing—providing stimuli, encouraging revision, and removing barriers. You may never think about a computer in the same way again.

*I didn't think I could use a computer, and I didn't think my students could.
But they can do it! Their reading is improving by leaps and bounds. And I
have to ask them to stop writing on one!*

Cheryl, a fifth-grade teacher

*I have seen a child move from total rejection of writing to an intense involvement
(accompanied by rapid improvement of quality) within a few weeks of beginning
to write with a computer.*

Seymour Papert (1980, page 30)

*The computer reads back what I write. I can hear my writing. And then, on
the computer it's real easy to change my story and make it better.*

Bryan, a third-grader

Five-year-old Maria sits in front of a computer. She says, "I walked to the store
with Mommy." As she speaks the words, they appear in written form on the
screen. Simultaneously, an animated picture of a girl and a woman walking to a
store appears above the writing. Maria says "Read" and the written words are
highlighted one by one as they are pronounced by the machine. Simultaneously,
the picture is reanimated. Satisfied, Maria contemplates the next sentence for her
story.

Except for the ability to recognize easily all of Maria's spoken words, computer
programs that provide slightly more limited experiences are now available. Teachers
are recognizing that computers are not complicated "number machines." Instead,
the area in which this technology may have the most profound impact on children's
learning is the language arts.

Seymour Papert, one of the creators of the educational computer language
Logo, asks that teachers view the computer as a pencil. The pencil is always there.
It's ready to be used for scribbling, writing, planning, arithmetic, drawing, erasing,
and breaking (for effect in moments of anger!). Similarly, the computer can be
used in many ways, serving teachers and children without dictating how they
should use it.

Used incorrectly, however, the computer can become a technological red
pencil, providing nothing more than the unmotivating, mechanical correction of
errors or worse. Critics decry the pernicious effect of computers on traditional
teaching. They warn that computers will take humanistic approaches out of the
humanities and artistic perspectives out of the language arts.

As we shall see, the resolution of this conflict is predictable. Computers are
neither a panacea nor a Pandora's box. Properly used, they can amplify good
teaching. They can empower children to communicate more effectively. They can
motivate both children and teachers and add to the joy of experiencing language.
What constitutes "proper use"? That's what this chapter is about.

As you prepare to study the uses of computers in reading and writing, examine

Box 12.1, which provides an introduction to computers and definitions of some of the most related common terms.

COMPUTERS AND READING

One of the most obvious ways to use computers is to have them *teach* reading directly. This approach, called *computer-assisted instruction* (CAI), is the most commonly used in schools. There are four different types of CAI programs, each with different purposes, strengths, and weaknesses. These programs are classified as *drill and practice, tutorial, simulation,* and *exploratory/games.*

CAI Programs

The most widely used type of computer program involves drill and practice. This application is easy for most people to understand because it is not unlike the use of flashcards or worksheets. For example, a series of computer programs from DLM Publishers was designed to give children practice in reading skills. In one program, *Construct-a-Word,* students must blend beginnings and endings to create words quickly and accurately. They both see and hear the words that they construct.

The greatest danger of using (or abusing) such approaches to reading lies in fragmenting reading into isolated skills. For example, games like *Construct-a-Word* provide context-independent word practice with consistent feedback. Before using a drill and practice program, however, you must ask:

Do students need practice on this skill?

Is the computer program incorporated into total reading program?

Have I planned for transfer of the skills taught in isolation to meaningful contexts?

The following is a summary of the characteristics of drill and practice computer programs (see Clements, 1985, for more details).

PURPOSE To provide practice on skills and (usually lower-level) knowledge to help children remember and use that which they have been taught.

METHODOLOGY 1. Linear (progresses in a "straight-ahead" fashion, without branching to explanations if a child's responses are incorrect).

2. Repetitious.

3. Format: computer presents exercise; child types in response; computer informs child if answer is correct (if correct, computer goes on to next exercise; if not, the computer asks the child to try again at least once before supplying the answer).

BOX 12.1

Introduction to Computers

A computer is a device that takes in information, stores or processes it according to specific instructions, and then shows the results. It first must take in those intructions, called a computer *program* (or *software*). Usually, a program is stored on a magnetic *disk*. A mechanical device called a *disk drive* reads (or *loads*) the program into the computer, much like a record player "reads" a record into a sound system.

Once stored, the program tells the computer what to do. For example, it might place a picture of a cat on the television-type screen (or *monitor*), then show "C—T," and finally ask the child to type the missing letter on the *keyboard*. It would determine if the letter the child typed were an "A." If so, it might be programmed to say "Good. C-A-T spells cat." If not, it might offer a hint. The following small glossary will help you become familiar with common computer terms.

CAI (computer-assisted instruction). A method of teaching that uses a computer to present instructional materials. Students interact with the computer in a learning situation that might involve drill and practice, tutorials, simulations, or the like.

CMI (computer-managed instruction). Use of computers in the management of instruction (as opposed to CAI programs that are designed to teach students). For example, computers could be used to keep records, test results, and progress reports, to generate materials, or to test students and prescribe appropriate work.

Computer. A device capable of accepting information, processing that information according to instructions, and producing the results of this processing: a general-purpose tool.

Cursor. A symbol, often blinking, that indicates where the next character will be displayed on the screen.

Disk (also diskette or floppy disk). A device used to store information such as a computer program or a word list. Permanently stored in a square jacket for protection, it resembles a phonograph record (especially a thin, flexible one).

Disk Drive. A mechanical device that can put information onto, and retrieve information from, a disk.

Documentation. Materials designed to aid the user of a computer program. It may include written directions and descriptions, examples, listings of the program, suggestions on use of the program in the classroom, and so on.

File. A collection of information that is treated as a unit.

Graphics. Any shapes, dots, lines, and colors that are drawn using a computer. These may involve pictures, graphs, maps, diagrams, or the like.

Hard Copy. Printout on paper of data, programs, or solutions.

Hardware. The physical equipment of a computer system, consisting of electrical, electronic, magnetic, and mechanical devices—for example, keyboards, monitors, disk drives, and printers.

Input/Output Devices (I/O Devices). The parts of a computer system that allow people to communicate with the central processing unit. Input devices insert data to be processed into the computer; for example, keyboards or card readers. Output devices include CRT's, printers, and card punchers.

Instructions. Symbols used to communicate with the computer that constitute orders or directions—computer programs.

Keyboard. An electric typewriter-like input device for typing information into a computer.

Load. To enter a computer program into the memory of a computer, usually from a disk.

Memory. A computer's storage.

Menu. A list of choices exhibited in a computer program to guide the user.

Modem (MOdulator/DEModulator). A device that allows information to pass from one computer to another over telephone lines.

Monitor. The display screen for a computer that is like the picture tube of a television set.

Network. Communication lines that connect various computer components together for large-scale computing and information sharing. A computer system consisting of a central computer and a number of users.

On-line. The connection of devices or information sources so that they are available to the computer.

Peripheral Devices. Accessories and/or extra equipment that are added to the computer system to increase its capabilities. For example; game paddles, voice synthesizers, any input/output device, or printers.

Printer. A device for printing information such as text onto paper.

Program. Instructions used to direct a computer to perform a specific set of operations so as to accomplish a given task, such as presenting a lesson or serving as an electronic typewriter. See also **Software.**

Read. See **Load.**

Software. Computer programs that are required to enable computers to process information. A good library of computer software is necessary for worthwhile educational use of computers.

Speech Synthesizer. A combination of electronic equipment and computer programs that enable a computer to produce human-like speech.

Word Processing. Computerized typing and composing, which can be used to rearrange words, sentences, paragraphs, and larger sections of text.

STRENGTHS
1. Efficient manner of building skills, due especially to individualization and feedback.
2. Interactive (the child must actively respond to the program; the program responds to the child).
3. Ensures child is practicing correct response.
4. Motivates child to perform what otherwise could be boring activity of repetitious practice, if well-constructed.
5. Easy to use.
6. May handle record keeping.
7. With programming experience, teachers can construct their own small CAI drill and practice routines.

WEAKNESSES
1. Usually addresses discrete sets of lower-level skills only.
2. Narrow range of teaching strategies.
3. May be boring if not well-constructed.
4. May reinforce incorrect concepts.
5. Necessitates considerable access to computer facilities (i.e., you need to have one or more computers available for periods of time that are long enough to provide sufficient hands-on experience for each child).

Emphasis on Tutorial. As you might expect, a tutorial CAI program instructs. It attempts to teach the child about some subject matter area in much the same way as a parent or teacher would do on a one-to-one basis. In fact, some of the better tutorial programs use a Socratic approach to teaching that directs a child's discovery through a carefully sequenced series of leading questions. The student then types a response, and the program gives appropriate feedback based on this response and either provides more information or asks further questions. To enable the program to respond appropriately, the original questions must have a limited range of possible responses.

Punctuation (Educational Activities) is an example of a simple tutorial. After a child types in her name, the computer writes her a letter without punctuation. The computer then prints:

```
WOW!
Something is missing.
What do you think it is,
Bonnie?
```

All the punctuation marks in these sentences then flash on and off several times. The screen clears, and displays:

```
Right, Bonnie.
It's punctuation.
.?,.?!,!,.?
```

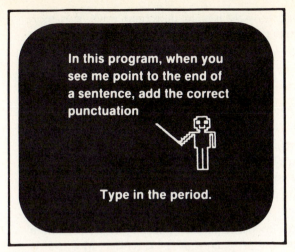

Figure 12.1 Sample Screen from a Simple Tutorial Program

> First let's look at periods. A period ends a sentence. When you see a period, you can stop and catch your breath. Sentences that end with periods just tell us something. Most sentences end with periods.

At this point, the screen shown in Figure 12.1 is displayed, and Bonnie is required to type a period. Different sound effects are used for each punctuation mark. When Bonnie types in the period, she hears a short beep. After this introduction, the first line of the letter was displayed again, with the figure pointing at the end of the first sentence. The program then continued to guide Bonnie to properly insert the needed periods. Of course, this is only one example. Tutorials differ widely; however, the following are characteristics shared by many.

PURPOSE   To teach the student about a particular topic.

METHODOLOGY 1. Linear progression with various amounts of branching.

2. Progression through a series of lessons.

3. Format: Socratic dialogue—presentation of information, questioning, and feedback dependent on the child's response; branching to explanations or review if child's responses indicate misconceptions.

STRENGTHS 1. A well-designed tutorial can effectively bring forth the child's active involvement and understanding of knowledge.

2. Can provide individualized, self-paced instruction.

3. Ensures that the child is participating in dialogue and responding correctly.

4. Although possibly limited in certain ways, it is more interactive than a lecture or textbook.

5. Can be an excellent means to provide students with review of concepts or to help students who have been absent to "catch up."

6. Easy to use.

WEAKNESSES 1. Narrow range of teaching strategies.

2. The intelligence of present-day tutorials is severely limited, especially compared to a teacher, who has considerable knowledge and intuition on which to rely. Therefore, the program's ability to respond to the child in a maximally helpful manner is also limited.

3. Similarly, to participate in a richer, more meaningful dialogue, the program must be extensive. Most microcomputers do not have enough memory to allow this. To respond intelligently to a child's open-ended responses also requires extensive field-testing, another reason why this type of tutorial is not often done. (Producers maintain that the programs sell without the expensive and time-consuming field testing.) Therefore most tutorials follow a restricted multiple-choice format.

4. Overused, this type of tutorial can become a game of "find out what the teacher wants and give it to her." It can also promote a shallow and narrow understanding of concepts.

5. Necessitates considerable access to computer facilities.

Emphasis on Simulation. Simulations are models of the world. Many popular games, such as "Life" and "Monopoly," are simulations. Computer simulations are also models of some part of the world. Children can learn a lot by pretending to be in that part or situation. Simulations are imaginary environments (albeit based on real-world facts) with a series of problems, often posed to a character who is under the child's control. Computer simulations have an advantage in that they can be programmed to respond in realistic ways based on real-world information. For instance, given a player's life choices such as going to college or getting a certain kind of job, a computerized game of "Life" could tell the player what his or her future would be like based on actual population statistics. This allows games to be more realistic and more powerful as learning tools.

A fourth-grade class, for example, was reading a basal story about a pioneer family's migration west. The teacher enriched this reading by having them reenact the journey using *Oregon* (MECC), a computer simulation of a family of five who attempt to complete the two thousand-mile trip along the Oregon Trail in five to six months. They have $700 and a wagon at the beginning of the trip. Children are then asked several questions. They type in their answers, which appear beside the question mark and in a column on the right (throughout the chapter, whatever students type is shown in boldface).

```
HOW MUCH DO YOU WANT TO SPEND ON
OXEN? 200                  200
FOOD? 50                    50
AMMUNITION? 100            100
CLOTHING? 200              200
MISC.SUPPLIES? 100       + 100
--------------            ----
              TOTAL = $ 650

     $700 SAVED
    -$650 SPENT
     ----
      $50 BALANCE

YOU HAVE $50 DOLLARS LEFT TO SPEND ALONG THE WAY....

PRESS SPACE BAR TO CONTINUE
```

The screen then shows a map of the Oregon Trail with a covered wagon at the beginning. The program shows how children have allotted their budgets, then asks questions about their itinerary.

```
MONDAY, MARCH 29, 1847   MILES = 0
-----------------------------------
FOOD  BULLETS  CLOTHING  MISC.  CASH
 50    5000      200      100    50
-----------------------------------
DO YOU WANT TO
1. STOP AT THE NEXT FORT
2. HUNT
3. CONTINUE

WHICH NUMBER?
```

If children choose to hunt, they must press a key in an attempt to shoot a deer. They are then asked questions such as

```
DO YOU WANT TO EAT
1. POORLY
2. MODERATELY
3. WELL

WHICH NUMBER?
```

If they choose number 3, the screen might show:

```
MONDAY, MARCH 29, 1847   MILES = 0
-----------------------------------
FOOD  BULLETS  CLOTHING  MISC.  CASH
 38    4976      200      100    50
-----------------------------------
```

Then a message might be displayed:

```
WAGON GETS SWAMPED FORDING RIVER--LOSE FOOD AND CLOTHES
```

The map is redisplayed, and the wagon moves along the trail. The screen then shows:

```
MONDAY, APRIL 29, 1847   MILES = 181
-------------------------------------
FOOD  BULLETS  CLOTHING  MISC.  CASH
  8     4976     180      100    50
-------------------------------------
YOU'D BETTER DO SOME HUNTING OR BUY SOME FOOD, AND SOON!
DO YOU WANT TO
1. HUNT
2. CONTINUE

WHICH NUMBER?
```

If students ignore the warning and choose number 2, they would read:

```
YOU RAN OUT OF FOOD AND STARVED TO DEATH.

DUE TO YOUR UNFORTUNATE SITUATION THERE ARE A FEW
FORMALITIES WE MUST GO THROUGH--WOULD YOU LIKE A
MINISTER?
```

If the same students played the game again, they might encounter hostile riders, heavy rains and other bad weather, rugged mountains, injuries to daughters and oxen, fires, fog, snakebites, wild animals, and so on. If they eat too well without having got adequate food, they will eventually starve; but if they eat too poorly, they may get sick. The simulation is based on historical information—the frequency of misfortunes, for example, is based on analyses of diaries of people who actually traveled the entire length of the trail.

The simulation is designed to help students learn about the westward movement, emigration, the Oregon Trail, the effects of natural events during migration, and the economic systems during the period. Students can also learn to discuss and solve problems in groups. This supplemented their reading of the basal story. Conversely, their teacher wisely used the basal reading story to develop an appreciation of the emotional impact of the tragedies that occurred in the simulation.

Not many simulations are specifically designed for the reading class. However, as *Oregon* demonstrates, students may develop both overall and content-area reading abilities. Simulations demand active, involved readers. They also promote the integration of reading with other subject matter areas and thus may develop background knowledge and related vocabulary. Most simulations share the following characteristics.

PURPOSE
To promote problem solving, develop an intuition or sense about a particular situation, facilitate the acquisition of skills and knowledge, and motivate interest in the subject and in learning.

METHODOLOGY
1. Non-linear.

2. Exploratory, discover-oriented.

3. Format: Provides a model of some part of the world through which children can learn by pretending, exploring, and manipulating.

STRENGTHS
1. Allows interaction with and study of events that would otherwise be inaccessible due to expense, danger, or time constraints.

2. Motivating and highly interactive.

3. Realistic (promotes transfer to out-of-school abilities).

4. Promotes social interaction and true discovery learning; children solve an actual problem.

5. Individualized in tems of a project approach.

6. Wide range of teaching strategies are possible (but not always built in).

7. One computer can easily serve the needs of an entire class.

8. Reflects real-world use of computers.

WEAKNESSES
1. Does not ensure students are responding correctly. (Because they are designed to allow children to explore "wrong" paths, this could be seen as a strength if properly managed by the teacher.)

2. Relatively more difficult to use effectively—an unfamiliar approach to education for many teachers.

3. If use is not well planned, can degenerate into little more than a "beat the computer" game.

4. Reading level may be high.

5. Is a copy of only some aspects of reality; if oversimplified or misused, may promote a misguided conception of real world situations and problems. If too complex, it may be inappropriate for children.

6. Does not include other important aspects of the real world, such as physical action and sensory impressions.

Emphasis on Exploratory Programs and Games. Exploratory programs and instructional games, like simulations, differ from the traditional modes of instruction with which most adults are familiar. However, teachers know that playful explorations and games are major ways young children learn. The term *games* here does not mean low-level drill and practice exercises transplanted to outer space. In the games discussed, the concepts or skills to be learned are intrinsic to the structure and content of the game.

In *M-ss-ng L-nks* (Sunburst), for example, one of several passages from classic children's literature is called to the screen. However, not all the letters will be there. Students choose a format: Only the consonants might be shown, only the first letters of each word, or only blanks and punctuation! Players try to fill in each blank. After a designated number of incorrect tries, the program fills in the letter. The object is to completely fill in the passage with as few tries as possible. The program demands that students use structural, comprehension, vocabulary, and spelling skills to decipher the text. Students can be heard saying, "Only a noun would make sense there," or "We know that story. Let's guess the names. . . ." Thus the program is more than just practice; it is about the nature of language. Sensitive teachers can use it as a springboard for helping children become aware of their intuitive knowledge about language.

The exploratory/game category is quite diverse in its characteristics. However, many share the following:

PURPOSE   To develop creativity, divergent thinking, and problem solving, facilitate the acquistion of skills and knowledge, and motivate interest in learning.

METHODOLOGY
1. Non-linear
2. Exploratory, discover-oriented.
3. Format: Provide a set of tools or a miniature (often fantasy) world that children use for explorations and productive play.

STRENGTHS
1. Utilizes and develops convergent and divergent abilities.
2. Motivating and highly interactive.
3. Promotes social interaction and true discovery learning; children solve an actual problem that they pose themselves.
4. Individualized in terms of self-directed learning.
5. Wide range of teaching strategies can be employed.
6. Can be used repeatedly.
7. Reflects real-world use of computers.

WEAKNESSES
1. Goals and objectives are not always clear.
2. Does not ensure students are responding correctly.
3. Relatively more difficult to use effectively.
4. If use is not well planned, can degenerate into little more than "playing with the computer."

5. Does not handle record keeping.

6. Variable on requirements for computer access.

There is one critical question that a teacher must ask about all computer programs, but especially about exploratory/game programs: "Why am I buying (or using) this program?" Not all interesting-looking games help children achieve important educational objectives. Studies have shown that the use of games raises achievement, *if* they are carefully selected to match curricular goals. Otherwise, they either make no difference or lower achievement (probably because children spend less time learning). The program should not be the goal, but a means of reaching an important educational goal.

CAI for Teaching Reading Skills

Special care must be taken in selecting software to be used for teaching reading skills. Some inappropriate characteristics of programs include overly competitive games, complex typing requirements, long and complicated setup procedures, and irrelevant and distracting graphics and sound (Clements, 1985). Just as important to the classroom teacher is that the programs not require inordinate amounts of adult supervision.

Worthwhile programs should teach significant concepts and skills in ways not possible *without the computer*. For example, *Juggle's Rainbow* is a graphically pleasing program that provides practice with the concepts of up, down, left, and right. However, the limited number of concepts taught and the availability (and possibly the superiority) of other, less expensive methods of teaching these concepts militate against purchasing this program. In addition, the concepts and skills taught must be *significant to the process of reading*. As discussed in Chapter 4, discriminating between shapes is not as useful for reading as discriminating between letters and words . . . and these skills are not as useful as reading words, sentences, and larger units of discourse.

Many CAI programs have been designed for specific areas of skill development: namely, word identification, phonic and structural analysis, vocabulary, and comprehension. To acquaint you with some of the programs, we have chosen two of these areas for discussion and analysis.

Vocabulary. Vocabulary development programs are intended to introduce words not previously known by the student. Because reading is a process of constructing meaning, expanding children's vocabulary is essential.

If vocabulary development consisted of a simple association between words and their definitions, then massive amounts of drill would be advised. Research suggests, however, that words are learned in meaningful contexts. Therefore the common software practice of matching new words to formal definitions may be inadequate. To encourage the establishment of meaning and retention, teachers and computer programs should strive toward:

using meaningful contextual setting and direct experiences whenever possible;

using synonyms and antonyms; and

providing for sufficient exposure that students master and use the words.

Many of the currently available computer programs do not meet these guidelines. They provide drill on isolated words. At least a few are being produced which are correlated more closely with the children's basal reader and/or allow teachers to write words they wish to teach into the program.

Comprehension. Much software that ostensibly teaches *comprehension* actually does not do so. It merely provides drill with feedback. Comprehension is a meaning-making process that does not always have simple "rights" and "wrongs." A related problem is the exclusive *skills* perspective of most of the software. Software that is built only upon a skills base often fragments the comprehension process.

Some of the limitations inherent in comprehension skills programs can be ameliorated partially by managing the social structure of children's use of computers. For example, have children work together on a subskills software program, taking turns reading and answering and asking their partner to justify his or her choices. *Comprehension Power* might be used that way. A large program covering twenty-five major comprehension skills, *Comprehension Power* includes literal understanding of details, evaluation of author's purpose, understanding persuasion, interpreting main idea, predicting outcomes, drawing conclusions, classifying, recognizing cause and effect, interpreting characters, and identifying mood and tone.

Another approach is to use software based on a holistic perspective. *The Puzzler* is designed to develop skill in hypothesis testing (Burnett and Miller, 1984). Students predict, confirm, and integrate. For instance, the program might ask children to generate divergent suppositions as to the identity of "an unusual friend" at numerous points during the story (the first point is immediately after reading the title!) Children must make several guesses before continuing with the story. There is no one correct answer, but as children read on, plausible answers become increasingly constrained (e.g., once they know the friend fits in a baseball mitt, guesses such as "my brother" or "a horse" are not as convincing). After group discussion, students write similar stories of their own for their friends to read (all on the computer).

Another instructional program, KRS, is based on a schema theory of reading and is designed to assist students in linking what they read to what they already know. The program is in the form of a newspaper. Students choose a newspaper (varying in readability level) and then an article from that newspaper. For one article, students might answer comprehension questions, selecting portions of it to justify their answers. The program offers feedback on the correctness of their answers. For other articles, they take the job of the editor, plagued by reporters who write passages with sentences that don't belong. Their job is to find and remove those sentences. Given an editorial, students might have to identify the author's point of view, find points of proof, evaluate whether the author addresses these points with fact or opinion, and finally, decide whether or not the argument was valid.

Literature, Computer Style

Until you can curl up comfortably with a version that costs five dollars or so, computerized literature is not likely to replace books. (Even then, the rationale for placing books on the computer without changing them is unclear!) Present-day programs are little more than simple comprehension tests designed to follow the reading of a book. Computer programs can, however, complement literature. Some interesting inroads in this direction are the development of "talking books" and interactive fiction.

The simplest "talking books" are those that read aloud. The *Magic Wand Speaking Reader* is a handheld device that translates specially coded texts into a humanlike voice for beginning readers. The child slides the wand along tracks printed beneath the text (of the books that accompany the wand). An optical scanner converts bar codes (which can be compared to the bar codes on supermarket products) into synthetic speech. Words, phrases, sentences, songs, and sound effects are produced. This allows children to re-read books and sentences as they wish. However, other types of interactive texts may be even more powerful.

In one system, readers who are stumped by a word have only to touch the word on the screen. The computer pronounces the word and underlines it so that readers can learn to read new words. On-line dictionaries providing definitions and explanations are also being constructed. They can "look up" works very quickly and can search for spellings with any letter(s) unknown—even the first! For the youngest children, the computer might be tied to a video disk that contains a picture dictionary. The word could also be pronounced. In the future, talking books will ask questions to ensure readers understand their content. If misunderstandings occur, extra help might be offered, or the text itself may be automatically altered to a less difficult level. In one project, students' gaze was monitored. When they looked at any word for an unusually long time, it was pronounced!

David Reinking and others at Rutgers University are using programs that allow readers to request that the computer provide context-specific definitions of any word with which they are not familiar. They may also ask to see a less technical version of the original passage, or further background information about the topic of the passage, which might include graphics. Finally, they might ask for information about the structure of the passage, such as the main idea of each paragraph. Research conducted with the program has indicated that students' comprehension can be positively affected by providing these options.

In interactive fiction, the child takes the role of one of the characters in a story, talking to other characters, making decisions that influence the plot sequence, and so on. This places children in motivating and intimate contact with the important features of a story: characters and their feelings, plot, sequences, and so on. An adventure game for elementary school children, *Dragon's Keep*, places the young reader near a magic house in and around which a magical dragon is holding sixteen animals captive. The child must find each animal and set it free. Children control where they go and what they do by selecting one of several choices. This program supplies practice in map reading (a map of the grounds is provided along with stickers of the animals) and reading comprehension, but does not tap higher-level understanding of plot and characterization. Other programs that involve the reader in all these levels are available, but unfortunately only for older students at present.

Another interesting approach is that of *Microzine*, a magazine-on-a-disk for students in grades four through eight. A kind of interactive *Weekly Reader*, it carries several different features. Ask Me allows students to interview famous young people by choosing questions they wish to ask. Other features permit them to create pictures, graphs, and the like.

Appendix E lists computer programs for various aspects of reading instruction along with publishers' addresses.

COMPUTERS AND WRITING

The computer's potential for language and literacy learning has only begun to be tapped. When children use computers to *compose*, they are engaged simultaneously in writing and reading. Therein lies the computer's great potential. In this section, we explore how computers connect reading and writing in a natural and powerful way. We also examine the role of the word processor as a scaffold in children's literacy development.

Connecting Writing and Reading

Using *Story Maker*, Bryan was constructing a story by selecting which of several paths should be followed. He had chosen the Haunted House story. After reading the first phrase, "Lace opened the front door and . . . ," he was given three possible ways to complete the sentence. The options he could choose were contained in the boxes at the second level of a "story tree"—a branching story design (see Figure 12.2). Bryan chose the second option. The computer placed the completed sentence on the screen: "Lace opened the front door and slipped into what looked like a bowl of spaghetti." It then offered Bryan the two options which are below the middle box in Figure 12.2. The whole story was constructed in this manner, with Bryan choosing the paths he preferred from each level of the "story tree." Each choice branched him to another set of choices, and so on. When the story was finished, he instructed the computer to print it out on paper.

The choices Bryan made determined not only the next sentence, but also what future paths would be available; his decisions had important consequences. He had to think about high-level aspects of the story such as story structure, the flow of the narrative, and characters' plans. Often, when children tackle new and complex challenges in writing, other areas in which they had been competent, such as handwriting and spelling, suffer (Graves, 1979; Rubin, 1982). *Story Maker* frees children of these details and allows them to concentrate fully on the meaning of their stories.

Children have been known to spend hours with *Story Maker*, printing out every possible story line. There is no right or wrong. Children receive meaningful responses, but not correction. If a more specific response *is* desired, children can

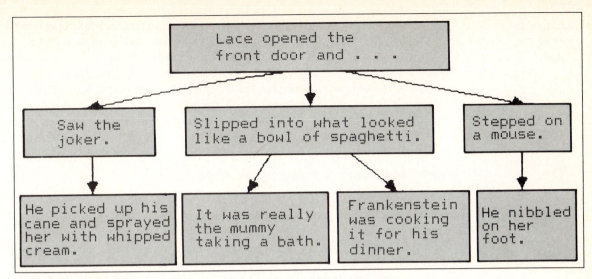

Figure 12.2 Example of a "Story Tree" from the *Story Maker* Program

elect to be given a goal at the beginning of the story. For instance, for the Haunted House story, the program might ask them to

```
WRITE A STORY IN WHICH
(1) LACE GETS A LION, AND
(2) LACE MEETS CATWOMAN
```

If Bryan had chosen the "saw the Joker" option (as any Batman afficionado would) but then had chosen the "whipped cream" and thus did not reach this goal, the program would have responded

```
WELL, BRYAN, YOU HAVE PARTIALLY SUCCEEDED.
YOU HAVE WRITTEN A STORY IN WHICH
(2) LACE MEETS CATWOMAN
BUT YOU HAVE NOT WRITTEN A STORY IN WHICH
(1) LACE GETS A LION.
IN A MOMENT, I WILL GIVE YOU A CHANCE TO TRY THIS STORY
AGAIN.
```

To reach the goal successfully, children must continually read for meaning, apply knowledge of story structure, infer, evaluate, and make predictions. Teachers can challenge children with other goals; for example, to construct a story that keeps the reader in suspense. Class discussions could be held in which children describe how they figured out how to reach the goal ("I thought that Catwoman would be in the story with the Joker, so I picked that branch first").

Finally, and perhaps most importantly, is the section called "Story Maker Maker," which demands that children create, plan, predict, and evaluate. Children add their own original story segments to an existing story tree or can make up a

355

completely new story tree. Teachers who use this program successfully encourage small groups of students to brainstorm about their story and write down all their ideas, often on index cards. They then lay these cards out, trying out different arrangements, and, finally, type in their best ideas. Some complex and fascinating stories have evolved from whole-class stories in which different groups contributed their own branches. Elementary school children have been observed to carry on independent conversations concerning story stucture after one remarked that another's effort was "not a story"!

Word Processing: A Powerful Scaffold

Computers provide *scaffolding* for young writers (Clements, 1983, 1984; Rosegrant, 1986a). Used in construction, scaffolds serve as supports, lifting up workers so that they can achieve something that otherwise would not have been possible. Educational scaffolds serve children as supports, helping them achieve personal communicative tasks that otherwise would have been impossible. Scaffolds do not simplify a task, but rather permit children to engage in complete reading or writing events. The child's *role* in the event is simplified and supported, not the event itself.

Scaffolds offer just enough assistance to enable the child to achieve a high level of ability and gain self-confidence. As a building takes shape, construction workers need less and less scaffolding to complete their work. As children's skill increases, the scaffolds are likewise removed—one bit at a time—allowing them increasing independence. Computer scaffolds, especially, allow the child to maintain a sense of competence: "I did it by myself." Importantly, scaffolding allows the child, right from the beginning, to use written language for a purpose. As in learning to talk and listen effectively, children do not participate in years of drills in meaningless skills. From the very beginning, children can experiment with letters and words without being distracted by the fine motor aspects of handwriting.

Perhaps the most powerful scaffold in a computerized writing system is a child-oriented text editor, or word processor. A word processor is merely a special program which, when loaded into the computer, allows the student to type in text (letters, words, sentences, etc.) and change it in any way desired. This allows children to "play" with written words just as freely as they play with oral language. Writers gradually shape and form their ideas, try out different ways to express themselves, and revise freely. The product is always neat and professional looking. Paper copies can be printed up easily at any stage of the writing process. A typical word processor features:

Wrap-around typing. You do not have to type a carriage return at the end of each line of text. If a word was going to be split at the end of a line, the computer automatically brings the whole word down to the next line. Conventions such as left-to-right and top-to-bottom are inherent.

Storage and retrieval of text. These are for later revision and printing.

Deletion. It is simple to delete letters, words, or sentences.

Insertion. You can insert letters, words, sentences, or paragraphs anywhere in the text. The rest of the writing is "moved over" automatically to make room for the insertion.

Finding and replacing. You can find any word or phrase anywhere in the text and if desired, change it. For example, if you decided to change your main character, you could instruct the computer to automatically find all the instances of "Henry" and change each to "Selma." You might then find all the instances of words such as "he" and "his" for possible replacement.

Block moves. If you decide your second paragraph, which starts dramatically, should really be your first, you can move the entire paragraph to the beginning of your composition. Other moves, of words, sentences, or multiple paragraphs, are handled the same way. Thus you can make large changes (e.g., rearranging paragraphs) or small ones (e.g., replacing a word) with ease without having to rewrite the entire composition.

Changing your mind. After deleting, inserting, replacing, or moving text, you can usually change your mind, automatically setting things back as they were.

Automatic formatting. Centering, paragraph indention, single- or double-spacing, and so on can be programmed automatically.

Appearance of text. Some word processors allow you to change the size, color, and "shape" (font) of the letters. *Magic Slate,* for example, includes underlining, italics, boldface, outline, superscript, and subscript. Probably more important, it has three versions: twenty columns (across the screen) with large letters for young children, and forty- and eighty-column versions for older students. With some programs you can combine pictures and a variety of typefaces.

Identifying errors. With typefaces rather than handwriting, spelling and punctuation are clearer. Therefore there is a greater chance that you will recognize errors. Easy deletion and insertion allows trial and error in this regard as well.

There are many different word processors available to children. Box 12.2 provides a list.

The Writing Workshop is an example of a flexible, multifaceted package that encompasses all three components of the writing process: pre-writing, writing, and postwriting. The program revolves around the Milliken Word Processor, an easy-to-learn program for young writers. The program enables students to complete the four fundamental tasks expected of any word processor: to compose and edit; to store and retrieve; to print; and to get help with any of these tasks. Each task is accomplished through a particular "mode" that the student chooses: Writing Tools, File Cabinet, Typewriter, or Help. The menu is represented on the first screen both textually and graphically—a tablet and pencil representing the writing mode; a typewriter representing the print mode, and so on (Figure 12.3). Before printing, the student may choose final features that include the numbers of characters per line, linespacing, page numbering, and margin sizes. While the Milliken Word Processor may not have the greatest number of features, it is one of the most intuitive programs designed for children.

BOX 12.2
Word Processors for Elementary School Children

Apple Writer II (Apple)

Bank Street Writer (Scholastic)

Blackboard (CTW)

Cut & Past (Electronic Arts)

Duxbury Braille Translator (Duxbury)

Easy Writer (Commodore)

Electric Pencil (IJG)

Easy Writer (IBM)

The Final Word (Mark of the Unicorn)

Friendlywriter (Friendlysoft)

Home Word (Sierra On-line)

Homework Helper: Writing (Spinnaker)

Kidtalk (CBS)

Listen to Learn (IBM)

Magic Slate (Sunburst)

Mega Writer (Megahaus)

Primary Editor (IBM)

psf: Write (Follette, Software Publishing)

Super Scriptsit (Tandy/Radio Shack)

Talking Screen Textwriter Program (Computing Adventures)

Volks Writer (Lifetree)

Wandah (Ruth Von Blum)

Word (Microsoft)

Word-pro IV Plus (Professional Software)

The Write Approach (Intellectual)

Writer's Assistant (Interlearn)

Writing Workshop (Milliken)

Word Processing and Speech. The addition of speech increases the interactivity of the computer as a writing tool. Students can hear what they write as it is spoken aloud. Jenny, a beginning kindergartner, loved to type in words on a computer equipped with a speech synthesizer. As Jenny typed *M*, she heard the letter *M* pronounced; the same went for *O* and another *M*. When she pressed the space bar, the computer would say "Mom." Over the course of several months, she worked up to sentences such as "I love my Mom, Dad, and cat." Hearing one's writing read back immediately is extremely motivating for students. More important, perhaps, it permits and even encourages revision.

In the *Talking Screen Textwriter Program* (TSTP), when text is read back, each word is highlighted in turn. This gives auditory support in that it allows children to hear letter names and words as they write and to hear any word, sentence, or story read aloud at any time. Often children will experiment with letters only, listening as the name of each is pronounced (Rosegrant, 1986a). Sometimes the speech synthesizer will mispronounce a word, such as a name (i.e., those words that are not in the synthesizer's dictionary and that are exceptions to phonics generalizations such as "Sheri"). Children can then fix, or change, the way this word is pronounced. To do this, they have to spell the word phonetically for the computer. Then "Sheri" remains on the screen, but the correct pronunciation is given. This can lead to meaningful explorations with letter-sound relationships. *Kidtalk* and *Listen to Learn* are other talking word processors.

Figure 12.3 Example of Mode Choice from the
Writing Workshop Program

With tools such as these, children can explore written language in several ways. For example, one group of first-graders discovered "special letters." When they typed *trp* and the space bar the computer said "t, r, p" (three separate letters). When they typed *trip* or *trap*, however, the computer said "trip" or "trap" (one word). They discovered that a "special letter"—a vowel—is necessary to pronounce a word. They later discovered that certain consonants and vowels, when combined, yield new sounds (e.g., digraphs such as *th*). Thus children can experiment with written language in much the same way as they experimented with and learned spoken language.

They also become more aware of certain features of language, such as rhyming patterns. One elementary-age student wrote the following poem with the *TSTP*:

```
The Fish
I saw a fish, that went swish swish,
Put it in the oven, it's not a tasty dish!
I ate him dry, I ate him fried,
And I am sorry that I died.
My mother cried. My father sighed.
I do not know if they cried and sighed
for my fish or I.
```

Some Advantages and Disadvantages of Word Processors. Working with word processors can have advantages and disadvantages. In one project parents were involved in teaching their children to compose with word processors. The director of the project describes how the computer can become a "tool" or a "trauma," depending on how it is used (Rosegrant, 1986b). For example, Jessica wrote a letter to one of her grandmothers and mailed it when she got home. Several days later her other grandmother called, jestingly demanding her own letter. During the next session, Jessica loaded in the old computer letter, typed the second grandmother's name over the first, added a "P.S. How's your eye?" and promptly mailed out the "new" letter. Jessica's mother joked, "My mother just got a form letter from her own grandchild!" She was, however, quite pleased with (and supportive of) her child's intelligent use of the tool.

On the other hand, Jane had to write thirteen identical thank-you letters following her birthday party. She, too, thought of using the same basic "file," altered appropriately. Her mother refused to let her take that shortcut, forcing her to type the same letter thirteen times. Needless to say, Jane's impressions of writing, the use of the computer as a tool, and the experience as a whole were opposite those of Jessica.

The following differences were found between parents who encouraged their children to use the computer as a tool (like Jessica's) and those who made the experience traumatic (like Jane's).

	As a tool	*As a trauma*
The computer . . .	facilitates communication	helps you get it "right"
The printer is used . . .	frequently, for several drafts, just for fun	only when the composition is correct (the computer is seen as a printing device)
The computer allows one to . . .	explore and experiment	be more accurate
The adult is a . . .	mentor	critic
The adult frequently . . .	supports and informs	intrudes and withholds

Teachers have similar effects. In the past, it was common to hear that computers would "change" teachers, teaching, students, and learning. Research does affirm a powerful effect, but in the opposite direction. Teachers have a strong effect on how the computer as a tool will be used. In one classroom, children load in prewritten computer files. Their job is to find and correct all the grammatical errors. In another, children use word processors to explore written language and to develop their communication abilities by writing stories with and for their classmates.

Take advantage of what the word processor can offer. The screen lends a public quality to writing that can encourage sharing and communication. It can encourage children to perceive text as flexible and malleable. It can increase teacher involvement in writing and, paradoxically, student independence.

Avoid some of the pitfalls of word processing. For some children and some writing tasks, the screen can become too public. Rearranging the setting can ameliorate this problem. Do not allow yourself to get carried away by over-editing children's writing. Avoid viewing any printout (as nice as it may look!) as a final draft. Finally, think about your students' ability to type. If they have insufficient typing skills, they may (at first) write less, be less spontaneous, or be loathe to delete!

Some Suggestions for Teaching Word Processing. Additional suggestions for teaching word processing follow:

Become familiar with the program yourself first. Use it for your own writing. While learning, you may wish to make a poster and/or duplicated sheet of major editing commands for your students.

Start simple. Teach only a few basic commands, then add more to students' repertoire as necessary.

Consider introducing word processing in a whole-class language experience story setting. As each command or key is pressed, discuss why it is needed and how to do it.

Work intensely with a small group to develop your first "experts." Post children's names with the instructions for using the program so that others can ask for help.

Continue presenting short, direct lessons to the class followed by work on the computer in pairs.

If few computers are available, rotate groups using the word processor for compositions. Or, have students write their first draft in pencil. When they are done, they can sign up for a twenty- to thirty-minute session at the computer. Working in pairs, one student types in her own composition as her friend reads it, suggesting changes along the way. (If possible, try to work for just a minute with students during this time; it is exciting to be a coach during the writing rather than a critic afterward.) The children then switch places. One teacher who had only one computer every third week had a parent volunteer type in students' work after school during the two weeks in which the class did not have access to the computer. In the third week, students would read and revise their programs. Although these methods are compromises to an extent, students can still benefit from using the computer, especially in reviewing and revising—the final, crucial step in writing.

Model and follow the writing process as described in Chapter 5.

Because students find themselves writing more, and more easily, on word processors, their work may be less organized and need more revision than paper-and-pencil writing. Fortunately, this free, continuous writing followed by reflection and revision is one of the best ways to compose. And the computer can help with revisions.

Compositions can be reviewed either as paper printouts or on the computer's screen. "Reviewing" should mean that both the teacher and other students read and react to a child's writing. The real advantage for students is the ease of making corrections. Rather than messy erasures, confusing lines and arrows, and unwelcome rewriting, editing on the computer is like a game. Press a key—poof!—a paragraph disappears. Move to an earlier spot in the composition and press another key—

the paragraph reappears in its new location. Or press a few keys and, in less than a second every "din't" becomes "didn't."

In sum, word processors, used correctly, can help children write. Words are not carved in stone; they are painted in light, a medium that encourages effortless manipulation. The more students intelligently manipulate text—the more they revise—the better writers they will become.

GUIDING STAGES IN THE WRITING PROCESS

In Chapter 5 we noted that children often rehearse before they write. They may talk, draw, or just imagine. Once they have produced a draft, children must also polish and clean up their writing before they have a "finished" piece. Computers should not replace, but may supplement, these kinds of activities.

Programs for Rehearsing

Prewriting programs include activities designed to help and encourage students to rehearse. Once they have done so, they usually move their text into a word processor for writing and revision.

The *Writing Adventure* is a motivating program for older students. The setting is an adventure story. Students progress through a series of adventure scenes (see Figure 12.4). They record their observations about the scene, useful objects, hidden treasures, and the like on notecards to gather information for their stories. Pictures, descriptive text, and prompting questions ("What sounds do you think you would hear?") stimulate rehearsal. As the main character, the child chooses

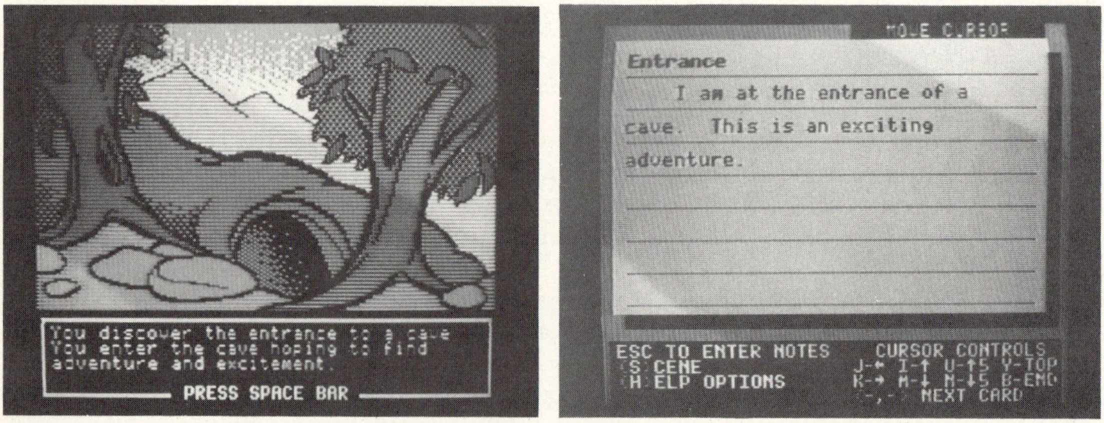

Figure 12.4 A Scene from the *Writing Adventure* Program

which option to take; for example, once in the cave, do they take the right, center, or left tunnel? After they have worked through one of the many possible sequences of scenes, they write a story with a built-in word processor, referring to the notecards they have written along the way. Each possible sequence has an open ending; students must write themselves out of a trap. In this way, the *Writing Adventure* guides students through the planning, drafting, and editing stages of writing.

The prewriting portion of the *Writing Workshop* contains three different programs designed to help young writers in the planning stage of their writing. The "Brainstorming" disk facilitates exploration of a topic through free association. The program has capabilities that then allow students to group the words they have generated and to name the various groups (Figure 12.5).

The "Branching" program is the reverse, guiding children from the general to the specific. After generating a topic, students decide upon up to four main ideas or categories suggested by the topic and then assign up to six details to each category. The "Brainstorming" and "Branching" activities offer various prompts if needed. If students have difficulty choosing a topic, a list of possible topics is provided. If they are unable to generate enough words or main ideas, the program asks questions such as "What good things does your topic make you think of?" or "What colors or smells do you associate with your topic?"

The final prewriting program, "Nutshelling," is designed to be more specific to a particular type of writing. Students may choose from writing forms such as the descriptive essay or letter. They are then asked key questions about purpose, audience, and tentative ideas.

Each of the prewriting programs includes management/authoring capabilities. The teacher or student may choose to change minimum requirements, to add a "Nutshelling" activity, or to replace one of the sets of default writing topics. In addition, the prewriting files may be expanded into composition form with the Milliken Word Processor.

Several programs to stimulate rehearsal are available, each with different activities. *Proteus Jr.* has five modules: Exploring, Narrowing, Listing, the 5 W's, and Describing. *Prewrite* asks students a series of questions designed to elicit their ideas:

```
Hi, what's your name?
Cheryl
Any ideas on what to write?
Yes, I want to write about lousy friends.
Okay. Now give me a one-to-five word title for your
topic. Here are some examples:
Feeling Blue,
Are Schoolyards Safe?
Flying Saucers.
What's your title?
Who's Really Your Friend?
What made you choose "Who's Really Your Friend?" to write
about?
Because Cindy was mean and I didn't deserve it, and . . .
```

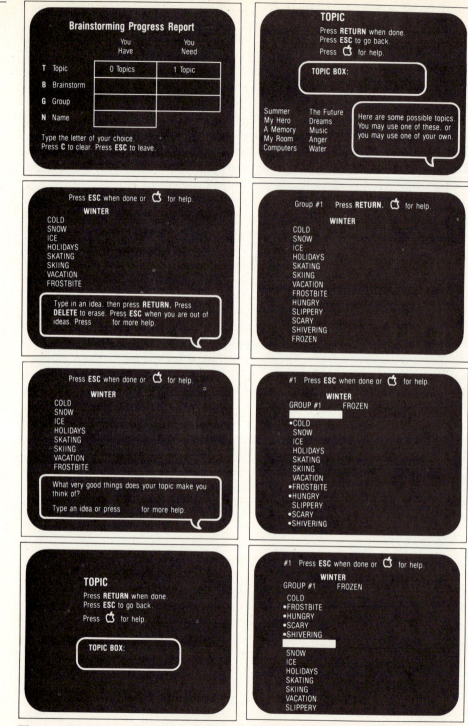

Figure 12.5 Brainstorming in the *Writing Workshop* Program

After answering the questions, students have notes on their purpose in writing, the main points they wish to make, important words to define, a sense of audience, and so on. One activity from *Quill*, "The Planner," asks questions to help students plan the structure of their composition. If they are writing a book report, they would choose the "book report planner." The program might ask them the name of the book, some of the characters, what type of book it was, whether they liked it, and the reasons they felt that way. Each planner is written by the teacher or by the teacher and students together. They brainstorm a list of prompting questions appropriate for a particular writing task. This list will be added to the activity as a new "planner" that writers can select.

For many children, drawing is a powerful rehearsal activity. Several programs allow students to create their own pictures and then write stories to accompany them. For example, *Kidwriter* allows even very young children to place, color, copy, and move a wide variety of pictures against different backgrounds. Once a picture is drawn, children use a simple word processor to write the accompanying text. See Box 12.3 for a listing of computer programs for rehearsing.

Programs for Editing and Proofreading

Once a draft is composed, the postwriting module of the *Writing Workshop* allows students to examine the piece of writing for editing and proofreading. The programs contained in the module assist children in turning a rough draft into a well-constructed, coherent manuscript free from errors. After composing a primary draft of the work, the postwriting disks act as a "teacher's aide," pointing out mechanical errors and areas of weakness in style and form. These programs, and others like them, are featured in this section.

Writers should be encouraged to leave these tasks for the final stage. This allows them to plan and write early drafts without undue concern for mechanical correctness—to concentrate on the generation of ideas and the full development of the topic. Several types of postwriting programs follow.

Spelling Checkers. A *spelling checker* locates spelling errors and brings them to students' attention. It works by matching the words that students type to its own computerized dictionary. Whenever a match cannot be found, it highlights that word and asks the students whether they want to change it or leave it as it is. If they change it, every occurrence of the misspelled word can be similarly replaced, if desired. Students can also choose to add the word to the dictionary. For example, they might add their names, so that whenever the spelling checker is used, it will recognize their names as correctly spelled words. Finally, students can ask the checker to "look up" words. In Figure 12.6, the *Hayden Speller* has highlighted *restrant* as a potentially misspelled word. The student chose "lookup" and the checker displayed a list of words that are spelled similarly. Because one of these words was the word intended, the student selected it by pointing the arrow. Automatically, *restrant* will be replaced by *restaurant*.

There are several advantages to students' use of spelling checkers. First, they learn about their mistakes. Bothersome typing errors are also easily located and

BOX 12.3

Programs for Rehearsing

Bank Street Story Book (Mindscape)

Branching (Milliken)

Brainstorming (Milliken)

CARIS, Computer Animated Reading Instruction System (Brittanica)

Compupoem (Steven Marcus)

Computer Chronicles (Interlearn)

Create-a-Story (Orange Cherry)

Early Childhood Learning Programs (Educational Activities)

Electric Poet (IBM)

Expository Writing (Interlearn)

First Liner (D'Adrian Software)

Flying Colors (Colorworks)

Friendly Filer (Grolier)

Just Imagine (Commodore)

Kermit's Electronic Storymaker (Simon & Shuster)

Kidwriter (Spinnaker)

The Letter Writer (Interlearn)

Madlibs Writer (SVE)

The Narrative Writing Tool (Interlearn)

Notecard Maker (Grolier)

Nutshelling (Milliken)

Outlining (Opportunities for Learning)

Playwriter series (Woodbury)

Poetry Express (Learning Well)

The Poetry Writer (Interlearn)

PFS File (Follette)

Playwriter (Woodbury)

Prewrite (Mimi Schwartz)

Proteus Jr. (Research Design Associates)

Quill (Heath)

Snoopy Writer (Random House)

Story Board (Data Command)

Story Machine (Spinnaker)

Story Maker (Bolt, Beranek, and Newman)

Story Maker: A Fact and Fiction Tool Kit (Scholastic)

Story Starter (Random House)

Story Tree (Scholastic)

That's My Story (Learning Well)

Think Tank (Living Videotext)

eliminated. Finally, students are encouraged to concentrate on composing, not spelling, at this stage of writing.

There are also disadvantages to spelling checkers: They often can't give proper spelling. Most do not recognize a word that is incorrect in a particular context if it is correct in another—for example, homonyms. Those with small dictionaries identify many correct words as misspelled.

All these problems can be overcome if the teacher carefully guides students in using the program. Used wisely, spelling checkers engender a sense of pride in spelling. Importantly, they focus attention on spelling at the proper stage in the writing process (postwriting) and they focus on those words a student generated in the communication process.

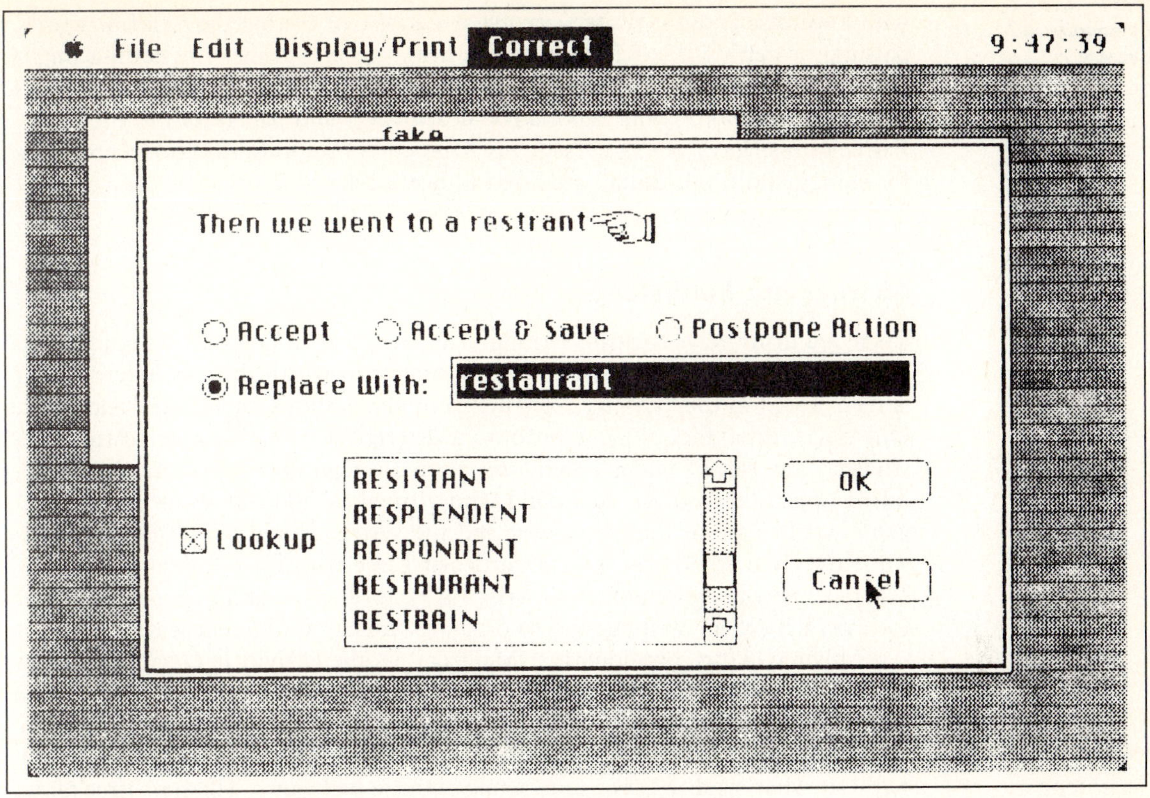

fake

Then we went to a restrant

○ Accept   ○ Accept & Save   ○ Postpone Action

● Replace With: **restaurant**

☒ Lookup

RESISTANT
RESPLENDENT
RESPONDENT
RESTAURANT
RESTRAIN

OK

Cancel

Figure 12.6   Spelling Example from the *Hayden Speller* Program

Thesauri. As one would think, electronic *thesauri*, such as *Webster's New World On-Line Thesaurus* (Simon & Schuster), allow the student or teacher to highlight a word and request synonyms. They are faster to use than book versions but serve approximately the same function. As yet, they are not widely available for elementary school students.

Grammar Checkers and Other Proofreading Programs. Most of these programs have been written for older writers. For example, *Sensible Grammar* checks for over one thousand commonly misused phrases, including clichés, informal, pompous, vague, wordy, repetitive, or sexist phrases, plus punctuation and capitalization errors. *Grammatik* searches for grammatical errors (e.g., *must of*) and repeated words (*to to*).

Some, however, are available for elementary school students. The postwriting module of the Writing Workshop includes several "Proofreader" activities. One encourages students to examine each of their sentences individually for flow and grammatical correctness. The "Mechanics Checker" scans the paper for tired words (e.g., *nice*) and tricky words (*their, they're, there*); specific pronoun problems; overuse of *and*; possible sentence fragments; and typos (e.g., sentences beginning

367

with lowercase letters). Writers are given a choice of editing the word or words, passing, or getting the help screen. The help screen explains why editing might be in order and how the problem could be corrected. The module also provides bar graph and word-count reports for all sentences and paragraphs in the paper. Extreme imbalances may signal sentence fragments or run-ons. Additional programs for editing and proofreading are listed in Box 12.4.

Sharing and Publishing

There are many ways to share writing. The "Library" in *Quill* allows students to store and retrieve information about any subject in which they are interested. It is then stored in the "Library," organized by the author's name, title, and topic. One class created files of game reviews. A description of each game, written by a student, was stored under several descriptive categories: video, arcade, home, board, sports, and so on. Any child who wanted to find out about an "arcade" game would type in that descriptor and the system would list all those games. Then the child could type in any particular game to get a full description. The "Library" encourages children to write for each other as well as for the teacher, to read each other's writing, and to organize writing in different ways.

Children like to communicate: "Mailbag," another activity in *Quill,* encourages written communication. It is an electronic combination of a post office, telephone system, and bulletin board. Written messages are sent via the computer to specific individuals, to a group ("soap opera watchers"), or to an open bulletin board. Let's say Matt sends a message to Craig about a ball game. The next time Craig uses the program, he is told he has mail waiting and can read the letter and respond immediately. The teacher might post a letter to "everyone interested in animals" concerning a movie the local library is featuring on Saturday.

With the proper equipment, students can communicate with others from all over the world using modems tied into telephone lines. For example, elementary school children in Southern California communicate with children in Alaska in one project (Levin, 1982). Students write messages which are sent over phone lines via computers in each school in the middle of the night (and therefore, inexpensively). The messages might be to "all video game lovers," to a list of people, or to a single person. Students are notified of messages they have received when they next use the computer. They can then peruse the messages, read them, print them out, send them to someone else, or throw them away. Not only does this facilitate and encourage meaningful and personal writing and reading, it prepares children to use electronic mail systems. Most importantly, children must make themselves understood in writing, or others who are far away are sure to ask them what they mean!

Publishing one's writing is a motivating way to share. *Newsroom* (Scholastic) simulates a real newspaper. It helps students with such features as the "Banner Work Area," "Copy Disk" (word processor), "Photo Lab," "Layout Disk," "Wire Service" (sending articles from one computer to another), and "Pressroom"

BOX 12.4

Programs for Editing and Proofreading

Grammar Checkers and Other Proofreading Programs

Ghost Writer (MECC)

Grammatik (Aspen Software)

Sensible Grammar (Sensible Software)

Word Proof (IBM)

The Writing Adventure (DLM)

Spelling Checkers

Bank Street Speller (Scholastic)

Benchmark Spelling Checker (MetaSoft)

Friendlyspeller (Friendlysoft)

Hayden Speller (Hayden Software)

Homeword Speller (Sierra On-Line)

Homework Helper: Writing (Spinnaker)

Lexicheck (Quark)

Magic Words (Artsci, Inc.)

Megaworks (Megahaus)

Random House Proofreader (Digital Marketing Corp.)

Spellworks (Advanced Logic Systems)

Sensible Speller (Sensible Software)

SpellStar (MicroPro)

Webster's New World Spelling Checker (Simon & Schuster)

Writing Workshop (Milliken)

(printing). These features are helpful, of course, but one can publish with general-purpose programs. One teacher used the *Writing Workshop* as the mainstay of her fourth-grade journalistic writing unit. The student reporters spent the week nosing out news stories, jotting down the facts in their spiral notebooks, and composing their stories on the classroom computer using the word processor on a rotating basis. On Fridays, the teacher wheeled three more computers into her room; loaded the word processor, the spelling checker, the mechanics checker, and the proofreader; and had her students edit, revise, and conference. After revision, each article was printed (the teacher was able to print out the articles in column form by instructing the program to print only thirty characters per line). Then the editorial staff for that week gathered to determine the placement of each article. After cutting and pasting, the students were able to see each article in newspaper form and how their individual articles fit into the paper as a whole. At this time, a final conference was held in which last-minute revisions could be suggested. The teacher was surprised to find that students who resisted making revisions in earlier drafts, claiming, "Nah! That's OK. I like it spelled that way!" were the first to insist that they be allowed to make corrections in their text and rushed back to the spelling checker. Except for the absence of cigar smoke and only the mildest forms of cursing, the atmosphere of an authentic newsroom pervaded the classroom. The children even began to wear loud ties. Of course, this cannot be directly attributed to Milliken.

A COMMENT ON EVALUATING COMPUTER PROGRAMS

The guidelines and examples presented here should provide the background knowledge needed to evaluate and select computer programs. It is often helpful to have checklists to guide such efforts (see Clements, 1985; Balajthy, 1986). Checklists can help remind you of important criteria. But taken to extremes, a "checklist mentality" is no more useful in evaluating software than it is in evaluating students.

Whether or not you use a checklist, remember the following essential questions:

On what model of reading is the software based—subskills only, or a holistic approach? Is this consistent with that of your classroom?

Does it address significant skills and knowledge in a valid way? (For example, tachistoscopic exercises have not proven useful off the computer. They are not useful on one.)

Does it help students learn better than they would using non-computer methods?

Are decoding, spelling, and other skills taught in context?

Is the text material meaningful to students?

Only if a program passes these tests would you ask computer-related questions.

How easy is it to use?

Can the student return to previous pages?

Is print size appropriate?

Does it display upper- and lowercase letters?

Are editing commands simple yet powerful?

Are commands (and help) available on the screen?

Can the program be legally copied or loaded into several computers at once?

Many sources contain reviews of software, including books (see Balajthy, 1986; Clements, 1985; Riedesel and Clements, 1985) and magazines (see *Electronic Learning*, the specialized *Computers, Reading and Language Arts,* and "The Printout" column in *The Reading Teacher*). But still, *you* must evaluate every program. First, of course, opinions differ. Second, a review out of the educational context in which the program will be used is of limited value. This problem is exacerbated by many reviewers' lack of knowledge concerning the reading process. Use published reviews to find out what is available and to narrow the field. Then choose the best package yourself.

SUMMARY

Balance is needed in the use of computers. They are not the mechanical, true/false antihumanistic Pandora's box that critics eschew. Neither are they a magical panacea filled with instant solutions. They will not solve educational problems nor—without careful teacher direction—will they significantly change reading and writing instruction. To provide direction, you must rely on your principles about education. You might build on the following (see also Balajthy, 1986; Clements, 1985):

> It is more important to help students learn than to use computers. If the software used is second-rate, students will be harmed rather than helped.

> It is more important to understand language and language learning than to understand computers. Most excellent applications of computers to the teaching of the language arts require a minimum of technological expertise and a maximum of teacher expertise. Although it may be beneficial in several areas, programming a computer is not a prerequisite to using it in the classroom.

> There are situations in which computers should be used and situations in which they should not. They should be used when they are consistent with, and complement, the goals and philosophy of the language arts program.

> Priority should be given to computer applications that place students in the role of active learners.

> Computer activities should be integrated into the curriculum.

> Teachers are the key to the successful use of computers.

THE WORKSHOP

In the Classroom

1. Describe several strengths and weaknesses of one of the following: *Story Maker, M-ss-ng L-nks, The Writing Workshop*. How would you build on the strengths and eliminate the weaknesses?

2. Participate in a classroom debate: Choose a side on both of the following issues and defend it.
   a. *Pro*: Revision on a computer will lead to more substantial, more meaningful changes and better writing.
      Con: Revision on a computer will make children lazy the way that calculators affected children with regard to arithmetic.
   b. *Pro*: Story starters are helpful and beneficial to beginning writers.
      Con: Children should be in control of the topics they write. They have plenty of deep personal importance to say if we encourage and allow them to say it.

3. Evaluate a reading or writing computer program in both computer terms and from a holistic perspective.

4. Work with three other students to build a curriculum unit around one promising computer program.

In the Field

1. Observe several children working on a reading or writing computer program.

Take notes. What is happening that appears positive? Negative? How could the interaction be improved?

2. Do a survey of the computer programs that are currently used in local schools. How would you evaluate them based on the criteria in this chapter?

3. Interview several practicing teachers who are using computers. Ask such questions as:
   a. With improved voice input and output, will speech and graphics via computers replace reading? What will be gained? Lost?
   b. Should reading presented on a computer be designed to urge students gently toward faster and faster rates of reading?
   c. Will children lose all the advantages of word processing if someone else types their compositions into the computer?
   d. What is your favorite piece of software? Why?

4. Word process a letter or other piece of writing yourself. Take notes on your reactions.

Part V

Making Decisions

Chapter 13

Assessing Reading Behavior and Performance

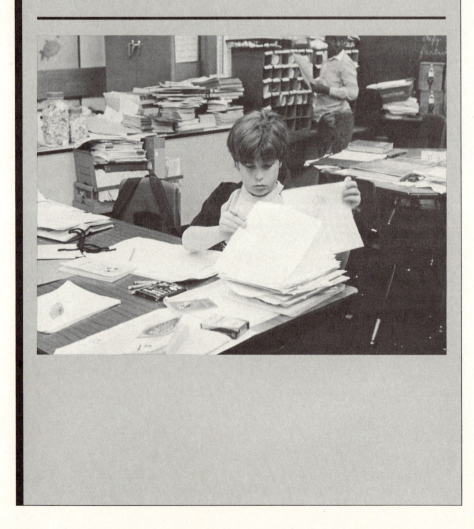

A retired teacher described the time he checked his blood pressure in a computerized machine. The read-out was alarmingly high, so he visited his doctor for more extensive testing. After several blood tests, a chest x-ray, an electrocardiogram, and several blood pressure readings before and after exercise, the doctor assured the teacher that his blood pressure was well within normal limits for a person his age. So what's the point of the story? How you judge a child's ability to read is much like evaluating the results of a blood pressure test. A reading test allows you to make inferences about performance, but it provides only a single perspective. Although these inferences can be useful in making instructional decisions, you must guard against confusing the test score with the phenomenon you seek to understand. How children read varies from context to context. This is why you must approach teaching diagnostically.

I personally think we overtest kids in my school. Too much testing takes time away from teaching. But my principal wants frequent assessments of students' skills. So I go along with the testing.

Mrs. Latham, a second-grade teacher

The teacher doesn't know how we read until the scores come back.

Janey, a nine-year-old

Harold doesn't make predictions. He needs to take more risks.

Mrs. Rainier, a fifth-grade teacher

Mrs. Latham gives her second-grade class "skill mastery" tests at the end of each unit of the basal reading program. Her principal urges teachers to follow the program closely. Among other things, this means making frequent checks on students' skill progress. Mrs. Latham administers tests frequently, even though she believes that too much testing takes time away from teaching and learning.

One of the tests that Mrs. Latham administered assessed students' ability to associate the hard and soft sounds of the letter *g*. John, one of her students, didn't reach mastery of this particular skill. In other words, he didn't score correctly on at least 80 percent of the items related to the skill objective; in fact, he had only answered six out of ten items correctly. This puzzled Mrs. Latham because just the day before John shared a part of a book he was reading. He read to her about a visit to the zoo which included seeing *g*iraffes and petting *g*oats. Mrs. Latham recalled other situations where John had little trouble reading *g* words. Although he failed to reach a level of mastery on the hard and soft sound of the letter *g*, John didn't experience difficulty reading passages containing words with soft and hard *g* sounds. She figured that either these words were in his sight vocabulary or he was able to recognize them in context.

John's performance on the test suggested that he would need additional skill work and review to reach mastery on the skill objective. However, Mrs. Latham decided not to use John's instructional time in this pursuit. Some may disagree with her decision. But the point to be underscored is that Mrs. Latham *made a decision about a child based on diagnostic teaching.*

In this chapter we emphasize the importance of diagnostic teaching in making decisions about instruction. This doesn't suggest that testing is unimportant. You need to know about formal and informal assessment and how to use test information to inform instruction. Diagnostic testing *and* teaching allow you to gather information in order to make inferences about children's reading ability and performance. In Mrs. Latham's case, she "knows" that John is capable of recognizing and distinguishing the *g* sound in *words that are in context and within his experiential grasp.* She weighed John's performance on a specific skill that was tested in isolation against her observations of a classroom reading situation. The test provided one perspective for becoming knowledgeable about a student's performance; the teaching situation provided another perspective. The information gathered from both situations helped to strengthen her decision. Let's examine why.

TOWARD A CORROBORATIVE FRAMEWORK FOR DECISION MAKING

Mrs. Latham's decision is another example of how teachers screen and filter information about children's performance through their concepts and beliefs about reading and learning to read. Mrs. Latham holds an interactive view of the reading process. She believes that reading acquisition involves coordinating and integrating many skills during actual reading situations. A child learns to read the way Mrs. Latham first learned to use a stick shift in a car with manual transmission. What needed to be learned was how to coordinate the use of the clutch pedal, gas pedal, brake, and stick in shifting from gear to gear. A beginner may practice pushing the clutch pedal in and out in isolated drill or simulate shifting from gear to gear. However, actually experiencing stick shifting in traffic makes the difference in learning how to coordinate and integrate the skills.

And so it is with John in his learning to become a fluent reader. When contrasting his performance on the test with his performance in a "real" reading situation, Mrs. Latham chose to weigh the information from the teaching situation more heavily than the score on the test. In fact, she decided that 60 percent accuracy on the skill when tested in isolation was a satisfactory score. Had John not been able to read words in context containing soft and hard *g* sounds, or if his test performance was poor, she probably would have made a different set of decisions.

Casey Stengel, manager of the New York Yankees in the 1950s and 1960s, was as renowned for his wonderful use of language as he was for winning baseball games. On one occasion after losing a hard-fought game, Stengel was quoted as saying, "You can know the score of the game and not know the real score." The "real score" involves understanding and appreciating the dynamics of what happens on the playing field during the game itself regardless of the outcome. In our estimation, the real score in reading always involves understanding and appreciating *how* children interact with print in various reading situations and *why*.

We advocate using multiple indicators of student performance for assessment. Any single indicator—whether it involves commercially prepared or teacher-made tests or observation—provides a perspective, one means of attesting to the accuracy of the score or phenomenon under examination. Multiple indicators, however, build a *corroborative framework* that strengthens decision making. As teachers we are constantly faced with making decisions. Multiple indicators of reading strengthen decision making because information from one data source builds on or is contrasted with information from other data sources. The result is a rich knowledge base for understanding how and why students perform in reading.

Because reading takes place inside the head, the process is not directly observable and, therefore, not directly measurable. Yet one of the important functions of reading tests, whether formal or informal, should be to help teachers understand a human process that is essentially hidden from direct examination. To what extent do standardized, criterion-referenced, informal, and teacher-made tests play a constructive role in the classroom? Why is diagnostic teaching such an invaluable part of classroom assessment? Let's read to find out answers to these broad but important questions.

FORMAL ASSESSMENT

Pressures for accountability have led many school districts to use formal reading tests as a means of assessment. Formal tests may be norm-referenced or criterion-referenced. In either case, however, they help to satisfy the public's concern for objective assessment. Norm-referenced tests, in particular, appear to fill the bill in this respect.

Standardized Tests

Standardized tests are machine scorable instruments that sample reading performance based on a single administration. Standardized test scores are useful in making comparisons among individuals or groups at the local, state, or national level. A norm-referenced test is constructed by administering it to large numbers of students in order to develop *norms*. It's inefficient and difficult, if not impossible, to test every student in an entire population. Norms, therefore, represent average scores of a sampling of students selected for testing according to factors such as age, sex, race, grade, or socioeconomic status. Once norm scores are established, they become the basis for comparing the performance of individuals or groups to the performance of those who were in the norming sample. These comparisons allow you to determine whether a child or group is making "normal" progress or performing in "normal" ways.

Normal progress or performance, of course, depends on the *representativeness* of the norming sample. Therefore, the norms of a test should reflect the characteristics of the population. Moreover, *it's important to make sure that the norming sample used in devising the tests resembles the group of students tested*. Some norm-referenced tests provide separate norms for specific kinds of populations (e.g., urban students). The technical manual for the test should contain information about the norming process, including a description of the norming group.

In developing norm-referenced tests, the scores in the norming sample are distributed along a *normal*, or *bell-shaped, curve*. That is to say, scores cluster symmetrically about the *mean,* the average of all scores. In Figure 13.1, notice that the majority of the scores (about 68 percent) are concentrated within one *standard deviation* above or below the mean. The standard deviation is an important measure because it represents the variability or dispersion of scores from the mean. The standard deviation, roughly speaking, can help you interpret a child's performance. You can judge how well a child performed on a test by examining a score in relation to the standard deviation. A score that falls more than one

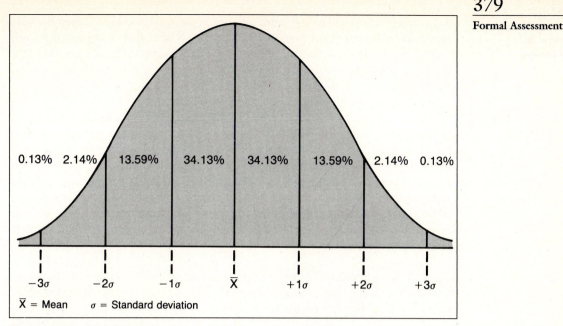

0.13%   2.14%   13.59%   34.13%   34.13%   13.59%   2.14%   0.13%

-3σ -2σ -1σ $\overline{X}$ $+1\sigma$ $+2\sigma$ $+3\sigma$

$\overline{X}$ = Mean σ = Standard deviation

Figure 13.1   A Bell Curve

standard deviation below the mean on a reading test would *probably* raise a red flag or be a cause for concern. Recognize, however, that standardized tests aren't error free: There are measurement problems with any test. Some tests, without question, are better than others in helping teachers to interpret performance. The more *valid* and *reliable* the reading test, the more likely it is to measure what it says it does.

   Reliability refers to the stability of the test. Does the test measure an ability consistently over time or consistently across equivalent forms? The reliability of a test is expressed as a correlation coefficient. Reliability coefficients can be found in examiners' manuals and are expressed in numerical form with a maximum possible value of +1.0. A reliability coefficient of +1.0 means that students' scores were ranked exactly the same on a test given on two different occasions or on two equivalent forms. If students were to take a test on Monday and then take an equivalent form or the same test on Thursday, their scores would be about the same on both tests, if they were indeed reliable. A test consumer should examine reliability coefficients given in the examiner's manual. A reliability coefficient of +0.85 or better is considered good, whereas a reliability coefficient below +0.70 suggests that the test lacks consistency.

   A statistic tied to the idea of reliability is the *standard error of measurement*. The standard error of measurement represents the range within which a subject's *true score* will likely fall. A true score is the score a test taker would have obtained if the test were free of error. Suppose the standard error of measurement was 0.8

for a reading test. If a student achieved a score of 4.0 on the test, then his true score would fall somewhere between 3.2 and 4.8. Rather than assume that a score received by a student is exactly accurate, the teacher should identify the standard error of measurement in the test manual and interpret each score as falling within a range.

Validity is probably the most important characteristic of a test. It refers to how well a test measures what it is designed to measure. A test developer will validate a test for general use along several fronts. First, the test should have *construct validity*. To establish contruct validity, the test developer must show the relationship between a theoretical construct such as *reading* and the test that proposes to measure the construct. Second, the test should have *content validity*. Content validity reflects how well the test represents the domain or content area being examined. Are there sufficient test items? Are the test items appropriate? Third, the test should have *predictive validity*. In other words, will it accurately predict future performance?

Types of Test Scores. To make interpretations properly you need to be aware of differences in the type of scores reported on a test. The raw, or obtained, score reflects the total number of correct items on a test. Raw scores are converted to other kinds of scores so that comparisons among individuals or groups can be made. A raw score, for example, may be converted into a *grade equivalency score*. This type of conversion provides information about reading performance as it relates to students at various grade levels. A grade equivalency score of 4.6 is read as "fourth grade, sixth month in school." Therefore a student whose raw score is transformed into a grade equivalency of 4.6 is supposedly performing at a level that is average for students who have completed six months of the fourth grade.

The idea behind a grade equivalency score is not flawless. When a score is reported in terms of grade level, it is often prone to misinterpretation. For example, don't be swayed by the erroneous assumption that reading growth progresses throughout the school year at a constant rate—that growth in reading is the same from month to month. Based on what is known about human development generally and language growth specifically, such an assumption makes little sense when applied to a human process as complex as learning to read.

One of the most serious misinterpretations of a grade equivalency score involves making placement decisions. Even though a child's performance on a test or subtest is reported as a grade level, this doesn't necessarily suggest placement in materials at that level. Suppose a student received a grade equivalency score of 2.8 on a comprehension subtest. The score may represent information about his ability to comprehend, but it doesn't mean that the student should be placed at the second grade, eighth month of basal reading or library materials. First, the standard error of the test indicates that there is a range within which 2.8 falls. Second, the test's norms were in all likelihood not standardized against the content and level of difficulty of the basal reading curriculum in a particular school or of library books. In 1981, the International Reading Association passed a resolution cautioning teachers on the misuse of grade equivalents and advocated the abandonment of grade equivalent scores for reporting students' performance. In place of grade level scores, the use of *percentile scores* and *standard scores* such as *stanines* provides a more appropriate vehicle for reporting test performance.

Percentiles refer to scores in terms of the percentage of a group the student has scored above. If several second-graders scored in the 68th percentile of a test, they scored as well as or better than 68 percent of the second-graders in the norming population. Whereas grade equivalency scores are normed by testing children at various grade levels, percentile norms are developed by examining performance only within a single grade level. Therefore, percentile scores provide information that helps teachers interpret relative performance within a grade level only. For this reason, percentiles are easily interpretable.

Stanine is one of several types of standard score. A standard score is a raw score that has been converted to a common standard to permit comparison. Because standard scores have the *same* mean and standard deviation, they allow teachers to make direct comparisons of student performance across tests and subtests. Specifically, stanine refers to a *standard nine*-point scale. When stanines are used to report results, the distribution of scores on a test is divided into nine parts. Therefore each stanine represents a single digit that ranges from 1 to 9 in numerical value. A stanine of 5 is the midpoint of the scale and represents average performance. Stanines 6, 7, 8, 9 indicate increasingly better performance; stanines 4, 3, 2, and 1 represent decreasing performance.

Types of Tests. Different norm-referenced tests have different purposes. Two broad types of tests are frequently used in schools. An assessment that is based on a *survey test* represents a measure of general performance only. It does not yield precise information about an individual's reading abilities. Survey tests are often used at the beginning of the school year as screening tests to identify children who may be having difficulties in broad areas of instruction. A survey test may be given to groups or individuals.

A standardized *diagnostic test*, on the other hand, is a type of formal assessment that is intended to provide more detailed information about individual students' strengths and weaknesses. The results of a diagnostic test are often used to profile a student's strengths and weaknesses of reading performance. Some diagnostic tests are individual; others are designed for group administration.

Most diagnostic tests are founded on a bottom-up, subskills view of reading. Therefore, diagnostic tests are characterized by a battery of subtests that uses large numbers of items to measure specific skills in areas such as phonics, structural analysis, word knowledge, and comprehension.

Although survey and diagnostic tests are designed to be informative, teachers need to know *why* they want to use tests and *for what* they are testing (Farr and Carey, 1985). Henk (1985, page 290) maintained that test selection should be guided by eight questions:

1. Are there distinct reasons why standardized tests would be more appropriate than informal ones?
2. Does a particular standardized test sufficiently measure the specific content, skills, and abilities relevant to the scope and sequence of the curriculum?

3. Will a general test tell me all I need to know, or should a more specialized instrument be used?

4. Is this a test I plan to give at the beginning of the year for screening purposes, or one that will be used at the end of the year to measure how much children have learned?

5. Is an individual test necessary to measure what I want, or will a group test suffice?

6. Would an oral or silent test yield the most important information for my purposes?

7. Is it absolutely necessary that the test be timed, or could I learn more about the children if it were not?

8. Will the time invested in the testing result in improved instruction?

In general, much controversy has surrounded the use of standardized achievement tests in American education, especially as they apply to culturally diverse populations. In the field of reading, the uses and misuses of standardized tests have also been debated.

Uses (and Misuses) of Test Results. Dorothy Watson's (1985) conversation with Janey, the nine-year old we quoted to begin the chapter, suggests that some youngsters are quite aware of the role tests play in school and hold some interesting notions about their use (or misuse). The conversation between Watson and Janey occurred in late September. When the topic turned to tests, Janey said, "We can't read until we finish our test. After that we can get in our groups; we can go to the library then, too. After the tests." When asked why this is the case, Janey explained, "He [the teacher] doesn't know how we read until the scores come back." We agree with Dorothy Watson: Janey's teacher has some unfounded, though prevalent, ideas about how formal tests scores are used.

Critics of formal testing tend to argue against the uses to which the standardized test information is put. As noted earlier, scores from formal testing shouldn't be used as the *only* source of information considered in making instructional decisions. But they often are.

Some critics call into question whether there is any worth at all to formal testing. For example, Goodman (1975) argued that such tests are mainly measures of intelligence and don't assess that which can be construed as reading. He contended that the reading measured on reading tests isn't the same as most "real-world" kinds of reading. Test passages are often very short and are accompanied by many questions. Seldom in real life would someone read a short passage and then be required to answer a series of questions about it.

Most test developers, however, assert that their tests can provide accurate and reliable information on groups of twenty-five or more. From their perspective, scores can show school-wide trends and differences among groups within a school. Standardized tests results can also be used to get an idea of how students in a school compare to other students across the country when assumptions about representativeness have been met. In addition, they will indicate if the school as a whole is increasing or decreasing in general reading achievement.

The assumptions underlying norm-referenced assessment are different from another kind of assessment often conducted in schools: criterion-referenced testing. Rather than comparing a student's test performance to that of a norming sample, performance on a criterion-referenced test hinges on mastery of specific reading skills. This, of course, was the case we described in Mrs. Latham's class in the beginning of the chapter. Let's examine criterion-referenced assessment and how test information is used in classroom decision making.

Criterion-Referenced Tests

Criterion-referenced tests have been used in formal situations for district-wide purposes and in classroom situations. The major premise behind criterion-referenced testing is that the mastery of reading skills should be assessed in relation to specific instructional objectives. Test performance is measured against a criterion, or acceptable score, for each of the objectives. Suppose, for example, that there are ten test items for each skill objective. Eight to ten correct items on the test would suggest a level of mastery as specified by the objective. A score of six or seven correct items would signal that additional practice and review of the skill under examination are needed. Fewer than six correct items would mean that a student is probably deficient in the skill and needs extensive reteaching to reach criterion or mastery.

Unlike a norm-referenced situation, performance on a criterion-referenced test is judged by what a student can or can't do with regard to the skill objectives of the test. The test taker isn't compared to anyone else. The rationale for assessment, then, is that it will indicate strengths and weaknesses in specific skill areas. Whereas norm-referenced test scores are used to screen students and to make general grouping decisions, results from a criterion-referenced assessment are used to make instructional decisions about reading skills development. For this reason, criterion-referenced tests have become part of the "standard operating procedure" of the reading skill management systems described in Chapter 2.

Reliability and Validity of Criterion-Referenced Tests. The reliability and validity of criterion-referenced tests have been called into question (Pearson and Johnson, 1975). It has been argued that test makers have tended not to establish statistical reliability and validity for criterion-referenced tests as they do for norm-referenced tests. As a result, users of criterion-referenced tests need to be aware of some of the important issues of reliability and validity surrounding the use of such tests.

Criterion-referenced tests often measure students' performance on a large number of objectives. Because the number of objectives tested is large, the number of items testing each objective may be as low as four or five. Such a practice leads to questions of how *reliable* the measurement of each skill can be with such a small number of items. It's possible that students who perform poorly on a criterion-referenced test won't perform poorly in another situation that assesses the same skill. For example, will a child who cannot count syllables in a word be unable to break down similar words into pronounceable parts when reading orally? Will a child who cannot answer inferential questions as directed on a test be unable to make inferences from a story in an oral retelling?

Test makers assume that mastery of specific skills leads to better reading ability. This is at best a tenuous assumption. A teacher must ask, "Do test items really measure what they are supposed to measure?" Smith and Johnson (1980) pointed out the problem in this respect:

> Test purchasers rightly assume that the tests provided for measuring attainment of objectives are valid indices of the skills at issue. However, if a test uses a paper-and-pencil task, then it ought, at the very least, to validate those measures by administering group and individual tests to a small sample of students. We are not convinced that identifying the initial consonant *f* from the distractor set *f, t, v, r* when given an oral stimulus is the same as saying /f/ when seeing *f*, or reading sentences which contain words starting with *f* (page 169).

Smith and Johnson's point is well taken, as is their concern for questions related to the concept of mastery. What does mastery performance mean on a criterion-referenced test? For example, are comprehension skills ever mastered? Or, as Smith and Johnson (1980) asserted, "We hope that no child could 'test out of' main ideas, or sequence . . . for if conceptual difficulty of words or contextual relationships were increased, the same child could fail to show mastery" (page 170). Comprehension is an ongoing, developing process, as we have maintained throughout this book. To test for mastery of a comprehension skill would provide a teacher with misleading information at best.

Criterion-referenced tests are similar to standardized diagnostic tests in the sense that both attempt to identify strengths and weaknesses in specific skill areas. As is the case with diagnostic tests, criterion-referenced tasks are part of a strong bottom-up approach to reading and learning to read. The teacher must recognize, however, that a criterion-referenced test provides only one perspective for understanding children's reading performance. Other indicators of reading should be weighed carefully in planning instruction.

INFORMAL ASSESSMENT

Informal tests of reading yield useful information about student performance. As the name implies, an informal assessment doesn't compare the performance of a tested group or individual to a normative population. Instead, informal tests may be given throughout the school year to individuals or groups for specific instructional purposes.

Informal reading tests gauge performance in relation to the student's success on a particular reading task or set of tasks. In this respect, they are similar to criterion-referenced measures. One of the best uses of informal tests is to evaluate how students interact with print in oral and silent reading situations. Rather than predicate the assessment on specific skill objectives as do criterion-referenced tests, informal tests analyze the interactive performance of children in situations that require passage level reading.

Informal reading inventories and teacher-made tests such as the cloze procedure are two important indicators of student performance. In the following sections, we explore how these measures can be used to inform decision making and strengthen inferences about children's reading behavior and performance.

Informal Reading Inventories

The Informal Reading Inventory (IRI) is an individually administered reading test. It usually consists of a series of graded word lists, graded reading passages, and comprehension questions. The passages are used to assess how students interact with print orally and silently. Johns (1981) claimed that learning how to use an IRI is an important part of a teacher's preparation. With the information gathered from an IRI you will be able to place students in appropriate instruction materials with some degree of confidence. Moreover, an analysis of oral reading miscues helps you to determine the *cueing systems* that students tend to rely on when reading. In short, IRI information can lead to instructional planning that will increase children's effectiveness with print.

IRIs are commercially available, although teachers can easily construct one. Selections from a basal reading series may be used to make an IRI. If you decide to make and use an IRI at least three steps are necessary:

1. Duplicate 100–200 word passages from basal stories. Select a passage for each grade level from the basal series, preprimer through grade eight. Passages should be chosen from the middle of each basal textbook to ensure representativeness.

2. Develop at least five comprehension questions for each passage. Be certain that different types of questions (based on question-answer relationships discussed in Chapter 6) are created for each graded passage. Avoid the following pitfalls:
   Questions that can be answered without reading the passage (except for "on your own" questions)
   Questions that require "yes-no" answers
   Questions that are long and complicated
   Questions that overload memory by requiring the reader to reconstruct lists (e.g., "Name four things that happened. . .")

3. Create an atmosphere conducive to assessment. Explain to the student prior to testing why you are giving the assessment. In doing so, attempt to take the mystery out of what can be a worrisome situation for the student.

Administering an IRI. Commercially published IRIs have graded word lists that can be used for several purposes: (1) to help determine a starting point for reading the graded passages, (2) to get an indication of the student's sight word proficiency (e.g., the ability to recognize words rapidly); and (3) to get an indication of the student's knowledge of sound-letter relationships to attack unfamiliar words.

When giving the IRI, the teacher may simply estimate placement in the graded passages instead of using word lists. Select a passage from the inventory that you believe the student can read easily and comprehend fully. A passage two grade levels below the student's present grade often fits the bill. If the passage turns out to be more difficult than anticipated, ask the student to read another one at a lower level. However, if the student reads the passage without difficulty, then progress to higher grade level passages until the reading task becomes too difficult.

Oral reading is usually followed by silent reading. In both oral and silent reading situations, the student responds to comprehension questions. However, an excellent variation is to first require students to retell everything that they recall from reading. Note the information given and then follow up with "aided recall" questions such as the following:

What else can you tell me about such and such?

What happened after such and such?

Where did such and such take place?

How did such and such happen?

Why do you think such and such happened?

What do you think the author might have been trying to say in this story?

Do not hurry through a retelling. When asking a question to aid recall, give the student time to think and respond.

Recording Oral Reading Errors. During the oral reading of the passage, the teacher notes reading errors such as mispronunciations, omissions, and substitutions. As the student reads, the teacher also notes how fluent the reading is. Does the student read in a slow, halting, word-by-word fashion? Or does he or she read rapidly and smoothly? Errors are recorded by marking deviations from the text on a copy of the passages read by the student. By *deviation,* we mean any difference that is observed between what the students says and the words on the page.

The following coding system can be used to mark errors:

1. *Omissions.* An omission error occurs when the reader omits a unit of written language, that is, a word, several words, parts of words, or a sentence(s). Circle the omitted unit of language.

   EXAMPLE   Jenny was (still) at school. She never played (after school)

2. *Substitutions.* A substitution error is noted when a real word (or words) is substituted for the word in text. Draw a line through the text word and write the substituted word above it.

   EXAMPLE   The ~~lion~~ *monkey* looked lonely.

3. *Mispronunciation*. A mispronunciation miscue is one in which the word is pronounced incorrectly. Follow the same procedure as a substitution error, writing the phonetic spelling above the word in text.

EXAMPLE   Because he was a frog, we called him Hoppy.

4. *Insertion*. The insertion miscue results when a word (or words) is inserted in the passage. Use a caret (∧) to show where the word was inserted and write the word.

EXAMPLE   She ran away.

5. *Repetition*. In repetition, a word or phrase is repeated. Treat the repetition of more than one word as a single unit, counting it as one miscue. Underline the portion of text that is repeated.

EXAMPLE   This is a tale about a man who is blind.

6. *Reversal*. The reversal error occurs when the order of a word (or words in the text) is transposed. Use a transpositional symbol (a curved mark) over and under the letters or words transposed.

EXAMPLE   He went to his trip.

"See you later," Sue said.

7. *Pronunciation*. A word (or words) is pronounced for the reader. Place the letter *P* over the word pronounced.

EXAMPLE   This was a startling development in his life.

In addition to marking errors, you should also code the reader's attempts to correct any errors made during oral reading. Self-correction attempts result in repetitions, which may have one of three outcomes:

1. *Successful correction*. The reader successfully corrects the error. Corrected miscues are coded in the following manner:

EXAMPLE   I did not know where I was going.

2. *Unsuccessful correction*. The reader attempts to correct an error but is unsuccessful. Unsuccessful correction attempts are coded in the following manner:

EXAMPLE   He felt compelled to leave.

3. *Abandoned correct form*. The student reads the text word or words correctly

but then decides to abandon the correct form for a different response. Code this behavior in the following manner:

$$\overset{\text{(AC)}\,\textit{wandered}}{}$$

EXAMPLE   Mike wondered if the tracks were made by a bear.

Familiarity with a coding system is important in marking oral errors. To ensure accurate coding, tape-record the student's reading. You can then replay the student's reading to check whether all errors are recorded accurately. Moreover, tape-recording will help in analyzing the student's responses to comprehension questions or a retelling of the material.

Determining Reading Levels.   The following reading levels can be determined for individual students by administering an IRI:

Independent level: The level at which the student reads fluently with excellent comprehension. The independent level has also been called the "recreational reading level" because not only will students be able to function on their own, but they often have high interest in the material.

Instructional level. The level at which the student can make progress in reading with instructional guidance. This level has been referred to as the "teaching level" because the material to be read must be challenging but not too difficult.

Frustration level. The level at which the student is unable to pronounce many of the words or is unable to comprehend the material satisfactorily. This is the lowest level of reading at which the reader is able to understand. The material is too difficult to provide a basis for growth.

Listening capacity level. The level at which the students can understand material that is read aloud. This level is also known as the "potential level" because if students were able to read fluently, they would not have a problem with comprehension.

The criteria used to determine reading levels have differed slightly among reading experts who have published IRIs. However, the most recommended over the years have been "the Betts criteria," so named for Emmett Betts (1946), who is generally considered to be the "father" of the IRI. These criteria are outlined in Table 13.1.

In making decisions about a student's reading level, teachers should be cognizant of two powerful correlates that determine whether children will find material difficult or not. First, there is a strong relationship between a student's interest in a topic and reading comprehension. Estes and Vaughan (1973), for example, found that children's reading levels fluctuated consistently between frustration and instructional levels depending upon their interest in the passage content of graded selections. Second, a strong case has been built throughout this book for the relationship that exists between background knowledge and reading comprehension. If children do poorly on a particular passage because they have limited knowledge or schema for its content, it's easy to err by underestimating reading level.

TABLE 13.1

Betts's Criteria for Determining Reading Levels

Reading Level	Behavioral Characteristics Commonly Observed	Word Recognition	Comprehension
Independent	Reads easily; comprehends fully; displays confidence; shows high interest	99 percent accuracy, or 1 error per 100 words	90 percent or greater accuracy
Instructional	Reads somewhat smoothly, occasionally word-by-word; understands and is challenged but not overwhelmed by the material; may seek help	95 percent accuracy, or 5 errors per 100 words	75 to 89 percent accuracy
Frustration	Often refuses to read or continue reading; lacks expression during oral reading; moves lips or finger points during silent reading. Lacks understanding of material	90 percent accuracy or less: 10 or more miscues per 100 words	Less than 50 percent accuracy
Capacity	Understands and is able to discuss material		75 percent accuracy or better

The point to remember is that reading levels are not chiseled in stone. Levels do fluctuate from material to material depending on a child's schema and interest in the passage content. The placement information that an IRI yields gives a "ball park" figure, an "indication." Therefore, placement decisions should rest on corroborative judgment, with IRI results providing one important source of information.

Analyzing Oral Reading Miscues

Oral reading errors are also called miscues. The terms *error* and *miscue* essentially describe the same phenomenon—a deviation or difference between what a reader says and the word on the page. Goodman (1973) believed that the term *error* signals something that is wrong or undesirable. In its place, he popularized the word *miscue* to reinforce a positive view of error in the reading process. A miscue provides a piece of evidence in an elaborate puzzle. Differences between what the reader says and what is printed on the page are not the result of random errors. Instead, these differences are "cued" by the thought and language of the reader, who is attempting to construct what the author is saying.

Miscues can be analyzed *quantitatively* or *qualitatively*. A quantitative analysis involves counting the number of errors; it pivots around a search for *deficits* in a student's ability to read accurately. A quantitative analysis is used, for example, to determine the reading levels previously discussed. In addition, a tallying of different types of errors has traditionally been a strategy for evaluating the strengths and weaknesses of a child's ability to analyze words. For example, does the reader consistently mispronounce the beginnings of words? An analysis based on this question helps to pinpoint specific difficulties. Does the reader consistently have trouble with single consonants? Consonant clusters?

In a quantitative analysis, each miscue carries equal weight, regardless of the contribution it makes to a child's understanding of the material read. A qualitative miscue analysis, on the other hand, offers a radically different perspective for exploring the strengths of students. A qualitative miscue analysis is a tool for assessing what children do when they read. It is not based on deficits related to word identification but rather on the *differences* between the miscues and the words on the page. Therefore some miscues are more significant than others.

A miscue is significant if it affects meaning—if it doesn't make sense within the context of the sentence or passage in which it occurs. Johns (1985, page 17) explained that miscues are generally significant when:

1. The meaning of the sentence or passages is significantly changed or altered and the student does not correct the miscue.
2. A nonword is used in place of the word in the passage.
3. Only a partial word is substituted for the word or phrase in the passage.
4. A word is pronounced for the student.

Miscues are generally *not* significant when:

1. The meaning of the sentence or passage undergoes no change or only minimal change.
2. They are self-corrected by the student.
3. They are acceptable in the student's dialect ("goed" home for "went" home; "idear" for "idea").
4. They are later read correctly in the same passage.

We agree with Johns that only significant miscues should be counted in determining reading levels according to Betts's criteria. He recommended subtracting the *total* of all *dialect miscues*, all *corrected miscues*, and all *miscues that do not change meaning* from the total number of recorded miscues.

Miscue analysis can be applied to graded passages from an IRI or to the oral reading of a single passage that presents the student with an extended and intensive reading experience. In the case of the latter, select a story or informational text that is at or just above the student's instructional level. The material must be challenging, but not frustrating.

Through miscue analysis, teachers can determine the extent to which the reader uses and coordinates graphic-sound, syntactic, and semantic information from the text. To analyze miscues, you should ask at least four crucial questions (Goodman and Burke, 1972):

1. *Does the miscue change meaning?* If it doesn't, then it's *semantically acceptable* within the context of the sentence or passage. Some examples of semantically acceptable miscues are:

I want to bring him *back* home.

Steve went to the ~~store~~ *shop*.

His feet are firmly planted ~~on~~ *to* the ground.

~~Mother~~ *Mom* works on Wall Street.

There were *(also)* phones for the car that worked with a small transistor.

Some examples of semantically unacceptable miscues are:

Bill went to ~~camp~~ *court* for the first time.

The mountain ~~loomed~~ *leaped* in the foreground.

The summer had been a ~~dry~~ *quiet* one.

2. *Does the miscue sound like language?* If it does, then it's *grammatically acceptable* within the context of a sentence or passage. Miscues are grammatically acceptable if they sound like language and serve as the same parts of speech as the text words. The above examples of semantically acceptable and unacceptable miscues also happen to be syntactically acceptable. Two examples of syntactically unacceptable miscues are:

Bill ~~reached~~ *carefully* for the book.

I have ~~a~~ *to* good idea.

In each example, the miscue doesn't sound like language when the text is read aloud.

3. *Do the miscue and the text word look and sound alike?* Substitution and mispronunciation miscues should be analyzed to determine how similar they are in approximating the graphic and pronunciation features of the text words. *High graphic-sound similarity* results when two of the three parts (beginning, middle, and end) of a word are similar, as in the miscue below:

He was ~~getting~~ *going* old.

Some *graphic-sound similarity* is present when one of three word parts is alike.

4. *Was an attempt made to self-correct the miscue?* Self-corrections are revealing because they demonstrate that the reader is attending to meaning and is aware that the initial miscuing did not make sense.

A profile can be developed for each reader by using the summary sheet in Figure 13.2. Study the passage that has been coded below. Then examine how each miscue was analyzed on the summary sheet.

walk
works
Sheep dogs ~~work~~ hard on a farm. They must © *lean* ~~learn~~ to take the sheep from place

© *mostly* *these*　*always*　*mostly*
to place. They ⌞must⌟ see that the sheep do not run ⟨away⟩. And they ~~must~~ see ⟨that⟩ the

loose and
sheep do not get ~~lost~~ ~~or~~ killed.

~~Something~~　*trying*　　*worker* © *learn*
Sometimes ⟨these⟩ dogs are ~~trained~~ to do other kind⟨s⟩ of farm work. They ~~learn~~ the

right to be called good helpers, too.

another working　　　　*coat*
Can you think of ~~one~~ ~~other~~ kind of ~~work~~ dog? He does not need a coat or strong

doesn't ~~leave~~　*and sleep*
legs like the sheep dog⟨s⟩. He ~~does~~ ~~not~~ learn to work ~~with~~ a sled in the deep, cold

doesn't ~~leave~~
snow. He ~~does~~ ~~not~~ learn to be a farm worker.

To determine the percentage of semantically acceptable miscues, count the number of "yes" responses in the column. Then count the number of miscues analyzed. (Do not tally successful self-corrections.) Divide the number of semantically acceptable miscues by the number of miscues analyzed and then multiply by 100.

To determine the percentage of syntactically acceptable miscues, proceed by counting the number of "yes" responses in the column. Divide that number by the number of miscues analyzed (less self-corrections) and then multiply by 100.

To determine the percentage of successful self-corrections, tally the number of "yes" responses in the column and divide that number by the number of self-correction attempts and then multiply by 100.

To determine the percentage of higher or some graphic-sound similarity, analyze mispronunciations and substitutions only. Divide the total of high-similarity words by the number of words analyzed and then multiply by 100. Follow the same procedure to determine whether some similarity exists between the miscues and text words.

Inferences can be made about oral reading behavior once the miscues are charted and the information summarized. Although the reader of the passage above miscued frequently, his strengths are apparent: He reads for meaning. More than half of his miscues were semantically acceptable. When attempting to self-correct, the reader was successful most of the time. Many of his miscues sounded like language. Moreover, the great majority of his substitution and mispronunciation miscues reflected knowledge of graphic-sound relationships.

Text	Miscue	Context Semantically Acceptable	Context Syntactically Acceptable	Self-Corrections	Graphic/Sound Similarity Beginning	Middle	Ending	Graphic/Sound Summary
work	walk	no	yes		X		X	high
learn	lean	—	—	yes	/////	/////	/////	/////
must	mostly	—	—	yes	/////	/////	/////	/////
the	these	yes	yes		X	X		high
away	always	—	—	yes	/////	/////	/////	/////
that		yes	yes		/////	/////	/////	/////
lost	loose	no	yes		X			some
or	and	no	yes					none
these		yes	yes		X	X	X	XXX
trained	trying	no	yes		X			some
kinds	kind	yes	yes		X	X		high
earn	learn	no	yes	no		X	X	high
helpers	helps	yes	yes		X	X		high
one other	another	yes	yes			X	X	
work	working	yes	yes		X	X		high
dog's	dog	yes	yes		X	X		high
learn	leave	—	—	yes	/////	/////	/////	/////
with	and	no	no					none
sled	sleep	no	yes		X			some
does not	doesn't	yes	yes		/////	/////	/////	/////

Percentage of semantically acceptable miscues   =   53 percent
Percentage of syntactically acceptable miscues   =   88 percent
Percentage of successful self-corrections   =   80 percent
Percentage of miscues with high graphic-sound similarity =   58 percent
Percentage of miscues with some graphic-sound similarity =   25 percent

Figure 13.2 Qualitative Miscue Analysis Summary Sheet

Seven significant miscues were made on the passage (which was slightly over one hundred words long). This indicates that the material bordered on frustration and probably is not appropriate for instruction. However, the reader has demonstrated strategies that get at meaning.

The Cloze Procedure

One of the most frequently recommended teacher-made tests for diagnostic purposes is the *cloze procedure*. "Cloze" refers to the psychological principle of closure, the human tendency to complete a familiar but not-quite-finished pattern. An example of the closure principle is for an individual to perceive a broken circle as a whole, or in the case of listening and reading, to supply a missing word in a familiar language sequence. The cloze procedure was originated by Wilson Taylor in 1953 as part of journalistic research to make newspapers more readable.

When developed by a teacher for classroom use, a cloze test evaluates how well students can read a particular text or reading selection as a result of their interaction with the material. The cloze procedure, therefore, is a method that systematically deletes words from a text passage and then assesses students' ability to accurately supply the words that were deleted. An assessment using a cloze passage should reveal the interplay between the prior knowledge that students bring to the reading task and their language competence. Knowing the extent of this interplay will be helpful in selecting materials and planning instructional procedures. Figure 13.3 presents an excerpt of a cloze test.

Constructing the Cloze Passage. The following steps can be used to develop a cloze passage for assessment:

1. Select a reading passage of approximately 275 words from material that students have not yet read but that you plan to assign.

2. Leave the first sentence intact. Starting with the second sentence, select at random one of the first five words. Delete every fifth word thereafter, until you have a total of fifty words for deletion. Retain the remaining sentence of the last deleted word. Type one more sentence intact. For children below grade four, deletion of every tenth word is often recommended.

3. Leave an underlined blank fifteen spaces long for each deleted word as you type the passage on a ditto master.

Administering the Cloze Passage. Three procedures are important to ensure that students understand the cloze task:

1. Inform students that they are not to use their textbooks or work together in completing the cloze passage.

2. Explain the task that students are to perform. Show how the cloze procedure works by providing several examples on the board.

3. Allow students as much time as they need to complete the cloze passage.

Directions: Read the following selection. Try to predict the missing words by using the context clues provided by the remaining words. Write the missing words on the lines.

The Bottle-Nosed Dolphin

The bottle-nosed dolphin is a star performer in many aquariums. Almost all the "porpoises" (1)_____

delight audiences with their (2)_____ are really bottle-nosed dolphins. (3)_____ dolphin can

be trained (4)_____ leap high into the (5)_____ to grab a fish (6)_____ its keeper's

hand. It (7)_____ also be taught to (8)_____ through a hoop and (9)_____

fetch a thrown ball (10)_____ stick.

　　Many scientists believe (11)_____ bottle-nosed dolphin is one (12)_____ the most intelligent

animals. (13)_____ think its intelligence ranks (14)_____ that of the dog (15)_____

of the chimpanzee, the (16)_____ intelligent animal. Others believe (17)_____ dolphin would

even outrank (18)_____ chimpanzee if (19)_____ animals were given the same (20)_____

test.

_____

ANSWERS

20. intelligence	15. and	10. or	5. air
19. both	14. between	9. to	4. to
18. the	13. Some	8. jump	3. This
17. the	12. of	7. can	2. tricks
16. most	11. the	6. from	1. that

Figure 13.3 Excerpt from a Cloze Passage

In all likelihood, students will be unfamiliar with the nature of the test. Staring at blank spaces and replacing missing words can be a formidable task for adults, let alone children. Do not expect a valid score the first several times that you administer a cloze test. Practice first with several cloze passages. Also, discuss the purpose of a cloze assessment and give students sufficient encouragement. Finally, make students aware of strategies they can use through "process discussions."

Scoring and Interpreting the Cloze Passage. Follow these steps to score and interpret a cloze test:

1. Count as correct every *exact* word students supply. *Do not* count synonyms even though they may appear to be satisfactory. Counting synonyms will not change the scores appreciably.

2. Multiply the total number of exact word replacements by two in order to determine the student's cloze percentage score.

3. Record the cloze percentage scores on a single sheet of paper for each class. For each class you now have from one to three instructional groups that can form the basis for differentiated assignments (see Figure 13.4).

The cloze test can be used to determine reading levels in much the same manner as an IRI. It yields the following levels:

1. *Independent level.* A score of above 60 percent indicates that the passage can be read with a great deal of competence by students. They may be able to read the material on their own without reading guidance.

2. *Instructional level.* A score of 40 to 60 percent indicates that the passage can be read with some competence by students. The material will challenge students if they are given some form of reading guidance.

3. *Frustration level.* A score below 40 percent indicates that the passage will probably be too difficult for students. They will need either a great deal of reading guidance to benefit from the material or more suitable material.

In making placement decisions, the performance of students who are on the border between two levels should be interpreted carefully. For example, if a student scored 38 percentage points on a cloze test, we suggest forsaking the admonition given above *not* to accept synonyms. If the student has a reasonably adequate number of synonyms (four or more) that were counted as errors, it is probably all right to place him or her in the instructional group, at least on a temporary basis. Then you can observe how he handles the material and interacts with others in the group.

As part of the process discussion suggested above, we recommend that students be aware of performance criteria. Discuss test results with the class in a general way. You need not reveal specific scores of individual students; however, explain the criteria for successful performance.

DIAGNOSTIC TEACHING

Observing how children interact with print while being taught is what diagnostic teaching is all about. The term *kidwatching* has been coined to dramatize the powerful role of observation in helping children grow and develop as language users. Yetta Goodman (1985) maintained that teachers screen their observations of children through their concepts and beliefs about reading and language learning.

In many classrooms, kidwatching is an ongoing, purposeful activity. Because language learning is complex, it's impossible to observe everything that happens in the classroom. The first essential, therefore, in observing children's reading and language use is to decide what to look for in advance.

Subject _____

Teacher _____

Period _____

Below 40 percent	Between 40 and 60 percent	Above 60 percent

Figure 13.4   Cloze Performance Chart

Mrs. Rainier, a fifth-grade teacher, is a kid-watcher. She uses what happens in the classroom to better understand and keep abreast of her children's literacy development and language growth. She makes a conscious effort to tune in to students' reading, writing, and language growth. Because she doesn't want to lose valuable insights, Mrs. Rainier has become a good listener and a good watcher. For her, professional observation is a natural outgrowth of teaching. She bases many of her instructional decisions on kidwatching and can zero in on what and how to teach in relation to literacy and language learning.

Mrs. Rainier is aware that the ability to listen and converse goes hand-in-hand with observation. Many of her students want to share their personal insights and happenings with her. They often talk about subjects that are seemingly unrelated to daily instructional routines. During informal moments such as these, Mrs. Rainier usually finds out about the student's background, problems, and interests. This type of conversation, in which she is an active listener, has been informative for planning lessons and guiding children's book selections. No wonder Mrs. Rainier makes herself available, before and after class, for discussion about general topics, lessons, and assignments.

On an instructional level, Mrs. Rainier believes that nothing replaces a good discussion of the material for assessing reading comprehension. For example, she regularly uses the Directed Reading-Thinking Activity (DRTA) as discussed in Chapter 6. Mrs. Rainier recognizes that prediction and inference-making are important aspects of reading comprehension. During DRTA discussions, Mrs. Rainier has been "keeping an eye" on Harold. In one lesson, Harold and his classmates read a part of a selection and then were asked to suggest what might happen next from the clues given. Mrs. Rainier listed their predictions on the board. The class then was asked to read on to find out if the text would confirm or refute the possibilities she had listed. Harold was reluctant to take risks throughout the activity. As the lesson progressed, most of his responses continued to come from previous experience rather than from what was actually portrayed in the story. Harold found it difficult to elaborate or clarify when he made certain predictions or inferences. Once committed, he did not want to change or refine his predictions, even when contradictory parts of the story were read aloud. As the DRTA lesson progressed, Harold relied more and more on Mrs. Rainier and his classmates for coaching and clues.

As you can see, Mrs. Rainier observed Harold as he interacted in a text learning situation. The DRTA discussion didn't have assessment as its primary purpose. Yet how Harold responded to the learning environment that was created yielded valuable *diagnostic* information about how he reads and interacts with peers and the teacher.

As Mrs. Rainier worked with Harold and his classmates, she formed questions that allowed her to concentrate on his development as a comprehender: To what extent does Harold take risks in making and supporting predictions? Does Harold use information from the text to support predictions? Does he begin to change or modify predictions as new information is gained? In this respect, Mrs. Rainier is not unlike other effective teachers. She responds to what unfolds before her and guides kidwatching by asking herself questions that reflect her instructional beliefs and objectives.

Observing

Many of the instructional strategies and procedures described in this book can be used diagnostically; that is, they can be used to observe and analyze students' reading behavior within the context of learning situations. Teachers can make instruction more effective by being alert to the way students respond to instruction and by adapting accordingly.

Observation is a tool that ranges from occasional notice of unusual student behavior to frequent anecdotal record keeping to checklists of students' behavior to interviews with students.

Anecdotal Notes. Anecdotal notes are intended to safeguard against the limitations of memory. Record observations in a journal, on charts, or on index cards. These jottings become your "field notes" and will aid you in classifying information, inferring behavior, and making predictions about individual students or instructional strategies and procedures.

It isn't necessary or even realistic to record anecdotal information every day for each student especially in classes with twenty-five or thirty children. However, over a period of time, focused observations for individual children will accumulate into a revealing and informative record of literacy and language learning.

Charts are particularly useful for keeping anecdotal records. Charts can be devised to record observations in instructional situations that are ongoing: participation in reading and writing activities, small and large group discussions, book sharing, silent and oral reading. For example, the chart in Figure 13.5 was developed to record observations of children's participation in journal writing sessions.

In addition, charts can be used to record certain behaviors across instructional activities. Examine the chart in Figure 13.6, devised to monitor and record evidence of risk taking.

A good strategy for developing a permanent record for each child in class is to cut observations apart from the individual charts. Then you can glue each student's anecdote into a permanent growth record. These can be used during conferences with students or with parents.

Some teachers find that writing anecdotal information can be unwieldy and time-consuming, especially if they are observing students over long stretches of time. An alternative to ongoing anecdotal notes is the use of checklists.

Checklists. Using a checklist is somewhat different from natural, open-ended observation. A checklist consists of categories that have been presented for specific diagnostic purposes. Individual items on the checklist guide the teacher's observations selectively. The DRTA checklist in Figure 13.7 can inform a teacher of

Mrs. Carter

Grade ___2___

Time Period: March 27–April 2

Name	Date	Behavior	Date	Behavior
George	3/27	*Frequently asks for assistance with spelling.*	4/2	*Appears to be writing more independently but still worries about correct spelling of words.*
Henry	3/27	*Revising draft of April Fool's story; has lots of ideas.*	3/29	*Writes fluently; ready to publish.*
Helen	3/28	*Copied a recipe from a cook book.*	4/2	*Wrote first original story; was very anxious to have story read; wanted to begin another story.*
Maxine	3/29	*Draws pictures to rehearse before writing; concentrates on handwriting and neatness.*	4/1	*Wrote a riddle; wants to share it with class.*

Figure 13.5 Observational Chart for Journal Writing

how particular groups of students are interacting with a text during a DRTA lesson.

If you plan to use the DRTA checklist, place a check next to each behavior that is observed during the lesson. An analysis quickly determines if certain students are not grouped appropriately.

Name	Date	Evidence of Risk Taking
Tony	10/11	Showed more willingness to try to spell independently.
Betty	10/12	Volunteered to be the recorder for Radio Reading.
Marie	10/11	Declined to reread portion of story being discussed; reluctant to participate in discussion.
Holly	10/13	Self-corrected miscues during oral reading; wasn't afraid to take guesses at unknown words.

Mrs. Metzger

Grade __4__

Week: October 11–October 15

Figure 13.6   Risk-taking Chart

Interviewing

Interviews tell you what children are thinking and feeling. Periodic student interviews can lead to a better understanding of (1) reading interests and attitudes, (2) how students perceive their strengths and weaknesses, and (3) how they perceive processes related to language learning. By way of example, two interviews are explained which explore students' perceptions of reading and learning to read.

Cecile Krause (1983) studied the perceptions of first-graders toward reading.

Teacher __Mr. Niece__

Grade __5__

Time Period: __Fourth period__

Group __Niece's Nikes__

	Student Name					
	Joe	Fred	JoAnne	Mary	Rich	Maude
Reading Behavior During DRTA						
<u>Reading Title of a Selection</u>						
1. Participates in predicting/is cooperative.	X	X			X	X
2. Makes some predictions with coaxing.	X					
3. Initiates own predictions eagerly after prompting with title.	X					
4. Low risk taking/ reluctant.		X		X		
5. Predictions are numerous.			X			
<u>After Reading Sections of a Selection</u>						
1. Retelling is accurate.	X		X		X	
2. Retelling is adequate.		X				X
3. Retelling is minimal.				X		
4. Confirms or refutes past predictions.	X		X			X

Figure 13.7   Directed Reading-Thinking Activity Checklist

	Student Name					
	Joe	Fred	JoAnne	Mary	Rich	Maude
5. Refines old and forms new predictions consistent with what has happened.					X	
6. Logical/probable/ realistic predictions.						
7. Explains predictions clearly.			X			X
Reading the End of a Selection 1. Shows awareness of story structure.	X					
2. Uses text throughout to justify predictions. a. Uses explicit information.	X		X			X
b. Uses implicit information.	X		X			X
3. Is able to converge thinking to decide on a main idea/ summary.	X		X			X

Figure 13.7   Directed Reading-Thinking Activity Checklist (*continued*)

She found that six- and seven-year-olds not only could verbalize their personal constructs of reading but that their perceptions reflected the way in which they interacted with print. Here are some of the questions that Krause asked the students in individual interviews:

1. Suppose someone from another planet happened to land on earth and saw you reading, and said to you, "What are you doing?" You would probably answer, "I'm reading." Then that person might ask, "What is reading?" How would you answer?

2. What would you do to teach someone to read?

Name: Date:
Classroom teacher: Reading level:
                                              Grade:

Directions: Introduce the procedure by explaining that you are interested in finding out
what children think about various reading activities. Tell the student that he or she will
be asked questions about his/her reading, that there are no right or wrong answers,
and that you are only interested in knowing what s/he thinks. Tell the student that if
s/he does not know how to answer a question s/he should say so and you will go on
to the next one.

General probes such as "Can you tell me more about that?" or "Anything else?" may
be used. Keep in mind that the interview is an informal diagnosic measure and you
should feel free to probe to elicit useful information.

1. What hobbies or interests do you have that you like to read about?
2. a. How often do you read in school?
   b. How often do you read at home?
3. What school subjects do you like to read about?

Introduce reading and content area books.

Directions: For this section use the child's classroom basal reader and a content area
textbook (social studies, science, etc.). Place these texts in front of the student. Ask
each question twice, once with reference to the basal reader and once with reference to
the content area textbook. Randomly vary the order of presentation (basal, content).
As each question is asked, open the appropriate text in front of the student to help
provide a point of reference for the question.

4. What is the most important reason for reading this kind of material?
   Why does your teacher want you to read this book?
5. a. Who's the best reader you know in _____?
   b. What does he/she do that makes him/her such a good reader?
6. a. How good are *you* at reading this kind of material?
   b. How do you know?
7. What do you have to do to get a good grade in _____ in your class?
8. a. If the teacher told you to remember the information in this story/chapter, what
      would be the best way to do this?
   b. Have you ever tried _____?
9. a. If your teacher told you to find the answers to the questions in this book what
      would be the best way to do this? Why?
   b. Have you ever tried _____?
10. a. What is the hardest part about answering questions like the ones in this book?
    b. Does that make you do anything differently?

Figure 13.8   Reading Comprehension Interview

Introduce at least two comprehension worksheets.

Directions: Present the worksheets to the child and ask questions 11 and 12. Ask the child to complete portions of each worksheet. Then ask questions 13 and 14. Next, show the child a worksheet designed to simulate the work of another child. Then ask question 15.

11. Why would your teacher want you to do worksheets like these (for what purpose)?
12. What would your teacher say you must do to get a good mark on worksheets like these? (What does your teacher look for?)

Ask the child to complete portions of at least two worksheets.

13. Did you do this one differently from the way you did that one? How or in what way?
14. Did you have to work harder on one of these worksheets than the other? (Does one make you think more?)

Present the simulated worksheet.

15. a. Look over this worksheet. If you were the teacher, what kind of mark would you give the worksheet? Why?
    b. If you were the teacher, what would you ask this person to do differently next time?

---

* Wixson, K., Bosky, A., Yochum, M. N., and Alverman, D. (1984). An interview for assessing students' perceptions of classroom reading tasks. *The Reading Teacher*, 37, pages 346–352. Reprinted with permission of the authors and the International Reading Association.

Figure 13.8   Reading Comprehension Interview (*continued*)

3. Who is the best reader you know? What makes her/him the best reader?

4. How did you learn to read?

5. What did your teacher do to help you learn?

6. If you are reading all by yourself and you come to a word you don't know, what do you do? Why? What do you do if that doesn't help? Why?

7. What should the teacher do when a person is reading out loud and says a word that is not the same as the word in the story?

8. Is it important for the teacher to teach you the new words before you read a story? Why or why not? (*If a conditional answer is given:*) When would it be important?

Karen Wixson (1984) and her colleagues developed an interview to probe students about the comprehension process. Designed for grades three through eight, the Reading Comprehension Interview (RCI) in Figure 13.8 takes about thirty minutes per student to administer in its entirety. The RCI explores students' perceptions of (1) the purpose of reading in different instructional contexts and content areas, (2) reading task requirements, and (3) strategies the student uses in different contexts. Its main uses are to help identify patterns of responses (for the whole group and individuals) that could then serve as guides to instruction and to analyze an individual's flexibility with different reading activities.

Interviews such as the RCI provide a rich source of information. When coupled with observations during teaching, interviews strengthen data from formal and informal tests of student performance. Moreover, interviews may reveal information that isn't possible from more traditional means of diagnostic assessment.

SUMMARY

Because reading takes place inside the head, it isn't directly observable or measurable. Observation and interview, informal reading inventories, miscue analysis, standardized, norm-referenced tests, criterion-referenced tests, and teacher-made tests such as the cloze procedure contribute to helping teachers understand a human process that's essentially hidden from direct examination. This is why teachers need to make instructional decisions based on multiple indicators of reading performance.

Norm-referenced and criterion-referenced tests are widely used in schools. In this chapter we examined how to interpret test scores and considered issues related to reliability, validity, and the uses of such tests. By way of contrast, we studied informal tests, whether commercially prepared or teacher-made. For example, informal reading inventories can be useful in placing children into appropriate materials and in determining how they interact with print in oral and silent reading situations.

Oral miscue analysis provides insight into the reading strategies children use to make sense out of text. Miscue analysis can be applied to any oral reading situation and, therefore, may be used in conjunction with informal reading inventories. The cloze procedure, developed by the teacher from classroom reading material, also provides teachers with an indication of a child's reading levels. Cloze tests performance can be analyzed to determine how well readers use their background knowledge and language competence in relation to specific reading material.

Diagnostic teaching involves observation, or kidwatching. It allows teachers to contrast test performance with children's ability to handle reading and learning activities within the context of classroom instruction. Anecdotal notes, checklists, and interviews are some of the techniques by which to better understand what children do, and why.

Throughout this chapter we have recommended caution toward any single indicator of reading performance. Decisions about individual students are always strengthened when teachers make use of diagnostic teaching and testing techniques.

THE WORKSHOP

In the Classroom

1. In small groups, decide how helpful each of the different types of assessment are for various kinds of decision making, using the following rating scale: 1 = very helpful; 2 = somewhat helpful; 3 = not helpful. Compare your ratings with those of other groups in the class.

Kinds of Decision Making

Types of Assessment	Placement	Daily Instruction	Long-range Instructional Planning
Standardized test			
Cloze test			
Criterion-referenced test			
Informal reading inventory			
Miscue analysis			
Observation			
Interview			
Checklists			
Anecdotal notes			

2. Suppose you were asked to address members of the school board on the merits of kid-watching in the district where you teach. Convince the board members that kid-watching is a slogan designed to legitimize the significance of professional observation in the classroom.

3. Develop an informal reading inventory, using graded passages and questions as suggested in the chapter.

4. Compare two published informal inventories from among those suggested by your instructor. How are they alike or different with respect to (a) placement criteria, (b) interpretation of errors, (c) questions accompanying passages, (d) ease of administration, and (e) diagnostic utility?

In the Field

1. Devise a cloze test and administer it to a child. Analyze the results for placement and the quality of word choices. What strengths does the child exhibit as a user of language?

2. Administer an informal reading inventory to a student and analyze the results. You

may use either a published inventory or the one you devised for classroom experience 3, above.

3. Interview a student, using the reading comprehension interview. Think about how you might use the information gained from the interview.

4. Plan a reading lesson with a teacher, then arrange to be the teacher's "eyes" and "ears." Watch what happens during the lesson, focusing on how much children are involved in learning. Discuss your notes with the teacher. What instructional decisions would you and the teacher make for the next lesson?

Chapter 14

Managing and Organizing the Effective Classroom

Remember the old saying, "There's a method to my madness"? Recalling some of the classrooms we've seen over the years, we'd be hard pressed to supply a comprehensive rationale for the ways in which they were organized and managed. Had we asked the teachers why they operated their classrooms as they did, we would have been given many different reasons. For teachers differ in their interpretations of what it means to provide effective reading instruction. In this chapter you'll read about how teachers use both new and old practices to organize and manage effective classrooms. You'll be given alternatives for arranging the physical environment, grouping students, allocating instructional time and materials, and then assembling the pieces. Use this as an opportunity to examine your own expectations and (potential) behaviors as you prepare to make decisions that may well reveal the method of your madness.

I have five classes of reading a day. That's 125 kids in and out of this room. We spend a lot of time getting ready and then cleaning up.

Jan, a seventh-grade reading teacher

Several of our elementary teachers wanted to start an individualized reading program after they took a children's literature course. I'm giving them all the support I can; however, getting together enough books is difficult.

Lois, a director of elementary instruction

I think reading class is okay. We do a lot of work. Once in awhile we get to have free reading.

Michelle, a fourth-grader

Classroom reading teachers probably wouldn't classify themselves as "managers." That term usually conjures up images of the business world where products are made, sold, and delivered. Managers are responsible for the orchestration of day-to-day company affairs. They are rated on their efficiency and effectiveness. The human element is there, but how can managers' responsibilities be compared to teachers' daily interactions with students? In many ways, they can't. The daily operations of classrooms are a world apart from business. Yet when reading teachers take control of the physical arrangement of their classrooms, the grouping of students for instruction, and the selection and use of materials, they are managing the classroom.

Once priorities have been established—most likely through district and school policy—and students have been assigned, the classroom becomes the focal point of instruction. Classroom management, then, is in the hands of the classroom teacher. What do teachers need to consider in order to effectively manage their classrooms? Teachers must conceptualize and organize classroom instruction, select classroom materials (as we discussed in Chapter 10), and achieve a physical organization in which all the pieces fit together.

To manage and organize classrooms efficiently and effectively, teachers deserve relevant, up-to-date information as well as traditional practices. We believe that this confluence of "new" or newly verified information with "old" or long-standing ideas provides an intelligent rationale for making classroom management decisions.

This chapter begins, then, with recent evidence from the *school improvement* efforts during the 1970s and 1980s. Researchers such as Ronald Edmunds (1979) asked many questions but focused on these: What kinds of schools are instructionally effective? What exactly is it that principals and teachers in effective schools and classrooms do?

The researchers identified a number of factors (discipline, time on task, direct instruction, teacher behavior, etc.) consistently linked to instructionally effective schools. Reading coordinators, specialists, and teachers should be cognizant of these factors because many of them *relate directly or indirectly to reading instruction.*

They are the "new" ingredients that contribute to *the effective classroom*. The "old" information stemming from a 150-year-old tradition is just as critical to good classroom management: *individualizing instruction*.

What began as individualized instruction spawned a set of procedures that are still associated with it today: self-selection, self-pacing, and self-interest. We use the term *individualizing* because it connotes the dynamic nature of reading instruction today. We believe the *majority of reading teachers are in the process of individualizing their instruction*. Due to the predominance of basal reader programs, most teachers do not formally or consciously select one approach over another for instruction. Most identify with the program already in place in their schools. The differences show up in the emphasis teachers place on instructional strategies (due to their beliefs) and time spent on those strategies. In other words, *teachers differ in their interpretations of and efforts at individualizing instruction in their own classrooms*.

CHARACTERISTICS OF EFFECTIVE CLASSROOMS

If you had the opportunity to spend a year visiting effective classrooms around the country, how would you describe what you observed? What, in the final analysis, would you cite as the major classroom characteristics?

As you've probably surmised, numerous studies such as this have been conducted. During the last decade researchers and teachers have collaborated to study those schools and classrooms in which effective instruction is happening. For example, schools in which inner-city children are *not* achieving far below national norms were identified as effective.

Factors reappeared in various studies; they were reiterated in reports on effective schools (Samuels, 1981; Wilder, 1977). Examine these factors in Table 14.1, "Managing Reading Instruction: Which Factors of Effectiveness Characterize Your Classroom?" Although the table displays a conglomeration of terms associated with categories of effectiveness, it is important to look at these in relation to reading instruction. How do these factors assist teachers in the management of their reading instruction?

More specifically, which factors relate to legitimate concerns of classroom teachers such as Jan at the chapter's beginning? Which factors seem to recur in the statements made by teachers with similar concerns about time wasted and student behavior? What kind of "work" is Michelle referring to if she's not reading? Is she one of the students described by Goodlad (1983) in his *Study of Schooling*?

> Students rarely planned or initiated anything, read or wrote anything of some length, or created their own products. They scarcely ever speculated on meanings, and most of the time they listened or worked alone (page 468).

When we are faced with alarming evidence such as the above description, we are reminded that many schools and classrooms don't show evidence of being effective learning environments. Thus it becomes doubly important that we select factors of effectiveness and relate them to the reading instruction we intend to provide. We'll consider several that cut across categories, such as discipline, time on task, and direct instruction, as well as teacher behavior and evaluation of students. Resources and classroom climate, two more factors contributing to the effective classroom, are considered later in the chapter.

Discipline

According to recent Gallup polls, school *discipline* is the major problem confronting our schools. Teachers too, whether they are beginning or experienced, are "acutely aware of the importance—and the difficulty—of maintaining good classroom discipline" (McDaniel, 1981, page 284).

We've all been in classrooms in which the only unruffled item was the bulletin board. Sometimes, if we dare to admit it, the classrooms were our own. How we interpreted test scores, how we distributed time on tasks, when we provided direct instruction in reading skills ... all paled in comparison to *getting the classroom under control.* According to Goodlad (1983), data revealed that teachers

were aware of the desirability of having students participate in setting their own goals, making choices, solving problems, working cooperatively with peers, and so on. But these views were tempered by conflicting ones having largely to do with maintaining

TABLE 14.1

Managing Reading Instruction: Which Factors of Effectiveness Characterize Your Classroom?

Teacher Behavior	Atmosphere or Climate	Instructional Emphasis	Evaluation	Resources
High expectations for all students	Orderly	Pupil acquisition of basic skills	Frequent	Flexible allocation to follow priorities
Confident, inventive	Quiet	Clear goals	Individual	Small classes, more adult volunteers
Flexible	Conducive to learning	Homogeneous groupings	Closely monitored student progress	Availability of extra personnel, time, and materials
Maintains discipline	High morale	Client-centered	Acceptance of test results as a measure of teacher performance	Supplementary materials
Task-oriented	Use of praise	More time invested in reading	Teacher-made tests	Close involvement of teachers and aides with pupils
Responsible	Focus on student achievement	Emphasis on cognitive development	Tests related to syllabus	Shared purposefulness among school persons and home
Experienced	Disciplined	Emphasis on homework and study	Test-taking skills stressed	
Provides structure	Traditional values of teaching and learning			
Emphasizes homework				

control. Those time-honored practices that appeared to help maintain control won out (pages 469–470).

Teachers, first and foremost, want disciplined classrooms and are willing to explore practical alternatives to punishment. They vote for "discipline" when asked which topic they'd prefer for an in-service day. Effective ways of working with students are in demand and must be the first order of business if constructive learning and teaching are to take place. How do teachers get students disciplined so that reading instruction is manageable?

Teachers' physical bearing in their classrooms can often set the tone. Body language is important. We communicate emotions such as confidence or fear by the way we hold ourselves (Verble, 1980). Who presents the more commanding figure—the teacher seated behind the desk or the teacher moving around the classroom? It is the one who is *moving* who is more likely to stimulate interest and hold students' attention. This is the teacher more closely aligned with several effective management behaviors reported by researchers (Kounin, 1970; Brophy, 1982).

Effective classroom managers respond to discipline problems, or better yet, to *potential discipline problems* by using "with-itness," "overlapping," and continuity and momentum (Kounin, 1970). What do these terms mean?

With-itness: The teacher knows what's going on *and* is able to communicate his or her awareness to the students. With-itness comes across in a nonthreatening manner and offers the student a way to "save face."

Overlapping: The teacher is able to pay attention to one activity such as a reading group *and* a deviating event at the same time. Overlapping permits the flow of activity to go uninterrupted, while at the same time defusing the situation. The teacher stays in control and the potential confrontation is avoided.

Continuity and Momentum: The teacher moves the class through different activities, keeps students' focus on a task, uses motivational comments, and presents variety and challenge during both seatwork and recitation (Emmer and Evertson, 1981).

The prevention of discipline problems and the notion of keeping the momentum going are particularly evident during reading instruction. If readers willingly participate in a reading activity, it's more likely they will *enjoy* that activity. If, on the other hand, readers pick up certain cues that tell them the activity is foisted on them, it's likely they will *not enjoy* that activity. Students who enjoy reading activities are motivated; they are a far cry from those whom we label "reluctant" readers. *Students who are motivated to read are able to stay that way in classrooms that are under control.*

Time on Task

Learning occurs through engagement; time spent on a task is a critical factor in effective reading instruction. How should children spend their instructional time in reading? More to the point, in what *kinds of reading activities* should they be engaged? A major recommendation of the Commission on Reading in *Becoming a Nation of Readers* (1985) is that "children should spend more time in independent reading," which is "associated with gains in reading achievement" (page 199).

In an earlier study, Leinhardt, Zigmond, and Cooley (1978) asked what teachers do that enables students to do things that help them learn. They observed 105 primary-grade children for twenty weeks and concluded that *certain kinds of reading activities are more important than others in producing achievement*. For example, the amount of time spent in silent reading was correlated with achievement (as measured by achievement tests), while activities such as traditional oral reading, story discussion, listening, and circling pictures with a common phonetic element were not. The investigators noted substantial variation from student to student and found *amount of teacher instruction* to be the strongest factor. To illustrate the connections among teacher behavior, student learning activities, and proficiency in reading:

> An increase of 5 minutes per day of silent reading time produced a one month gain in achievement (in Guthrie, 1982, page 768).

It is critical that reading teachers provide enough "opportunity to learn" certain skills if they wish children to show gains in achievement tests assessing those skills. Large differences in the numbers of minutes students are actually engaged in reading instruction is a matter of great practical importance to reading teachers. An excellent illustration of a large disparity in time (from four to fifty-two minutes!) was reported in the Beginning Teacher Evaluation Study (Marliave, Fisher, and Filby, 1977):

> If 50 minutes of reading instruction per day is allocated to a student who pays attention only about a third of the time and only one-fourth of the student's reading time is at a high level of success, then the student will experience only about 4 minutes of engaged reading at a high success level. Similarly, if 100 minutes per day are allocated to reading for a student who pays attention 85 percent of the time, at a high level of success for almost two-thirds of that time, then she or he will experience about 52 minutes (Berliner, 1981, page 215).

Effective teachers of reading want to improve student reading behaviors; they want to provide them the opportunity to learn. Guthrie (1982) suggested these three ways teachers could begin to do this: (1) increase the amount of time students spend reading; (2) reduce the amount of time students spend waiting and on other off-task behaviors; and (3) assist those individual students who are less engaged, that is, who are detached.

Teachers who try to implement any of these three suggestions will probably find it necessary to reexamine their classroom organization and management system. Some quick yet pertinent questions need to be answered:

When is the best time in the day to have a silent (or oral) reading activity?

Are there enough materials such as books and magazines to sustain each student's interest?

When are students most likely to spend time waiting? What activity are they finishing, beginning, or in the middle of?

Is the room arranged to make access to reading materials easy?

Who are the students who seem most detached during reading?

Are they detached during other activities as well? Are they in locations where the teacher can reach them within minimal time?

Finally, our consideration of time on task in relation to reading instruction leads us back to the basic business of dealing with and setting instructional priorities. Time is precious, and what we decide to do with classroom time reveals much about what we value.

We have different beliefs about reading, different philosophies which "result in different beliefs about what is important for children to learn" (Berliner, 1981, page 206). Very real differences in instruction occur because of the way teachers allocate time on task. A clear illustration of this is Berliner's summation of his end-of-year tabulations of four fifth-grade classes for reading:

> Classroom C spends dramatically more time on comprehension in reading than any of the other three fifth grade classes. In classroom D silent reading and spelling were emphasized, as judged from the dramatically greater allocation of time to those content areas, in contrast to the average amount of time each student of classes A, B, and C received. And oral reading hardly seemed to be of interest to the teacher of class B (page 206).

Direct Instruction

Direct instruction is the "second half" or corresponding piece to any consideration of time on task. It involves deciding *what* instruction for *which* students and in *what ways*. Berliner's (1981) description best summarizes the logic behind direct instruction:

> If the tests they use are matched to the curriculum they teach, then elementary school teachers who find ways to put students into contact with the academic curriculum, and keep them in contact with that curriculum, while maintaining a convivial classroom atmosphere, are successful in promoting reading achievement (page 218).

Do reading teachers abide by their district's reading curriculum? There is recent evidence to confirm that they do. First, there is little variance from district to district in the content of the reading curricula. Second, neither is there much difference between the intended curriculum as written and that which is explicitly taught. In effect, there is a

> sameness of form in the substance and design of the curriculum . . .

> The fit between the intended curriculum of textbooks and the taught curriculum of the classroom was rather neat (Goodlad, pages 467, 468).

The differences, then, as in so many other aspects of reading instruction, are subtle. They are found in the emphasis of classroom teachers who direct instruction;

who *find ways* to put students in contact with the reading curriculum (including the text).

The question becomes a pragmatic one to the reading teacher: How is instruction delivered? According to Table 14.1, *homogeneous grouping* is a characteristic of effective instruction. Grouping students together for a purpose is an accepted practice. The *size* of the group, however, is still cause for some disagreement.

Samuels (1981), who reported characteristics of exemplary reading programs, included these statements about the Direct Instruction Model:

> Maintain student attention. This is done through rapid paced, teacher-directed, *small group* instruction. It is more efficient than one-to-one instruction and allows for better supervision than large group instruction (pages 262, 263).

Others describe direct instruction as a teacher-centered focus with little student choice and frequent *whole class* presentations. It is "more effective for some purposes and students than for others" (Peterson, 1979, page 46). We need to decide ways to group based on need.

The *key* to direct instruction, we believe, is not that teachers consistently prefer small or large groups, but rather, that they remain *flexible* in forming and disbanding groups.

If our purpose is to increase gains in achievement test scores, as in the silent reading example previously used, students may perform slightly better on these tests with direct or traditional teaching. If our purpose is to develop creativity and problem-solving or to improve students' attitudes, independence, and curiosity, students may do somewhat better with less traditional teaching.

Depending on the nature of the students—their sense of personal control and their ability—direct instruction varies in effectiveness. Students who are external, that is, have a locus of control that matches a closely directed teaching situation, will benefit while those who are internal and frustrated in a situation where they have little control will not. Students of high ability do better in less direct approaches such as small group instruction. Low-ability students apparently need the greater direction and help provided by the teacher in large group instruction.

In other words, teachers of reading need to decide (1) what the desired outcome is, and (2) what the type of student(s) is. For example, if you plan on teaching "making inferences" from a text selection to twenty high-ability fifth-graders, you may decide to form several small groups for instruction. If, on the other hand, you plan to reinforce a word analysis skill such as "dividing words into syllables" with fifteen third-graders below the criterion, you may decide to instruct them directly as a total group.

Revival of Large Group Instruction. In many schools today we are witnessing the comeback of large group homogeneous grouping for reading instruction. For example, in Figure 14.1, ten average fifth-grade readers from Room A join fifteen average fifth-grade readers in Room B. The teacher in Room B instructs the whole group of twenty-five students, using the same level basal reader, for the forty-five-minute period.

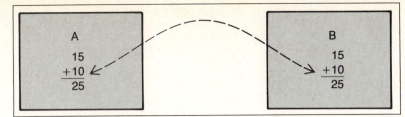

Figure 14.1   Interclass Grouping

It is worth noting that this comes at a time in our country when teachers have been making significant progress in individualizing their instruction. Whether this trend toward combining groups into a single larger, more homogenous one is a step forward bears investigating by teachers and principals. We need to reflect on the ways grouping can affect students.

Learning to read is a social activity for children, especially in the early grades. There is evidence that teachers differ in their treatment or focus with better and poorer readers. They correct errors of poor readers almost three times more than errors of good readers and interrupt poor readers more than good readers at the point of error (Allington, 1978). Teachers also help children read the right word in different ways: They give more decoding cues to poor readers and more context cues to better readers. One implication, then, is whether teachers unwittingly increase reading problems of children by hindering their self-correcting behaviors.

A more positive social consequence of the return to homogeneous large group instruction concerns the relationship between student perceptions and reading comprehension. It seems that students who perceive competitiveness, difficulty, and friction are less likely to show gains on a standardized reading test (Talmage and Walberg, 1978). On the other hand, students "involved in cross-class or interclass grouping for reading would find themselves with others of similar reading ability . . . . Such a situation might lend itself to a less competitive atmosphere than the more commonly found intraclass grouping situation might" (Walberg, Chou Hare, and Pulliam, 1981, page 155).

Figure 14.2 illustrates the prevailing grouping for reading arrangements in elementary classrooms. Twenty-three fourth-graders, divided into three groups, move alternately to designated seats in the reading area or circle and are instructed directly by the teacher. Each group of eight or so may take their chairs with them or find chairs already arranged or sit on a carpeted area off to one side. The two remaining groups are working independently on reading-related assignments, usually involving writing. Type of group organization, then, depends often on the preference teachers voice for managing their program. Next, how are students typically assigned to a reading group?

Evaluation of Students

Scores from standardized achievement tests are often relegated to the bottom drawer of the principal's or teacher's desk. If you have this kind of data available,

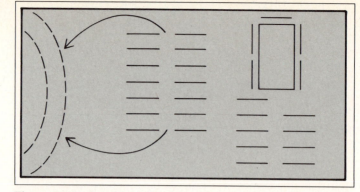

Figure 14.2 Intraclass Grouping

why not make use of it? Test results can supply one more piece of information to help teachers make decisions, especially with regard to classroom management and assigning students to groups. Test scores, when combined with other information, can help teachers evaluate materials and students' placement in reading groups.

Baumann and Stevenson (1982) devised a procedure for making decisions about students' instructional programs. They charted each student's name, reading score, aptitude score (I.Q.), testing ability (handling of testing situation), placement, progress in reading program, and instructional decision. We adapted this chart (see Table 14.2), eliminating the "aptitude score" category because accurate I.Q. information is simply not easily obtained. The usefulness of the chart and, hence, the standardized scores is in the assessment of whether or not each student's reading program placement accommodates his or her needs.

Taking the time to follow through with a procedure such as this can result in more efficient use of time later in the school year. In addition to validating (or invalidating) the student's test performance itself, a teacher can recommend further diagnostic testing for students and build an ongoing classroom assessment profile in reading.

This puts the teacher in the driver's seat when it comes to providing information about pupil achievement. Decisions about students are made, verified, reassessed, and become the basis for future planning. Part of a classroom evaluation, documentation of students, is accounted for. The next part of total classroom evaluation is information on teacher behavior. Who gathers this, what does it entail, and how can it be used *by teachers*?

TEACHER BEHAVIOR

Teacher behavior, its influence on students and instruction, is pervasive. Certainly, learning more about teachers is central to understanding all other factors in the effective classroom. Thus we focus on discipline, or *the teacher's use of discipline*.

TABLE 14.2

Grade Four—Mr. Argyle

Name	Reading Score	Testing Ability	Reading Placement	Program Progress	Instructional Decision
Don	42	Good	Level 5 Basal	Making good effort; having some difficulty	Consider a move to Level 4 reader due to material's difficulty.
Marie	94	Excellent	Level 6 Basal	Far and away the best reader	Verify instructional level with an IRI; develop individualized reading program with Marie.
Gigi	51	Satisfactory	Level 4	Capable, consistent student	Keep in present materials.

We focus on direct instruction, or *the teacher's grouping for direct instruction*. We focus on time on task, or *the teacher's selection of reading activities*. There is a need to pay close attention to teacher behavior. Principals who observe their teachers, students who learn in their teachers' classrooms, and teachers themselves—all need to better understand teacher behavior. How do principals and supervisors, teachers and students view the behaviors of teachers in the classroom, especially the reading classroom?

As the Principal Sees It

Assume the role of elementary principal for a minute or two right now. You have the profiles of student achievement tests and last marking period's printouts. It's time to evaluate the teacher's methodology.

You're aware from a recent series of administrator in-service sessions that certain components are associated with successful reading programs. You read the articles that every so often appear in your mailbox, compliments of the reading supervisor. You know that in successful reading programs, principals should:

Be knowledgeable about commercial reading materials and different approaches to reading.

Assist teachers in the selection of materials.

Encourage parent-teacher conferences.

Encourage recreational reading and sharing children's literature.

Once inside the classroom, it will be helpful to follow some guidelines as you observe the reading instruction. Examine these two forms in Boxes 14.1 and 14.2,

BOX 14.1

Teacher Observation Form A

	Never	Rarely	Sometimes	Usually	Always
1. Teacher demonstrates a genuine liking for students by					
A. complimenting students for completing tasks successfully	1	2	3	4	5
B. being sensitive to students when making suggestions for improvement	1	2	3	4	5
C. respecting students' choices of pleasure reading materials	1	2	3	4	5
D. _____ Other	1	2	3	4	5
2. Teacher demonstrates efficient planning by					
A. structuring specific time periods for instructional activities	1	2	3	4	5
B. using supplemental resources to teach needed skills	1	2	3	4	5
C. using teacher-made materials related to students' specific skill needs	1	2	3	4	5
D. _____ Other	1	2	3	4	5
3. Teacher helps students to improve their ability to attend by					
A. supplying students with appropriate pleasure reading materials	1	2	3	4	5
B. providing meaningful purposes related to reading assignments	1	2	3	4	5
C. praising students	1	2	3	4	5
D. _____ Other	1	2	3	4	5
4. Teacher guides students to respond to each other in groups by motivating them to					
A. share ideas for projects	1	2	3	4	5
B. discuss aspects of stories	1	2	3	4	5
C. provide tutorial support during skill activities	1	2	3	4	5
D. _____ Other	1	2	3	4	5

	Never	Rarely	Sometimes	Usually	Always

5. Teacher focuses on students' specific reading needs by
   A. using strategies directly related to students' strengths and weaknesses 1 2 3 4 5
   B. minimizing attention to factors that do not enhance students' reading 1 2 3 4 5
   C. _____ 1 2 3 4 5
   Other

6. Teacher makes students aware of their progress by
   A. presenting students with a profile of pre- and post-assessment information that shows improvement 1 2 3 4 5
   B. playing the first and second tape recordings of students' oral reading so that students can realize their improved performance 1 2 3 4 5
   C. _____ 1 2 3 4 5
   Other

7. Teacher stimulates responses at varied levels of understanding by
   A. asking questions related to the literal level of cognition 1 2 3 4 5
   B. asking questions related to the interpretive level of cognition 1 2 3 4 5
   C. asking questions related to the applied level of cognition 1 2 3 4 5
   D. _____ 1 2 3 4 5
   Other

BOX 14.2
Teacher Observation Form B

1. Communicates with clarity
   _____ Points made clearly.
   _____ Student questions answered completely.
   _____ Little time is spent answering student questions that are necessitated by lack of clarity.
   _____ Directions or procedures given clearly.

   _____ _____
   (other)
   _____ _____

2. Efficient use of instructional time
   _____ Discipline required within the group.
   _____ Discipline required outside the group.
   _____ Absence of confusion.
   _____ Materials needed are present.
   _____ Teacher interacts at appropriate times.
   _____ Task routines are specified.

   _____ _____
   (other)
   _____ _____

3. Feedback
   _____ Praise and/or adult positive feedback.
   _____ Criticism and/or adult negative feedback.
   _____ Accepting student response.
   _____ Acting on student response.

   _____ _____
   (other)

which we excerpted (Sanacore, 1981; Bagford, 1981), and which may be further adapted as you see fit.

Both of these sets of guidelines are useful in that they provide a common ground for principals and teachers to talk. They include items that relate to successful lessons and, as such, are positive means to communicate about observations. A word of caution: Look for *patterns*. Don't expect to observe once or twice and witness all of these behaviors. The fact remains that frequent informal classroom visits provide principals with the most useful information over time.

As the Student Sees It

In the past, did your teacher's opinion of you matter to you? If not your teacher's opinion of *you*, what about his or her opinion of your *work*? Chances are you have

4. Rate/level of student
    _____ Teacher encourages student(s) to elaborate on answers (probes).
    _____ Utilizes student responses.
    _____ Asks literal, narrow questions.
    _____ Asks higher-order, open-ended questions.
    _____ Question elicits response from a number of students.
    _____ A number of different students are given a response opportunity.

    _____ _____
    (other)

    _____ _____

5. An encouraging environment
    _____ Accepts student feeling.
    _____ Praises/encourages students about their reading.
    _____ Uses student comparisons.
    _____ Creates a positive environment.
        _____ book displays   _____ reading hardware
        _____ tapes/tape recorders   _____ reading hardware
        _____ films/strips/loops   _____ interest centers/stations
        _____ overhead projections

    _____ _____
    (other)

    _____ _____

Group starting time _____ ending time _____
("off task" = nonreading activity)
Student off task (minutes) _____
Group off task (minutes) _____

said yes to one or perhaps both of these questions. Why do teachers' opinions matter so much to students (of all ages) and what effect does this produce?

Teachers' attitudes and behaviors, as perceived by students, seem to have a noticeable effect on students' self-concepts. Since our self-concept affects how we feel about a situation, in this case a learning situation, it's important to think about teachers' behaviors. Quandt (1972) identified teacher behaviors that are especially significant in improving or keeping intact students' self-concepts: minimizing differences between reading groups; comparing the student's progress against herself rather than with the group; utilizing student interests; and using carefully chosen materials that the student can read.

Students know that their teachers are more important than the techniques, approaches, and materials used. *Teacher expectations* for their students' success or lack of it are often revealed in their general behaviors in the classroom. Teacher expectations are lived up to—or down to—by students. Yet these are intangibles; they are not obvious. How can teachers, who are closest to their own behaviors, deal with them constructively?

To date, most of the research on teachers' expectations has focused on their expectations for student achievement (Good, 1982, page 31). Yet there is "need for more information about student's perceptions and judgments of classroom events" (page 30). Do students observe and assess teacher behaviors and classroom assignments in ways that are consistent with teachers' intentions?

As the Teacher Sees It

This time we don't have to pretend or try to recall what is was like. Most readers are teachers or will soon be teachers. We know better than anyone what it is like. The cover of one introductory teacher education textbook captured the essence of this view (Anglin et al., 1981): It depicts rows of student desks and the top of a teacher's desk as seen from *behind* the teacher's desk. We often have that vantage, looking out at the classroom and seeing our students. Let's try to look within.

First, as teachers we need to analyze our own attitudes and behaviors to find out whether or not they are conducive to forming positive attitudes in students. As you read each statement (adapted from Quandt, 1972) in Box 14.3, think of your verbal and nonverbal signals, the classroom atmosphere, and the expectations that you may be communicating. For each "yes" response, give at least one example, either from your past experiences or projected ones.

Second, teachers need to identify basic instructional practices in reading. Basic in this case means in positively affecting students' attitudes through the standard combination of *interests* plus *needs*. Which of the suggestions in Box 14.4 are you already implementing? Check "yes" for those; check "perhaps" if you are interested in finding ways to implement the suggestion; check "no" if you are not now implementing it and are not interested in finding ways to do so.

Finally, teachers need to realize that many times it is the overwhelming pressure of factors *outside school* that win out. In spite of the care taken to examine educational and attitudinal factors as well as our reflections on differing perspectives, our efforts at creating a responsive, well-organized, effective classroom won't always pay off. Relationships in families, nutrition, illness, abuse, economic hardship, and community pressures can and do override school factors. The important point for us as teachers is to make certain that we keep our expectations high and provide many opportunities for students to reach *up* to them.

INDIVIDUALIZING INSTRUCTION

The term *individualizing*, more than *individualized*, connotes the process of providing differentiated instruction to students. It is the accumulation of previous knowledge and direct experiences in reading classrooms over the years. We believe that most teachers of reading still ascribe to this process which originated as the individualized instruction approach.

BOX 14.3
Teacher Self-Analysis

1. I respect each student's efforts at becoming a better reader and value each one as a reader.

   Example: _____

   _____

2. I permit students to express their fears and dislikes even when they are directed at me.

   Example: _____

   _____

3. I consider the feelings of my students by giving immediate attention to their needs and interests.

   Example: _____

   _____

4. I convince my students they don't have to be afraid of making mistakes.

   Example: _____

   _____

5. I believe that each student can achieve some measure of success with reading.

   Example: _____

   _____

6. When student progress indicates that my methods and materials are not producing desired results, I change the methods or materials.

   Example: _____

   _____

7. I am aware of ways, verbal and nonverbal, in which I communicate my feelings about reading to my students.

   Example: _____

   _____

Individualized Instruction: Confusions and Misunderstandings

The term *individualized instruction* has to be one of the all-time "ten most misunderstood terms in education." Naturally, it means different things to different people. To some, it means programmed, prescriptive instruction; to others, it

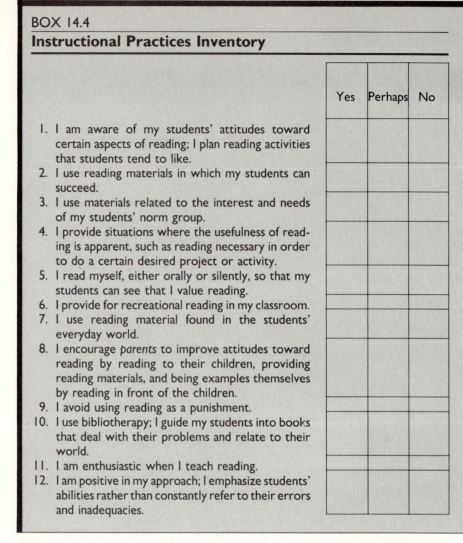

BOX 14.4

Instructional Practices Inventory

	Yes	Perhaps	No
1. I am aware of my students' attitudes toward certain aspects of reading; I plan reading activities that students tend to like.			
2. I use reading materials in which my students can succeed.			
3. I use materials related to the interest and needs of my students' norm group.			
4. I provide situations where the usefulness of reading is apparent, such as reading necessary in order to do a certain desired project or activity.			
5. I read myself, either orally or silently, so that my students can see that I value reading.			
6. I provide for recreational reading in my classroom.			
7. I use reading material found in the students' everyday world.			
8. I encourage *parents* to improve attitudes toward reading by reading to their children, providing reading materials, and being examples themselves by reading in front of the children.			
9. I avoid using reading as a punishment.			
10. I use bibliotherapy; I guide my students into books that deal with their problems and relate to their world.			
11. I am enthusiastic when I teach reading.			
12. I am positive in my approach; I emphasize students' abilities rather than constantly refer to their errors and inadequacies.			

means one-to-one teaching or tutoring; to yet others, it means flexible grouping for instruction. Often educators disagree over the definitions of terms but the disagreement doesn't cause any harm.

Sometimes, however, failure to be on the same wavelength can result in unintended educational *disservice*. As a case in point, we remember sitting in an audience of school administrators and directors of Title I in a midwestern state in the mid-seventies. The person in charge of disbursing funds at the state level as well as enforcing and interpreting the accompanying rules and regulations was speaking. Director Watts vacillated on several issues that were raised, but stood firm when he declared that "individualized instruction is not an approved form of instruction and will not be condoned." Glances were quickly exchanged around the room and collective eyebrows raised, but his remarks went unchallenged.

Most in the audience were quick to catch his rather narrow definition of individualized instruction: one-on-one, that is, one teacher or tutor per one Title I student. Watts may even have evoked sympathy from some of us who sensed his fear of the projected costs of such instruction! However, one valuable, pragmatic lesson was learned by all that day: Design any instructional grouping patterns you wish, but don't refer to *any* of them as individualized instruction.

What Is Individualized Instruction in Reading?

This is the key question for those interested in classroom organization because it can help us clarify the major ways we choose to deliver reading instruction: in small groups, whole class, or one-to-one.

Individualized instruction evolved out of a 150-year-old American goal of providing free schooling for everyone. Its biggest impetus came with the development of reading tests in the early part of the twentieth century. It spawned many experiments in education such as ability grouping, flexible promotions, and differentiated assignments. Many of the plans followed the ideas outlined in the Dalton and the Winnetka plans which allowed children to work in reading and content areas at their own pace (Smith, 1965, page 194).

Gradually, individualized instruction went beyond children's learning rates and reading achievement. The child's interest in reading, attitude toward reading, and personal self-esteem and satisfaction in reading expanded the goal of instruction (Smith, 1965, page 378). Terms associated with individualization ranged from *individual progression* in the 1920s to *individualized instruction in reading*, to *self-selection in reading*, to *personalized reading*. Today, we might add *objective-based* and *prescriptive* learning.

An interesting irony is that originally, procedures used in individualized classrooms did not vary widely, whatever the adopted term. Read the following classic description; does it conjure up a reasonable picture of individualized instruction in your mind?

> Each child selects a book that he wants to read. During the individual conference period the teacher sits in some particular spot in the room as each child comes and reads to her. As he does so, she notes his individual needs and gives him appropriate help. Finally she writes what the child is reading, his needs, and strengths on his record card. Then another individual conference is held, and so on. If several children need help on the same skills, they may be called together in a group for such help (Smith, 1965, page 379).

The above scenario does, after all, seem like a plausible description of individualized instruction. How it's actually *applied* in reading classrooms around the country is another matter entirely. In practice, two variations of the original individualized approach to instruction are often found in today's classroom: (1) Individualized procedures are one part of the total reading program (i.e., one day a week); or (2) parts of individualized reading are integrated into another reading approach (i.e., self-selection during free reading).

Thus while individualized instruction as an approach to or program for reading instruction is not as widespread as others, its *influence* on reading teachers has been pervasive. *Teacher assessment of individual readers' strengths and weaknesses* is the very core of effective reading instruction. This is not peculiar to individualized instruction, but a tenet that cuts across the delivery of reading instruction, regardless of the organization pattern used.

Influences of Individualized Instruction

The term *individualized instruction* in reading has waxed and waned. Models of prescriptive and of personalized individualized programs such as skills management systems and literature-thematic units have come and gone. What are we left with? What historical influences of the individualized instruction movement helped shape the delivery of reading instruction today?

As Gates stated in a 1964 correspondence, "I have always believed that if one accepts the theory that the basal reading program must be used it should be adjusted to individual needs and that each child should be encouraged to move on into wider and more advanced material as rapidly as possible" (Smith, 1965, page 240). Individualization of instruction is not contrary to basal reader programs. However, it has gone beyond the traditions of ability grouping.

Durrell, in the 1950s, suggested as much when he challenged teachers of reading to provide for individual differences of students. Teachers should be "providing suitable materials; individual conferences; extensive individual silent reading; long-range assignments; workbooks, standard test lessons and other self-administering materials; small grouping of 5 to 6 pupils" (Smith, 1965, page 294).

Let's examine further two major ramifications of individualizing instruction in reading that evolved out of a long tradition, yet still coincide with effective classroom management.

Groups. The concept of creating and disbanding groups of differing sizes, abilities, and interests for the purpose of providing specific instruction is germane to effective classroom instruction. Yet while grouping is used to organize the teaching of content subjects (such as math and social studies), reading instruction is historically associated with grouping. The reading group or circle is indigenous to reading.

Can you remember your old reading group? We might joke about having been a bluebird, robin, eagle, maybe even a buzzard. Whether such memories are amusingly nostalgic or painful, few of us ever lose them completely. It's probably just as well that we do remember, because reading groups today are as prevalent as they ever were. One of the reasons for this lack of change, according to Goodlad (1983), is that "the circumstances of teaching make it difficult for teachers to do other than what they have already learned to do" (page 469).

Consequently, we observe daily reading circles gathering for round-robin oral reading from basal readers. Or, for other purposes, small groups may gather for story discussions and questions. Large groups of whole classes may stay intact for silent reading and writing; books may be reported in individual conferences.

What are some consequences of placing students in groups? As we discussed earlier, under direct instruction, teachers' behaviors toward children assigned to "low" groups differ from their behaviors toward those assigned to the "high" group. Teachers are less likely to ask the lower group to answer higher-level comprehension questions (Allington in Good, 1982, page 27). In addition to how group placement affects students' performance, "we need to understand much more thoroughly the consequences of placing students into groups" as it affects students' expectations.

A corollary to grouping, as we see it, is awareness of the *physical environment* of the classroom. What do the space, materials, and decision-making capabilities of students and teachers reveal about the classroom as a place for learning? If someone took a snapshot of your classroom, how would you describe the composition of student groups and the nature of activities in progress?

From the *Study of Schooling*, you will recall that researchers found little variation in curricular form and teaching methods:

> Indeed, the range in these presumed-to-be-central aspects of schooling was markedly less overall than in such characteristics as classroom climate, school climate, staff relationships and school/home relations (Goodlad, 1983 page 469).

Their findings, did, however, reveal that "schools differ in their ambience" (page 469).

This recognition, that classroom climates or *classroom environments* are distinct and that the classroom is the sum total of all its organizational components, has grown through the years. Further, we have come to acknowledge that this physical environment embodies the goals of the classroom and the teacher's role. Teachers have learned to combine their knowledge about reading and learning to read to create as conducive a learning environment as possible.

Materials. The endorsement of a wide variety of reading materials has become accepted practice across school districts, as we discussed in Chapter 10. Originally provided for the purpose of matching up students with materials on their reading level, the concept of material variety quickly expanded. Now there are diverse materials to meet students' interests and to provide instructional variety as well. Reference books, catalogs, paperback books, and magazines are found in corner shelves for free and silent reading. Skill cards from kits, along with workbook pages and dittos, are self-checked by students; hardcover basal readers and softcover high-interest, low-vocabulary series move from shelf to circled readers to desks and back again to the shelf.

Materials are involved in most of the instructional day. Based on the results of observations of 1,016 classrooms, Goodlad and associates (1983) determined that, at the elementary level, 70 percent of class time is spent on instruction. How is the student's time distributed across the array of activities in a day? At the elementary level, 60 percent of classroom time is spent "preparing for and cleaning up after assignments, listening to teachers explain or lecture, and fulfilling written assignments" (page 467).

When many reading teachers speak about presenting a skill, reinforcing the skill, testing for its mastery, and perhaps reteaching the skill, they are assuming that *materials* accompany each one of these steps. They are probably right. Teachers at the other end of the spectrum—those whose programs revolve around independent reading of personally selected books and short stories and poems—also have legitimate views.

This leads to another factor related to materials: *record-keeping* and the amount of teacher time required to keep records. Record-keeping refers to the necessity of keeping records on individual readers' total and daily performance in relation to skill needs and reading strategies, materials used, completed and projected activities, assigned groups, grades and test scores received, and recommendations for future instructional placement. Teachers are always seeking efficient ways of accumulating, recording, and synthesizing this kind of information. Publishing companies frequently promote built-in record-keeping components for both students and teachers.

We have established that many materials are a must for reading teachers. They are also something of a paradox. If you manage individual reading, you need a variety of materials. On the other hand, if you have a lot of materials, you need to effectively manage your classroom.

PUTTING IT ALL TOGETHER: CLASSROOM ORGANIZATION

We have considered a number of factors necessary to manage classroom reading instruction. Getting the classroom under control, keeping students engaged with direct instruction, and examining our own behaviors and expectations helped us deal with the task of organization. The ramifications of individualizing instruction, along with the basic need to orchestrate children and materials and our beliefs with some degree of efficiency, bring us to a final consideration: putting the pieces together.

Unfortunately—or fortunately, depending on your point of view—designing a functional classroom is not the same as designing a family room or a new house. There are no scaled drawings from which to choose. Classroom teachers have to make do with what is already there. The result is a potpourri of elementary classroom designs ranging from traditional row after row to open modular groupings to cozy carpets and cubbyholes.

Creating a Physical Environment

"Behind the classroom door." No, this isn't the title of a new miniseries about the clandestine adventures of an ambitious reading teacher. It does, however, leave a lot to the imagination. What actually goes on in the classroom once the door is closed? Any experienced teacher will acknowledge that, within the confines of one's own classroom, there is a certain degree of autonomy that outside pressures don't penetrate. The physical arrangement of the classroom, given an understanding custodian, is one expression of a teacher's autonomy. The way the furniture is arranged contributes to the reading program's organization.

Years ago, when one of the authors was taking her first course in reading as an undergraduate, the term *moveable furniture* appeared on the midterm exam. Arranging desks, chairs, materials, and so forth can contribute a great deal to the organization of an entire semester or year-long reading program. The *physical structure* put into place by the reading teacher can support the goals or underlying structure of the reading program. It can work for the teacher as much as if not more than any other component in the total program and total classroom environment.

Experienced teachers realize this eventually. Perhaps, if more prospective and practicing teachers were exposed to philosophies such as Herbert Kohl's in *The Open Classroom* (1969), they would do even more behind the classroom door:

> The placement of objects in space is not arbitrary, and rooms represent in physical form the spirit and souls of places and institutions. A teacher's room tells us something about who he is and a great deal about what he is doing.
>
> It is important for teachers to look at the spatial dimensions of their classrooms, to step back, so they may see how the organization of space represents the life within it (page 35).

Stepping Back. When you do step back and look carefully at your reading classroom, what do you see? Shuman (1982) wrote about strategies to interest reluctant readers and, in doing so, described "the reading classroom." He believed this environment could have a positive effect on learning outcomes:

> Reading areas . . . set apart from the rest of the classroom . . . Bookcases . . . shag carpet . . . furniture can be more home-like. The reading area . . . crammed with reading materials of every sort . . . at least 100 books . . .
>
> Class libraries . . . used paperbacks and magazines. Print should cover the walls . . . posters, cartoons, comic strips, newspaper articles, student writing and recipes.
>
> . . . Air, rail, bus schedules; store catalogs; newspapers; telephone directories; driver's license manuals . . . (page 727).

Another perspective to take as you look around the room is to examine it for *space usage,* or books, nooks, and crannies. For example, do you see a space suitable for a reading loft? Such a loft might hold four or five readers on top and house a mini-library underneath. Is there any room for a reading fort made of empty carpet-roll tubes? How about creating student "offices" by using partitions to divide a table into three or four separate areas? If these aren't feasible ways to use space, you might consider establishing several "special reading spots"—such as chair, carpet, cupboard, or sofa.

Still another scan of your classroom might be made with *storage techniques* in mind. Boxes, labeled shelves, bulletin boards, and pegboards are multipurpose and inexpensive. Boxes make good filing cabinets; students, too, might like their own filing drawers. Thorough and visible labeling helps students know where to return materials around the room. Bulletin boards can be used to store activity cards, forms, and record sheets, to name a few possibilities. Pegboards can be used for hanging heavier items (Stahl and Anzalone, 1970). One of the most unusual storage techniques observed was three rows of eight cylinders each . . . ten-gallon cardboard ice cream containers! They were sturdy and, if nothing else, contributed to positive student attitudes (or memories)!

We asked a fifth-grade teacher whose classroom we admired and whose teaching always seemed to be carried out with purpose and reflection this question: "What do you *call* your room arrangement, Wanda?" She responded, "I don't know; it doesn't really have a name, but it works." We asked her to describe what and how her reading classroom is organized. Box 14.5 is Wanda's description of her classroom and how it came into being.

Creating a physical environment is important, but it is not an end in itself. A teacher's underlying concern for processes of learning is the heart of the matter.

> Getting rid of desks, setting up refrigerator cartons, installing area rugs, and utilizing all kinds of material for partitioning and for storage are useful only if they are intended to maximize children's learning and to capture their interest (Thomas, 1975, page 208).

The physical environment teachers of reading create can set the stage for a productive reading program. Children's literature programs and the use of literature in the elementary and early childhood classroom have been studied and serve to illustrate the connection between physical environment and program. Morrow (1982) reported a definite relationship between children's frequency of use of literature and physical design or program characteristics. Yet library corners were neither carefully designed nor valued as an important area of the classroom (page 344).

Teachers who make books accessible to children by making changes in time and physical design of their classrooms are contributing to the development of readers. Ideas for keeping records or just "keeping track of things" follow.

Ideas for Getting Organized

Ideas for getting your classroom organized run the gamut from deciding to establish learning centers to designing a system to record books students read. Some pertain to the classroom as a whole and others to individual students in selected activities. They are all ways of bringing order and organization to the classroom.

Learning Centers. Several advantages to setting up learning centers are that they allow more pupil movement, more and diverse opportunities for pupils to work in small groups or independently, and more pupil choice, commitment, and responsibility.

BOX 14.5

Doing Away with Desks

A fascinating experience in class arrangement took place in my classroom one year—all because one of my student's father worked for a cardboard box factory.

He came to me one day with the free offer of fifty heavy-duty, double-strength cardboard boxes approximately 2 x 2 x 2 feet in size. Could I use them? The price was right, so of course I said yes.

Now, how could I use this terrific gift? And then the answer came to me one day when a student said, "Mrs. Rogers, I haven't sat in my own seat since the first five minutes of today!" I gave this some thought and realized that with the flexible grouping we were constantly using, the children actually did spend very little time in their own desks. So I asked, "Why not do away with desks?" And we did.

Each student was given a box which was to house books, supplies, and so on. We stacked the boxes two tall and they provided instant dividers to make separate spaces in the room for small groups to meet.

Much of our class instruction was done in small groups with different groupings for each subject. By removing "desk ownership," we eliminated territorial problems. No more did we hear, "Jim wrote all over my desk during reading class." "You can't sit here. I don't want your cooties all over my desk." "Mrs. Rogers, Judy stole my pencil out of my desk when she was sitting there."

Desks were viewed as workbenches and storage areas for learning activities equipment and materials. By removing student-desk associations, the desks themselves became more flexible for rearranging to meet different organizational needs.

An unexpected benefit was that students became more involved. Because they no longer had a desk for retreat where they could wile away time unproductively or daydream, they tended to "find something to do" when they finished a task; kibbitz in on another group of students, use the library or resource center, take a book to a corner, or involve themselves in a listening or hands-on activity in special areas set up for that purpose. They learned to move themselves from one task to another, rather than "sit in *their* seats" and wait to be told what to do by the teacher.

One of the best advantages was that it opened new vistas of classroom organization for me as a teacher. I found myself less restricted and more creative and efficient. I could arrange the management of an activity without the confines of "desk ownership."

Why teachers choose to use learning centers is important because their purpose should determine the type of center. An illustration of this is the Guide to Learning Centers in Table 14.3, adapted from Thomas (1975).

One type of center doesn't preclude carryover to another type; students may experience motivation in a prescription center, for example. As your purposes become more specific, the types of learning centers possible expand. Specific types of centers might include these:

TABLE 14.3

Guide to Learning Centers

Purpose	Type	Objective
1. Arouse students' interests	Motivational	Determined by teacher
2. Find out what students know	Diagnostic	Determined by teacher
3. Guide skills development	Prescriptive	Determined by teacher and students
4. Broaden experiences	Enrichment	Determined by students

Subject: Language arts, math, social studies, science, music

_____

Interest: Sports, records, insects, food, rocks, cultures, airplanes

_____

Inquiry: "Are camels still used on the desert?"

_____

Problem-solv-ing: "You're visiting a friend overnight. You wake up and smell smoke; what do you do?"

_____

Theme: Appearance and reality
("Is Wilbur, in reality, a terrific pig?")

_____

Construction: Building models, making films
("Construct a six-petal flower using LOGO turtle graphics.")

_____

We've added a blank line to each type above. Can you add more examples to each type and then think of more types and examples to list below?

_____   _____

_____   _____

_____   _____

_____   _____

Room Diagrams. One of the most useful ideas for organizing any classroom, whether you have learning centers or other formats, is a diagram of the classroom. This serves three simple yet essential purposes: (1) It helps the teacher keep track of where and how various activities are taking place and with whom; (2) it helps parents and other teachers acclimate to your classroom whether they are visiting or presiding over another class or study hall (the diagram becomes a handy seating chart); and (3) it gives students an opportunity to see what is available for them to do now and anticipate what other activities are in store for them.

There are many "activity" and "idea" books on the market today, and most seem to contain room arrangement diagrams. Some offer elaborate configurations whereas others present more easily attainable plans. We believe that room diagrams are just as useful to the teacher who is beginning to use optional activities or centers as they are to the teacher who has scrapped traditional formats completely. To illustrate, the rooms outlined in Figure 14.3 are traditional elementary classrooms in which learning centers are separated from "regular" instructional areas either around the periphery or off to one side. While classrooms that have distinct areas for diverse activities tend to have certain days or times set aside for their use, other classrooms have alternatives integrated into their daily routines.

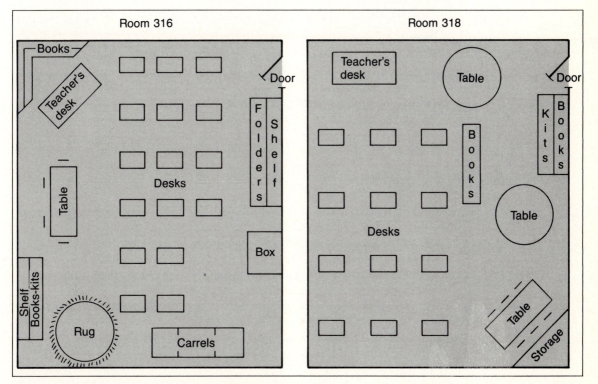

Figure 14.3 Traditional Classrooms with Activity Centers

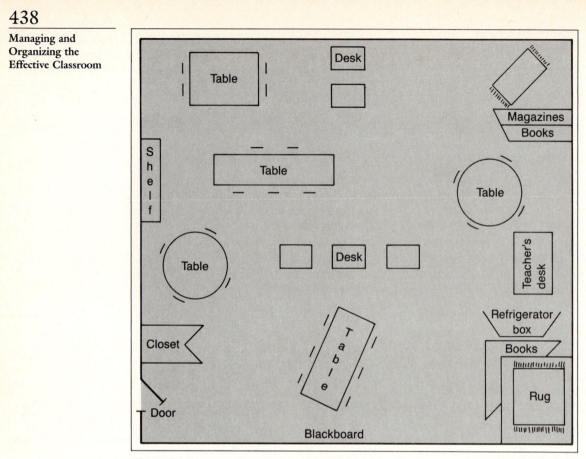

Figure 14.4 Learning Center Classroom

Figure 14.4 outlines a room in which learning or activity areas are the centers for all classroom learning.

Student Schedules. The secret to effective implementation of classroom learning centers is teacher organization and the scheduling of students to designated activities. Arranging each student's schedule is time-consuming. In order to develop an *individual schedule* such as Julie's in Figure 14.5 for a five-week unit, teachers need to consider where and when and in what combinations they want students at the various stations. A student who needs extensive work in a particular area, such as composition or listening, is given more time at that numbered station. All students, regardless of their strengths and weaknesses, usually want "equal" time at certain popular areas, such as games or free-reading stations.

In addition to, or instead of, individual student schedules, teachers may develop *small group schedules* to rotate groups of students to stations. This type of schedule is often called *rotational* (Duval et al., 1977). Figure 14.6 illustrates a

Week	Monday	Tuesday	Wednesday	Thursday	Friday
	Schedule (January 4 to February 1)			Name _____Julie A._____	
	Special Comments: Use Level <u>D</u> in <u>Reading for Concepts</u> (#7); do your book inventory cards at #8.				
A	—	1	2	3	7
B	7	3	9	5	5
C	8	1	4	5	5
D	6	4	4	8	5
E	9	8	1	4	3

Figure 14.5   Individual Student Unit Schedule

schedule designed for second-graders to follow during their language arts hour each morning for a week to ten days.

The names of stations that the teacher believes are important enough to merit a block of time during language arts are put in the outer, stationary circle. Names

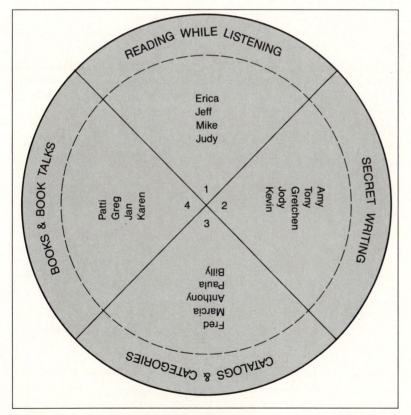

Figure 14.6   Small Group Student Schedule

of students are listed in the inner circle that can be rotated daily or more or less frequently. In some grades, teachers may decide to let the students decide when to go the next station.

A third way of scheduling students is through *contracting*. Ideally, this is a contractual agreement between student and teacher in which the student makes a commitment to assume responsibility for a learning experience. The amount of teacher input needed varies from student to student. Independent students will more readily participate in this kind of decision making than other, more dependent ones.

Successful contracting is looked at as a process that begins during teacher-student conferences. First, the interests of the student are uncovered through discussion or observation and discussion. Next, the teacher confers with the student about what will be needed to follow up on the interest, and a contract is drawn up and signed. Materials are searched out and organized as the student carries out the plan of study. Then the teacher helps as needed by answering questions and giving some direct instruction in skills. The process continues and the contract is completed when the student achieves her goals.

Contracts, then, are potentially the most individual and personal of schedules. They should not be done en masse. They do vary in their complexity (Thomas, page 275). Two contracts are illustrated in Figure 14.7, the one on the left for a second-grader and the one on the right for a fifth-grader.

Inventories. Keeping track of books and stories read by students and materials used by students is a problem for many teachers. It is not feasible for teachers to take on the task of recording who read what, in what level, and what was it all about. Parent volunteers and teacher aides are ideal assistants. However, the most valuable assets to any organized classroom are the students themselves.

Any classroom that has a reading/library corner or that includes sustained silent reading in its reading program should also have a system to record what

My name: _____
Today is: _____
1. I will read _____ stories in the library corner.
2. I will write _____ stories in my special book.
3. I will copy _____ new words on my words cards.

Signed, __(me)_____

_____
(teacher)

Name _____ Date _____
    I'm interested in finding out about _____.
To do this, I will spend _____hours a week at the _____ and _____ hours at the _____.
    From my notes, I will prepare a _____ and do a _____ which I will share with the class on _____.

Signed, __(student)_____

_____
(teacher)

Figure 14.7   Individual Student Contracts

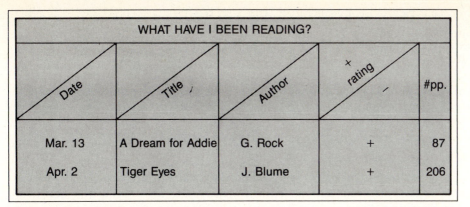

Figure 14.8   Individual Reading Chart

students are reading. One system is to have cards or charts attached to the inside back cover of a student folder as shown in Figure 14.8.

Another uncomplicated and valuable inventory system is interest inventory cards (Vacca, 1977). Each time a student reads a book or story, either in school or out, she fills out a five-by-eight-inch card as shown in Figure 14.9. The main purpose, along with keeping tabs on what students read, is to provide a way for sharing with the entire class. If the cards are stored in an easily accessible box, students will use it frequently.

A third and more personal system for keeping abreast of students' reading interests is the conference, or personal interview. At least once every week to ten days, the teacher should talk with each student privately about his or her reading. Attempt to get at the student's thoughts and feelings about what he or she read as well as the major concepts. In fact, conferences in which the students do most

Category → or Topic	SPORTS		Jennifer L.	← Student's Name
Title →	PAPER LION	GEORGE PLIMPTON		← Author's Name
	# ____ pages			
	This book tells of the real experience of the author. Although he is a writer, not a . . .			← Important Ideas

Figure 14.9   Interest Inventory Card

of the talking are the most successful ones. It's best to avoid any temptation to remind students of their failure to turn in past assignments, to discuss their rude behavior during lunch, or to ask them to read a short passage aloud.

Some techniques that have worked for us during conferences are:

1. Mention an activity the student has done well in or seemed to like doing in the classroom. Ask why he liked it. Ask how we could get other students interested in it.

2. Ask about favorite parts of a story or book; ask about her least favorite parts. Probe about why in both cases.

3. Use items from an interest inventory (friends, trips, hobbies, TV, movies, wishes, etc.) and ask about them orally rather than having the student fill them out. Meet again and share results of your "analysis" with the student. Have you been accurate in your determination of his major interests?

4. If the third technique is successful, a reading contract in which the student actually decides to do some reading and makes plans to do it is a good possibility. This automatically brings the focus back to the topic of interest.

5. Ask the student to fill out a self-evaluation form (see Figure 14.10). Although this type of evaluation works well with groups of students at the end of a unit, it "may result in the kind of real communication you have been promoting in a conference situation but did not quite achieve" (Vacca, 1976, page 567).

Keeping track of materials used by students has been a courtesy extended by the teacher in one grade to the teacher in the next grade for years. Now that there's more to this than "Sarah has worked well in the Level 12 reader this year," teachers need the assistance of their students. Brief, clear lists of materials and activities can often be filled in for each individual student at the end of a unit or semester or year.

Planning Charts. The final and most comprehensive way to organize all the "things" in your classroom is to construct a chart that allows you to see at a glance what you've got to work with. Table 14.4 is an example of a chart that was developed for a seventh-grade classroom that employed an integrated learning stations format (Vacca, 1976, page 565). The second column is left blank to emphasize the flexibility in materials, especially when entire class sets are not ordered in favor of a variety at different levels.

CLASSROOM SCENARIOS

Anything is possible when teachers, putting it all together, design and implement reading instruction in their own classrooms. We've selected three scenarios to share here because they all involve some teacher-made, student-produced materials; they are uncomplicated, appropriate for early or intermediate grades; and, above all, they emphasize reading as a meaningful and meaning-getting activity.

Name ______________________

Date ______________________

Period ______________________

Directions: Answer Yes or No in each box.

		Stations 1	2	3	4	5	6	7	8	9	10	11
1.	Did I improve in this activity?											
2.	Did I understand and follow directions?											
3.	Did I write neatly and accurately?											
4.	Did I do as much as I could?											
5.	Did I learn anything new?											

6. The activities I did my best work on were ______________________ and ______________

   It was my best work because ______________________

7. The activities that I had difficulty with were ______________________ and ______________

   They were difficult because ______________________

8. The activity I like most is ______________________

9. The activity I dislike most is ______________________

Comments about your program: ______________________

Figure 14.10 Self-Evaluation Form

Scenario 1: Beginning Reading with "The Gingerbread Man"

Joy Mossburg (1982) tells about the third week in December several years ago:

> The basic skills lessons were competing unsuccessfully with "visions of sugarplums." To cope, I realized that I must change procedures. This was my strategy:
>
> 1. One afternoon a familiar story was told: "The Gingerbread Man." The children were encouraged to chime in on the redundancy.
> 2. All the children engaged in a story play. Standing in a large circle, they helped me retell the story. At appropriate times everyone assumed the actions of the different characters. Everyone became the little old lady when she made the gingerbread, the little boy when he sniffed the aroma, and the various characters when the great chase began.

3. I rewrote the story on the board as members of the class dictated. The passage was read from the board several times. A narrator read the informational portions and various children spoke for the characters.

4. The story was copied onto a ditto master. Enough copies were made so that each child could have a copy.

5. That evening, I made preparations for the next day. Enough warm water was mixed with two packages of gingerbread cake mix to make a stiff cookie dough. The dough was divided into twenty-six ball-like portions (enough for twenty-five children and the teacher). The dough was covered with plastic wrap and refrigerated overnight.

Day Two with the Gingerbread Man

With the gingerbread dough, a box of raisins, three cookie sheets, a roll of aluminum foil and waxed paper, I set out for school the next morning. Intent upon taking every advantage to involve the children in language activities, the following directions were written on the board:

TABLE 14.4

Stations Implementation Chart (SIC)

Type of Activity	Available Materials	Number of Students per Class Period	Criteria for Placement	Days Operating
Skills game or audiovisual		Two to five	Affective	Monday to Friday
Creative writing or language experience		Two to six	Affective/random	Monday to Friday
Sustained silent reading (SSR)		Whole class		One to four
DRTA (Directed Reading-Thinking Activity)		Four to eight	Reading level	Two to three
Basal workbook		Two to five	Reading level	Monday to Friday
High interest–low vocabulary		Two to five	Reading level	Monday to Friday
Skill kit		Two to five	Random	Monday to Friday
Free reading		Two to four	Affective/random	Monday to Friday
Learning center or library		One to three	Random	Monday to Friday
Conference		One to two	Class list	Two to three
Listening for fun		Whole class		One or two

Reprinted from Vacca, J. L., & Vacca, R. T. (1976). Learning stations: How to in the middle grades. *Journal of Reading, 19,* 563–567.

1. Wash your hands with soap and water.
2. Make the gingerbread man's body.
3. Make the gingerbread man's head.
4. Make the gingerbread man's legs.
5. Make the gingerbread man's arms.
6. Use the raisins to make his eyes, mouth, nose and buttons.
7. Bake him in the oven.

Watch out! He might escape!

Before the children did anything with their dough, I demonstrated what they were to do, always referring to the directions step-by-step. I scrubbed my hands as if I were readying for surgery.

Each child was given a $5'' \times 8''$ piece of aluminum foil. Their portion of the dough and a handful of raisins were placed on a piece of waxed paper. With their instructions on the board, they knew exactly what they were to do. No questions!

This class had engaged in creative dramatics frequently; I wasn't surprised when I began to hear several of the children carrying on dialogues with their gingerbread man. "I'm going to stop you!" "You'll not run away from me!" Some spoke for the gingerbread man, "I'll get away from all of you!"

When the children finished, each gingerbread man, riding on his piece of foil, was placed on a cookie sheet. One cookie sheet accommodated nine gingerbread men. I had earlier obtained permission to use the large oven in the lunchroom. So-o-o-o with three pans of gingerbread men, the books that had been copied the evening before and several sets of magic markers to illustrate the books while the cookies baked, an enthusiastic troop made their way happily down the hall. The principal, whom they happened to meet in the hall was cautioned, "Be on the lookout for escaping gingerbread men!"

While the gingerbread men underwent their transformation in the oven, the children personalized their books. They were excited at the idea of having a book they could read so well to take home with them.

It wasn't long before a spicy smell penetrated the school. Several people came in sniffing. The children, of course, were most eager to relate what was taking place. When I opened the oven door, I was almost expecting to be run over by a small army of little men. They lay obediently, however, each on his own little piece of foil.

There was just enough time to finish illustrating the books while the cookies cooled. Everyone enjoyed the next event—devouring their gingerbread men!

Then came a discussion of possibilities. *What if the gingerbread men had tried to escape?* Later that day, each child wrote a personal version of what might have happened. The following is an example of one of the stories with the child's own spelling:

I mad a jnjrbred man.
He had to iz a noz and a mowth
The tchr put him in the uvn
When we opund the uvn he jumpt rit out and start
to run down the hall.
I chast aftr him
The prnsupl chast him
The jm tchr chast him too

He got uway nehow
Im glad

Before the children left that day, I obtained permission to copy their stories into a big book for the classroom reading corner. I was given permission to correct spellings and add necessary punctuation marks so that the stories could be enjoyed by others.

In the *Big Book of Gingerbread Men* (the name later chosen for this classroom treasure), the original story the children had dictated to me was included, along with the directions for making gingerbread men, a summary of all that had taken place, and most important of all—each child's own story of what might have happened. Luckily, I laminated the pages. The book became one of the most popular with the children.

On the last day of school, many months after making gingerbread men, the class was asked what they liked best about first grade. The response was overwhelming—making gingerbread men! I had to admit that I felt pretty good about the entire experience, too (Mossburg, 1982, pages 30–32).

Scenario 2: Primary-Grade Experiences and the Microcomputer

What could be more relevant in the current age of computer games than a computer or microcomputer approach to recording the verbal responses of students in the language experience approach? As we noted in Chapter 12, the use of the microcomputer in the classroom for this purpose is feasible if:

1. A word processing system is available for your microcomputer (Apple, Commodore Pet, TRS-80, or other brand). Easy-to-use word processing systems available for the Apple, Commodore Pet, and TRS-80, respectively, are Bank Street Writer, Paper Mate, and Scripsit. Each has its advantages, but the important point is that there are inexpensive and easy-to-use word processing programs for the three most popular microcomputers used in education.

2. A printer is available in the school office, learning resource center, or teachers' workroom which can be connected to the brand of microcomputer available to the reading teacher.

Given the solution of those two conditions, a microcomputer can be used successfully to enhance the language experience approach to teaching reading.

Here's How. Imagine a scenario in which primary students have returned from a field trip. Usually, as the children discuss their experiences, the teacher will write the students' responses on a large flip chart or on the blackboard. In the microcomputer enhancement mode of using the language experience approach, the teacher will type the children's answers on the microcomputer keyboard and they will be displayed on the video screen.

Things to consider include:

Typing input is immediately visible on video screen.

Upper- and lowercase letters are needed in the video image.

Upper- and lowercase letters are needed in the print image.

Double-size print for primary-level children is available on most microcomputers for video screen display.

Before purchasing a printer, samples of the quality of print should be requested.

Using a printer makes possible a take-home or class booklet.

Permanent printed copies would be much easier than present requirement for the teacher to copy from the blackboard or the flipchart.

The flipchart is more permanent and larger than the video screen image.

Microcomputer responses never need to be copied again by the teacher since they can be saved on cassette tape or on a disk.

A larger screen than is typically used with some microcomputers should be used with large class groups.

An audiovisual cart that elevates the video monitor should be used.

The blackboard is no more permanent that a video screen.

Student writing of blackboard or flipchart words may be minimized by microcomputer printer availability.

Could have students type in responses instead of a parent volunteer (Judd and Walker, 1982, pages 11–13).

Scenario 3: Intermediate-Grade Classroom Newspaper

An ideal way to involve elementary students in worthwhile communication is the production of a classroom newspaper.

Organizing a class newspaper project may begin with a field trip through the local newspaper office. This should be followed with a study of newspaper reporting and writing techniques. Students will be eager to learn the various techniques because they will want to have a part on the newspaper staff. A field trip to the local high school journalism class is another possibility for giving students insight in producing a newspaper. While necessary skills are being developed students should begin setting up their staff. Reporters, editors, proofreaders, and even a circulation manager will be needed. Students will need to learn how to collect news items and to become aware of deadlines for preparing stories. Editors must develop effective techniques for discovering spelling and other errors. The actual typing of the stencils may be done by the classroom teacher, a school secretary, an interested parent, or perhaps a student. When the spirit masters are ready the paper is almost ready for the circulation department to staple and distribute.

With the production of a newspaper the class begins to feel they are rendering a service to the entire school. Such things as a lost and found column, classified ad section, and an activity calendar will help students realize that other students are reading their paper and depending on it for much-needed services. Children enjoy conducting surveys, and establishing school-wide contests which can be initiated and reported in the paper at school. The newspaper becomes a way to keep all students informed about interesting issues and holidays. It is an excellent way to promote better understanding in the area of public relations between the home and the school. The newspaper allows interested parents to see the kinds of work students are doing, and what is happening at school. It allows school principals and other interested officials to become aware of student thinking and ability.

When a class is involved in producing a newspaper its members are functioning as a group. Students develop greater skills in group dynamics and learn to cooperate with a total group. They learn first hand the difference in opinion and fact when they write editorials and news stories. They become more interested in the world around them as they develop the habit of looking for information to go in the paper. They develop a greater appreciation for other newspapers.

A newspaper in the elementary school is a very rewarding project. Watching boys and girls develop and grow in communication skills, observing the pride in the eyes of the parents, and being able to share classroom activities with colleagues make the project very appealing. You might like to consider this creative project for your own classroom (Whitfield and Whitfield, 1982, pages 23–24).

SUMMARY

In this chapter, we considered what teachers need to do in order to effectively manage and organize their classrooms for reading instruction. A great deal that we do to manage reading instruction, to organize our classrooms and materials, can be traced back through the evolution of individualized instruction. The school improvement movement of the late seventies and early eighties introduced new information but the goal of reading instruction has remained constant: to produce independent readers.

Several factors are associated with effective learning environments: discipline, time spent on a task, direct instruction, grouping, and evaluation. We paid close attention to teacher behavior as central to understanding all other factors in an effective classroom. How a teacher manages and organizes a classroom while attempting to individualize instruction depends heavily on the teacher's daily decisions.

To this end, we considered the ways in which teachers put everything together. This is the atmosphere, the environment, the climate, the overall sense of structure or togetherness you feel when you enter a classroom. This too is a changeable area; most teachers want to create a classroom environment conducive to learning. How they schedule students, balance activities and materials, and test and keep records differs from teacher to teacher. Just as teachers individualize in various ways, their classroom environments vary from straight-row traditional to flexible-seating open arrangements. Learning stations—how to organize this type of classroom and materials—were explained and several classrooms profiled.

Whatever the students, the priorities, the reading program, or the approach, each individual teacher must manage her or his classroom. How we manipulate and use our physical environment determines our effectiveness.

THE WORKSHOP

In the Classroom

1. Describe how you would organize "your" classroom to support the goals of your school's reading program. Develop a room diagram to illustrate how you would arrange furniture, materials, student activities, storage, and so on. Label the diagram and share it with other students in the class.

2. Team up with another class member and complete the abridged learning stations implementation chart, first deciding what grade level or type of class you are teaching.

Type of Activity	Available Materials	Number of Students	Criteria for Placement	Days Operating
1.				
2.				
3.				
4.				
5.				

In the Field

1. Reexamine the two teacher observation forms included in the chapter. Make any improvements you think are necessary before piloting either Form A or B, observing during the language arts block or reading period in the same classroom at approximately the same time for at least three days.

2. Look for patterns in the behaviors and classroom dynamics you observed in the above field exercise. Write these down and bring your analysis to class to share and compare with colleagues. (You need not have observed in the same classroom.)

Chapter 15

Adapting Instruction to Meet Individual Needs

by Nancy D. Padak

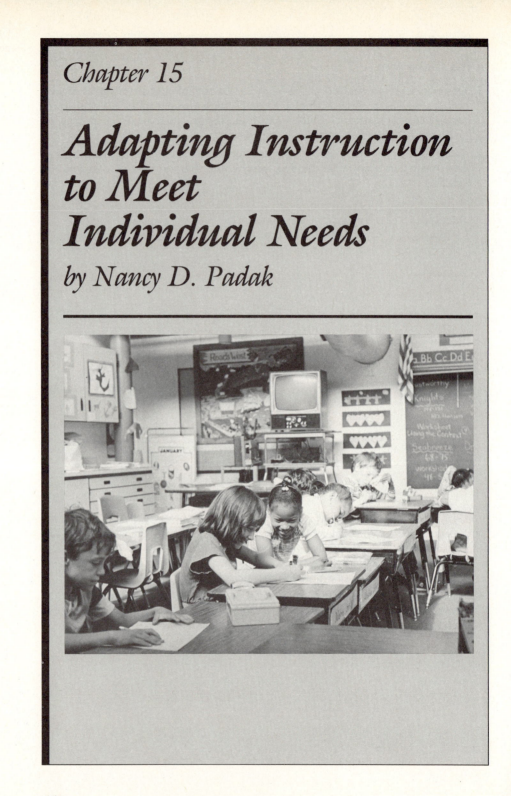

In this chapter, you will be challenged to think like a linguist and an anthropologist. But for now, think like a journalist: Ask, Who? What? When? Where? How? Why? Effective teachers consider all these questions as they make decisions about their classroom reading programs. Decisions should be based on teachers' theories of reading and knowledge about instructional strategies, but it is equally important to consider children's needs as instruction is planned and delivered. Children learn at different rates and in different ways. Many classrooms include children from diverse linguistic and cultural backgrounds. Instructional adaptations based on children's needs can provide a foundation for successful literacy growth. In this chapter, we provide information and instructional guidelines that may help you adapt instruction to meet the needs of all the students in your classroom.

*I know Jenny's trying to do her best work. She really seems to want to learn.
And she can be successful, but it takes her such a long time.*

> George, a first-grade teacher

*Reading has always been difficult for Charley. In the past, he's really tried,
but this year he seems different. I think he's giving up.*

> Lori, a fifth-grade teacher

*I don't know what to do about Jane. She just sits there. She never finishes her
work. I feel she should be contributing much more to the class, but her thoughts
are a thousand miles away.*

> Bonnie, a fourth-grade teacher

*Tony's reading ability is really amazing! I'm not really sure what he can learn
from our basal, but I do keep him with the top group. I don't want him to
miss any skills.*

> Gary, a second-grade teacher

Each child is unique. Superficial differences are obvious—height, hair color, and
the like. Others are more subtle. Children's interests and experiences may vary,
for example, as well their strengths, weaknesses, and needs as readers. Diversity,
rather than uniformity, is the "norm" in classrooms and in all other places where
human beings gather. Planning a learning environment that acknowledges and
capitalizes on this diversity is one of the most exciting challenges teachers face.

If we accept the notion of diversity among students, does it follow that each
child has "individual needs" in reading? Strictly speaking, the answer is probably
yes. Attempting to fashion instruction based on a careful determination of each
child's special needs in reading, however, would leave very little time for teaching.
To resolve this dilemma, most teachers plan instruction based instead upon their
assessment of group needs; in most cases, this decision-making strategy works
quite well. Each year, however, teachers encounter children who truly *do* have
special needs in reading. Some of these children learn very quickly; some learn
very slowly; and others may learn best in atypical ways. Some may have language
backgrounds that differ from the majority. Effective teachers adapt their classroom
reading programs to meet these needs.

Throughout this chapter, we will describe students who may benefit from
adapting instruction. We will also suggest teaching and practice activities that
represent effective instructional adaptations for children with special needs. First,
however, we need to define an important term.

WHAT DOES IT MEAN TO ADAPT?

If you were to look up *adapt* in a dictionary, you'd find a definition something like this: to modify so as to suit new conditions; to adjust. Turning to *adjust*, you would find: to bring things into proper relation through the use of skill or judgment. When considered in relation to adapting reading instruction in the classroom, these definitions suggest the need to change certain aspects of instruction in order to provide appropriate learning experiences for children. They also suggest that such changes are the result of teacher skill and judgment.

Accepting change as part of adapting instruction is easy; the tricky part is deciding what to change, for whom to change, and how to change. Reconsidering the connections between theory and practice may help teachers determine the "what" of adapting instruction. For example, should beliefs about reading or about instruction be adapted when considering children with special needs? Should teachers' implicit theories about reading be adapted? Probably not. In most cases, teachers' beliefs about reading and about instruction are expansive enough to encompass all children's needs. The following instructional beliefs and attitudes are representative of such broadness:

Believing in the importance of evaluating and refining one's theories about reading; continuing to refine instructional practices in accordance with beliefs.

Believing that all children can grow as readers; communicating this expectation to children.

Providing instructional environments that emphasize global reading behaviors.

Using instructional strategies that promote reading as a thinking, problem-solving process.

Basing instructional decisions on both implicit models of reading and an understanding of students' needs.

Ideas such as these can form the core of literacy instruction for all students, including those with special needs.

If beliefs about reading and models of reading need not be changed as teachers consider adapting instruction, what *should* be adapted? In Chapter 2, we presented a diagram that illustrates the relationship between theory and practice. Below, we add another layer to the diagram (Figure 15.1) which provides direction for adapting instruction.

In order to adapt instruction to children's needs, the classroom teacher begins by developing his or her powers of observation, connecting observations to theories, making practical plans, and seeking assistance from colleagues. Skillful observation is developed through a willingness to understand the learning process, practice in working with children, and getting knee-deep in teaching. Relating observations to theories comes as a result of thinking about why we do do what we do. Finally, literacy instruction, especially in providing for children with special needs, cannot be a solitary venture. Literacy instruction is a social as well as professional experience shared with colleagues in the school community. The

Step 1 ↓	What are your beliefs about how students learn to read?
Step 2 ↓	How do your beliefs reflect models of reading?
Step 3 ↓	What are the major approaches to reading instruction?
Step 4 ↓	Which instructional strategies will you decide to use?
Step 5 ↓	What are students' special needs in reading?
Step 6	How can instruction be adapted to meet the needs of individual students?

Figure 15.1   Making Decisions About Adapting Instruction

astute teacher forms a network of support for literacy instruction by capitalizing on the many support services available within the school or district and by drawing on the wisdom of colleagues.

WORKING WITH COLLEAGUES TO MEET SPECIAL NEEDS

Not too long ago, we were involved in a series of in-service workshops for teachers in an elementary school. Several teachers asked us to visit their classrooms so that we could observe them trying new strategies with their students. Finding a time to visit, though, was an interesting challenge. A conversation with one teacher went something like this: "You can't come on Monday, Wednesday, or Friday mornings because four of my children are in the L.D. resource room. Michael and Bonnie are at gifted all day on Tuesdays, and six kids go to Chapter I every day at 1:30. How about Thursday morning? No, wait—Melissa and Chad see the speech therapist then."

This teacher's classroom is not unusual. On most days the door to the regular classroom is like a turnstile, a constant rotation of children going in and out. Trying to meet children's special needs can be a scheduling nightmare. The special teacher must schedule around myriad others, often has to cut instructional time short because of special events in the regular classroom or building, and sometimes has to remind others about the importance of the support service to the child's total educational program.

As we have become increasingly aware of learning differences among children, we have felt the responsibility to plan instruction that meets children's needs.

Classroom teachers have a great deal of this responsibility, but they often cannot do it alone.

Networking

Most school districts have attempted to resolve this dilemma by offering various pull-out and pull-in programs for children with special needs. *Pull-out programs* might include Chapter I, L.D. resources, special classes for gifted students, or speech and language sessions. *Pull-in* generally refers to mainstreaming, or providing some instruction for special education students in the regular classroom. All these programs have the same goals: to meet individual needs and to acknowledge the human right to learn. Problems can arise, however, when support services are not integrated carefully with regular classroom activities. The child with special needs may go in one direction with the special teacher and another with the regular teacher or may feel totally segregated from classroom life. This lack of integration between special services and regular classrooms is a problem in some classrooms, but it's not insurmountable.

Through careful planning and frequent communication, teachers can plan a diversified yet consistent delivery system for children with special reading needs. This system should present an integration of methods, materials, goals, and aims between support personnel and regular classroom teachers. In other words, a form of instructional networking is needed. Put simply, to network is to *share* responsibility, ideas, information, and resources. To make the pull-in/pull-out system work, classroom teachers need to focus on inclusion rather than exclusion. Resource personnel need to be pulled into classroom instructional planning. Regular and special teachers need to collaborate and organize instructional content and schedules as a team.

Such an approach to meeting individual needs is already practiced in many school districts. For example, multidisciplinary or teacher-assistance teams are sometimes formed at a building level. These teams may consist of the principal, several classroom teachers, and various support personnel (e.g., reading specialist, school psychologist, social worker). When a student experiences difficulty, the team analyzes the problem and discusses alternatives for attempting to solve it. Such an approach has several advantages:

The ownership of the student's problem is shared by the classroom teacher and the support personnel. The classroom teacher maintains responsibility for solving the problem but has the benefit of others' expertise.

Teams provide opportunities for creative problem-solving, as well as for examining possible causes of and solutions for learning difficulties from several different points of view.

Students benefit from quick attention to their learning problems and carefully planned assistance.

Another way to conceptualize the relationships between classroom teachers and support personnel is to visualize support possibilities as a pyramid (Olson,

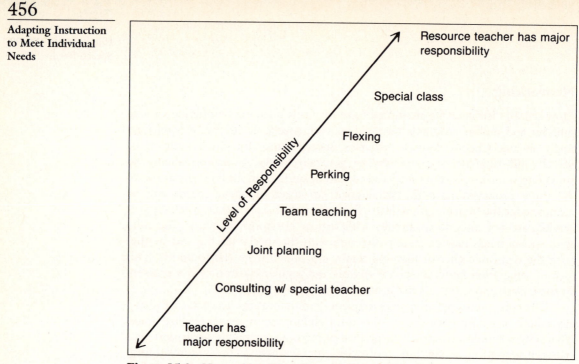

Figure 15.2 Networking/Teaming with Support Personnel

1985; see Figure 15.2). At the broadest level, the classroom teacher has total responsibility for the child's reading growth and utilizes resource personnel in a consultant capacity. This may occur frequently and informally as teachers converse and share concerns with support personnel in the building. Depending on the severity of the child's reading needs, the classroom teacher may share responsibility with resource personnel in many other ways:

Joint planning and evaluating of student progress.

Team teaching certain units, or for certain segments of the instructional period. This may take place in the regular classroom or in the special teacher's classroom.

Having resource personnel provide brief study sessions that perk learning in certain skill areas for a specific group.

Using flexible scheduling plans for resource teachers to meet with certain groups.

Having the special teacher provide daily reading instruction, either in conjunction with the regular classroom teacher or alone. In this latter instance, the classroom teacher provides supplementary reading instruction when the child is in the regular classroom. At this level, the classroom teacher has least responsibility for the child's reading program.

Regardless of the way in which the classroom teacher and the special teacher interact, their joint goal should be to provide effective and consistent reading instruction for children with special needs.

Mainstreaming

U.S. Public Law 92-142, the Education of the Handicapped Act, became a law in 1975. It mandates free, appropriate, public education for all handicapped children between the ages of five and eighteen, and encourages service for preschoolers and those in the eighteen to twenty-one age range. Specific provisions of the act include individualized educational plans (IEPs) for all handicapped students, periodic reviews of their progress, and instruction in the least restrictive environment. Pull-in programs, or mainstreaming practices, were developed to provide instruction in the least restrictive environment.

In this chapter we provide some suggestions for helping children with special needs grow toward reading maturity. We focus on four types of children for whom instruction may need to be adapted: gifted readers, learning-disabled readers, linguistically diverse students, and those who speak English as a second language. For each of these groups of children, we first attempt to describe what their special reading needs might be. Included in these sections are definitions of terms (e.g., IEP, LD, LEP, ESL) often associated with these students. We then describe ways in which reading instruction may be adapted to meet these children's special needs. Finally, we provide suggestions for working with special teachers.

ADAPTING INSTRUCTION FOR GIFTED READERS

Many schools and districts have some special programs for academically talented younsters, but teachers have primary responsibility for providing appropriate reading instruction for the gifted readers in their classrooms. Gifted readers have special needs that often cannot be met without adapting instruction. Some knowledge of the characteristics of gifted readers is necessary, however, in order to make effective decisions about adaptations.

Who Are Gifted Readers?

Some gifted readers are easy to spot: They read voraciously and well above their grade levels; their vocabularies are quite advanced; they do well on tests. Others, however, are not so easy to identify: They fail tests; they don't do homework; they daydream. One prominent characteristic of the gifted learner is the capacity for high performance because of outstanding abilities. Gifted readers, then, are either present or potential high achievers in reading. They are children who are reading substantially above grade level or who possess the ability to make rapid progress in reading when given proper instruction.

Many children later identified as gifted readers can read before they begin school. These children learn to read without formal instruction. Rather, their reading abilities develop naturally in environments where reading is a valued and frequent activity and where they have many opportunities to use language (Durkin, 1966). Not all gifted children are early readers, though. In one study, for example, only 17 to 23 percent of gifted prekindergartners were already reading (Cassidy and Vukelich, 1980). Because of above-average ability and task commitment, however, gifted readers who are not reading when they enter school ordinarily progress at a rapid rate.

As a general rule, gifted readers also have advanced language abilities when compared to others their own age. They often have extensive vocabularies and can use words in new and innovative contexts. "The typical gifted child uses words easily, accurately, and creatively" (Bonds and Bonds, 1983, page 4). Their conversations are often sprinkled with complex sentences and complicated syntactic forms.

Finally, gifted readers often show evidence of other remarkable cognitive abilities. They may perceive relationships, solve problems, and grasp abstract ideas quickly, for example. They may demonstrate keen observational skills and acute awareness of subtle elements in their environments. They may be question-askers and risk-takers who often find unconventional responses to conventional tasks (Witty, 1971).

All these are generalizations, of course, and may not apply to all gifted readers. Furthermore, gifted readers may not show academic talent in any other area. Conversely, a child might have special abilities in another academic area (e.g., math), but not be a gifted reader. Nonetheless, children who fit some or all of the characteristics described above may possess outstanding learning ability in reading; they may be gifted readers.

Instruction for Gifted Readers: Avoiding Some Traps

Working with readers of such tremendous ability and potential can possibly be unnerving for the classroom teacher. In order to provide effective instruction for gifted readers, teachers must first avoid two traps related to these children.

One common though misguided belief is that gifted readers will learn on their own and therefore need no instructional attention or guidance (Carr, 1984). This is an easy trap to fall into in the daily hustle and bustle of the classroom, but it can be a hazardous one for several reasons. Because gifted readers can perform well above grade level, some teachers tend not to worry about their progress. In such instances, children may begin to "take it easy." Not even intellectual and creative talent can survive educational neglect and apathy, however. Children's progress should be monitored periodically so that they are encouraged to grow.

Teachers also need to monitor the reading interests of gifted readers. Because of their curiosity about the world around them, gifted readers often choose to read deeply in an area of interest (Witty, 1985). Certainly, a great deal of independent reading should be encouraged. Efforts should also be made to encourage reading in a wide range of areas, attempting challenging topics, and diversifying interests and skills (Cassidy, 1979; Moller, 1984).

Just as slow-learning students may experience negative feedback because they are on the bottom of the academic ladder, gifted readers may experience some difficulty because they are on the top. (One fifth-grader we know was quite upset because a classmate called him "professor." Sometimes it's hard to understand children's pejoratives.) Relationships with peers may be frustrating; expectations of adults may be overwhelming. Sometimes it may seem safer to quit than to risk failure; or it may be more satisfying to be one of the crowd than to stand out academically. Observant teachers notice such difficulties and provide guidance when appropriate. They realize that gifted readers need understanding "others" in their lives, and that being gifted can sometimes mean being lonely.

Another trap to avoid when making decisions about gifted readers is the "skills trap." Some teachers, especially in the primary grades, fail to realize that gifted children's special learning abilities demand different instructional emphases. They tend to hold gifted readers back or require them to complete all basal materials "so they won't miss any skills." This may even be done by well-intended teachers who are aware of children's advanced reading levels.

Adapting instruction for gifted readers means adjusting content and pacing as well as activities. Gifted readers who are reading upon entrance to school should be encouraged to read from a variety of sources in order to apply and develop their abilities (Witty, 1985). Because of their high verbal and reasoning abilities, gifted readers can often comprehend material well beyond the grasp of so-called average readers. Given such considerations, it makes little sense to limit instruction to the "basal routine." In short, gifted readers' progress ought not to be thwarted by being "taught" (or by having to practice) skills they have already mastered. Like other children with special needs, gifted readers will thrive in a supportive, print-rich environment that provides many opportunities for exploration through reading.

Reading Instruction for Gifted Readers

Gifted readers often have instructional levels that are well beyond their grade placement. They tend to learn new skills rapidly and easily, often without any direct instruction and certainly without the seemingly endless drill provided in most basal reading series. Thus it may be inappropriate to routinely include gifted readers among the three or four instructional reading groups that operate in the classroom. Not even the "above-average" group is challenging enough for the gifted reader. Challenging gifted readers on a daily basis can itself be a challenge for teachers, who must locate materials, structure lessons, stay one step ahead, and find time to do it all. Yet some adaptation of the classroom reading program is necessary to meet the needs of these talented readers. Decisions about adaptation should focus upon creating both enrichment and acceleration opportunities for gifted readers. Because of the variety among teachers, gifted readers, and instructional contexts, however, specific decisions about adaptation probably need to be made on a case-by-case basis. There are nevertheless some broad guidelines for making decisions about adaptation (see below). Included with each are some activities that may themselves be adapted to meet the needs of the gifted readers in your classroom.

Gifted Readers Should Be Encouraged to Read from a Variety of Sources That Are Individually Suitable and Appealing. The concept of "readability" means little when working with gifted readers; in many respects, the sky's the limit. Gifted readers should be guided toward exploring all types of reading material. They might be encouraged to study poetry and drama, for example. In addition to fostering literary appreciation, the study of poetry and drama can be used as a springboard for further study. With the teacher's guidance, children can analyze poems and plays in order to learn the artist's craft. They can be led to discover the literary devices that poets and playwrights use to communicate through words. Such study leads quite naturally to encouraging children to write their own poems and plays. Preparing a dramatic adaptation of a favorite novel might be an interesting project. Children's poetry collections and plays can be "published" and added to the classroom library.

Reading of nonfiction should also be encouraged. Children should learn that reading news magazines, for example, can be an effective way to satisfy their curiosity. A written or oral presentation entitled "What Happened This Week" might be a good way to share such knowledge. One instructional goal for gifted readers, then, is to provide reading and writing experiences with diverse materials.

Instruction for Gifted Readers Should Focus on Reading as a Thinking, Problem-solving Process. Wide reading in a topic of interest can easily lead to comparative reading activities (Boothby, 1980)—uncovering similarities and differences in different accounts of the same subject and speculating about why differences, in particular, might exist. A gifted reader who is interested in American history, for example, might read several accounts of Thomas Jefferson's life. The child might then be encouraged to explore how the accounts differ and to speculate about why that might be so. Differing accounts of current events can also be analyzed. Children might collect articles about an important event from as many different sources as possible. Again, children can be encouraged to compare the differing accounts to hypothesize about reasons for differences.

Another interesting comparative reading project for gifted readers is wide reading in a specific type or genre of literature. Children might collect and read fairy tales, folk tales, or international myths. They could then compare and contrast the stories in an effort to discover their common elements. Finally, they might write their own versions and make a book for the classroom library.

Gifted readers should be encouraged and guided in the use of research methods when putting their reading and writing ideas into action. Many teachers have found this six-step procedure (Gensley, 1975) helpful for guiding gifted readers through the research process:

1. Form your purpose or hypothesis.

2. Gather the information or materials you will need.

3. Read and think about the information. You may wish to write down some of the things you find as you read and think.

4. Process the information. If doing an experiment, make sure you understand the directions. Put everything down in your own words.

5. Do the project or experiment.

6. Discuss the project with your classmates and teacher. Evaluate the project and yourself. Ask questions.

Another instructional goal for gifted readers, then, is to encourage critical and comparative reading. All readers, including the gifted, need to understand reading as a thinking process.

Encourage Gifted Readers to Explore the Nature of Language: Its History, Development, and Variations. The study of language itself can be an interesting focus for the reading and writing activities of gifted readers (Heimberger, 1980). For example, children might find out where their first and last names originated and what they mean, or they can learn and use the names for common objects in another language and compare these words to their English counterparts. They can also collect words borrowed from other languages and read to discover the circumstances surrounding the borrowing. Finally, they can collect commonly used foreign expressions (e.g., hors d'oeuvres). They can devise their own language codes and use them to write secret messages or stories, or they can collect new words (e.g., *space shuttle, microchip*) or words that have become obsolete (e.g., *trolley, icebox*). Children can interview people (e.g., lawyers, police) to learn about the special "languages" of occupations. Finally, they can explore regional dialect variations in pronunciation, syntax, and word choice.

Gifted children are often intensely curious about phenomena others might take for granted. Activities such as these can foster interest in a very important aspect of everyday living—the English language itself.

Instruction for Gifted Readers Should Include Ample Opportunity for Creative Expression. For young children, teachers can encourage dramatic play such as taking phone messages, writing lists of all sorts, or making an inventory of the classroom grocery store that involves reading and writing. Older children might be encouraged to write plays or put on puppet shows. Reader's theater and other creative drama activities can also be beneficial.

Multimedia projects can provide effective instruction for gifted readers. Children can set poetry to music or create illustrations for their favorite poems. They can investigate children's literature and then write and illustrate books for younger children. They can explore cartooning by collecting a variety of cartoons, reading about cartooning, and creating their own cartoons. Finally, they can explore film-making techniques: They can write and produce films, TV shows, or slide shows about topics of interest. Activities such as these can encourage creative expression through reading and writing.

Instruction for Gifted Readers Should Include Opportunities for Meaningful Social and Academic Interaction with Others. Because of their advanced reading ability and parallel outstanding ability to accumulate and retain information, gifted readers begin the year at a higher level and advance more quickly than their classmates. As the years go by, this situation intensifies: Their abilities and interests often lead gifted readers farther and farther away from their peers. These special talents should certainly be fostered, but parents and teachers are often rightfully concerned about isolating gifted readers from their peers. Furthermore, effective teachers realize the need for all learners, including the gifted, to interact intellectually and socially in the classroom. Thus the reading program for gifted learners should include group as well as independent work.

Most classroom reading programs include many opportunities for gifted readers to work with their classmates. All students benefit from shared book experiences, for example, and all should participate in sustained silent reading. Gifted readers can also be included in classroom language experiences and can participate in story discussions based on holistic instructional strategies such as the DRTA. In short, teachers should include gifted readers in whole or small group instructional activities whenever appropriate.

Gifted readers can be valuable resources for other children in the classroom. They might serve occasionally as peer tutors, for example. (Some guidelines for establishing a peer tutoring program are provided in the next selection.) Teachers should also encourage gifted readers to share the results of their individual inquiries with others.

Networking and Teaming to Enhance Instruction

In order to plan and deliver effective instruction for gifted readers, teachers should seek advice and assistance from colleagues and other resource personnel. Reading specialists can be valuable in program preparation since they often have access to up-to-date information about materials, strategies, and evaluation procedures.

Some schools or school districts have pull-out programs for gifted readers. In such cases, the classroom teacher should work with the resource teacher to provide consistent and enriched instruction for children. It's important to avoid fragmentation in programming: for example, the resource teacher launching off in one direction and the classroom teacher in another. Unfortunately for children, fragmentation occurs all too often (Olson, 1985). It can be avoided through cooperative planning and frequent communication. Both teachers might decide upon a common instructional plan, for example; then each could take responsibility for different portions of it.

Gifted readers benefit from instructional adaptations that enrich the regular reading program. They also need an accelerated program that differs from the norm in both content and pacing. By utilizing the human resources available through networking and teaming as well as other material resources (e.g., see

Lukasevich, 1983), the classroom teacher can provide an effective, consistent, and continuous program for the gifted reader.

ADAPTING INSTRUCTION FOR CHILDREN WITH LEARNING DISABILITIES

Children with learning disabilities constitute a second group of students for whom adaptation of reading instruction may prove beneficial. Special education teachers generally assume major responsibility for the literacy instruction of children with severe learning disabilities. These children are often mainstreamed for other portions of the school day so that they can interact with their peers. Children with milder disabilities, however, may stay in the classroom for reading instruction and receive tutoring or resource help from a learning disabilities teacher. In either case, the classroom teacher needs to understand characteristics of learning disabled (L.D.) children in order to make effective decisions about adapting instruction.

Who Are the Learning Disabled?

Put simply, *learning disabled children* demonstrate significant gaps between ability or potential to learn and actual achievement. Children with learning disabilities are not slow learners; neither are they developmentally handicapped. Their problems with learning are much more subtle and perhaps in some ways much more frustrating than those of other special education students.

The Association for Children with Learning Disabilities (1985, page 1) has defined the term *specific learning disability* as "a chronic condition of presumed neurological origin which selectively interferes with the development, integration, and/or demonstration of verbal or nonverbal activities." This broad and somewhat abstract definition suggests that the L.D. child's academic difficulties stem from deficits in basic psychological processes, such as attention, perception, or conceptual reasoning. In other words, the child's learning problems are constitutionally rather than environmentally caused. Learning disabled students generally have average or above-average ability (as measured by standardized tests) and demonstrate severe discrepancies between their low levels of achievement and their apparent potential (Harris, 1980).

Two primary behaviors characterize the L.D. youngster: *indiscrimination* and *impulsiveness* (Kirk, Kliebhan, and Lerner, 1978). All children are indiscriminate and impulsive from time to time. But these behaviors may be prolonged and exaggerated in some children due to an immaturity in neural development.

Indiscrimination is rooted in the inability to note likenesses and differences and to synthesize these observations into meaning. The L.D. child may have difficulty separating, differentiating, and integrating sensations and observations; disorganization and disorder may result. One teacher described an L.D. student in her classroom like this: "Janet can't get down to work. She's busy putting her lunch away, hanging up her jacket, talking to her neighbor, tying her shoelace, which does not seem to be tight enough and has to be retied, noticing that Alfred did not put his lunch away in the right spot and that there's a funny groove on the floor next to a crack in the linoleum, and then she's occupied chasing a fly" (Smith, 1979, page 17). Notice that Janet's teacher began by saying that Janet *couldn't* get down to work, rather than *wouldn't*. That's an important distinction. L.D. children's classroom behavior may be inappropriate at times, but teachers must remember that these children are not willfully misbehaving.

The source of impulsiveness often observed in L.D. students is an inability to prioritize sensory messages. All messages are given equal importance, and the child's attempts to focus are futile. The L.D. child often cannot ignore "the footsteps in the hall, the light tumbling through the venetian blinds, the hand of his neighbor fixing her hair, the jangling earrings of his teacher . . ." (Smith, 1979, page 16). Distractibility results.

Obviously, disorganization and distractibility are inappropriate behaviors for successful academic growth. Classroom teachers can ordinarily spot these behaviors in children quickly. Other behaviors associated with the learning disabled include erratic, inconsistent, unpredictable behavior (has good days and bad days); poor attention span (tires quickly, gives up easily); forgetfulness (does not finish work or does so carelessly, is extremely disorganized, loses place easily); unusual or inappropriate behavior (has temper tantrums, acts "silly," daydreams, overreacts to common events); and language difficulties (mixes words up, recalls with difficulty, has difficulty following sequence).

Characteristics such as these can assist teachers in identifying children who may need referral for further testing. Descriptions of characteristics can also help teachers understand how children's disabilities may manifest themselves in the classroom. A word of caution is in order, however. Like all other groups of children, the learning disabled are both similar and dissimilar to each other. They may be homogeneous in their inability to profit from "normal educational experiences," but they are heterogeneous in that their problems vary in both type and degree. In other words, we should be knowledgeable about children's strengths and weaknesses but careful not to label children or make unwarranted assumptions about them.

Reading Instruction for the Learning Disabled

A classroom climate for the L.D. student is a fine blend of structure and challenge. Many adaptations appropriate for the slow learner can benefit the L.D. child as well. Interestingly, some adaptations for the gifted learner can also be appropriate. In fact, many learning disabled children have creativity or unusual talent in other areas (Labuda and James, 1985). It makes sense to adapt instruction to capitalize on the strengths of L.D. children whenever possible so that they can produce results that peers, parents, and teachers recognize as outstanding. Positive feedback can confirm children's ability to learn and can be highly motivating. Motivation, of course, can facilitate further growth.

No one program or approach will be effective with all L.D. students. Nonetheless, the broad guidelines provided below may assist teachers in adapting instruction to meet the needs of the L.D. children in their classrooms.

The Learning Environment Should Be Structured and Predictable. Because of their disorganization and distractibility, L.D. students often benefit from extra structure in their learning environments. The amount of extra structure needed should probably be determined on a case-by-case basis, but teachers might help children by *structuring time and space*. If possible, seat the child out of the line of traffic, facing in a direction where distractions are at a minimum, and close to the teacher's desk so he or she can receive eye messages and be reassured. Help the child organize his or her work space. Prepare a daily schedule and highlight it with color. Use visual and nonverbal cues to help the child stay on task (checklists, nods of the head, gestures, etc.). The teacher can also *set limits*. Make sure the classroom rules are clearly understood by the disabled learner. Do not be creative in applying consequences for inappropriate behavior. Be predictable and consistent with discipline. Finally, teachers can *establish a routine*. Schedule a regular time during reading/writing instruction to meet with the disabled learner individually or as part of a small group. Prepare the child for transitions, such as going to resource classes, the library, or the gym. Warn children of changes in routine well in advance. Make sure children know about assemblies, for example, almost as soon as you do (Smith, 1979).

Instruction for Disabled Learners Should Preserve Their Self-Esteem. The day-to-day instruction for the L.D. child is fraught with tensions—talking out, demanding attention, interrupting, and so forth. This can be exhausting and anxiety producing for both the child and the teacher. We can best help children clarify and deal with their frustration and feelings of inadequacy by talking with them and demonstrating that we understand and want to help. Smith (1979, pages 110–111) suggests several discussion starters: "When you are frustrated, it helps to tell about it, and then we can help you deal with it." "That's not appropriate behavior. It doesn't fit this situation because _____. This is the appropriate behavior. Let's try it." "First, let's look at what you are good at and what you *can* do. Then we'll be better able to tackle what you can't do."

Teachers too can feel frustrated and inadequate in their attempts to assist L.D. children. If the teacher begins to feel like a failure, it won't be long before the child's feelings of worthlessness are reinforced. Teachers can avoid such a negative cycle by observing the child carefully, soliciting help for solving problems, and maintaining a sense of humor. In short, both teachers and children should adopt an "I can do it" attitude. It can be contagious.

Establishing Independence Should Be an Instructional Goal. Because L.D. children often have difficulty sorting out and organizing their perceptions, they need to be taught precisely how to do what they are supposed to do in as concrete and clear a manner as possible. Recognition of subtlety may be difficult for the learning disabled. The classroom teacher can serve as a model for how to approach situations, how to treat others, how to say things, and how to work through problems. The road to self-regulation for the learning disabled can be long and arduous; eventual success depends on patience and persistence. Everyone working with the child needs to demonstrate strategies for exercising control and problem solving so that the child can eventually internalize the overall strategy: What is the problem/situation/event? What do I already know about this? What do I want to happen? How can I make this happen? What can I do/say? What happened? What was the result? What did I learn?

L.D. children should also be encouraged to monitor their own behavior and to evaluate their progress through an activity as they go along. One teacher taught his L.D. students never to say they had finished a piece of work until they had said to themselves: "Look carefully at what I have done. Now look again. Did I do what I was asked to do? Am I satisfied?" (Smith, 1979, p. 129).

The L.D. student may be able to grasp concepts quickly yet be unable to express them effectively. Talking through problem-solving steps and verbalizing thinking processes may help the L.D. child discover a pathway for expressing what he or she knows.

Help Children Be Successful by Adapting Assignments and Making Instructions Clear. Some adaptations in the amount of reading given to children at one time may help them be more successful. If possible, teachers might break assignments into shorter tasks for L.D. children. Teachers should attempt to teach the abstract through the concrete, perhaps by using pictures, objects, the child's sense, movement, or drama. Having children take tests in several shorter sessions rather than one long one may also help. In addition, content area reading assignments might be adapted so that the L.D. child works only with the material that's absolutely necessary to learn.

Practice adaptations can also be beneficial. Children can make things with different materials; use puppets, learning games, or manipulatives; or use audio-visual equipment. Visual cues such as charts, pictographs, or rebus clues may be helpful additions to practice materials. Finally, listening to tape-recorded stories, songs, or in-class oral presentations can provide needed support (Labuda and James, 1985).

Instructions and other directions sometimes confuse L.D. students. Teachers can help by speaking slowly when giving oral directions and by limiting the number given at any one time. It also helps to encourage focusing: "Eyes on me. Now think through what you'll need." or "Are you ready? Concentrating? Good!" or "Slow down. Organize. We have time." After instructions or directions have been given, the child might be asked to repeat them. Another possibility is to pair the L.D. child with a peer helper, who can write down and explain assignments or read directions or essential information to the child.

Instruction for L.D. Students Should Include Social and Academic Interaction with Others. The classroom teacher should include L.D. children in whole group activities whenever possible. Story time, SSR, shared book experiences, and language-experience activities are times for all children to work together. Cooperative learning procedures can also benefit mainstreamed children by promoting positive peer relationships and by providing opportunities for integrating language arts instruction (Maring et al., 1985). Heterogeneous groups of children might survey a content area reading assignment and select key terms, for example, and then work together to prepare semantic maps or structured overviews for the concepts. Children might also work together to read and rewrite difficult portions of text. Activities such as these can challenge the intellect and creativity of all children, including the learning disabled.

Networking and Teaming to Enhance Instruction

There are no easy answers for helping children with learning disabilities grow as readers. The classroom teacher struggles with his or her own sense of adequacy when trying to meet their needs; a crisis in confidence can result. The astute teacher brings all the resources of the school to bear on the development of an instructional plan. For example, the psychologist may provide much needed counseling for the child and may consult with the teacher as well; the nurse can assist in monitoring medication; the principal can be an ally in maintaining discipline; the supervisor can assist in program planning.

For the most seriously disabled, a teacher specializing in learning disabilities generally provides the bulk of literacy instruction. The classroom teacher needs to work closely with this individual in order to provide supportive and enriching activities which complement the core program. Discipline procedures and instructional strategies should also be compatible with those used by the resource teacher.

For those with milder disabilities, the classroom teacher may provide the majority of instruction with the resource teacher giving supplementary support. In these instances, the resource teacher can serve as a consultant about instructional sequences, strategies, and materials. He or she may also be a valuable sounding board for problems and concerns. Instructional networking for children with learning disabilities can serve as an inspiration and a salvation for the classroom teacher.

Helping the L.D. child is indeed a team effort, and the classroom teacher is an essential member of the team. Children with learning disabilities qualify for special education programming that has been legally defined and regulated. A special vocabulary has emerged as a result of these regulations. Teachers need to understand the technical terms and abbreviations used by special educators. Several of these terms are defined in Box 15.1.

ADAPTING INSTRUCTION FOR THE LINGUISTICALLY DIVERSE

Before reading this section, answer the questions in Box 15.2. Did you find one answer in each case that sounded best or most natural to you? Did some of the others sound strange? Probably so. If you had grown up in another part of the country, however, your responses might have been different. If you're an easterner, for example, you may have answered "soda" for question 3. Midwesterners probably answered "pop," and in some parts of the South, the "best" answer would be "Coke." Researchers use questions like these to learn about *dialects*, or

BOX 15.1

Definitions of Special Education Terms

hyperactive Behavior characterized by abnormal, excessive activity or movement.

hypoactive Behavior showing an obvious loss or absence of physical activity.

IEP (individualized education plan) A component of P.L. 94-142 (see below) that requires a written plan of instruction for each child receiving special services. The plan must include the child's present levels of educational performance, annual goals, short-term objectives, specific services needed by the child, dates when these services will begin, and other related information. IEPs are developed by a team and must include parent involvement.

learning disability Severe achievement difficulties in a specific learning area as compared to individuals with similar mental ability. Learning areas include oral expression, listening comprehension, written expression, basic reading skills, reading comprehension, mathematics calculation, and mathematics reasoning.

least restrictive environment The concept developed by the courts in the 1970s that disabled persons should be educated or served in the best possible environment for each individual. If an individual can function with less structure or restraint, he or she should have that opportunity. This notion led to the concept of mainstreaming.

mainstreaming The concept of serving the handicapped within the regular classroom, with support personnel and services, rather than placing children in self-contained special classes.

P.L. 94-142 (Education for All Handicapped Children Act of 1975) A federal law that has been described as the "Bill of Rights for the handicapped" and which includes many provisions and special features, including free appropriate public education, definitions of various handicaps, priorities for special education services, protective safeguards, and procedures for developing the mandatory IEP.

special education A broad term covering programs and services for exceptional children who deviate so far physically, mentally, or emotionally from the normal that they require unique learning experiences, techniques, or materials in order to be maintained in the regular classroom, and specialized classes and programs if the problems are severe.

varieties of spoken language used by particular groups, communities, or regions. Studies conducted by anthropologists, educators, linguists, sociologists, and others have yielded a great deal of information about linguistic diversity. It is important for teachers to understand how and why language varies so that they can adapt instruction for the linguistically diverse learners in their classrooms.

BOX 15.2
Linguistic Diversity

---

1. Taken together, reading, writing, speaking, and listening are often called the *language arts*. The word *arts* is pronounced:
   a. arts
   b. awts
   c. ahts

2. Another way of saying 6:45 is quarter _____ 7.
   a. of
   b. till
   c. to

3. Pepsi, 7-Up, and root beer can also be called:
   a. Cokes
   b. pop
   c. sodas
   d. soft drinks
   e. tonics

Who Are the Linguistically Diverse?

The answer is simple: We all are. Each of us has a style and manner of speaking that differs from all others. Our individual dialects, or idiolects, have been influenced by a variety of factors, such as geographical location, socioeconomic status, ethnic origin, educational level, age, and even occupation. Many aspects of the speaking situation also affect language use. We choose different ways of speaking according to where we are, how well we know the person with whom we're speaking, how familiar we both are with the topic, and so forth. As adults, we are competent and flexible language users who can vary our oral language patterns as needed. We don't speak in exactly the same way on every occasion, nor should we.

Such language variation is also evident among our students. In most cases, children's first language is learned at home, although peer interactions influence language learning as well (Dale, 1972; Labov, 1970). By the time they enter school, children's language is quite sophisticated in terms of phonology, syntax, and vocabulary. As teachers, we need to acknowledge and build on these strengths in order to help children grow as language users.

Children's spoken language may vary considerably from the teacher's. Some of this variation is related to level of language development. "Bisketti" (spaghetti) and "eckscape" (escape) are examples of this. Saying "goed," "comed," or "seed" (for went, came, or saw) is another. At one stage in their language development, children typically overgeneralize the "-ed" rule for forming past tenses in English. Linguists speculate that this overgeneralization is rooted in the child's attempt to internalize the rule (Dale, 1972); parents and teachers know that the overgeneralization is stubbornly resistant to correction, as are pronunciations like "bisketti."

Linguistic diversity in the classroom may be the result of other factors as well. Children who move from one region of the country to another, for example, are likely to speak differently than their peers or teacher. The spoken language of bilingual children or those for whom English is a second language will also differ. (This issue is explored in more detail in the next section of this chapter.) Social variation in language may also be evident. Social variation is often discussed in terms of standard English—the oral language of the majority of educated speakers in a community—and nonstandard English—the language system of speakers with less formal education (Barnitz, 1980).

Regardless of the source of variation, dialects differ from each other in at least three ways: in pronunciation or phonology, in grammar or syntax, and in vocabulary or lexicon. Teachers should expect children's language to differ, then, in the way words sound, in the way words go together to form sentences, and in the specific vocabulary used to express ideas. Dialect differences have been studied extensively. Researchers report that the linguistic systems of various dialects, though different in some respects from standard English, are sophisticated, regular, and rule-governed (Padak, 1981). From a linguistic point of view, no dialect of English is any better or any worse than any other.

For a variety of reasons, teachers often find a great deal of linguistic diversity among the children in their classrooms. Because reading is a language-based activity, it is important for teachers to consider how (or if) children's home language or dialects may affect their growth as readers.

Reading Instruction for Linguistically Diverse Learners

In a very real sense, language variations face all readers. No one talks like books are written. The conventions of oral language differ from the conventions of written language. Very few published materials are simply "talk written down." In addition, we've all read authors like Mark Twain and Shakespeare, though none of us talks like Huck Finn or Hamlet. As readers, we can understand different language forms, even though we might never use them in our own speech. In other words, we don't need to abandon our oral language patterns in order to read. The same is true of our students, of course. When making decisions about reading instruction for linguistically diverse learners, it's wise to remember that one doesn't have to talk like a book in order to read one.

Linguistic differences should not be viewed as impediments to literacy growth. In fact, doing so may create problems for students where none need exist. "The only special disadvantage which speakers of low status dialects suffer in learning to read is one imposed by teachers and schools" (Goodman and Buck, 1973, page 6). Rather than viewing linguistic diversity as a disadvantage or barrier, teachers should incorporate respect for diversity into literacy instruction. Our goal for all students should be growth toward flexible language use. Such flexibility can be achieved in classrooms that encourage communication in a variety of settings and ways. The guidelines that follow can help teachers establish this kind of learning environment.

Teachers and Students Must Understand and Value Linguistic Diversity. Reading should be taught as part of an entire language arts program that emphasizes how language *is* used rather than prescribing how it *should be* used. We should provide students with opportunities to "try out" different ways of speaking. Our aims should be to foster risk taking with language and, thus, to help students become flexible language users. In other words, linguistically diverse learners should come to view standard oral and written English as useful, yet they should never regard their own dialects as inferior (Wheat, Galen, and Norwood, 1979).

Experimentation with different ways of speaking is best accomplished in a trusted environment where students feel their language is accepted by others, including the teacher. Teachers might explore their own language attitudes by thinking about questions like the following (Wheat, Galen, and Norwood, 1979): What do I know about language? What do terms such as *different, inferior, right,* and *wrong* mean in the study of language? What do I know about my own language? Do I use different styles of language in different situations? What do I know about this child's language? How does it differ from mine?

The teacher's attitude about linguistic diversity set the tone for the classroom. Teachers should help students understand that there are several, equally valid ways of expressing the same thought. In short, teachers must understand that speaking standard English is not a prerequisite to learning to read standard English. Knowing and accepting each child's oral language is crucial if teaching and learning are to be effective (Padak, 1981).

Children Should Have Natural Opportunities to Use Language. Developing an accepting climate for learning is a necessary first step toward adapting instruction for linguistically diverse learners. In doing so, teachers will need to resolve an underlying instructional dilemma: preserving appreciation for children's dialects while at the same time providing natural opportunities for approximating the standard. Achieving this balance is a challenge that demands careful thought, planning, and communication. For example, teacher's guides and other curriculum materials seldom acknowledge linguistic diversity. As a result, teachers may need to look elsewhere for instructional suggestions. Furthermore, concerned parents may also exert some pressure, some advocating preservation of the dialect and others just the opposite. The teacher needs to plan instruction that nurtures the child's self-concept in the classroom community as well.

Providing natural opportunities for language use can help resolve this dilemma. All children benefit from listening to language, experimenting with language, and practicing with text. Teachers can model standard English naturally during conversation and daily oral reading. Choosing selections for oral reading that are written in different dialects can help all children learn to appreciate linguistic diversity. Frequent opportunity for conversation and interaction with peers also provides children with different language models. Sociodramatic activities, such as role-playing, creative drama, puppetry, or pantomime, can be beneficial as well. Activities such as these, coupled with abundant opportunities to explore print, can provide a secure base for experimentation with language. The focus of these activities should be communication, not correction. Linguistically diverse children need to learn about their options as language users without feeling that their preferred dialect is inadequate or inferior.

Reading Instruction Should Be Grounded in Meaning. Reading is fundamentally a meaning-based process. Conscious awareness of this belief can assist teachers in planning instruction for linguistically diverse learners. Over the years, educators have approached instruction in three basic ways (Barnitz, 1980).

The first is delaying reading instruction until standard spoken English is learned. This option was quickly abandoned and is not recommended currently. We know that one need not speak a dialect in order to understand it, whether in conversation or in reading. In fact, learning to speak a second dialect is influenced by a variety of factors beyond the teacher's control, such as desire to become a part of that dialect group (Granger, 1976). Furthermore, some sociolinguists believe that children are not even aware of the prestige associated with standard English until adolescence (Shuy, 1969; Labov, 1970). Finally, peer groups may influence language use more than families or schools (Labov, 1970; Dale, 1972).

The second is changing the text to match children's oral language patterns. Several large urban areas (e.g., Chicago, Detroit, and Washington, D.C.) created "dialect basals" in the early 1970s, but this solution, too, was fraught with difficulties. In some cases, community disapproval led to abandoning the project. The cost involved with local development was also a prohibiting factor. Finally, informal speech patterns change relatively quickly, and it was difficult to keep the basals current in this regard.

If the language experience approach (LEA) is used instructionally, of course, text changes are unnecessary, since children's oral language patterns are preserved. We recommend the LEA for the initial instruction of linguistically diverse children. Seeing their own language in print helps children make the meaning connection that is so important to reading growth. In addition, the LEA capitalizes on children's language competence, which can enhance children's self-concepts and sense of worth (Wheat, Galen, and Norwood, 1979).

The third method is encouraging children to read standard English texts in their own dialect patterns. The use of home dialects in oral reading is natural, and dialect-involved miscues seldom interfere with the reader's quest for meaning (Goodman and Buck, 1973). In fact, dialect miscues should be viewed positively, since they demonstrate that the child has understood the text. Without such understanding, the dialect transformation would not be possible.

In order to distinguish between dialect miscues and those made for other reasons, teachers must learn the important features of children's dialects. Dialects may vary in homonym pairs, for example. In some dialects, the following are homonyms: test/tess, poke/pork, tar/tire, poor/pore, all/oil. Miscues of this nature do not affect meaning. The phonological differences that exist across dialects also mean that the nature of phonics generalizations may vary. In the examples cited above, the final /t/ in *test* and the /r/ in *pork* are silent letters.

Syntactic differences among dialects should also be explored. Transformations such as "I asked did he do it" for "I asked if he did it" are the result of syntactic differences. Learning the features of a dialect can help teachers recognize its systematic nature and points of divergence from standard English. This, in turn, can help teachers develop more sensitive and effective instructional strategies (Padak, 1981).

In sum, effective instruction for linguistically diverse learners is based on language growth and flexibility, not change. Teachers must recognize that children may read in their own dialects and write in patterns that reflect their dialects. Instruction should capitalize on children's strengths in comprehension and expression and should minimize attention to differences.

Networking and Teaming to Enhance Instruction

In order to explore their options as language users, children need a stable and secure learning environment. If linguistically diverse learners take part in special reading programs, such as Chapter 1, the classroom teacher should make every effort at cooperation and communication with the special reading teacher so that children's overall instruction is comprehensive and integrated. Teachers can also work together to learn about the features of children's dialects, perhaps by reading and discussing texts on the subject (e.g., Labov, 1970; Bryen, Hartman, and Tait, 1978).

Volunteers and peer tutors can also enhance instruction for linguistically diverse learners. Volunteers can assist with shared book activities, taking dictation, listening to children read, and so forth. Peer tutors can offer different language models for children in an informal setting. All these extra helpers should understand the importance of accepting children's dialects.

Finally, we should strive for parental involvement and support. Teachers might encourage parents to contribute to their children's literacy efforts by reading aloud to them and encouraging reading and writing at hme. Parents too may need to understand the relationship between spoken language patterns and reading growth. Teachers should be prepared to discuss such issues with parents so that they understand the basis for instructional decisions.

All in all, adapting attitudes may be more important than adapting instruction when working with linguistically diverse children. We challenge you to uncover and recognize your own language biases. Doing so will help you learn to accept your students' dialects, which in turn provides the foundation for effective instruction.

ADAPTING INSTRUCTION FOR BILINGUAL LEARNERS

America is a nation of immigrants; relatively few of us are native Americans. At some point in the recent or distant past, our ancestors immigrated to the United States from other parts of the world. In most cases, our immigrant ancestors faced the need to learn a new language and culture while maintaining their own cultural heritage. Ours is truly a multicultural society, and schools can play a major part in fostering understanding and appreciation of cultural diversity.

"Culture" is a broad term that refers to all aspects of life within a society. Anthropologists typically study five major components of culture: language, diet, costume, socialization patterns, and ethics (Jaramillo, 1973). While all of these components of culture are important, language differences are often a major concern for classroom teachers. This is especially true when we consider literacy instruction. What adaptions of reading instruction will benefit children whose native language is not English? How can we help these children learn to understand and use the English language? How can we foster respect for linguistic and cultural diversity among all our students? There are no easy answers to these questions, of course, but we need to consider each carefully. As with the other groups of learners discussed in this chapter, bilingual learners can grow toward language proficiency when instruction is adapted to meet their special needs.

Who Are Bilingual Learners?

According to the reauthorization of the Bilingual Education Act of 1978, bilingual learners are those who have limited proficiency in English and speak another language fluently. In most cases, this other language is the first language the child learns and English is the second. In 1983, an estimated 3.6 million children aged five to fourteen living in the United States fit this definition; 62 percent of these children lived in three states: California, New York, and Texas (Ohio Department of Education, 1983). Demographic projections suggest increased growth among school-aged bilingual learners well into the next decade (Toch, 1984).

The federal government has regulated certain aspects of bilingual education since the mid-1960s. Despite this regulation, a great deal of controversy persists about instructional methods, goals, and other issues related to bilingual education. Some argue for English language and native language instruction so children can maintain their cultural identity. Others maintain that schools have the primary responsibility for the transmission of the "American culture" and that all students should be instructed in English only. In short, the issues related to bilingual education are sociological and political, as well as pedagogical. As teachers, we must be aware of these issues in order to plan effective instruction for all of our students.

First-Language and Second-Language Learning. In order to make instructional adaptations for bilingual students, teachers must first develop an understanding of the relationship between first- or native-language learning and second-language learning. Box 15.3 provides definitions for some important terms related to second-language learning.

Some children are truly bilingual. If the two languages are acquired early enough (usually birth through age five or six), the two languages develop simultaneously, and children are equally fluent in both. No particular instructional adaptations are necessary for these children, but they represent only a small percentage of bilingual learners.

Most bilingual children are more proficient in their native language than they

---

BOX 15.3

Terminology Related to Second-Language Learning

bilingualism The capability of speaking more than one language fluently.

bilingual education The use of two languages for instruction in all subject matters; in the United States, one of these must be English.

ESL English as a second language. *tutoring in english*

LEP Limited English proficiency, ESL students whose English language proficiency is not great enough to learn independently in classrooms where English is the only language of instruction.

native language The first language that a person learns as a member of a certain cultural group.

second language A language learned after the basics of the native language have been acquired.

---

are in English. For these children, the first language is learned naturally in infancy and early children. The native language may always seem more natural than English, and it may be used more often than English.

Native-language learning can be used as a point of reference for second-language learning. Children have already acquired a language and have, in the process, learned a great deal about how language works. A large part of the second-language learner's task is to learn new labels for concepts that are already known. Syntactic or work order differences between the first and second languages must also be learned. Teachers can promote positive transfer from native to second language by encouraging hypothesis-testing and providing an instructional environment in which children feel comfortable taking such risks.

Certain aspects of native language knowledge can interfere with second-language learning. Syntactic differences in the two languages can cause confusion. For example, native Japanese speakers expect to find negation at the end of a sentence rather than close to the verb, as occurs in English. Native speakers of Romance languages, like Spanish and French, may expect adjectives to follow nouns rather than precede them (Barnitz, 1982).

Certain types of vocabulary words may cause difficulty for second-language learners as well. In general, content words that represent things, actions, or qualities are acquired more easily than function words, such as auxiliaries, prepositions, conjunctions, articles, and pronouns (Sinatra, 1981). Learning to use articles can be particularly troublesome. Consider the following pairs of sentences:

Turn on Second Street.   Turn on the second street.
He's a tall boy.   He's tall.
It's water.   It's the water.

Though function words are relatively few in number, they are frequently used and fairly abstract. Teachers who work with bilingual children should learn about the major contrasts or points of difference between children's native language(s) and English. Such knowledge can help teachers help children acquire English successfully.

As children acquire a second language, conversational fluency nearly always precedes written language fluency. Children may be able to converse on the playground, for example, yet still have difficulty using the academic language of the classroom or understanding written English. Teachers must be careful not to make unwarranted assumptions about children's English language competence based on observations in informal, conversational situations. Conversational fluency should not be confused with academic language or written language fluency. For the second-language learner, the three are not the same.

Language and Culture. Teachers who work with bilingual learners need to learn to think like anthropologists. They need to listen and observe carefully in order to be aware of and alert to possible cultural misunderstandings in the classroom (McLeod, 1976). For example, how would you describe a child who averted her eyes rather than looking directly at you? Would you assume that the child was ashamed and had something to hide or that she was being polite and respectful? Your assumptions about the child's behavior are based on the nonverbal communication customs of your own culture. In some cultures, averting one's eyes is a sign of respect, and looking directly at an "authority" figure like a teacher is considered improper. Much of nonverbal communication is culture-specific. Differences in nonverbal customs can cause misunderstandings in the classroom unless teachers understand this aspect of their students' cultures.

Other cultural differences can affect what happens in the classroom as well. Mitigation rules, which stipulate who should talk and when, often differ among cultures. Even the reasons for achieving can be culture-specific. In some cultures children are taught to achieve for individual advancement, while in others individual achievement is desirable only if it benefits a group. Finally, cross-cultural differences may affect children's comprehension since comprehension is closely tied to past experiences (Barnitz, 1982).

Learning a new language and culture can be a formidable task for a child. Sensitive teachers understand this and endeavor to facilitate the child's growth by learning about possible sources of linguistic conflict and cultural misunderstanding. This information provides the basis for effective instructional adaptations for bilingual learners.

Reading Instruction for Bilingual Learners

Many school districts offer special instructional support for bilingual learners. Children in some schools may be taken from the regular classroom for bilingual or ESL instruction. In other instances, tutors or aides may provide support for children in the regular classroom; sometimes no extra support is available at all. The classroom teacher's responsibility for literacy instruction varies according to available support services, of course. The instructional guidelines provided below, however, can help teachers decide about instructional adaptations whether they bear primary responsibility for literacy instruction or supplement the efforts of other teachers.

Reading Instruction for Bilingual Learners Should Foster Natural, Meaningful Language Opportunities. Second-language learners can form new language habits through frequent participation in meaningful oral language activities. Opportunities for conversation and informal sharing should be abundant, since they provide children with the chance to practice English and to learn informally from their peers. Speech situations should be authentic; a real message should be transmitted. Lanuage learning should relate to immediate needs in the school and community.

Bilingual children can also benefit from exposure to natural English-speaking situations through listening activities. The teacher should frequently read aloud, with children close by so that they can see the pictures and the print. Favorites can be reread and tape-recorded so children can listen to tapes and follow along in the books (Hough, Nurss, and Enright, 1986). Play activities and role-playing can also provide opportunities for listening to English in natural situations. Repeated exposure to meaningful language is necessary for maximal second language acquisition. The language-experience approach is perhaps the best alternative for teaching reading to bilingual learners. Concept understanding is insured, since children are dictating about their own experiences. In addition, LEA accounts are linguistically and culturally appropriate. Those who take dictation from children should remember that the child's ideas are a more appropriate focus than the form used to express them. Our goal should be the transmission of meaning rather than rote memorization. We need not necessarily *teach* English, but we must make it possible for children to acquire English.

Reading Instruction for Bilingual Learners Should Foster Multicultural Appreciation. A culturally diverse classroom affords all children excellent opportunities to learn about the world around them. Children can learn about and celebrate holidays from different cultures. Songs can be learned and sung. Ethnic cooking can be studied, prepared, and enjoyed. Children from different cultures can make bulletin boards to illustrate the significant aspects of their cultures. Bilingual learners can write short dialogues in their native languages and teach them to the rest of the class (McLeod, 1976). Activities such as these demonstrate respect for children's heritages while fostering multicultural understanding among all children.

Children whose language and culture are different from the majority may feel set apart from others. This problem can be solved, in part, through books that illustrate significant aspects of children's cultures. Many children's books from other lands have been translated into English. (See Box 15.4 at the end of this chapter for bibliographies of such books.) All children should have the opportunity to hear about and read about different cultures.

Bilingual children need opportunities to use and hear their native languages

BOX 15.4

Booklists: Diversity in the Classroom

Each of the articles or books listed below contains an annotated bibliography of children's trade books. Teachers may find the bibliographies helpful for establishing a classroom library that reflects the diversity of the classroom.

Ethnic and Cultural Diversity

Aoki, Elaine M. "'Are You Chinese? Are You Japanese? Or Are You Just a Mixed-up Kid?' Using Asian American Children's Literature." *The Reading Teacher*, 34 (January, 1981), 382–385.

Buttlar, Lois, and Lubomyr Wynar. *Building Ethnic Collections: An Annotated Guide for School Media Centers and Public Libraries.* Littleton, Colo.: Libraries Unlimited, 1977.

Carlson, Ruth K. *Emerging Humanity: Multiethnic Literature for Children and Adolescents.* Dubuque, Iowa: Brown, 1972.

Cox, Juanita, and Beth S. Wallis. "Books for the Cajun Child: Lagniappe, or a Little Something Extra for Multicultural Teaching." *The Reading Teacher,* 36 (December 1982), 263–266.

Gilliland, Hap. "A New View of Native Americans in Children's Books." *The Reading Teacher,* 35, (May 1982), 912–916.

May, Jill P. "To Think Anew: Native American Literature and Children's Attitudes." *The Reading Teacher,* 36 (April 1983), 790–794.

Povsic, Frances F. "Czechoslovakia: Children's Fiction in English." *The Reading Teacher,* 33 (March 1980), 686–691.

———. "Poland: Children's Fiction in English." *The Reading Teacher,* 33 (April 1980), 806–815.

———. "The Ukraine: Children's Stories in English." *The Reading Teacher,* 35 (March 1982), 716–722.

———. "Yugoslavia: An Annotated Guide to Children's Fiction in English." *The Reading Teacher,* 33 (February 1980), 559–566.

in the classroom. Children from similar language backgrounds might discuss in their native language what they have read in English, for example. Teachers can interject clarifying words from children's native languages into instruction. The child, a parent, or another community member might teach the teacher some important words and phrases that can aid in the instructional process: "Do you understand?" "Do you need help?" "Good work!"

Finally, teachers should capitalize upon opportunities to teach the new culture through reading. Newspapers and magazines transmit culture through print. Children can study advertisements, read advice columns, enjoy cartoons, and read or listen to news about their community and the nation. Idioms and current slang deserve instructional attention, too, since they are such integral parts of conver-

Ethnic and Cultural Diversity (*continued*)

Radencich, Marguerite C. "Books That Promote Positive Attitudes Toward Second Language Learning." *The Reading Teacher,* 38 (February 1985), 528–530.

Reid, Virginia M., ed. *Reading Ladders for Human Relations.* 5th ed. Washington, D.C.: American Council on Education, 1972.

Schon, Isabel. "Recent Outstanding Books for Young Readers from Spanish-Speaking Countries." *The Reading Teacher,* 36 (November 1982), 206–209.

————. "Remarkable Books in Spanish for Young Readers." *The Reading Teacher,* 38 (March 1985), 668–670.

Schon, Isabel, and Patricia Kennedy. "Noteworthy Books in Spanish for Children and Young Adults from Spanish-Speaking Countries." *The Reading Teacher,* 37 (November 1983), 138–142.

Wagoner, Shirley A. "Mexican-Americans in Children's Literature Since 1970." *The Reading Teacher,* 36 (December 1982), 274–279.

Exceptional Children

Baskin, Barbara H., and Karen H. Harris. *Notes from a Different Drummer: A Guide to Juvenile Fiction Portraying the Handicapped.* New York: Bowker, 1977.

Korth, Virginia. "The Gifted in Children's Fiction." *The Gifted Child Quarterly,* 21 (Summer 1977), 246–260.

Lass, Bonnie, and Marcia Bromfield. "Books About Children with Special Needs: An Annotated Bibliography." *The Reading Teacher,* 34 (February 1981), 530–533.

Tway, Eileen. "The Gifted Child in Literature." *Language Arts,* 57, (January 1980), 14–20.

Wagoner, Shirley A. "The Portrayal of the Cognitively Disabled in Children's Literature." *The Reading Teacher,* 37 (February 1984), 502–508.

sation, particularly among children. With some planning and preparation, teachers can transform classrooms into cultural exchanges. All children benefit from such activities.

Reading Instruction for Bilingual Learners Should Focus on the Visual and the Concrete. Bilingual learners need comprehensible, concrete referents for their vocabularies to grow. Concrete manipulatives (e.g., story boards) can be beneficial. Filmstrips, picture books, magazines, newspapers, cartoons, and the like also provide children with pictorial reinforcement. Well-illustrated books provide additional context for the second-language learner. All of this visual support facilitates learning a new language.

Teachers can support children's language-learning efforts by providing verbal and nonverbal cues to maximize their understanding. While reading aloud or speaking to children, teachers can use pauses for effect or to signal changes in episode. Volume changes can signal the moods of stories read or represent different characters. Pointing, gesturing, and varying facial expressions can also provide the second-language learner with clues to meaning (Hough, Nurss, and Enright, 1986).

With some planning, story reading can be a powerful language development tool for LEP students. Listening to stories can help children develop vocabulary and concepts, oral fluency, and sense of story. Listening also provides the opportunity to learn grammar patterns and to make predictions about the content and form of written material. Teachers can encourage predictions by using the directed listening–thinking activity (see Chapter 6) when reading to children. Children's initial responses may be gestures or other means of nonverbal communication. Teachers should encourage response but should not expect comments from all. Many children work through a period of silent, receptive second language acquisition before they feel comfortable expressing themselves. It's important to nurture this process, but not to rush it (Hough, Nurss, and Enright, 1986).

As a rule, meaningless pronunciation drills should be avoided. All instruction and practice should provide opportunities for natural, meaningful communication. Teachers may also need to adapt phonics instruction for second-language learners. Phonological contrasts between the child's native language and English may complicate phonics instruction. These differences may make it difficult or impossible for the child to use English phonic knowledge as a decoding tool. During the initial stages of instruction, vocabulary development within meaningful oral and written contexts should be the goal. At all levels, the ability to understand what another has said or written is much more important than pronunciation.

Children can practice by reading predictable pattern books. Teachers can encourage children to repeat the refrain or complete the pattern. The consistency of plot and language patterns in these books allows interesting and meaningful practice in both vocabulary and language patterns. Repetitious poetry with strong rhythms can also provide meaningful practice for children (Hough, Nurss, and Enright, 1986).

Opportunities for language practice permeate the school day. Children can retell or dramatize what they've read or heard. Multisensory activities, such as role-playing, art work, and writing activities can also enhance language growth (Elley and Mangubhai, 1983). Concrete experiences like field trips or content area projects provide natural opportunities for language growth. Even television can be an effective instructional tool. Children need lots of opportunities to hear meaningful language and to use what they've heard.

Reading Instruction for Bilingual Learners Should Include Meaningful Social and Academic Interaction with Others. A climate of acceptance allows children to experiment with and explore their second language and culture. Teachers can nurture such acceptance by encouraging informal interaction in the classroom. All children benefit from opportunities to work together toward a common goal and to share thoughts and feelings with each other. For bilingual children, these opportunities serve a dual purpose: They learn more about the English language and develop a sense of belonging in the classroom community. Both, of course, should be major instructional goals.

Children can also share through writing. Interaction during writing conferences can lead to additional language learning and provide meaningful practice. Children should be encouraged to read each other's writing as well. If the authors' names are prominently displayed on student-made books, children can consult the authors for help with incomprehensible language patterns or unknown vocabulary. First languages are acquired naturally because children want to understand and be understood by those around them. Second-language learning can be facilitated in the same sort of environment. Bilingual learners benefit from an abundance of opportunities to explore print and to interact with peers in literacy activities.

Networking and Teaming to Enhance Instruction

In districts with large populations of LEP students, the regular classroom teacher probably will not be solely responsible for children's literacy instruction. Bilingual learners may spend part (or all) of the school day in bilingual classrooms working with bilingual teachers. School districts may also provide ESL instruction to LEP students to help them acquire the English skills they need to be successful in school. These programs may be the principal component of the special language instruction for children or may complement bilingual instruction. As with all other "pull-out" programs, coordination and communication between the regular classroom teacher and the special language teacher is an essential ingredient for success.

Current laws mandate some form of extra instructional assistance in instances where at least twenty children from a common language background attend the same school. In cases where no such concentration exists or in schools with a few students each from many language backgrounds, the classroom teacher may be responsible for literacy instruction. In such instances, teachers should seek assistance, information, resources, and ideas from colleagues and specialists in the school setting. By working together, school personnel can help LEP children grow successfully toward bilingualism.

Teachers might also find community resources helpful for planning and implementing literacy instruction for LEP students. Social or religious agency personnel often have valuable information about the cultures and needs of minority language groups. In addition to providing background information for the teacher, community resource persons might visit classrooms to share their knowledge with children. Some volunteers may also be willing to assist in the classroom on a regular basis. Bringing the community in to the classroom can enhance instruction for all students and can foster multicultural understanding and appreciation.

SUMMARY

Understanding and accepting children's differences has been a common thread throughout this chapter. Diversity among learners is a fact of life in classrooms. Ignoring this creates unnecessary difficulties and frustrations for both students and teachers. Embracing it, on the other hand, leads to effective instructional adaptations in reading.

Gifted readers are children who are reading substantially above grade level and/or who possess the ability to make rapid progress in reading. Instructional adaptations for these children should focus upon both enrichment and acceleration of the regular curriculum. Gifted readers should read widely and should come to view reading as a thinking, problem-solving process. They might be encouraged to explore the nature of language. Ample opportunities for creative expression and inquiry through reading will help gifted readers grow. Skills instruction should be provided on an "as needed" basis; children should not be "taught" or required to practice skills that they have already mastered. Finally, instruction for gifted readers should include opportunities for meaningful social and academic interaction with others.

Children with learning disabilities that affect reading also require instructional adaptations. L.D. students generally have average or above-average ability but demonstrate significantly low levels of achievement. These children often benefit from assistance in structuring their learning—in understanding the classroom routine and their own responsibilities as learners. We can help them become successful, independent readers by adapting assignments and making instructions clear. All instruction should preserve children's self-esteem. Of course, instruction for learning disabled students should include social and academic interaction with others.

Linguistic diversity in the classroom may be the result of a variety of factors. Dialects differ from each other in phonology, syntax, and lexicon. Rather than viewing linguistic diversity as a disadvantage or barrier, teachers and students must understand and value linguistic diversity. Children should have many natural opportunities to use language so that they can experiment with language and discover their options as language users. Teachers must recognize that children may read in their own dialect patterns, but these dialect miscues seldom interfere with the child's quest for meaning. Instruction for linguistically diverse learners should capitalize on children's strengths in comprehension and expression. Our goals for children should center upon language growth and flexibility, not change.

Finally, bilingual or LEP students benefit from instructional adaptations. Teachers working with bilingual learners must remember that oral language proficiency precedes written language proficiency. Natural opportunities for language learning and practice can help children refine their expressive and receptive communication skills in English. Teachers should encourage language sharing and interaction during all of every school day. Communicating meaning through language is a more appropriate instructional focus than language drill or rote memorization.

Teachers who adopt instruction effectively use their understanding of children's needs and their beliefs about reading to make instructional decisions. They recognize that whatever the adaptation, meaning must be the heart of reading instruction. They also facilitate meaningful interaction among all students whenever possible. Finally, their decisions convey the uniqueness and value of each individual in the classroom. Their classroom libraries contain books that reflect the diversity among us all. (The booklist in Box 15.4 contains many helpful resources for establishing such a library.) Their reading to children, discussions with them, and instructional choices help children grow as readers and grow in their understanding of those around them.

THE WORKSHOP

In the Classroom

1. Effective instructional adaptations for the children described in this chapter are dependent, in part, on your own attitudes about what's important for reading growth. Talk with your classmates about the questions provided below. Concentrate on what you believe and try to articulate reasons for your beliefs.
   a. Is the basal reader an appropriate instructional core for gifted readers? Why?
   b. Is the basal reader an appropriate instructional core for L.D. students? Why?
   c. How should teachers respond to oral dialect differences or language differences in the speech of LEP students? Why?
   d. When taking dictation, should the teacher preserve the child's oral language patterns? Why?
   e. How can teachers help children accept and respect diversity in the classroom?

2. Read some children's books about or from another culture. Prepare annotated bibliographies of the books that you can share with your classmates.

3. Examine a basal manual for the grade level you teach or hope to teach. Decide upon the types of instructional adaptations necessary for the groups of children described in this chapter.

In the Field

1. Observe a teacher working with some of the "special needs" learners we have described. Take field notes during your observation that focus on instructional adaptations. Evaluate the effectiveness of the teacher's decisions and talk with the teacher to determine his/her perceptions.

2. Find out about the language and culture of minority groups that live in your community. Explore the resources available through social agencies as well. Share this information with your classmates.

3. Keep a log of your work with "special needs" children, evaluating your instructional adaptations and recording suggestions for improvement.

4. Observe in a classroom for an entire day. Keep a running record of children's opportunities to interact with each other throughout the school day. Afterward, evaluate the interactions and decide on other times when interaction might have been encouraged.

Appendix A

GUIDELINES FOR ANALYZING CONCEPTUAL FRAMEWORKS OF READING INTERVIEWS

Directions: Use the following summary statements as guidelines to help analyze your responses to the questions in the interview.

Question 1: Main instructional goals

Bottom-Up Responses:

Increase children's ability to blend sounds into words or ability to sound out words.

Increase knowledge of phonetic sounds (sound-letter associations).

Build sight vocabulary.

Increase ability to use word attack skills.

Top-Down Responses:

Increase students' ability to read independently by encouraging them to read library or other books that are easy enough for them on their own.

Increase enjoyment of reading by having a lot of books around, reading aloud to children, and sharing books I thought were special.

Improve comprehension.

Increase ability to find specific information, identify key ideas, determine cause-and-effect relationships, and make inferences. (Although these are discrete skills, they are categorized as top-down because students use higher-order linguistic units—phrases, sentences, paragraphs—in accomplishing them.)

Question 2: Teacher responses when students make oral reading errors

Bottom-Up Responses:

Help students sound out the word.

Tell students what the word is, and have them spell and then repeat the word.

Top-Down Responses:

Ask "Does that make sense?"

Don't interrupt; one word doesn't "goof up" the meaning of a whole passage.

Don't interrupt; if students are worried about each word, they won't be able to remember what is read.

Don't correct if the error doesn't affect the meaning of the passage.

If the error affects the meaning of the passage, ask students to reread the passage, tell students the word, ask "Does that make sense?"

Question 3: Teacher responses when students do not know a word

Bottom-Up Responses:

Help students sound out the word.

Help them distinguish smaller words within the word.

Help them break the word down phonetically.

Help them sound the word out syllable by syllable.

Tell them to use work attack skills.

Give them word attack clues; for example, "The sound of the beginning consonant rhymes with _____."

Top-Down Responses:

Tell students to skip the word, go on, and come back and see what makes sense.

Ask "What makes sense and starts with _____?"

Question 4 and 5: Most important instructional activities

Bottom-Up Responses:

Working on skills.

Working on phonics.

Working on sight vocabulary.

Vocabulary drill.

Discussing experience charts, focusing on the words included and any punctuation needed.

Tape-recording students' reading and playing it back, emphasizing accuracy in word recognition.

Top-Down Responses:

Actual reading, silent reading, and independent reading.

Comprehension.

Discussion of what students have read.

Book reports.

Tape-recording students' reading and playing it back, emphasizing enjoyment of reading or comprehension.

Question 6: Ranking of parts of the Directed Reading Procedure

Bottom-Up Responses:

The following are most important:

> introduction of vocabulary
>
> activities to develop reading skills

The following are least important:

> setting purposes for reading

reading

reaction to silent reading

introduction of vocabulary, when the teacher stresses students' using word attack skills to sound out new words

Top-Down Responses:

The following are most important:

setting purposes for reading

reading

reaction to silent reading

The following are least important:

introduction of vocabulary

activities to develop reading skills

Question 7: Introducing new vocabulary words

Bottom-Up Responses:

Introducing new vocabulary is important because students need to know what words they will encounter in order to be able to read a story.

Previewing new vocabulary isn't necessary; if students have learned word attack skills, they can sound out unknown words.

Introducing new words is useful in helping students learn what words are important in a reading lesson.

Vocabulary words should be introduced if students don't know the meanings of the words; otherwise it isn't necessary.

Top-Down Responses:

Vocabulary words need not be introduced before reading because students can often figure out words from context.

Question 8: What a reading test should do

Bottom-Up Responses:

Test word attack skills.

Test ability to name the letters of the alphabet.

Test sight words.

Test knowledge of meanings of words.

Test ability to analyze letter patterns of words missed during oral reading.

Test visual skills such as reversal.

Top-Down Responses:

Test comprehension: Students should be able to read a passage orally, look at the errors they make, and use context in figuring out words.

Test whether students are able to glean the meanings of words from context.

Answer questions like the following: Do students enjoy reading? Do their parents read to them? Do their parents take them to the library?

Have students read passages and answer questions.

Have students read directions and follow them.

Question 9: What students should do when they come to an unknown word during silent reading

Bottom-Up Responses:

Sound it out.

Use their word attack skills.

Top-Down Responses:

Look at the beginning and the end of the sentence and try to think of a word that makes sense.

Try to think of a word that both makes sense and has those letter sounds.

Skip the word; often students can understand the meaning of the sentence without knowing every word.

Use context.

Question 10: Who is the best reader?

Reader A	*Reader B*	*Reader C*
Miscue is similar both graphically and in meaning to the text word.	Miscue is a real word that is graphically similar but not meaningful in the text.	Miscue is a nonword that is graphically similar.

Bottom-Up Responses:

Reader C, because *cannal* is graphically similar to *canal*.

Reader B, because *candle* is a real word that is graphically similar to *canal*.

Top-Down Responses:

Reader A, because *channel* is similar in meaning to *canal*.

Appendix B

NEWBERRY AWARD BOOKS

1986   MacLachlan, *Sarah Plain and Tall* (Harper & Row)
1985   McKinley, *Hero and the Crown* (Greenwillow)
1984   Voigt, *Dicey's Song* (Atheneum)
1983   Clary, *Dear Mr. Henshaw* (Monroe)
1982   Willard and Provenson, *William Blake's Inn* (Harcourt Brace Jovanovich)
1981   Paterson, *Jacob Have I Loved* (Crowell)
1980   Blos, *A Gathering of Days: A New England Girl's Journal, 1830–1832* (Scribner's)
1979   Raskin, *The Westing Game* (Dutton)
1978   Paterson, *Bridge to Terabithia* (Crowell)
1977   Taylor, *Roll of Thunder, Hear My Cry* (Dial)
1976   Cooper, *The Grey King* (Atheneum)
1975   Hamilton, *M. C. Higgins, the Great* (Macmillan)
1974   Fox, *The Slave Dancer* (Bradbury)
1973   George, *Julie of the Wolves* (Harper & Row)
1972   O'Brien, *Mrs. Frisby and the Rats of NIMH* (Atheneum)
1971   Byars, *Summer of the Swans* (Viking)
1970   Armstrong, *Sounder* (Harper & Row)
1969   Alexander, *The High King* (Holt, Rinehart & Winston)
1968   Konigsburg, *From the Mixed-up Files of Mrs. Basil E. Frankweiler* (Atheneum)
1967   Hunt, *Up a Road Slowly* (Follett)
1966   de Trevino, *I, Juan de Pareja* (Farrar, Straus & Giroux)
1965   Wojciechowska, *Shadow of a Bull* (Atheneum)
1964   Neville, *It's Like This, Cat* (Harper & Row)
1963   L'Engle, *A Wrinkle in Time* (Farrar, Straus & Giroux)
1962   Speare, *Bronze Bow* (Houghton Mifflin)
1961   O'Dell, *Island of the Blue Dolphins* (Houghton Mifflin)
1960   Krumgold, *Onion John* (Crowell)
1959   Speare, *Witch of Blackbird Pond* (Houghton Mifflin)
1958   Keith, *Rifles for Waitie* (Crowell)
1957   Sorensen, *Miracles on Maple Hill* (Harcourt, Brace)
1956   Latham, *Carry On, Mr. Bowditch* (Houghton Mifflin)
1955   de Jong, *The Wheel on the School* (Harper & Row)
1954   Krumgold, *And Now Miguel* (Crowell)
1953   Clark, *The Secret of the Andes* (Viking)

1952 Estes, *Ginger Pye* (Harcourt, Brace)
1951 Yates, *Amos Fortune, Free Man* (Dutton)
1950 de Angeli, *The Door in the Wall* (Doubleday)
1949 Henry, *King of the Wind* (Rand McNally)
1948 du Bois, *The Twenty-one Balloons* (Viking)
1947 Bailey, *Miss Hickory* (Viking)
1946 Lenski, *Strawberry Girl* (Lippincott)
1945 Lawson, *Rabbit Hill* (Viking)
1944 Forbes, *Johnny Tremain* (Houghton Mifflin)
1943 Gray, *Adam of the Road* (Viking)
1942 Edmonds, *Matchlock Gun* (Dodd, Mead)
1941 Sperry, *Call It Courage* (Macmillan)
1940 Daugherty, *Daniel Boone* (Viking)
1939 Enright, *Thimble Summer* (Holt)
1938 Seredy, *The White Stag* (Viking)
1937 Sawyer, *Roller Skates* (Viking)
1936 Brink, *Cadie Woodlawn* (Macmillan)
1935 Shannon, *Dobry* (Viking)
1934 Meigs, *Invincible Louisa: Anniversary Edition* (Little, Brown)
1933 Lewis, *Young Fu of the Upper Yangtze* (Holt)
1932 Armer, *Waterless Mountain* (McKay)
1931 Coatsworth, *The Cat Who Went to Heaven* (Macmillan)
1930 Kelly, *The Trumpeter of Krakow* (Macmillan)
1929 Field, *Hitty: Her First Hundred Years* (Macmillan)
1928 Mujkerji, *Gay Neck* (Dutton)
1927 James, *Smoky the Cowhorse* (Scribner's)
1926 Christmas, *Shen of the Sea* (Dutton)
1925 Finger, *Tales from Silver Lands* (Doubleday)
1924 Hawes, *The Dark Frigate* (Little, Brown)
1923 Lofting, *The Voyages of Dr. Dolittle* (Lippincott)
1922 van Loon, *The Story of Mankind* (Liveright)

Appendix C

CALDECOTT AWARD BOOKS

1986   Van Allsburg, *Polar Express* (Houghton Mifflin)
1985   Hodges and Human, *Saint George and the Dragon* (Little, Brown)
1984   Provenson, *The Glorious Flight* (Viking)
1983   Brown, *Shadow* (Scribner's)
1982   Van Allsburg, *Jumanji* (Houghton Mifflin)
1981   Lobel, *Fables* (Harper & Row)
1980   Hall and Cooney, *The Ox-Cart Man* (Viking)
1979   Goble, *The Girl Who Loved Wild Horses* (Bradbury)
1978   Spier, *Noah's Ark* (Doubleday)
1977   Musgrove, *Ashanti to Zulu: African Traditions* (Dial)
1976   Aardema, *Why Mosquitoes Buzz in People's Ears* (Dial)
1975   McDermott, *Arrow to the Sun* (Viking)
1974   Zemach, *Duffy and the Devil* (Farrar, Straus & Giroux)
1973   Mosel, *The Funny Little Woman* (Dutton)
1972   Hogrogian, *One Fine Day* (Macmillan)
1971   Haley, *A Story, a Story* (Atheneum)
1970   Steig, *Sylvester and the Magic Pebble* (Simon & Schuster)
1969   Ransome, *Fool of the World and the Flying Ship* (Farrar, Straus & Giroux)
1968   Emberley, *Drummer Hoff* (Prentice-Hall)
1967   News, *Sam Bangs and Moonshine* (Holt, Rinehart & Winston)
1966   Leadhas and Hogrogian, *Always Room for One More* (Holt, Rinehart & Winston)
1965   de Regniers, *May I Bring a Friend?* (Atheneum)
1964   Sendak, *Where the Wild Things Are* (Harper & Row)
1963   Keats, *The Snowy Day* (Viking)
1962   Brown, *Once a Mouse* (Scribner's)
1961   Robbins, *Baboushka and the Three Kings* (Parnassus)
1960   Ets and Labastida, *Nine Days to Christmas* (Viking)
1959   Cooney, *Chanticleer and the Fox* (Crowell)
1958   McCloskey, *Time of Wonder* (Viking)
1957   Udry and Simont, *A Tree Is Nice* (Harper & Row)
1956   Langstaff and Rojankovsky, *Frog Went A-Courtin'* (Harcourt, Brace)
1955   Brown, *Cinderella* (Scribner's)
1954   Bemelmans, *Madeline's Rescue* (Viking)

1953 Ward, *The Biggest Bear* (Houghton Mifflin)

1952 Nicolas, *Finders Keepers* (Harcourt, Brace)

1951 Milhous, *The Egg Tree* (Scribner's)

1950 Politi, *Song of the Swallows* (Scribner's)

1949 Hader, *Big Snow* (Macmillan)

1948 Tresselt and Duvoisin, *White Snow, Bright Snow* (Lothrop)

1947 MacDonald and Weisgard, *Little Island* (Doubleday)

1946 Petersham, *Rooster Crown* (Macmillan)

1945 Field and Jones, *Prayer for a Child* (Macmillan)

1944 Thurber and Slobodkin, *Many Moons* (Harcourt, Brace)

1943 Burton, *Little House* (Houghton Mifflin)

1942 McCloskey, *Make Way for Ducklings* (Viking)

1941 Lawson, *They Were Strong and Good* (Viking)

1940 d'Aulaire, *Abraham Lincoln* (Doubleday)

1939 Handforth, *Mei Li* (Doubleday)

1938 Lathrop, *Animals of the Bible* (Lippincott)

Appendix D

A BIBLIOGRAPHY OF PREDICTABLE BOOKS*

Adams, Pam. *This Old Man*. New York, N.Y.: Grossett and Dunlap, 1974.
Alain. *One, Two, Three, Going to Sea*. New York, N.Y.: Scholastic, 1964.
Aliki. *Go Tell Aunt Rhody*. New York, N.Y.: Macmillan, 1974.
Aliki. *Hush Little Baby*. Englewood Cliffs, N.J.: Prentice-Hall, 1968.
Aliki. *My Five Senses*. New York, N.Y.: Thomas Y. Crowell, 1962.
Asch, Frank. *Monkey Face*. New York, N.Y.: Parents' Magazine Press, 1977.
Balian, Lorna. *The Animal*. Nashville, Tenn.: Abingdon Press, 1972.
Balian, Lorna. *Where in the World Is Henry?* Scarsdale, N.Y.: Bradbury Press, 1972.
Barohas, Sarah E. *I Was Walking Down the Road*. New York, N.Y.: Scholastic, 1975.
Baum, Arline, and Joseph Baum. *One Bright Monday Morning*. New York, N.Y.: Random House, 1962.
Becker, John. *Seven Little Rabbits*. New York, N.Y.: Scholastic, 1973.
Beckman, Kaj. *Lisa Cannot Sleep*. New York, N.Y.: Franklin Watts, 1969.
Bellah, Melanie. *A First Book of Sounds*. Racine, Wis.: Golden Press, 1963.
Bonne, Rose, and Alan Mills. *I Know an Old Lady*. New York, N.Y.: Rand McNally, 1961.
Brand, Oscar. *When I First Came to This Land*. New York, N.Y.: Putnam's Sons, 1974.
Brandenberg, Franz. *I Once Knew a Man*. New York, N.Y.: Macmillan, 1970.
Brown, Marcia, *The Three Billy Goats Gruff*. New York, N.Y.: Harcourt Brace Jovanovich, 1957.
Brown, Margaret Wise. *Four Fur Feet*. New York, N.Y.: William R. Scott, 1961.
Brown, Margaret Wise. *Goodnight Moon*. New York, N.Y.: Harper and Row, 1947.
Brown, Margaret Wise. *Home for a Bunny*. Racine, Wis.: Golden Press, 1956.
Brown, Margaret Wise. *Where Have You Been?* New York, N.Y.: Scholastic, 1952.
The Bus Ride, illustrated by Justin Wager. New York, N.Y.: Scott, Foresman, 1971.
Carle, Eric. *The Grouchy Ladybug*. New York, N.Y.: Thomas Y. Crowell, 1977.
Carle, Eric. *The Mixed Up Chameleon*. New York, N.Y.: Thomas Y. Crowell, 1975.
Carle, Eric. *The Very Hungry Caterpillar*. Cleveland, Ohio: Collins World, 1969.
Charlip, Remy. *Fortunately*. New York, N.Y.: Parents' Magazine Press, 1964.
Charlip, Remy. *What Good Luck! What Bad Luck!* New York, N.Y.: Scholastic, 1969.

* Reprinted with permission of Lynn K. Rhodes and the International Reading Association from "I Can Read! Predictable Books as Resources for Reading and Writing Instruction." *The Reading Teacher, 34*, 1981, 511–518.

Cook, Bernadine. *The Little Fish That Got Away*. Reading, Mass.: Addison-Wesley, 1976.

de Regniers, Beatrice Schenk. *Catch a Little Fox*. New York, N.Y.: Seabury Press, 1970.

de Regniers, Beatrice Schenk. *The Day Everybody Cried*. New York, N.Y.: The Viking Press, 1967.

de Regniers, Beatrice Schenk. *How Joe the Bear and Sam the Mouse Got Together*. New York, N.Y.: Parents' Magazine Press, 1965.

de Regniers, Beatrice Schenk. *The Little Book*. New York, N.Y.: Henry Z. Walck, 1961.

de Regniers, Beatrice Schenk. *May I Bring a Friend?* New York, N.Y.: Atheneum, 1972.

de Regniers, Beatrice Schenk. *Willy O'Dwyer Jumped in the Fire*. New York, N.Y.: Atheneum, 1968.

Domanska, Janina. *If All the Seas Were One Sea*. New York, N.Y.: Macmillan, 1971.

Duff, Maggie. *Jonny and His Drum*. New York, N.Y.: Henry Z. Walck, 1972.

Duff, Maggie. *Rum Pum Pum*. New York, N.Y.: Macmillan, 1978.

Emberley, Barbara. *Simon's Song*. Englewood Cliffs, N.J.: Prentice-Hall, 1969.

Emberly, Ed. *Klippity Klop*. Boston, Mass.: Little, Brown, 1974.

Ets, Marie Hall. *Elephant in a Well*. New York, N.Y.: The Viking Press, 1972.

Ets, Marie Hall. *Play with Me*. New York, N.Y.: The Viking Press, 1955.

Flack, Marjorie. *Ask Mr. Bear*. New York, N.Y.: Macmillan, 1932.

Galdone, Paul. *Henny Penny*. New York, N.Y.: Scholastic, 1968.

Galdone, Paul. *The Little Red Hen*. New York, N.Y.: Scholastic, 1973.

Galdone, Paul. *The Three Bears*. New York, N.Y.: Scholastic, 1972.

Galdone, Paul. *The Three Billy Goats Gruff*. New York, N.Y.: Seabury Press, 1973.

Galdone, Paul. *The Three Little Pigs*. New York, N.Y.: Seabury Press, 1970.

Ginsburg, Mirra. *The Chick and the Duckling*. New York, N.Y.: Macmillan, 1972.

Greenberg, Polly. *Oh Lord, I Wish I Was a Buzzard*. New York, N.Y.: Macmillan, 1968.

Hoffman, Hilde. *The Green Grass Grows All Around*. New York, N.Y.: Macmillan, 1968.

Hutchins, Pat. *Good-Night Owl*. New York, N.Y.: Macmillan, 1972.

Hutchins, Pat. *Rosie's Walk*. New York, N.Y.: Macmillan, 1968.

Hutchins, Pat. *Titch*. New York, N.Y.: Collier Books, 1971.

Keats, Ezra Jack. *Over in the Meadow*. New York, N.Y.: Scholastic, 1971.

Kent, Jack. *The Fat Cat*. New York, N.Y.: Scholastic, 1971.

Klein, Lenore. *Brave Daniel*. New York, N.Y.: Scholastic, 1958.

Kraus, Robert. *Whose Mouse Are You?* New York, N.Y.: Collier Books, 1970.

Langstaff, John, and Feodor Rojankovsky. *Frog Went A-Courtin'*. New York, N.Y.: Harcourt Brace Jovanovich, 1955.

Langstaff, John. *Gather My Gold Together: Four Songs for Four Seasons*. Garden City, N.Y.: Doubleday, 1971.

Langstaff, John. *Oh, A-Hunting We Will Go*. New York, N.Y.: Atheneum, 1974.

Langstaff, John. *Over in the Meadow*. New York, N.Y.: Harcourt Brace Jovanovich, 1957.

Laurence, Ester. *We're Off to Catch a Dragon*. Nashville, Tenn.: Abingdon Press, 1969.

Lexau, Joan. *Crocodile and Hen*. New York, N.Y.: Harper and Row, 1969.

Lobel, Anita. *King Rooster, Queen Hen*. New York, N.Y.: Greenwillow, 1975.

Lobel, Arnold. *A Treeful of Pigs*. New York, N.Y.: Greenwillow, 1979.

Mack, Stan. *10 Bears in My Bed*. New York, N.Y.: Pantheon, 1974.

Martin, Bill. *Brown Bear, Brown Bear*. New York, N.Y.: Holt, Rinehart and Winston, 1970.

Martin, Bill. *Fire! Fire! Said Mrs. McGuire*. New York, N.Y.: Holt, Rinehart and Winston, 1970.

Mayer, Mercer. *If I Had. . . .* New York, N.Y.: Dial Press, 1968.

Mayer, Mercer. *Just for You*. New York, N.Y.: Golden Press, 1975.

McGovern, Ann. *Too Much Noise*. New York, N.Y.: Scholastic, 1967.

Memling, Carl. *Ten Little Animals*. Racine, Wis.: Golden Press. 1961.

Moffett, Martha. *A Flower Pot Is Not a Hat*. New York, N.Y.: E. P. Dutton, 1972.

Peppe, Rodney. *The House that Jack Built*. New York, N.Y.: Delacorte, 1970.

Polushkin, Maria. *Mother, Mother, I Want Another*. New York, N.Y.: Crown Publishers, 1978.

Preston, Edna Mitchell. *Where Did My Mother Go?* New York, N.Y.: Four Winds Press, 1978.

Quackenbush, Robert. *She'll Be Comin' Round the Mountain*. Philadelphia, Pa.: J.B. Lippincott, 1973.

Quackenbush, Robert. *Skip to My Lou*. Philadelphia, Pa.: J.B. Lippincott, 1975.

Rokoff, Sandra. *Here Is a Cat*. Singapore: Hallmark Children's Editions, no date.

Scheer, Jullian, and Marvin Bileck. *Rain Makes Applesauce*. New York, N.Y.: Holiday House, 1964.

Scheer, Jullian, and Marvin Bileck, *Upside Down Day*. New York, N.Y.: Holiday House, 1968.

Sendak, Maurice. *Where the Wild Things Are*. New York, N.Y.: Harper and Row, 1963.

Shaw, Charles B. *It Looked Like Spilt Milk*. New York, N.Y.: Harper and Row, 1947.

Shulevitz, Uri. *One Monday Morning*. New York, N.Y.: Scribner's, 1967.

Skaar, Grace. *What Do the Animals Say?* New York, N.Y.: Scholastic, 1972.

Sonneborn, Ruth A. *Someone Is Eating the Sun*. New York, N.Y.: Random House, 1974.

Spier, Peter. *The Fox Went Out on a Chilly Night*. Garden City, N.Y.: Doubleday, 1961.

Stover, JoAnn. *If Everybody Did*. New York, N.Y.: David McKay, 1960.

Tolstoy, Alexei. *The Great Big Enormous Turnip*. New York, N.Y.: Franklin Watts, 1968.

Welber, Robert. *Goodbye, Hello*. New York, N.Y.: Pantheon, 1974.

Wildsmith, Brian. *The Twelve Days of Christmas*. New York, N.Y.: Franklin Watts, 1972.

Wolkstein, Diane. *The Visit*. New York, N.Y.: Alfred A. Knopf, 1977.

Wondriska, William. *All the Animals Were Angry*. New York, N.Y.: Holt, Rinehart and Winston, 1970.

Zaid, Barry. *Chicken Little*. New York, N.Y.: Random House, no date.

Zemach, Harve. *The Judge*. New York, N.Y.: Farrar, Straus and Giroux, 1969.

Zemach, Margot. *Hush, Little Baby*. New York, N.Y.: E. P. Dutton, 1976.

Zemach, Margot. *The Teeny Tiny Woman*. New York, N.Y.: Scholastic, 1965.

Zolotow, Charlotte. *Do You Know What I'll Do?* New York, N.Y.: Harper and Row, 1958.

Appendix E

COMPUTER PROGRAMS FOR READING INSTRUCTION AND ADDRESSES OF PUBLISHERS

Programs for the Young Child

Alphabet Arcade (Program Design)
Alphabet Beasts & Co. (Software Productions)
Alphabet/Keyboard (Random House)
Alphabet Song (Edu-Soft)
Alphabetization (Milliken)
Alphabetizing I-II (Aquarius People Materials)
Bop-a-bet (Sierra On-Line)
Bouncy Bee Learns Letters (IBM)
Charlie Brown's ABC's (Random House)
Children's Carrousel (Dynacomp)
Customized Alphabet Drill (Random House)
Early Games for Young Children (Springboard)
Early Learning Fun (Triton)
Easyreader (American Educational Computer)
Get Set for Writing to Read (IBM)
Getting Ready to Read and Add (Sunburst)
Juggle's Rainbow (The Learning Company)
Kids' Stuff (Stone Software)
Kinder Koncepts (Midwest)
KinderComp (Spinnaker)
Leaps and Bounds (Muse)
Letter Recognition (Hartley)
Letters and Numbers (Teaching Tools)
Look 'n' Hook the Learning Line
My First Alphabet (Atari)
My Letters, Numbers and Words (Stone Software)
Missing Letters (IBM)
Preschool IQ Builder (Program Design)
Primary Math/Prereading (MECC)
Stickybear Reading (Weekly Reader)

496

Talking Teacher (Imagic)
Working with the Alphabet (Orange Cherry)

Programs for Literature

Dragon's Keep (Sierra On-Line)
Fairy Tales (Orange Cherry)
Great American Folk Heroes (Orange Cherry)
The Magic Wand Speaking Reader (Texas Instruments)
Newberry Winners (Sunburst)
Tales of Discovery (Information Technology Design)

Programs for Comprehension

Active Reader—World of Nature Series (Orange Cherry)
Adventures Around the World (Orange Cherry)
Cloze Plus (Milliken)
The Cloze Technique for Developing Comprehension (Orange Cherry)
Comprehension Power Program (I/CT)
Diascriptive Reading (Educational Activities)
Extra, Extra (Media Materials)
Fables and Poems (Intellectual Software)
Fact or Opinion (Learning Well)
Fantasy Land ("reading between the lines"; Learning Well)
Galaxy Search (predicting outcomes; Learning Well)
Getting the Main Idea (Learning Well)
Missing Links (Sunburst)
Myths (Intellectual Software)
Our Wild and Crazy World (Educational Activities)
PAL (Universal Systems for Education)
Prime Suspect Reading Adventure (Orange Cherry)
Puzzler (Sunburst)
Reading and Thinking (Intellectual Software)
Reading Around Words (context analysis; I/CT)
Reading Comprehension (American Educational Computers)
Reading Comprehension (Dorsett)
Reading Comprehension (Intellectual Software)
Reading Comprehension Skills (IBM)
Reading for Information (IBM)
Reading for Meaning (IBM)
Reading Series (CSR)

Programs for Vocabulary Development

Analogies Tutor (Hartley)
Antonyms/Synonyms (Hartley)
Chambers of Vocab (Reader's Digest)
Game Show (Advanced Ideas)
Interactive Text (Rutgers University)

Language Development Series (Scott, Foresman)
Mind Bind (Princeton Educational Software)
Quizit (Regents/ALA)
Snake-O-Nyms (Milliken)
Spell Bound (World Book)
Trickster Coyote (Reader's Digest)
Vocabulary (Personal Computer Products)
Vocabulary Baseball (J & S)
Vocabulary Series (Intellectual Software)
Vocabulary Word Builder (American Educational Computer)
Word Player (World Book)

Programs for Word Identification

Boppie's Great Word Chase (DLM)
Bouncy Bee Learns Words (IBM)
Construct-a-Word (DLM)
Cross Clues (SRA)
Don't Fall (Apple)
Early Games for Young Children (Springboard)
Fry Instant Words Program (Jamestown)
Hint and Hunt Series (DLM)
Instant Zoo (CTW)
Kids on Keys (Spinnaker)
Language/Reading Development Program (Software Technology for Computers)
Letters and First Words (C & C)
Odd One Out (Sunburst)
Picture Place! (CTW)
The Reading Machine (SouthWest EdPsych)
Spelling Bee and Reading Primer (Edu-Ware)
Syllasearch (DLM)
Teach Me Words (SVE)
Verb Viper (DLM)
Word Families (Hartley)
Word Memory Programs (I/CT)
Word Pictures (Orange Cherry)
Word Radar (DLM)
Word Wise (TIES)
Word Wiz (Alphanetics)
Wordman (DLM)

Phonics Programs

Alphabet Sounds (Orange Cherry)
Chomp (Denis)
Consonant Combo (McCarthy-McCormack)
Consonant-Vowel-Consonant (CBS)
Construct-a-Word Series (DLM)
Fundamental Phonics and Word Attack (Random House)

Fundamental Word Focus (Random House)
Game Power for Phonics, Plus (Spin-a-test)
Hint and Hunt Series (DLM)
Learn About Sounds in Reading (American Educational Computer)
Learn to Read (American Educational Computer)
Old MacDonald's Farm Vowels (TEKSYM)
Phonet (MECC)
Phonics (American Educational Computer)
Phonics (Dorsett)
Phonics (SRA)
Reading Development (Dorsett)
Reading Readiness (Orange Cherry)
Rhyming
    Beginning Reader (Intellectual Software)
    Hinky-Pinky (22nd Avenue Workshop)
    Roll-a-Word (CTW)
Vowel Sounds (Orange Cherry)
Word Families (Hartley)
Wordspinner (The Learning Company)

Structural Analysis Programs

Antonyms and Synonyms (Hartley)
Contractions (Educational Activities)
Prefixes (*Elementary*, Vol. 5; MECC)
Homonyms (Hartley)
Homonyms (Milliken)
Homonyms in Context (Random House)
Learn About Words in Reading (American Educational Computer)
Pet/Pit/Put (Data Command)
Root Words and Suffixes (CBS)
Roots/Affixes (Hartley)
Tank Tactics (Data Command)
Tennis Anyone—Plurals (Data Command)
Vocabulary Skills: Prefixes, Suffixes, and Root Words (Media Materials)
Word Division (Ahead Designs)
Word Master (homonyms; DLM)

Context Clues

Cloze Encounters (Intellectual Software)
Cloze-Plus (I/CT)
Cloze Technique for Developing Comprehension (Orange Cherry)
Context Clues (Learning Well)
Context Clues (Milton Bradley)
Monkeynews (Artworx)

PUBLISHERS OF SOFTWARE

The addresses of many of the main producers of reading software are listed below. If a particular publisher is not found here, refer to listings in computer magazines and books, references such as the *Classroom Computer News Directory of Educational Computing Resources*, or ask for assistance at your local computer store or library. Note that some publishers, such as Dynacomp, Follet, Hammett, Opportunities for Learning, Orange Cherry Media, Queue, Scholastic, and SVE, carry software from many publishers. They might also be contacted.

Advanced Ideas, Inc.
2550 Ninth Street, Suite 104
Berkeley, CA 94710

Ahead Designs
699 North Vulcan, No. 88
Encinitas, CA 92024

Alphanetics
P.O. Box 339
Forestville, CA 95436

American Educational Computer
2450 Embarcadero Way
Palo Alto, CA 94303

Apple Computer, Inc.
20525 Mariani Avenue, Dept. MS: 22Y
Cupertino, CA 95014

Aquarius People Materials, Inc.
P.O. Box 128
Indian Rocks Beach, FL 33535

Artworx Software Co., Inc.
150 North Main Street
Fairport, NY 14450

Atari, Inc.
1265 Borregas Avenue
Sunnyvale, CA 94086

C & C Software
5713 Kentford Circle
Wichita, KS 67220

CBS Software
383 Madison Avenue
New York, NY 10017

CSR (Computer Systems Research, Inc.)
P.O. Box 45
Avon, CT 06001

CTW (Children's Television Workshop)
One Lincoln Plaza
New York, NY 10023

Data Command
P.O. Box 548
Kankakee, IL 60901

Davidson & Associates
6069 Groveoak Place, No. 12
Rancho Palos Verdes, CA 90274

DLM (Developmental Learning Activities)
P.O. Box 4000
One DLM Park
Austin, TX 75002

Dorsett Education Systems, Inc.
P.O. Box 1226
Norman, OK 73070

Dynacomp, Inc.
1427 Monroe Avenue
Rochester, NY 14618

Educational Activities Inc.
1937 Grand Avenue
Baldwin, NY 11510

Edu-Soft
P.O. Box 2560
Berkeley, CA 94702

Edu-Ware Services, Inc.
28035 Dorothy Drive
Agoura Hills, CA 91301-0522

Follet Library Book Co.
4506 Northwest Highway
Crystal Lake, IL 60014

J. L. Hammett Co.
P.O. Box 545
Braintree, MA 02184

Hartley Courseware
123 Bridge
Dimondale, MI 48821

Hayden Software
600 Suffolk Street
Lowell, MA 01854

IBM Software
P.O. Box 1328
1000 Northwest 51st Street
Boca Raton, FL 33432

I/CT
Taylor Associates
10 Stepar Place
Huntington Station, NY 11746

Intellectual Software
562 Boston Avenue
Bridgeport, CT 06610

Jamestown Pub.
P.O. Box 6743
Providence, RI 02940

J & S Software
14 Venderventer Avenue
Port Washington, NY 11050

K-12 Micro Media
P.O. Box 17
Valley Cottage, NY 10989

The Learning Company
545 Middlefield Road, Suite 170
Menlo Park, CA 94025

Learning Consultants, Inc.
690 Lafayette Road
Medina, OH 44256

Learning Well
200 South Service Road
Roslyn Heights, NY 11577

MECC (Minnesota Educational Computing
  Consortium)
2520 Broadway Drive
Saint Paul, MN 55113

Media Materials
2936 Remington Avenue
Baltimore, MD 21211

Midwest Publications
P.O. Box 448
Pacific Grove, CA 93950

Milliken Publishing Co.
1100 Research Boulevard
St. Louis, MO 63132

Muse
347 North Charles Street
Baltimore, MD 21201

Opportunities for Learning
20417 Nordhoff Street, Room VC
Chatsworth, CA 91311

Orange Cherry Media
P.O. Box 427
Dept. 9
Bedford Hills, NY 10507

Personal Computer Products
1400 Coleman Avenue, Suite C-18
Santa Clara, CA 95050

Program Design, Inc.
11 Idar Court
Greenwich, CT 06830

Queue
5 Chapelhill Drive
Fairfield, CT 06423

Random House School Division
2970 Brandywine Road
Atlanta, GA 30341

Reader's Digest
Microcomputer Software Department
Pleasantville, NY 10570

Regents/ALA
Two Park Avenue
New York, NY 10016

Scholastic Inc.
P.O. Box 7503
2931 East McCarty Street
Jefferson City, MO 65102

Scott, Foresman and Company
1900 East Lake Avenue
Glenview, IL 60025

Sierra On-Line
Sierra On-Line Building
Coarsegold, CA 93614

Software Productions
2357 Southway Drive
P.O. Box 21341
Columbus, OH 43221

SouthWest EdPsych Services
P.O. Box 1870
Phoenix, AZ 85001

Spin-a-test Pub. Co.
3177 Hogarth Drive
Sacramento, CA 95827

Spinnaker Software
215 First Street
Cambridge, MA 02139

Springboard Software
7807 Creekridge Circle
Minneapolis, MN 55435

SRA (Science Research Associates, Inc.)
927 Woodrow Avenue
North Canton, OH 44720

Stone Software
7910 Ivanhoe Avenue, Suite 319
La Jolla, CA 92037

Sunburst Communications Inc.
39 Washington Avenue, Room YB7
Pleasantville, NY 10570

SVE (Society for Visual Education)
1345 Diversey Parkway, Dept. 106-FD
Chicago, IL 60614

Tandy Corporation/Radio Shack
1800 One Tandy Center
Fort Worth, TX 76102

TCS/Houghton Mifflin Company
One Beacon Street
Boston, MA 02108

Teaching Tools
P.O. Box 12679
Research Triangle Park, NC 27709

TEKSYM
145404 County Road 15
Minneapolis, MN 55441

Triton Products Co. (has assumed marketing
of all TI software)
P.O. Box 8123
San Francisco, CA 94128

The 22nd Avenue Workshop
P.O. Box 3425
Eugene, OR 97403

Universal Systems for Education, Inc.
2120 Academy Circle, Suite E
Colorado Springs, CO 80909

Weekly Reader Family Software
Xerox Educational Publications
245 Long Hill Road
Middletown, CT 06457

World Book Discovery Electronic Products
Merchandise Mart Plaza, 5th Floor
Mail Station 13
Chicago, IL 60654

Bibliography

Aaron, R. L., & Anderson, M. K. (1981). A comparison of values expressed in juvenile magazines and basal reader series. *The Reading Teacher, 35,* 305–313.

ACLD Newsbriefs, 58. (1985, January/February).

Allington, R. (1978, March). Are good and poor readers taught differently? Is that why poor readers are poor readers? Paper presented at the annual meeting of the American Educational Research Association, Toronto.

Anderson, R. C., & Freebody, P. (1981). Vocabulary knowledge. In J. T. Guthrie (Ed.), *Comprehension and teaching: Research perspectives.* Newark, Del.: International Reading Association.

Anglin, L., Goldman, R., & Anglin, J. (1982). *Teaching: What is it all about?* New York: Harper & Row.

Arbuthnot, M. H. (1968). In S. Sebesta (Ed.), *Ivory, apes, and peacocks: The literature point of view.* Newark, Del.: International Reading Association.

Armbruster, B. B., & Anderson, T. H. (1981). *Content area textbooks.* Reading Education Report No. 23. Urbana: University of Illinois Center for the Study of Reading.

Artley, A. S. (1975). Words, words, words. *Language Arts, 52,* 1067–1072.

Artley, A. S. (1980). Reading: Skills or competencies? *Language Arts, 57,* 546–549.

Ashton-Warner, S. (1959). *Spinster.* New York: Simon & Schuster.

Ashton-Warner, S. (1963). *Teacher.* New York: Simon & Schuster.

Ashton-Warner, S. (1972). *Spearpoint: Teachers in America.* New York: Knopf.

Atkinson, R. C. (1975). Mnemotechnics in second-language learning. *American Psychologist, 30,* 821–828.

Atwell, N. (1985). Everyone sits at a big desk: Discovering topics for writing. *English Journal, 74,* 35–39.

Aukerman, R. C. (1981). *The basal reader approach to reading.* New York: Wiley.

Aulls, M. W. (1978). *Developmental and remedial reading in the middle grades.* Boston: Allyn & Bacon.

Aulls, M. W. (1982). *Developing readers in today's elementary school.* Boston: Allyn & Bacon.

Ausubel, D. P. (1968). *Educational psychology: A cognitive view.* New York: Holt, Rinehart & Winston.

Ausubel, D. P., Novak, J. D., & Hanesian, H. (1978). *Educational psychology: A cognitive view.* 2nd ed. New York: Holt, Rinehart & Winston.

Bagford, J. (1981). Evaluating teachers on reading instruction. *The Reading Teacher, 34,* 400–404.

Baker, R. (1979). A publisher views the development and selection of reading programs. In T. Hatcher & L. Erickson (Eds.), *Indoctrinate or Educate*. Newark, Del.: International Reading Association.

Balajthy, E. (1986). *Microcomputers in reading and language arts*. Englewood Cliffs, N.J.: Prentice-Hall.

Barnitz, J. G. (1980). Black English and other dialects: Sociolinguistic implications for reading instruction. *The Reading Teacher, 33,* 779–786.

Barnitz, J. G. (1982). Orthographies, bilingualism and learning to read English as a second language. *The Reading Teacher, 35,* 560–567.

Barron, R. (1968). The use of vocabulary as an advance organizer. In H. Herber & P. Sanders (Eds.), *Research in reading in the content areas: First report*. Syracuse, N.Y.: Syracuse University Reading and Language Arts Center.

Barron, R., & Earle, R. (1973). An approach for vocabulary development. In H. Herber & R. Barron (Eds.), *Research in reading in the content areas: Second report*. Syracuse, N.Y.: Syracuse University Reading and Language Arts Center.

Baumann, J., & Stevenson, J. (1982). Using scores from standardized reading achievement tests. *The Reading Teacher, 35,* 528–532.

Beck, I. L., & McKeown, M. G. (1983). Learning words well: A program to enhance vocabulary and comprehension. *The Reading Teacher, 36,* 622–625.

Beck, I. L., McKeown, M. G., McCaslin, E., & Burket, A. (1979). *Instructional dimensions that may affect reading comprehension: Examples of two commercial reading programs*. Pittsburgh: University of Pittsburgh Language Research and Development Center.

Beck, I. L., Perfetti, C. A., & McKeown, M. G. (1982). Effects of long-term vocabulary instruction on lexical access and reading comprehension. *Journal of Educational Psychology, 74,* 506–521.

Becoming a nation of readers: The report of the commission on reading (1985). Washington, D.C.: National Institute of Education.

Benton, M. (1984). The methodology vacuum in teaching literature. *Language Arts, 61,* 265–275.

Berliner, D. C. (1981). Academic learning time and reading achievement. In J. Guthrie (Ed.), *Comprehension and teaching: Research reviews*. Newark, Del.: International Reading Association.

Betts, E. A. (1946). *Foundations of reading instruction*. New York: American Book Company.

Bingham, A. (1982). Using writing folders to document student progress. In T. Newkirk & N. Atwell (Eds.), *Understanding writing: Ways of observing, learning and teaching*. Chelmsford, Mass.: Northeast Regional Exchange.

Bissex, G. L. (1980). *Gnys at wrk: A child learns to write and read*. Cambridge: Harvard University Press.

Bloom, B. (1956). *Taxonomy of educational objectives: Cognitive domain*. New York: McKay.

Bloomfield, L., & Barnhart, C. (1961). *Let's read*. New York: Holt, Rinehart & Winston.

Blume, J. (1970). *Are you there, God? It's me, Margaret*. New York: Dell.

Bonds, C. W., & Bonds, L. T. (1983). Reading and the gifted student. *Roper Review, 5,* 4–6.

Boothby, P. R. (1980). Creative and critical reading for the gifted. *The Reading Teacher, 33,* 674–676.

Bransford, J. D., & Johnson, M. K. (1973). Considerations of some problems of comprehension. In W. C. Chase (Ed.), *Visual information processing*. New York: Academic.

Bright ideas (1984). Kent, Ohio: Writing Process Demonstration Project, Kent State University.

Britton, J. N., Burgess, T., Martin, N., McLeod, A., & Rosen, H. (1975). *The development of writing abilities (11-18)*. London: Macmillan Education.

Brophy, J. (1982). Classroom management and learning. *American Education, 18,* 20–23.

Bruckerhoff, C. (1977). What do students say about reading instruction? *The Clearing House, 51,* 103–107.

Bruner, J., Goodnow, J. J., & Austin, G. A. (1977). *A study of thinking.* New York: Science Editions.

Brutton, D. (1974). How to develop and maintain student interest in reading. *English Journal, 63,* 74–77.

Bryen, D. M., Hartman, C., & Tait, P. (1978). *Variant English.* Columbus, Ohio: Merrill.

Burnett, J. D., & Miller, L. (1984). Computer-assisted learning and reading: Developing the product or fostering the process? *Computer Education, 8,* 134–150.

Calkins, L. M. (1983). *Lessons from a child.* Portsmouth, N.H.: Heinemann Educational Books.

Calkins, L. M. (1986). *The art of teaching writing.* Portsmouth, N.H.: Heinemann Educational Books.

Carr, K. S. (1984). What gifted readers need from reading instruction. *The Reading Teacher, 38,* 144–146.

Cassidy, J. (1979, January). What about the talented reader? *Teacher,* 76–80.

Cassidy, J. (1981). Inquiry reading for the gifted. *The Reading Teacher, 35,* 17–21.

Cassidy, J., & Vukelich, C. (1980). Do the gifted read early? *The Reading Teacher, 33,* 578–582.

Cazden, C. (1972). *Child language and education.* New York: Holt, Rinehart & Winston.

Chall, J. S. (1958). *Readability: An appraisal of research and application.* Columbus: Ohio State University Bureau of Educational Research.

Chall, J. S. (1967). *Learning to read: The great debate.* New York: McGraw-Hill.

Chaplin, M. T. (1982). No more reading "reading." *Reading World, 21,* 340–346.

Chenfield, M. (1978). *Teaching language arts creatively.* New York: Harcourt Brace Jovanovich.

Chomsky, C. (1970). Reading, writing, and phonology. *Harvard Educational Review, 40,* 287–309.

Chomsky, C. (1976). After decoding: What? *Language Arts, 53,* 288–296, 314.

Chomsky, C. (1979). Approaching reading through invented spelling. In L. B. Resnick & P. A. Weaver (Eds.), *Theory and practice of early reading,* Vol. 2. Hillsdale, N.Y.: Erlbaum.

Chow, L. T. (1969). What teachers read to pupils in the middle grades. Ph.D. diss., Ohio State University.

Clark, M. M. (1976). *Young fluent readers.* London: Heinemann Educational Books.

Clay, M. M. (1979a). *Concepts about print test.* Portsmouth, N.H.: Heinemann Educational Books.

Clay, M. M. (1979b). *Reading: The patterning of complex behavior.* 2nd ed. Auckland, New Zealand: Heinemann Educational Books.

Clements, D. H. (1984–85). Supporting young children's Logo programming. *The Computing Teacher, 11,* 24–30.

Clements, D. H. (1985). *Computers in early and primary education.* Englewood Cliffs, N.J.: Prentice-Hall.

Cohen, D. (1968). The effect of literature on vocabulary and reading achievement. *Elementary English, 45,* 209–213, 217.

Coody, B., & Nelson, D. (1982). *Teaching elementary language arts.* Belmont, Calif.: Wadsworth.

Cramer, R. L. (1975). Reading to children: Why and how. *The Reading Teacher, 28,* 460–463.

Cramer, R. L. (1978). *Children's writing and language growth.* Columbus, Ohio: Merrill.

Criscuolo, N. P. (1977). Book reports: Twelve creative alternatives. *The Reading Teacher, 30,* 893–895.

Criscuolo, N. P. (1979). Twenty-five ways to motivate the reluctant reader. *School and Community, 65,* 13–16.

Criscuolo, N. P. (1981). Creative homework with the newspaper. *The Reading Teacher, 34,* 921–922.

Cunningham, J. W. (1979). An automatic pilot for decoding. *The Reading Teacher, 32,* 420–424.

Cunningham, P. (1975–76). Investigating a synthesized theory of mediated word recognition. *Reading Research Quarterly, 11,* 127–143.

Cunningham, P. (1981). A teacher's guide to materials shopping. *The Reading Teacher, 35,* 180–184.

Cunningham, R. T. (1971). Developing question-asking skills. In J. Weigand (Ed.), *Developing teacher competencies.* Englewood Cliffs, N.J.: Prentice-Hall.

Dale, E. (1969). *Audiovisual methods in teaching.* 3rd ed. New York: Holt, Rinehart & Winston.

Dale, P. S. (1972). *Language development.* Hinsdale, Ill.: Dryden.

Davis, D. C. (1973). *Playway: Education for reality.* Minneapolis: Winston.

Davis, F. B. (1944). Fundamental factors of comprehension in reading. *Psychometrika, 9,* 185–197.

Davison, M. M. (1983). Classroom bibliotherapy: Why and how. *Reading World, 22,* 103–107.

Degler, L. S. (1978). Using the newspaper to develop comprehension skills. *Journal of Reading, 21,* 339–342.

DeHaven, E. P. (1983). *Teaching and learning the language arts.* 2nd ed. Boston: Little, Brown.

Deighton, L. (1970). *Vocabulary development in the classroom.* New York: Teachers College Press.

Dillon, J. T. (1983). *Teaching and the art of questioning.* Bloomington, Ind.: Phi Delta Kappa Educational Foundation.

Downing, J. (1979). *Reading and reasoning.* New York: Springer-Verlag.

Downing, J., (1982). Reading: Skill or skills? *Reading Teacher, 35,* 534–537.

Downing, J., Ayers, D., & Shaefer, B. (1982). *Linguistic awareness in reading readiness (LARR) test.* Slough, Berks.: NFER-Nelson.

Dryer, S. S. (1981). *The book finder: A guide to children's literature about the needs and problems of youth, ages 2-15.* Vol. 2. Circle Pines, Minn.: American Guidance Service.

Duffelmeyer, F. (1980). The influence of experience-based instruction in learning word meanings. *Journal of Reading, 24,* 35–40.

Dupuis, M. M., & Snyder, S. L. (1983). Develop concepts through vocabulary: A strategy for reading specialists to use with content teachers. *Journal of Reading, 26,* 297–305.

Durkin, D. (1966). *Children who read early.* New York: Teachers College Press.

Durkin, D. (1978–79). What classroom observations reveal about reading comprehension instruction. *Reading Research Quarterly, 14,* 481–538.

Durkin, D. (1980). *Teaching young children to read.* 3rd ed. Boston: Allyn & Bacon.

Durrell, D. D. (1958). Success in first-grade reading. *Journal of Education,* 1–8.

Earle, R. (1976). *Teaching reading and mathematics.* Newark, Del.: International Reading Association.

Edmunds, R. (1979). Effective schools for the urban poor. *Educational Leadership, 36,* 15–27.

Elbow, P. (1973). *Writing without teachers.* New York: Oxford University Press.

Elkind, D. (1981). *The hurried child: Growing up too fast, too soon.* Reading, Mass.: Addison-Wesley.

Elkonin, D. B. (1973). Methods of teaching reading: USSR. In J. Downing (Ed.), *Comparative reading: Cross-national studies of behavior and processes in reading and writing.* New York: Macmillan.

Elley, W., & Mangubhai, F. (1983). The impact of reading on second-language learning. *Reading Research Quarterly, 19,* 53–67.

Emberley, E. (1977). *The great thumbprint drawing book.* Boston: Little, Brown.

Emmer, E. T., & Evertson, C. M. (1981). Synthesis of research on classroom management. *Educational Leadership, 38,* 342–347.

Estes, T. H., & Johnstone, J. (1977). Twelve easy ways to make readers hate reading (and one difficult way to make them love it). *Language Arts, 54,* 891–897.

Estes, T. H., & Vaughan, J. L., Jr. (1973). Reading interest and comprehension: Implications. *The Reading Teacher, 27,* 149–152.

Estes, T. H., & Vaughan, J. L., Jr. (1985). *Reading and learning in the content classroom.* 2nd ed. Boston: Allyn & Bacon.

Farr, R., & Carey, F. (1986). *Reading: What can be measured?* 2nd ed. Newark, Del.: International Reading Association.

Farr, R., & Rosner, N. (1979). *Teaching a child to read.* New York: Harcourt Brace Jovanovich.

Feeley, J. (1974). Television and reading in the seventies. Paper presented at the annual meeting of the International Reading Association, New Orleans.

Fitzgerald, G. G. (1979). Why kids can read the book but not the workbook. *The Reading Teacher, 32,* 930–932.

Fowler, G. L. (1982). Developing comprehension skills in primary students through the use of story frames. *The Reading Teacher, 36,* 176–179.

Freedman, G., & Reynolds, E. G. (1980). Enriching basal reader lessons with semantic webbing. *The Reading Teacher, 33,* 677–684.

Fry, E. B. (1968). A readability formula that saves time. *Journal of Reading, 11,* 513–516, 575–578.

Fry, E. B. (1977). Fry's readability graph: Clarifications, validity and extension to level 17. *Journal of Reading, 21,* 242–252.

Fry, E. B. (1980). The new instant word list. *The Reading Teacher, 34,* 284–290.

Gagné, R. M. (1977). *The conditions of learning.* 3rd ed. New York: Holt, Rinehart & Winston.

Gambrell, L. B. (1985). Dialogue journals: Reading-writing interactions. *The Reading Teacher, 38,* 512–515.

Gans, R. (1963). *Common sense in teaching reading.* New York: Bobbs-Merrill.

Gensley, J. (1975). Let's teach the gifted to read. *The Gifted Child Quarterly, 19,* 21–22.

Gentry, J. R., & Henderson, E. H. (1980). Three steps to teaching beginning readers to spell. In E. H. Henderson & J. W. Beers (Eds.), *Developmental aspects of learning to spell: A reflection of word knowledge.* Newark, Del.: International Reading Association.

Gillet, J., & Kita, M. J. (1979). Words, kids and categories. *The Reading Teacher, 32,* 538–542.

Gillet, J., & Temple, C. (1986). *Understanding reading problems.* 2nd ed. Boston: Little, Brown.

Gipe, J. P. (1980). Use of relevant context helps kids learn new word meanings. *The Reading Teacher, 33*, 398–402.

Goff, B. (1969). *Where is Daddy? The story of divorce*. Boston: Beacon.

Gonzales, P. C. (1980). What's wrong with the basal reader approach to language development? *The Reading Teacher, 33*, 668–673.

Good, T. (1982). How teachers' expectations affect results. *American Education, 18*, 25–32.

Goodlad, J. (1983). A study of schooling: Some findings and hypotheses. *Phi Delta Kappan, 64*, 465–470.

Goodman, K. S. (1973a). *Miscue analysis: Application to reading instruction*. Urbana, Ill.: National Council of Teachers of English.

Goodman, K. S. (1973b). Psycholinguistic universals in the reading process. In F. Smith (Ed.), *Psycholinguistics and reading*. New York: Holt, Rinehart & Winston.

Goodman, K. S. (1975). Do you have to be smart to read? Do you have to read to be smart? *The Reading Teacher, 28*, 625–632.

Goodman, K. S. (1986a). Basal readers: A call for action. *Language Arts, 63*, 358–363.

Goodman, K. S. (1986b). *What's whole in whole language?* Ontario: Scholastic-TAB.

Goodman, K. S., & Buck, C. (1973). Dialect barriers to reading comprehension revisited. *The Reading Teacher, 22*, 6–12.

Goodman, Y. M. (1978). Kid-watching: An alternative to testing. *National Elementary Principal, 10*, 41–45.

Goodman, Y. M., & Burke, C. L. (1972). *Reading miscue inventory manual: Procedure for diagnosis and evaluation*. New York: Macmillan.

Gordon, C. J., & Braun, C. (1983). Using story schemata as an aid to reading and writing. *The Reading Teacher, 37*, 116–121.

Gough, P. B. (1972). One second of reading. In J. F. Kavanaugh & I. G. Mattingly (Eds.), *Language by eye and ear*. Cambridge: MIT Press.

Gove, M. K. (1981). The influence of teachers' conceptual frameworks of reading on their instructional decision making. Ph.D. diss., Kent State University.

Granger, R. C. (1976). The nonstandard speaking child: Myths past and present. *Young Children, 31*, 479–485.

Graves, D. (1975). An examination of the writing processes of seven-year-old children. *Research in the Teaching of English, 91*, 227–241.

Graves, D. (1979). Research update: What children show us about revision. *Language Arts, 56*, 312–319.

Graves, D. (1982). *Writing: Teachers and children at work*. Portsmouth, N.H.: Heinemann Educational Books.

Gruenberg, R. (1948). Poor Mr. Fingle. In *More favorite stories*. New York: Doubleday.

Guilford, J. P. (1956). The structure of intellect. *Psychological Bulletin, 53*, 267–293.

Guthrie, J. T. (1982). Effective teaching practices. *The Reading Teacher, 35*, 766–768.

Halliday, M. A. K. (1975). Learning how to mean: Exploration in the development of language. London: Arnold.

Hansen, J. (1981). An inferential comprehension strategy for use with primary children. *The Reading Teacher, 34*, 665–669.

Harman, S. (1982). Are reversals a symptom of dyslexia? *The Reading Teacher, 35*, 424–428.

Harris, A. J. (1980). An overview of reading disabilities and learning disabilities in the U.S. *The Reading Teacher, 33*, 420–425.

Harris, L. A., & Smith, C. B. (1980). *Reading instruction: Diagnostic teaching in the classroom*. 3rd ed. New York: Holt, Rinehart & Winston.

Harste, J. C., & Burke, C. L. (1977). A new hypothesis for reading teacher research. In P. D. Pearson & J. Hansen (Eds.), *Reading: Theory, research and practice*. Clemson, S.C.: National Reading Conference.

Harste, J. C., Burke, C. L., & Woodward, V. A. (1982). Children's language and world: Initial encounters with print. In J. Langer & M. Smith-Burke (Eds.), *Bridging the gap: Reader meets author*. Newark, Del.: International Reading Association.

Heathington, B. S., & Alexander, J. E. (1984). Do classroom teachers emphasize attitudes toward reading? *The Reading Teacher*, *37*, 484–488.

Heilman, A. W. (1977). *Phonics in proper perspective*. 3rd ed. Columbus, Ohio: Merrill.

Heilman, A. W., Blair, T. R., & Rupley, W. H. (1986). *Principles and practices of teaching reading*. 6th ed. Columbus, Ohio: Merrill.

Heimberger, M. J. (1980). *Teaching the gifted and talented in the elementary classroom*. Washington, D.C.: National Education Association.

Henderson, E. H., & Beer, J. W. (Eds.) (1980). *Developmental and cognitive aspects of learning to spell: A reflection of word knowledge*. Newark, Del.: International Reading Association.

Henk, W. A. (1985). Assessing children's reading abilities. In L. W. Searfoss & J. E. Readence (Eds.), *Helping children learn to read*. Englewood Cliffs, N.J.: Prentice-Hall.

Henry, G. (1974). *Teaching reading as concept development*. Newark, Del.: International Reading Association.

Hepler, S. I. (1982). Patterns of response to literature: A one-year study of a fifth- and sixth-grade classroom. Ph.D. diss., Ohio State University.

Hepler, S. I., & Hickman, J. (1982). The book was okay. I love you—Social aspects of response to literature. *Theory into Practice*, *21*, 278–283.

Herber, H. L. (1978). *Teaching reading in content areas*. 2nd ed. Englewood Cliffs, N.J.: Prentice-Hall.

Herber, H. L., & Nelson, J. (1975). Questioning is not the answer. *Journal of Reading*, *18*, 512–517.

Hickman, J. (1983). Classrooms that help children like books. In N. Roser & M. Frith (Eds.), *Children's choices*. Newark, Del.: International Reading Association.

Hittleman, D. (1973). Seeking a psycholinguistic definition of readability. *The Reading Teacher*, *26*, 783–789.

Holdaway, D. (1972). *Independence in reading*. Sydney: Ashton Scholastic.

Holdaway, D. (1979). *The foundations of literacy*. Portsmouth, N.H.: Heinemann Educational Books.

Holdaway, D. (1982). Shared book experience: Teaching reading using favorite books. *Theory into Practice*, *23*, 293–300.

Hong, L. K. (1981). Modifying SSR for beginning readers. *The Reading Teacher*, *34*, 888–891.

Hoskisson, K. (1975). The many facets of assisted reading. *Elementary English*, *52*, 312–315.

Hough, R. A., Nurss, J. R., & Enright, D. S. (1986). Story reading with limited English speaking children in the regular classroom. *The Reading Teacher*, *39*, 510–514.

Hunt, L. C. (1970). Effect of self-selection, interest, and motivation upon independent, instructional, and frustrational levels. *The Reading Teacher*, *24*, 146–151.

Hunter, E. (1977). Changing the dynamics of the classroom. *Theory into Practice*, *16*, 290–295.

Hymes, D. (1974). *Foundations in sociolinguistics: An ethnographic approach*. Philadelphia: University of Pennsylvania Press.

Hymes, J. L. (1958). *Before the child reads.* Evanston, Ill.: Row, Peterson.

Ignoffo, M. (1980). The thread of thought: Analogies as a vocabulary building method. *Journal of Reading, 23,* 519–521.

Irwin, J. W., & Davis, C. A. (1980). Assessing readability: The checklist approach. *Journal of Reading, 24,* 124–130.

Jacobson, M. L., & Freeman, E. B. (1981). A comparison of language use in basal readers and adolescent novels. *Reading World, 21,* 50–58.

Jaramillo, M. L. (1973). Cultural differences in the ESOL classroom. *TESOL Quarterly, 7,* 51–60.

Johns, J. L. (1985). *Basic reading inventory.* 3rd ed. Dubuque, Iowa: Kendall-Hunt.

Johnson, B., & Lehnert, L. (1984). Learning phonics naturally: A model for instruction. *Reading Horizons, 24,* 90–98.

Johnson, D. D., & Pearson, P. D. (1978). *Teaching reading vocabulary.* New York: Holt, Rinehart & Winston.

Judd, H., & Walker, J. E. (1982). Use of the microcomputer to enhance the language experience approach to teaching reading. *Ohio Reading Teacher, 17,* 11–13.

Kamil, M. L., & Pearson, P. D. (1979). Theory and practice in teaching reading. *New York University Education Quarterly,* 10–16.

Kaplan, E. M., & Tuckman, A. (1980). Vocabulary strategies belong in the hands of learners. *Journal of Reading, 24,* 32–34.

Kelly, L., & Vergason, G. (1978). *Dictionary of special education and rehabilitation.* Denver: Love.

Kirby, D., & Liner, T. (1981). *Inside out: Developmental strategies for teaching writing.* Montclair, N.J.: Boynton/Cook.

Kirk, S. A., Kliebhan, J. M., & Lerner, J. W. (1978). *Teaching reading to slow and disabled learners.* Boston: Houghton Mifflin.

Klein, M. L. (1985). *The development of writing in children: Pre-K through grade 8.* Englewood Cliffs, N.J.: Prentice-Hall.

Kohl, H. (1969). *The open classroom: Teaching in elementary schools.* West Nyack, N.Y.: Parker.

Kounin, J. (1970). *Discipline and group management in classrooms.* New York: Holt, Rinehart & Winston.

Kraus, C. (1983). The influence of first-grade teachers' conceptual frameworks of reading on their students' perceptions of reading and reading behavior. Ph.D. diss., Kent State University.

Laberge, D., & Samuels, S. J. (1976). Toward a theory of automatic information processing in reading. In H. Singer & R. Ruddell (Eds.), *Theoretical models and processes of reading.* 2nd ed. Newark, Del.: International Reading Association.

Labov, W. (1970). *The study of nonstandard English.* Urbana, Ill.: National Council of Teachers of English.

Labuda, M., & James, H. J. (1985). Fostering creativity in children who differ. In M. Labuda (Ed.), *Creative reading for gifted learners.* 2nd ed. Newark, Del.: International Reading Association.

Lamme, L. L. (1984). *Growing up writing.* Washington, D.C.: Acropolis.

Lang, H. (1983). Selecting trade books with children. In N. Roser and M. Frith (Eds.), *Children's choices.* Newark, Del.: International Reading Association.

Lass, B. (1982). Portrait of my son as an early reader. *The Reading Teacher, 36,* 20–29.

Lass, B. (1983). Portrait of my son as an early reader II. *The Reading Teacher, 36,* 508–517.

Lauritzen, C. (1982). A modification of repeated readings for group instruction. *The Reading Teacher, 35,* 456–458.

Levin, J. A. (1982). Microcomputer communication networks for education. *The Quarterly Newsletter of the Laboratory of Comparative Human Cognition, 4.*

Levine, S. G. (1984). USSR: A necessary component in teaching reading. *Journal of Reading, 27,* 394–400.

Liberman, I. Y., Shankweiler, D., Fisher, F. W., & Carter, B. (1974). Explicit syllable and phoneme segmentation in the young child. *The Journal of Experimental Child Psychology, 18,* 201–212.

Liberman, I. Y., Shankweiler, D., Liberman, A., Fowler, C., & Fischer, F. (1977). Phonetic segmentation and recoding in the beginning reader. In A. Reber & D. Scarborough (Eds.), *Toward a psychology of reading.* Hillsdale, N.J.: Erlbaum.

Lindemann, E. (1982). *A rhetoric for writing teachers.* New York: Oxford University Press.

Lukasevich, A. (1983). Three dozen useful information sources on reading for the gifted. *The Reading Teacher, 36,* 542–548.

Lundsteen, S. (1976). *Children learn to communicate.* Englewood Cliffs, N.J.: Prentice-Hall.

Luria, A. (1977). The development of writing in the child. *Soviet Psychology, 16,* 65–113.

Macdonald, J. B. (1966). Individual versus group instruction in first-grade reading. *The Reading Teacher, 19,* 643–647.

MacGinitie, W. H. (1976). When should we begin to teach reading? *Language Arts, 53,* 878–882.

Macrorie, K. (1970). *Uptaught.* Rochelle Park, N.J.: Hayden.

Mandler, J., and Johnson, N. (1977). Remembrance of things parsed: Story structure and recall. *Cognitive Psychology, 9,* 111–151.

Mangieri, J. M. (1980). Characteristics of an effectively organized classroom. In D. Lapp (Ed.), *Making reading possible through effective classroom management.* Newark, Del.: International Reading Association.

Manzo, A. V. (1969). The request procedure. *Journal of Reading, 11,* 123–126.

Manzo, A. V. (1981). Subjective approach to vocabulary acquisition. *Reading Psychology, 2,* 1–6.

Manzo, A. V., & Shirk, J. K. (1972). Some generalizations and strategies for guiding vocabulary learning. *Journal of Reading Behavior, 4,* 78–89.

Marchbanks, G., & Levin, H. (1965). Cues by which children recognize words. *Journal of Educational Psychology, 56,* 57–61.

Maring, G. H., Furman, G. C., & Blum-Anderson, J. (1985). Five cooperative learning strategies for mainstreamed youngsters in content area classrooms. *The Reading Teacher, 39,* 310–313.

Marliave, R. N., Fisher, C. W., & Filby, N. N. (1977, April). Alternative procedures for collecting instructional time data. Paper presented at the annual meeting of the American Educational Research Association, New York City.

Mason, G. E., Blanchard, J. S., & Daniel, D. B. (1983). *Computer applications in reading.* 2nd ed. Newark, Del.: International Reading Association.

Mavrogenes, N. A., & Galen, N. D. (1979). Cross-age tutoring: Why and how. *Journal of Reading, 22,* 344–353.

McCracken, R. A. (1971). Initiating sustained silent reading. *Journal of Reading, 14,* 521–524, 582–583.

McCracken, R. A., & McCracken, M. J. (1978). Modeling is the key to sustained reading. *The Reading Teacher, 31,* 406–408.

McDaniel, T. R. (1981). Exploring alternatives to punishment: The keys to effective discipline. In S. Elam (Ed.), *Cream of the Kappan*. Bloomington, Ind.: Phi Delta Kappa Educational Foundation.

McDonald, F. J. (1965). *Educational psychology*. Belmont, Calif.: Wadsworth.

McDonnell, G. M., & Osburn, E. B. (1978). New thoughts about reading readiness. *Language Arts, 55,* 26–29.

McLeod, B. (1976). The relevance of anthropology to language teaching. *TESOL Quarterly, 10,* 211–219.

McNeil, J. D. (1974). False prerequisites in the teaching of reading. *Journal of Reading Behavior, 6,* 421–427.

Meyer, B. J. F. (1975). *The organization of prose and its effect on memory*. Amsterdam: North-Holland.

Meyer, B. J. F., Brandt, D., & Bluth, G. (1979). Use of top-level structure in text: Key for reading comprehension of ninth-grade students. *Reading Research Quarterly, 16,* 72–103.

Moffett, J. (1975). An interview with James Moffett. *Media and Methods, 15,* 20–24.

Moldofsky, P. B. (1983). Teaching students to determine the central story problem: A practical application of schema theory. *The Reading Teacher, 36,* 740–745.

Moller, B. (1984). An instructional model for gifted advanced readers. *Journal of Reading, 27,* 324–327.

Morphett, M. V., & Washburne, C. (1931). When should children begin to read? *Elementary School Journal, 31,* 496–503.

Morris, D., & Perney, J. (1984). Developmental spelling as a predictor of first-grade reading achievement. *The Elementary School Journal, 84,* 441–457.

Morrow, L. M. (1982). Relationships between literature programs, library corner designs and children's use of literature. *Journal of Educational Research, 75,* 339–344.

Mossburg, J. (1982a). First-grade teachers love their reading workbooks. *The Reading Teacher, 35,* 842–843.

Mossburg, J. (1982b). The gingerbread man: A lesson that smells of success. *Ohio Reading Teacher, 17,* 30–32.

Murray, D. M. (1985). *A writer teaches writing*. 2nd ed. Boston: Houghton Mifflin.

Neisser, U. (1976). *Cognition and reality: Principles and implications of cognitive psychology*. San Francisco: Freeman.

Nelson, J. (1978). Readability: Some cautions for the content area teacher. *Journal of Reading, 21,* 620–625.

Neuman, S. B. (1982). Television viewing and leisure reading: A qualitative analysis. *Journal of Educational Research, 75,* 299–304.

Niles, O. (1965). Organization perceived. In H. Herber (Ed.), *Developing study skills in secondary schools*. Newark, Del.: International Reading Association.

Nolte, R. Y., & Singer, H. (1985). Active comprehension: Teaching a process of reading comprehension and its effects on reading achievement. *The Reading Teacher, 39,* 24–28.

Norton, D. E. (1980). *The effective teaching of language arts*. Columbus, Ohio: Merrill.

Ohnmacht, D. C. (1969, April). The effects of letter knowledge on achievement in reading in the first grade. Paper presented at the annual meeting of the American Education Research Association, Los Angeles.

Olson, L. (1985, January 11). Programs for the gifted fragmented, inadequate, study says. *Education Week, 4,* 5.

Osborn, J. (1984). *Evaluating workbooks*. Reading Education Report No. 52. Urbana: University of Illinois Center for the Study of Reading.

Padak, N. D. (1981). The language and educational needs of children who speak Black English. *The Reading Teacher, 35,* 144–151.

Pany, D., & Jenkins, J. (1977). *Learning word meanings: A comparison of instructional procedures and effects on measures of reading comprehension with learning disabled students.* Technical Report No. 25. Urbana: University of Illinois Center for the Study of Reading.

Pearson, P. D. (1982). *Asking questions about stories.* Columbus, Ohio: Ginn.

Pearson, P. D., & Johnson, D. (1978). *Teaching reading comprehension.* New York: Holt, Rinehart & Winston.

Pellegrini, A. D., & Galda, L. (1982). Effects of thematic-fantasy play training on the development of children's story comprehension. *American Educational Research Journal, 19,* 443–452.

Peterson, P. (1979). Direct instruction: Effective for what and for whom? *Educational Leadership, 36,* 46–48.

Piaget, J. (1973). *The language and thought of the child.* New York: World.

Pieronek, F. T. (1980). Do basal readers reflect the interests of intermediate students? *The Reading Teacher, 33,* 408–412.

Pikulski, J. (1978). Readiness for reading: A practical approach. *Language Arts, 55,* 192–197.

Pressley, M., Levin, J. R., & Miller, G. E. (1981). How does the keyword method affect vocabulary comprehension and usage? *Reading Research Quarterly, 16,* 213–226.

Protheroe, D. (1979). Gi-Go: The content of content area reading. In R. T. Vacca & J. A. Meagher (Eds.), *Reading through content.* Storrs: University Publications and the University of Connecticut Reading-Language Arts Center.

Quandt, I. (1972). *Self-concept and reading.* Newark, Del.: International Reading Association.

Raphael, T. E. (1982). Question-answering strategies for children. *The Reading Teacher, 36,* 186–191.

Raphael, T. E. (1986). Teaching question-answer relationships, revisited. *The Reading Teacher, 39,* 516–622.

Read, C. (1971). Preschool children's knowledge of English phonology. *Harvard Educational Review, 41,* 1–34.

Read, C. (1975). *Children's categorization of speech sounds in English.* Urbana, Ill.: National Council of Teachers of English.

Reid, D., Hresko, W., & Hammill, D. (1981). *Test of early reading ability.* Chicago: Stoelting.

Riedesel, C. A., & Clements, D. H. (1985). *Coping with computers in the elementary and middle school.* Englewood Cliffs, N.J.: Prentice-Hall.

Rose, K. (1982). *Teaching language arts to children.* New York: Harcourt Brace Jovanovich.

Rosegrant, T. J. (1986a). Using the microcomputer as a scaffold for assisting beginning readers and writers. In J. Hoot (Ed.), *Computers in early childhood education: Issues and practices.* Englewood Cliffs, N.J.: Prentice-Hall.

Rosegrant, T. J. (1986b, April). Adult-child communication in writing. Paper presented at the annual meeting of the American Education Research Association, San Francisco.

Rosenblatt, L. (1982). The literary transaction: Evocation and response. *Theory into Practice, 21,* 268–277.

Rubin, A. (1982). The computer confronts language arts: Cans and shoulds for education. In A. C. Wilkinson (Ed.), *Classroom computers and cognitive science.* New York: Academic.

Rudman, M. K. (1976). *Children's literature: An issues approach.* Lexington, Mass.: Heath.

Rumelhart, D. E. (1975). *Toward an interactive model of reading.* Technical Report No. 46. San Diego: Center for Human Information Processing.

Rumelhart, D. E. (1982). Schemata: The building blocks of cognition. In J. Guthrie (Ed.), *Comprehension and teaching: Research reviews*. Newark, Del.: International Reading Association.

Rupley, W. H., Garcia, J., & Longnion, B. (1981). Sex role portrayal in reading materials: Implications for the 1980s. *The Reading Teacher, 34*, 786–791.

Samuels, S. J. (1972). The effect of letter-name knowledge on learning to read. *American Educational Research Journal, 1*, 65–74.

Samuels, S. J. (1976). Hierarchical subskills in the reading acquisition process. In J. T. Guthrie (Ed.), *Aspects of reading acquisition*. Baltimore, Md.: Johns Hopkins University Press.

Samuels, S. J. (1979). Method of repeated readings. *The Reading Teacher, 32*, 403–408.

Samuels, S. J. (1981). Characteristics of exemplary reading programs. In J. Guthrie (Ed.), *Comprehension and teaching: Research reviews*. Newark, Del.: International Reading Association.

Sanacore, J. (1981). Guidelines for observing remedial reading lessons. *The Reading Teacher, 34*, 394–399.

Savage, J. F., & Mooney, J. F. (1979). *Teaching reading to children with special needs*. Boston: Allyn & Bacon.

Schacter, S. W. (1978). An investigation of the effects of vocabulary instruction and schemata orientation on reading comprehension. Ph.D. diss., University of Minnesota.

Schramm, W., Lyle, J., & Parker, E. (1961). *Television in the lives of our children*. Stanford: Stanford University Press.

Shields, C., & Vondrak, L. (1980). Good news about newspapers. *Journal of Reading, 24*, 259–260.

Shuman, R. B. (1982). Reading with a purpose: Strategies to interest reluctant readers. *Journal of Reading, 25*, 725–730.

Shuy, R. W. (1969). Some language and cultural differences in a theory of reading. In K. S. Goodman & J. T. Fleming (Eds.), *Psycholinguistics and the teaching of reading*. Newark, Del.: International Reading Association.

Sinatra, R. (1981). Using visuals to help the second-language learner. *The Reading Teacher, 34*, 539–546.

Singer, D., Singer, J., & Zuckerman, D. (1981). *Getting the most out of TV*. Santa Monica: Goodyear.

Singer, H. (1978). Active comprehension: From answering to asking questions. *The Reading Teacher, 31*, 901–908.

Singer, H., & Ruddell, R. (Eds.). (1985). *Theoretical models and processes of reading*. 3rd ed. Newark, Del.: International Reading Association.

Sirota, B. S. (1971). The effect of a planned literature program of daily oral reading by the teacher on the voluntary reading of fifth-grade children. Ph.D. diss., New York University.

Smith, F. (1976). Learning to read by reading. *Language Arts, 53*, 297–299, 322.

Smith, F. (1977). The uses of language. *Language Arts, 54*, 6, 638–644.

Smith, F. (1979). *Reading without nonsense*. New York: Teachers College Press.

Smith, L. B. (1982). Sixth graders write about reading literature. *Language Arts, 59*, 357–366.

Smith, N. B. (1965). *American reading instruction*. Newark, Del.: International Reading Association.

Smith, R. J., & Johnson, D. D. (1980). *Teaching children to read*. Reading, Mass.: Addison-Wesley.

Smith, S. (1979). *No easy answers: Teaching the learning disabled child.* Cambridge, Mass.: Winthrop.

Snyder, G. V. (1979). Do basal characters read in their daily lives? *The Reading Teacher, 33,* 303–306.

Snyder, G. V. (1981). Learner verification of reading games. *The Reading Teacher, 34,* 686–691.

Sowers, S. (1982). Six questions teachers ask about invented spelling. In T. Newkirk & N. Atwell (Eds.), *Understanding writing: Ways of observing, learning and teaching.* Chelmsford, Mass.: Northeast Regional Exchange.

Spache, G. (1974). *Good reading for poor readers.* Ill.: Garrard.

Spearitt, D. (1972). Identification of subskills in reading comprehension by maximum likelihood factor analysis. *Reading Research Quarterly, 8,* 92–111.

Spiegel, D. L. (1981a). *Reading for pleasure: Guidelines.* Newark, Del.: International Reading Association.

Spiegel, D. L. (1981b). Six alternatives to the directed reading activity. *The Reading Teacher, 34,* 914–922.

Squire, J. R. (1984). Composing and comprehending: Two sides of the same basic process. In J. M. Jensen (Ed.), *Composing and Comprehending.* Urbana, Ill.: National Conference on Research in English.

Stahl, D. K., & Anzalone, D. (1970). *Individualized teaching in elementary schools.* West Nyack, N.Y.: Parker.

Stahl, S. A. (1982). Differential word knowledge and reading comprehension. Ph.D. diss., Harvard University.

Stahl, S. A. (1983, October). Vocabulary instruction and the nature of word meanings. Paper presented at a meeting of the College Reading Association, Atlanta.

Stauffer, R. G. (1969). *Directing reading maturity as a cognitive process.* New York: Harper & Row.

Stauffer, R. G. (1970). *The language experience approach to the teaching of reading.* New York: Harper & Row.

Stauffer, R. G. (1975). *Directing the reading-thinking process.* New York: Harper & Row.

Stein, N., & Glenn, C. (1979). An analysis of story comprehension in elementary school children. In R. Freedle (Ed.), *New directions in discourse processing.* Norwood, N.J.: Ablex.

Stennett, R. G., Smythe, P. C., & Hardy, M. (1975). Hierarchical organization of reading subskills: Statistical approaches. *Journal of Reading Behavior, 7,* 223–228.

Stewig, J. W. (1980). *Read to write.* 2nd ed. New York: Holt, Rinehart & Winston.

Stoodt, B. (1981). *Reading instruction.* Boston: Houghton Mifflin.

Strang, R., McCollough, C. M., & Traxler, A. E. (1967). *The improvement of reading.* 4th ed. New York: McGraw-Hill.

Strategies for developing language programs for national origin minority students (1983). Columbus: Ohio Department of Education.

Strickland, R. (1962). *The language of elementary school children: Its relationship to the language of reading textbooks and the quality of reading of selected children.* Bloomington: Indiana University School of Education.

Sutherland, Z. (1976). *The Arbuthnot anthology of children's literature.* Chicago: Scott, Foresman.

Sutherland, Z. (Ed.) (1980). *The best in children's books: The University of Chicago guide to children's literature* (1973–78). Chicago: University of Chicago Press.

Swaby, B. (1983). *Teaching and learning reading.* Boston: Little, Brown.

Tabs, H. (1975). *Teacher's handbook for elementary social studies.* Reading, Mass.: Addison-Wesley.

Talmage, H., & Walberg, H. (1978). Naturalistic, decision-oriented evaluation of a district reading program. *Journal of Reading Behavior, 10*, 185–195.

Tanner, N. (1983). Phonics. In J. E. Alexander (Ed.), *Teaching reading*. 2nd ed. Boston: Little, Brown.

Taylor, N. E., & Vanter, J. (1978). Helping children discover the functions of written language. *Language Arts, 55*, 941–945.

Taylor, W. (1953). Cloze procedure: A new tool for measuring readability. *Journalism Quarterly, 30*, 415–433.

Tchudi, S., & Yates, J. (1983). *Teaching writing in content areas: Elementary school*. Washington, D.C.: National Education Association.

Teale, W. H. (1978). Positive environments for learning to read: What studies of early readers tell us. *Language Arts, 55*, 922–932.

Thomas, J. (1975). *Learning centers: Opening up the classroom*. Boston: Holbrook.

Thorndyke, P. (1977). Cognitive structures in comprehension and memory of narrative discourse. *Cognitive Psychology, 9*, 77–110.

Thurstone, L. L. (1946). A note on a reanalysis of Davis' reading tests. *Psychometrika, 11*, 185–188.

Tierney, R. J., Readence, J. E., & Dishner, E. K. (1985). *Reading strategies and practices*. 2nd ed. Boston: Allyn & Bacon.

Toch, T. (1984, February 8). The emerging politics of language. *Education Week, 3*, 20.

Torrey, J. W. (1969). Learning to read with a teacher: A case study. *Elementary English, 46*, 550–556, 658.

Trelease, J. (1985). *The read-aloud handbook*. New York: Penguin.

Tuinman, J. T., & Brady, M. C. (1974). How does vocabulary account for variance on reading comprehension tests? A preliminary instructional analysis. In P. Nacke (Ed.), *Interaction: Research and practice in college-adult reading*. Yearbook of the National Reading Conference, 23. Clemson, S.C.: National Reading Conference.

Tway, E. (1984). The resource center: Children's literature. *Language Arts, 61*, 312–315.

Tway, E. (Ed.) (1981). *Reading ladders for human relations*. 6th ed. Washington, D.C.: American Council on Education.

Vacca, J. L. (1977). Including attitude assessment in the classroom reading program. *Illinois Reading Council Journal, 5*, 8–10.

Vacca, J. L., and Vacca, R. T. (1976). Learning stations: How to in the middle grades. *Journal of Reading, 19*, 563–567.

Vacca, R. T., & Vacca, J. L. (1983). Two less than fortunate consequences of reading research in the 1970s. *Reading Research Quarterly, 18*, 382–383.

Vacca, R. T., & Vacca, J. L. (1986). *Content area reading*. 2nd ed. Boston: Little, Brown.

Veatch, J., & Acinapuro, P. (1966). *Reading in the elementary school*. New York: Owen.

Veatch, J., Sawicki, F., Elliot, G., Flake, E., & Blakey, J. (1979). *Key words to reading*. 2nd ed. Columbus, Ohio: Merrill.

Venezky, R. L. (1978). Reading acquisition: The occult and the obscure. In F. B. Murray & J. J. Pikulski (Eds.), *The acquisition of reading*. Baltimore: University Park Press.

Verble, M. (1980). *Dealing in discipline: Study guide*. Lincoln, Neb.: University of Mid-America Press.

Yvgotsky, L. S. (1962). *Thought and language*. Cambridge: MIT Press.

Vygotsky, L. S. (1978). *Mind in society*. Cambridge: Harvard University Press.

Walberg, H., Chou Hare, V., & Pulliam, C. (1981). Social-psychological perceptions and reading comprehension. In J. Guthrie (Ed.), *Comprehension and teaching: Research reviews*. Newark, Del.: International Reading Association.

Walton, S. (1984, February 8). Research and the quest for "effective" bilingual methods. *Education Week, 3,* 18–20.

Watson, D. (1978). Reader selected miscues: Getting more from sustained silent reading. *English Education, 10,* 75–85.

Watson, D. (1985). Watching and listening to children read. In A. Jaggar & M. T. Smith-Burke (Eds.), *Observing the language learner.* Newark, Del.: International Reading Association.

Wechsler, D. (1958). *The measurement and appraisal of adult intelligence.* Baltimore: Williams & Wilkins.

Whaley, J. F. (1981). Story grammar and reading instruction. *The Reading Teacher, 34,* 762–771.

What works: Research about teaching and learning. (1986). Washington, D.C.: U.S. Department of Education.

Wheat, T. E., Galen, N. D., & Norwood, M. (1974). Initial reading experiences for linguistically diverse learners. *The Reading Teacher, 33,* 28–31.

Whitfield, E., and Whitfield, C. (1982). Developing a classroom newspaper. *Ohio Reading Teacher, 16,* 23–24.

Wilder, G. (1977). Five exemplary reading programs. In J. Guthrie (Ed.), *Cognition, curriculum and comprehension.* Newark, Del.: International Reading Association.

Wittrock, M. D., Marks, C., & Doctorow, M. (1975). Reading as a generative process. *Journal of Educational Psychology, 67,* 481–489.

Witty, P. A. (1971). *Reading for the gifted and creative student.* Newark, Del.: International Reading Association.

Witty, P. A. (1985). Rationale for fostering creative reading in the gifted and the creative. In M. Labuda (Ed.), *Creative learning for gifted learners.* 2nd ed. Newark, Del.: International Reading Association.

Wixson, K., Bosky, A., Yochum, M. N., & Alvermann, D. (1984). An interview for assessing students' perceptions of classroom reading tasks. *The Reading Teacher, 37,* 346–353.

Wolf, J. (1985). Teaching young writers to revise. *The Ohio Reading Teacher, 19,* 28–30.

Wolf, J., & Vacca, R. T. (1985). *Teaching the writing process: A resource guide for elementary classroom teachers.* Kent, Ohio: Writing Process Demonstration Project, Kent State University.

Yawkey, T. D. (1980). Why play? *Educational Research Quarterly, 5,* 74–77.

Acknowledgments (continued from page iv)

Chapter 4

Figure 4.1 Spellings of Three Kindergarteners. Reprinted with permission of Dr. J. Richard Gentry and the International Reading Association. Figure 1 from "Three Steps to Teaching Beginning Readers to Spell," J. R. Gentry and E. H. Henderson, *Developmental and Cognitive Aspects of Learning to Spell: A Reflection of Word Knowledge,* E. H. Henderson and J. W. Beers, editors.

Box 4.2 Reading-Readiness Checklist. Reprinted with permission of Macmillan Publishing Company from *Reading Instruction: Diagnostic Teaching in the Classroom,* 4th ed., by L. A. Harris and C. B. Smith. Copyright © 1984 by Macmillan Publishing Company.

Questions for Checklist on Reading Readiness. From Gloria McDonnell and E. Bess Osburn, "New Thoughts on Reading Readiness," pp. 27–29 in *Language Arts,* Vol. 55, #1, January 1978. Copyright © 1978 by the National Council of Teachers of English. Reprinted by permission of the publisher. Reprinted by permission of *Language Arts* Magazine and the National Council of Teachers of English.

Chapter 5

Quotations from Robert Frost poem. Last stanza from "The Road Not Taken." From *The Poetry of Robert Frost* edited by Edward Connery Lathem. Copyright 1916, © 1969 by Holt, Rinehart and Winston. Copyright 1944 by Robert Frost. Reprinted by permission of Henry Holt and Company and Jonathan Cape Ltd.

Figure 5.1 An Early Scribbling Sample. Reprinted with permission from *Growing Up Writing,* by Linda Leonard Lamme, Ph.D., copyright © Highlights for Children, 1984, published by Acropolis Books Ltd., 2400 17 St., NW, Washington, DC 20009, $8.95.

Jessica's "Pollushein" Drafts and "Pollution" Revision. From "Teaching Young Writers to Revise" by Judi Wolf in *Ohio Reading Teacher,* Vol. 19, No. 4, July 1985, pp. 28–30. Reprinted with permission of *Ohio Reading Teacher.*

Chapter 6

People of the Third Planet by Dale Crail. Adapted from "People of the Third Planet" by Dale Crail. Copyright © 1968 by Scholastic, Inc. Reprinted by permission of Scholastic, Inc.

Figure 6.3 Potential Stopping Points in a DR-TA. Reprinted with permission of Gerald L. Fowler and the International Reading Association. Figure 6 from "Developing Comprehension Skills in Primary Students Through the Use of Story Frames," Gerald Fowler, *The Reading Teacher,* November 1982, p. 178.

"Understanding the Language of the Dog." From Mongillo, *Reading About Science.* Copyright 1981. McGraw-Hill Book Company. Reproduced with permission of McGraw-Hill Book Company.

Chapter 7

Figure 7.1 Dale's Cone of Experience. From *Audiovisual Methods in Teaching,* Third Edition, by Edgar Dale. Copyright © 1946, 1954, 1969 by Holt, Rinehart and Winston. Reprinted with permission of Holt, Rinehart and Winston.

Chapter 8

Box 8.1 The Instant Words: First Hundred, Second Hundred, Third Hundred. From *Elementary Reading Instruction* by Edward Fry, Ph.D. McGraw-Hill Book Company, 1977. Reprinted with permission of Edward Fry, Ph.D.

Dinosaur Poem. Poem from *The Story Box,* p. 2. Reprinted with permission of The Wright Group, 10949 Technology Place, San Diego, CA 92126.

Chapter 10

Figure 10.2 Scope and Sequence Chart. From *Winterfall Teacher's Resource Book,* Level 16 Keytext Program. The Economy Company, pp. xxii, 1984. Reprinted with permission of The Economy Company.

Figure 10.3 Program Scope and Sequence Chart. Page T28, "Program Scope and Sequence," from *Sky Climbers Teacher's Edition,* Level 10, Copyright 1985. Reprinted with permission of Scott, Foresman and Company.

Figure 10.5 Instructional Sequence. From *Winterfall Teacher's Resource Book,* Keytext Program. The Economy Company, pp. xii, 1984. Reprinted with permission of The Economy Company.

Chapter 11

Box 11.1 General Textbook Readability Checklist. Reprinted with permission of J.W. Irwin and the International Reading Association. Readability Checklist from J. W. Irwin and C. A. Davis, "Assessing Readability: A Checklist Approach." *Journal of Reading*, November 1980.

Box 11.2 Fry Readability Graph. From *Elementary Reading Instruction* by Edward Fry, Ph.D. McGraw Hill Book Company, 1977. Reprinted with permission of Edward Fry, Ph.D.

Figure 11.1 Reading Signals. From Richard T. Vacca and JoAnne L. Vacca. *Content Area Reading*, 2nd ed., p. 33. Copyright © 1986 by Richard T. Vacca and JoAnne L. Vacca. Reprinted by permission of Little, Brown and Company.

Figure 11.2 Structured Overview. Developed by Janice Mark. Reprinted by permission of Janice Mark.

Anticipation Guide for "Plants in the Environment." Developed by Carolee Henderson. Reprinted by permission of Carolee Henderson.

Box 11.3 Anticipation Guide for "Chimp Who Learned Language." Developed by Elizabeth Martin. Reprinted by permission of Elizabeth Martin.

Box 11.4 Anticipation Guide for "Androclus and the Lion." Developed by Elizabeth Martin. Reprinted by permission of Elizabeth Martin.

Box 11.5 Pattern Guide for "Why Mosquitos Buzz in People's Ears." Developed by Rose Mary Burns. Reprinted by permission of Rose Mary Burns.

Figure 11.2 Structured Overview. Developed by Janice Mark. Reprinted by permission of Janice Mark.

Figure 11.3 Semantic Web on Magnetism. Developed by Janice Mark. Reprinted by permission of Janice Mark.

Figure 11.4 Variability of a Content Unit. From Richard T. Vacca and JoAnne L. Vacca, *Content Area Reading*, 2nd ed., p. 363. Copyright © 1986 by Richard T. Vacca and JoAnne L. Vacca. Reprinted by permission of Little, Brown and Company.

Chapter 12

Figure 12.1 Sample Screen from a Simple Tutorial Program. Tricky Trip program screen shot and punctuation photograph used by permission of Educational Activities, Inc.

Figure 12.2 Example of a "Story Tree" from the Story Maker Program. Story Maker slide used by permission of Scholastic Software, Inc. Math Shop slide and Success with Reading slide used by permission of Scholastic Software, Inc.

Figure 12.3 Example of Mode Choice from the Writing Workshop *Program*. Writing Workshop slides used by permission of Milliken Publishing Company.

Figure 12.4 A Scene from the Writing Adventure *Program, 12.5 Brainstorming in the* Writing Workshop *Program, and 12.6 Spelling Example from the* Hayden Speller *Program*. From *The Writing Adventure* by Panda Learning Systems. © 1986 DLM Teaching Resources, a division of DLM, Inc., Allen, TX 75002.

Chapter 13

Figure 13.9 Reading Comprehension Interview. Reprinted with permission of Karen K. Wixson and the International Reading Association. From "An Interview for Assessing Students' Perceptions of Classroom Reading Tasks," Karen Wixson, A. B. Bosky, M. N. Yochum, and D. E. Alvermann, *The Reading Teacher,* January 1984.

Chapter 14

Box 14.1 Teacher Observation Form A. Reprinted with permission of Dr. Joseph Sanacore and the International Reading Association. From "Guidelines for Observing Remedial Reading Lessons," Joseph Sanacore, *The Reading Teacher*, January 1981.

Box 14.2 Teacher Observation Form B. Reprinted with permission of Dr. Jack Bagford and the International Reading Association. From "Evaluating Teachers on Reading Instruction," Jack Bagford, *The Reading Teacher*, January 1981.

Figure 14.4 Guide to Learning Centers. Reprinted by permission of Professor John Thomas. From "Categories of Learning Centers," John Thomas, *Learning Centers,* Holbrook Press, Inc., Allyn and Bacon Publishers, 1975.

Box 14.5 Dowing Away with Desks. Developed by Wanda Rogers. Reprinted by permission of Wanda Rogers.

Figure 14.12 Self-Evaluation Form. Reprinted by permission of JoAnne Vacca and the International Reading Association. From *Journal of Reading*, April 1976.

Figure 14.14 Stations Implementation Chart. Reprinted by permission of JoAnne Vacca and the International Reading Association. From *Journal of Reading, 19,* 1976.

Scenario #1 Beginning Reading with The Gingerbread Man. Reprinted with permission of *Ohio Reading Teacher*. From The "Gingerbread Man" lesson in Idea X Change by Joy Mossburg on pages 30–32 of *Ohio Reading Teacher*, Vol. 17, No. 1, October 1982.

Scenario #2 Primary Grade Experiences and the Use of the Microcomputer. Reprinted with permission of *Ohio Reading Teacher*. From "Use of the Microcomputer to Enhance the Language Experience Approach to Teaching Reading," by D. Judd & J. Walker on pages 11–13 of *Ohio Reading Teacher*, Vol. 17, No. 1, October 1982.

Scenario #3 Intermediate-Grade Classroom Newspaper. Reprinted with permission of *Ohio Reading Teacher*. From the "Developing a Classroom Newspaper," by E. Whitfield & C. Whitfield in Idea X Change on pages 23–24 of *Ohio Reading Teacher*, Vol. 16, No. 3, April 1982.

Appendix D

A Bibliography of Predictable Books. Reprinted with permission of Lynn K. Rhodes and the International Reading Association from "I Can Read! Predictable Books as Resources for Reading and Writing Instruction." *The Reading Teacher*, Vol. 34, No. 5, February 1981, pp. 511–518.

Index

Aaron, I., 317
Aaron, R., 268, 280
Acinapuro, P., 43
Adaptation. *See* Individualized instruction
Advance organizer, 152–154
Aesthetics, 258–260
Alexander, J., 238
Aliteracy, 239, 294
Allington, R., 419, 431
Analogies, 200–201
Analytic phonics, 40
Anderson, M., 280
Anderson, R., 176, 268
Anderson, T., 307
Anglin, L., 426
Anticipation guides, 319–322
Antonyms, 192–193
Anzalone, D., 297, 434
Applied level of comprehension, 164
Aptitude hypothesis, 176
Armbruster, B., 307
Arnsdorf, V., 317
Artley, S., 36, 182
Ashton-Warner, S., 211
Assessment
    formal. *See* Tests
    informal. *See* Informal assessment
Association for Children with Learning
        Disabilities, 463
Atwell, N., 118, 123
Aukerman, R., 277
Aulls, M., 81, 163, 165
Ausubel, D., 80
Authoritative/contractual use of language, 9
Automaticity, 13
Ayers, D., 223

Baker, R., 290–291
Balajthy, E., 370
Barnhart, C., 39–40
Barnitz, J., 470, 475, 476
Barron, R., 319, 327

Basal instruction, terms of, 274–276
Basal readers, 42, 266–267
    alternative lessons with, 286–287
    appearance of, 279
    history of, 267–273
    illustrations in, 279
    instructional methods with, 285–289
    language style of, 281–282
    lesson framework of, 283–284
    modern, 273, 277
    stereotyping in, 279–281
    workbooks and, 282–283
Bass, H., 317
Baumann, J., 420
Beck, I., 145, 174, 176, 183, 184
Beer, J., 88, 111
Beginning readers, Sustained Silent Reading
        and, 254–255
Beginning reading behavior, checklist for, 96
Beginning reading instruction, 80–94
    activities contributing to, 70–73
    goals of, 81–82
    reading readiness and, 79–80
    timing of, 78–80
Behavior
    student, 414–417
    teacher, 420–426
Bell-shaped curve, 378
Benton, M., 259
Berliner, D., 416, 417
Betts, E., 388, 389
Bilingual learners, 473–481
    cultural factors affecting, 476, 477–478
    first- and second-language learning of, 474–
        476
    networking and teaming to benefit, 481
    peer interaction for, 480–481
    phonics drills and, 480
    reading instruction for, 476–481
    visual emphasis in instruction to benefit,
        479–480
Bissex, G., 63, 111
Blanchard, J., 41, 42

Bloom, B., 163
Bloomfield, L., 39–40
Blume, J., 244
Bookmaking, 132–133, 134–135
Book reports, 250–251
Boothby, P., 460
Bottom-up conceptual framework, 20–21
Bottom-up models of reading instruction, 10,
    13–15, 59
Brady, M., 176
Brainstorming, 322–323
    computer programs for, 363
Bransford, J., 11
Braun, C., 149
Britton, J., 123
Brophy, J., 415
Brown, M., 247
Bruckerhoff, C., 237
Brutton, D., 237
Bryen, D., 473
Brzeinski, J., 317
Buck, C., 470, 472
Buggey, J., 317
Burke, C., 18, 48, 69, 390
Burnett, J., 352

CAI. *See* Computer-assisted instruction;
    Reading; Writing
Caldecott Award books, 491–492
Calkins, L., 105, 120
Carey, R., 381
Carr, K., 458
Carter, B., 90
Cassidy, J., 458
Categorization, 196–197
Cause and effect, 317
Censorship, 293
Chall, J., 37–38
Chaplin, M., 283
Chenfield, M., 71
Chomsky, C., 104, 112, 229
Chôu Hare, V., 419
Clark, M., 61–62
Classroom(s)
    computer use in, 446–447
    direct instruction in, 417–419
    discipline in, 414–415
    effectiveness of, 413–414
    furniture in, 433, 435
    group instruction in, 418–419, 430
    individualized instruction in, 426–432
    inventory, 439, 441–442
    learning centers in, 434–436
    materials in, 431–432
    newspaper publishing in, 447–448
    organization of, 432–442
    physical environment in, 432–434
    planning charts for, 442
    room diagram for, 437–438
    scenarios in, 442–448
    scheduling students in, 438–439

space usage in, 433
storage in, 433–434
student evaluation in, 419–420
teacher behavior in, 420–426
time on task in, 415–417
Clay, M., 80, 91, 104, 111, 223
Clements, D., 341, 351, 356, 370
Cloze passage(s), 149, 216
    administering, 394–395
    constructing, 394
    defined, 394
    modified, 215–216
    scoring and interpreting, 395–396
Clymer-Barrett battery, 95
Code emphasis, 274
Cognition, reading and, 7
Cohen, D., 243
Commission on Reading, 38, 218–219,
    416
Communicative competence, 10
Comparative reading, 460–461
Comparison and contrast, 197, 317
Competence, communicative, 10
Comprehension
    computer-assisted instruction and, 352
    levels of, 163–164
    questions and, 161–165
    strategy for teaching, 287–289
    teaching and testing of, 287
Computer-assisted instruction, 41–42
    comprehension and, 352
    dangers of, 340, 341
    defined, 342
    drill and practice for, 341, 344
    editing and, 365–368, 369
    evaluating programs for, 370
    exploratory programs for, 349–351
    games for, 349–351
    grammar checkers and, 367
    in literature, 353–354
    methodology of, 341
    primary grade use of, 446–447
    proofreaders and, 367–368
    publishing aids used with, 368–369
    purpose of, 341, 345, 349, 350
    for reading, 341, 343–354, 496–499
    simulation in, 346–349
    spelling checkers and, 365–366
    strengths of, 344, 345–346, 349, 350
    tutorial programs for, 344–346
    vocabulary development with, 351–352
    weaknesses of, 344, 346, 349, 350–351
    word processing and. *See* Word processors
    for writing, 354–369
    writing process and, 362–369
Computer programs for reading instruction,
    341, 343–354, 496–499
Computer terms, 342–343
Concept circles, 197
Concept development
    strategies for, 186–201
    vocabulary and, 174–175

Concepts
  hierarchy of, 179–181
  words and, 177–181
Concepts About Print Tests, 223
Conceptual Framework of Reading Interview,
  16–25
  analyzing, 485–488
Conceptual knowledge, 175
Conceptually driven models. *See* Top-down
  models
Cone of Experience, 178, 187–188
Conferencing, 126
Consonant blends, 221, 224
Consonant digraphs, 221, 224
Consonants, 220–221, 224
Construct validity, 380
Content validity, 380
Context
  analysis of, 215–217
  reading and, 214–218
Contextual knowledge, 182
Continuous progress, 274
Controlled vocabulary, 274
Conventional spelling, 111
Coody, B., 251, 333
Cooley, 416
Correction of reading errors, 387
Corroborative framework for decision making,
  377–378
Cramer, R., 66, 91, 115–116
Creating, and beginning reading instruction,
  70–71
Criscuolo, N., 250, 298–299
Criterion-referenced tests, 274
  defined, 383
  reliability of, 383–384
  validity of, 384
Cryptography, 216–217
Cueing, 385
Cultural diversity, 476, 477–478
Cunningham, P., 224, 297
Cunningham, R., 164
Curriculum
  home-centered, 64–65
  language-centered, 65

Dale, E., 150, 178, 187–188, 469, 472
Dancing, and beginning reading instruction, 71
Daniel, D., 41, 42
Data driven models. *See* Bottom-up models
Davis, C., 246, 307
Davis, F., 175
Decoding, 208
Definitional knowledge, 175, 182, 191
DeHaven, E., 300
Deighton, L., 186
Developmental Spelling Assessment, 223
Diagnostic teaching, 396–406
  checklists for, 399–400
  field notes and, 399
  interviewing and, 401–406
  observation in, 399

Diagnostic tests, 381–382
Dialects, 467–468
  acceptance of in classroom, 472
Dillon, J., 161–162
Direct instruction in classroom, 417–419
Directed Reading Activity, 42, 284
  background building for, 284
  follow-up and enrichment of, 285
  guided reading and, 284
  motivation in, 284
  skill development and practice in, 284
Directed Reading-Thinking Activity, 147,
  157–159, 287, 292, 398, 402–403
Discipline, 414–415
Divertive use of language, 9, 85
Downing, J., 36, 93, 223
DRA. *See* Directed Reading Activity
Drafting an essay, 125
Drama
  and beginning reading instruction, 72–73
  response to literature through, 260
  and vocabulary development, 190
DRTA. *See* Directed Reading-Thinking
  Activity
Dufflemeyer, F., 190
Dupuis, M., 186
Durkin, D., 60, 83, 87, 210, 458
Durrell, D., 92, 429
Duval, 438

Earle, R., 327, 333
Early readers, 59–63
Echo reading, 228
Editing, 129, 132
  computer programs for, 365–368, 369
Edmunds, R., 412
Education for All Handicapped Children Act
  of 1975, 468
"Electric Company," 92
Elkind, D., 79
Elkonin, D., 89
Elley, W., 480
Emmer, E., 415
English as a second language. *See* Bilingual
  learners
Enright, D., 477, 480
Enumeration, 317
Environment
  influence of on reading, 56–63
  influence of on writing, 115–117
Errors
  abandonment of correct form, 387–388
  correction of, 387
  insertion, 387
  mispronunciation, 387
  omission, 386
  pronunciation, 387
  repetition, 387
  reversal, 387
  substitution, 386
ESL. *See* Bilingual learners

Estes, T., 34, 334, 388
Evaluation, student, 419–420
Evertson, C., 415
Extended reading, 274

Farr, R., 44, 78, 79, 381
Feeley, J., 300
Filby, N., 416
Fischer, F., 90
Fisher, C., 416
Fitzgerald, G., 282
Formal assessment. *See* Tests
Fowler, G., 152
Freebody, P., 176
Freeman, E., 281
Free word association, 191
Freewriting, 123, 125
Fries, 40
Frost, R., 104
Frustration reading level, 388, 396
Fry, E., 210, 309, 314
Fry Readability Graph, 309, 314
Functional illiteracy, 294

Galda, L., 260
Galen, N., 471, 472
Gambrell, L., 123
Gans, R., 10
Gates, 430
Gates-MacGintie tests, 95
Gauch, P., 291
Gensley, J., 460–461
Gentry, J., 89
Gifted readers
  choice of reading matter for, 460
  comparative reading and, 460–461
  creative expression and, 461–462
  defined, 457–458
  linguistic instruction of, 461
  misconceptions about, 458–459
  networking and teaming for, 462–463
  peer relations of, 459, 462
  reading instruction for, 459–463
  skills-oriented instruction and, 459
  supervision needs of, 458
Gillet, J., 111, 194
Gipe, J., 184
Glenn, C., 143
Gonzales, P., 282
Good, T., 426, 431
Goodlad, J., 413, 414, 429, 430
Goodman, K., 38, 282, 285, 382, 389, 390, 396, 470, 472
Gordon, C., 149
Gough, P., 13
Gove, M., 17, 45
Grade equivalency score, 380
Grammar, story, 143–145
Granger, R., 472
Graphic organizer, 152
Graphic-sound similarity, 391

Graphophonemics, 9, 13
Graves, D., 115, 119, 126, 354
Gray, W., 269
Group instruction, 418–419
Gruenberg, R., 247
Guilford, J., 163
Guthrie, J., 416

Halliday, M. A. K., 8, 9
Hammill, D., 223
Hansen, J., 160
Hardy, M., 37
Harris, A., 72, 463
Harris, L., 298
Harrison-Stroud profile, 95
Harste, J., 18, 48, 69
Hartman, C., 473
Heathington, B., 238
Heilman, A., 218
Heimberger, M., 461
Henderson, E., 88, 89, 111
Henk, W., 381
Henry, G., 185
Hepler, S., 248–249
Herber, H., 163, 324
Heuristic use of language, 9
Hickman, J., 240–241, 244, 248–249
Hinton, S., 291
Hittleman, D., 309
Holdaway, D., 58, 59, 64, 67, 239
Holistic approach to reading instruction, 34–38
Home, influence of on reading, 56–63, 64–66
Hong, L. 254
Hoskisson, K., 68
Hough, R., 477, 480
Hresko, W., 223
Hunt, L., 251–252
Hunter, E., 49
Hymes, D., 10, 57
Hyperactivity and hypoactivity, 468

IEPs. *See* Individualized education plans
Ignoffo, M., 201
Illiteracy, 294
Illustrations, in basal readers, 279
Imaginative use of language, 9
Improvisation as response to literature, 260
Independent reading level, 388, 396
Individualized education plans, 457, 468
Individualized instruction
  defined, 429–430
  for gifted readers, 457–463
  influence of, 430–432
  misconceptions about, 427–429
  for special needs students, 454–457
Individualized-personalized approach to instruction, 43–44
Individualized-prescriptive approach to instruction, 39–42
Inferential strategy, 160–161

Informal assessment, 384–396
Informal Reading Inventory
   administration of, 385–386
   defined, 385
   reading level criteria for, 388–389
   recording oral reading errors in, 386–388
Insertion errors, 387
Instructional aids, 275
Instructional materials, 290–300
   beliefs about, 292
   choosing, 292–294
   evaluating, 294–297
   games as, 298
   newspapers as, 298–299
   student-produced, 297–300
   teacher-made, 297–300
   television as, 299–300
Instructional methods, 285–289
Instructional reading level, 388, 396
Instructional strategies, 44–49
Instrumental hypothesis, 176
Instrumental use of language, 9, 84–85
Interactional use of language, 9
Interactive models, 11, 16
International Reading Association, 380
Interpretive level of comprehension, 163
Interviews
   as diagnostic aid, 401–406
   as writing tool, 122
Invented spelling, 110–114
   advantages of, 112–113
Inventories, 439, 441–442
IQ testing, 420
IRI, 395
Irwin, J., 307

Jackson, D., 317
Jacobsen, M., 281
James, H., 466
Jaramillo, M., 474
Jenkins, J., 176
Johns, J., 385, 390
Johnson, B., 225
Johnson, D., 165, 182, 198, 383, 384
Johnson, M., 11
Johnson, N., 143
Johnstone, J., 34
Joint Committee on Reading, 65
Journal writing, 123, 125
Jovanovich, 160
Judy and Judy, 133

Kamil, M., 16, 34, 35
Keyword method, 189–190, 211, 214
Kirby, D., 132, 133
Kirk, S., 463
Kita, M., 194
Klein, M., 106
Kliebhan, J., 463
Knowledge
   definitional, 191

definitional vs. conceptual, 175
definitional vs. contextual, 182
Knowledge hypothesis, 176
Kohl, H., 433
Kounin, J., 415
Krause, C., 401, 403

Laberge, D., 13
Labov, W., 469, 472, 473
Labuda, M., 466
Lamme, L., 106
Language
   experiencing, 69–73
   of instruction, 93–94
   reading as aspect of, 7
   social bases of, 8–9
   uses of, 9, 82–86
Language arts, 277
Language Experience Approach, 43, 472
Language experience stories, 86–88
Lass, B., 63
Lauritzen, C., 230
LD. See Learning disabled children
LEA. See Language Experience Approach
Learning centers, 434–436
Learning disabled children
   adaptation for, 466
   behavior of, 463–464
   defined, 463, 468
   fostering independence of, 465–466
   giving directions for, 466
   impulsiveness of, 463
   indiscrimination of, 463
   networking and teaming to benefit, 467
   peer relations and, 466–467
   reading instruction of, 464–467
   self-esteem of, 465
   structured environment for, 465
Lee-Clark test, 95
Lehnert, L., 225
Leinhardt, 416
LEP. See Limited English Proficiency
Lerner, J., 463
Letter recognition, 92–93
   and sound association, 89–90
Levels of readers, 275
Levin, H., 209
Levin, J. A., 368
Levin, J. R., 189
Levine, S., 252
Liberman, I., 90–91
Limited English Proficiency, 475, 481
Lindemann, E., 121
Liner, T., 132, 133
Linguistic diversity, 466–473
   defined, 469–470
   effects of on instruction, 472
   networking and teaming to cope with, 473
   reading instruction and, 470
   understanding, 471
   value of, 471–472

Listening
  as component of vocabulary, 177
  capacity level of, 388
Literal level of comprehension, 163
Literature
  aesthetics of, 258–260
  in basal readers, 277
  classroom, 240–242
  computer-assisted instruction in 353–354
  evaluation of, 242–243
  listening to, 243–245
  response to, 257–261
  selection of for children, 248–249
  for storytelling, 246–247
LOGO, 340
Lukasevich, A., 463

McCracken, M., 252
McCracken, R., 252, 253
McDaniel, T., 414
McDonald, F., 36
Macdonald, J., 44
McDonnell, G., 94
McGuffey, W., 267
McKeown, M., 174, 176, 183
McLeod, B., 476, 477
McNeil, J., 37
Macro-cloze story, 149. *See also* Cloze
    passage(s)
Mainstreaming, 457, 468
Management, 275, 277
Mandler, J., 143
Mangieri, J., 297
Mangubhai, F., 480
Manzo, A., 155, 186, 190
Maping, 145–147
  Semantic, 197–199
Marchbanks, G., 209
Maring, G., 466
Marliave, R., 416
Mason, G., 41, 42, 283
Mean, 378
Meaning emphasis, 275
"Memory" reading, 67
Metropolitan Readiness Test, 95
Meyer, B., 317
Michel, A., 321
Miller, G., 189
Miller, L., 352
Miscues
  analysis of, 390–393
  corrected, 390, 391
  dialect, 390
  grammatically acceptable, 391
  graphic-sound similar, 391
  semantically acceptable, 390–391
Mispronunciation, 387
Modified cloze passage, 215–216
Moffett, J., 58
Moldofsky, P., 148
Morphett, M., 78

Morris, D., 223
Morrow, L., 434
Mossburg, J., 282, 443, 446
Motivation, 236–250
  of aliterate individuals, 239
  book reports and, 250–251
  classroom literature and, 240–242
  Directed Reading Activity and, 284
  encouraging response to literature, 257–261
Murphy, B., 291
Murphy-Durell analysis, 95

Neisser, U., 11
Nelson, D., 251, 333
Nelson, J., 309
Networking, 455–457, 462–463, 467, 481
Neuman, S., 300
New England Primer, 268–269
Newberry Award books, 489–490
Newspaper, classroom publishing for, 447–448
Niles, O., 316
Nolte, R., 155
Normal curve, 378
Norms, 378
Norton, D., 245, 246
Norwood, M., 471, 472
Nurss, J., 477, 480

Observation
  checklists for, 399–400
  field notes and, 399
Ohnmacht, D., 92
Olson, L., 455–456, 462
Omission errors, 386
Oral reading strategies, 228–230
  echo reading, 228
  repeated readings, 229–230
  simultaneous listening and reading, 228–229
Organizer, advance, 152–154
Osborn, J., 282, 283
Osburn, E., 94
Overview, structured, 152

Padak, N., 470, 471, 473
Pany, D., 176
Papert, S., 340
Parents, as providers of reading assistance, 67–
    69
Pattern guides, 326
Pattern recognition, 227
Patterns of organization, 317–318
Pearson, P., 16, 34, 35, 149, 165, 383
Pellegrini, A., 260
Percentile score, 381
Perfetti, C., 176
Perney, J., 223
Perpetuating use of language, 9, 83–84
Personal use of language, 9, 85–86
Peterson, P., 418
Phonemic segmentation, 90–92
Phonemic spelling, 111

Phonic analysis, 88–92, 208
Phonic elements
  consonant blends, 221, 224
  consonant digraphs, 221, 224
  consonant-influenced vowels, 222
  consonants, 220–221, 224
  phonograms, 222
  syllables, 222–223, 224
  vowel digraphs, 221–222, 224
  vowel diphthongs, 222, 224
  vowels, 221, 224
Phonics, 40–41
  analytic, 219–220
  reading and, 218–219
  synthetic, 220
Phonics instruction
  listening and listing, 226
  pattern recognition and, 227
  tests used in, 223
  word building and, 226
Phonograms, 222
Piaget, J., 8
Pictures, and vocabulary development, 188–
    190
Pieronek, F., 277
Pikulski, J., 56
PL 94–142 (Education for All Handicapped
    Children Act of 1975), 468
"Predictable" books, 493–495
Predictive validity, 380
Prephonemic spelling, 111
Prereading preparation, 150–154
Pressley, M., 189
Prewriting, computer programs for, 362–363
Primers, 273, 275
Problem solution, 317
Pronunciation errors, 387
Proofreading, 132
  computer programs for, 367–368
Protheroe, D., 175
Psycholinguistics, 9
Publishing, 132–133
  computer-assisted, 368–369
Pulliam, C., 419

Quandt, I., 425, 426
Question-answer relationships, 165–170
Question continuum, 164–165
Questioning
  alternatives to, 162–163
  comprehension and, 161–165
  discussion and, 161
  reciprocal, 155–156
  student-generated, 154–157

Raphael, T., 165
RCI, 404–406
Read, C., 88, 111
Readability, Fry graph of, 309, 314
Readability formulas
  limitations of, 309

usefulness of, 309
Reader-response theory, 258–259
Readers, early, 59–63
Readiness to read, 79–80, 94–97
Reading
  aesthetic, 258–260
  aloud. See Reading to children
  approaches to, 38–44
  beginning, 443–446
  cognition and, 7
  comparative, 460–461
  as component of vocabulary, 177
  computer programs for teaching, 341, 343–
    354, 496–499
  decision making about strategies for, 377–
    378
  echo, 228
  errors in, 386–388
  extended, 274
  free time for, 256–257
  groups, 430
  guided, 284
  home influence on, 56–63, 64–66
  instructional materials for. See Instructional
    materials
  interaction with text, 157–161, 323–327
  language and, 7
  language experience and, 69–73
  language experience stories, 86–88
  levels of. See Reading level
  materials, selection of for classroom, 431–
    432
  meaning as ground for, 472–473
  "memory," 67
  models of, 10–16
  motivation for. See Motivation
  oral, 228–230
  parents and, 67–69
  as process, 38
  psycholinguistics and, 9
  purpose and use of, 82–86
  readiness for, 79–80, 94–97
  reading-like behavior and, 94–95
  sociolinguistics and, 9
  sustained silent. See Sustained Silent Reading
  tests of, 378–384
  textbooks for. See Textbooks
  of textbooks, 318–332
  theories of, 5–6
  vocabulary for, 208
Reading Comprehension Interview, 404–406
Reading level, 388–396
Reading readiness, 273
  checklist for, 98–99
Reading to children, 66, 243–246. See also
    Storytelling
  follow-ups to, 246
Regulatory use of language, 9, 84
Rehearsing
  computer programs for, 362–365, 366
  for writing, 122–125

Reid, D., 223
Reinforcement, 275
Reinking, D., 353
Reliability of tests, 379–380
Repeated readings, 229–230
Repetition errors, 387
Repetition of favorite stories, 67
Representational use of language, 9
ReQuest. *See* Questioning, reciprocal
Reversal errors, 387
Revising, 126
Riedesel, C., 370
Role playing, and beginning reading
    instruction, 72
Rose, K., 72, 261
Rosegrant, T., 356, 358, 359
Rosenblatt, L., 257–259
Rosner, N., 44, 78, 79
Rubin, A., 354
Rudman, M., 280
Rumelhart, D., 11
Rupley, W., 280, 281

Samuels, S., 13, 37, 92, 229, 413, 418
SAV, 190–191
Scenarios, classroom, 442–448
Schachter, S. W., 176
Schaefer, B., 223
Scheduling, 438–439
Schemata, 11, 142–157
    activating, 154–157
    building, 150–154
    mapping, 145–147
    story grammar, 143–145
Schramm, W., 299
Scope and sequence charts, 270–271, 276
Scrambled story, 149–150
Scribbling, 106–108
    controlled, 106–107, 108
    name, 107
Semantic mapping, 197–199
Semantics, 9
Semantic system, 11–12
Semantic webs, 331–332
"Sesame Street," 92
Shankweiler, D., 90
Shields, C., 299
Shirk, J., 186
Shoephoerster, H., 317
Shuman, R., 433
Shuy, R., 472
Sight words, 209
    high-frequency, 210–211
    instruction in, 209
    recognition of, 208
Silence, effective use of, 162–163
Silent reading, 251–253. *See also* Sustained
    Silent Reading
Simultaneous Listening and Reading, 228–229
Sinatra, R., 475
Singer, D., 299

Singer, H., 154–155
Singing, and beginning reading instruction, 71
Sirota, B., 243
Skills
    building of, 276
    maintenance of, 276
    management of, 40–41
SLR, 228–229
Smith, C., 298
Smith, F., 8–9, 15, 59, 464, 465, 466
Smith, L., 249
Smith, N., 269, 429, 430
Smith, R., 182, 198, 384
Smythe, P., 37
Snyder, S., 186, 277, 298
Sociolinguistics, 9
Software, publishers of, 496–501
Sowers, S., 113
Speaking, as component of vocabulary, 177
Spearitt, D., 175
Special education, list of terms used in, 468
Special needs instruction, 454–457
    networking in, 455–457
Spelling
    computer checkers for, 365
    invented, 110–114
Spiegel, D., 250, 256, 257
Squire, J., 104
SSR. *See* Sustained Silent Reading
Stahl, S., 182, 183, 297, 434
Standard deviation, 378
Standard error, 379–380
Standardized tests, 378–383
    diagnostic, 381–382
    misuse of, 382–383
    norms on, 378
    reliability of, 379–380
    scoring of, 380–381
    survey of, 381–382
    types of, 381–382
    uses of, 382–383
    validity of, 380
Stanines, 381
Stauffer, R., 43
Stein, N., 143
Stengel, C., 377
Stennett, R., 37
Stereotypes, 280
    analyzing, 281
Stevenson, J., 420
Stewig, J., 242, 243, 246, 247
Stoodt, B., 224
Story(ies)
    macro-cloze, 149
    schema for. *See* Schemata
    scrambled, 149–150
    structure of, 148–149
    treatment of in classroom, 148–149
Story frames, 150
Story grammar, 143–145
Story mapping, 145–147

Storytelling, 246–248
   literature for, 246–247
   multimedia, 248
   preparation for, 247
Strands of instruction, 276, 277
Strickland, R., 281
Structural analysis, 208
Structured overview, 152, 319
Study, units of, 332–335
Studying
   graphic aids to, 329
   semantic webs in, 331–332
   strategies for, 328–332
   survey technique of, 328–329
Subjective Approach to Vocabulary, 190–191
Subskills approach to reading instruction, 34–38
Substitution errors, 386
Suess, Dr., 85
Survey technique, 328–329
Survey tests, 381–382
Sustained Silent Reading, 292
   beginning readers and, 254–255
   benefits of, 255–257
   goals of, 252–253
   implementation of, 253–254
   less able readers and, 254–255
Swaby, B., 152
Syllables, 222–223, 224
Synonyms, 191–192
Syntactic system, 12–13
Syntax, 9
Synthetic phonics, 40

Taba, H., 163
Tait, P., 473
Talking, and beginning reading instruction, 70
Talmage, H., 419
Tanner, N., 224
Taylor, N., 83
Taylor, W., 394
Teachers
   behavior of, 420–426
   evaluation of, 422–425
   expectations of, 425
   observation of by principal, 421–425
   relation of with students, 424–426
   self-analysis by, 426, 427
Teale, W., 59–61
Temple, C., 111
Test of Early Reading Ability, 223
Test of Linguistic Awareness, 223
Tests
   criterion-referenced, 274, 383–384
   IQ, 420
   readiness, 95
   reading ability, 223
   skill mastery, 376
   standardized, 378–383
Test scores
   grade equivalency, 380

percentile, 381
standard, 381
stanine, 381
Textbook reading
   anticipation guides for, 319–322
   background knowledge for, 318–319
   brainstorming and, 322–323
   pattern guides for, 326
   structured overviews for, 319
   studying and, 328–332
   three-level reading guides for, 324–326
   vocabulary reinforcement in, 326–327
Textbooks
   difficulty of, 306–308
   interestability of, rating, 308
   organization of, 313–318
   patterns of organization in, 317–318
   previewing of, 313, 315–316
   readability of, 308–313
   reading of, 318–332
   skimming of, 316
   structure of, 316–318
   understandability of, rating, 307–308
   usability of, rating, 308
Thesauri, electronic, 367
Thomas, J., 435, 439
Thorndyke, P., 143
Three-level reading guides, 324–326
Thurstone, L., 175
Time on task, 415–417
Time order, 317
Toch, T., 474
Tokenism, 280
Tom, C., 243
Top-down conceptual framework, 21
Top-down models of reading instruction, 10–11, 15
Torrey, J., 62
Transitional spelling, 111
Trelease, J., 66
Tuinman, J., 176
Tway, E., 248

Units of study, 332–335

Vacca, J. L., 38, 184, 193, 441, 442, 444
Vacca, R. T., 38, 193, 444
Validity of tests, 380
Van Allen, R., 43
Vanter, J., 83
Vaughan, J., 334, 388
Veatch, 43, 214
Venezky, R., 92
Verble, M., 415
Visual arts, response to literature and, 260
Vocabulary
   analogies and, 200–201
   categorization of words in, 196–197
   classifying words in, 193–201
   comparison and contrast and, 197
   components of, 177

comprehension and, 175–177
computer-assisted instruction and, 351–352
concept circles for, 197
concept development and, 174–175
controlled, 274
cumulative nature of, 176–177
defined, 177
development of, 276
dramatization as tool for developing, 190
experience and, 187–188
hypotheses about, 176–177
instruction principles, and, 183–186
keyword method for, 189–190, 211, 214
personal associations and, 190–191
pictures as tool for developing, 188–190
reading and, 208
reinforcement activities for, 326–327
semantic mapping of, 197–199
sight, 208
strategies for developing, 186–201, 289
subjective approach to, 190–191
word meanings and, 191–193
word sorts and, 194–196
Vondrak, L., 299
Vowel digraphs, 221–222, 224
Vowel diphthongs, 222, 224
Vowels, 221, 224
    consonant-influenced, 222
Vukelich, C., 458
Vygotsky, L., 8, 105

Walberg, H., 419
Washburne, C., 78
Watson, D., 217, 382
Wechsler, D., 176
Whaley, J., 149
Wheat, T., 471, 472
Whitfield, C., 448
Whitfield, E., 448
Whole-word method, 276
Wilder, G., 413
Williams, M., 245
Witty, P., 458–459
Wixson, K., 405
Wolkoff, J., 291
Woodward, V., 69
Word analysis, 208
Word attack, 208
Word identification. *See also* Phonics
    configuration and, 209

context and, 214–218
decoding in, 208
defined, 207
immediate, 208
"instant" words, 212–213
mediated, 208
phonic and structural analyses in, 208
reader selected miscue strategy for, 218
recognition and, 207–208
Word meanings
    antonyms, 192–193
    multiple, 193
    synonyms, 191–192
Word processors, 356–362
    advantages of, 359–360
    disadvantages of, 359–360
    features of, 356–357
    speech and, 358–359
    teaching use of, 361–362
Words, concepts and, 177–181
Word sorts, 194–196
Workbooks, 276, 282–283
Writing
    classroom guidelines for, 119–121
    computer programs for teaching, 354–369
    development of, 105–115
    environment and, 115–117
    reading and, 354–356
    response to literature and, 260–261
    routine for, 117–119
    vocabulary and, 177
Writing process
    bookmaking, 132–133, 134–135
    choosing a topic, 122–123
    computers, use of in, 362–369
    conferencing, 126
    drafting, 125
    editing, 129, 132
    freewriting, 123, 125
    proofreading, 132
    publishing, 132–133
    rehearsing, 122–125
    revising, 126
Written expression, 106
    scribbling, 106–108

Yawkey, T., 260

Zigmond, 416